Handbook of Early
Literacy Research

Handbook of
Early Literacy
Research

Edited by

Susan B. Neuman
David K. Dickinson

THE GUILFORD PRESS

New York   London

© 2002 The Guilford Press
A Division of Guilford Publications, Inc.
72 Spring Street, New York, NY 10012
www.guilford.com

Paperback edition 2003

Library of Congress Cataloging-in-Publication Data

Handbook of early literacy research / edited by Susan B. Neuman, David K. Dickinson.
     p. cm.
  Includes bibiographical references and index.
  ISBN 1-57230-653-X (hc.)   ISBN 1-57230-895-8 (pbk.)
  1. Language arts (Early childhood)—Handbooks, manuals, etc.   2. Reading (Early childhood)—Handbooks, manuals, etc. 3. Language arts (Early childhood)—Research—Handbooks, manuals, etc. 4. Children—Language—Handbooks, manuals, etc. I. Neuman, Susan B. II. Dickinson, David K.

LB1139.5.L35 H37 2001
372.6—dc21   2001033004

About the Editors

❖

Susan B. Neuman, PhD, is Professor of Educational Studies at the University of Michigan and the Director of the Center for the Improvement of Early Reading Ability (CIERA). Her interests include beginning reading and writing, family literacy, and parent involvement. Formerly, she was a Professor at Temple University for 10 years, where she coordinated the Reading and Language Arts Program. She has published over 100 articles in journals including *Reading Research Quarterly, American Educational Research Journal, Early Childhood Research Quarterly,* and *The Reading Teacher.* Among her most recent books are *Learning to Read and Write: Developmentally Appropriate Practice, Children Achieving: Best Practices in Early Literacy, Literacy in the Television Age,* and *Language and Literacy in Early Childhood.*

David K. Dickinson, PhD, is a Senior Research Scientist at the Education Development Center (EDC) in Newton, Massachusetts. Prior to joining EDC he was an elementary school teacher in Philadelphia for 5 years. He then served as Director of Teacher Education at the Child Study Department at Tufts University and the Education Department at Clark University. He moved to EDC to direct the New England Research Center on Head Start Quality, one of four Quality Research Centers funded by Head Start. Since 1994, he and colleagues at EDC have been developing and studying an approach to helping preschool teachers more effectively support children's language and literacy. He has reported his research in over 50 articles and chapters and edited *Bridges to Literacy: Children, Families and Schools.* His longitudinal research is reported in *Beginning Literacy with Language: Young Children Learning at Home and School,* a book that he cowrote with Patton Tabors. He also cowrote *The Early Language and Literacy Classroom Observation,* a tool for describing the quality of classroom support for language and literacy.

Contributors

❖

Marilyn J. Adams is the author of *Beginning to Read*. Ms. Adams chaired the planning committee and served on the study committee for the National Research Council's 1998 report, *Preventing Reading Difficulties in Young Children*. Dr. Adams is a Visiting Scholar at Harvard University.

W. Steven Barnett, Professor in the Graduate School of Education and the Graduate School of Public Policy at Rutgers University in New Brunswick, New Jersey, has broad interests in the economics of education and the ecology of human development. Much of his research is concerned with the long-term effects of early education for children disadvantaged by poverty or disabilities. Dr. Barnett directs the Center for Early Education Research (CEER) at Rutgers University, where his work includes field studies of best practices, research on the development of early childhood care and education policy, studies of the opportunities and experiences of young children in low-income urban areas, and benefit–cost analysis of preschool programs and their long-term effects. Dr. Barnett's recent publications include *Lives in the Balance* and, with Sarane Spence Boocock, *Early Care and Education for Children in Poverty*.

Margaret R. Burchinal is a Senior Scientist at the Frank Porter Graham Child Development Center and a Research Associate Professor of Developmental Psychology at the University of North Carolina at Chapel Hill. She is a methodologist who specializes in longitudinal methods, and has served as the primary statistician for many child development projects, including the NICHD Study of Early Child Care and the OERI National Center for Early Development and Learning. Dr. Burchinal is the author of more than 50 articles and chapters.

Her current research interests are in the area of identifying risk and protective factors for social and cognitive development.

Adriana G. Bus is Associate Professor at Leiden University, The Netherlands. A former reading specialist at a reading clinic, she teaches courses in reading, writing, and learning problems at the undergraduate and graduate levels. She was involved in several Dutch projects to stimulate literacy in preschool, kindergarten, and first grade, and was the founding president of the Dutch division of the International Reading Association. Dr. Bus is the author of a Dutch monograph about emergent literacy and has published articles in leading journals in the fields of education, educational psychology, and child development.

David K. Dickinson (*see* About the Editors).

Dionne R. Dobbins is a Research Analyst at the American Institutes for Research, in Washington, DC, an educational research firm. She recently completed a postdoctoral fellowship at the University of North Carolina at Chapel Hill as part of the National Center for Early Development and Learning. She served as Program Coordinator for the Carolina Family Literacy Studies, a longitudinal study of family literacy programs. Her research focuses on interventions for low-income, minority, and immigrant families.

Anne Haas Dyson is Professor of Language, Literacy, and Culture in the School of Education at the University of California, Berkeley, and a recent recipient of the University of California, Berkeley's, Distinguished Teaching Award. A former teacher of young children, she studies the social lives and literacy learning of schoolchildren. Among her publications are *The Need for Story: Cultural Diversity in*

Classroom and Community (coedited with Celia Genishi), *Social Worlds of Children Learning to Write in an Urban Primary School,* which was awarded NCTE's David Russell Award for Distinguished Research, *What Difference Does Difference Make?: Teacher Reflections on Diversity, Literacy, and the Urban Primary School* (with the San Francisco East Bay Teacher Study Group), and *Writing Superheroes: Contemporary Childhood, Popular Culture, and Classroom Literacy.* She is a coeditor of the new international *Journal of Early Childhood Literacy.*

Linda B. Gambrell is Professor and Director of the School of Education at Clemson University. She has written books on reading instruction and numerous articles that have been published in journals such as *Reading Research Quarterly, The Reading Teacher,* and *Journal of Educational Research.* Dr. Gambrell served as a Principal Investigator at the National Reading Research Center, as an elected member of the Board of Directors for the International Reading Association (IRA), and as coeditor of *The Journal of Reading Behavior,* and she received the IRA Outstanding Teacher Educator in Reading Award. Currently, she serves as President of the National Reading Conference and the College Reading Association. Her research interests include reading comprehension strategy instruction and literacy motivation.

Javier Gayan is a Research Assistant at the Institute for Behavioral Genetics and the Department of Psychology at the University of Colorado at Boulder. His research is based on the behavior genetics of reading disability, and includes twin analyses that separate the genetic and environmental influences on reading and reading disability, and genetic linkage analyses to identify genes that influence reading disability.

James Paul Gee has taught at Hampshire College in Amherst, Massachusetts, Boston University, and the University of Southern California. He also served as the Jacob Hiatt Professor of Education at Clark University in Worcester, Massachusetts. In 1998, he became the Tashia Morgridge Professor of Reading at the University of Wisconsin at Madison. He has published widely in journals in linguistics, psychology, the social sciences, and education. His books include *Sociolinguistics and Literacies, The Social Mind, Introduction to Human Language, The New Work Order* (with Glynda Hull and Colin Lankshear), and *An Introduction to Discourse Analysis.*

Virginia Goatley is an Associate Professor in the Reading Department of the University at Albany, State University of New York. A former classroom teacher, she currently teaches graduate courses on literacy difficulties, writing, and curriculum issues. She has published several articles and chapters about students experiencing literacy difficulties. Dr. Goatley is a Project Director in the National Research Center for English Learning and Achievement, which is conducting a longitudinal study on elementary students in classrooms using integrated instruction.

Claude Goldenberg is Professor of Teacher Education and Associate Dean of the College of Education, California State University, Long Beach. He is also a Research Psychologist at the University of California, Los Angeles, and a Principal Investigator for the Center for Research in Diversity and Education. He has taught junior high school in San Antonio, Texas, and first grade in a bilingual elementary school in Los Angeles. Dr. Goldenberg was a National Academy of Education Spencer Fellow in 1986 to 1988 and in 1993 was a co-recipient of the International Reading Association's Albert J. Harris Award. In 1997, he produced *Settings for Change,* a video describing a 5-year school improvement project that raised academic achievement in a largely Latino, bilingual elementary school. Dr. Goldenberg has served on the National Research Council's Head Start Research Roundtable and the Committee for the Prevention of Early Reading Difficulties in Young Children. His publications have appeared in numerous professional and research books and journals. He is currently involved in a number of projects focusing on Latino children's academic development and the processes and dynamics of school change.

Usha Goswami is Professor of Cognitive Developmental Psychology at the Institute of Child Health, University College London. Her research interests focus on the role of analogical reasoning in cognitive development, reading development, and language development. She originally trained as a teacher, and has received a number of career awards, including the British Psychology Society Spearman Medal, the Norman Geschwind–Rodin Prize (Sweden), and fellowships from the National Academy of Education (USA) and the Alexander von Humboldt Foundation (Germany). She advised on the UK National Curriculum and the UK National Literacy Project, and is on the editorial boards of the *Journal of Ex-*

perimental Child Psychology, Applied Psycholinguistics, Dyslexia, Cognitive Development, Developmental Science, and the *Journal of Child Psychology and Psychiatry.*

Carol Scheffner Hammer is an Assistant Professor of communication disorders at The Pennsylvania State University, University Park. Her research interests include language and literacy development in African American and Hispanic populations, parental beliefs about and parental support of language and literacy development, and the relationship between environmental factors and language and literacy development in children from diverse contexts and children with language impairments. Her longitudinal research investigates the language and literacy development of bilingual children attending Head Start and the relationship between the environment and bilingual preschoolers' language and literacy outcomes. This project is funded by the National Institutes of Health—National Institute of Child Health and Human Development.

Suzannah Herrmann is a doctoral student in the Educational Leadership Program in the School of Education at the University of North Carolina at Chapel Hill. For the past 2 years she has served as a project coordinator of the Carolina Family Literacy Studies, a research study of family literacy programs in North Carolina. She also has served as project coordinator for the state evaluation of the North Carolina Even Start Family Literacy Programs. Her research interests focus on family literacy, service integration, and federal education policy. She is currently conducting research on service integration in family literacy programs.

Elfrieda H. Hiebert is Professor of Literacy, Language, and Culture in the School of Education at the University of Michigan. Dr. Hiebert has worked in the field of early reading acquisition for more than 25 years, first as a teacher of primary-level students in central California and next, as a teacher educator and researcher at the University of Kentucky, the University of Colorado–Boulder, and the University of Michigan. She has published over 100 research articles and chapters on how instructional and assessment practices influence literacy acquisition, especially among low-income children. She currently has research grants to investigate the difficulty of current beginning reading textbooks and to design curricula and texts for English language learners. Professor Hiebert was awarded an Alumni

Achievement Award from the University of Wisconsin in 2000.

Marcia A. Invernizzi is an Associate Professor of Reading Education at the University of Virginia's (UVA) Curry School of Education, where she is also Director of the McGuffey Reading Center. She is the author of numerous articles in a variety of professional journals, including *The Reading Teacher, Language Arts,* the *Elementary School Journal, Annals of Dyslexia,* and the *Journal of Reading Behavior.* Her current research interests focus on early childhood prevention programs and flexible, ongoing reading interventions. She is a coauthor and the Principal Investigator of PALS, the screening tool used for Virginia's Early Intervention Reading Initiative, and Project Coordinator for UVA's America Reads program. She is also cofounder of Book Buddies, which received the 1997 Virginia State Reading Association's Literacy Award for community service.

Peter H. Johnston is a Professor at the University at Albany, State University of New York, where he is Chair of the Reading Department, and a Senior Scientist at the National Center on English Learning and Achievement. He has worked as an elementary classroom teacher and as a reading teacher. He serves on the editorial boards of *Reading Research Quarterly, Journal of Literacy Research, Elementary School Journal, The Reading Teacher,* and *Literacy, Teaching and Learning.* Dr. Johnston chaired the International Reading Association (IRA) and National Council of Teachers of English (NCTE) Joint Task Force on Assessment to produce their position monograph *Standards for the Assessment of Reading and Writing* (1994). He has written over 40 articles and three books and has been recognized with the Albert J. Harris Award by IRA for work on reading disability (1987) and "The Outstanding Learned Article" of the Educational Press Association (1996). His current research interests include literacy assessment and its consequences, and the development of a democratic literacy.

Christopher J. Lonigan is an Associate Professor of Clinical Psychology at Florida State University. Dr. Lonigan serves on the editorial board of several journals and is a member of the Executive Committee for the Division of Clinical Child and Adolescent Psychology of the American Psychological Association. The majority of his current research focuses on identifying preschool predictors of reading acquisition, evaluating preventive interventions for children at risk of reading difficulties, and examining the overlap of reading disabilities and attention-deficit/hyperactivity disorder. Much of this work, supported through grants from NICHD and DHHS, has been directed at developing and validating measures of preschool phonological processing abilities and identifying efficacious early preschool interventions for phonological processing skills.

Elizabeth Manlove is an Assistant Professor of Human Development at The Pennsylvania State University. Her research interests focus on young children and the adults who care for them, particularly fathers and child-care providers. She is currently working with Dr. Lynne Vernon-Feagans on a longitudinal study of infants who enter child care before 1 year of age. She is also working as a child-care specialist on a large-scale ethnography of low-income working families and families on public assistance. Dr. Manlove has published a number of articles on child care and child-care providers.

Leigh Ann Martin is a doctoral student at the University of Michigan School of Education. She received her master's in education (1998) from the University of Michigan and her bachelor's in computer science (1984) from Brigham Young University. Her research interests center around early reading development and the texts that support beginning readers.

Anne McGill-Franzen teaches at the University of Florida, Gainesville, where she is Associate Professor of Literacy, and co-directs several projects at the National Research Center for English Learning and Achievement, University at Albany, State University of New York. Her recent work is published in journals such as *Reading Research Quarterly, Journal of Educational Research, The Reading Teacher,* and *Educational Research.* She is the recipient of the International Reading Association's Nila Banton Smith Award for her study of the development of literacy in young children and co-recipient of the Albert J. Harris Award for research in reading disabilities.

Adele Miccio is an Assistant Professor of Communication Disorders at The Pennsylvania State University, University Park. Her research interests include phonological development in children at risk for communicative disorders, the relationship between early phonological development and later literacy problems, and intervention efficacy. Her longi-

tudinal research projects that examine the effects of chronic otitis media on early phonological development and the relationship between bilingual phonological development and emerging literacy are funded by the National Institutes of Health —National Institute of Child Health and Human Development. She is reviews editor for *Clinical Linguistics and Phonetics* and an editorial consultant for the *Journal of Speech, Language, and Hearing Research* and the *American Journal of Speech–Language Pathology.*

Lesley Mandel Morrow is Professor and Chair of the Department of Learning and Teaching at the Graduate School of Education at Rutgers University, where she is coordinator of the PhD program in Literacy. She began her career as a classroom teacher and later became a reading specialist. Her area of research deals with early literacy development with an emphasis on physical and social contexts to motivate reading. Dr. Morrow has more than 200 publications to her credit. Her articles have appeared in journals such as *Reading Research Quarterly, Journal of Educational Psychology,* and *The Reading Teacher.* Her most recent books are *Literacy Development in the Early Years: Helping Children Read and Write* and *The Literacy Center: Contexts for Reading and Writing.* She received the Rutgers University awards for research, teaching, and service, and the International Reading Association's Outstanding Teacher Educator or Reading Award from Fordham University. She also served as an elected member of the International Reading Association.

Susan B. Neuman (*see* About the Editors).

Rebecca S. New is currently an Associate Professor of Child Development and Director of Teacher Education at the Eliot–Pearson Department of Child Development at Tufts University. She joined the field of early education in the late 1960s as a primary school teacher in Florida public schools, where she developed interests in home–school relations, multicultural education, and collaborative curricula. Her research interests in the cultural psychology of child development and early education have focused primarily on Italian early care and education. She played a major role in critiquing and revising the NAEYC document on developmentally appropriate practice, and coedited (with Bruce Mallory) *Diversity and Developmentally Appropriate Practices: Challenges for Early Childhood Education.* Other recent and/or ongoing professional activities include consultation with Early Head Start programs and the National Research Council's Committee on Early Childhood Pedagogy, and participation in the 12-nation review of early care and education policies sponsored by the Organization for Economic and Cooperative Development.

Richard K. Olson is Professor of Psychology at the University of Colorado at Boulder, Associate Director of the Center for the Study of Learning Disabilities, and President Elect of the Society for the Scientific Study of Reading. His research has focused on the genetic and environmental etiology of reading disabilities through the comparison of identical and fraternal twins' behavior and DNA, and on the use of talking computers in the schools for the remediation of reading disabilities.

A. D. Pellegrini is a Professor of Educational Psychology at the University of Minnesota, where he teaches courses on research methods and on peer relations and aggression. Recent honors include election as a Fellow of the American Psychological Association (Educational and Developmental) and as an Honorary Professor of Human Development at Cardiff University (UK). His recent research interests center around two areas: social interaction bases of cognition and social dominance.

Donald J. Richgels is a Professor in the Department of Literacy Education at Northern Illinois University, where he teaches undergraduate and graduate courses in language arts, reading, and language development. He is the coauthor, with Lea McGee, of *Literacy's Beginnings: Supporting Young Readers and Writers*. Dr. Richgels's work has appeared in *Language and Speech, Reading Research Quarterly, Journal of Reading Behavior, The Reading Teacher, Journal of Educational Research*, and *Early Childhood Research Quarterly*. His current research interests are preschool and kindergarten classroom practice and the relationship between spoken language acquisition and literacy development.

Joanne E. Roberts is a Senior Scientist at the Frank Porter Graham Child Development Center at the University of North Carolina at Chapel Hill (UNC) and a Research Professor of Pediatrics and Speech and Hearing Sciences at UNC. Dr. Roberts has written over 55 articles and book chapters on the speech and language development of at-risk children and children with disabilities published in speech–language, pediatric, and early childhood journals and books. She currently serves as Principal Investigator of grants on the communication skills of young children funded by the National Institute on Deafness and Other Communication Disorders and the Maternal and Child Health Bureau. Her current research focuses on the relationship of otitis media to children's later language and school performance, the early language and literacy skills of African American children, and the communication skills of young males with fragile X syndrome.

Rebecca Rogers is Assistant Professor of Education at Washington University in St. Louis. She has worked as a reading teacher in both elementary and adult basic education classrooms. Dr. Rogers was awarded a Lillian Barlow Scholarship for Women to support research on the intersection of gender, literacy, and identity. She was also awarded the 2000 National Reading Conference "Student Researcher of the Year" award. Dr. Rogers teaches undergraduate and graduate courses in reading assessment and discourse, and ethnography at Washington University.

Kathleen Roskos is a Professor in Education at John Carroll University, where she teaches courses in reading instruction and reading diagnosis. Her research includes early literacy development, teacher cognition, and the design of professional education for teachers. She has published research articles on these topics in leading journals and also has coauthored or coedited books in these areas. Currently, Dr. Roskos is coordinating a state-wide project that seeks to enhance the professional teaching of reading through school-based professional development and learning.

Terry Salinger is a managing research associate at the Pelavin Research Center of the American Institutes for Research (AIR) in Washington, DC. Dr. Salinger is currently project director for the development of kindergarten through grade-10 tests for the school district of Philadelphia and co-project director for the federally funded project evaluating the effectiveness of Goals 2000 initiatives in reading and language arts. She served as deputy director for test development for the Voluntary National Tests. Prior to joining AIR, Dr. Salinger was the director of research at the International Reading Association (IRA). Among her responsibilities at IRA was project leadership for the IRA/NCTE National Standards for English Language Arts. She is widely published in the areas of early literacy and assessment

Donna M. Scanlon recently joined the faculty in the Department of Reading and Special Education at the College of St. Rose, where she is involved in the preparation of reading teachers. She is also the Associate Director of the Child Research and Study Center at the University at Albany, State University of New York. Her research has centered on the cognitive characteristics of children who experience substantial difficulty in learning to read and on the efficacy of various instructional approaches in reducing the incidence of long-term reading difficulties. Most of this research has been supported by grants from the National Institute of Child Health and Human Development. The results of this programmatic research have been presented in numerous book chapters and in a variety of journals.

Hollis S. Scarborough is a developmental psychologist whose primary research focus is the relationship between spoken and written language from the preschool years through adulthood. Her published work includes reviews and empirical studies of the preschool antecedents of reading disabilities, the prediction of reading achievement, the assessment of children's language abilities, and related topics. She recently served on the National Research Council's Committee on the Prevention of Reading Difficulties in Young Children, and is currently on the governing board of the Society for the Scientific Study of Reading and on the editorial boards of the *Journal of Learning Disabilities, Applied Psycholinguistics,* and the *Annals of Dyslexia.* She is a Senior Research Scientist at Haskins Laboratories and holds faculty appointments at the City University of New York and at Bryn Mawr College.

Catherine E. Snow is the Henry Lee Shattuck Professor in Human Development and Psychology at the Harvard Graduate School of Education. She teaches graduate courses in language development, bilingualism, and writing development. She served as president of AERA (1999–2000), is editor of *Applied Psycholinguistics,* and is chair of the Rand–OERI Reading Study Group. Dr. Snow has written more than 100 articles, chapters, monographs, and books. Her current research interests include how language skills relate to literacy and second-language literacy acquisition. She is also involved in collaborative efforts to rethink the content needs of teacher education around literacy.

Kimberley E. Sprague is a Research Associate at the Center for Children and Families at the Education Development Center (EDC). She was trained in research methods at Harvard's Graduate School of Education and Abt Associates, Inc., where she was an analyst. Ms. Sprague is now leading the analysis work of the New England Quality Research Center at EDC. Prior to her work at EDC and Abt, she was a preschool teacher.

Steven A. Stahl is Professor of Reading Education at the University of Georgia and is Co-Director of the Center for the Improvement of Early Reading Achievement. He also is the Director of the University of Georgia Reading Clinic. Dr. Stahl was a consultant to the National Reading Panel and a principal investigator at both the Center for the Study of Reading and the National Reading Research Center. Dr. Stahl's research interests center around the effective instruction of reading. Recently, he has concentrated on issues in beginning reading, especially decoding and phonological awareness instruction.

Dorothy S. Strickland is the State of New Jersey Professor of Reading at Rutgers University. A former classroom teacher, reading consultant, and learning disabilities specialist, she is past president of both the International Reading Association (IRA) and the IRA Reading Hall of Fame. She is active in the National Council of Teachers of English (NCTE), in which she has held numerous offices, and in the National Association for the Education of Young Children. Dr. Strickland received IRA's Outstanding Teacher Educator of Reading Award, NCTE's award as Outstanding Educator in the Language Arts, and the NCTE Rewey Belle Inglis Award as Outstanding Woman in the Teaching of English. Included among her publications are *Families: Poems Celebrating the African American Experience; The Administration and Supervision of Reading Programs; Emerging Literacy: Young Children Learn to Read and Write; Language, Literacy, and the Child; Teaching Phonics Today;* and *Beginning Reading and Writing.*

Patton O. Tabors has been a Research Associate at the Harvard Graduate School of Education since 1987. During that time she has been involved in research related to language and literacy acquisition of both English-speaking and second-language-learning children. Dr. Tabors has been the research coordinator for the Home–School Study of Language and Literacy Development, the MDRC/Child Trends Embedded Observational Study of

Mother–Child Interaction, and the Harvard Language Diversity Project, a subproject of the New England Quality Research Center on Head Start. Dr. Tabors is the author of *One Child, Two Languages: A Guide for Preschool Educators of Children Learning English as a Second Language* and the coeditor, with David Dickinson, of *Beginning Literacy with Language: Young Children Learning at Home and School.*

Frank R. Vellutino currently holds joint appointments in the Department of Psychology, the Department of Educational and Counseling Psychology, and the Program in Linguistics and Cognitive Science (Department of Anthropology) at the University at Albany, State University of New York. He is also Director of the Child Research and Study Center at the University at Albany. His research has been devoted to developing an understanding of the cognitive underpinnings of literacy development with special emphasis on the causes and correlates of difficulties in learning to read. His most recent work has been concerned with the use of early identification and early intervention to reduce the incidence of protracted reading difficulties in beginning readers and to assist in developing more accurate criteria for identifying children at risk for reading difficulties and diagnosing reading disability. Though his research has been supported by a variety of public and private funding agencies, most of his research funding has been provided by the National Institute of Child Health and Human Development. Dr. Vellutino is the author of numerous research publications, including a scholarly text, many journal articles, numerous book chapters, and several invited reviews and position papers.

Lynne Vernon-Feagans is Associate Dean for Research and Professor of Human Development at The Pennsylvania State University. Her area of interest over the last 25 years has been young children at risk for language and literacy problems. Her research has examined children with learning disabilities, children in poverty, and children who have chronic problems with otitis media. She is currently directing a $3 million NICHD-funded longitudinal study of infants who enter day care before 1 year of age. The focus of the grant is to understand the health, language, and social processes at home and in day care that lead to school readiness and adjustment. She is also one of the Associate Editors of the *International Journal of Behavioral Development.* Dr. Ver-

non-Feagans has published widely and is the author of a recent book on the transition to school for a group of low-income African American children, which focuses on language at home and at school.

Barbara Hanna Wasik is a psychologist on the faculty of the School of Education at the University of North Carolina at Chapel Hill (UNC). She is also a Fellow of the UNC Frank Porter Graham Child Development Center and the Director of the UNC Center for Home Visiting. She has devoted most of her professional career to the study of prevention and intervention programs for young children at risk for social or academic difficulties. She currently directs the Carolina Family Literacy Studies project, a longitudinal study of intergenerational family literacy programs. She is a member of the Board of Educational Affairs of the American Psychological Association, Chair of the American Psychological Association Task Force on Early Education and Care, a member of the National Advisory Board of the Parents as Teachers National Center, and a member of the National Academy of Science's Committee on Early Childhood Pedagogy. She is the author of over 80 publications, including books, chapters, and journal articles.

Rita Watson currently holds the Wolens Chair in Educational Research at the School of Education, the Hebrew University of Jerusalem, and was formerly Associate Professor of Educational Psychology at the University of British Columbia, Canada. Her current primary area of research and teaching is the development and interrelation of language and cognition, particularly as they are influenced by cultural and social contexts. Her papers on the consequences of pragmatics and literacy for definitions and cognition in general have been published in the *Journal of Child Language* and other journals and edited collections.

Grover J. Whitehurst is Leading Professor of Psychology, Professor of Pediatrics, and Chairman of the Department of Psychology at the State University of New York at Stony Brook. His research focuses on the prevention of reading problems in children from low-income backgrounds and the nature and consequences of early language delay. He has developed a shared-picturebook reading technique with young children, called Dialogic Reading, widely used by parents and teachers in the United States and other countries. Dr. Whitehurst serves on a number of national panels and advisory groups, including the National Research Council's Committee on Early Childhood Pedagogy and the U.S. Department of Health and Human Services' Committee on Head Start Research and Evaluation. He cur- rently directs nationwide projects to enhance emergent literacy and prevent reading difficul- ties for the National Center for Learning Dis- abilities and the Public Library Association. He is a recipient of the Microsoft Innovators in Higher Education Award.

Contents

I. WAYS OF CONCEPTUALIZING EARLY LITERACY DEVELOPMENT

II. STRANDS OF EARLY LITERACY DEVELOPMENT

III. HOME AND COMMUNITY INFLUENCES

IV. SCHOOLING INFLUENCES: THE PRESCHOOL YEARS

V. INSTRUCTIONAL MATERIALS AND CLASSROOM PRACTICES

VI. SPECIAL INTERVENTION EFFORTS

I
WAYS OF CONCEPTUALIZING EARLY LITERACY DEVELOPMENT

1

Introduction

❖

SUSAN B. NEUMAN
DAVID K. DICKINSON

This is an exciting time for research in early literacy development. Consider the major strides in recent years in our understanding of children's development as literacy learners. Holding a grip on the profession for over 50 years, the reading-readiness perspective, the view that learning to read was a product of development, is now widely discredited. Moreover, the emergent literacy perspective, the understanding that literacy development begins long before children start formal instruction, is now largely taken for granted. Today, there is consensus, strikingly demonstrated by the degree of convergence in recent reports, that children are doing critical cognitive work in literacy development from birth through 6 and that quality instruction makes a vital contribution in these years to children's success as readers and writers.

This handbook represents what we would consider the now-and-future phase of work in early literacy. Perhaps less dazzling than the changes in perspective of the last century, yet no less important, researchers are beginning to fine-tune their understandings of literacy and development. Whereas once there were perspectives, now researchers are generating theory—complicated understandings of cognitive processing models in oral and written language, sociocultural models that focus on the integration of context and cognition, and ecological and environmental theories that examine children's formal and informal learning of written language development in school and nonschool settings. And, theory development in early literacy is not a minor accomplishment. Unlike the perspectives of the past, these theories have provided us with an understanding of the complexity of literacy learning as well as some tangible evidence for better understanding how it can be developed, nurtured, and taught. At this same time, it provides us with a daunting list of challenges for understanding how literacy achievement can be a right and not a privilege for all children.

Clearly this handbook signals that the study of early literacy has come of age. The chapters are authored by some of the most prestigious researchers of written language development for young children. They come from a variety of disciplinary perspectives—child development, psychology, linguistics, reading, and social policy. And this was by design. When first considering a handbook, it became clear that early literacy crossed the traditional boundaries of discipline; it could not be adequately addressed by one field or by a limited group of scholars. Thus the strength of this volume is the complex, varied, and multidisciplinary views it brings to the study of young children and their understandings of print.

Across the chapters in this volume, we see several points of particular energy around theoretical and practical issues, all of which we anticipate will be active areas for the advancement of theory and practice in the coming years. The fact that such concentrations have appeared reflects the maturing of the study of early literacy; theoretical positions are emerging and instructional approaches are taking shape and are being subjected to serious empirical scrutiny. But as increasingly well-articulated perspectives mature, the challenge of keeping abreast of developments in related, yet distinct, areas grows. We hope that this volume will help promote cross-fertilization of theories and practices among those who are addressing similar issues from distinct perspectives. To this end we first discuss several major themes and then briefly review key points made in each of the chapters in the volume in the hope that they will help readers locate those chapters with material of interest to them.

One trend evident in several chapters is interest in identifying the literacy-related cognitive and linguistic capacities that emerge during the preschool years. There is general agreement about the relevant set of abilities needing study and, in particular, broad recognition of the significance of phonemic awareness to early reading. Efforts now are under way to understand the emergence of and long-term contributions to reading and writing of varied oral language abilities. Oral language has long been assumed to play a role in reading and writing; now researchers are examining these links more fully as they strive to understand the relationships between various aspects of language and literacy. Although there is general agreement that vocabulary plays a central role in reading, the picture for syntax and discourse-level skills is far less clear. Our ignorance of the role of oral language in literacy is especially evident when one considers second-language learners.

Another noteworthy and heartening development in the area of early literacy studies is the appearance of theories that provide theoretical descriptions of the causal mechanisms that support or impede various aspects of literacy functioning and development. One example of such work is the lexical restructuring hypothesis, which posits that the emergence of phonological awareness is driven by the child's level of lexical

development in conjunction with the phonological and lexical structure of his or her language. Cognitive models of the reading process also are being developed by cognitive science; these hold promise both for providing explanations of reading and for guiding instructional practice. On a different front are efforts to understand the biological mechanisms that underpin literacy. Such work is progressing at varied levels, ranging from genetic studies to examination of brain functioning to consideration of the sensory system and theories of how biological malfunctions might interfere with literacy functioning and development.

As some are constructing increasingly sophisticated cognitive models, others are turning their attention to the social context and developing theories that articulate the place of the social world in literacy and its development. Some researchers who work from the sociocultural approach are demonstrating how careful examination of literacy in use reveals the depth to which the social context and children's attitudes and beliefs about themselves determine how to make sense of and to employ literacy. Others place literacy development in broader contexts, as they seek to understand ways in which literacy practices have evolved over the centuries. Far and away the most common way that the role of social context is considered is examination of the impact of children's experiences with peers and families on their emerging literacy capacities. The energy that is going into research on the links between children's experiences and literacy development reflects the sense of urgency that results from an awareness of the serious gap in achievement between children from different social, racial, and linguistic backgrounds.

This sense of urgency is being increasingly fueled by growing evidence of remarkable and sobering long-term stability in children's literacy-related skills from the preschool years until high school. We have little understanding of the dynamics that help to account for this stability and are only beginning to learn whether there is greater malleability in the early years, and the extent to which early interventions can affect changes that endure.

The amount of research and instructional effort being expended in efforts to ameliorate the achievement gap give testimony to the widespread recognition of the need of our society to understand and address the needs of children who are falling behind. Research reported in many chapters reveals how recognition of the urgent need to enrich the learning opportunities of young children has been translated into interventions that draw on understanding of the cognitive and linguistic dimensions of reading as well as understanding of the importance of social dynamics context. Broadgauged interventions designed to enhance children's development in the preschool years are being found to have beneficial effects. These costly omnibus approaches that have been employed with preschool-age children now are being augmented by efforts that target language and literacy skills and are delivered through the family, home visitors, and preschool teachers.

As we have become increasingly aware of the long-term impact of initial reading success in first grade, a number of intensive interventions have been developed to assist struggling beginning readers. Some address children's needs with one-on-one tutoring, others consider the extent to which classrooms provide children needed phonics, and still others emphasize the importance of providing children carefully selected reading materials as well as varied opportunities for meaningful uses of literacy.

Increasingly, instructional innovations are being subjected to careful scrutiny. As a result, we have solid data indicating that children are reading better as a result of improved classroom materials, increased use of phonics instruction in classrooms that include writing and reading, and one-on-one tutoring delivered by trained professionals as well as volunteers and paraprofessionals. However, we have reason for only cautious optimism because often interventions that initially appear to hold great promise later turn out to have limitations in the breadth, amount, or longevity of impact. Similarly, laudatory public efforts to bring about major changes by sweeping legislation or mandating accountability through testing have proved to have mixed results at best.

As we enter the 21st century, we carry with us recognition that the preschool years play a critical role in children's long-term literacy success, emerging theories designed to explain how development occurs, and a growing array of interventions designed to bolster children's growth prior to school entry and to support those who struggle as they face the daunting challenges of early decoding. Increasingly we can ground our efforts to support children's growth in theoretical explanations of literacy and its development. Despite these hopeful signs, we also must acknowledge that we are far from understanding the intricacies of literacy development, and we have only an imperfect grasp of the complex interplay between children's culturally laden experiences in their homes and communities and their capacity to succeed with the literacy demands of school. The intellectual energy displayed by the authors of these chapters and the dedication of practitioners reflected in the work reported give testimony to the fact that, in the coming decade, we will assuredly make enormous intellectual strides that are linked to important advances in our ability to meet the literacy needs of all children.

Contents of the Volume

We have grouped the chapters into sections that reflect similar sets of issues. In many cases the placement of chapters was relatively straightforward, but in other cases a single chapter addresses issues that are germane to several sections. To aid the readers in finding their way among those chapters that most interest them, we provide some cross-referencing between chapters, highlighting those that may appear in other sections but which address related issues. To further assist the readers in locating material we briefly review each chapter, emphasizing one or two key elements.

Part I, "Ways of Conceptualizing Early Literacy Development," contains chapters that address broad questions about the nature of early literacy development from different theoretical perspectives. In Chapter 2, Grover J. Whitehurst and Christopher J. Lonigan discuss the development of literacy from the emergent literacy period into the primary grades. Adopting a cognitive perspective, they identify two clusters of skills: inside-out, phonological and print-related knowledge from the printed word that is employed to translate sounds to print and print to sounds, and outside-in, lexical and conceptual knowledge that is brought from outside the written text and used to construct meaning. They trace the developmental pathways of these clusters and describe high levels of stability within clusters and, using these data, stress the need to intervene during the preschool years.

Chapter 3 presents a contrasting theoretical perspective, as James Paul Gee, working from a sociocultural perspective, introduces the concepts rooted in the New Literacy Studies approach to language and literacy. He stresses the extent to which literacy is intertwined with attitudes, beliefs, and ways of talking and behaving, arguing that literacy is not a general capacity; rather, people adopt varying socially constrained ways of using language and print as they construct meaning. He employs core concepts from this approach as he works through a detailed example that illustrates insights one can gain from using this approach.

In Chapter 4, Rita Watson also draws on a sociocultural approach, placing literacy within historical and developmental perspectives. First she draws on historical and cultural explanations, considering claims about the impact of literacy on thought and discourse and arguing that literacy practices have the capacity to amplify sets of existing cognitive characteristics. Then, she examines claims about the relationships between children's oral language skills and literacy acquisition and concludes that the verdict is still out on the impact of selected language skills on literacy but that there is strong evidence of the impact of literacy practices on language.

In Chapter 5, Anthony D. Pellegrini addresses themes earlier raised by both Gee and Watson, as he considers the impact of social contexts on literacy development. In contrast to Watson, he argues that early skill using "literate language" plays an important role in supporting later literacy skills. Similar to Gee, he argues that to develop adequate understanding of language and literacy, we need to attend to the contexts of interaction. Drawing on ethological theory and methodology he illustrates how these tools can be used to help researchers understand the contexts of literacy acquisition.

In Chapter 6, Marilyn J. Adams reviews relationships between phonemic awareness, phonics instruction, and reading and employs a cognitive science perspective as she shows how the parallel distributed processing models help explain the reading process and also help explain the cognitive base for some common misconceptions about the nature of reading. She addresses the critical difference between initial learning of new patterns and practicing previously established connections and uses her theoretical approach to help elucidate why enjoyable activities and games play such a prominent and effective role in supporting children's grasp of phonemic awareness.

Part I ends with Richard K. Olson's discussion of the data that make clear the contributions to literacy that are made by biology. In Chapter 7, Olson reviews data from twin studies and draws the conclusion that they point to the heritability of reading skills, with phonemic awareness being especially strongly influenced by genetic factors. Further evidence of the impact of genetic factors on reading comes from DNA studies. Finally, Olson discusses efforts to link reading behavior to biological functioning through examination of brain morphology and activity.

Part II, "Strands of Early Literacy Development," includes chapters that examine various strands of knowledge and skills that emerge as children become literate. In Chapter 8, Hollis S. Scarborough examines continuities and discontinuities in language skills and links between language and reading ability from the preschool years into the early grades. She points to data illustrating clear evidence of long-term stability in language skills and argues that current conceptions of the causes of reading difficulties need to be reconsidered. Drawing on medical analogies, she outlines two alternatives to the causal chain models typically employed. She also argues that we need to recognize that development may occur in fits and starts and that this uneven pattern of growth may have important consequences for researchers and diagnosticians.

In Chapter 9, Usha Goswami examines phonological development, its connections to oral language development, and its relationship to literacy. Taking a cognitive science approach, she reviews research on the lexical restructuring hypothesis, which is that vocabulary growth is causally related to phonological awareness because it precipitates a restructuring in how lexical items are stored, leading to storing of words in smaller units which can be examined and compared. She then discusses how phonological awareness and early reading are related, drawing on the lexical restructuring theory, and concludes by showing how the same approach can help explain the impact of environments on phonological awareness development.

In Chapter 10, Anne Haas Dyson examines children's writing as a process of meaning construction that draws on the full range of symbolic and textual resources at a child's disposal. Dyson analyzes the ways in which children come to understand the written symbolic system while learning to construct meaning within the social world of classrooms. Writing development, she argues, involves differentiation of the elements of the written symbol system and understanding of the new social practices of school and their underlying ideological values. She argues that her perspective can enable classrooms to value the cultural and linguistic resources of children from diverse backgrounds.

Part II concludes with Chapter 11, in which Donald Richgels provides a historical perspective on research and classroom practices since the 1970s. Using Charles Read's seminal article on invented spelling, he traces key notions such as the insight that spelling is a developmental phenomena and investigations of "language awareness" that later focused on phonemic awareness. Richgels then examines the intertwined history of research on phonemic awareness, writing development and classroom practices and argues that hopeful new directions in research and practice may flow from recent studies that examine the value of phonics instruction that is closely tied to writing and writing instruction.

Part III, "Home and Community Influences," includes chapters on the compelling issues of language acquisition and language diversity, and children's prospects for literacy achievement. Patton O. Tabors and Catherine E. Snow, in Chapter 12, describe bilingual development for children from birth to age 8 and examine the multiple pathways and multiple influences for literacy acquisition. Their research indicates that some approaches involve consistent support for a child's bilingualism while others, although leading to the acquisition of English language and literacy skills, may be dead-ends for bilingualism or biliteracy. They offer guidelines for educators in developing programs for young bilingual children.

In Chapter 13, Adriana G. Bus examines the rich research base for reading aloud to children frequently and conversationally. From the theoretical lens of the attachment hypothesis, she describes how relationships between caregiver and child, secure or insecure, influence the types and qualities of the conversation in storybook reading. These qualitative differences are related to children's developing understanding of decontextualized language and their motivation to read.

Chapters 14 and 15 focus on the challenges we face in making schools work for all children. Lynne Vernon-Feagans and her colleagues, in Chapter 14, describe the skills and experiences of children in poverty, highlighting research from the preschool Abecedarian project. Their findings cut across many of the issues described in other chapters, related to the causal factors related to poor school achievement. Like Tabors and Snow, they argue that any causal explanation of the poor performance in reading of poor children must take into account multiple factors, including the biological/health factors, the environments in which poor children live, and the discrimination created by the schools and larger society. Following on this theme, Claude Goldenberg, in Chapter 15, suggests that although progress has been made, achievement remains elusive for far too many children from low-income families. His research examines the home and neighborhood of urban and rural children from African American and Hispanic families, examining similarities and differences that exist cross-culturally and between socioeconomic groups with respect to the preliteracy language experience and skills most privileged in these cultures. Both of these chapters emphasize the importance of looking beyond educational interventions to the integration of programs, policies, and services in the community, with the schools being one of but many agencies to serve families and children.

Part III ends with a thoughtful analysis by Joanne E. Roberts and Margaret R. Burchinal, in Chapter 16, of the complex interplay between biology and environment. In contrast to Vernon-Feagan's findings from the Abecedarian project on the lasting effects of otitis media on language and literacy acquisition, Roberts reports on the mediating effects of instruction. Conducting several longitudinal studies, she and her colleagues find that high-quality, intensive instruction may overcome initial delays in language development, with children eventually reading at grade level. This chapter essentially argues, as many in this section, that effective programs that are carefully targeted to the special needs of these learners can ameliorate language and literacy differences.

Part IV, "Schooling Influences: The Preschool Years," examines instruction in the early years. Rebecca S. New, in Chapter 17, emphasizes a situated perspective, viewing literacy as a context-specific, sociocultural activity. Spending much time in Italy, she supports her image of early-childhood education with the Italian belief of schooling as a system of relations with parents and community. Here, literacy is not seen as an end in itself but, rather, as a starting point to consider individual and social educational goals and actions. Thus, literacy activity is a dynamic process and not to be defined as achievement on test scores.

David K. Dickinson and Kimberley E. Sprague in Chapter 18 examine the nature of care children receive in the preschool years, and the impact quality has on children's language and literacy development. Converging results from three studies suggest that deficits in language can be improved in preschool settings. High-quality language experiences in preschool classrooms affect the vocabulary and early literacy development, especially for those children from low-income families; thus qualitative changes in these settings may have enduring effects possibly lasting well into the middle school years.

In Chapter 19, Kathleen Roskos and Susan B. Neuman focus on a particular aspect of quality in early literacy classrooms for preschoolers—the physical and social environment. Through a series of intervention studies, they develop basic principles for the placement of props in settings to foster more complex literacy interactions, which may be applied generally to other preschool classrooms. These studies provide evidence for the power and the limitations of the physical environment, leading to a more complex interpretation of environment as activity setting. They argue that activity setting, which includes the physical environment, the social environment, and goal-directed activity, may enhance the quality of language interactions and vocabulary and provide better understandings of the purposes and functions of literacy.

Frank R. Vellutino and Donna M. Scanlon in Chapter 20 take a cognitive perspective, viewing literacy impairment as a result of limitations in early reading experiences or quality instruction, which is highly amenable to early intervention. They argue that the majority of children who experience early reading difficulties can become functional readers if they are provided with early and intensive remediation tailored to their individual strengths and needs, providing confirmation that reading difficulties are caused by experiential and instructional deficits rather than by neurodevelopment deficits.

Thus, chapters in Part IV emphasize how preschool programs may be tailored to different definitions of literacy, and how children may learn from these specialized environments.

Part V, "Instructional Materials and Classroom Practices," digs deeper into specific instructional practices and constituent skills that support literacy attainment for children who have difficulty in reading. Dorothy S. Strickland, in Chapter 21, examines the shift in emphasis from remedial programs for educating young African American children to early-intervention programs. She describes a number of research-based representative programs and argues, as others in this volume, that the coordination of social services along with the quality of learning experiences with clear and focused guidelines is necessary to improve instruction, not only for young African American children but for all children judged to be at high risk for academic difficulty.

In Chapter 22, Steven A. Stahl addresses the important role of phonics and phonological awareness teaching in the early years. He takes an historical perspective, looking at Jeanne Chall's, *Learning to Read: The Great Debate,* and suggests that some of the recent concerns about phonics teaching are remarkably similar to those years ago. For example, he indicates that the recent furor over the research findings by Barbara Foorman and her colleagues at the University of Texas, is not unlike the research findings of Chall (i.e., that systematic, synthetic approaches to phonics instruction tends to be more powerful than other approaches). Reviewing different approaches to teaching phonics and phonological awareness, Stahl emphasizes critical teaching principles for young struggling readers.

But the issue of balance, providing skill instruction with opportunities to enjoy and develop critical understandings from books, continues to concern many researchers. Lesley Mandel Morrow and Linda B. Gambrell, in Chapter 23, argue for the benefits of literature-based instruction, particularly in these early years. These researchers suggest that literature provides special motivation to read and to learn skills in the context of real reading. However, professional development opportunities are critical for quality implementation. Teachers' knowledge of quality literature and their understanding of genre, use, and functions of literature in content areas are necessary for effective practice.

Elfrieda H. Hiebert and Leigh Ann Martin, in Chapter 24, bring these issues of phonological awareness, phonics, and literature-based instruction to bear in reviewing the texts for beginning readers. The researchers tackle the question of how reading acquisition may be facilitated or hindered by different types of texts, looking at systematic phonics instruction and how different words are acquired through these texts. Examining the research on current texts recently published, and the match between the texts and patterns from word-learning studies, Hiebert and Martin show rather dramatic shifts in textbooks over the past 20 years. Without systematic research on text features, they suggest that the vacillation evident in textbooks over the past 20 years is likely to continue.

The final two chapters in this section offer contrasting views of assessment in early literacy. Peter H. Johnston and Rebecca Rogers, in Chapter 25, make a strong case

for document assessment, the broad repertoire of behaviors involved in noting, recording, and interpreting children's behaviors and performances. Contrary to standardized measurement, documentation is interpretive, focused on better understanding the child and his or her developing identity as a literacy learner. Because teachers are the primary assessment agents in early childhood, Johnston and Rogers suggest that we need to create a community of teachers who are sensitive observers/listeners and able to document a child's development without resorting to a discourse of disability and deficit.

Terry Salinger, on the other hand, in Chapter 26, sees a role for objective-based measurement. Describing the many purposes for assessment, she argues for multiple assessments, or systems to more accurately calibrate children's progress both within classrooms and across classroom boundaries. Scoring collected evidence can help teachers move beyond their intuitive interpretations, having far-reaching effects on the early-childhood instructional program. Both arguments in Chapters 25 and 26 are persuasive and provide evidence for the reasons that assessment has remained such a controversial topic in early literacy.

This volume concludes with Part VI, "Special Intervention Efforts," with Chapter 27 by W. Steven Barnett, providing a review of the literature on the impact of child care, preschool, and early-intervention programs on children's development. After briefly discussing evidence of short-term effects, Barnett examines in more detail 37 studies that meet stringent criteria, including that children be followed from the preschool years beyond age 8. He argues that what appears to be a fading out of effects in the later primary grades actually reflects methodological weaknesses. Rather than fading effects, he claims that available evidence points to enduring impact of early-care environments on children's reading skills and achievement without continuing school-age interventions.

In Chapter 28, Barbara Hanna Wasik and her colleagues discuss family literacy programs and the complex issues that surround such programs. They review research on programs that strive to foster children's development by enhancing the literacy skills of parents and conclude that there is only limited empirical evidence for the effectiveness of these efforts. However, they point to hopeful findings that program intensity and direct child services are consistently important aspects of family literacy programs. Then, using a typology of approaches to work with, they describe those programs that coach families in valued practices and those that strive to understand a family's world view and create interventions that build on parents' strengths.

In Chapter 29, Marcia A. Invernizzi discusses the use of one-on-one tutoring programs. Noting that between 20 and 45% of the children in school systems are identified as having reading difficulties, she argues that these numbers can be reduced significantly through tutoring programs. She discusses trade-offs involved with various tutorial approaches and, drawing on the experiences of two programs that use volunteers and paraprofessionals, argues that such tutors can be effective when provided appropriate training and support. She closes with a case study of a school-based tutoring program that shows how tutoring efforts can be integrated with the broader instructional program of a school.

The final chapter in this section and the book (Chapter 30) is by Anne McGill-Franzen and Virginia Goatley, who examine the evolution of Title 1 and Special Education from 1965 to the present. They trace the shift from simple distribution of resources to use of funds to deliver services within classrooms, to support schoolwide reform efforts, and for programs that serve children in preschool through first grade. Acknowledging that many teachers lack needed skills, they point to evidence of the beneficial effects of the Early Literacy Project, a professional development effort found to improve classroom instruction and children's learning. They conclude by discussing organizational changes that may have beneficial effects.

Thus, these chapters suggest that research in early literacy has come far in this past decade. Although acknowledging these advances, still critical challenges remain for the future. Among them:

• Great concern over the achievement gap between children from middle- and low-income minority communities. Despite our increasing knowledge base in the skills and strategies predictive of achievement, it remains unclear whether we have found ways to improve and sustain reading success over the long term.

• Clearly, there are no easy answers to improving children's achievement, no magic bullets, and no inoculations. Basing early interventions on skills without greater sensitivity to the purposes and practices and developing identities of children is likely not to be effective in the long run.

• We must acknowledge different theories of learning and recognize that individual children are likely to learn in different ways. Because there tend to be multiple reasons for children's lack of success in learning to read, there must be multiple pathways to ensure that they do.

• Those children who struggle most in school are likely to need help from a number of different social agencies, school specialists, teachers, and health care providers. Coordination of school, family, and social services is critical for the well-being, growth, and development of children.

• Professional development of teachers and specialists is the most important factor for ensuring quality instruction. We are likely to remain a nation of haves and have-nots until we provide the knowledge, skills, and resources necessary to professionalize our work force in the early-childhood years.

2

Emergent Literacy: Development from Prereaders to Readers

❖

GROVER J. WHITEHURST
CHRISTOPHER J. LONIGAN

Learning to read is a key milestone for children living in a literate society. Reading skills provide a critical part of the foundation for children's academic success. Children who read well read more and, as a result, acquire more knowledge in numerous domains (Cunningham & Stanovich, 1998; Echols, West, Stanovich, & Zehr, 1996; Morrison, Smith, & Dow-Ehrensberger, 1995). Nagy and Anderson (1984, p. 328) estimated that the number of words read in a year by a middle-school child who is an avid reader might approach 10,000,000, compared to 100,000 for the least motivated middle-school reader. By virtue of the sheer volume read, substantial advantages in vocabulary and content knowledge accrue to children who are avid readers. In contrast, children who lag behind in their reading skills receive less practice in reading than do other children (Allington, 1984), miss opportunities to develop reading comprehension strategies (Brown, Palincsar, & Purcell, 1986), often encounter reading material that is too advanced for their skills (Allington, 1984), and acquire negative attitudes about reading itself (Oka & Paris, 1987). Such processes lead to what Stanovich (e.g., 1986) termed a "Matthew effect" (i.e., the rich get richer while the poor get poorer) such that those children with poor reading skills fall further and fur-

ther behind their more literate peers in reading as well as in other academic areas (Chall, Jacobs, & Baldwin, 1990).

More than one in three children experience significant difficulties in learning to read (Adams, 1990; Shaywitz, Escobar, Shaywitz, Fletcher, & Makuch, 1992), and there is strong continuity between the skills with which children enter school and their later academic performance. Those children who experience early difficulties in learning to read are unlikely to catch up to their peers (Baydar, Brooks-Gunn, & Furstenberg, 1993; Francis, Shaywitz, Stuebing, Shaywitz, & Fletcher, 1996; Stevenson & Newman, 1986; Torgesen, Wagner, Rashotte, Alexander, & Conroy, 1997; Tramontana, Hooper, & Selzer, 1988). For instance, Juel (1988) reported that the probability that children would remain poor readers at the end of the fourth grade if they were poor readers at the end of the first grade was .88. Children who enter school with limited reading-related skills are at high risk of qualifying for special education services. In fact, the majority of school-age children who are evaluated for special education services are referred because of unsatisfactory progress in reading (Lentz, 1988). Of those children who experience serious problems with reading, from 10 to 15% eventually drop out of high school and only 2% complete a 4-year college program. Surveys of adolescents and young adults with criminal records show that about half have reading difficulties. Similarly, about half of youths with a history of substance abuse have reading problems (National Institute of Child Health and Human Development [NICHD], 2000a). (For additional discussion of developmental continuities see Scarborough, Chapter 8.)

Children from low-income families are at particular risk for reading difficulties (e.g., Dubow & Ippolito, 1994; Juel, Griffith, & Gough, 1986, Smith & Dixon, 1995) and are more likely to be slow in the development of oral language skills (e.g., Juel et al., 1986; Lonigan & Whitehurst, 1998; Whitehurst, 1996), letter knowledge, and phonological processing skills prior to school entry (Bowey, 1995; Lonigan, Burgess, Anthony, & Barker, 1998; MacLean, Bryant, & Bradley, 1987; Raz & Bryant, 1990). Socioeconimic-status-linked differences in phonological processing skills relate to later differences in word decoding skills (e.g., Raz & Bryant, 1990).

Based on a diverse body of research evidence, it now seems clear that learning to read is affected by the foundation skills of phonological processing, print awareness, and oral language. Children with more of these skills profit more from reading instruction, learn to read sooner, and read better than do children with less of these skills (Whitehurst & Lonigan, 1998). Many children, particularly those from low-income families, are not prepared for the reading instruction they will receive in first grade. They are likely to fail, with catastrophic results. It is not an exaggeration to say that the prevention of reading difficulties is a matter of survival for many children. We will examine recent research on paths of influence on learning to read that begin in the preschool period. If interventions designed to increase reading readiness and prevent reading difficulties are informed by this research, children should benefit. (For further discussion of the impact of home and community background factors, see Chapters 12–16 and 22.)

Emergent Literacy

Emergent literacy refers to the developmental precursors of formal reading that have

their origins early in the life of a child. This conceptualization departs from an older perspective on reading acquisition that sees the process of learning to read as beginning with formal school-based instruction in reading or with reading readiness skills taught in kindergarten, such as letter recognition. This reading readiness approach creates a boundary between the "real" reading that children are taught in educational settings and everything that comes before. In contrast, an emergent literacy perspective views literacy-related behaviors occurring in the preschool period as legitimate and important aspects of the developmental continuum of literacy. Current inquiry into emergent literacy represents a broad field with multiple perspectives and a wide range of research methodologies. It is complicated by changing conceptualizations of what constitutes literacy; for instance, recent years have seen the concept of literacy extended to any situation in which an individual negotiates the environment through the use of a symbolic system (e.g., maps, bus schedules, store coupons, and television advertisements). We restrict our focus to more conventional forms of literacy (i.e., the reading or writing of alphabetic texts). The majority of research on emergent literacy has been conducted with English-speaking children learning an alphabetic writing system; consequently, the extent to which these concepts of emergent literacy extend to children learning writing systems or languages other than English is not clear. Our approach in this chapter is to highlight those selected areas of emergent literacy that research has shown to be linked with later reading and that might be most relevant for early-intervention programs designed to affect children's literacy skills. We focus here on how these emergent literacy abilities develop over time and how they affect each other.

Two Domains of Literacy

Whitehurst and Lonigan (1998) proposed that emergent and conventional literacy are derived from individuals' ability to utilize information from two interdependent domains of information: *outside-in* and *inside-out*, as represented in Figure 2.1. The out-

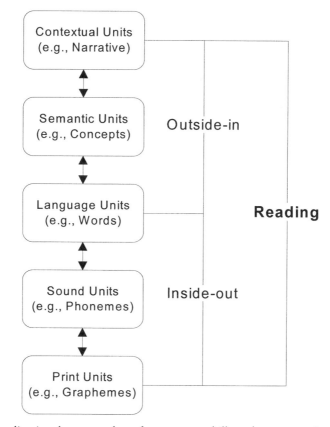

FIGURE 2.1. Fluent reading involves a number of component skills and processes. A reader must decode units of print into units of sound and units of sound into units of language. This is an inside-out process. However, being able to say a written word or series of written words is only a part of reading. The fluent reader must understand those auditory derivations, which involves placing them in the correct conceptual and contextual framework. This is an outside-in process. The bidirectional arrows in the figure illustrate that there is cross-talk between different components of reading. For example, the sentence context affects the phonological rendering of the italicized letters in these two phrases: "a *lead* balloon," "*lead* me there."

side-in units in the figure represent sources of information from outside the printed word that directly support children's understanding of the meaning of print (e.g., vocabulary, conceptual knowledge, and story schemas). The inside-out units represent sources of information within the printed word that support children's ability to translate print into sounds and sounds into print (e.g., phonemic awareness and letter knowledge). These sources of information are labeled outside-*in* and inside-*out,* rather than simply outside and inside to denote that in mature readers information from each domain penetrates into the processing of information from the other.

As an example of this distinction, imagine a child trying to read the sentence, "She sent off to the very best seed house for five bushels of lupine seed" (Cooney, 1982, p. 21). The ability to decode the letters in this sentence into correct phonological representations (i.e., being able to say the sentence) depends on knowing letters, sounds, links between letters and sounds, punctuation, and sentence grammar, as well as cognitive processes, such as being able to remember and organize these elements into a sequence. These are inside-out processes, which are based on and keyed to sources of information that are available at the level of individual printed words and short sequences of words at the sentence level. However, a child could know how to process all the word-level print information in this sentence (i.e., be able to read the sentence aloud) and still not read it successfully. What does the sentence mean? Meaningful comprehension of all but the simplest of writing depends on knowledge that cannot be found in the word or sentence itself. Who is the "she" referred to in the earlier sentence? Why is she sending away for seed? Why does she need five bushels? What is lupine? In short, what is the narrative, conceptual, and semantic context in which this sentence is found, and how does the sentence make sense within that context? Answering these questions depends on outside-in information involving knowledge of the world, semantic knowledge, and knowledge of the written context in which this particular sentence occurred. Outside-in and inside-out sources of information are both essential to successful reading and are used simultaneously in readers who are reading well.

This distinction between outside-in and inside-out information sources is related to but different from a distinction in the psychological literature between top-down and bottom-up processing. "Top-down" and "bottom-up" are terms taken from the literature on perception. They refer to whether an individual perceives a stimulus (e.g., recognizing a person's face) by noticing separate defining features of the stimulus and assembling them into a recognizable pattern (bottom-up), or perceives a stimulus by use of the context and what is already known about the situation (top-down). Outside-in sources of information for reading can support top-down processing, while inside-out sources of information can support bottom-up processing; thus in this way the distinctions are superficially similar. However, top-down and bottom-up are alternative routes to the same destination. Thus we can recognize the person who has just entered the room as "Joe" because he is the person we are all waiting for (top-down), or because he is the person with the bushy eyebrows and red hair (bottom-up). However, a successful reader cannot use either outside-in or inside-out sources of information to read: Both are essential. Further, inside-out and outside-in refer to sources of information that have to be processed rather than to specific psychological or neurological processing mechanisms, as in the case for bottom-up and top-down. Because outside-in and inside-out are sources of information to be processed, it is possible for top-down and bottom-up processing to occur within each of these domains of information. Thus, within the inside-out domain of information, a reader's ability to sound out or decode a particular printed word will depend on the bottom-up process of translating letters to their corresponding phonemes as well as on top-down, contextual processing (e.g., a competent reader will process the "e" in "read" differently than the "e" in "red" because of the effect of the surrounding context of letters). Likewise, within the outside-in domain of information, a reader's ability to understand a newspaper story about Bill Gates buying *The New York Times* will depend on a bottom-up assembly of information in the story as well as on top-down influences from cultural knowledge about Bill Gates.

In summary, the inside-out domain comprises the sources of information about which a reader must develop skills and knowledge that allow a translation of print into phonological representations, and vice versa. The outside-in domain comprises the sources of information to which the reader must apply skills and knowledge that enable understanding of phonological representations. Inexpensive software for personal computers is readily available that will render print into speech (i.e., that can process inside-out information). However, a computer that can understand what it reads is still to be found only in science fiction. Although understanding of print is the goal and requires complex human cognitive abilities and experience, neither a computer nor a human can understand print that it cannot decode. Thus learning to decode (i.e., to smoothly, effectively, and effortlessly process inside-out information in print) is a critical step in learning to read for meaning.

Components of Emergent Literacy

Elsewhere we have reviewed research on emergent literacy with respect to each of the elements in Figure 2.1 (Whitehurst & Lonigan, 1998). Here we focus on two inside-out elements (phonological processing and print awareness) and one outside-in element (oral language) about which the evidence for a link to conventional literacy is strongest. After reviewing evidence on the effects of phonological processing, print awareness, and oral language on learning to read, we present a conceptual and empirically tested model of the developmental interrelationships among these aspects of emergent literacy.

Phonological Processing Skills

Within the past two decades, a strong consensus has emerged concerning the role of phonological processing in the acquisition of reading and spelling in alphabetic languages (Adams, 1990; Wagner & Torgesen, 1987). Phonological processing refers to activities that require sensitivity to, manipulation of, or use of the sounds in words. Prior research has identified three interrelated clusters of phonological processing abilities: phonological sensitivity, phonological naming, and phonological memory (Wagner & Torgesen, 1987).

1. *Phonological sensitivity* refers to the ability to detect and manipulate the sound structure of oral language. Phonological sensitivity might be revealed by a child's ability to identify words that rhyme, blend spoken syllables or phonemes together to form a word, delete syllables or phonemes from spoken words to form a new word, or count the number of phonemes in a spoken word. For example, assessing sensitivity to phonemes might involve asking the child to count the number of phonemes in the word "donut," or to say what word results when the sounds /b/ . . . /a/ . . . /t/ are put together. It is important to understand that phonological sensitivity is an oral language skill that can develop without any exposure to print or letters. It is not phonics, which is a teaching method that emphasizes the relationship between letters and corresponding sounds.

The developing phonological sensitivity of young children progresses from sensitivity to large and concrete units of sound (i.e., words and syllables) to subsyllabic units of onset (i.e., the initial consonant or consonant cluster in a syllable) and rime (i.e., the vowel and final consonant or consonant cluster in a syllable) to small and abstract units of sound (i.e., phonemes) (Adams, 1990; Anthony et al., 2000; Fox & Routh, 1975; Loningan, Burgess, & Anthony, 2000; Lonigan et al., 1998). Phonological sensitivity promotes the development of decoding skills because graphemes in written language correspond to speech sounds at the level of phonemes. If children cannot perceive the individual sounds in spoken words, they will have difficulty identifying the correspondence between print and the language it represents.

2. *Phonological memory* refers to short-term memory for sound-based information (Baddeley, 1986) and is typically measured by immediate recall of verbally presented material. For example, phonological memory might be assessed by having a child repeat nonwords of increasing length (e.g., "weem" and "nokyisms"), repeat increasingly longer sentences (e.g., "The big dog" and "The cat in the hat stood on the chair."), or repeat lists of digits that increase in length (e.g., "4 . . . 3" and "5 . . . 2 . . . 8 . . . 4"). Efficient phonological memory enables children to maintain an accurate representation of the phonemes associated with the letters of a word while decoding and, therefore, devote more cognitive resources to decoding and comprehension processes.

3. *Phonological naming* refers to the efficiency of retrieval of phonological information from permanent memory. Two measures of phonological naming have been used, isolated naming and serial naming. In isolated naming, the child is presented with a picture of a single object and the time to begin a pronunciation is measured. Performance on serial-naming tasks for older children is typically measured as the time it takes for all individual elements in an array of letters, digits, or colors to be named. In younger children, performance on a serial-naming task might be measured by asking the child to name a sequence of pictures of objects (e.g., rat, man, house, tree, and snake) as fast as he or she can. Efficiency in phonological access might influence the ease with which a child can retrieve the phonological information associated with letters, word segments, and whole words and increase the likelihood that he or she can use phonological information in decoding (Bowers & Wolf, 1993; Wolf, 1991).

These three phonological processes are strongly related to subsequent decoding abilities (e.g., the ability to sound out words), and, in the absence of intervention, individual differences in these processes are highly stable from the late preschool period forward (Burgess & Lonigan, 1998; Lonigan et al., in press; Torgesen & Burgess, 1998; Wagner, Torgesen, & Rashotte; 1994; Wagner, Torgesen, Laughon, Simmons, & Rashotte, 1993; Wagner et al., 1997). For example, Wagner et al. (1994) reported that year-to-year stability coefficients for phonological sensitivity ranged from .83 (from kindergarten to first grade) to .95 (from second grade to third grade and from third grade to fourth grade).

Poor phonological processing skills are the hallmark of poor readers. There is a core phonological deficit (i.e., sensitivity or access) in nearly all poor readers, and there are deficits in other reading-related skills (e.g., vocabulary) in some poor readers depending on the degree to which their level of reading is discrepant from their level of general cognitive and academic functioning (Stanovich, 1988; Stanovich & Siegel, 1994). In other words, a poor reader may exhibit low levels of phonological processing skills compared to his or her same-age peers but have oral-language skills and general cognitive abilities that are consistent with age expectations (i.e., the condition typically referred to as dyslexia). In contrast, a poor reader may exhibit low levels of phonological processing skills, oral language, and general cognitive abilities compared to his or her same-age peers (i.e., a condition sometimes referred to as garden-variety poor reading). Both types of poor readers have deficient phonological processing. Children who have what is sometimes called a double deficit (i.e., poor performance on both phonological sensitivity and phonological naming tasks relative to same-age peers) tend to be at the very bottom of the distribution of reading ability (Bowers, 1995; Bowers & Wolf, 1993; McBride-Chang & Manis, 1996).

The majority of work concerning pre-readers' phonological processing skills has examined phonological sensitivity. Individual differences in preschool and kindergarten children's phonological sensitivity are related to early reading acquisition (e.g., Bradley & Bryant, 1983, 1985; Bryant, MacLean, Bradley, & Crossland, 1990; Lonigan et al., in press; Stanovich, Cunningham, & Cramer, 1984). Children who are better at detecting rhymes, syllables, or phonemes are quicker to learn to read, and this relation is present even after variability due to factors such as IQ, vocabulary, memory, and social class are removed statistically (Bryant et al., 1990; MacLean et al., 1987; Raz & Bryant, 1990; Wagner & Torgesen, 1987; Wagner et al., 1994, 1997).

Experimental demonstrations that training children in phonological sensitivity positively affects reading support a causal relation between phonological sensitivity and early reading skills (e.g., Bradley & Bryant, 1985; Brady, Fowler, Stone, & Winbury, 1994; Byrne & Fielding-Barnsley, 1991a, 1993). For example, Byrne and Fielding-Barnsley (1991a) taught preschool children to identify a limited number of phonemes in the initial and final positions of words. These children scored higher on measures of phonological sensitivity than did a control group, and their ability to decode words was also higher.

Print Principles

Knowledge of the alphabet at school entry is one of the single best predictors of eventual reading achievement (Adams, 1990; Stevenson & Newman, 1986). In alphabetic writing systems, decoding text involves the translation of units of print (graphemes) to units of sound (phonemes), and writing involves translating units of sound into units of print. At the most basic level, this task requires the ability to distinguish letters. A beginning reader who cannot recognize and distinguish the individual letters of the alphabet will have difficulty learning the sounds those letters represent (Bond & Dykstra, 1967; Chall, 1967; Mason, 1980). In some cases, the task of learning letter–sound correspondence is facilitated by letter names that are the same as one of the phonemes that the letter represents. For example, the name of the letter "e" is the sound made by that letter in words such as "be." In other cases letter names are different from the phonemes those letters map onto. For example, the word "not" would be pronounced as "en-ot" if the name of the letter "n" was the sound linked to that letter.

The potentially confusing nature of letter–name to letter–sound correspondence has led developers of some curriculum materials to avoid letter names entirely when teaching children (e.g., Lindamood, 1995; McGuinness, 1997), preferring instead to teach directly that different letter shapes make different sounds; for example, the letter shape "a" makes two sounds (long "a" and short "a"). However, no research to date has evaluated the degree to which teaching the names of letters is helpful or harmful to children compared to leaving out letter names and teaching the connection between letter shapes and sounds directly. Studies of the early development of decoding and phonological sensitivity have generally found that letter–name knowledge is a stronger predictor of growth in these skills than is letter–sound knowledge (e.g., Burgess & Lonigan, 1998; Wagner et al., 1994). Letter names provide relevant information about the sounds they represent (e.g., the /t/ in "tee," /k/ in "kay"), and beginning readers appear to use this information in reading and writing (Ehri & Wilce, 1985; Read, 1971; Treiman, 1993).

In addition to its direct role in facilitating text decoding, letter knowledge appears to play an influential role in the development of phonological sensitivity, both prior to and after the initiation of formal reading instruction. Higher levels of letter knowledge are associated with children's abilities to detect and manipulate phonemes (e.g., Bowey, 1994; Johnston, Anderson, & Holligan, 1996; Stahl & Murray, 1994) but not rhyme and syllables (Naslund & Schneider, 1996). Wagner et al. (1994, 1997) reported the results of a longitudinal study that explicitly tested the influence of letter knowledge on subsequent phonological sensitivity development. They found that individual differences in kindergarten and first-grade letter knowledge were significantly related to measures of phonological sensitivity 1 and 2 years later. Likewise, Burgess and Lonigan (1998) found that preschool children's letter knowledge was a unique predictor of growth in phonological sensitivity across one year.

Despite these strong links between letter knowledge and later reading, interventions that teach children letter names alone do not seem to produce large effects on reading acquisition (Adams, 1990). Interventions designed to promote emergent inside-out skills are most powerful when training in both phonological sensitivity and letter knowledge is included in the intervention (e.g., Bradley & Bryant, 1985). For example, combining training in phoneme identity by classifying words based on their initial sounds (e.g., bat, ball, beach, bell, and bill all start with the /b/ sound) with training to identify the initial letter of words (i.e., words that start with the /b/ sound such as bat, ball, and beach, begin with the letter "b") appears to produce stronger effects on subsequent reading skills than the sound categorization training alone.

Emergent Writing

Another route to print awareness and letter knowledge is through writing and invented spelling. Behaviors such as pretending to write and learning to write one's name are examples of emergent writing. Many adults have had the experience of seeing a young child scribble some indecipherable marks on paper and then ask an adult to read what it says. The child is indicating that he or she knows print has meaning without yet knowing how to write. There have been a number of descriptive studies of children's emergent writing (e.g., Ferreiro & Teberosky, 1982; Harste, Woodward, & Burke, 1984; Sulzby, 1986). Most of these studies converge on a common developmental pattern of children's emergent writing. It appears that very young children treat writing in a pictographic sense that includes using drawing as writing or using scribble-like markings with meaning only to the child. Later, children begin to use different letters, numbers, and letter-like forms to represent the different things being written about. In this phase, children may reorder relatively few symbols to stand for the different words. Often in this phase, characteristics of the thing written are encoded into the word (e.g., a bear is bigger than a duck, therefore, the word "bear" has to be bigger than the word "duck"). For many children in the late preschool period, letters come to stand for the different syllables in words, and from this stage children finally begin to use letters to represent the individual sounds (e.g., phonemes) in words.

When prereaders use letters to represent individual sounds, they often do so in an idiosyncratic way (e.g., representing only the first and last sounds of a word as in the spelling "BK" for the word "bike"). This type of writing has been termed "invented spelling," which consists of writing words following a more or less phonological, rather than orthographic, strategy. Invented spelling appears to be a vehicle through which many children grapple with and begin to understand the alphabetic principle (that letters represents sounds) (Clarke, 1988; Ehri, 1988). For example, Torgeson and Davis (1996) found that a pretest measure of kindergarten children's ability to engage in invented spelling was the strongest and most consistent predictor of their progress in a phonological training curriculum. Clarke (1988) found that first-graders who were encouraged to invent spellings of words for which they did not know the correct spelling showed more progress in spelling and decoding than children who were not encouraged to invent spellings. The longitudinal research of Whitehurst and colleagues, summarized subsequently in Figure 2.2, indicates that the relatively advanced writing skill of invented spelling has developmental origins in acts such as drawing pictures of objects and writing one's name. Because of the demonstrated effects of emergent writing on children's acquisition of the alphabetic knowledge, and because drawing and scribbling are expressive acts that are well suited to the proclivities of preschoolers, activities that encourage writing at the preschool level are promising avenues for interventions to enhance emergent literacy.

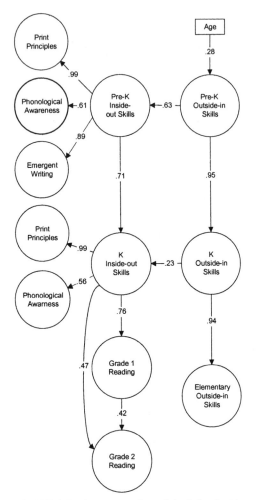

FIGURE 2.2. A structural model of the development of inside-out and outside-in skills from pre-K through second grade. A sample of 367 children was followed annually. The CFI fit index for the model is .92.

Oral Language Skills

Reading is a process of translating visual codes into meaningful language. In the earliest stages, reading in an alphabetic writing system involves decoding letters into corresponding sounds and linking those sounds to single words. In more advanced stages, reading involves complex synthesis of linguistic meaning from the inside-out and outside-in domains of information. The developmental links between oral language skills and read-

ing have generally been ignored in the literature, from which it is possible to form the impression that vocabulary and other oral linguistic skills are positively and causally related to reading at all levels of a child's development of reading. Thus we have the National Research Council's conclusion that the majority of reading problems could be prevented by, among other things, increasing children's oral language skills (Snow, Burns, & Griffin, 1998), and the conclusion of the National Reading Panel that vocabulary is critically important in oral reading instruction (NICHD, 2000b).

Consistent with these conclusions, a number of studies demonstrate positive correlations between individual differences in oral language skills and later differences in reading (e.g., Bishop & Adams, 1990; Butler, Marsh, Sheppard, & Sheppard, 1985; Pikulski & Tobin, 1989; Scarborough, 1989; Share, Jorm, MacLean, & Mathews, 1984). In other words, children who have larger vocabularies and greater understanding of spoken language have higher reading scores. However, simple correlations between vocabulary size and reading scores may reflect nothing more than the influence of third variables, such as the quality of a child's home environment, on both vocabulary and reading. We review recent research indicating that the connection between oral language and reading is conditional on the child's stage of development in language, as well as literacy, and is causally complex. We start the review with older elementary school children, (readers) then move to preschoolers (prereaders), and finally consider children who are just learning to decode in early elementary school (beginning readers).

Among older readers (e.g., fourth- and fifth-graders) the relationship between reading and language comprehension is direct and bidirectional. Thus children with more semantic knowledge are better able to comprehend what they are reading (Gillon & Dodd, 1994; Mason, 1992; Share & Silva, 1982; Snow, Barnes, Chandler, Hemphill, & Goodman, 1991; Tunmer & Hoover, 1992; Tunmer, Herriman, & Nesdale, 1988; Vellutino, Scanlon, & Tanzman, 1991). The relationship flows the other way as well: Children who read more frequently and fluently develop larger vocabularies and stores of concepts and facts (Cunningham & Stanovich, 1991, 1998; Stanovich & West, 1989; West, Stanovich, & Mitchell, 1993). In older children, reading generates knowledge, and knowledge supports reading comprehension.

Skipping from older readers to the other end of the developmental range, prereaders, one of the most interesting findings of recent research on emergent literacy is the relationship between vocabulary size and phonological sensitivity. Children with larger vocabularies have more developed phonological sensitivity (Wagner et al.,

1993, 1997). This relationship begins early in the preschool period (Burgess & Lonigan, 1998; Chaney, 1992; Lonigan et al., 1998, 2000).

Vocabulary growth appears to be causal in children's movement from global to segmented representations for words (e.g., "homework" to "home" - "work"). As children learn more words, it becomes more efficient to remember words in terms of their constituent parts rather than as wholes. Children who have small vocabularies are limited in their phonological sensitivity because they have not yet been forced by the sheer size of the vocabulary to move from global to segmented representations of words: Vocabulary development sets the stage for the emergence of phonological sensitivity (Fowler, 1991; Metsala & Walley, 1998, see Goswami, Chapter 9, for more on this topic).

A Structural Model of the Development of Emergent Literacy

The two relationships we have described, between oral vocabulary size and phonological awareness in prereaders and between oral vocabulary and comprehension in older readers, are captured in research by Whitehurst and colleagues that we described subsequently (Whitehurst & Fischel, 2000; Whitehurst & Storch, in press). This research also addresses the relationship between oral language and reading among beginning readers, demonstrating that the relationship is indirect (i.e., mediated by phonological sensitivity and other inside-out skills acquired in the preschool period). This has clear implications for the timing and focus of interventions to support emergent literacy.

The project followed several hundred children from low-income families from their entry into Head Start, when they had just turned 4, to their exit from fifth grade as 10-year-olds. Measures of outside-in and inside-out skills were collected at Head Start exit and at kindergarten exit. Measures of reading ability and oral language ability were collected annually at the end of first through fifth grades. Results through grade 2 are summarized here.

We used structural equation modeling (SEM) to examine causal possibilities within the data from the assessments described previously. Although SEM is at the core of modern statistical approaches to correlational data and has become relatively accessible to researchers, it is still sufficiently new that a brief primer may be useful (Byrne, 1994). SEM begins with what is a conceptual rather than a statistical component: causal modeling. A causal model is an hypothesis about the field of variables that affect one or more dependent variables of interest, presented formally as a path diagram. The diagram in Figure 2.2 represents causal hypotheses with respect to the links between emergent literacy and literacy skills for the children from low-income backgrounds. The second step in SEM is to develop a measurement model that corresponds to the constructs specified in the causal model. Whenever possible, multiple indicators of a given ability or construct are used, thereby introducing a distinction between latent variables and observed variables. When a particular construct, such as reading ability, is measured with multiple indicators, it is represented in path diagrams as a circle or an oval (i.e., as a latent variable, e.g., Grade 2 Reading in Figure 2.2). In contrast, when a construct is measured with only one test or instrument, it is represented in path diagrams as a square or rectangle (i.e., as a measured variable, e.g., Age in Figure 2.2). Relations between variables in SEM, whether the variables are latent or measured, are represented by path diagrams, which are collections of variables connected by lines and arrows. If variables are connected by a line with a single arrowhead, the variable with the arrowhead pointing into it is being modeled as determined by the variable with the line leading out of it (e.g., Grade 2 Reading in Figure 2.2 is modeled as determined in part by Grade 1 Reading). The third step in SEM is to assess the model against the data that have been collected. The statistical assessment of a model generates one or more measures of the degree of fit between the model and the matrix of correlations between the variables to which the model has been applied. The Bentler comparative fit index (CFI) is a frequently used measure of fit (Bentler, 1995). The CFI ranges from 0 to 1, with values around .9 or above traditionally viewed as indicating relatively close fit

between a model and the underlying data. Along with a measure of fit come weight estimates for each of the paths in the model. These are related to standardized betas in multiple regression or correlation coefficients in simple correlation. They provide a standardized estimate of the strength of influence of a given path. However, unlike simple regression or correlation coefficients, each path weight is conditional on and takes into account all the other variables in the model. Thus a high simple correlation between two variables (e.g., oral language scores in pre-K and reading scores in second grade) might diminish or be shown to be mediated or moderated by other variables in full structural model.

Figure 2.2 represents the structural equation model applied to the data from Head Start children described earlier. The focus in this model is the measurement and development of inside-out and outside-in skills, not in the variables in the child's environment, such as literacy practices in the home, that might influence the development of those skills. A consideration of environmental and background variables can be handled easily once the skill sequence is well mapped. We have reported such data elsewhere (e.g., Whitehurst & Fischel, 2000). The CFI index for the model in Figure 2.2 is .92. Thus the fit between the model and the data is good, particularly given the number of variables and time span involved.

The model is arranged in temporal order from the top to the bottom of the figure. The temporal ordering of the variables in the model corresponds both to when the data were collected and when the variables in the model are assumed to be operating. The inside-out variable at pre-K (Head Start) is composed of three latent variables, Print Principles, Phonological Awareness, and Emergent Writing. These are the three principle domains of inside-out abilities previously described in this chapter. These three latent variables are defined by measured variables that are subtests of the Developing Skills Checklist (CTB/McGraw-Hill, 1990). Emergent Writing is dropped from the model at K (kindergarten), not because it is unimportant but because the measures employed (e.g., the child's ability to write his or her name) have generally been mastered by children in our sample by the end of kindergarten. The outside-in variable at pre-K and K represents separate measures of receptive vocabulary (the Peabody Picture Vocabulary Test— Revised; Dunn & Dunn, 1981) and expressive vocabulary (the Expressive One-Word Picture Vocabulary Test; Gardner, 1990) taken each year. The outside-in variable in elementary school represents measures of receptive vocabulary (the Peabody Picture Vocabulary Test—Revised) taken separately in grade 1 and Grade 2. Grade 1 Reading is a latent variable defined in by scores on three tests of reading, the Stanford Achievement Test Word Reading subscale (Psychological Corporation, 1989), the Wide Range Achievement Test Word Reading subscale (Jastak & Wilkinson, 1984), and the Woodcock Word Attack subscale (Woodcock, 1987). Grade 2 Reading is similar, with the Stanford Achievement Test Comprehension subscale substituted for the Wide Range Achievement Test Word Reading subscale. Age is entered in the model because raw scores or their equivalents were used for all measures in Figure 2.2 rather than age-standardized scores. It makes sense to use raw scores because children within a particular grade are generally held to the same standards whether they are younger or older members of their class, and all children were tested at the end of each school year. Further, we are interested in how skills develop over time, which is difficult to detect when children's scores are adjusted for their ages. However, chronological age still affects outcomes, particularly for outside-in language skills, as shown in Figure 2.2 and in previous research on this sample (Crone & Whitehurst, 1999).

Note three findings that are illustrated in Figure 2.2:

1. There is striking continuity within the outside-in and inside-out dimensions of emergent literacy, with betas (correlations) in the .90s for the outside-in skills, and a beta of .71 between inside-out skills in pre-K and the same skills in kindergarten. Thus individual differences among children on these skills are set very early (by age 4) and children's degree of skill in these domains relative to other children in the sample is quite stable thereafter.

2. Inside-out emergent literacy skills in kindergarten predict reading in second grade directly and with greater strength (beta = .47) than reading in first grade predicts reading in second grade (beta = .42). Thus emergent literacy skills in kindergarten such as phonological awareness and letter recognition are as important or more important than the child's actual reading success in first grade in predicting later reading outcomes.

3. The relationship between inside-out and outside-in skills is very strong in the pre-K period (beta = .63), but this relationship becomes weak in kindergarten (beta = .23) and is nonsignificant in first and second grade. Thus during early elementary school when children are learning to read, their knowledge of language and concepts (outside-in skills) and their reading and prereading skills (inside-out skills) are modular; that is, having a larger vocabulary in first grade does not directly help a child learn to read. The influence of vocabulary size is indirect and mediated by the child's earlier acquisition of inside-out skills.

The most important practical issue that can be addressed with the data analyses that are reflected in Figure 2.2 is the origins of differences in how well children from low-income families learn to read. The picture that emerges is remarkably clear and consistent with the conceptual distinction between inside-out and outside-in skills presented previously: Reading success through the end of second grade is directly and strongly dependent on the inside-out skills that children bring to the task of reading from the preschool and kindergarten period. Note that 58% of the variance in reading outcomes in grade 1 can be accounted for by the child's inside-out skills at the end of kindergarten (derived by squaring the path weight). In turn, 50% of the variance in inside-out skills in kindergarten can be accounted for by inside-out skills from the preschool period. The stability in language trajectories is even higher, with 90% of the variance in outside-in skills in kindergarten accounted by outside-in skills at the end of pre-K, and 88% of the variance in outside-in scores in grades one and two accounted for by outside-in skills at the end of kindergarten. Children who start school behind in these areas are likely to stay behind.

The model we have found to fit the data

from our sample through the end of second grade is surprising in that it suggests that inside-out and outside-in processes are connected in the preschool period but become substantially separate and modular in kindergarten, first, and second grade. Thus interventions that hope to impact outside-in skills such as vocabulary and knowledge of narrative structure need to occur early in the preschool period if they are to have later effects during the decoding stages of learning to read.

Environments That Encourage the Development of Emergent Literacy

Given the findings in Figure 2.2, what do we know of interventions and environments that support the growth of emergent literacy? The prototypical and iconic aspect of home literacy, shared book reading, provides a potentially rich source of information and opportunity for children to learn language in a developmentally sensitive context (e.g., DeLoache & DeMendoza, 1987; Ninio, 1980; Pellegrini, Brody, & Sigel, 1985; Sénéchal, Cornell, & Broda, 1995; Wheeler, 1983). For instance, Wells (1985) found that approximately 5% of the daily speech of 24-month-old children occurred in the context of storytime, and Ninio and Bruner (1978) reported that the most frequent context for maternal labeling of objects was during shared reading. Shared reading and print exposure foster vocabulary development in preschool children (e.g., Cornell, Sénéchal, & Broda, 1988; Elley, 1989; Jenkins, Stein, & Wysocki, 1984; Sénéchal & Cornell, 1993; Sénéchal, LeFevre, Hudson, & Lawson, 1996; Sénéchal, Thomas, & Monker, 1995), and print exposure has substantial effects on the development of reading skills at older ages when children are already reading (e.g., Allen, Cipielewski, & Stanovich, 1992; Anderson & Freebody, 1981; Cunningham & Stanovich, 1991, 1998; Echols et al., 1996; Nagy, Anderson, & Herman, 1987).

Sénéchal et al. (1996) reported that other aspects of the home literacy environment (e.g., number of books in the home, library visits, and parents' own print exposure) were related to children's vocabulary skills;

however, only the frequency of library visits was related to children's vocabulary after controlling for the effects of children's print exposure. Payne, Whitehurst, and Angell (1994) found that adult literacy activities in low-income households (e.g., the amount of time a parent spends reading for pleasure) were not significantly related to children's oral language, which was best predicted by activities that directly involved the child (i.e., frequency of shared reading, number of children's books in the home, frequency of library visits with child). Other aspects of adult–child verbal interactions have also been implicated in the acquisition of some emergent literacy skills. For example, Dickinson and Tabors (1991; see also Beales, DeTemple, & Dickinson, 1994) reported that features of conversations among parents and children during meals and other conversational interactions (e.g., the proportion of narrative and explanatory talk) contributed to the development of children's decontextualized language skills.

Most existing studies do not support a direct link between shared reading and growth in phonological skills (Lonigan, Dyer, & Anthony, 1996; Raz & Bryant, 1990; Whitehurst, 1996). For example, Lonigan et al. (1996) found that growth in preschool phonological sensitivity was related to parental involvement in literacy activities in the home (i.e., frequency of parents' reading for pleasure and children observing parents reading), but growth in phonological sensitivity was not associated with shared reading frequency. Similarly, Sénéchal, LeFevre, Thomas, and Daley (1998) reported that kindergarten and first-grade children's written language knowledge (i.e., print concepts, letter knowledge, invented spelling, and word identification) was associated with parental attempts to teach their children about print but not exposure to storybooks. In contrast, children's oral language skills were associated with storybook exposure but not parents' attempts to teach print. Some evidence suggests that exposure to alphabet books may increase children's letter knowledge and phonological processing skills (Baker, Fernandez-Fain, Scher, & Williams, 1998; Murray, Stahl, & Ivey, 1996). Some studies find a relation between experiences with word games in the home and the development of phonological processing (Fernandez-Fain & Baker, 1997), but other studies do not (Raz & Bryant, 1990).

Emergent Literacy Interventions

A number of interventions have been developed to enhance children's oral language skills through shared reading. The most widely researched and validated of these interventions is called dialogic reading (Whitehurst & Lonigan, 1998). Dialogic reading involves several changes in the way adults typically read books to children. Central to these changes is a shift in roles. During typical shared reading, the adult reads and the child listens, but in dialogic reading the child learns to become the storyteller. The adult assumes the role of an active listener, asking questions, adding information, and prompting the child to increase the sophistication of descriptions of the material in the picture book. A child's responses to the book are encouraged through praise and repetition, and more sophisticated responses are encouraged by expansions of the child's utterances and by more challenging questions from the adult reading partner. For 2- and 3-year-olds, questions from adults focus on individual pages in a book, asking the child to describe objects, actions, and events on the page (e.g., "What is this? What color is the duck? What is the duck doing?"). For 4- and 5-year-olds, questions increasingly focus on the narrative as a whole or on relations between the book and the child's life (e.g., "Have you ever seen a duck swimming? What did it look like?").

Dialogic reading has been shown to produce larger effects on the oral language skills of children from middle- to upper-income families than a similar amount of typical picture book reading (Arnold, Lonigan, Whitehurst, & Epstein, 1994; Whitehurst et al., 1988). Studies conducted with children from low-income families attending child care demonstrate that child-care teachers, parents, or community volunteers using a 6-week small-group center-based or home dialogic reading intervention can produce substantial positive changes in the development of children's language as measured by standardized and naturalistic measures (Lonigan, Anthony, Bloomfield, Dyer, & Samwel,

1999; Lonigan & Whitehurst, 1998; Valdez-Menchaca & Whitehurst, 1992; Whitehurst, Arnold, et al., 1994) that are maintained 6 months following the intervention (Whitehurst, Arnold, et al., 1994). A large-scale longitudinal study of the use of dialogic reading over a year of a Head Start program for 4-year-olds showed large effects on emergent literacy skills at the end of Head Start that were maintained through the end of kindergarten; however, these positive effects did not generalize to reading scores at the end of second grade (Whitehurst, Epstein, et al., 1994, Whitehurst et al., 1999).

Experimental studies of programs designed to teach children phonological sensitivity show positive effects on children's reading and spelling skills (e.g., see Bus & van IJzendorn, 1999, for review). Phonological sensitivity training programs that have included letter knowledge training produced larger gains than did phonological sensitivity training alone (Ball & Blackman, 1988; Bradley & Bryant, 1985). The majority of these programs teach children how to categorize objects on the basis of certain sounds (e.g., initial phonemes). Other programs explicitly teach children phonemic analysis and synthesis skills. For example, Torgesen, Morgan, and Davis (1992) found that a 7-week group training program that taught children both analysis (e.g., identify initial, final, or middle sounds in words) and synthesis skills (e.g., say words after hearing their phonemes in isolation) resulted in larger gains in both phonological sensitivity and a reading analogue task than did training in synthesis skills alone. In addition, they found that both training groups performed better than did a group of control children who had listened to stories, engaged in discussions about the stories, and answered comprehension questions for an equivalent period.

Whereas most phonological sensitivity training studies have been conducted with children at the beginning stages of learning to read (i.e., kindergarten or first grade), Byrne and Fielding-Barnsley (1991a) found that preschool children (mean age = 55 months) exposed to 12 weeks of their *Sound Foundations* program (Byrne & Fielding-Barnsely, 1991b) demonstrated greater increases in phonological sensitivity than did a group of control children exposed to storybook reading and a semantic categorization program, and some of these gains were maintained through the first and second grades (Byrne & Fielding-Barnsley, 1993, 1995). This intervention program consisted of teaching children six phonemes in the initial and final positions of words by drawing attention to the sound in words, discussing how the sound is made by the mouth, reciting rhymes with the phoneme in the appropriate position, and encouraging children to find objects in a poster that had the sound in the initial (or final) position. Worksheets in which children identified and colored items with the phoneme in the correct position were used, and the letter for the phoneme was displayed. A final stage of training introduced children to two card games that required matching objects on the basis of initial or final phonemes.

Evidence also points to the potential effectiveness of software designed to teach phonological sensitivity skills to children (Barker & Torgesen, 1995; Foster, Erickson, Foster, Brinkman, & Torgesen, 1994; Lonigan et al., 2000; Olson, Wise, Ring, & Johnson, 1997; Wise, Olson, Ring, & Johnson, 1998). Foster et al. (1994) conducted two experiments in which preschool and kindergarten children were randomly assigned to receive either their standard school curriculum or between 5 and 8 hours of exposure to DaisyQuest (Erickson, Foster, Foster, Torgesen, & Packer, 1992), a computer program designed to teach phonological sensitivity in the context of an interactive adventure game. Children in the experimental group in both studies demonstrated significant and large gains in phonological skills compared to the children in the no-treatment control group.

Lonigan et al. (2000) evaluated the effectiveness of an 8-week intervention using DaisyQuest with children attending Head Start. Compared to children who received the standard Head Start curriculum, children in the experimental group experienced significant growth in their ability to identify rhyme and to perform analysis tasks. Barker and Torgesen (1995) also examined the effectiveness of the DaisyQuest program with a group of at-risk first grade children who were randomly assigned to either an experimental or control group. Children in the experimental group received approximately 8 hours of exposure to the program, and children in the control group received an equal amount of exposure to computer programs designed to teach early math skills or other reading skills. Exposure to the DaisyQuest program produced significant and large improvements in children's phonological sensitivity and word identification skills compared to the control groups.

Conclusions

Children know a lot about reading before they begin formal reading instruction, and this knowledge provides the building blocks for learning to read and write. The developmental precursors of reading skills are already organized into outside-in and inside-out domains during the preschool period. Knowledge of print and phonological awareness is closely connected within the domain of inside-out skills and shows strong continuity over time, whereas oral vocabulary operates within a separately organized outside-in domain which shows even stronger developmental continuity. Although the outside-in and inside-out domains are connected (i.e., they covary) during the preschool years, by the time children are involved in formal reading instruction in first and second grade, the influence of the outside-in domain has waned and become indirect. The strong, direct correlates of reading success from the kindergarten period are inside-out skills.

Different aspects of the home literacy environment differentially affect outside-in versus inside-out skills. Shared reading, for example, primarily affects oral vocabulary, while rhyming, word–sound games, and exposure to alphabet materials primarily affect inside-out skills. Future efforts to prevent reading problems need to be sensitive to the differences between the inside-out and outside-in domains of emergent literacy and their developmental relationships.

Acknowledgments

Preparation of this work was supported in part by grants to Grover J. Whitehurst from the Administration for Children and Families (No. 90-YD-

0026) and to Christopher J. Lonigan from the National Institute of Child Health and Human Development (No. HD36067, HD36509) and the Administration for Children and Families (No. 90-YF-0023). Views expressed herein are the authors' and have not been cleared by the grantors.

References

Adams, M. J. (1990). *Learning to read: Thinking and learning about print.* Cambridge, MA: MIT Press.

Allen, L., Cipielewski, J., & Stanovich, K. E. (1992). Multiple indicators of children's reading habits and attitudes: Construct validity and cognitive correlates. *Journal of Educational Psychology, 84,* 489–503.

Allington, R. L. (1984). Content, coverage, and contextual reading in reading groups. *Journal of Reading Behavior, 16,* 85–96.

Anderson, R. C., & Freebody, P. (1981). Vocabulary knowledge. In J. Guthrie (Ed.), *Comprehension and teaching: Research reviews* (pp. 77–117). Newark, DE: International Reading Association.

Anthony, J. L., Lonigan, C. J., Burgess, S. R., Bacon, K. D., Phillips, B. M., & Cantor, B. G. (2000). *Structure of preschool phonological sensitivity: Overlapping sensitivity to rhyme, words, syllables, and phonemes.* Manuscript submitted for publication.

Baddeley, A. (1986). *Working memory.* New York: Oxford University Press.

Baker, L., Fernandez-Fein, S., Scher, D., & Williams, H. (1998). Home experiences related to the development of word recognition. In J. L Metsala & L. C. Ehri (Eds.), *Word recognition in beginning literacy* (pp. 263–287). Mahwah, NJ: Erlbaum.

Ball, E. W., & Blachman, B. A. (1988). Phoneme segmentation training: Effect on reading readiness. *Annals of Dyslexia, 38,* 208–225.

Barker, T. A., & Torgesen, J. K. (1995). An evaluation of computer-assisted instruction in phonological awareness with below average readers. *Journal of Educational Computing Research, 13,* 89–103.

Baydar, N., Brooks-Gunn, J., & Furstenberg, F. F. (1993). Early warning signs of functional illiteracy: Predictors in childhood and adolescence. *Child Development, 64,* 815–829.

Beals, D. E., DeTemple, J. M., & Dickinson, D. K. (1994). Talking and listening that support early literacy development of children from low-income families. In D. K. Dickinson (Ed.), *Bridges to literacy: Children, families, and schools* (pp. 1–15). Cambridge, MA: Blackwell.

Bentler, P. M. (1995.). *EQS structural equations program manual.* Los Angeles: BMDP Statistical Software.

Bishop, D. V. M., & Adams, C. (1990). A prospective study of the relationship between specific language impairment, phonological disorders and reading retardation. *Journal of Child Psychology and Psychiatry and Allied Disciplines, 31,* 1027–1050.

Bond, G. L., & Dykstra, R. (1967). The cooperative research program in first-grade reading instruction. *Reading Research Quarterly, 2,* 5–142.

Bowers, P. G. (1995). Tracing symbol naming speed's unique contributions to reading disabilities over time. *Reading and Writing, 7,* 189–216.

Bowers, P. G., & Wolf, M. (1993). Theoretical links among naming speed, precise timing mechanisms and orthographic skill in dyslexia. *Reading and Writing, 5,* 69–85.

Bowey, J. A. (1994). Phonological sensitivity in novice readers and nonreaders. *Journal of Experimental Child Psychology, 58,* 134–159.

Bowey, J. A. (1995). Socioeconomic status differences in preschool phonological sensitivity and first-grade reading achievement. *Journal of Educational Psychology, 87,* 476–487.

Bradley, L., & Bryant, P. E. (1983). Categorizing sounds and learning to read—A causal connection. *Nature, 301,* 419–421.

Bradley, L., & Bryant, P. (1985). *Rhyme and reason in reading and spelling.* Ann Arbor: University of Michigan Press.

Brady, S., Fowler, A., Stone, B., & Winbury, N. (1994). Training phonological awareness: A study with inner-city kindergarten children. *Annals of Dyslexia, 44,* 26–59.

Brown, A. L., Palincsar, A. S., & Purcell, L. (1986). Poor readers: Teach, don't label. In U. Neisser (Ed.), *The school achievement of minority children: New perspectives* (pp. 105–143). Hillsdale, NJ: Erlbaum.

Bryant, P. E., MacLean, M., Bradley, L. L., & Crossland, J. (1990). Rhyme and alliteration, phoneme detection, and learning to read. *Developmental Psychology, 26,* 429–438.

Burgess, S. R., & Lonigan, C. J. (1998) Bidirectional relations of phonological sensitivity and prereading abilities: Evidence from a preschool sample. *Journal of Experimental Child Psychology, 70,* 117–141.

Bus, A. G., & van IJzendoorn, M. H. (1999). Phonological awareness and early reading: A meta-analysis of experimental training studies. *Journal of Educational Psychology, 91,* 403–414.

Butler, S. R., Marsh, H. W., Sheppard, M. J., & Sheppard, J. L. (1985). Seven-year longitudinal study of the early prediction of reading achievement. *Journal of Educational Psychology, 77,* 349–361.

Byrne, B. M. (1994). *Structural equation modeling with EQS and EQS/Windows.* Thousand Oaks, CA: Sage.

Byrne, B., & Fielding-Barnsley, R. F. (1991a). Evaluation of a program to teach phonemic awareness to young children. *Journal of Educational Psychology, 82,* 805–812.

Byrne, B., & Fielding-Barnsley, R. F. (1991b). *Sound foundations.* Artarmon, New South Wales, Australia: Leyden.

Byrne, B., & Fielding-Barnsley, R. F. (1993). Evaluation of a program to teach phonemic awareness to young children: A one year follow-up. *Journal of Educational Psychology, 85*, 104–111.

Byrne, B., & Fielding-Barnsley, R. (1995). Evaluation of a program to teach phonemic awareness to young children: A 2- and 3-year follow-up and a new preschool trial. *Journal of Educational Psychology, 87*, 488–503.

Chall, J. S. (1967). *Learning to read: The great debate.* New York: McGraw-Hill.

Chall, J. S., Jacobs, V., & Baldwin, L. (1990). *The reading crisis: Why poor children fall behind.* Cambridge, MA: Harvard university Press.

Chaney, C. (1992). Language development, metalinguistic skills, and print awareness in 3-year-old children. *Applied Psycholinguistics, 13*, 485–514.

Clarke, L. K. (1988). Invented versus traditional spelling in first graders' writings: Effects on learning to spell and read. *Research in the Teaching of English, 22*, 281–309.

Cooney, B. (1982). *Miss Rumphius.* New York: Puffin Books.

Cornell, E. H., Sénéchal, M., & Broda, L. S. (1988). Recall of picture books by 3-year-old children: Testing and repetition effects in joint reading activities. *Journal of Educational Psychology, 80*, 537–542.

CTB/McGraw-Hill. (1990). *Developing Skills Checklist.* Monterey, CA: McGraw-Hill.

Crone, D. A., & Whitehurst, G. J. (1999). Schooling effects on emergent literacy and early reading skills. *Journal of Educational Psychology, 91*, 604–614.

Cunningham, A. E., & Stanovich, K. E. (1991). Tracking the unique effects of print exposure in children: Associations with vocabulary, general knowledge, and spelling. *Journal of Educational Psychology, 83*, 264–274.

Cunningham, A. E., & Stanovich, K. E. (1998). Early reading acquisition and its relation to reading experience and ability 10 years later. *Developmental Psychology, 33*, 934–945.

DeLoache, J. S., & DeMendoza, O. A. P. (1987). Joint picturebook interactions of mothers and one-year-old children. *British Journal of Developmental Psychology, 5*, 111–123.

Dickinson, D. K., & Tabors, P. O. (1991). Early literacy: Linkages between home, school, and literacy achievement at age five. *Journal of Research in Childhood Education, 6*, 30–46.

Dubow, E. F., & Ippolito, M. F. (1994). Effects of poverty and quality of the home environment on changes in the academic and behavioral adjustment of elementary school-age children. *Journal of Clinical Child Psychology, 23*, 401–412.

Dunn, L. M., & Dunn, L. M. (1981). *Peabody Picture Vocabulary Test—Revised.* Circle Pines, NM: American Guidance Service.

Echols, L. D., West, R. F., Stanovich, K. E., & Zehr, K. S. (1996). Using children's literacy activities to predict growth in verbal cognitive skills: A longitudinal investigation. *Journal of Educational Psychology, 88*, 296–304.

Ehri, L. C. (1988). Movement in word reading and spelling: How spelling contributes to reading. In J. Mason (Ed.), *Reading and writing connections.* Newton, MA: Allyn & Bacon.

Ehri, L., & Wilce, L. (1985). Movement into reading: Is the first stage of printed word learning visual or phonetic? *Reading Research Quarterly, 20*, 163–179.

Elley, W. B. (1989). Vocabulary acquisition from listening to stories. *Reading Research Quarterly, 24*, 174–187.

Erickson, G. C., Foster, K. C., Foster, D. F., Torgesen, J. K., & Packer, S. (1992). *DaisyQuest.* Scotts Valley, CA: Great Wave Software.

Fernandez-Fein, S., & Baker, L. (1997). Rhyme and alliteration sensitivity and relevant experiences in preschoolers from diverse backgrounds. *Journal of Literacy Research, 29*, 433–459.

Ferreiro, E., & Teberosky, A. (1982). *Literacy before schooling.* Exeter, NH: Heinemann.

Foster, K. C., Erickson, G. C., Foster, D. F., Brinkman, D., & Torgesen, J. K. (1994). Computer administered instruction in phonological awareness: Evaluation of the DaisyQuest Program. *Journal of Research and Development in Education,*

Fowler, A. E. (1991). How early phonological development might set the stage for phoneme awareness. In S. A. Brady & D. P. Shankweiler (Eds.), *Phonological processes in literacy* (pp. 97–117). Hillsdale, NJ: Erlbaum.

Fox, B., & Routh, D. K. (1975). Analyzing spoken language into words, syllables, and phonemes: A developmental study. *Journal of Psycholinguistic Research, 4*, 331–342.

Francis, D. J., Shaywitz, S. E., Stuebing, K. K., Shaywitz, B. A., & Fletcher, J. M. (1996). Developmental lag versus deficit model of reading disability: A longitudinal, individual growth curve analysis. *Journal of Educational Psychology, 88*, 3–17.

Gardner, M. F. (1990). *Expressive One-Word Picture Vocabulary Test—Revised.* Novato, CA: Academic Therapy.

Gillon, G., & Dodd, B. J. (1994). A prospective study of the relationship between phonological, semantic and syntactic skills and specific reading disability. *Reading and Writing, 6*, 321–345.

Harste, J. E., Woodward, V. A., & Burke, C. L. (1984). *Language stories and literacy lessons.* Portsmouth, NH: Heinemann.

Jastak, S., & Wilkinson, G. S. (1984). *Wide Range Achievement Test—Revised.* Wilmington, DE: Jastak Associates.

Jenkins, J. R., Stein, M. L., & Wysocki, K. (1984). Learning vocabulary through reading. *American Educational Research Journal, 21*, 767–787.

Johnston, R. S., Anderson, M., & Holligan, C. (1996). Knowledge of the alphabet and explicit awareness of phonemes in prereaders: The nature of the relationship. *Reading and Writing: An Interdisciplinary Journal, 8*, 217–234.

Juel, C. (1988). Learning to read and write: A longitudinal study of 54 children from first through fourth grades. *Journal of Educational Psychology, 80,* 437–447.

Juel, C., Griffith, P. L., & Gough, P. B. (1986). Acquisition of literacy: A longitudinal study of children in first and second grade. *Journal of Educational Psychology, 78,* 243–255.

Lentz, F. E. (1988). Effective reading interventions in the regular classroom. In J. L. Graden, J. E. Zins, & M. J. Curtis (Eds.), *Alternative educational delivery systems: Enhancing instructional options for all students.* Washington DC: National Association of School Psychologists.

Lindamood, P. (1995). Lindamood-Bell Learning Processes overview. In C. W. M. J. S. Pickering (Ed.), *Clinical studies of multisensory structured language education* (pp. 97–99). Salem, OR: International Multisensory Structured Language Education Council.

Lonigan, C. J., Anthony, J. L., Bloomfield, B. G., Dyer, S. M., & Samwel, C. S. (1999). Effects of two preschool shared reading interventions on the emergent literacy skills of children from low-income families. *Journal of Early Intervention, 22,* 306–322.

Lonigan, C . J., Bacon, K. D., Phillips, B. M., Cantor, B. G., Anthony, J. L., & Goldstein, H. (2000). *Evaluation of a computer-assisted instruction phonological sensitivity program with preschool children at-risk for reading problems.* Manuscript submitted for publication.

Lonigan, C. J., Burgess, S. R., Anthony, J. L., & Barker, T. A. (1998). Development of phonological sensitivity in two- to five-year-old children. *Journal of Educational Psychology, 90,* 294–311.

Lonigan, C. J., Burgess, S. R., & Anthony, J. L. (2000). Development of emergent literacy and early reading skills in preschool children: Evidence from a latent variable longitudinal study. *Developmental Psychology, 36,* 596–613.

Lonigan, C. J., Dyer, S. M., & Anthony, J. L. (1996, April). *The influence of the home literacy environment on the development of literacy skills in children from diverse racial and economic backgrounds.* Paper presented at the Annual Convention of the American Educational Research Association, New York.

Lonigan, C. J., & Whitehurst, G. J. (1998). Examination of the relative efficacy of parent and teacher involvement in a shared-reading intervention for preschool children from low-income backgrounds. *Early Childhood Research Quarterly, 13,* 263–290.

MacLean, M., Bryant, P., & Bradley, L. (1987). Rhymes, nursery rhymes, and reading in early childhood. *Merrill–Palmer Quarterly, 33,* 255–282.

Mason, J. M. (1980). When children do begin to read: An exploration of four year old children's letter and word reading competencies. *Reading Research Quarterly, 15,* 203–227.

Mason, J. M. (1992). Reading stories to preliterate children: A proposed connection to reading. In P. B. Gough, L. C. Ehri, & R. Treiman (Eds.), *Reading acquisition* (pp. 215–243). Hillsdale, NJ: Erlbaum.

McBride-Chang, C., & Manis, F. R. (1996). Structural invariance in the associations of naming speed, phonological awareness, and verbal reasoning in good and poor readers: A test of the double deficit hypothesis. *Reading and Writing, 8,* 323–339.

McGuinness, D. (1997). *Why our children can't read and what we can do about it: A scientific revolution in reading.* New York: Free Press.

Metsala, J. L., & Walley, A. C. (1998). Spoken vocabulary growth and the segmental restructuring of lexical representations: Precursors to phonemic awareness and early reading ability. In J. L Metsala & L. C. Ehri (Eds.), *Word recognition in beginning literacy* (pp. 89–120). Mahwah, NJ: Erlbaum.

Morrison, F. J., Smith, L., & Dow-Ehrensberger, M. (1995). Education and cognitive development—A natural experiment. *Developmental Psychology, 31,* 789–799.

Murray, B. A., Stahl, S. A., & Ivey, M. G. (1996). Developing phoneme awareness through alphabet books. *Reading and Writing, 8,* 307–322.

Nagy, W. E., & Anderson, R. C. (1984). How many words are there in printed school English? *Reading Research Quarterly, 19,* 304–330.

Nagy, W. E., Anderson, R. C., & Herman, P. A. (1987). Learning word meanings from context during normal reading. *American Educational Research Journal, 24,* 237–270.

Naslund, J. C., & Schneider, W. (1996). Kindergarten letter knowledge, phonological skills, and memory processes: Relative effects on early literacy. *Journal of Experimental Child Psychology, 62,* 30–59.

National Institute of Child Health and Human Development. (2000a). *Report of the national reading panel. Teaching children to read: Reports of the subgroups.* Available online at http://www. nichd. nih. gov/publications/nrp/ch4-I. pdf .

National Institute of Child Health and Human Development. (2000b). *Why children succeed or fail at reading. Research from NICHD's program in learning disabilities.* Available online at http:// www. nichd. nih. gov/publications/pubs/readbro. htm.

Ninio, A. (1980). Picture book reading in mother–infant dyads belonging to two subgroups in Israel. *Child Development, 51,* 587–590.

Ninio, A., & Bruner, J. S. (1978). The achievement and antecedents of labeling. *Journal of Child Language, 5,* 1–15.

Oka, E., & Paris, S. (1987). Patterns of motivation and reading skills in underachieving children. In S. Ceci (Ed.), *Handbook of cognitive, social, and neuropsychological aspects of learning disabilities* (vol. 2, pp. 115–145). Hillsdale, NJ: Erlbaum.

Olson, R. K., Wise, B. W., Ring, J., & Johnson, M. (1997). Computer-based remedial training in phoneme awareness and phoneme decoding: Effects on post-training development of word recognition. *Scientific Studies of Reading, 1,* 235–253.

Pellegrini, A. D., Brody, G. H., & Sigel, I. (1985). Parent's book-reading habits with their children. *Journal of Educational Psychology, 77,* 332–340.

Pikulski, J. J., & Tobin, A. W. (1989). Factors associated with long-term reading achievement of early readers. In S. McCormick, J. Zutell, P. Scharer, & P. O'Keefe (Eds.), *Cognitive and social perspectives for literacy research and instruction* (pp. 123–133). Chicago: National Reading Conference.

Psychological Corporation. (1989). *Stanford achievement test—Eighth edition.* Orlando, FL: Harcourt Brace.

Raz, I. S., & Bryant, P. (1990). Social background, phonological awareness and children's reading. *British Journal of Developmental Psychology, 8,* 209–225.

Reid, C. (1971). Pre-school children's knowledge of English phonology. *Harvard Educational Review, 41,* 1–34.

Scarborough, H. (1989). Prediction of reading dysfunction from familial and individual differences. *Journal of Educational Psychology, 81,* 101–108.

Sénéchal, M., & Cornell, E. H. (1993). Vocabulary acquisition through shared reading experiences. *Reading Research Quarterly, 28,* 360–375.

Sénéchal, M., Cornell, E. H., & Broda, L. S. (1995). Age-related differences in the organization of parent–infant interactions during picture-book reading. *Early Childhood Research Quarterly, 10,* 317–337.

Sénéchal, M., LeFevre, J., Hudson, E., & Lawson, E. P. (1996). Knowledge of storybooks as a predictor of young children's vocabulary. *Journal of Educational Psychology, 88,* 520–536.

Sénéchal, M., LeFevre, J., Thomas, E. M., & Daley, K. E. (1998). Differential effects of home literacy experiences on the development of oral and written language. *Reading Research Quarterly, 13,* 96–116.

Sénéchal, M., Thomas, E. H., & Monker, J. A. (1995). Individual differences in 4-year-old children's acquisition of vocabulary during storybook reading. *Journal of Educational Psychology, 87,* 218–229.

Share, D. L., Jorm, A. F., MacLean, R., & Mathews, R. (1984). Sources of individual differences in reading acquisition. *Journal of Educational Psychology, 76,* 1309–1324.

Share, D. L., & Silva, P. (1987). Language deficits and specific reading retardation: Cause or effect? *British Journal of Disorders of Communication, 22,* 219–226.

Shaywitz, S. E., Escobar, M. D., Shaywitz, B. A., Fletcher, J. M., & Makuch, R. (1992). Evidence that dyslexia may represent the lower tail of the normal distribution of reading ability. *New England Journal of Medicine, 326,* 145–150.

Smith, S. S., & Dixon, R. G. (1995). Literacy concepts of low- and middle-class four-year-olds entering preschool. *Journal of Educational Research, 88,* 243–253.

Snow, C. E., Barnes, W. S., Chandler, J., Hemphill, L., & Goodman, I. F. (1991). *Unfulfilled expectations: Home and school influences on literacy.* Cambridge: Harvard University Press.

Snow, C. E., Burns, M. S., & Griffin, P. (Eds.). (1998). *Preventing reading difficulties in young children.* Washington, DC: National Academy Press.

Stahl, S. A., & Murray, B. A. (1994). Defining phonological awareness and its relationship to early reading. *Journal of Educational Psychology, 86,* 221–234.

Stanovich, K. E. (1986). Matthew effects in reading: Some consequences of individual differences in the acquisition of literacy. *Reading Research Quarterly, 21,* 360–407.

Stanovich, K. E. (1988). Explaining the differences between the dyslexic and the garden-variety poor reader: The phonological-core variable-difference model. *Journal of Learning Disabilities, 21,* 590–612.

Stanovich, K. E, Cunningham, A. E., & Cramer, B. B. (1984). Assessing phonological awareness in kindergarten children: Issues of task comparability. *Journal of Experimental Child Psychology, 38,* 175–190.

Stanovich, K. E., & Siegel, L. S. (1994). Phenotypic performance profile of children with reading disabilities: A regression-based test of the phonological-core variable-difference model. *Journal of Educational Psychology, 86,* 24–53.

Stanovich, K. E., & West, R. F. (1989). Exposure to print and orthographic processing. *Reading Research Quarterly, 24,* 402–433.

Stevenson, H. W., & Newman, R. S. (1986). Long-term prediction of achievement and attitudes in mathematics and reading. *Child Development, 57,* 646–659.

Sulzby, E. (1986). Writing and reading: Signs of oral and written language organization in the young child. In W. H. Teale & E. Sulzby (Eds.), *Emergent literacy: Reading and writing* (pp. 50–87). Norwood, NJ: Ablex.

Torgesen, J. K., & Burgess, S. R. (1998). Consistency of reading-related phonological processes throughout early childhood: Evidence from longitudinal–correlational and instructional studies. In J. L Metsala & L. C. Ehri (Eds.), *Word recognition in beginning literacy* (pp. 161–188). Mahwah, NJ: Erlbaum.

Torgesen, J. K., & Davis, C. (1996). Individual difference variables that predict response to training in phonological awareness. *Journal of Experimental Child Psychology, 63,* 1–21.

Torgesen, J. K., Morgan, S., & Davis, C. (1992). Effects of two types of phonological awareness training on word learning in kindergarten children. *Journal of Educational Psychology, 84,* 364–370.

Torgesen, J. K., Wagner, R. K., Rashotte, C. A., Alexander, A. W., & Conroy, T. (1997). Preventative and remedial interventions for children with severe reading disabilities. *Learning Disabilities, 8,* 51–62.

Tramontana, M. G., Hooper, S., & Selzer, S. C. (1988). Research on preschool prediction of later academic achievement: A review. *Developmental Review, 8,* 89–146.

Treiman, R. (1993). *Beginning to spell.* New York: Oxford University Press.

Tunmer, W. E., Herriman, M. L., & Nesdale, A. R. (1988). Metalinguistic abilities and beginning reading. *Reading Research Quarterly, 23,* 134–158.

Tunmer, W. E., & Hoover, W. A. (1992). Cognitive and linguistic factors in learning to read. In P. B. Gough, L. C. Ehri, & R. Treiman (Eds.), *Reading acquisition.* Hillsdale, NJ: Erlbaum.

Valdez-Menchaca, M. C., & Whitehurst, G. J. (1992). Accelerating language development through picture book reading: A systematic extension to Mexican day-care. *Developmental Psychology, 28,* 1106–1114.

Vellutino, F. R., Scanlon, D. M., & Tanzman, M. S. (1991). Bridging the gap between cognitive and neuropsychological conceptualizations of reading disability. *Learning and Individual Differences, 3,* 181–203.

Wagner, R. K., & Torgesen, J. K. (1987). The natural of phonological processing and its causal role in the acquisition of reading skills. *Psychological Bulletin, 101,* 192–212.

Wagner, R. K., Torgesen, J. K., Laughon, P., Simmons, K., & Rashotte, C. A. (1993). The development of young readers' phonological processing abilities. *Journal of Educational Psychology, 85,* 1–20.

Wagner, R. K., Torgesen, J. K., & Rashotte, C. A. (1994). Development of reading-related phonological processing abilities: New evidence of bidirectional causality from a latent variable longitudinal study. *Developmental Psychology, 30,* 73–87.

Wagner, R. K., Torgesen, J. K., Rashotte, C. A., Hecht, S. A., Barker, T. A., Burgess, S. R., Donahue, J., & Garon, T. (1997). Changing relations between phonological processing abilities and word-level reading as children develop from beginning to skilled readers: A 5-year longitudinal study. *Developmental Psychology, 33,* 468–479.

West, R. F., Stanovich, K. E., & Mitchell, H. R. (1993). Reading in the real world and its correlates. *Reading Research Quarterly, 28,* 34–51.

Wheeler, M. P. (1983). Context-related age changes in mother's speech: Joint book reading. *Journal of Child Language, 10,* 259–263.

White, K. (1982). The relation between socioeconomic status and academic achievement. *Psychological Bulletin, 91,* 461–481.

Whitehurst, G. J. (1996). Language processes in context: Language learning in children reared in poverty. In L. B. Adamson & M. A. Romski (Eds.), *Research on communication and language disorders: Contribution to theories of language development.* Baltimore, MD: Brookes.

Whitehurst, G. J., Arnold, D. H., Epstein, J. N., Angell, A. L., Smith, M., & Fischel, J. E. (1994). A picture book reading intervention in daycare and home for children from low-income families. *Developmental Psychology, 30,* 679–689.

Whitehurst, G. J., Epstein, J. N., Angell, A. C., Payne, A. C., Crone, D. A., & Fischel, J. E. (1994). Outcomes of an emergent literacy intervention in Head Start. *Journal of Educational Psychology, 86,* 542–555.

Whitehurst, G. J., & Fischel, J. E. (2000). A developmental model of reading and language impairments arising in conditions of economic poverty. In D. Bishop & L. Leonard (Eds.), *Speech and language impairment: From theory to practice* (pp. 53–71). East Sussex: Psychology Press.

Whitehurst, G. J., & Lonigan, C. J. (1998). Child development and emergent literacy. *Child Development, 68,* 848–872.

Whitehurst, G. J., & Storch, S. A. (in press). The role of family and home in the developmental course of literacy in children from low income backgrounds In J. Brooks-Gunn & P. R. Britt (Eds.), *New directions for child and adolescent development: Family literacy environments.* San Francisco: Jossey-Bass.

Whitehurst, G. J., Zevenbergen, A. A., Crone, D. A., Schultz, M. D., Velting, O. N., & Fischel, J. E. (1999). Outcomes of an emergent literacy intervention from Head Start through second grade. *Journal of Educational Psychology, 91,* 261–272.

Wise, B. W., Olson, R. K., Ring, J., & Johnson, M. (1998). Interactive computer support for improving phonological skills. In J. L Metsala & L. C. Ehri (Eds.), *Word recognition in beginning literacy* (pp. 189–208). Mahwah, NJ: Erlbaum.

Wolf, M. (1991). Naming speed and reading: The contribution of the cognitive neurosciences. *Reading Research Quarterly, 26,* 123–141.

Woodcock, R. W. (1987). *Woodcock reading mastery tests—Revised.* Circle Pines, MN: American Guidance Service.

3

A Sociocultural Perspective on Early Literacy Development

❖

JAMES PAUL GEE

This chapter develops a sociocultural approach to early literacy, a perspective rooted in the "New Literacy Studies" (hereafter "NLS"; Gee, 1996; Street, 1995). The chapter is organized as follows: I first spell out what constitutes (one version of) an NLS perspective. This leads to a question about whether we should sharply distinguish between the development of oral language and literacy. This question allows me to introduce some key theoretical notions, namely, "core grammar," "social languages," and "genres." I then discuss some of the implications of social languages and genres for the study of early literacy. The next two sections introduce the last of our theoretical notions, namely "Discourses" (with a capital "D") and "cultural models," followed by a brief note on the sociocultural view of learning. The final section uses the theoretical notions developed in the earlier sections to study a specific early literacy event. The analysis in this section is meant both to apply the theory developed here and to bring out some of its implications for the study of early literacy.

A "New Literacy Studies" Perspective

An NLS perspective places language and literacy in their full array of cognitive, social,

cultural, institutional, and historical contexts (for overviews and full citations to the literature, see Barton, 1994; Gee, 1996; Street 1995). From an NLS perspective, there really is no such general thing as "literacy." Rather, people adopt different "ways with printed words" within different sociocultural practices for different purposes and functions (Heath, 1983; Scollon & Scollon, 1981; Street, 1984). In these practices, humans are always meaning producers, not just meaning consumers (Kress, 1996).

Literacy is something different when a Los Angeles Latino street gang member writes a piece of graffiti on an urban wall to memorialize a recent event than when an elementary teacher writes a note in her journal about one of her students. It is different again when a child reads her own story written in invented spelling to her classmates than when she reads a decodable text in a small group with her teacher. It is different yet again when it is inside physics than when it is inside literary criticism.

Furthermore, "ways with printed words" within such sociocultural practices are always integrally and inextricably integrated with ways of talking, thinking, believing, knowing, acting, interacting, valuing, and feeling. We cannot just take the "print bits" out and forget the rest. The gang member's graffiti or the teacher's journal note are embedded in different ways of talking, thinking, believing, knowing, acting, interacting, valuing, and feeling. In turn, these differences are rooted in different *socially situated identities,* whether these be a Los Angeles Latino gang member or a first-grade progressivist teacher.

Finally, sociocultural practices that embed "ways with printed words" almost always involve human beings *both* coordinating and getting coordinated by other people, as well as forms of language, nonverbal images and symbols, objects, tools, technologies, sites, and times (Latour, 1987, 1991). Such practices are a "dance" in which people are simultaneously active (coordinating) and passive (getting coordinated), a dance in which they get "in synch" with other people and with forms of language, images, symbols, objects, tools, technologies, sites, and times. We cannot leave images, objects, and tools out of the literacy picture either (all of these are sometimes referred to as mediating devices; Wertsch, 1998).

It may, at first, seem odd to talk about a human being getting coordinated by (having to get in synch with) a piece of language, a symbol, an image, an object, a tool, technology, a place, or a time. But each of these things have "affordances" and place constraints on what we humans can and cannot do. Think about how a hammer offers itself ("comes to hand") to us in a certain way. So do words, phrases, symbols, images, technologies, and times and places. Think, for example, about the affordances of personal narratives as a language form (as opposed to, say, expository reports)— what they are good at getting done and what they are not particularly good at getting done. The affordances of a new tool ("mediating device") often give a learner more new "intelligence" than any internal mental change, though mental changes follow from the acquisition of new tools (Wertsch, 1998).

As an example of what I mean by coordinating and getting coordinated, consider a second-grade classroom engaged in research on fast-growing plants. A small group of girls in this class (Rosebery, Puttick, & Bodwell, 1996) wanted to find out what light conditions made plants grow best. Here the literacy events (notes, graphs, descriptions, reports, explanations, etc.) were all part of a great dance. In this dance, the girls used their bodies and minds, as well as their oral and written words to coordinate—and, in turn, got them coordinated by—other children, the teacher, various forms of language, symbols, and images, plants, lights, rooms, spaces, and various scientific tools. When the girls wrote "light makes plants greener" on a note pad it became a "tentative hypothesis" rather than, say, a factual assertion, only within the context of the whole dance. One does not know exactly how to read it outside the dance.

From an NLS perspective, all that I have said thus far about "ways with printed words" is just as true of "ways with oral words." There really is no such thing as "language" in general, no such thing even as "English" in general. Rather, people adopt different ways with oral words within different and specific sociocultural practices. Within these practices, these ways with oral words are always integrally and inextricably integrated with ways of talking, thinking, believing, knowing, acting, interacting, valuing, and feeling associated with specific socially situated identities. Here, too, we cannot just take the "oral bits" out and forget the rest. Finally, in the case of sociocultural practices that embed ways with oral words it is true, too, that they almost always involve human beings both coordinating and getting coordinated by not just language but other people, nonverbal images and symbols, objects, tools, technologies, sites, and times as well.

Thus, in the end, the NLS suggests that if someone wants to know about the development of literacy, he or she should not ask how literacy and language develop. Rather, he or she should ask how a specific sociocultural practice (or related set of them) embedded in specific ways with printed words develops. Immediately we can see that this is *equally* a question about individuals ("How does this child acquire this sociocultural practice?") and about groups ("How does this sociocultural practice acquire this child as a participant?") (Varenne & McDermott, 1999). The individual and the social are not in conflict here.

A Question: The Distinction between Oral and Written Language

Core Grammar

The perspective we have developed thus far suggests a question (see Gee, 1994, for discussion): Given that the written and the oral are inextricably linked to each other and to nonverbal "stuff" (i.e., minds, bodies, feelings, and objects), how important is the distinction between oral and written language (literacy)? This question, it turns out, is fatally ambiguous. The distinction is important if what we mean by "oral language" is what I will call "core grammar." The distinction is not crucial if what we mean by "oral language" is what I will call a "social language." First I discuss core grammar and then go on to discuss social languages.

Core grammar is the biologically specified *basic design* of a given human oral or signed language such as English or American Sign Language (Chomsky, 1986, 1995). It is the basic set of grammatical properties of a language as these are instantiated in native (first) language acquisition. For example, it is part of the core grammar of English that the head of a relative clause occurs before the relative clause (e.g., "the person who loves me," where "the person" is the head of the relative clause "who loves me"), while it is part of the core grammar of Japanese that the head of the relative clause occurs after the relative clause (e.g., something like "who loves me, the person").

The acquisition of core grammar is guided by a human biological capacity for language (Chomsky, 1986, 1995; Pinker, 1994). Basically, human biology sets the basic pattern any human language can take, leaving certain fairly restricted parameters open to be determined by experience with specific languages. Thus, relative clauses across languages share a good deal of their grammatical properties. The choice of where the head is located is left open to be determined by the language data to which the child is exposed. The English child sets the parameter of head before relative clause and the Japanese child sets it as head after relative clause. This choice is not conscious and is directed by the human child's innate unconscious knowledge of what relative clauses can look like and what parameters need to be set.

Barring quite serious disorders, all human children acquire the full core grammar of their native language. It just does not happen that Susie, a rich child, ends up having relative clauses in her grammar and Alice, a poor child, does not. Furthermore, although there are individual differences and dialect differences, from the point of view of core grammar, these are irrelevant. Every speaker/hearer of (core grammar) English, regardless of dialect, has control of an equally complex and rule-governed grammar. That is, whether one's dialect says "he's tired" or "he tired" (as in some dialects of English), both forms are equally good expressions of the core grammar of English, which allows diminution of the auxiliary verb "be" in just such grammatical environments, in one case realized as a contraction ('s) and in the other realized as deletion of the auxiliary verb (Rickford, 1999).

While core grammar is acquired with biological help, no form of literacy is. Oral language has been around long enough in human history to be "wired" into our genes. But literacy has not been around long enough to be so wired (it is at best 10,000 years). Thus, however forms of literacy are acquired, this process must, in some important respects, be different from how the core grammar of a language is acquired.

Social Languages

That is the "core grammar" story. But, as we said previously, there is another sense of the term "oral language." By oral language we can mean not the basic biologically driven design of English grammar but *language in use*. Language in use always comes, not in some generic "English" but in some *specific variety* of English *customized* to and for the specific context in which it is being used. Such different varieties are sometimes called registers (Halliday, 1994; Halliday & Hasan, 1989), but I here call them social languages (Gee, 1996, 1999).

Social languages are varieties of a language that are associated with specific *socially situated identities* ("*who* is talking/writing/acting") and specific *socially situated activities* ("*what* is being done"). An urban gang member warning another gang member off his turf uses a different social language than does a cutting-edge molecular biologist warning another molecular biologist off her research turf. The social languages they use both reflect and construct *who* they are (at that time and place) and *what* they are doing (Wieder & Pratt, 1990).

What makes one social language different from another? Each social language draws on the grammatical resources of a language such as English differently (and here I use "grammar" broadly to mean phonological, lexical, morphological, syntactic, semantic, discourse, and pragmatic devices). First, in a given social language, some resources (e.g., simple clauses) may be used and others may not (e.g., relative clauses). Second, some resources (e.g., relative clauses) may be used more frequently in one social language than in another. And, third, and most important, what defines the grammar of a social language is not just what grammatical resources it uses or how frequently it uses them but the *patterning* of different grammatical resources together.

Let me give an example of what I mean by a *pattern of grammatical elements* characterizing the grammar of a social language. Consider an example from Greg Myers's important work (1990, p. 150) on writing in science: Biologists, and other scientists, write differently in professional journals than they do in popular science magazines. These two different ways of writing do different things and display different identities. Thus, consider the following examples from the same scientist:

Professional science journal

Experiments show that *Heliconius* butterflies are less likely to oviposit on host plants that possess eggs or egg-like structures. These egg-mimics are an unambiguous example of a plant trait evolved in response to a host-restricted group of insect herbivores.

Popular science magazine

Heliconius butterflies lay their eggs on *Passiflora* vines. In defense the vines seem to have evolved fake eggs that make it look to the butterflies as if eggs have already been laid on them.

The two passages pattern grammatical elements together quite differently. The professional passage names things in terms of the role they play in the scientific *theory* of coevolution (e.g., "host plants," "egg-like structures," "egg-mimics," "plant trait," and "a host-restricted group of insect herbivores"). The popular passage names things as they are in the world (e.g., "vines" and "butterflies"). The professional passage uses as the subjects of its sentences elements of science (e.g., "experiments" and "egg-mimics"). The popular passage uses as the subjects of its sentences elements of the world ("butterflies "vines"). The professional passage uses more technical terms than the popular one (e.g., note "oviposit" rather than "laid"). The professional passage uses a type of complex noun phrase (i.e., "an unambiguous example of a plant trait evolved in response to a host-restricted group of insect herbivores") that has no equivalent in the popular passage.

We could go on and on. What matters is the way in which these different grammatical elements *pattern* within each text to make one one social language and the other another. For example, we would not expect someone to mix and match features from each social language (e.g., naming in terms of the role they play in a scientific theory but exclusively using real-world terms as subjects of sentences). If this happened, it would mark either incompetence or the creation of a new hybrid social language, one usable for different purposes within a different practice.

One should not think that social languages are relevant only to writing or academic styles of speaking. In fact, we all regularly vary our talk in everyday circumstances to enact different socially situated identities and activities. For example, an upper-middle-class, Anglo American young college student (Gee, 1996), talking about the same story she had read, said to her parents at dinner: "Well, when I thought about it, I don't know, it seemed to me that Gregory should be the most offensive. . . . He was hypocritical, in the sense that he professed to love her, then acted like that." But to her boyfriend later, she said: "What an ass that guy was, you know, her boyfriend. I should hope, if I ever did that to see you, you would shoot the guy. He uses her and he says he loves her. Roger never lies, you know what I mean?"

Genres

Another notion is relevant here to our discussion of social languages: the notion of "genres." Genres are more or less fixed patterns of language associated with more or less fixed patterns of actions and interactions (Martin, 1985; Miller, 1984). For example, a greeting ritual ("How are you?"; "Fine"; "And you?"; "Fine") is a genre. It is relatively fixed, though, of course, it still allows for some variation. Genres are the ways different socioculturally defined groups of people get their "routine" social business done. Similar genres can be enacted in different social languages, though some social languages are more closely associated with some genres than they are with others.

As an example of genres, consider a common social practice in some homes. Parents read books to a child who cannot yet "really read." They, in turn, invite the child to read (or the child offers). The child picks up a book and pretends to read. Following is an example of just such a pretend reading. I have placed it in lines and stanzas to show how patterned this piece of oral language is (Gee, 1996):

STANZA 1 (Introduction)
1. This is a story
2. About some kids who were once friends
3. But got into a big fight
4. And were not

STANZA 2 (Frame)
5. You can read along in your story book
6. I'm gonna read aloud
[story-reading prosody from now on]

STANZA 3 (Title)
7. "How the Friends Got Unfriend"

STANZA 4 (Setting: Introduction of Characters)
8. Once upon a time there was three boys 'n three girls
9. They were named Betty Lou, Pallis, and Parshin, were the girls
10. And Michael, Jason, and Aaron were the boys
11. They were friends

STANZA 5 (Problem: Sex Differences)
12. The boys would play Transformers
13. And the girls would play Cabbage Patches

STANZA 6 (Crisis: Fight))
14. But then one day they got into a fight on who would be which team
15. It was a very bad fight
16. They were punching
17. And they were pulling
18. And they were banging

STANZA 7 (Resolution 1: Storm)
19. Then all of a sudden the sky turned dark
20. The rain began to fall
21. There was lightning going on
22. And they were not friends

STANZA 8 (Resolution 2: Mothers punish)
23. Then um the mothers came shooting out 'n saying
24. "What are you punching for?
25. You are going to be punished for a whole year"

STANZA 9 (Frame)
26. The end
27. Wasn't it fun reading together?
28. Let's do it again
29. Real soon!

This little girl's oral performance has one genre embedded inside another: The genre of a "literary child's-book story," with its own typical structure, is embedded inside a genre we can label "parent reads to child." Note, in the case of the "literary" story, that the weather turning dark and stormy when something "bad" has happened is part of the genre of certain sorts of literary stories. The particular type of "parent reads to child" genre the little girl uses here (and she is playing the role of the parent) is a typical "routine" of language and action used by certain sorts of families. This genre includes introducing the story (Stanza 1); instructions to follow along (Stanza 2); giving the title (Stanza 3); starting the story (Stanza 4: "Once upon a time . . ."); reading the story (Stanzas 4–8); and closing the event and commenting on it (Stanza 9).

Within her story (Stanzas 4–8), the child uses a literary social language (another child may have used a different sort of social language) that involves a good deal of syntactic parallelism and repetition pat-terned together with literary syntax. Of course, this sort of social language is a generic convention of certain sorts of (e.g., literary) texts and activities. As I said previously, certain sorts of genres and certain sorts of social languages are often associated (for historical reasons).

Implications of Social Languages and Genres

Now here is the "bite" of social languages and genres: Unlike core grammar, social languages and genres are not a product of a human biological capacity; rather, they are creatures of history and culture. The social languages that nuclear physicists speak and write—or, for that matter, the social languages that Los Angeles urban Latino gang members speak and write—have not been around long enough in human history to get a biological boost. And genres, like the particular form of the genre "parent reads to child" that the little girl used, are, of course, the outcome of repeated experiences of rituals or routines used by specific sociocultural groups. Biology is irrelevant here.

When we talk about social languages and genres, oral and written language are inextricably mixed. Some social languages are written; some are spoken. Some have both spoken and written versions, and written and spoken versions are often mixed and integrated within specific social practices. Genres often mix written and spoken language, as well as actions and interactions (e.g., bedtime reading to children). The little girl's pretend-reading story earlier was spoken, but its language shares more features with some forms of written language than it does with her everyday vernacular.

In the end, from an NLS perspective, what is important is not the distinction between written and oral language but specific sociocultural practices, social languages, and genres. Within these there is a complex interplay of written language, oral language, action, and interaction. In turn, the issue for early literacy is not "learning to read" but how the child—at home, in the community, and at school—does or does not acquire specific social practices, social languages, and genres that involve "ways with printed words," along with much else.

Here is another part of the bite of social languages and genres: Both inside and outside school, most social languages and genres are clearly not acquired by "direct instruction." While some forms of (appropriately timed) scaffolding, modeling, and instructional guidance by mentors appear to be important, immersion in meaningful practice is essential. Social languages and genres are acquired by processes of socialization.

Discourses

But, now we must ask: socialization into what? When people learn new social languages and genres—at the level of being able to produce them and not just consume them—they are being socialized into what I will call "Discourses" with a big "D" (I use "discourse" with a little "d" to mean just "language in use"; Gee, 1996, 1999; see also Clark, 1996). Even when people learn a new social language or genre only so that they can consume (interpret it), but not produce it, they are learning to recognize a new Discourse. Related, but somewhat different, terms others have used to capture some of what I am trying to capture with the term "Discourses" are communities of practice (Wenger, 1998), actor–actant networks (Latour, 1986, 1991), and activity systems (Engestrom, Miettinen, & Punamaki, 1999; Leont'ev, 1978).

Discourses always involve language (i.e., they recruit specific social languages), *but they always involve more than language* as well. Social languages are embedded within Discourses and only have relevance and meaning within them. A Discourse integrates ways of talking, listening, writing, reading, acting, interacting, believing, valuing, and feeling (and using various objects, symbols, images, tools and technologies) in the service of enacting meaningful socially situated identities and activities. Being-doing a certain sort of physicist, gang member, feminist, first-grade child in Ms. Smith's room, special ed ("SPED") student, regular at the local bar, or "gifted upper-middle-class child engaged in emergent literacy" are all Discourses.

We can think of Discourses as "identity kits." It is almost as if we get a "tool kit" full of specific devices (i.e., ways with words, deeds, thoughts, values, actions, interactions, objects, tools, and technologies) in terms of which we can enact a specific identity and engage in specific activities associated with that identity. For example, think of what devices (in words, deeds, clothes, objects, attitudes, etc.) an individual would get in a Sherlock Holmes identity kit (e.g., there is *no* "Say No to Drugs" bumper sticker in this kit; one does get both a pipe and lots of logic). The Doctor Watson identity kit is different. And, we can think of the Sherlock Holmes identity kit ("Discourse") and the Doctor Watson identity kit ("Discourse") as themselves parts of a yet larger Discourse, the Holmes–Watson Discourse, because Watson is part of Holmes's identity kit and Holmes is part of Watson's. Discourse can be embedded one inside the other.

Think, also, of the devices the little girl is leveraging from her "emergent literacy identity kit" in terms of which she is enacting the Discourse of a particular sort of *emergently literate upper-middle-class child of educated parents.* As this description makes clear, Discourses need not have any overt label that their participants know and use. An overt label is not important—all that is important is that people can recognize (consciously or unconsciously) that in word and deed someone is being a "certain kind of person" (*who*) engaged in a certain kind of activity (what).

One Discourse can mix or blend two others. For example, Karen Gallas (1994) created in her classroom a sharing-time Discourse (a way of being a recognizable sharer in her classroom) that mixed Anglo and African American styles. Discourses can be related to each other in relationships of alignment or tension. For example, the Discourse in which the little girl mentioned previously is engaged is well aligned with practices and values in various school-based Discourses (e.g., creative literature). On the other hand, Scollon and Scollon (1981) have pointed out that school-based Discourses which incorporate essayist practices and values conflict with the values, attitudes, and ways with words embedded in some Native American home and community-based Discourses (i.e., ways of being a

Native American of a certain sort). These latter Discourses value communicating only when the sender knows the receiver of the communication and his or her context and do not value the sorts of "fictionalizing" (generalizing) of sender and receiver that essayist practices involve.

Cultural Models

Within their socialization into Discourses (and we are all socialized into a great many across our lifetimes), people always acquire "cultural models" (D'Andrade & Strauss, 1992; Gee, 1999; Holland, Lachicotte, Skinner, & Cain, 1998; Holland & Quinn, 1987; Shore, 1996; Strauss & Quinn, 1997). Cultural models are everyday "theories" (i.e., storylines, images, schemas, metaphors, and models) about the world that people socialized into a given Discourse share. Cultural models tell people what is "typical" or "normal" from the perspective of a particular Discourse (or related/aligned set of them).

For example, certain types of middle-class people in the United States hold a cultural model of child development that goes something like this (Harkness, Super, & Keefer, 1992): A child is born dependent on her parents and grows up by going through stages (often disruptive) toward greater and greater independence (and independence is a high value for this group of people). This cultural model plays a central role in this group's Discourse of parent–child relations (i.e., enacting and recognizing identities as parents and children).

On the other hand, certain sorts of working-class families (Philipsen, 1975) hold a cultural model of child development that goes something like this: A child is born unsocialized and with tendencies to be selfish. The child needs discipline from the home to learn to be a cooperative social member of the family (a high value of this group of people). This cultural model plays a central role in this group's Discourse of parent–child relations.

These different cultural models, connected to different (partially) class-based Discourses of parenting, are not "true" or "false." Rather, they focus on different aspects of childhood and development. Cultural models define for people in a Discourse what counts as "normal" and "natural" and what counts as "inappropriate" and "deviant." They are, of course, thereby thoroughly value-laden.

Cultural models come out of and, in turn, inform the social practices in which people in a Discourse engage. Cultural models are stored in people's minds (by no means always consciously), though they are supplemented and instantiated in the objects, texts, and practices that are part and parcel of the Discourse. For example, many "guidebooks" supplement and instantiate the foregoing middle-class cultural model of childhood and stages. On the other hand, many religious materials supplement and instantiate the above working-class model of childhood.

Figure 3.1 summarizes our discussion so far, defining each of our theoretical tools and showing how they are related to each other.

Discourses: Ways of combining and coordinating words, deeds, thoughts, values, bodies, objects, tools, and technologies, and other people (at the appropriate times and places) so as to enact and recognize specific socially situated identities and activities.

Social Languages: Ways with words (oral and written) within Discourses that relate form and meaning so as to express specific socially situated identities and activities.

Genres: Combinations of ways with words (oral and written) and actions that have become more or less routinized within a Discourse in order to enact and recognize specific socially situated identities and activities in relatively stable and uniform ways (and, in doing so, we humans reproduce our Discourses and institutions through history).

Cultural Models: Often tacit and taken-for-granted schemas, storylines, theories, images, or representations (partially represented inside people's heads and partially represented within their materials and practices) that tell a group of people within a Discourse what is "typical" or "normal" from the point of view of that Discourse.

FIGURE 3.1. Summary of tools for understanding language and literacy in sociocultural terms.

Learning and Communities of Practice

The sociocultural perspective I have developed encourages us to take a particular perspective on learning. A view of learning that only focuses on changing representations in people's heads fails to engage with the full range of material, social, and cultural factors that we have heretofore stressed. The approach to learning most compatible with a sociocultural perspective on language and literacy is one that defines learning as *a change in how one participates in specific social practices within specific Discourses.* Such changes always imply changes in socially situated identities, because these identities flow from how marginally or centrally a person participates in specific social practices within specific Discourses.

This view of learning requires us to see that people operating within Discourses often constitute a "community of practice" (Lave 1996; Lave & Wenger 1991; Rogoff 1990; Wertsch 1985, 1991), that is, they are ongoingly engaged in and bonded together through a common set of endeavors within which they may have distinctive but overlapping functions. These might be people in an elementary school classroom, members of a street gang or an academic discipline, affiliates of a "cause" (e.g., "greens"), or participants in a specific business organization. Such communities of practice reproduce themselves through "apprenticing" newcomers, in thought, word, and deed, to their characteristic social languages, cultural models, and social practices.

I do not have space here to elaborate this view of learning, which is, in any case, well spelled out in the sources I have cited in the last paragraph. But let me note, because the matter has generated so much controversy, that an NLS perspective on language, learning, and literacy is neither "pro" nor "anti" skills (or, e.g., phonics) in any general way. Rather, such a view cautions that skill-based learning is not some general thing, but a different thing with different effects (good, bad, or neither) as it is differently situated inside different specific social practices and Discourses (recruiting specific socially situated identities, social languages, and cultural models). Furthermore, the child is always acquiring much more than the skills or phonics, namely, specific socially situated identities, values, attitudes, norms, ways with words, deeds, and tools, and so forth.

Studying Early Literacy as Fully Socioculturally Situated Practice

I turn now to a specific event involving early literacy from my own research. I want to show how the theoretical apparatus developed thus far forces us to see such events as socioculturally specific. The event is this: An upper-middle-class, highly educated father approaches his 3-year-old (3 years, 10 months) son who is sitting at the kitchen table. The child is using an activity book in which each page contains a picture with a missing piece. A question is printed under the picture and the space left for the missing piece. The child uses a "magic pen" to rub the space and "magically" uncovers the rest of the picture. The part of the picture that is uncovered is an image that constitutes the answer to the question at the bottom of the page, though, of course, the child must put this answer into words.

In the specific case I want to discuss here, the overt part of the picture was the top half of the bodies of Donald and Daisy Duck The question printed at the bottom of the page was this: In what are Donald and Daisy riding? (Note the social language in which this question is written. It is not the more vernacular form: "What are Donald and Daisy riding in?"). The child used his pen to uncover an old fashioned Model T sort of car with an open top. Donald and Daisy turn out to be sitting in the car.

The father, seeing the child engaged in this activity, asks him, after he has uncovered the car, to read the question printed below the picture. Notice that the father has not asked the child to give the answer to the question, which is a different activity. The father is confident the child could answer this latter question and has a different purpose here. His purpose is, in fact, to engage in an indirect "reading lesson," though one of a special and specific sort.

The father is aware that the child, although he knows the names of the letters of the alphabet and can recognize many of them in words, cannot decode print. He is also aware that the child has on several pre-

vious occasions, in the midst of various literacy-related activities, said that he is "learning to read." However, in yet other activities, at other times, the child has said that he "cannot read" and thereafter seemed more reluctant to engage in his otherwise proactive stance toward texts. This has concerned the father, who values the child's active engagement with texts and the child's belief, expressed in some contexts and not others, that he is not just learning to read but is, in fact, "a reader."

We might say that the father is operating with a however tacit theory (cultural model) that a child's assuming a certain identity ("I am a reader") facilitates the acquisition of that identity and its concomitant skills. In fact, I believe this sort of model is fairly common in certain sorts of families. Parents co-construct an identity with a child (attribute, and get the child to believe in, a certain "competence") before the child can actually fully carry out all the "skills" associated with this identity ("competence before performance").

So, the father has asked the child "to read" the printed question below the picture of Donald and Daisy Duck sitting in the newly uncovered car. Following is the printed version of the question and what the child offered as his "reading" of the question:

Printed version: In what are Donald and Daisy riding?
Child's reading: What is Donald and Daisy riding on?

After the child uttered the foregoing sentence, he said: "See, I told you I was learning to read." He seems to be well aware of the father's purposes. The child, the father, the words, and the book are all here "in synch" to pull off a specific practice. And this is a form of "instruction," but a form that is typical of what goes on inside socialization processes.

The father and son have taken an activity that is for the child now a virtual genre—namely, uncovering a piece of a picture and on the basis of it answering a question—and incorporated it into different *metalevel activity*. That is, the father and son use the original activity not in and for itself but as a platform with which to "discuss" reading or, perhaps better put, to co-construct a cultural model of what reading is. The father's question and the son's final response ("See, I told you I was learning to read") clearly indicate that they are seeking to demonstrate to and for each other that the child "can read."

Figure 3.2 (partially) analyzes this event in terms of the theoretical notions we have developed above.

From a developmental point of view, then, what is going on here? Nothing so general as "acquiring literacy." Rather, something much more specific is going on.

First, the child is acquiring, amidst immersion and adult guidance, a piece of a particular type of *social language*. The question he has to form—and he very well knows this—has to be a *classificatory question*. It cannot be, for instance, a narrative-based question (e.g., something like "What are Donald and Daisy doing?" or "Where are Donald and Daisy going?"). Classificatory questions (and related syntactic and discourse resources) are a common part of many school-based (and academic) social

languages, especially those associated with nonliterary content areas (e.g., the sciences).

The acquisition of this piece of a social language is, in this case, scaffolded by a genre the child has acquired, namely, uncover piece of picture, form a classificatory question to which the picture is an answer (when the parent is not there to read the question for the child), and give the answer. This genre bears a good deal of similarity to a number of different nonnarrative language and action genres (routines) used in the early years of school.

We may note, finally, in regard to social languages, that the child's question is uttered in a more vernacular style than the printed question. So syntactically it is, in one sense, in the wrong "style" (though it is perfectly grammatical from a core grammar perspective, despite what school grammars might say). However, from a discourse perspective (in terms of the function its syntax carries out), it is in just the right style; that is, it is a classificatory question. And it is a mainstay of child language development that the acquisition of a function often precedes acquisition of a fully "correct" form (in the sense of "contextually appropriate," not necessarily in the sense of "grammatically correct").

In addition to acquiring a specific piece of certain sorts of social languages, the child is, also, as part and parcel of the activity, acquiring different cultural models. One of these is a cultural model about what reading is. The model is something like this: Reading is not primarily letter-by-letter decoding but the proactive production of appropriate styles of language (e.g., here a classificatory question) and their concomitant meanings in conjunction with print. This is a model that the father (at some level quite consciously) wants the child to adopt, both to sustain the child's interest in becoming a "reader" and to counteract the child's claims, in other contexts, that he "cannot read." Of course, the child's claim that he "cannot read" in those other contexts reflects that, in other activities, he is acquiring a different cultural model of reading, namely, one something like this: Reading is primarily the ability to decode letters and words and one is not a reader if meaning is not primarily driven from decoding print.

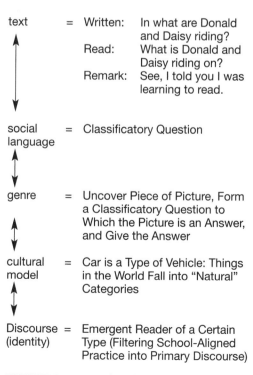

text	=	Written:	In what are Donald and Daisy riding?
		Read:	What is Donald and Daisy riding on?
		Remark:	See, I told you I was learning to read.
social language	=	Classificatory Question	
genre	=	Uncover Piece of Picture, Form a Classificatory Question to Which the Picture is an Answer, and Give the Answer	
cultural model	=	Car is a Type of Vehicle: Things in the World Fall into "Natural" Categories	
Discourse (identity)	=	Emergent Reader of a Certain Type (Filtering School-Aligned Practice into Primary Discourse)	

FIGURE 3.2. Partial analysis of a literacy event.

Of course, as his socialization proceeds, the child will acquire yet other cultural models of reading (or extend and deepen ones already acquired).

The genres, social languages, and cultural models present in this interaction between father and son existed, of course, in conjunction with ways of thinking, valuing, feeling, acting, and interacting and in conjunction with various mediating objects (e.g., the book and the "magic pen"), images (the pictures of Donald, Daisy, and the car), sites (kitchen table), and times (morning as father was about to go to work). In and through the social practices which recruit these genres, social language, and cultural models, the 3-year-old is acquiring a Discourse. The father and the child are co-constructing the child as a reader (and, indeed, a person) of *a particular type;* that is, one who takes reading to be the proactive production of appropriate styles of language and meanings in conjunction with print. This socially situated identity involves an orientation to oneself as an active producer (not just consumer) of "appropriate" meanings in conjunction with print, meanings that, in this case, turn out to be school and academically related.

However, this Discourse is not unrelated to other Discourses the child is or will be acquiring. I have repeatedly pointed out earlier how the social language, genre, and cultural models involved in this social practice are in full alignment with some of the social languages, genres, cultural models, and social practices the child will confront in the early years of school (here construing schooling in fairly traditional terms).

At the same time, this engagement between father and child, beyond being a moment in the production of the Discourse of "a certain type of reader," is also a moment in the child's acquisition of what I call his "primary Discourse." The child's primary Discourse is the ways with words, objects, and deeds that are associated with his primary sense of self formed in and through his (most certainly class-based) primary socialization within the family (or other culturally relevant primary socializing group) as a "person like us." In this case, the child is learning that "people like us" are "readers like this."

Now consider what it means that the child's acquisition of the reader Discourse (being–doing a certain type of reader) is simultaneously aligned with (traditional) school-based Discourses and part of his acquisition of his primary Discourse. This ties school-related values, attitudes, and ways with words, at a specific and not some general level, to his primary sense of self and belonging. This will almost certainly affect how the child reacts to, and resonates with, school-based ways with words and things.

If one accepts a connectionist (network, associational) view of the mind/brain (Clark, 1993; Gee, 1992), it may also affect how the child stores in his or her mind/brain the elements of early school-based or school-related literacy practices in relation to his initial experiences in and of the world. Elements of literacy practices become incorporated into the initial mental networks through which the child learns to experience the world and his initial sense of who he and his family is.

For example, the same child we have been discussing, when he was 2 years old and on his first hike in a forest, saw a squirrel and said "like Henry's forest" (from a picture in a *Thomas the Tank Engine* book). The child was interrelating, in one mental network, a book forest and a real forest, and, in fact, was interpreting the real forest partially through the book forest. Intertextuality in the sense of text–world relations (where the world is treated almost like a text) is built right into the child's initial experiences of world and family.

On the other hand, for another child, elements of early school-based or school-related literacy practices (though not necessarily the elements of culturally specific non-school-related literacy practices) may be stored quite separately from the affective and cognitive elements associated with early learning in the midst of acquiring one's primary Discourse. One can well imagine that this implies that teachers of such children may very well need to find associational "bridges" between the child's primary Discourse and early school-based Discourses if literacy practices and school Discourses are to resonate with the child's experience of the world and initial sense of self.

In conclusion, I have already several times earlier pointed out some of the implications of an NLS perspective for the study of early literacy. I can rephrase these here by saying the following: An NLS perspective implies that only when we understand a child's "multiple literacies" (i.e., different "ways with words" embedded in different social practices and Discourses) in as specific and situated a way as we tried to do with the 3-year-old can we really understand and appropriately assess a child's language and literacy development. This most certainly means understanding children's culturally specific "ways with words" that, while rooted in home or community-based Discourses, are not "school aligned" (and, in fact, children from all cultural groups have these, though some have many more than others). It means, as well, questioning the rather general way in which literacy is treated in school, much academic research, and in assessing children.

References

Barton, D. (1994). *Literacy: An introduction to the ecology of written language.* Oxford, UK: Blackwell.

Chomsky, N. (1986). *Knowledge of language.* New York: Praeger.

Chomsky, N. (1995). *The minimalist program.* Cambridge, MA: MIT Press.

Clark, A. (1993). *Associative engines: Connectionism, concepts, and representational change.* Cambridge, UK: Cambridge University Press.

Clark, H. H. (1996). *Using language.* Cambridge, UK: Cambridge University Press.

D'Andrade, R., & Strauss, C. (Eds.). (1992). *Human motives and cultural models.* Cambridge, UK: Cambridge University Press.

Engestrom, Y., Miettinen, R., & Punamaki, R-L. (Eds.). (1999). *Perspectives on activity theory.* Cambridge, UK: Cambridge University Press.

Gallas, K. (1994). *The languages of learning: How children talk, write, dance, draw, and sing their understanding of the world.* New York: Teachers College Press.

Gee, J. P. (1992). *The social mind: Language, ideology, and social practice.* New York: Bergin & Garvey.

Gee, J. P. (1994). First language acquisition as a guide for theories of learning and pedagogy, *Linguistics and Education, 6,* 331–354.

Gee, J. P. (1996). *Social linguistics and literacies: Ideology in Discourses* (2nd ed.). London: Taylor & Francis.

Gee, J. P. (1999). *An introduction to discourse analysis: Theory and method.* London: Routledge.

Halliday, M. A. K. (1994). *An introduction to functional grammar* (2nd ed.). London: Edward Arnold.

Halliday, M. A. K., & Hasan, R. (1989). *Language, context, and text: Aspects of language as a social-semiotic perspective.* Oxford, UK: Oxford University Press.

Harkness, S., Super, C., & Keefer, C. H. (1992). *Learning to be an American parent: How cultural models gain directive force.* In R. D'Andrade & C. Strauss (Eds.), *Human motives and cultural models* (pp. 163–178). Cambridge, UK: Cambridge University Press.

Heath, S. B. (1983). *Ways with words: Language, life, and work in communities and classrooms.* Cambridge, UK: Cambridge University Press.

Holland, D., Lachicotte, W., Skinner, D., & Cain, C. (1998). *Identity and agency in cultural worlds.* Cambridge, MA: Harvard University Press.

Holland, D., & Quinn, N. (Eds.). (1987). *Cultural models in language and thought.* Cambridge, UK: Cambridge University Press.

Kress, G. (1996). *Before writing: Rethinking paths into literacy.* London: Routledge.

Latour, B. (1987). *Science in action.* Cambridge, MA: Harvard University Press.

Latour, B. (1991). *We have never been modern.* Cambridge, MA: Harvard University Press.

Lave, J. (1996). Teaching, as learning, in practice. *Mind, Culture, and Activity, 3,* 149–164.

Lave, J., & Wenger, E. (1991). *Situated learning: Legitimate peripheral participation.* Cambridge, UK: Cambridge University Press.

Leont'ev, A. N. (1978). *Activity, consciousness, and personality.* Englewood Cliffs, NJ: Prentice-Hall.

Martin, J. R. (1985). *Factual writing: Exploring and challenging social reality.* Geelong, Victoria, Australia: Deakin University Press.

Miller, C. R. (1984). Genre as social action. *Quarterly Journal of Speech, 70,* 151–167.

Myers, G. (1990). *Writing biology: Texts in the social construction of scientific knowledge.* Madison: University of Wisconsin Press.

Philipsen, G. (1975). Speaking "like a man" in Teamsterville: Culture patterns of role enactment in an urban neighborhood, *Quarterly Journal of Speech, 61,* 26–39.

Pinker, S. (1994). *The language instinct: How the mind creates language.* New York: William Morrow.

Rickford, J. R. (1999). *African American vernacular English: Features, evolution, educational implications.* Oxford, UK: Blackwell.

Rogoff, B. (1990). *Apprenticeship in thinking: Cognitive development in social context.* New York: Oxford University Press.

Rosebery, A. S., Puttick, G. M., & Bodwell, M. B. (1996). *"How much light does a plant need?": Questions, data, and theories in a second grade classroom.* Portsmouth, NH: Heinemann.

Scollon, R., & Scollon, S. W. (1981). *Narrative, literacy, and face in interethnic communication.* Norwood, NJ: Ablex.

Shore, B. (1996). *Culture in mind: Cognition, cul-*

ture, and the problem of meaning. New York: Oxford University Press.

Strauss, C., & Quinn, N. (1997). *A cognitive theory of cultural meaning.* Cambridge, UK: Cambridge University Press.

Street, B. (1995). *Literacy in theory and practice.* Cambridge, UK: Cambridge University Press.

Street, B. (1995). *Social literacies: Critical approaches to literacy in development, ethnography and education.* London: Longman.

Varenne, H., & McDermott, R. (1999). *Successful failure: The school America builds.* Boulder, CO: Westview.

Wenger, E. (1998). *Communities of practice: Learn-ing, meaning, and identity.* Cambridge, UK: Cambridge University Press.

Wertsch, J. V. (1985). *Vygotsky and the social formation of mind.* Cambridge, MA: Harvard University Press.

Wertsch, J. V. (1991). *Voices of the mind: A sociocultural approach to mediated action.* Cambridge, MA: Harvard University Press.

Wertsch, J. V. (1998). *Mind as action.* Oxford, UK: Oxford University Press.

Wieder, D. L., & Pratt, S. (1990). On being a recognizable Indian among Indians. In D. Carbaugh (Ed.), *Cultural communication and intercultural contact* (pp. 45–64). Hillsdale, NJ: Erlbaum.

4

Literacy and Oral Language: Implications for Early Literacy Acquisition

❖

RITA WATSON

Two kinds of claims about the relation between literacy and oral language have been made. One is that the acquisition of literacy, and its increasingly sophisticated use over many generations, creates new kinds of thought and discourse. More simply, the claim is that literacy influences the forms of oral language. Evidence for this kind of claim is necessarily historical and cultural. While cultural explanation should be compatible with psychological explanation (cf. Kornblith, 1987; Sperber, 1996), cognitive factors alone cannot account for cultural–historical phenomena.

The second kind of claim, actually two related claims, follows from the first. It is that forms of oral language associated with literacy can be orally transmitted and, once acquired, facilitate the acquisition of literacy-related skills and success in formal education. More simply, this claim is that forms of oral language influence literacy acquisition. Evidence for the second kind of claim is necessarily psychological in nature in that it deals with the competence and performance of individuals. The contexts of acquisition and performance are, however, unalterably cultural and social (cf. Tomasello, Kruger, & Ratner, 1993).

This bidirectionality, in which literacy is claimed to both influence and be influenced by a form of oral language, invites articulation. The goal of this chapter is to approach a more coherent account of this relation. Some of the arguments that have been advanced in support of the two claims above are discussed. A pragmatic analysis suggests that while the use of written language is fundamentally similar to that of oral language, the requirements of text-based understanding could lead to an increase in metalinguistic, abstract, and paradigmatic forms in oral language. The oral transmission of these discourse forms and their influence on the early acquisition of literacy-related skills is then discussed with reference to a pragmatic theoretical framework. (For the most closely related discussions see Gee, Chapter 2; Whitehurst, Chapter 3; and Pellegrini, Chapter 4).

Literacy and Oral Language

Metalanguage

One of the most central and influential claims about the influence of literacy is that it creates new conceptions of language in its users (Olson, 1994). That is, the effect of literacy is to render the elements of language opaque, to bring them into conscious awareness. Texts heighten attention to the specific words used and to the linguistic code. Olson argues that this is because writing "fixes" a representation of the language, allowing reflection and interpretation. Language thereby becomes the object of thought. Olson uses the term "metalanguage" to refer to discourse which takes any aspect of written or spoken language as its object.

The argument that literacy increases metalinguistic awareness has a long tradition. Vygotsky (1962) argued that writing brings awareness to speech, Goody and Watt (1968) and Luria (1976) that it enabled formal logical thought, such as syllogistic reasoning, by allowing linguistic premises to be explicitly represented, preserved and operated on; Goody (1987) that writing makes speech objective by preserving statements and opening them up for critical inquiry; and Ong (1982) that writing raises consciousness in general, and consciousness of language in particular. Halliday (1987) claims that consciousness is the single most important element distinguishing the use of texts from the use of oral language, in that a higher level of consciousness of what one is trying to say underlies text revision and concern with clarity and structure in written documents.

Some of the clearest empirical evidence of an effect of literacy on conceptions of language is work on phonemic segmentation. The phonemic segmentation performance of alphabetic literates corresponds to alphabetic orthographic units, or letters. For example, they will identify three separable phonemes in words such as "bat" (b-a-t) and "cat" (c-a-t). Preliterates and nonalphabetic literates usually segment words into nonalphabetic phonemic units, such as onsets and rimes (cat: c = onset, -at = rime, c + at = onset + rime), which are more syllabic in nature (Goswami, 1986, 1991; Goswami & Bryant, 1990; Liberman, Shankweiler, Fisher, & Carter, 1974; Treiman, 1985, 1991, 1992).

The conceptual categories with which the phonemic segmentation task is accomplished, it seems clear, are influenced by the properties of the orthography acquired in learning to read. But this change is not a development from inadequate to adequate abilities for the same reason that alphabetic

literacy is no longer viewed as the end point of a historical progression toward better orthographies (Harris, 1986; Olson, 1994). The alphabetic–phonemic conceptual categories constructed by the users of alphabetic scripts are constructed because they are needed to read and write. Nonalphabetic literates show preferences that correspond to the elements of their own nonalphabetic orthography (Read, Zhang, Nie, & Ding, 1986), and there is evidence that cuneiform literates in the preclassical period developed the conception of "orthographic element," sometimes organizing texts on the basis of their syllabic orthographic properties alone rather than on the basis of semantic or referential properties. The users of logographic or syllabic scripts appear to form the conceptual categories of their spoken language that correspond to the orthographic elements that they use in order to read and write.

Any orthography, then, necessarily creates conceptual categories for thinking about language in that it requires the user to segment the stream of speech into units that can be described with that orthography. Orthographies, then, can be thought of as theories of the language they are created or adapted to represent (Watson, 2000). Such theories can be relatively simple, restricted to rules for how the stream of speech can be segmented into orthographic representation. Over time, and with increasingly sophisticated uses of texts, theories of language can become more sophisticated and include explicit formulations of such things as word meanings and grammatical form.

The metalinguistic claim, and more general claims about the role of literacy in raising awareness or consciousness of representation, has been criticized and some good evidence has been presented against it. Metalanguage is not a unique consequence of literacy. Feldman (1991) points out that traditional preliterate cultures have oral language forms, such as the poetry of the Wana culture and myths of the Ilongot, that are, in effect, fixed. These remembered oral forms could be reflected upon and interpreted much in the same way that members of Western literate societies would reflect on or interpret a written text. Narasimhan (1991) similarly argues that the ancient Rigveda texts in India, traditional oral literature, were fixed oral forms, and extensive oral commentaries on them were constructed. Carruthers (cited in Olson, 1994, p. 16) also makes the claim that writing something down cannot change our representation of it.

While there is strong evidence that orthographies influence conceptions of language, it is thus difficult to maintain that literacy has a causal role in the emergence of metalanguage or basic human metacognition. Literacy is too recent, from an evolutionary perspective, to have caused such a fundamental change in the representational capacities of the human brain (cf. Cosmides & Tooby, 1994), and developmentally, young children evidence metarepresentational abilities before they are literate (Astington, 1993). It is more likely that if literacy does have an effect on metarepresentational capacities, it is in the nature of an amplification of existing abilities. Metalanguage, although not caused by literacy, may be enhanced by literacy and may become more highly developed in a literate cultural tradition.

Decontextualization

Another widely held assumption about literacy is that it creates a distinctive mode of thought and language or genre of discourse. The most obvious way in which a written text is distinct from ordinary oral discourse is the absence of two engaged interlocutors, a speaker and a hearer, who share an immediate physical context. This observation has been the basis for claiming that writing has its effect by lifting speech out of its context (Ong, 1982) and thereby turning it into an object of thought and interpretation. This process has been characterized by many as decontextualization.

A number of features of language have been argued to distinguish a literate or decontextualized genre of discourse. One is detachment or distance. This can be marked by an increased use of the passive voice, avoidance of the first-person pronoun, and use of abstract subjects (Chafe & Danielewicz, 1987). These features reduce a sense of personal involvement in the discourse. The language of ordinary conversation shows more interpersonal involvement markers whereas "literate" language focuses on the code and content of the message (Tannen, 1985).

Decontextualization may also be marked by deictics, words that require immediate context in order to be understood. English has fewer spatial deictics than the languages of preliterate traditional societies (Denny, 1991). English deictics, "here, there, this, and that," encode only a single spatial variable, nearness or distance from the speaker. The languages of simpler, preliterate societies, notably Kikuyu and Eskimo, have deictic systems that express four and six spatial variables, respectively, showing a higher level of dependence on the nonlinguistic context for interpretation. The use of relative clauses and subordination also can indicate decontextualization (Ong, 1982) by providing linguistic cues for foregrounding or backgrounding content and marking how information is to be taken, cues that are provided by the nonlinguistic context in ordinary oral discourse. Other features, such as metaphor, can serve a similar "self-contextualizing" function, making texts more autonomous or decontextualized (cf. Halliday, 1987; Olson, 1977).

It is important to note that "literate language" and its corresponding features are not a consequence of using a written modality. Chafe and Danielewicz (1987) show that written letters to a friend contain elements of an "oral" style, whereas spoken formal lectures contain more features of detachment and could be characterized as more "literate." It is thus not the modality that is used, oral or written, that determines the presence or absence of these features. Rather, it is a pattern of language use, a kind of discourse that can manifest in either oral or written modes of production.

The above suggests that any distinctiveness that can be associated with "literate" or decontextualized discourse must be based on the frequency with which the above features appear. Use of passives and subordination is not exclusive or defining, since they appear in other forms of discourse. Like metalanguage, these features are not a unique consequence of literacy. The notion of a decontextualized or literate genre of discourse, then, while descriptively useful, may not take us far beyond description. The characterization of such a genre as "decontextualized" may also be misleading.

All communication takes place in a context of some description.

Abstraction and Paradigmatic Thought

It is difficult to address the linguistic consequences of literacy without addressing cognitive consequences. The "abstract topics" said to characterize literate discourse refer to its propositional or representational content, what it is about. The content of discourse is grounded in cognition.

One aspect of thought has long been associated with higher levels of literacy in a society. Luria (1976; Vygotsky, 1962) claimed that literates used taxonomic classification more frequently in sorting tasks and word definitions, whereas nonliterates preferred to group objects or define words according to functions. Levi-Strauss (1962) claimed that hierachical classification was more in evidence in literate Western societies, while some traditional societies showed binary opposition preferences in their cognitive organization. Bruner (1986) developed the theory that a hierarchical, paradigmatic mode of organization in language and thought is associated with a literate or scientific cognitive orientation, in contrast to a narrative mode, which is more cognitively basic and personally authentic. Narrative is the form of autobiographical memory and experience, whereas paradigmatic/hierachical organization characterizes analytic–reflective thought. An individual does not function exclusively in either mode but, rather, uses one or the other depending on the context of an activity or on a communicative goal.

Again, it seems that the consequence of a literate cultural tradition is one of increasing development or amplification of existing cognitive structures or discourse forms. Hierarchical taxonomic structures, as has become clear on both cross-cultural (Atran, 1990) and developmental (Bauer & Mandler, 1989; Markman, 1987) accounts, are universal in cognition. A literate cultural tradition could enhance or amplify this form of organization but does not cause it.

It is also important to note that the simple presence of literacy in a culture is not sufficient for a higher manifestation of paradigmatic thought to appear in either sorting or definition tasks. Vai literates whose activi-

ties with text were limited to personal use such as letter writing and account keeping showed no such effect (Scribner & Cole, 1981). It seems instead that it is the uses to which literacy is put, the cumulative effects of a literate scientific tradition, that create a bias in thought and language (Olson, 1994; Scribner & Cole, 1981).

Text-Based Understanding

On the accounts discussed above, the influence of literacy on oral language appear to be in the nature of enhancement or amplification of a particular set of existing characteristics, since most of the features that define literate genres of discourse or modes of thought are descriptive and nonunique. This gives rise to the question of how far such conceptions can take us toward a coherent or precise account of the relation between literacy and oral language.

It may be useful to entertain an alternate conceptualization. It may be that the disparate range of features associated with literate discourse or literate modes of thought could actually be predictable consequences of the sustained requirements of text-based understanding. It seems apparent that they are all nonunique to literate cultures, that they are grounded in the universal characteristics of human cognition and language and retain their imprint. What, then, does text understanding require that is unique?

Writing as Communication

Recent theories of writing suggest that historically, writing systems were invented not to transcribe speech but to convey information (Gaur, 1987; Harris, 1986). That is, texts are primarily communicative in nature. The degree to which written language fulfills its function lies in its communicative adequacy with respect to the messages that it is designed to convey rather than its representational adequacy with respect to the linguistic code. The standard account of the consequences of literacy is code-based. It claims that the representational adequacy of postclassical alphabetic orthography was largely responsible for substantial cultural and cognitive change (Goody & Watt, 1963; McLuhan, 1962; Olson, 1977; Ong,

1982). A communicative or pragmatic account suggests, rather, that any consequences of literacy on language and cognition are more likely event-based, a result of cumulative text-understanding events.

In current pragmatic theory, communication is seen as an inferential process (Blakemore, 1987; Sperber & Wilson, 1995). The derivation of meaning, whether from an utterance or a text, is accomplished on the basis of assumption schemas in the cognitive environment of the hearer or reader, including assumptions about the speaker's or writer's communicative and informative intentions. The process of inferential understanding, potentially lengthy and complex, is constrained by the principle of relevance. The hearer does not process all the explicatures and implicatures of an utterance, only enough to derive a relevant enough interpretation, that is, relevant to him or her. The most relevant interpretation is the one in which the minimum amount of effort yields the maximum contextual (cognitive) effects. On a pragmatic account, then, a reader's goal is similar to a hearer's. Both want to recover an interpretation that is relevant enough to warrant the effort invested.

Context

On a relevance-theoretic account, contexts are selected, not given. The hearer/reader selects a context, or a set of assumptions, within which an utterance or text is maximally relevant to him or her. Context is not limited to the shared physical environment of speaker and hearer. It consists in the entire set of assumptions that a hearer/reader brings to bear in the interpretation process. The difference between text understanding and utterance understanding is not a "lack of context" but, rather, a change in the sources of inference available to a reader. The hearer of an utterance can appeal to a number of sources to enrich his cognitive environment, including his interlocutor and their immediate shared environment. The reader of a text, in contrast, has fewer options. When communication fails, the reader is more heavily dependent on the written message for a resolution of the difficulty.

Beyond what is represented in the code, however, a reader must draw on his own assumptions about the text and about the intentions of the author in constructing a context for interpretation. The heightened role of the code is due to the nature of the interpretive process, not to an "absence of context." Any text understanding event has a "con-text," all nontext features that define the cognitive environment in which the interpretive process takes place. From a cognitive perspective, then, the inferential process is the same whether a comprehender is using a written code or an oral utterance as a source of input. Any difference lies in the sources of information that can be brought to bear in the inferential–interpretive process.

On the standard account, the increase in the importance of the code in written communication is a consequence of its presence as a fixed or permanent representation of language. On a pragmatic account, the importance of the code is limited to occasions on which the representational demands of text interpretation are high, when extra processing must be done to arrive at a relevant interpretation, as in cases of ambiguity or complexity. The role of the linguistic code necessarily becomes more prominent in these cases because of the difficulties of interpretation and the limitations on other sources of inference. The pragmatic account is consistent with the findings that Vai literates whose use of texts was restricted to personal goals such as letter writing showed no "consequences" of literacy as predicted by the standard account (Scribner & Cole, 1981). The representational and interpretive demands on these uses of literacy are not high enough, and the simple presence and use of an orthography does not have a significant effect.

Interpretation and Abstraction

It is exactly the cases of ambiguity or complexity, cases in which ordinary interpretation fails, that give rise to reflection and abstraction, on a pragmatic account. We saw above that neither reflection nor abstraction is a unique consequence of text understanding, but there is some suggestion that they are both amplified by texts. A reason for this emerges on the above account. In the case of failure to arrive at a relevant interpretation of a text, as in cases of ambiguity or complexity, the reader returns to the code, considering what alternate readings might be possible. Thinking of what the writer could have meant by a particular expression would lead to an enumeration of all the possible meanings that might be encoded by that expression.

This is a process of reflection on what the writer could possibly have meant, and a process of abstraction of possible meanings from a linguistic expression. The more complex and extended the text, the more reflection and abstraction would be necessary and the higher the abstract representational demand would be on the reader. Personal letters would have a low representational demand, since the reader has rich assumptions about a personal acquaintance to draw on and could also reasonably assume that ambiguities would be resolved during a subsequent personal encounter with the writer. A philosophical text, in contrast, puts an extremely high representational demand on a reader who cannot draw on personal knowledge of the writer. The degree of reflection and abstraction, then, is a consequence of the nature and uses of text, not simply the presence of the written code.

Orthographies, it was argued above, necessarily create conceptions of language that they are used to represent. Learning how an orthography segments the stream of speech into phonemic elements is like acquiring an explicit theory of a language. When the uses of that orthography remain simple, the theory remains simple. But when the uses of text become complex and sophisticated, theories necessarily develop to include concepts such as interpretation and meaning. Philosophers recognized the need for word definitions when it became evident that the senses underlying ordinary oral language understanding were not precise enough for philosophy (Olson, 1994; Watson & Olson, 1987; Watson, 2000). Explicit word definitions function as axioms in the sort of explicit, sophisticated theories of interpretation that complex texts require. They are abstract expressions of the meanings of words in natural language.

Sophisticated or opaque interpretation may itself be the mechanism by which such forms come about and, more generally, the mechanism by which literacy has its effects on language and cognition (Olson, 1994). Sophisticated interpretation recruits cognition and language in particular ways that underwrite its requirements, and by doing so repeatedly could cause the development of those cognitive and linguistic capacities.

Paradigmatic Organization

On a pragmatic inferential account of text-based understanding, it also becomes clearer why paradigmatic, hierarchical organization in thought and language may be more dominant in a literate culture. Hierarchical or superordinate category terms are inferentially rich, conveying a lot of information about underlying conceptual organization in a single word (Markman, 1987). The ability to support many inferences would make them more relevant in code-based inference. The expression "A cat is an animal" allows far more inferences about a cat, and more accurate ones, than the expression "A cat has four legs," which could also be true of a table. Using a category term in a definition, explanation, or description or classifying a picture of a cat with another animal in a sort task reflects an understanding of this inferential richness, and therefore relevance, of categorical information.

It has been shown that the taxonomic category bias in word definitions is a consequence not simply of conceptual organization but also of communicative requirements, specifically relevance (Watson, 1995). When children use superordinate category terms in definition, they almost invariably express them first. This illustrates a recognition of their relevance: They are maximally informative, are inferentially rich, and allow immediate disambiguation and reference assignment in the hearer/reader. Children increasingly use these terms as they get older. The claim that this development reflects communicative requirements rather than conceptual change is supported by the concurrent finding that functional predicates, earlier emerging developmentally and also central to conceptual understanding, continue to be expressed in definition. They are simply displaced by the increase in taxonomic expressions at the beginning of the utterance. Functional predicates are increasingly seen as less "defining," less relevant, and are relegated to the role of secondary information.

These findings suggest that what Luria (1976), Levi-Strauss (1962), and others argued was a change in the basic form of conceptual organization as a consequence of literacy is more probably a change in how conceptual organization is recruited in communicative events. The increasing dominance of taxonomic organization in word definition or classification tasks is a manifestation of their relevance to text-based or code-based inference. The same literate subjects that demonstrate it may favor functional explanation if faced with a different task environment. Similarly, the lack of taxonomic preference displayed by nonliterates on these tasks is unlikely to indicate a lack of taxonomic cognitive organization. All evidence suggests that taxonomic organization is universal and early emerging. It is more likely that the preferences such as those displayed by the unschooled Vai (Scribner & Cole, 1981) reflect their noncomplex uses of text. In the absence of text-based understanding with high representational demands, there would be no reason to develop an increased reliance on inferentially rich paradigmatic organization.

This discussion suggests that a literate cultural tradition has some influence on the development of oral language and thought. Metalanguage, abstraction, and paradigmatic organization are all present in traditional oral societies and are not caused by literacy. The representational demands of sophisticated text interpretation, however, do increase their relevance. Metalanguage is needed to map orthographies onto the stream of speech, to recognize the elements of grammar and to clarify the meanings of the lexicon. In short, metalanguage is necessary to solve a range of problems created by written communication. Reflection and abstraction are the necessary consequences of an increased reliance on the code in the disambiguation of complex written expressions. An increase in paradigmatic organization reflects the inferential richness and communicative economy afforded by a taxonomic category label. The influence is event-based, a cumulative consequence of sophisticated text-based interpretation events. The presence of a written code is in

itself not enough to create any significant change (cf. Scribner & Cole, 1981).

Oral Transmission

A number of scholars have claimed that the characteristics of oral language associated with higher levels of literacy can be orally transmitted (Heath, 1983; Mehan, 1979; cf. Olson, 1994; Scollon & Scollon, 1981; Wells, 1981). The argument is that the oral language developed in literate cultural traditions is passed on to children in daily interaction. The shared reading of books by parent and child has been implicated as a prime context for this kind of cultural transmission (Bus & van IJzendoorn, 1988; Ninio & Bruner, 1978; Snow, 1983; Watson, 1989a). Continuities between these forms of discourse in the home and the forms of discourse typical of schools is compelling and has been argued to influence the ease with which children make the transition to school and acquire cognitive and literacy skills (Heath, 1983; Scollon & Scollon, 1981; Watson & Shapiro, 1988; Wells, 1981).

A key example of this kind of talk is the known information question identified by Mehan (1979). A common discourse pattern in schools is a three-part sequence consisting of a question (Q) to which the teacher already knows the answer, the child's response (R), and an evaluative reaction (E) by the teacher, such as:

Q: What is a crocodile?

R: A crocodile is an animal with a big mouth and lots of teeth.

E: Yes that's right.

There is observational and ethnographic evidence that patterns like this are more common in middle-class homes and much less evident in working-class homes (Heath, 1983; Wells, 1981). Heath (1983) observes that even if children with no experience grasp the basic nature of the known information question, they have difficulty in understanding the underlying intention: Why would someone ask a question about something they already know?

There is also observational evidence of a bias toward paradigmatic organization in classroom discourse episodes (Watson, 1985):

Q: What is a lullaby?
A: It helps you to go to sleep at night.
Q: But what is it?
A: It's a song.
E: That's right.

Similarly, picture book "reading" between parent and child frequently includes requests for labels, descriptions, or explanations in a similar kind of triadic discourse structure (Ninio & Bruner, 1978):

MOTHER: What's that?
CHILD: Ouse.
MOTHER: Mouse, yes. That's a mouse.

MOTHER: What's that?
CHILD: Fishy.
MOTHER: Yes, and what's he doing?

The discourse pattern elicited by books, even the simple picture books shared by parent and child, thus appear to have something in common with the kinds of discourse found in schools, at least schools in the Western cultural tradition. They are both occasioned not by lived events and their necessities but by the interpretive requirements of texts and other forms of representation.

It is interesting that in school contexts, real objects can engender the same kind of discourse as books. This is shown by the following typical show-and-tell episode with a 5-year-old (Watson, 1989a):

TEACHER: What's that?
CHILD: It's an enchanted egg.
TEACHER: What does enchanted mean?
CHILD: It means there's something inside it.

When the child successfully supplies a label for the object, she is asked to define the label. The object becomes an occasion for generating explanations and definitions rather than play or action. The discourse is organized around signification and interpretation rather than enactment or experience. What the child can do with the object is less important that the verbal reports she can produce. In show-and-tell one must be able to say what one knows, to provide a verbal explanation, description, or definition.

These examples indicate that in situations such as shared book reading or show-and-tell, children are asked to interpret, define, or explain, patterns of discourse that reflect the requirements of text-based understanding. The parents and teachers in the above episodes, consciously or not, are equipping their children with the interpretive forms that they will need in order to succeed in a literate culture. These episodes are examples of oral transmission of these forms.

Cultural Learning

The examples of oral transmission given above are forms of cultural learning (Tomasello et al., 1993). The examples suggest that the oral forms argued above to be amplified by literacy, metalanguage, abstraction, and paradigmatic organization are present in the language of literate adults to their children. That this can occur even in the absence of texts, as in the show-and-tell episode, suggests that they are cultural forms rather than one-off reactions of an individual to a text. This raises the question, What is learned?

Cognition

There is some evidence that parents' speech is correlated with children's cognitive organization. The frequency with which parents use hierarchical–taxonomic labels in book-reading discourse is significantly and positively correlated to their children's subsequent category organization as revealed by picture sort tasks, sort rationale, and use of category terms in receptive language comprehension tasks and word definition tasks (Watson, 1989a, 1989b). Metalinguistic and mental state terms in parents' language—cognitive verbs such as "think, know, remember, understand" and speech verbs such as "tell, say, mean"—are similarly correlated to children's performance on these tasks.

These results show a relation between the frequency of metalanguage and paradigmatic organization in parent's talk and children's subsequent cognitive and expressive language performance on a number of tasks. The more metalanguage and paradigmatic features appear in parent's talk, the more likely it is that children will display category preferences in picture sort and rationale tasks and use hierarchical–taxonomic terms in their word definitions.

Early Literacy Skills

Whether familiarity with "literate" language influences the acquisition of print-related skills is a thornier question. A relation has been found between the use of inner-state words and metalinguistic terms in parent–child book-reading discourse and children's early concepts about print (Watson & Shapiro, 1988). A consistent relation between use of generic expressions in parent–child discourse and children's symbolic and print skills has also been found (Watson, 1996). Generic expressions are generalizations over individuals and events, such as "People ride horses," "If you put red and white together you get pink," "We get milk from cows." Weaker evidence has also been found that talk about nonpresent, past, or future events is related to preliteracy skills, and that parental responsiveness—encouragement without direct teaching or corrective feedback—is related to children's acquisition of preliteracy and early literacy skills (Watson, 1996).

Although these correlational data cannot support causal interpretation, it is highly unlikely that they are due to chance. The sheer variability of oral language makes the probability of finding such correlations unlikely. When they are found consistently in successive longitudinal analyses and across different theoretically motivated comparisons, the argument that they reflect meaningful relations is strengthened. It is, however, extraordinarily difficult to draw unequivocal conclusions from this kind of result.

The primary difficulty of exploring this question empirically is the intractable problem of differentiating oral language variables from a large number of other factors that could simultaneously influence a child's acquisition of literacy. Many factors interact with oral language, and parents who use the discourse forms above may also manifest other characteristics that could influence their child's success. Socioeconomic status, intelligence, and motivation are some obvious candidates, and biological, temperamental, and heritability factors may also be important.

Literacy itself takes many definitions. Beyond acquiring a set of basic skills for decoding and producing written symbols, children must develop an interpretive competence with many forms of representation and communication. Advancement in the institutions of a literate culture requires more than being able to read and write. It requires sophisticated interpretation and the advanced uses of texts and other forms of representation. Specific studies of skill acquisition, traditional learning studies, and experimental investigation of the processes underlying basic literacy all contribute to our understanding of aspects of this complex achievement. A causal account of the acquisition of literacy, however, waits on a better understanding of exactly what needs to be explained.

Conclusion

The influence of oral language on children's early acquisition of literacy seems obvious on ethnographic and observational accounts and is supported by correlational evidence. But these do not constitute proof. The suggestion that talking to children in a particular way will cause them to acquire literacy more easily is not warranted by the available data.

It does, however, seem warranted to conclude that texts influence the way in which language and cognition are recruited in interpretive and communicative processes. There are incontrovertible pragmatic reasons why metalanguage, abstraction, and paradigmatic organization play a greater role in the process of text understanding than in ordinary oral language comprehension. It is not an accident that they manifest more frequently in the task performance of Western-schooled literates, and the explanation for it is not culture-centric. It is simply a consequence of repeated text-based communicative events involving increasingly complex, sophisticated uses of text and the attendant interpretive requirements.

Metalanguage, abstraction, and paradigmatic organization are basic, universal features of human cognition that assume much greater importance in literate cultural traditions because of the interpretive and communicative requirements of text-based understanding. The evidence for oral transmission suggests that they become cultural forms. The definitional data suggest that they have their effects not by changing cognitive organization but by recruiting language and cognition in ways that are relevant to the task at hand.

On the theory and data discussed above, the relation of oral language to literacy and the significance of oral language transmission for the early acquisition of literacy are best characterized by the principle of relevance. A literate cultural tradition increases the relevance of metalanguage, abstraction, and paradigmatic organization in interpretation. Communicative events manifest the relevance of these forms. Children participate in these communicative events, acquire an understanding of the relevance of these forms, and subsequently use them in text-related understanding and literacy-related skills. In this way, oral language may have a broad-based influence on the acquisition of the competence that is necessary to succeed in the institutions of a literate culture. It gives children an understanding of how to recruit their knowledge in ways that are relevant to text-based understanding.

References

Astington, J. W. (1993). *The child's discovery of the mind.* Cambridge, MA: Harvard University Press.

Atran, S. (1990). *Cognitive foundations of natural history: Towards an anthropology of science.* New York and Cambridge, UK: Cambridge University Press.

Bauer, P. J., & Mandler, J. (1989). Taxonomies and triads: Conceptual organization in one-to-two year olds. *Cognitive Psychology, 21,* 156–184.

Blakemore, D. (1987). *Semantic constraints on relevance.* Oxford, UK: Blackwell.

Bruner, J. S. (1986). *Actual minds, possible worlds.* Cambridge, MA, and London: Harvard University Press.

Bus, A., & Van IJzendoorn, M. (1988). Mother–child interaction, attachment and emergent literacy. *Child Development, 59,* 1262–1272.

Chafe, W., & Danielewicz, J. (1987). Properties of spoken and written language. In R. Horowitz & J. Samuels (Eds.), *Comprehending oral and written language* (pp. 83–112). London and San Diego, CA: Academic Press.

Cosmides, L., & Tooby, J. (1994). Origins of domain specificity: The evolution of functional organization. In L. A. Hirschfeld & S. A. Gelman (Eds.), *Mapping the mind: Domain specificity in cognition and culture* (pp. 85–116). New York: Cambridge University Press.

Denny, J. P. (1991). Rational thought in oral culture and literate decontextualization. In D. R. Olson & N. Torrance (Eds.), *Literacy and orality* (pp. 66–89). Cambridge, UK: Cambridge University Press.

Feldman, C. (1991). Oral metalanguage. In D. R. Olson & N. Torrance (Eds.), *Literacy and orality* (pp. 47–65). Cambridge, UK: Cambridge University Press.

Gaur, A. (1987). *A history of writing.* London: The British Library

Goody, J. (1987). *The interface between the oral and the written.* Cambridge, UK: Cambridge University Press.

Goody, J., & Watt, I. (1963). The consequences of literacy. In J. Goody (Ed.). *Literacy in traditional societies.* Cambridge, UK: Cambridge University Press.

Goswami, U. (1986). Children's use of analogy in learning to read: A developmental study. *Journal of Experimental Child Psychology, 42,* 73–83.

Goswami, U. (1991). Learning about spelling sequences: The role of onsets and rimes in analogies in reading. *Child Development, 62,* 1110–1123.

Goswami, U., & Bryant, P. (1990). Rhyme, analogy, and children's reading. In P. B. Gough, L. C. Ehri, & R. Treiman (Eds.), *Reading acquisition* (pp. 49–64). Hillsdale, NJ: Erlbaum.

Halliday, M. A. K. (1987). Spoken and written modes of meaning. In R. Horowitz & J. Samuels (Eds.), *Comprehending oral and written language* (pp. 55–82). New York: Academic Press.

Harris, R. (1986). *The origin of writing.* London: Duckworth.

Heath, S. (1983). *Ways with words.* Cambridge, UK: Cambridge University Press.

Kornblith, H. (1987). *Naturalizing epistemology.* Cambridge, MA, and London: MIT Press.

Levi-Strauss, C. (1962). *The savage mind.* Chicago: University of Chicago Press.

Liberman, I. Y., Shankweiler, D., Fisher, F. W., & Carter, B. (1974). Explicit syllable and phoneme segmentation in the young child. *Journal of Experimental Child Psychology, 18,* 201–212.

Luria, A. (1976). *Cognitive development: Its cultural and social foundations.* Cambridge, UK: Cambridge University Press.

Markman, E. (1987). How children constrain the possible meanings of words. In U. Neisser (Ed.), *Concepts and conceptual development.* Cambridge, UK: Cambridge University Press.

McLuhan, M. (1962). *The Gutenberg galaxy.* Toronto: University of Toronto Press.

Mehan, H. (1979). *Learning lessons.* Cambridge MA: Harvard University Press.

Narasimhan, R. (1991). Literacy: Its characterization and implications. In D. R. Olson & N. Torrance (Eds.), *Literacy and orality* (pp. 177–197). Cambridge, UK: Cambridge University Press.

Ninio, A., & Bruner, J. S. (1978). The achievement and antecedents of labeling. *Journal of Child Language, 5*, 1–15.

Olson, D. R. (1977). From utterance to text: The bias of language in speech and writing. *Harvard Educational Review, 47*(3), 257–281.

Olson, D. R. (1994). *The world on paper.* Cambridge, UK: Cambridge University Press.

Ong, W. (1982). *Orality and literacy: The technologizing of the word.* London: Methuen.

Read, C. A., Zhang, Y., Nie, H., & Ding, B. (1986). The ability to manipulate speech sounds depends on knowing alphabetic reading. *Cognition, 24*, 31–44.

Scollon, R., & Scollon, S. (1981). *Narrative, literacy and face in interethnic communication.* Norwood, NJ: Ablex.

Scribner, S., & Cole, M. (1981). *The psychology of literacy.* Cambridge, UK: Cambridge University Press.

Sperber, D. (1996). *Explaining culture: A naturalistic approach.* Oxford, UK, and Cambridge, MA: Blackwell.

Sperber, D., & Wilson, D. (1995). *Relevance: Communication and cognition.* (2nd ed.). Oxford, UK, and Cambridge, MA: Blackwell. (Original work published 1986)

Snow, C. (1983). Literacy and language: Relationships during the preschool years. *Harvard Educational Review, 53*(2), 165–189.

Tannen, D. (1985). Relative focus on involvement in oral and written discourse. In D. R. Olson, A. Hildyard, & N. Torrance (Eds.), *Literacy, language and learning: The nature and consequences of reading and writing* (pp. 124–127). Cambridge, UK: The Cambridge University Press.

Tomasello, M., Kruger, A. C., & Ratner, H. H. (1993). Cultural learning. *Behavioral and Brain Sciences, 16*, 495–552.

Treiman, R. (1985). Onsets and rimes as units of spoken syllables: Evidence from children. *Journal of Experimental Child Psychology, 39*, 161–181.

Treiman, R. (1991). Phonological awareness and its role in learning to read and spell. In D. J. Sawyer & B. J. Fox (Eds.), *Phonological awareness in reading: The evolution of current perspectives* (pp. 159–189). New York: Springer-Verlag.

Treiman, R. (1992). The role of intrasyllabic units in learning to read and spell. In P. B. Gough, L. C. Ehri, & R. Treiman (Eds.), *Reading acquisition* (pp. 65–106). Hillsdale, NJ: Erlbaum.

Vygotsky, L. (1962). *Thought and language.* Cambridge, MA: MIT Press.

Watson, R. (1989a). Literate discourse and cognitive organization: Some relations between parent's talk and 3-year-olds' thought. *Applied Psycholinguistics, 10*, 221–236.

Watson, R. (1989b, April). *Saying and knowing: The development of taxonomic organization in children's expressions of meaning.* Paper presented to the Society for Research in Child Development, Kansas City, KS.

Watson, R. (1995). Relevance and definition. *Journal of Child Language, 22*, 211–222.

Watson, R. (1996). Talk about text: Literate discourse and metaliterate knowledge. In K. Reeder, J. Shapiro, R. Watson, & H. Goelman (Eds.), *Literate apprenticeships: The emergence of language and literacy in the preschool years* (pp. 81–100). Norwood, NJ: Ablex.

Watson, R. (2000). Cognition and the lexicon in the environment of texts. In J. W. Astington (Ed.), *Minds in the making* (pp. 62–79). London: Blackwell.

Watson, R., & Olson, D. R. (1987). From meaning to definition: A literate bias on the structure of word meaning. In R. Horowitz & J. Samuels (Eds.), *Comprehending oral and written language* (pp. 329–354). London and San Diego, CA: Academic Press.

Watson, R., & Shapiro, J. (1988). Discourse from home to school. *Applied Psychology: An International Review, 37*, 395–409.

Wells, G. (1981). *Learning through interaction.* Cambridge, UK: Cambridge University Press.

5

Some Theoretical and Methodological Considerations in Studying Literacy in Social Context

❖

A. D. PELLEGRINI

The social context in which literacy develops is a central theme in much of the current research in early literacy. Clearly, however, what constitutes social context is a vast territory, and theoretical, and corresponding methodological, guidance is needed to specify those aspects of the social context which support the development of literacy in young children. To date, however, most of the work in this area treats social context as a rather undifferentiated construct. For example, social context can be defined as children interacting with more competent others (e.g., Reeder, Shapiro, Watson, & Goelman, 1996) or interacting with peers (Pellegrini, Galda, Bartini, & Charak, 1998). Each of these traditions has generated important insights into the ways in which social context influences literacy learning, but it is clearly time to advance beyond this general level of understanding of social context and its role in early literacy learning.

Specifically, we need to advance beyond general conceptualization of social contexts, such as peers versus adults, and specify more exactly the nature of each of these social contexts which relate to early literacy development. With few exceptions (e.g., Bus & van IJzendoorn, 1988; Daiute, Hartup, Shool, & Zajac, 1993; Pellegrini & Galda,

1998), researchers have not attended to qualitative differences within peer or adult–child contexts and the corresponding implications for early literacy development. Further, much research pits one model or approach against the other, much of which is quite adversarial, implying that there is only one correct path to literacy.

In this chapter I discuss theoretical models of social influences on literacy drawn from sociology and ethology. Theory is needed to specify those specific aspects of social context which are relevant as it is not enough to simply say that we must look more specifically at social context or that behavior varies by context: Different theories specify the importance of different aspects of social context, and correspondingly, each sees different phenomena as relevant. Kagan's (1994) simple but cogent example of how theory determines what is considered relevant for scientific inquiry is informative: A cow and those attributes considered to be relevant for study will differ if one is, for example, an economist (cow as commodity) or a theologian (cow as sacred object). In this chapter I specify what I see as relevant in social context. Next, I address some specific methodological issues associated with studying literacy in social context.

A basic premise of this chapter is that the use of a specific oral language register, which I call literate language, is fundamental to becoming literate in school. Further, as I (e.g., Pellegrini & Galda, 1998) and others (Dickinson & Moreton, 1991; Olson, 1977; Snow, 1983) have argued elsewhere, literate language is a developmental precursor to traditional school-based literacy and a robust predictor of early school-based literacy (Pellegrini & Galda, 1998; Pellegrini et al., 1998). This is probably due to the fact that literate language shares many of design features with the oral language of literacy instruction (Cook-Gumperz, 1973; Heath, 1983) and with the written language of school-based literacy events (Olson, 1977). The correspondence of this register to school-based literacy is one of social convention, a convention that is implicitly or explicitly taught in many families and in most schools.

School-Based Literacy Is Taught, Not Acquired

As Scribner and Cole (1978) have illustrated, there are many different forms of literacy, and being literate in one area often does not transfer (in the psychological sense) to another area. There are instances in which children and mothers are literate in one area but not facile with school-based texts (Pellegrini, Perlmutter, Galda, & Brody, 1990). For example, lower socioeconomic mothers and their children may be facile at reading and talking about newspaper advertisements but not at reading an alphabet book (Pellegrini et al., 1990).The similarity and familiarity of the two formats (newspapers vs. trade books) seem to be responsible for the differences. This degree of similarity between home and school literacy events predicts success in school-based literacy.

In short, literacy is something that must be taught either implicitly or explicitly. It is not "acquired" in the same sense that oral language is acquired. Virtually all individuals (under conditions ranging from highly supportive to highly restrictive) develop dimensions of oral language that render them functional, whereas many individuals, even under relatively supportive conditions, do not become literate. Further, no scholar, to

my knowledge, has suggested a biological program for literacy as they have for oral language development (e.g., the Language Acquisition Device). Where literacy seems to be learned "naturally," as in cases of precocious readers described by Durkin (1966) and Clark (1976), features of the home environments in which literacy is learned are close to the features of school literacy events. For example, these children are read to frequently by parents, the books that are read are similar to those used in school literacy events, and the sort of talk that surrounds home literacy events is similar to the talk of school literacy events (Bernstein, 1960, 1972; Cook-Gumperz, 1977; Heath, 1983; Scollon & Scollon, 1981). In short, children are most successful in becoming literate when their socialization history is isomorphic to the socialization practice of school.

From this view, school-based literacy is only one, very specific variety of literacy. Intrinsically, it is no better or worse than other types of literacy; it just happens to be used by a certain social group. Access to this register is probably necessary, but certainly not sufficient, for success in school and probably in society at large. I make the case here that specific dimensions of children's social environments afford opportunity to learn literate language.

Design Features of Literate Language

The type of literacy taught in schools has often been described as "decontextualized" (e.g., Olson, 1977) in the sense that meaning is conveyed primarily through linguistic means, with minimal reliance on contextual cues and shared assumptions. If a speaker, for example, wanted to identify a car in a car park, literate language would encode critical information about the car (make, year, color) as well as the location (lot A, aisle 5, in the middle). More contextualized language might rely on shared knowledge (e.g., It's in the place we parked yesterday) or context (e.g., pointing to the location).

Literacy also entails the decontextualization of the "self" (Scollon & Scollon, 1981). This involves treating one's self, as well as others, as generalized others, with whom one shares little knowledge. The communicative implication of this stance is that meaning must be "lexicalized," or explicitly encoded in language. This ability to distance from and reflect on one's audience is crucial to literacy (Applebee, 1978). The literate communicator conveys meaning so that this generalized other can comprehend the message. Because of the generalized and distant nature of one's audience, communicative strategies which rely on shared knowledge assumptions and gestures do not effectively communicate meaning. Literate events in school, or those events during which individuals interact around print, too, are typically characterized by "literate language." The language of the books that children read and the language that children produce, both in writing and while talking with teachers and peers, during literacy events are "literate."

To produce and comprehend the sorts of language that minimally rely on context and maximally rely on linguistic features, children must choose from a variety of linguistic options to realize their meaningful intentions. Importantly, decontextualization and fictionalized self features of literate language should have the correlated benefit of stimulating children's metalinguistic and metacognitive awareness, or awareness of the rules and options governing language and their use in social context. That is, as children reflect on the demands of the communicative situation, they are also reflecting on the nature of language and thought processes to be used. Children's awareness of language, thought, and literacy can be inferred from their use of terms about language and thought (e.g., "talk," "say," and "think") and literacy events (e.g., "book," "pencil," and "read") (Pellegrini, Galda, Shockley, & Stahl, 1995). As is well documented, the ability to reflect on language is an important developmental precursor to school-based literacy (Adams, 1990).

Two Social Routes to Learning Literate Language

In this section I outline two possible social routes to literacy learning: (1) through exposure to a variety of social roles and (2) through a few, close, relationships. In each case, I stress the social contextual variables

supporting the learning and maintenance of literate language.

Certain developmental assumptions guide this discussion, however. First, different individuals can reach similar developmental hallmarks, such as literacy, through a variety of routes (e.g., Bateson, 1976). Given the diversity of environments into which individuals are born it would not be adaptive for there to be only one specific route to development.

Another basic developmental assumption guiding this discussion is that despite the regularity which characterizes development, there are also individual differences which mediate individuals' transitions with the environment. Further, accounting for individual differences helps us avoid the trap of presenting the individual as a passive responder to the environment. Models which do not make such provision often reduce learning and development to some variant of learning theory and social transmission (see Tooby & Cosmides, 1992, for extended discussions). Individual differences inherent to the child interact with the specific socialization environments to influence developmental trajectories. In short, individuals and environments influence each other in a recursive manner.

Path 1: Variety of Social Contacts

That children's cognitive and linguistic processes can be affected by a varied social network is well situated in theoretical traditions in sociology and ethology. Here I briefly discuss relevant aspects of each theory.

SOCIOLOGY OF EDUCATION

Sociologists, of course, are interested in social processes and, at least since Durkheim and G. H. Mead, have been interested in the ways in which social processes map onto language and cognitive processes. Following the Durkheimian tradition, the English sociologist of education, Basil Bernstein (1960, 1971, 1972, 1982), developed one of the most thorough, and perhaps most controversial, theories relating social context to literate language. At the most general level, Bernstein proposed, like Halliday (1973), that the structure, or form, of language follows the function for which it is used. Bernstein suggested, specifically, that children's ability to use literate language (though he used the term "elaborated code") was a result of their socialization experiences at home. The socialization practices of middle-class homes, he argued, resembled those of most schools. Thus, the relative status of middle-class children in their facility with school language and achievement is a result of the isomorphism between middle and school socialization practices, as I argued earlier.

Bernstein specified four socialization contexts at home and at school: the regulative context (where the child is made aware of moral order and rules), the instructional context (where children learn skills and about objects and people), the imaginative context (where child is encouraged to experiment and re-create the world in his or her own terms), and the interpersonal context (where the child becomes aware of his or her own and others' affective states). Children in different groups are socialized to take different roles in each of these contexts.

These different socialization practices have direct implications for children's language use. Take the regulative context. If children are treated according to a "positional" orientation, their language and social experiences are limited to culturally determined roles (e.g., children should always obey parents, without question or explanation). Caregivers set out guidelines without providing rationales or expecting feedback from children. The implication of this orientation is that children do not have to verbally explicate meaning to be understood: Meaning can be conveyed by virtue of one's assigned social role—not through verbal explanation. Such limited role experiences (they are only recipients of orders) and the language they use in these situations may evidence a paucity of appeals based on reasoning and causal conjunctions (e.g., "Do this *because* it's your turn"). These sorts of socialization contexts are typified by strictly defined power relationships. Caregivers and parents, by definition of their roles, give orders and children, correspondingly, comply without question; this is exemplary of Bernstein's notion of strong classification (Bernstein, 1982).

By contrast, a person-centered orientation involves a looser power relationship. Roles are based on reasoning, not on assigned position. Consequently, in a regulative context children must define their social roles by appropriate social and linguistic behavior; they cannot merely step into a positionally defined role. Part of the process of defining a role, according to Bernstein (1972), entails making role relationships opaque. Children in these circumstances reflect on their roles and those of the interlocutors and follow role-appropriate social and linguistic rules. In short, the person-centered orientation socializes children to a "fictionalized self" orientation, to verbally explicate meaning, and to reflect on the rules of different speech events.

When children from positional and person-oriented traditions go to school they often encounter an institution that does not encourage (or indeed tolerate) deviations from accepted social behaviors and registers; this is Bernstein's (1982) notion of a strong frame. Thus, children who have learned the language of school are speaking the socially accepted register of school; other language varieties are not tolerated. The implications for school success then becomes painfully clear and predictable.

That these socially accepted registers can be learned in school and in the community, even if they have not been learned initially at home, is an important dimension of Bernstein's theory. Unlike more fatalistic theories (e.g., Gee, 1989), which put forth a variant of the "critical period hypothesis" (i.e., If you haven't been socialized to learn school language by the time you enter school, it is nearly impossible to learn it), children can and do learn the school register if the frame and classification systems in schools (Cazden, 1995) and other socialization contexts (e.g., churches and youth groups) is weakened.

As I noted earlier, Bernstein's theory was very controversial when it was introduced. Much of the controversy related to discussions of class differences and socialization contexts. The heart of the controversy related to the perception that elaborated code and its speakers were superior to restricted code and its speakers (Hymes, 1995). I say "perception" because many scholars (e.g., Halliday, 1973, 1995; Hymes, 1995), myself included, believe that much of the criticism was unjust. Rather than saying one code was superior to another, Bernstein was saying, I think, that language structure and form are determined by social processes. One variant of language is no better or worse than another; they merely reflect language used in different settings. Schooling and elaborated code represent one socialization context and one variety of language. This variant of language, however, has been given high status by our society.

Bernstein's theory stimulated a massive amount of research in the United Kingdom (e.g.,Tizzard & Hughes, 1984; Wells, 1981) and in the United States (Hess & Shipman, 1965), and in many cases the hypothesized class differences (in the United Kingdom) and in the United States were not supported. The more basic dimension of the theory has been supported, however: Children's socialization contexts affect social behavior, language, and school success. This point was clearly made by Heath (1983) in her longitudinal ethnography in the American South. Here I present another, and perhaps less familiar, example which also supports this position.

Drawing from the literature on family interaction, recent research has shown that children reared in *authoritative* families (Baumrind, 1989) are more socially competent and achieve in school at higher levels than do children in other socialization arrangements. Authoritative parenting practices are generally defined as responsive to children's needs yet demanding. Steinberg and colleagues (Steinberg, Dombusch, & Brown, 1992) have further illustrated that autonomy granting and democratic orientations within an authoritative style are particularly important in predicting school success. Examples of democratic and autonomy granting orientations include parent–child joint decision making. This orientation is strikingly similar to Bernstein's person-oriented socialization style.

ETHOLOGY

Ethologists are biologists who study animal behavior from an evolutionary perspective (Tinbergen, 1963). To accomplish this study, ethologists rely on in-depth observations of animals in natural and experimental contexts. While the mainstay of ethological research involves careful description, an important dimension of ethological research involves making inferences about the cognitive processes of animals from their social behaviors (Bjorklund & Pellegrini, in press; Smith, 1998).

One branch of ethology also stresses the importance of interacting with a varied social network in maximizing cognitive and linguistic development (see Tomasello & Call, 1998, for an extended discussion). At a general level, ethological theory posits that primate cognition evolved in the context of individuals having to keep track of conspecifics in their immediate group (Bjorklund & Pellegrini, in press; Dunbar & Spoor, 1995; Humphrey, 1976; Jolly, 1966). This level of recordkeeping is necessary to recognize allies and enemies. Enemies are remembered for their negative acts or alliances. Similarly, allies are remembered for their help; thus individuals know they can be cooperative with these individuals as their cooperation will likely be reciprocated. This sort of social knowledge has been naturally selected for because it relates to individuals' survival and reproduction. It is clearly dangerous to be too trusting of enemies. Similarly, cooperation should be reciprocated because it benefits all parties involved (Axelrod & Hamilton, 1981).

As the variety and number of social contacts increase, so too must the complexity of the cognitions necessary to keep track of individuals and their actions. This proposition leads to the hypothesis that experience with a varied, or a diverse, group of peers should relate to cognitive development generally and the use of literate language specifically. A more modularized version of this hypothesis holds that intelligence generally is not affected by social interaction, but only a specific social intelligence module is affected (Cosmides & Tooby, 1992; Tomasello & Call, 1998).

A test of the hypothesized relation between the variety of children's social contacts and literacy learning was conducted by Pellegrini and colleagues (1995) with a group of first-graders. The variety of children's social contacts at home was measured three times a week across the whole school year using child literacy diaries. The variety of children's social contacts in their classrooms was assessed across the whole year using diaries taken home by children and direct observations of children in their classrooms.

Findings support the variety hypothesis to the extent that the variety of social contacts at home was positively and significantly correlated with the variety at school; both variety measures were positively and significantly correlated with cognitive perspective taking and literate language. Literate language was, in turn, correlated with measures of metalinguistic awareness and school-based literacy, such as Clay's Concepts about Print. Of course, a longitudinal research design is necessary to establish directionality and causality: Is it intelligence, or social intelligence, that affects a variety of social contacts or vice versa.

Path 2: Close Relationships

SOCIOLOGY

There is tradition in sociology, associated with the Chicago school, most notably Cooley and Mead, whereby individuals come to know themselves, and to have knowledge about their social and cognitive understanding of the world, by interacting with "significant others." Unlike the Piagetian position, which holds that knowledge about self develops from the inside out, this position posits that children come to reflect on their knowledge of social, cognitive, and linguistic processes by interacting with others who are close (i.e., familiar, trusting, and emotionally involved with) to them, such as friends and siblings (Dunn, 1988). These close interactions, which often involve bouts of conflict, elicit high levels of emotionality. In the process of trying to "cool" these emotions, children typically talk about them by verbally encoding emotion state words, such as "sad" and "happy." This process, in turn, results in children reflecting not only on their emotional states, but also on the social and linguistic processes involved in those interactions (Pellegrini, Galda, Flor, Bartini, & Charak, 1997). One realization of this "meta" process is children's use of literate language.

ETHOLOGY

That close relationships may foster cognitive and linguistic development is also con-

sistent with some ethological theory. This notion is an extension of kin selection theory (Trivers, 1972, 1985), a branch of evolutionary biology which states that individuals will cooperate with kin and, by extension, familiar and close peers, such as friends (Tomasello & Call, 1996), relative to unfamiliar and psychologically distant peers. Cooperation is more likely to be observed with close, familiar others for two reasons. First, in the environment of evolutionary adaptedness kin comprise a sizable portion of one's social group (Tomasello & Call, 1998). Indeed, even in contemporary society, kin, relative to nonkin, comprise a sizable portion of individuals' supportive social networks (Dunbar & Spoor, 1995). Kin cooperate with each other in the interest of promoting their own survival. Moving beyond cooperation with kin to cooperation with familiar, close peers, such as friends, cooperation is adaptive because of the high likelihood that it will be reciprocated by familiar others, in a *quid pro quo* fashion (Axelrod & Hamilton, 1981).

Close relationships, such as sibling relationships, friendships, and attachment relationships, are characterized by trust and emotional investment. This emotional component may be particularly important for children learning literate language to the extent that these relations afford opportunities to disagree and resolve disagreement. These, in turn, allow children to reflect on the social interactive process and corresponding language forms (Pellegrini & Galda, 1998; Pellegrini et al., 1997, 1998): Children in close relationships tend to monitor and remember the details of their interactions and disagreements (Dunn & Slomkowski, 1992). Evidence of children's monitoring of the social interactive processes includes children's talk about "internal states," such as emotions and language.

A direct test of the effects of friendship groupings on children's use of literate language and literacy was conducted by Pellegrini and colleagues (1997, 1998). Groups of kindergarten children were observed in one of two conditions across a whole school year: with reciprocally nominated friends or with acquaintances. Results suggest that although friends and acquaintances did not vary in number of conceptual conflicts, friends were more likely to resolve the conflicts. In addition, friends, compared to non-friends, exhibited more emotional terms and literate language. Using structural equation modeling, we (Pellegrini et al., 1997) supported the hypothesized process from conflicts and resolutions to the use of emotional terms then to literate language. Literate language, in turn, predicted school-based literacy.

To my knowledge, a direct test of the relative effect of close versus varied social contacts with children of different temperaments has not been conducted. Such a test is clearly needed as the extant work on diverse social contacts is correlational and the directionality is unclear. It could be the case that facility with literate language enables children to interact with a varied social network. Currently, Edward Melhuish at Cardiff University, Ithel Jones at Florida State University, and I are testing experimentally the relative effects of close and varied peer groupings on Welsh infant schoolchildren's literate language.

Methodological Issues Associated with Studying Literacy in Social Context

Standard Methods in Studying Early Literacy

The study of early literacy is characterized by a wide variety of methodological approaches, ranging from psychological procedures used by Snow, Dickinson, and their colleagues to ethnographic studies.

The dominant psychological theory in the study of early literacy is derived from Vygotsky's sociohistorical theory. In this model, as we all know, children learn specific skills in the context of interacting with a more competent tutor (see Mason & Sinha, 1993, for a thorough review of this literature). Given the context sensitivity of much of this work, interactions between children and their parents are typically recorded in their homes.

In addition, observations between children and their teachers are also conducted in their classrooms. Oral language and social behavior is typically sampled and recorded and related to induced or preexist-

ing measures of literacy. Children's social relationships are typically measured through some form of sociometric nomination or rating system.

In this section, I discuss observational methods used by ethologists to study children's social behavior. As noted previously, ethologists use observational methods to describe behavior in its natural habitat. To this end, behavioral categories are often induced to index the behavioral repertoires of their focal children. I limit my discussion of the use of observational methods to address the measurement of variety and quality of social relationships as those dimensions are theoretically relevant to the arguments presented earlier.

I discuss sampling and recording rules which are used in direct and indirect observational methods. Direct methods are used for "live" observations, where observers sample and record behavior from the ongoing streams of behavior. Indirect methods, such as diary techniques, involve a research participant or his or her teacher or parent sampling and recording relevant behavior from a distance. Use of indirect methods is often dictated by the inaccessibility of the participants or the targeted behavior. For example, diary methods are especially useful in gathering information on literacy practices at home.

Specification of sampling and recording rules are especially important to discuss. For example, specific sampling and recording rules are necessary to collect frequency data. Frequencies of social interactants and variety of social partners are relevant measures for the theories discussed previously. Similarly, in using observational methods to measure closeness, only certain sampling and recording rules are appropriate.

Direct Observations of Children

Sampling rules refer to the procedures we follow to sample behavior from its ongoing stream. Recording rules refer to the principles used to encode them. Both sets of rules should be followed to minimize biases of various sorts (Martin & Bateson, 1996; Pellegrini, 1996). For example, sampling rules minimize biases associated with observers attending to the closest and most visible participants and behaviors. Importantly, the choice of recording rules, further influences the sorts of measures which can be derived from our observation. If, for example, we are interested in recording information on "closeness" (a dimension of intensity) or "frequency," we would be limited to specific recording rules. Table 5.1 presents a matrix of sampling and corresponding recording rules, as well as associated measures.

Ad lib sampling is not systematic to the extent that no rules are followed. It merely has an observer looking at the people and events in which he or she is interested. Although this type of sampling is rife with possibilities for bias (e.g., an observer may unintentionally spend disproportionate amounts of time observing a limited set of children or in a limit space) it is useful at the beginning of a project. For example, an observer and the participants can get used to each other during the initial stages of a project.

Focal child sampling involves choosing a specific child to observe in a predetermined order for a specific time. By varying the order in which children are observed, this sampling procedure minimizes biases associated with observing a specific set of children, such as those most visible or those in close proximity to the observer. It can be paired with any of the three recording rules: continuous (where the behavior of an individual is recorded continuously for a speci-

fied period of time, the sampling interval), 0/1 (where an occurrence, marked by a 1, or 0 for the nonoccurrence of behavior, during the sampling interval), or instantaneous recording (where behavior is recorded at the instance where the sampling interval is marked). With 0/1, recording frequencies cannot be derived because a 1 is entered if a behavior occurs 1 time or 20 times during an interval. Instantaneous recording can also be used with focal child sampling. It involves recording the behavior of interest at the instant that a signal (e.g., a beeper on a watch) occurs. Focal child sampling with continuous recording is an excellent choice for observing social interactions of children across time. Importantly, frequencies can *only* be derived from continuous recording.

Scan sampling involves scanning each individual in a whole group rapidly, and repeatedly; thus only instantaneous recording is used. For example, a classroom could be scanned, where an observer looks at each child for 1 second and records attention/inattention. Numbers scans can be conducted across specified periods to increase the representativeness of the sampled behavior.

Event, or behavior, sampling is used when we are especially interested in a relatively rare or infrequently occurring event, such as aggression. We observe until that event occurs; then we record it continuously from beginning to end (with continuous recording) or merely mark 1 if it occurred (with 0/1 recording).

As can also be seen in Table 5.1, we can only derive frequencies from continuously recorded data. Similarly, with this recording rule we can also derive durations, or how long specified behaviors last (e.g., how long children play together continuously), latencies, or time from the presentation of a stimulus, (e.g., presentation of a flash card, and a response, reading the word on the card), pattern, or how a series of related behaviors unfolds across time (e.g., an adult reader asks a child a question about the text, the child answers correctly, and the adult, then asks a clarification question). Finally, measures of intensity, or magnitude, can also be derived from continuous recording; for example, one dimension of intensity might include "closeness" of children's relationships. Notoriously difficult to quantify, intensity

TABLE 5.1. Sampling and Recording Rules

	Recording rules		
	Continuous	0/1	Instantaneous
Sampling rules			
Ad lib			
Focal child	X	X	X
Scan			X
Event	X	X	
Measures			
Frequency	X		
Duration	X		
Latency	X		
Pattern	X		
Intensity	X	X	X

ratings are often derived by adding the components of a category to come up with a score. For example, closeness might be defined in terms of reciprocal interactions, positive affect, physical proximity, and mutual gaze exchange. A "high" rating of closeness might have all four components of the category and a low rating would have one. Of course, this approach assumes that all components are equally interesting, which may or may not be true. This component definition of closeness might be particularly useful in conjunction with a duration measure, such as time spent together, or the durations associated with each behavioral dimension.

A variant of this approach was used to study the variety of children's social partners in a study of first-graders' literacy (Pellegrini et al., 1995). In this study, the variety of peers with whom focal children interacted in their classrooms was continuously recorded across the whole year. This measure was related to other measures of social competence (e.g., variety of social partners at home) and to perspective taking. Diary measures were used to measure the variety of social participants in home-based literacy events.

The use of observational methods to study close relationships (e.g., children's friendship) is less common. As noted earlier, friendship is typically measured by having children nominate peers as friends and a friendship relationship is typically defined as reciprocally nominated pairs. In some cases the use of nominations is questioned by schools and parents. It is assumed that asking children to nominate peers makes some children feel excluded, though there is no evidence, to my knowledge, to support this claim.

Observational methods can be used to measure friendship by incorporating criterial dimensions of friendship: reciprocity, mutuality, propinquity, and emotional investment (Hartup, 1996). For example, reciprocity can be observed in terms of equality of the roles taken by children. Mutuality can be observed in terms of sharing. Propinquity can be measured by physical proximity and duration of time spent together. The validity of the observational measure of friendships was evidenced by the positive correlations between behavior measures and friendship nominations.

Using Diaries to Sample and Record Behavior

Previously described methods are most frequently applied to "live" or "direct" observations. We typically conduct these observations in public places and places to which researchers have easy access. This is probably why so much of the child development and early literacy research has been conducted in classrooms and so little has been conducted in those places in which children spend the majority of their time: in their communities. Clearly, we need to know about children's experiences outside school to help us understand their behavior in school. This is abundantly clearly from the theoretical and empirical work of Bernstein (1971, 1972, 1982) and Heath (1983). The difficulties and expenses associated with conducting observational research in the community, however, are powerful deterrents.

Diary or indirect methods (Pellegrini, 1996) are a family of measures whereby social interaction can be sampled and recorded. Indeed, diary methods have a long and interesting history in child study, psychology, and education. For example, Darwin (1877) used a diary to record observations of his child. Further, classic studies in child language used this method (Brown, 1973). More recently we have used diaries to record first-grade children's literacy-related behaviors and the people at home with whom they interact in literacy events (Pellegrini et al., 1995) and the peers with whom young adolescents interact before and after school (Pellegrini & Bartini, 2000).

Sampling and recording rules must also be kept in mind when using diaries. Specific to sampling rules, it is imperative for the researcher to specify the time he or she wants the data to be recorded (e.g., record for the period from 3 P.M. yesterday to 7 A.M. today). In other instances, we can use time-, rather than event-based, sampling rules to spot-sample children, as Bloch (1989) did when she called children or their parents at home during various parts of the day to sample who they are playing with and where. Similarly, Csikszentmihalyi and Larsen (1984) provided participants with preprogrammed "beepers"; when the beepers sound, the participants record the behaviors of interest. Clearly, a varied and extensive sampling plan is necessary for reliable and valid data.

Recording rules can also influence the reliability and validity of data collected from diaries. I have found that providing respondents with a set "glossary" of words from which to answer specific diary questions maximizes data validity. For example, in our work on children reading books at home (Pellegrini et al., 1995), we listed the possible participants with whom they could have interacted. More recently, in our work on adolescent aggression (Pellegrini & Bartini, 2000), we have provided specific words as possible responses for each question (e.g., How did this make you feel? Sad? Happy? Proud? Foolish? I'm not sure?). Of course, the lists of words can only be generated after less structured pilot work, to identify possible categories.

In this latter work, we found that diaries correlated significantly with other measures which tapped feelings and events, such as self-reports and peer responses. The diaries did not correlate significantly with direct observations or with teachers' ratings. It is probably the case that different methods are complementary, not overlapping. We concluded that the diaries, self-reports, and peer measures related to "insider" views of behavior and the direct observations and teacher rating were indicative of the outsider, public view. Both perspectives are clearly necessary to understand children in schools.

Conclusions

In this chapter I suggested that children's socialization experiences, both in the home and with their peer groups, have important implications for the social roles and rules they learn. These socialization experiences, in turn, affect children's learning of literate language. In one sort of socialization experience, the varied route, we find that children socialize to take on different roles and interact with a variety of people develop literate language as a consequence of these varied social experiences.

In another social context, the closeness route, the quality of the social relationship is important rather than just diverse experiences. In close peer relationships (e.g., friendships) children learn to monitor the interactive process such that they treat the rules of literacy as opaque and consequently are capable of "going meta" on these rules. This "meta" ability is crucial in school-based literacy learning.

These findings are relevant to both the theory and the practice surrounding school-based literacy. Regarding theory, these results point out the importance of recognizing that children attain developmental hallmarks through different routes. That there is no one "royal route" to competence is a logical, and empirical, extension of the position that children are born into a wide variety of niches and that survival necessitates adaptation to those different niches.

At the level of practice, these findings provide at least two different social contexts which support early literacy. Application of a specific social grouping practice might result from children's preferences. For example, it might be the case that certain children (e.g., shy/inhibited children) are more likely to engage in conceptual conflict-resolution cycles and to reflect on corresponding emotional and linguistic processes when with friends than when with acquaintances (Pellegrini et al., 1997).

Future research should document the extent to which individual differences in children (e.g., differences in sociability and shyness) bias them toward certain social grouping in different contexts. It may be the case, for example, that shy children pursue close relationships and sociable children choose to interact with a more diverse social field.

I also outlined a variety of methods by which these matters of social context could be studied. It is especially important that we extend our studies of children's social context beyond those already studied thoroughly: the classroom and the mother–child book-reading dyads. To this end, it is probably necessary to observe children directly in their communities or to use diary methods when this approach is too expensive.

Acknowledgment

I acknowledge the helpful comments of David Dickinson on an earlier draft of this chapter.

References

Adams, M. J. (1990). *Beginning to read.* Cambridge, MA: MIT Press.

Applebee, A. (1978). *The child's concept of story.* Chicago: University of Chicago Press.

Axelrod, R., & Hamilton. W. D. (1981). The evolution of cooperation. *Science, 211,* 1390–1396

Bateson, P. P. G. (1976). Rules and reciprocity in behavioral development. In P. P. G. Bateson & R. A. Hinde (Eds.), *Growing points in ethology* (pp. 410–421). New York: Cambridge University Press.

Baumrind, D. (1989). Rearing competent children. In W. Damon (Ed.), *Child development today and tomorrow* (pp. 349–378). San Francisco: Jossey-Bass.

Bernstein, B. (1960). Language and social class. *British Journal of Sociology, 2,* 217–276.

Bernstein, B. (1971). *Class, codes, and control* (vol. 1). London: Routledge & Kegan Paul.

Bernstein, B. (1972). Social class, language, and socialization. In P. Giglioli (Ed.), *Language and social context* (pp. 157–178). Hammondsworth, UK: Penguin.

Bernstein, B. (1982). Codes, modalities and the process of cultural reproduction: A model. In M. Apple (Ed.), *Cultural and production in education.* Boston: Routledge.

Bjorklund, D., & Pellegrini, A. D. (in press). *Phylogeny and ontogeny: The emergence of evolutionary developmental psychology.* Washington, DC: American Psychological Association.

Bloch, M. (1989). Young girls' and boys' play at home and in the community. In M. Bloch & A. D. Pellegrini (Eds.), *The ecological context of children's play* (pp. 120–154). Norwood, NJ: Ablex.

Brown, R. (1973). *A first language.* Cambridge, MA: Harvard University Press.

Bus, A. G., & van IJzendoorn, M. (1988). Mother–child interaction, attachment, and emergent literacy. *Child Development, 59,* 1262–1272.

Cazden, C. B. (1995). Visible and invisible pedagogies in literacy education. In P. Atkinson, B. Davies, & S. Delamont (Eds.), *Discourse and reproduction* (pp. 159–172). Cresskill, NY: Hampton Press.

Clark, M. (1976). *Young fluent readers.* London: Heinnemann.

Cook-Gumperz, J. (1973). Situated instructions: Language socialization of school aged children. In S. Ervin-Tripp & C. Mitchell-Kernan (Eds.), *Child discourse* (pp. 103–124). New York: Academic Press.

Cosmides, L., & Tooby, J. (1992). Cognitive adaptations for social exchange. In J. H. Barkow, L. Cosmides, & J. Tooby (Eds.), *The adapted mind: Evolutionary psychology and the generation of culture* (pp. 163–228). New York: Oxford University Press.

Csikszentmihalyi, M., & Larsen, R. (1984). *Being adolescent.* New York: Basic Books.

Daiute, C., Hartup, W., Sholl, W., & Zajac, R. (1993, April). *Peer collaboration and written language development.* Paper presented at the biennial meetings of the Society for Research in Child Development, New Orleans.

Darwin, C. (1877). Biographical sketch of an infant. *Mind, 2,* 285–294.

Dickinson, D., & Moreton, J. (1991). *Predicting specific kindergarten literacy skills from three-year-olds preschool experience.* Paper presented at the biennial meetings of the Society for Research in Child Development, Seattle.

Dunbar, R. I. M., & Spoor, M. (1995). Social networks, support cliques, and kinship. *Human Nature, 6,* 273–290.

Dunn, J. (1988). *The beginnings of social understanding.* Cambridge, MA: Harvard University Press.

Dunn, J., & Slomkowski, C. (1992). Conflict and the development of social understanding. In C. U. Shantz & W. W. Hartup (Eds.), *Conflict in child and adolescent development* (pp. 70–97). New York: Cambridge University Press.

Durkin, D. (1966). *Children who read early: Social bases of early literacy.* New York: Teachers College Press.

Gee, J. P. (1989). Literacy, discourse, and linguistics *Journal of Education, M*(1, whole number).

Halliday, M. A. K. (1973). The functional basis of language. In B. Bernstein (Ed.), *Class, codes, and control* (vol. 2, pp. 343–366). London: Routledge & Kegan Paul.

Halliday, M. A. K. (1995). Language and the theory of codes. In A. R. Sadovnik (Ed.), *Knowledge and pedagogy* (pp. 127–143). Norwood, NJ: Ablex.

Hartup, W. W. (1996). The company they keep: Friendships and their developmental significance. *Child Development, 67,* 1–13.

Heath, S. B. (1983). *Ways with words.* New York: Cambridge University Press.

Hess, R. D., & Shipman, V. C. (1965). Early experience and the socialization of cognitive modes in children. *Child Development, 30,* 369–386.

Humphrey, N. K. (1976). The social function of intellect. In P. P. G. Bateson & R. A. Hinde (Eds.), *Growing points in ethology* (pp. 303–317). Cambridge, UK: Cambridge University Press.

Hymes, D. (1995). Bernstein and poetic. In P. Atkinson, B. Davies, & S. Delamont (Eds.), *Discourse and reproduction* (pp. 1–24). Cresskill, NY: Hampton Press.

Jolly, A. (1966). Lemur social behavior and primate intelligence. *Science, 153,* 501–506.

Kagan, J. (1994). On the nature of emotion. In N. Fox (Ed.), The nature of emotion regulation. *Monographs of the Society for Research in Child Development, 59*(2–3, Serial No. 240).

Martin, P., & Bateson, P. (1996). *Measuring behavior.* London: Cambridge University Press.

Mason, J., & Sinha, A. (1993). Emerging literacy in the early childhood years. In B. Spodek (Ed.), *Handbook of research on the education of young children* (pp. 137–150). New York: Macmillan.

Olson, D. R. (1977). From utterance to text. *Harvard Educational Review, 47,* 257–281.

Pellegrini, A. D. (1996). *Observing children in the*

natural worlds: A methodological primer. Mahwah, NJ: Erlbaum.

Pellegrini, A. D., & Bartini, M. (2000). An empirical comparison of methods of sampling aggression and victimization in school settings. *Journal of Educational Psychology, 92,* 360–366.

Pellegrini, A. D., & Galda, L. (1998). *The development of school-based literacy: A social ecological perspective.* London: Routledge.

Pellegrini, A. D., Galda, L., Bartini, M., & Charak, D. (1998). Oral language and literacy learning in context: The role of social relationships. *Merrill-Palmer Quarterly, 44,* 38–54.

Pellegrini, A. D., Galda, L., Flor, D., Bartini, D., & Charak, D. (1997). Close relationships, individual differences and early literacy learning. *Journal of Experimental Child Psychology, 7,* 409–422.

Pellegrini, A. D., Galda, L., Shockley, B., & Stahl, S. (1995). The nexus of social and literacy experiences at home and school: Implications for primary school oral language and literacy. *British Journal of Educational Psychology, 65,* 273–285.

Pellegrini, A. D., Perlmutter, J. C., Galda, L., & Brody, G. H. (1990). Joint reading between Head Start children and their mothers. *Child Development, 61,* 51–67.

Reeder, K., Shapiro, J., Watson, R., & Goelman, H. (1996). *Literate apprenticeships.* Norwood, NJ: Ablex.

Scollon, R., & Scollon, S. (1981). *Narrative and face in inter-ethnic communication.* Norwood, NJ: Ablex.

Scribner, S., & Cole, M. (1978). Literacy without schooling. *Harvard Educational Review, 48,* 448–461.

Smith, P. K. (1998). Ethological methods in early childhood education. In B. Spodek, O. Saracho, & A. D. Pellegrini (Eds.), *Issues in early childhood educational research* (pp. 93–112). New York: Teachers College Press.

Snow, C. (1983). Literacy and language. *Harvard Educational Review, 53,* 165–189.

Steinberg, L., Dornbusch, S. M., & Brown, B. B. (1992). Ethnic differences in adolescent achievement. *American Psychologist, 47,* 723–729.

Tinbergen, N. (1963). On the aims and methods of ethology. *Zeitschrift fur Tierpsychologie, 20,* 410–433.

Tizzard, B., & Hughes, M. (1984). *Young children learning.* Cambridge, MA: Harvard University Press.

Tomasello, M., & Call, J. (1998). *Primate cognition.* New York: Oxford University Press.

Tooby, J., & Cosmides, L. (1992). The psychological foundations of culture. In J. H. Barkow, L. Cosmides, & J. Tooby (Eds.), *The adapted mind: Evolutionary psychology and the generation of culture* (pp. 19–136). New York: Oxford University Press.

Trivers, R. (1972). Parental investment and sexual selection. In B. Campbell (Ed.), *Sexual selection and the descent of man* (pp. 136–179). Chicago: Aldine.

Trivers, R. (1985). *Social evolution.* Menlo Park, CA: Benjamin/Cummings.

Wells, G. (1981). *Learning through interaction.* London: Cambridge University Press.

6

Alphabetic Anxiety and Explicit, Systematic Phonics Instruction: A Cognitive Science Perspective

❖

MARILYN J. ADAMS

The invention of the alphabet has been broadly hailed as perhaps the most intellectually liberating invention in the social history of the world. Historian David Diringer (1968) described it as "the creation of a 'revolutionary writing' a script which we can perhaps term 'democratic' (or, rather, a 'people's script', as against the 'theocratic' scripts that preceded it" (p. 161). After all, a language may embrace thousands upon thousands of words. In contrast, the number of symbols in an alphabetic system are few enough to be learned by almost anyone and once learned and understood are adequate for reading and writing any speakable expression in the language.

Beyond any such arguments about the benefits of the alphabetic principle in theory is a wealth of research and scholarship affirming its fundamental importance in practice. Nevertheless, issues of whether and how to teach the alphabetic basics to young readers are, even today, the most divisive and disruptive topics in all of education. (For related discussions of basic development see Goswami, Chapter 9, and Whitehurst, Chapter 2, for related discussions of instructional methods, see Stahl, Chapter 23, and Hiebert, Chapter 25.)

Over the last several decades, as provoked by this debate, the public has three times sponsored comprehensive reviews of the professional literature in this domain, beginning with Jeanne Chall's classic, *Learning to Read: The Great Debate* (1967). Although, as permitted by research, the more recent efforts have increasingly emphasized instructional support of the linguistic, semantic, and metacognitive capacities on which reading comprehension depends (Adams, 1990; Committee on Prevention of Reading Difficulties in Young Children, 1998), the major conclusions of all three reports are the same. First, all three of these reports urged that from the start children be fully and actively engaged in the kinds of thoughtful and supported reading and writing activities through which reading comprehension must grow. Second, all three of these reports firmly concluded that providing beginning readers with explicit, well-organized instruction in the alphabetic basics, including phonics, is of special value toward helping them learn to read.

As it happens, virtually no one objects to the notion of supporting young readers' comprehension development. Nor should they: The purpose of teaching children to read, after all, is to afford them reflective access to the information and modes of thought that text offers. On the other hand, the recommendations of these reports concerning the importance of alphabetic and phonics instruction have invariably been met with vigorous and rancorous protest from within the field of reading education.

A common argument in such antialphabetic diatribes is that no single study is sufficient to permit any sound conclusion about the value of such instruction for children in general (e.g., Allington & Woodside-Jiron, 1999; Coles, 2000; Dressman, 1999; Taylor, 1998; Taylor, Anderson, Au, & Raphael, 2000). But this makes no sense. First, if any single factor can be held responsible for the prodigious amount of research directed to issues of decoding over the last several decades, it is the overabundance of evidence that comprehension is effectively precluded except to the extent that children can read the words. Second, research on the methods and impact of comprehension instruction per se is strikingly sparse compared to the information our field has compiled on the nature and importance of effective phonics instruction. Moreover, evidence documenting the importance of systematic, explicit alphabetic instruction goes legions beyond any small set of studies.

Charged with evaluating the status of research-based knowledge on reading instruction, the recent National Research Panel (2000) located 52 different, soundly designed, and peer-reviewed experimental studies of the value of phonemic awareness instruction on children's reading and spelling growth. In fact, the results of these studies were uniformly positive. Yet, the panel was able to appraise their collective implications more closely through statistical meta-analysis (which is essentially a procedure for treating whole experiments as though they are individual subjects). In terms of its impact on reading growth—where that includes reading comprehension as well as word recognition—explicit instruction of phonemic awareness was shown to be of significant and lasting benefit for all students, "including normally developing readers, children at risk for future reading problems, disabled readers, preschoolers, kindergartners, 1st graders, children in 2nd through 6th grades (most of whom were disabled readers), children across various SES levels, and children learning to read in English as well as in other languages" (p. 5). Such instruction was

also shown to accelerate spelling growth significantly in all children except those with established learning disabilities. Further—if not surprisingly (see Adams, Treiman, & Pressley, 1997)—these positive effects were especially pronounced when phonemes were methodically coupled with letters during instruction.

In the same manner, the National Research Panel (2000) was able to conclude that both reading and spelling growth are significantly and positively influenced by systematic phonics instruction. The panel's meta-analysis of 38 different experimental studies published since 1970 affirmed this conclusion across students' socioeconomic backgrounds and especially when such instruction was provided at the outset of children's reading careers, in kindergarten and grade 1. Also of note, the benefits of such instruction accrued regardless of the particular program of systematic phonics in study and regardless of the type of less methodical or less "phonicsy" instruction received by the comparison groups (e.g., basals, whole language, and whole word).

In full complement to such studies on effective instruction are the results of those on ineffective learning. Research on entering students has repeatedly shown poor grasp of the alphabetic basics—letter knowledge and phonemic awareness—to be an extremely strong harbinger of difficulty in learning to read (see Scarborough, 1998). Similarly, among older students, poor working knowledge of phonics, as evidenced in decoding or spelling, is the signature of reading delay and disability (e.g., Lyon & Moats, 1997; Rack, Snowling, & Olson, 1992; Shankweiler et al., 1995; Stanovich & Siegel, 1994).

In short, and contrary to the suggestions of some detractors, the force of such findings is not about endorsing any particular program of instruction or discrediting any other. Nor are the benefits of such instruction restricted to any particular category of students. Rather, the inescapable points of such research are that (1) to learn to read, all students must know the letters of the alphabet, understand their linguistic significance (phonemic awareness), and learn the logic and conventions governing their use (phonics); and (2) ensuring students' grasp of these basics must be a serious goal of any responsible program of beginning reading instruction.

The evidence is compelling. Despite that, many continue to deny and decry its message. Of those who demur, moreover, are some who are in prime position to shape the instruction of our children and the belief systems of our profession. Toward resolving this debate, a key question, therefore, is why such alphabetic anxiety persists.

The Academic Case against Phonics

Among academics, two major arguments have been made against systematic phonics instruction. The first is philosophical or, perhaps, epistemological, and runs essentially as follows: The reason we send children to school is not merely to help them read and write; rather, we teach them to read and write because we want them to be truly literate. We want them to internalize the kinds of knowledge and perspective that text offers, and we want them to gain the disposition to expand, share, and explore their knowledge and thoughts in the ways that text affords. Phonics, in contrast, would seem to be an exercise in rank paired-associated learning. How misguided, how shortsighted, perhaps how counterproductive to lead children in their very introduction to school to believe that education—worse, literacy—is about the kind of learning and thinking that rats and pigeons can do.

Looking through history, from Horace Mann to G. Stanley Hall to Frank Smith, the academics' stated case against phonics has continually centered on this cognitive incongruity. But, again, erudite as they may sound, these protests make little sense. First, the message from research is that phonics be taught in support of—*not* instead of—developing children's language and literary stance. Second, in any complex endeavor, children must learn to walk before they run. Learning must start somewhere: if not with letters and phonemes, then where? The variously "preferred" alternatives to letters and phonemes seem only to magnify the learning task—indeed, many times over. According to Foshay (1990), research on the so-called look–say approach indicated that, on

average, children required 57 exposures to a word to learn it holistically by sight—and there are thousands and thousands of words to be learned. How long might it take them to visually master a reasonably serviceable inventory of whole, multiword "idea units," as Frank Smith (1973) suggested they do?

The second major argument against phonics instruction is psychological. That is, what distinguishes skilled from less skilled readers is not merely the richness of the interpretive response they build from text but the rapidity with which they do so. Reading at a comfortable pace, mature readers can course through text at rates exceeding five words per second. Considering speed alone, the notion that skillful reading might involve recognizing, sounding, and blending together the separate letters of each word of text seems flatly preposterous. Moreover, if the utility of the alphabetic principle to mature readers is marginal at best, then dwelling on it with beginners seems unproductive—at best.

In contrast to the philosophical objections to alphabetic teaching and learning, these psychological objections do make sense—given their premises. It is therefore these psychological arguments on which I will focus for the remainder of this chapter. I first argue that the core problem with these arguments derives from their obsolete premise that the processes involved in word recognition and reading must proceed in series, one at a time. Second, I suggest that the intuitive appeal for these arguments is rooted in how the unifocal nature of human attention hides the many-layered and interactive dynamics of reading and writing from introspection. Third, I argue that it is this same interplay between knowledge and attention that compels both the cognitive importance of learning to recognize words easily and accurately and the pedagogical value of explicit, systematic phonics instruction.

The Alphabetic Principle and the Nature of Skillful Reading

Over the last few decades, both the quantity and the quality of scientific information about the actual processes of reading have increased exponentially. It turns out that when reading for meaning, skillful readers do indeed briefly dwell or fixate their eyes on nearly every content word of text. Further, during the fraction of a second that they do so, they visually process the full spelling of the word; nearly as quickly, they register both its pronunciation and its contextually appropriate meaning (for reviews, see Just & Carpenter, 1987; Rayner, 1997; Rayner & Pollatsek, 1989). As modern technology began to reveal such facts, researchers were baffled. Within their traditional theories, each of the subprocesses of reading had been conceived as happening one by one, each finishing up its job before passing its product to the next. Clearly, these long-held theories were hopelessly incapable of explaining the sheer speed much less the rich interactivity of the word recognition process.

Introduced a decade or so ago by Jay McClelland and David Rumelhart (McClelland & Rumelhart, 1986; Rumelhart & McClelland, 1986), the connectionist or parallel distributed processing (PDP) framework has all but displaced the traditional models in the scientific dialogue on reading. Realized through sophisticated computer simulations, these models were quickly shown to mimic both strengths and weaknesses of human beings in such reading-related tasks as learning to pronounce printed English (Plaut, McClelland, Seidenberg, & Patterson, 1996; Seidenberg & McClelland, 1989), learning tense and agreement for English verbs (Plunkett & Marchman, 1993), the resolution of lexical ambiguity (Kawamoto, 1993), and even generating explanation and analogy in studies of literature and science (Holyoak & Thagard, 1989). Though originally developed by psychologists in the interest of understanding the perception and learning or written and spoken language by humans, the power of these models was quickly recognized in the other sciences, and they have since become the basis for such advanced computing applications as recognizing tumors in CAT (computerized axial tomography) scans; discerning submarines from whales in sonar returns; and computer recognition of speech, fingerprints, handwriting, faces, voices, and other such informationally noisy and multilayered patterns. To be sure, refinement and extension of these powerful models will continue to constitute a highly active domain of research and development for some time to come. At present, however, I wish to focus on but a few of their fundamental structural assumptions, many levels removed from current research on their optimal inner workings.

First and foremost, in contrast with the traditional models of human learning and information processing, the subprocesses in the PDP models do not operate one by one in series. Instead, as schematized in Figure 6.1, they operate in concert, each simultaneously sending and receiving hypotheses to and from each other such that the final output of each is influenced by all. With respect to the "great debate," one significant upshot of this shift from serial to parallel processing is that it gives us a way of conceiving how good readers manage to go from the letterwise messiness of English spellings to cogent, context-sensitive interpretations in the split second that they may accord to each word. Equally important, however, the dynamic of the PDP models renders moot all discussions of whether the reading process is driven top-down, from meaning to print, or bottom-up, from print to meaning: All levels of processing are assumed to be active and interactive at once, working in mutual coordination with each other.

For a better understanding of how the model works, imagine, as depicted in Figure 6.2, that the reader has fixated the printed word "cat." As indicated by arrow 1, it is the visual recognition of a printed word that sets the reading response in motion. Recognition is the process by which any perceived event will automatically activate or "turn on" a person's memories of similar events past. Because the experienced reader has seen the word "cat" so many times, it will be recognized almost at once. The visual memory of letter features, letters, and letter patterns that is involved in print recognition is represented by the oval labeled *Orthographic Processor*.

Yet, memory is associative. That is, to the extent that any sight you see evokes in your mind a memory of itself, it will also evoke your memories of what else you sensed, of how you felt, and of how you responded to it on each prior encounter (for a reading-relevant review, see Anderson & Pearson,

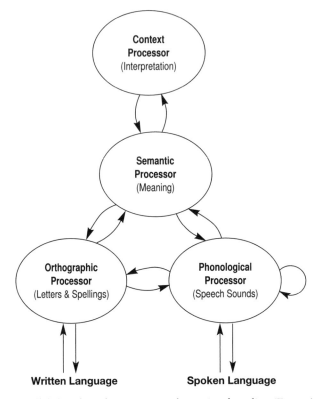

FIGURE 6.1. A parallel-distributed processing schematic of reading (From Adams, 1990).

1984). For the skilled reader, then, the sight of a familiar word will automatically evoke its personal history of usage and interpretations in print and, through that, its previously experienced meanings in general: As represented by arrow 2a, leading from the Orthographic Processor to the *Semantic Processor,* the sight of the word "cat" will automatically activate the reader's accumulated knowledge about cats. Note, too, that to the extent that the word in fixation has been primed or anticipated by context (arrow 5a), the meaning in quest will already be partially activated. In turn, because thoughts of cats have so frequently been coupled with language of cats, these catful memories will trigger the memory for the spoken word /cat/, as shown by arrow 3a which leads from the Semantic Processor to the *Phonological Processor.*

Arrow 2b, leading from the Orthographic Processor to the Phonological Processor, represents the learned associations from print to speech. Through these associations, sight of the written word "cat" will auto-matically activate or recall memory for the spoken word, /cat/. In turn, because the spoken word /cat/ has become so thoroughly associated with sights and thoughts of cats, the Phonological Processor's activation will, in course, be passed on to the Semantic Processor, as shown by arrow 3b. Interestingly, research shows that for English, in which the arrangement of symbols that comprise a word correlate far more tightly with pronunciation than meaning, it is this indirect input from the Phonological Processor that generally dominates readers' initial semantic responses to a word (Lukatela & Turvey, 1994). For written Chinese, by contrast, input to the Semantic Processor from the Orthographic Processor is generally faster and stronger (Hu & Catts, 1998; Perfetti & Zhang, 1995).

Next, notice the arrows labeled 4a and 4b, that lead to the Orthographic Processor from the Phonological and Semantic Processors. With respect to learning, the effect of these feedback loops is one of reinforcing or strengthening the tie between the ortho-

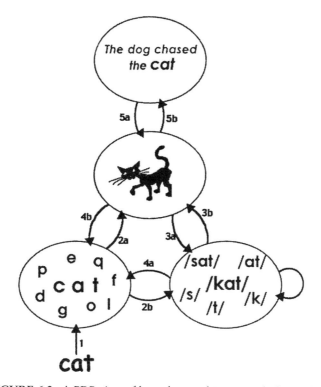

FIGURE 6.2. A PDP view of how the word "cat" might be read.

graphic response and its pronunciation and meaning. The result for the reader is that every word read will be recognized relatively quickly if encountered again a few lines down and, albeit less so, forever after. By the same mechanism, accessibility is generally faster for words that are encountered often than for those that are not.

Yet, in any network as complex as this, these sorts of feedback loops are still more important for controlling the flow of activation. Recall that when excited, any given memory (and each of its parts) will pass activation to others with which it has been associated previously. Necessarily, however, most of these many associations are false leads. Importantly, then, those that will dominate or be taken to matter in any given context are largely determined by which of them most strongly answers back. In this example, the correct meaning and pronunciation of the word "cat" will answer most loudly because both have been stimulated from both directions. Further, as the feedback from the Phonological and Semantic Processors add to the activation of the Or-

thographic response, the activation that the Orthographic response sends back to them is increased in turn. The net result is that a mutually reinforcing pattern of resonance is set off between compatible responses. Moreover, as soon as any given set of memories reaches a critical level of activation dominance, it shuts off all competitors in winner-take-all fashion.

Finally, consider the collective effect of these bidirectional connections between spelling, sound, and meaning. If you back your perspective off a level, you will see that in addition to the circuits they create between any pair of processors, they create two large circuits through all three, one going clockwise and one going counterclockwise. Provided that all the processors respond and that all agree, the excitation traveling around each of these circuits serves only to boost and speed the excitation carried by the others until—winner take all— the sight, sound, and meaning of the word "cat" seem to "pop" to mind at once. For the skilled reader, this happens very quickly and almost effortlessly, given a mere glance at the word, as the sheer result of prior learning and experience.

Automatic versus Controlled Processing

The amount of effort that one must invest in any mental task is conceptualized by psychologists to lie on a continuum. "Automatic processes," such as those by which skilled readers recognize most words, lie on one end of this continuum. The term given to the other end of the continuum is "controlled processing." Where a task lies along the continuum between automatic and controlled processing is determined by its familiarity and, in turn, determines its demands on active attention, its speed, and its accessibility to conscious reflection (for reviews, see Schneider, 1999; Shiffrin, 1988).

First, where a cognitive task lies on this continuum depends on its degree of familiarity. Only tasks that are extremely familiar and extremely well practiced can be completed automatically. In effect, the responses attendant to automatic processes have been overlearned and elaborated to the point of becoming built-in components of the recognition cycle such that they tend to be triggered by the right context even contrary to intentions. In contrast, to the extent that any task is less than overlearned, its successful completion depends on controlled processing. Such tasks are necessarily deliberate. They require concerted mental effort or even, at the extreme, intense concentration (Shiffrin & Schneider, 1977).

Even the most complex processes—determining competitive moves from the lay of a chessboard, piloting high-performance aircraft, sight reading piano music—are shown to become nearly automatic given sufficient practice. The automaticity of word recognition is evidenced by the Stroop effect: Good readers find themselves unable to avoid reading and understanding the words on a page even when asked to attend to and report only to the color of the ink in which they are printed. Alternatively, I suggest an "authentic" experiment: Next time you are driving down the highway, make an effort to ignore the words on the signs and billboards that you pass; despite your efforts, you are likely to find that that you cannot shut them out but, instead, that you irrepressibly hear their words shouting at your mind's ear, their sight, sound, and meaning, "popping" to consciousness at once. In contrast, if a word's recognition dead-ends or diffuses at any level—be it orthographic, phonological, or semantic—the automatic, upward flow of information will short-circuit and abort. A word can be recognized automatically only if its spelling, pronunciation, and meaning are securely represented and interconnected in memory: All are necessary; none is sufficient.

Second, active attention or thought is unifocal and indivisible; it can be allocated to only one mental process (perception, thought, decision, response, action, etc.) at any moment in time. Because of this, the mind can entertain only one controlled process at a time. In contrast, the only constraint on the concurrent execution of automatic processes is that they not interfere with one another at the level of receptor (e.g., eyes and ears), effector (e.g., hands and tongue), or memory resources (Wickens, 1984). Because automatic responses do not require active attention, they can be executed in parallel with each other and/or with a concurrent activity that does require active attention and effort. During reading, the tasks of creating and monitoring understanding place a continual demand on active attention. Thus, whenever and to whatever extent the word recognition process requires attention, it can only be at the cost of comprehension.

Faced with more than one task that requires any amount of attentional control, people can cope only by switching their active attention back and forth between them. However, even for trivial tasks, such attentional "multiplexing" is shown to exact a measurable cost in terms of mental efficiency (Broadbent, 1958). The mental cost of shifting attention back and forth between comprehension and word recognition snags is held to be a major cause of the strong relationship between measures of reading fluency and comprehension (Samuels, Schermer, & Reinking, 1992). At the extreme, when a child labors long and hard over the words of a text, this trade-off is abundantly evident. Yet even when word-level difficulties are relatively minor, their cumulative toll can be significant. Thus, Foorman,

Francis, Shaywitz, Shaywitz, and Fletcher (1997) have shown that even among mainstream high school students, 40% of the variance in comprehension can be traced to differences in word recognition facility. This may also be the explanation for the fact that listening comprehension is shown to exceed reading comprehension until students can read above the sixth-grade level.

Third, automatic processing is extremely rapid, with mental responses to a stimulus requiring as little as 2 milliseconds. Controlled responses, by comparison, take hundreds or even thousands of times longer. By itself, the minimum time required to shift active attention from one mental focus to another is several hundred milliseconds (Reeves & Sperling, 1986). On top of that, and especially to the extent that difficult discriminations or considered contrasts of the alternatives are involved, a controlled response may take orders of magnitude more time. Thus, it is not only that children who are uncomfortable with the words will get less out of a text when they read it but, further, that it may take them many times longer to get through it.

Fourth, only to the extent that tasks are accorded the active, thoughtful attention of controlled processing do they leave a trace in memory that can be consciously recalled. Thus to the extent that a task is well automatized, people are notoriously unreliable at "knowing" whether or not they did it ("I usually put the keys in my purse, but . . . ?"). Indeed, one of the reasons that automated processing has been so prominent an area of research is that failures to resume, or to properly resume, interrupted response routines (such as pilots' checklists) are a major cause of industrial accidents (Norman, 1983). Given that automated tasks are, by definition, extremely familiar, their remarkable resistance to conscious reflection or inspection may be their most counterintuitive property. Training people to proficiency on complex, dynamic decision tasks does not facilitate their ability to describe the considerations and conditions that necessarily govern their performance (Berry & Broadbent, 1984). Conversely, though experts are often found able and willing to provide detailed and confident accounts of how they go about such tasks, their descriptions typically bear little correspondence to physical records of their actual performance.

Introspective versus Objective Analyses of Reading

The same sort of mismatch between introspective and objective analyses of the reading process is arguably the major cause for the divisiveness about what is involved in reading and what ought to be involved in its instruction. Objective, empirical research has proven over and over, using a wide array of methods and instrumentation, that given an alphabetic script, the skillful reader's ability to read with fluency and reflective comprehension depends, integrally and incontrovertibly, on deep, detailed, and ready working knowledge of the spellings and spelling–sound correspondences of the words on the page (Adams, 1990; Committee on the Prevention of Reading Difficulties, 1998). Nevertheless and directly contrary to such hard evidence, the very relevance of the lower-level dimensions of print are sometimes denied even by people who claim the mantle of authority:

> An unfortunate consequence of the alphabetic principle for the fluent reader is the widespread conviction that because words are constructed of letters, letters must be identified in order for words to be read—a misconception that could have created havoc in written language communication if our instinctive behavior in reading was not to ignore individual letters. (Smith, 1973, p 124).

Intuitions, unfortunately, mislead. It is, after all, only because the processes of word recognition are so highly automatized that skillful readers can focus their active attention on the necessarily thought-intensive tasks of comprehension. To the same extent, however, it is only the processes of comprehension that can remain available for introspective examination. For the skillful reader, the lower-level processes of word recognition are far too fast and much too deeply embedded in the mental machinery of reading to be felt.

Whole language, the word method, the sentence method, look–say, psycholinguistic guessing, discovery through immersion: The particulars and labels have wandered a bit across eras but—guided, no doubt, by the introspective musings of the mature readers who thought them up—the emphasis of each of these approaches has been on finding a way to anchor reading directly on comprehension and, thereby, to finesse direct instruction on the letter- or wordwise structure of text. Attendant to most of these approaches has been the assumption that as the inevitable product of repeated exposure, students would acquire what they needed to know about the orthographic structure of words while reading for meaning.

But here is the catch-22. As discussed earlier, repetition can do no more than strengthen that which has already been learned. Learning, in contrast, depends on the active thought and attention of controlled processing. One cannot cause children to learn about the lower-level dimensions of print through activities that direct their attention away from them.

Becoming a Reader

Beyond giving us a way to explain the nature of skillful reading and the cognitive basis for its inscrutability, the PDP models may be still more useful in helping us to understand certain of the most reliable—and most controversial—findings in beginning reading research. Specifically, what is it about *systematic* and *explicit* instruction that makes it differentially effective?

Within the PDP models, learning about a new pattern or concept is the result of attending to new relations between its recognized parts and pieces. From this premise, two key implications about learning follow directly: (1) what one *can* learn from a situation depends on the prior familiarity of its parts and pieces; (2) what one *does* learn from a situation depends on the relations among its parts to which one attends. Herein lie both the useful interpretation of the terms "systematic" and "explicit," respectively, as well as the explanation for their instructional power.

The meanings of the word "systematic," according to *Merriam-Webster's Ninth Collegiate Dictionary* (1983, p. 1199), are relating to or consisting of a system; presented as a coherent body of principles; methodical in procedure or plan; and concerned with

classification. Consistent with these definitions, the power of systematic phonics instruction lies in organizing the lessons so that they reveal the logic of the alphabetic system, including its broadly useful categories of spelling patterns and conventions, and so that they progress manageably in complexity. The goal of systematic instruction is one of maximizing the likelihood that whenever children are asked to learn something new, they already possess the appropriate prior knowledge and understandings to see its value and to learn it efficiently and productively.

Given these definitions of systematic instruction, the priority importance of ensuring that beginners can comfortably recognize the letters is axiomatic. Inasmuch as the letters are the smallest units of print, they are the basic building blocks of orthographic knowledge. Unless and until a child can reliably recognize the letters, the memorability of printed words is limited and phonics and spelling instruction are out of reach, because unless and until a child can reliably recognize the letters, the mind cannot possibly build stable connections between them. Moreover, to the extent that children must devote attention to identifying the letters of a word, they can have little capacity left for noticing the relations between them. Thus, it is not just the accuracy of letter identification that is found prognostic of reading success but also its ease or speed (Biemiller, 1977–1978; Blachman, 1984).

Similarly, unless and until children have a basic awareness of phonemes, demanding that they learn the letters' sounds is a useless exercise. It is not, after all, memorizing the sounds that matters but connecting the letters to the sounds of one's own speech. Indeed, pedagogically speaking, this is a good example of one of the most significant differences between the newer models of learning and their traditional forebears. A fundamental tenet of traditional learning theory was that any new relationship—for example, between a letter and a sound or between a word and its meaning—could and would be learned given sufficient exposure, and from this there follows the theoretical justification both for drill and skill and for implicit learning approaches, from Bloomfield and Barnhart's (1961) linguistic readers to the storybook immersion practices of the 1990s. The PDP models hold that practice or repeated encounters will boost the strength or robustness of anything that has already been learned well enough to be recognized. In contrast to the older models, however, the PDP models hold that *initial* learning is indifferent to repeated exposures except given the prior knowledge and attention on which such learning depends. Moreover, by virtue of their assumption that learning consists of building new connections between the established parts and pieces of a percept, the PDP models embody a structural explanation for such familiar, child-centered constraints as "developmental appropriateness" and Vygotsky's "zone of proximal development." In plain English, if the same thing has been said 17 times, the problem is not that the child has not heard it. The remedy to this situation lies not in saying or displaying whatever it is again, but in figuring out what it is that the child is not understanding and whether that misunderstanding is due to lack of knowledge or misplaced attention.

Many systematic phonics programs begin word recognition instruction by establishing a degree of comfort with short vowel monosyllables before introducing more complex orthographic conventions. In theory, this too seems a sensible approach. First, it secures the basic left-to-right, letter-to-phoneme logic of the alphabetic principle at the outset of learning. Second, it tacitly recognizes that the child cannot effectively focus attention on, for example, the final "e" while struggling to represent and hold the rest of the letter ensemble in mind. Third, it allows for such conventions to be taught and learned, not as cognitively confusing instances but as understandable generalities; that is, if it is clear to the child that "hat" says /hat/ and "slim" says /slim/, then the significance of the "e" on "hate" and "slime" becomes attentionally worthwhile. Again, the purpose of layering instruction in such ways is one of clearly revealing the logic and order of the alphabetic principle and its conventions. The goal is one of reducing the learning task from zillions of little things that must be rote memorized to relatively few big ones that the child can reasonably be asked to understand and think about.

Here, too, stemming from their interactive dynamic, lies a second welcome pedagogical emphasis of these newer theories. Though the logic and structures of the orthographic system may be most efficiently built layer by layer, bottom up, from simple to complex, they are useful only as connected at every step to the child's top-down knowledge of language and meaning. Thus, even when the force of instruction is on phonemic awareness, decoding, or spelling, its value depends integrally on ensuring that students understand and think about (attend to) the meaning and use of each word in focus. It goes without saying that such ongoing linguistic support warrants special care when working with students with limited proficiency in English. However, it is no less important when working with native English speakers, for research affirms that children do not reliably alert to the meanings of even very familiar words when they are presented in isolation (Ehri, 1979)—perhaps the way you may find yourself failing to recognize a perfectly familiar word while browsing in the dictionary. In short, if the objective of systematic instruction is one of maximizing the ease and impact of learning, then the lessons must be child-centered *and* goal-directed, at once.

The meaning of "explicit," according to the *Merriam-Webster's Ninth Collegiate Dictionary,* (1983, p. 438) is "fully revealed or expressed without vagueness, implication, or ambiguity: leaving no question as to meaning or intent (explicit instructions)." The goal of explicit instruction is one of helping children to focus their attention on the relations that matter, because, again, that which one learns depends on that to which one attends.

The special benefit of explicit instruction in phonemic awareness relates to the fact that in normal speaking and listening situations, one's attention is properly focused on meaning and message. As we were so often—and eloquently—reminded by Alvin Liberman (e.g., 1999), not only are the phonemes deeply embedded in the machinery of speech production and perception, but, even for the young child, they are thoroughly automatized or listening and speaking for meaning would not be possible. In effect, then, understanding the logic of an alphabetic system requires that children learn to attend to that which they have learned not to attend to—and therein lies the benefit of phonemic awareness activities. Phoneme isolation activities are valuable because they cause the child to notice the existence and nature of the phonemes. Oral blending and segmenting activities are valuable because they explicitly and actively engage the child in discovering that *every word can be conceived as a sequence of phonemes*. It is this discovery—this *insight*—to which the term "phonemic awareness" refers; without it, neither phonics nor spelling can make any sense.

In this context, I ask the reader to pause and consider why it should be that games figure so prominently among activities for developing phonemic awareness (see, e.g., Adams, Foorman, Lundberg, & Beeler, 1997). An obvious answer is that games are more engaging and more appropriate developmentally for young children than, say, lectures or worksheets. This is important, for unless children can be persuaded to pay attention, they won't learn a thing. Even so, there is a more compelling rationale. Specifically, in conducting phonemic awareness activities, the teacher is not trying to cause children to *learn* something; at some level, after all, the children already know the phonemes. Rather, the goal in conducting phonemic awareness activities is to induce children to *understand* something: A child can parrot responses perfectly without having a clue as to what they mean; however, a child cannot get a joke or answer a riddle without understanding what it is about.

To be sure, gaining an awareness of phonemes and their alphabetic relevance is more difficult for some children than for others. Nevertheless, once children "get it" with two or three letters, they need barely a word to transfer that understanding to the rest (Byrne, 1992). There is, in short, no sense in which phonemic awareness training should increase classroom "drill and skill." On the contrary, explicit phonemic awareness training is about developing in children the attentional and metacognitive control that renders unnecessary the drill and skill of traditional phonics.

In similar spirit, setting storybooks aside to provide focused work on decoding and spelling can be seen as helpful in two ways. First, removing the attentional lure of meaningful context makes it far easier to focus the children on the structural properties of the words themselves. Second, teaching decoding and spelling in isolation affords the opportunity to select the words in study on the basis of their structural properties. A frequent instructional strategy in systematic, explicit phonics programs is one of exploiting minimal contrasts in such word play (e.g., If this spells "cat," how do you spell "bat"? "hat"? "had"? "sad"? "mad"? "map"? "cap"? "clap"? "clip"? "flip"? "lip"? . . .). An obvious advantage of thus holding the bulk of the spelling constant from word to word is that it lightens the encoding task so that the child has relatively more capacity to attend to what is different about each one. In theory, however, the underlying advantage of such activities is still greater. On one hand, repeating a recognized spelling–sound pattern from word to word should reinforce or strengthen its representation in memory. On the other hand, changing an element of these patterns from word to word should enrich their representations in a way that makes them inherently generalizable, so that rather than becoming holistically tied to any specific word, they will piecewise respond to other, similar words—"rat," "ham," "hit," "slip," "slap," "flat," "flop"—that the child may encounter beyond the lesson. Ultimately, the goal is to set up the child's orthographic knowledge so that it will respond quickly and accurately to any well-spelled word that is encountered, freeing the reader to think about what the word means rather than what it says. Indeed, difficulty in decoding orthographically regular pseudowords is a potent correlate of reading disability and delay (Rack et al., 1992).

More generally, the reason for teaching phonics is to enable children to expand their word recognition and spelling repertoires on their own. For this to be a reasonable expectation, however, children must be given activities and materials that reward them for trying.

Toward this end, encouraging children to write independently is of proven value (see Adams et al., 1997). And no wonder this is so: Asking children to generate their own spellings is a way of engaging them in thinking actively and reflectively about the sounds of words in relation to their written representations. When regular opportunities for independent writing are complemented by systematic spelling instruction, the benefits are especially marked and extend to reading as well as writing growth (Shatil, Share, & Levin, 2000).

In the reading domain, decodable texts are the analog to independent writing opportunities. For both, the implicit message is as follows: "If you don't already know a word, try sounding it out." The very process of sounding a word out requires controlled attention to its separate letters and letter–sound correspondences as well as to the relationships among them that collectively determine the word's overall pronunciation and meaning. Thus each time a child sounds a word successfully, it leaves an elaborate trace in memory to be used again for the same word or to be modified for any similarly spelled new one. Yet, if there are too many words that must be sounded, the children will get worn out even as they lose the meaningful thread of the text (Perfetti, 1985). Similarly, if the new words are by and large beyond the children's decoding ability, many will conclude that it is generally not worth trying (see Juel & Roper-Schneider, 1985).

If children are expected to sound out new words while reading, the text must be considerately designed and leveled with that in mind. The text must be manageable in terms of content, vocabulary, and sentence structure, and its potentially new words must be appropriately spaced throughout the text to allow the child to maintain or regain comprehension with reasonable ease. In addition, its potentially new words must be consistently selected to be within the child's decoding capacity and collectively chosen and varied to reinforce attention to every letter position—not just the first. Thus, notwithstanding frequent citations by detractors, neither can texts that are dominated by sentences such as "Dan can fan a tan van" be seen as instructionally useful decodables—many an intelligent child will quickly figure out that the efficient way to deal with such patterns is to sound just the first letter and go for it. Indeed, Thompson (Thompson, Cottrell, & Fletcher-Finn, 1996; Thompson & Fletcher-Finn, 1993) has shown that, regardless of instruction on isolated letter–sound correspondences,

young readers' ability to decode pseudo-words depends strongly on the number of times they have previously encountered its graphemes in the same position and similar spellings while reading (e.g., success in decoding "ob" was influenced the number of times they had encountered such words as "job," "crab," "cab," "rib," etc.).

But again, it hardly matters how many times any spelling shows up if children do not attend to it. In addition to giving children texts in which new words can be decoded, therefore, it is important to make it clear to them that they are expected to do so. This, too, has been a bone of contention in the field of beginning reading, and not without reason. Research affirms the observations of many practitioners: Beginners who are taught to stop and decode new words while reading tend to read more slowly and to commit more nonword errors than those who are not (Chall, 1967; Elder, 1971; Lesgold, Resnick, & Hammond, 1985). Slow reading is burdensome reading, and nonword errors would seem flatly incongruous with ongoing comprehension. A reasonable interpretation of these differences is that encouraging children to attend to phonics while reading may inhibit their reading growth.

To investigate this issue, Connelly, Johnston, and Thompson (1999) worked with first- and second-graders from four different schools, two in Scotland and two in New Zealand. In the Scottish schools, the children received a systematic program of explicit phonics instruction complemented with lesson-appropriate decodable texts. In the New Zealand schools, children were taught the letter names but not their sounds. Phonics was not taught, neither synthetic nor analogical, but children were asked to write regularly, using inventive spelling. In reading, the emphasis was on meaning from the outset, and children were taught to rely on context, to think ahead and make predictions, and, only as necessary, to use initial letters as help in identifying words. The reading materials in the New Zealand schools consisted of a finely graded series of predictable texts. And, significantly, the children's progress through them was individually controlled by the teacher through systematic monitoring of their word reading accuracy.

Connelly et al. (1999) chose 41 second-graders from each location who were matched in age, vocabulary, memory, and—importantly—word–reading attainment, and carefully analyzed their performance on a standardized passage comprehension test (Neale, 1989). As anticipated, the phonics-taught children read far more slowly, averaging 10 months behind age norms; by comparison, the reading speed of the children without phonics was 4 months ahead of the age norms. Not as anticipated, however, the phonics-taught children showed better comprehension, averaging 1 month below norms as compared to 5 months below for the others. (We are reminded of the difference between measuring children's comprehension on what they can read and measuring it on what they *ought* to be able to read to keep up with school demands.) Most informative, I think, was Connelly et al.'s (1999) analysis of the children's word errors during passage reading. In terms of the overall number of errors, the two groups were wholly comparable, which was to be expected given that they were matched on word–reading ability in the first place. In terms of the nature of the children's errors, however, the differences were marked. As observed by others, the phonics-taught children did indeed produce significantly more nonword errors than the meaning-first group. However, the meaning-first group skipped or refused to read far more words than the phonics-taught group; fully 46% of their errors were refusals as opposed to 11% for the phonics group. Analyses of the children's performance on a test (Elliott, Murray, & Pearson, 1979) of isolated words yielded similar results. Not only did the errors of meaning-first children include far more refusals (49% vs. 6%), but their misreadings, whether words or nonwords, showed significantly less graphic similarity to the test word than did those of the phonics-taught group.

Although skipping or minimizing attention to difficult words may allow a child to read more quickly, it commensurately forfeits the opportunity to learn—and importantly, the word that might as well be guessed in today's text may well be a critical part of the context in tomorrow's. Underscoring this point, Byrne, Freebody, and Gates (1992) found that regardless of their ability to recognize real words in second grade, those who were poor at decoding nonwords lost standing in both word recognition and comprehension by third grade. In contrast, and even if they were relatively poor at recognizing real words in second grade, the word–reading and comprehension proficiency of those who were good at decoding nonwords grew significantly by a third.

It should go without saying that a major consideration in selecting reading materials for children is that they be both understandable and worth understanding. However, neither should we need to remind ourselves that among reasons that we ask young children to read any text is to make them better able to learn and profit from the next. The reason for teaching children to pause and attend to unfamiliar words in one text is so they will not need to in the next. The reason for asking them to decode each new word they encounter is to make it easier for them to decode and learn the next. The goal of helping children learn to recognize words quickly and easily is to ensure that word recognition will feed rather than compete with comprehension. The goal of explicitly and systematically teaching children to understand and use phonics is to bring them to that point faster by supporting the efficiency and robustness of their learning as well as the independence with which it can be nurtured through their own independent efforts and thoughtfulness.

References

Adams, M. J. (1990). *Beginning to read: Thinking and learning about print.* Cambridge, MA: MIT Press.

Adams, M. J., Foorman, B. R., Lundberg, I., & Beeler, T. (1997). *Phonemic awareness in young children: A classroom curriculum.* Baltimore: Brookes.

Adams, M. J., Treiman, R., & Pressley, M. (1997). Reading, writing, and literacy. In I. Sigel & A. Renninger (Eds.), *Mussen's handbook of child psychology: Vol. 4. Child psychology in practice* (pp. 275–356). New York: Wiley.

Allington, R. L., & Woodside-Jiron, H. (1999). The politics of literacy teaching: How "research" shaped educational policy. *Educational Researcher, 28*(8), 4–13.

Anderson, R. C., & Pearson, P. D. (1984). A schema-theoretic view of basic processes in reading. In P. D. Pearson, R. Barr, M. L. Kamil, & P. Moshenthal (Eds.), *Handbook of reading research* (pp. 255–291). New York: Longman.

Berry, D. C., & Broadbent, D. E. (1984). On the relationship between task performance and associated verbalizable knowledge. *Quarterly Journal of Experimental Psychology, 36,* 209–231.

Biemiller, A. (1977–1978). Relationships between oral reading rates for letters, words, and simple text in the development of reading achievement. *Reading Research Quarterly, 13,* 223–253.

Blachman, B. A. (1984). Relationship of rapid naming ability and language analysis skills to kindergarten and first-grade reading achievement. *Journal of Educational Psychology, 76,* 610–622.

Bloomfield, L., & Barnhart, C. L. (1961). *Let's read.* Detroit: Wayne State University Press.

Broadbent, D. E. (1958). *Perception and communication.* London: Pergamon Press.

Byrne, B. (1992). Studies in the acquisition procedure for reading. In P. B. Gough, L. C. Ehri, & R. Treiman (Eds.), *Reading acquisition* (pp. 1–34). Hillsdale, NJ: Erlbaum.

Byrne, B., Freebody, P., & Gates, A. (1992). Longitudinal data on the relations of word-reading strategies to comprehension, reading time, and phonemic awareness. *Reading Research Quarterly, 27,* 140–151.

Chall, J. S. (1967). *Learning to read: The great debate.* New York: McGraw-Hill.

Coles, G. (2000). *Misreading reading: The bad science that hurts children.* Portsmouth, NH: Heinemann.

Committee on the Prevention of Reading Difficulties in Young Children. (1998). *The prevention of reading difficulties in young children.* Washington, DC: National Academy Press.

Connelly, B., Johnston, R. S., & Thompson, G. B. (1999). The influence of instructional approaches on reading procedures. In G. B. Thompson & T. Nicholson (Eds.), *Learning to read: Beyond phonics and whole language* (pp. 103–123). New York: Teachers College Press.

Diringer, D. (1968). *The alphabet.* London: Hutchinson.

Dressman, M. (1999). On the use and misuse of research evidence: Decoding two states' reading initiatives. *Reading Research Quarterly, 34,* 258–285.

Ehri, L. C. (1979). Linguistic insight: Threshold of reading acquisition. In T. Waller & G. MacKinnon (Eds.), *Reading research: Advances in theory and practice* (vol. 1, pp. 63–111). New York: Academic Press.

Elder, R. D. (1971). Oral reading achievement of Scottish and American children. *Elementary School Journal, 71,* 216–230.

Elliott, C., Murray, D., & Pearson, L. (1979). *British Ability Scales.* Windsor, Birkshire, UK: NFER-Nelson.

Foorman, B., Francis, D., Shaywitz, S., Shaywitz, B., & Fletcher, J. (1997). The case for early reading intervention. In B. Blachman (Ed.), *Foundations of reading acquisition and dyslexia* (pp. 243–264). Mahwah, NJ: Erlbaum.

Foshay, A. W. (1990). Textbooks and the curriculum during the progressive era, 1930–1950. In D. L. Elliott & A. Woodward (Eds.), *Eighty-ninth yearbook of the National Society for the Study of Education, part 1: Textbooks and schooling in the United States* (pp. 23–41). Chicago: University of Chicago Press.

Holyoak, K. J., & Thagard, P. (1989). Analogical mapping by constraint satisfaction. *Cognitive Science, 13,* 295–355.

Hu, C.-F., & Catts, H. W. (1998). The role of phonological processing in early reading ability: What we can learn from Chinese. *Scientific Studies of Reading, 2,* 55–79.

Juel, C., & Roper-Schneider, D. (1985). The influence of basal readers on first grade reading. *Reading Research Quarterly, 20,* 134–152.

Just, M. A., & Carpenter, P. A. (1987). *The psychology of reading and language comprehension.* Boston: Allyn & Bacon.

Kawamoto, A. M. (1993). Nonlinear dynamics in the resolution of lexical ambiguity: A parallel distributed processing account. *Journal of Memory and Language, 32,* 464–473.

Lesgold, A., Resnick, L. B., & Hammond, K. (1985). Learning to read: A longitudinal study of word skill development in tow curricula. In G. E. MacKinnon & T. G. Waller (Eds.), *Reading research: Advances in theory and practice* (Vol. 4, pp. 107–138). New York: Academic Press.

Liberman, A. M. (1999). The reading researcher and the reading teacher need the right theory of speech. *Scientific Studies of Reading, 3,* 95–112.

Lukatela, G., & Turvey, M. T. (1994), Visual Lexical access is initially phonological: 1. Evidence from associative priming by words, homophones, and pseudohomophones. *Journal of Experimental Psychology: General, 123,* 107–128

Lyon, G. R., & Moats, L. C. (1997). Critical conceptual and methodological considerations in reading intervention research. *Journal of Learning Disabilities, 30,* 578–588.

McClelland, J. L., & Rumelhart, D. E. (Eds.). (1986). *Parallel distributed processing, vol. 2.* Cambridge, MA: MIT Press.

Merriam-Webster's ninth new collegiate dictionary. (1983). Springfield, MA: Merriam-Webster.

National Research Panel. (2000). *Teaching children to read: An evidence-based assessment of the scientific research literature on reading and its implications for reading instruction.* Rockville, MD: National Institutes of Health.

Neale, M. D. (1989). *The Neale analysis of reading ability* (rev. British ed.). Windsor, Berkshe, UK: NFER-Nelson.

Norman, D. A. (1983). Design rules based on analyses of human error. *Communications of the ACM, 26,* 254–258.

Perfetti, C. A. (1985). *Reading ability.* New York: Oxford University Press.

Perfetti, C. A., & Zhang, S. (1995). The universal word identification reflex. In D. I. Medin (Ed.),

The psychology of learning and motivation (vol. 33, pp. 159–189). San Diego, CA: Academic Press.

Plaut, D. C., McClelland, J. L., Seidenberg, M. S., & Patterson, K. (1996). Understanding normal and impaired word reading. Computational principles in quasi-regular domains. *Psychological Review, 103,* 56–115.

Plunkett, K., & Marchman, V. (1993). From rote learning to system building: Acquiring verb morphology in children and connectionists nets. *Cognition, 48,* 21–69.

Rack, J. P., Snowling, M. J., & Olson, R. K. (1992). The nonword reading deficit in developmental dyslexia: A review. *Reading Research Quarterly, 26,* 28–53.

Rayner, K. (1997). Understanding eye movements in reading. *Scientific Studies of Reading, 1,* 317–341.

Rayner, K., & Pollatsek, A. (1989). Eye movements in reading: A tutorial review. In M. Coltheart (Ed.), *Attention and performance XII: The psychology of reading* (pp. 327–362). London: Erlbaum.

Reeves, A., & Sperling, G. (1986). Attention gating in short-term visual memory. *Psychological Review, 93,* 180–206.

Rumelhart, D. E., & McClelland, J. L. (1986). *Parallel distributed processing (vol. 1).* Cambridge, MA: MIT Press.

Samuels, S. J., Schermer, N., & Reinking, D. (1992). Reading fluency: Techniques for making decoding automatic. In S. J. Samuels & A. Farstrup (Eds.), *What research has to say about reading instruction* (pp. 123–144). Newark, DE: International Reading Association.

Scarborough, H. S. (1998). Early identificiation of children at risk for reading disabilities. In B. K. Shapiro, P. J. Accardo, & A. J. Capute (Eds.), *Specific reading disability* (pp. 75–199). Timonium, MD: York Press.

Schneider, W. (1999). Automaticity. In R. A. Wilson & F. C. Keil (Eds.), *The MIT Encyclopedia of the cognitive sciences* (pp. 63–63). Cambridge, MA: MIT Press.

Seidenberg, M. S., & McClelland, J. L. (1989). A distributed, developmental model of word recognition and naming. *Psychological Review, 96,* 523–568.

Shankweiler, D., Crain, S., Katz, L., Fowler, A. E., Liberman, A. M., Brady, S. A., Thornton, R., Lundquist, E., Dreyer, L., Fletcher, J. M., Stuebing, K. K., Shaywitz, S. E., & Shaywitz, B. A. (1995). Cognitive profiles of reading-disabled children: Comparison of language skills in phonology, morphology, and syntax. *Psychological Science, 6,* 149–156.

Shatil, E., Share, D. L., & Levin, I. (2000). On the contribution of kindergarten writing to grade 1 literacy: A longitudinal study in Hebrew. *Applied Psycholinguistics, 21,* 1–21.

Shiffrin, R. M. (1988). Attention. In R. C. Atkinson, R. J. Herrnstein, G. Lindzey, & R. D. Luce (Eds.), *Stevens' handbook of experimental psychology* (vol. 2, pp. 739–811). New York: Wiley.

Shiffrin, R. M., & Schneider, W. (1977). Controlled and automatic information processing: II. Perceptual learning, automatic attending, and a general theory. *Psychological Review, 84,* 127–189.

Smith, F. (1973). *Psycholinguistics and reading.* New York: Holt, Rinehart & Winston.

Stanovich, K. E., & Siegel, L. S. (1994). Phenotypic performance profile of children with reading disabilities: A regression-based test of the phonological-core variable-difference model. *Journal of Educational Psychology, 86,* 24–53.

Taylor, B., Anderson, R. C., Au, K. H., & Raphael, T. E. (2000). Discretion in the translation of research to policy: A case from beginning reading. *Educational Researcher, 29,* 16–26.

Taylor, D. (1998). *Beginning to read and the spin doctors of science.* Urbana, IL: National Council of Teachers of English.

Thompson, G. B., Cottrell, D. S., & Fletcher-Flinn, C. M. (1996). Sublexical orthographic–phonological relations early in the acquisition of reading: The knowledge sources account. *Journal of Experimental Child Psychology, 62,* 190–222.

Thompson, G. B., & Fletcher-Flinn, C. M. (1993). A theory of knowledge sources and prcedures for reading acquisition. In G. B. Thompson, W. E. Tunmer, & T. Nicholson (Eds.), *Reading acquisition processes* (pp. 20–73). Clevedon, UK: Multilingual Matters.

Wickens, C. D. (1984). *Engineering psychology and human performance.* Columbus, OH: Charles F. Merrill.

7

Brains, Genes, and Environment in Reading Development

❖

RICHARD K. OLSON
JAVIER GAYAN

The editors of this volume offered an initial title, "Biological Factors," for this chapter. Expansion of the title was encouraged. Our inclusion of "brains" and "genes" would seem to fit under the biological-factors category, but why add "environment" when environmental factors are addressed in many of the other chapters? We leave the environmental details to those chapters, but we argue here that individual differences in the development of literacy and related language skills are caused by genes and two separable environmental influences: shared environment and unique environment. Our argument is based primarily on evidence from behavioral–genetic studies with identical and fraternal twins that explore the balance of genetic, shared-family environment and nonshared environmental influences on reading disability and on individual differences in reading across the normal range. The evidence from twins for genetic influences on individual differences in reading ability will then be reinforced by results from recent linkage studies of DNA in children and adults with deficits in reading and related language skills. Finally, we review some recent studies of genetic influences on brain anatomy and studies of differences in brain anatomy and function in good and poor readers. (For discussion of related research see Scarborough, Chapter 7.)

Nearly all the relevant evidence discussed in this chapter for genetic influences on literacy and for reading-related differences in brain activity has come from subjects who were at least 8 years of age. This is unfortunate for a volume that is focused on early literacy development, but little direct evidence is available for younger children. At the end of the chapter we discuss the likely relevance of results from older children for early literacy development. We also briefly discuss a new preschool longitudinal twin study that will provide more direct evidence on the genetic and environmental etiology of early literacy and related language skills.

Before discussing the genetic and brain imaging results, we address three important preliminary questions about how reading-related genes might have evolved, why reading-related genes may have relatively little to do with much of the literacy problem in the United States, and how reading-related genes may in part influence individuals' selection of their reading environment.

Reading-Related Genes and Evolution

How could reading be influenced by genetic variation when it is a relatively recent and culturally dependent practice? The question is posed for genetic influences on within-species (human) individual differences, but the answer may begin with the genes that make humans different from other primates. It is estimated that humans and our nearest primate relatives differ in only about 2% of their entire genome, though this 2% must include some very important genes. Some of these genes must influence the development of brain and vocal-tract structures related to complex speech production and comprehension. Humans, unless socially isolated or severely hearing impaired, nearly always develop a complex spoken language. The specific phonological structure and lexical entries vary across languages and subcultures, but in contrast with writing and reading, speaking and listening are basic and nearly universal human characteristics. Of course, there are significant individual differences in developmental rate and adult achievement in speaking and listening. We will see that there is evidence for genetic influence on these individual differences in certain aspects of language development, and that these genetic influences on language are largely shared with those for reading development. This may be a partial answer to the foregoing question: Genes that influence subtle individual differences in language may have more profound effects on learning to read.

Important Cultural Sources of Reading Failure in the United States

A challenge to genetic influences on individual differences in reading has been raised by those who are legitimately concerned about the strong effects in the United States from cultural differences in children's first language, socioeconomic level, and educational opportunity (cf. Coles, 1987). For example, many children struggle to read in a second language, and many children in extreme poverty may have little support for literacy development in their homes and schools. Environmental factors may play a dominant role in explaining reading failure in such situations. Before considering the behavioral–genetic evidence, we need to think about how the environmental range for reading in a population might influence the proportional estimates of genetic and environmental influences on individual dif-

ferences in reading within that population. Imagine a culture that arbitrarily sent half the children to good schools and the other half to work in the fields without formal or home schooling. There would be extreme differences in literacy between these subgroups, and variation across the population would be mostly due to the extreme environmental differences imposed by the culture. On the other hand, imagine a culture that provided nearly every child with good reading instruction in school and worked to ensure family support for reading development. No doubt the variation in literacy development would be considerably reduced compared to the first example and there would be far fewer nonreaders, but there would still be significant individual differences in rate of reading growth. With considerably less environmental variation in the second example, genetic effects would likely account for a larger proportion of the variation in the population. In a hypothetical and impossible scenario where there was *no* environmental variation, genes would account for *all* the variance in the population.

In the behavioral–genetic studies of reading disability described in this chapter, the restriction of environmental range is a deliberate choice based on commonly accepted definitions of "specific reading disability" or "dyslexia" (cf. Lyon, 1995). The Colorado Learning Disabilities Research Center (CLDRC; DeFries et al., 1997) has been supported by the National Institutes of Health to study the genetic and environmental etiology of specific learning disabilities, including attention-deficit/hyperactivity disorder (ADHD) and reading disability. The CLDRC definition of reading disabilities excludes the many Hispanic and other children in Colorado who are learning to read English as a second language. A large proportion of these children are poor readers, but learning to read English as a second language and other correlated cultural conditions were seen as environmental circumstances that would be responsible for the English as a Second Language (ESL) group's generally poor reading. If ESL children had been included in the CLDRC twin studies, it is possible that the proportional population estimates for shared-family environment influences would have been higher, and the proportion of genetic influence would have been reciprocally lower. It is important to keep this in mind when interpreting the results of behavioral–genetic studies. Because the samples in these studies are often not a random sample of the whole population, they may not accurately reflect the relative importance of environmental and genetic factors in literacy development across the whole population.

Equal Shared-Environment and Genetic Assumptions in Twin Studies

The interpretation of data from identical and fraternal twins reared together depends on assumptions of genetic differences and shared-environment similarities (Plomin, DeFries, & McClearn, 1990). The genetic differences for identical and fraternal twins are well established: Identical twins share all their genes, whereas fraternal twins share half their segregating genes (those genes that make us different as individuals), on average. On the other hand, the equal shared-environment assumption for identical and fraternal twins is not as clear and is often misunderstood (cf. Coles, 1987). Both types of twin pairs live in the same family and go to the same schools in the CLDRC and similar twin studies, but there are likely to be greater *self-selected* environmental differences within fraternal twin pairs that are influenced by their different genes (Plomin, DeFries, & Loehlin, 1977; Scarr & McCartney, 1983). Imagine that a genetically influenced reading disability is present in one fraternal twin but not the other. The twin with the genetically influenced reading disability might experience frustration and failure in learning to read and be less likely to practice reading than the normal member of the pair. (The twin with reading disability may need much *more* reading practice to reach the functional level of the normal twin, but this is not a likely outcome for most children with reading disabilities.) This scenario suggests that fraternal twins' self-selected reading environments are more likely to be different, compared to identical twins, in relation to a genetically influenced reading disability. Genetic influences on self-selection in the reading environment and their reciprocal influence on reading de-

velopment are assumed to be part of the genetic influence revealed in twin studies. Twin studies also assume that there is no significant *externally* imposed difference in shared environment that is based on twin type. For example, in the CLDRC studies, there is no significant difference in the degree to which identical and fraternal twins are assigned to the same elementary school classes, which is less than 20% for both types of twin pairs.

Twin Methods for Estimating Genetic and Environmental Influences on Group Deficits in Reading

Modern twin studies have accepted the reality that reading disability is not a categorical disorder, and that reading ability is normally distributed in populations with broad public schooling (Rodgers, 1983; Shaywitz, Escobar, Shaywitz, Fletcher, & Makuch, 1992). Recognition of the normal distribution of reading ability in broadly educated populations has required the development of new statistical methods that are appropriate for assessing the etiology of group membership in the tails of the distributions for different skills (DeFries & Fulker, 1985). A detailed description of modern behavioral–genetic methods is beyond the scope of this chapter, but a brief overview can provide a basic understanding of how estimates of genetic, shared-environment, and nonshared environment are derived for deviant group membership on a normally distributed dimension such as reading. First, one must have some indication of the distribution of performance in the reference population, and then the performance of twins with and without reading disability must be described in relation to that population distribution. This is accomplished in the CLDRC twin studies by identifying both normal-range twin pairs without a school history for reading disability and twin pairs where at least one member has a school history for a reading problem. Both types of twin pairs are then tested extensively in the laboratory to establish the normal distribution for the various measures across age and to define deviant groups relative to age norms on these measures. One and a half standard deviations (SDs) below the local population mean, approximately the lower 10%, is a common criterion for deviant group membership in the CLDRC studies.

Twins in the deviant group are called "probands." The average genetic and environmental etiology for proband-group membership is determined by the status of the second member of the pair, the "cotwin," which may also be a "proband" if they fall below the −1.5 SD criterion. For example, if group membership in the low tail for reading were entirely due to genetic influence, both members of an identical twin pair would be probands in the deviant group, whereas the cotwins of fraternal-twin probands would regress halfway toward the population mean, on average, because they share half their segregating genes, on average. In contrast, if shared environment were the only cause of deviant group membership, then all fraternal and identical cotwins of probands would also be probands, regardless of their genetic similarity status. Actual results fall between these extremes, reflecting the balance of genetic and shared-environment influence on deviant group membership.

It is important to emphasize that estimates of genetic and shared-environment influence are for the *group* average, not for individuals within the group. The relative importance of genetic and environmental factors may vary widely across individuals within the deviant group. Behavioral–genetic analyses are based on population statistics and cannot determine genetic effects at the individual level. Later in the chapter, we discuss linkage analyses of subjects' DNA that may ultimately lead to evidence for genetic etiology at an individual level.

Proportional estimates of nonshared environment effects, including test error, can be derived simply by noting differences between members of identical twin pairs: Because identical twins share both their genes and their family environment, nonshared environment or test error would be the only reason for a within-pair difference. If some nonshared environmental event such as a random head injury were the only cause for reading disability, cotwins of both identical and fraternal twin probands would be expected to regress nearly all the way to the population mean, on average, constrained only by the 10% (if that is the severity criterion for reading disability in the population) of cotwins who might also have had a head injury and developed reading disability.

Genetic and Environmental Influences on Reading Disability and Relations to IQ

DeFries, Fulker, and LaBuda (1987) reported the first twin analyses of reading disability that used the DeFries and Fulker (1985) regression method to estimate genetic influence on deviant group membership. Reading disability was defined as approximately the lower 10th percentile on a composite measure that was based on the word recognition, reading comprehension, and spelling subscales from the Peabody Individual Achievement Test (PIAT; Dunn & Markwardt, 1970). The group heritability for this definition of reading disability was estimated to be a modest but statistically significant 29% from small samples of 64 identical and 55 fraternal twin pairs between 8 and 18 years of age. The most recently published analyses of the PIAT composite reading measure with much larger samples of identical ($n = 223$) and fraternal ($n = 169$) same-sex twin pairs from the CLDRC yielded a higher estimate of group heritability (58%), and a very high level of statistical significance ($p < 10^{-12}$) (Wadsworth, Olson, Pennington, & DeFries, 2000). This result should leave little doubt that there is substantial genetic influence on the group deficit in reading within the sampled population of 8- to 18-year-olds with English as a first language in the Colorado schools.

Wadsworth et al. (2000) emphasized a significant qualification of the above group-heritability estimate for reading disability: The level of heritability for the group deficit in reading was significantly related to probands' Wechsler (1974) full-scale IQ scores. Group heritabilities were 43% for probands with IQ scores below 100, and 72% for probands with IQ scores of 100 and above. Thus, environmental influences on reading deficits were more important for children with lower IQ scores, and accounted for 57% of that group's defcit. Olson, Datta, Gayan, and DeFries (1999) found a similar pattern of results for IQ and the genetic etiology for the group deficit in isolated word recognition.

The role of IQ in the definition of reading disability and in the determination of eligibility for remedial and special education services has been quite controversial. Public law has required a discrepancy between reading and IQ scores, but there is little evidence that the core phonological reading problems in children with reading disability are different for low- and high-IQ groups (Siegel 1989; Stanovich & Siegel, 1994), and there is little or no relation between IQ and children's response to reading remediation (Vellutino, Scanlon, & Lyon, 2000). A policy that denies remedial services for children with low IQ scores would add to the substantial environmental constraints on their reading development that have been documented in our behavioral–genetic studies with twins (Olson et al., 1999; Wadsworth et al., 2000).

Genetic and Environmental Influences on Component Skills in Reading and Language

Olson, Wise, Conners, Rack, and Fulker (1989) explored the genetic etiology for group deficits in isolated word recognition, two component reading skills in word recognition, and a related language measure of phoneme awareness. The component skills in word reading were phonological decoding, measured by subjects' accuracy and speed in reading nonwords (e.g., calch, tegwop, and framble), and orthographic coding, measured by subjects' accuracy and speed in discriminating a word from a phonologically identical foil (e.g., rain rane; sammon salmon). The phonological decoding task was similar to several standardized measures of "word attack," though the addition of a speed requirement was novel and important for its genetic etiology. The orthographic task was designed so that regardless of children's phonological decoding skills or their application in the task, they would have to depend on their memory for the target word's specific orthographic pattern.

The initial theoretical rationale for employing the phonological and orthographic tasks was based on dual-route models of printed word recognition (cf. Olson, 1985; Patterson, Marshal, & Coltheart, 1985). The idea was that there were separable indirect and direct routes to the lexicon. The indirect route was based on "sounding out" and blending grapheme–phoneme correspondences to identify the word. This phonological decoding of print was viewed as a slow process that was particularly important in the early stages of reading development and in later encounters with unfamiliar printed words. As words were repeatedly read, it was assumed that a faster "direct" route to the lexicon was established for the words' specific orthographic patterns.

The dual-route model seemed to fit with many intuitive notions of how children learn to read. It also seemed to fit with evidence for different subtypes of acquired dyslexia due to brain damage. Some patients labeled "phonological" or "deep dyslexics" were relatively weak in reading unfamiliar nonwords compared to their reading of regular and exception words they had seen before (Marshal & Newcombe, 1966). More rarely, there were other patients called "surface dyslexics" who displayed the opposite pattern: They could read nonwords and regular words without too much trouble but had greater difficulty reading exception words that would require specific memory for their unusual orthographic–phonological correspondences (e.g., said and yacht) (Patterson et al., 1985). Presumably, the surface dyslexics would also have great difficulty with our orthographic coding task that employed phonologically identical foils and required memory for a word's specific orthographic pattern (e.g., rain rane).

The dual-route model has faced several serious challenges in recent years. Among these challenges are findings indicating that phonological processing of print is much faster and automatic than previously assumed (Van Orden, Pennington, & Stone, 1990), that brain-damage evidence for independence of the two supposed routes is really not very clear either behaviorally or anatomically, and that computer simulations of reading development in connectionist models do not require separate mechanisms for reading nonwords and exception words (Plaut, McClelland, Seidenberg, &

Patterson, 1996; Seidenberg & McClelland, 1989). The latter finding has been extended most recently in connectionist models that suggest problems with the precision of phonological representations on the input side in phonological dyslexics and problems with the number of "hidden units" in surface dyslexics (Harm & Seidenberg, 1999; Manis, Seidenberg, Doi, McBride-Chang, & Petersen, 1996). These theoretical issues are too complex for a complete discussion in this chapter. A very lucid review can be found in Pennington (1999). The theoretical issues surrounding dual-route theory are introduced here because behavioral–genetic data and brain imaging can provide a new source of evidence about shared and/or independent etiologies of individual differences in orthographic and phonological coding skills. Before turning to this data, we discuss a basic language skill that may be uniquely important for learning the grapheme–phoneme correspondences required for phonological decoding.

Learning to phonologically decode printed words may depend on children's ability to isolate and manipulate the abstract phonemes of their language. "Phoneme awareness" is thought by many to be a prerequisite language skill for learning to read (cf. Liberman, Shankweiler, Fisher, & Carter, 1974), though there is a strong reciprocal influence on phoneme awareness from learning to read (Morais, Cary, Alegria, & Bertelson, 1979). The measure of phoneme awareness used in the Olson et al. (1989) twin study was a modification of the game many know as "Pig Latin." In this game, children are asked to move the initial consonant or consonant cluster sound to the end of a spoken word and add the "ay" sound. Thus, "pig" would become "igpay." There is no reference to letters in the task instructions, though a few children report using orthographic images.

Prior to their genetic analyses of the foregoing component reading and language skills, Olson et al. (1989) matched a group of older poor readers (mean age 15 years) to a group of younger normal readers (mean age 10 years) on a standard measure of word recognition, and then compared the groups on phonological decoding, phoneme awareness, and orthographic coding. They found that on average, the older poor readers were similar to the younger normal readers in orthographic coding accuracy. However, the older poor readers were significantly lower, on average, than the younger normal readers in both phonological decoding and phoneme awareness (see Rack, Snowling, & Olson, 1992, for a review of similar results in other studies). This result seemed to suggest that language deficits in phoneme awareness and closely related reading deficits in phonological decoding may play a causal role in slowing the reading growth of most children with reading disability. Olson et al. (1989) suggested that the disabled readers' word reading tended to be better than expected from their poor phonological skills because they had more exposure to the advanced words on the test than did the much younger comparison group of normal readers.

Results from behavioral–genetic analyses in Olson et al. (1989) seemed to fit the foregoing hypothesis of a special role for phoneme awareness and phonological decoding in reading disability: Group deficits in both these skills and in word recognition were significantly heritable. In contrast, the group deficit in orthographic coding was not significantly heritable. This result seemed to support the etiological separation of phonological (direct) and orthographic (indirect) pathways to the lexicon. However, it is now clear in larger samples that the group deficit in orthographic coding accuracy is also highly heritable, at nearly the same level as phonological decoding. A more recent behavioral–genetic analysis by Gayan and Olson (1999) of group deficits in the foregoing component skills was performed with much larger samples of identical and fraternal twin pairs tested in the CLDRC. This more powerful analysis revealed highly significant evidence for substantial genetic etiology on all the measures. Table 7.1 presents the results for genetic (h_g^2), shared environment (c_g^2), and nonshared environment (e_g^2) influences on low-group membership.

Note that *both* genetic and shared-environment influences were significant for all measures, though the balance of genetic and shared-environment influences seems to vary somewhat across the measures. Genet-

TABLE 7.1. Estimates of Genetic Shared-Environment and Nonshared-Environment Influences and Standard Errors for Group Deficits

Task	Genetic influences h_g^2 (SE)	Shared environment c_g^2 (SE)	Nonshared environment e_g^2 (SE)
Word recognition	.45 (.08)*	.49 (.10)*	.06
Phonological decoding	.61 (.12)*	.24 (.12)*	.15
Phoneme awareness	.56 (.14)*	.24 (.13)*	.20
Orthographic coding	.58 (.12)*	.20 (.12)*	.22

Note. Data from Gayan and Olson (1999). Standard errors (*SE*s) are in parentheses.
*$p < .05$.

ic influence was lower and shared-environment influence was higher for the group deficit in word recognition. Perhaps shared environmental influences related to print exposure have a greater impact on measures of word recognition than on phonological decoding and on the precise memory for specific spellings required in the orthographic coding task.

The fact that group deficits in different reading-related skills have significant genetic influences does not imply that their genetic influences are caused by the same genes. Even when two heritable reading-related variables are correlated, it is possible that their correlation is largely due to environmental rather than genetic influence. Direct evidence for common genetic influence was obtained by the selection of twin probands for deficits in word recognition and comparing identical and fraternal cotwin regression to the mean on phonological decoding, phoneme awareness, or orthographic coding (Olson, Forsberg, & Wise, 1994). For all three variables, there was significantly greater regression to the population mean for fraternal compared to identical cotwins, indicating significant common genetic etiologies with deficits in word recognition. Separate analyses determined that there was significant common genetic influence on group deficits in phonological decoding and orthographic coding and particularly strong common genetic influences on group deficits in phonological decoding and phoneme awareness.

While the foregoing bivariate analyses have shown that there is some common genetic etiology for group deficits across different measures, there may also be some in-

dependent genetic influence on each measure. Different statistical methods have been developed to assess both shared and independent genetic and environmental influences on individual differences in different skills (Neale, 1997). Olson et al. (1999) used these methods to show that individual differences in phonological decoding and orthographic coding were due to *both* common and independent genetic influences. The behavioral–genetic evidence for partly independent genetic influences on these two component skills in word recognition has led to attempts to confirm their independence in linkage studies of DNA and in measures of brain function. We first review the evidence from linkage analyses with DNA and then turn to anatomical and functional imaging of the brain.

Linkage Analyses of Reading Disability

Genetic influences on a complex cognitive process such as reading are most likely mediated by the activity of many different genes, interacting with the environment, during pre- and postnatal development. However, it is possible that a few genes may have effects that are strong enough in the general population, or in extended families with a history of reading disabilities, that are detectable against the background of other gene influences. This view of multiple genetic influences on reading disability is different from the distinct disease models and single-gene effects that have been linked to disorders such as Huntington's disease or cystic fibrosis. Nevertheless, the method of

DNA linkage analysis can be used to find regions on the chromosomes that are statistically "linked" in the sample with the expression of a quantitative disorder such as reading disability. These locations are "quantitative trait loci" (QTLs; Plomin et al., 1990).

Linkage is typically established for a region of DNA on a chromosome that may contain many genes. Markers indicating the presence of specific sequences of base pairs can be used to determine whether two family members inherited the same segment of DNA from a relative. The relatives' behavioral data are then compared to their DNA markers to see whether those who share the disorder have inherited the same segment of DNA.

Linkage for reading disability has been detected at statistically significant levels in several different locations that have replicated across different studies. Evidence for statistically significant linkage has been found in a region on the short arm of chromosome 6 for samples of fraternal twins (Cardon et al., 1994; Gayan et al., 1999), ordinary sibling pairs (Fisher et al., 1999), and extended families (Grigorenko et al., 1997; Grigorenko, Wood, Meyer, & Pauls, 2000; Smith, Kimberling, & Pennington, 1991).

Smith et al. (1991) and Grigorenko et al. (1997) also found linkage evidence for deficits in word recognition on the long arm of chromosome 15q, and Morris (2000) reported an association between a marker and reading disability in the same area. Finally, two studies of extended families have reported significant linkage of reading disability to chromosome 1 (Grigorenko, Wood, Meyer, & Pauls, 1998; Rabin et al., 1993). Overall, the results from extended family studies suggests that the genes influencing reading disability may vary across families (Smith et al., 1991).

In addition to differences in genetic transmission across different families, there is limited evidence that deficits in different component reading skills might have partly different genetic etiologies. Grigorenko et al. (1997) found evidence suggesting that whereas deficits in phonological skills were more significantly linked to chromosome 6, deficits in word recognition were more significantly linked to chromosome 15. However, the contrasts in linkage strengths on chromosomes 6 and 15 for the different measures in Grigorenko et al. (1997) were not statistically significant. Similarly, Gayan et al. (1999) found significant linkage on chromosome 6 for deficits in phoneme awareness, phonological decoding, and orthographic coding but not for word recognition. Again, the differences in linkage strength for these different measures were not statistically significant.

In view of the previous discussion of both shared and independent genetic etiologies for deficits in phonological and orthographic coding (Olson et al., 1994, 1999), their shared linkage on chromosome 6 is notable (Fisher et al., 1999; Gayan et al., 1999). The linkage for orthographic coding appeared to be stronger than that for phonological decoding in both studies, but again these differences in linkage strength were not statistically significant. Much larger samples of siblings and/or extended families will be needed to confirm any differential linkage for different component reading and language skills.

Linkage evidence can only indicate that there is a statistical relation between a region of DNA and reading disability or deficits in related component skills. It does not specify the gene (or genes) involved, or that a particular person's reading disability is due primarily to genetic influence. Evidence for linkage ultimately needs to be followed up with the fine mapping of genes in the region of DNA that has been linked with reading disability. When a gene is finally located that is responsible for the linkage results, the next steps are to clone the gene, determine the protein that is coded by the gene, and understand the expression of that gene and its protein in brain development in interaction with the environment. These are big steps that will likely prove to be far more difficult than the initial discovery of statistical linkage of reading disability to various regions of the genome. Before these steps are accomplished, it may be possible to use genetic markers that are on or extremely close to a responsible gene to assess an individual's genetic risk for developing reading disability, and this information might be used to prescribe early environmental intervention to compensate for any negative genetic influence.

Genetic and Environmental Influences on Brain Morphology and Function

Although we cannot currently identify specific genes related to reading disability and their association with differences in brain development, data from identical and fraternal twins have been used to see if there are unspecified genetic influences on measures of brain morphology. Some of the twin pairs from the CLDRC have had their brains scanned with magnetic resonance imaging (MRI) (Pennington et al., 2000; Pennington et al., 1999). Volume data for 13 individual brain structures was then factor-analyzed. This analysis yielded "cortical" and "subcortical" factors for each hemisphere that accounted for 64% of the total variance. Total cerebral volume was also computed. The identical twin correlations for each of these five volume scores ranged from .78 to .98, while those for fraternal twins ranged from .32 to .65. The pattern of identical and fraternal twin correlations indicated that 56% to 97% of individual variation on the five volume scores was due to genetic factors, while shared environmental influences accounted for 0% to 37% of individual variation. (The sample size was too small to reveal significant differences in these percentages across the different volume measures.) Thus, the evidence for some genetic influence on brain morphology was quite strong (Pennington et al., 2000).

Pennington et al. (1999) compared each of the 13 brain-structure volumes for twins with and without reading disability. They found that the insula and callosal thickness were significantly smaller in children with reading disability. No other reading-group differences in brain volume were found among the different structures, including the planum temporale that had been reported to differ in autopsy data from a few seriously dyslexic adults (Galaburda, 1988). The results from other MRI studies of reading disability and the planum temporale have been inconsistent (cf. Larsen, Hoien, & Odegard, 1990; Rumsey, Donohue, et al., 1997). In fact, *no* finding of structural differences between disabled and normal readers' brains has replicated consistently across studies (Pennington, 1999).

Possible differences in brain morphology related to reading disability are intriguing, but even if they exist, they do not provide evidence on possible functional differences in the different structures that are either correlated with or independent from brain morphology. There is currently a great deal of research using functional magnetic resonance imaging (FMRI) and positron emission tomography (PET) methods that reflect the amount of blood flow and/or metabolic activity in different areas of the brain while subjects perform different tasks. One of these studies found that activity in the left insula was significantly lower in children with reading disability compared to activity in normal readers during reading-related tasks (Paulesu et al., 1996). This result may be related to the Pennington et al. (1999) finding that the insula was significantly smaller for the group of twins with reading disability. The role of the insula in reading is not entirely clear at this point, but it seems to be part of a pathway between cortical regions involved in the initial visual processing of words and regions involved more in their semantic and phonological representations.

Pugh et al. (in press) reviewed the results of their own and other recent neuroimaging studies comparing good and poor readers. The details of the methods and results vary somewhat across studies, but there were some common findings when good and poor readers were engaged in reading and related tasks that required phonological assembly: Compared to good readers, poor readers tended to show lower activation in and lower correlations between the left dorsal (temporal–parietal) and left ventral (occipito–temporal) areas, and the poor readers showed relatively greater activation in the inferior frontal and right hemisphere posterior regions. For normal readers, Pugh et al. (in press) argued that activation of the left posterior dorsal area by pseudowords and low-frequency words was associated with the analysis of grapheme–phoneme correspondences and the integration of phonological and lexical semantic features. The normal readers' activation of the left posterior ventral area by highly familiar words was thought to reflect that area's role in fluent reading of word forms, whose development is dependent on prior processing in the left posterior dorsal area. For poor readers, their greater activation of the inferior frontal gyrus is thought to reflect a compensatory shift to articulatory coding in support of phonological analysis, and their greater activation of posterior right hemisphere areas is thought to reflect the additional and dissociated development of nonphonologicaly based visuosemantic pattern recognition, which is less efficient for fluent reading.

Pugh et al. (in press) commented on the potential value of using neuroimaging to monitor the effects of remediation programs on brain function. Several such projects are currently under way in different laboratories. A recent and highly publicized study by Richards et al. (2000) claimed that a "phonologically based" remediation program resulted in the normalization of lactate metabolism in the left anterior quadrant (overlapping the inferior frontal gyrus discussed in Pugh et al., in press) in the brains of eight dyslexic children. The study imaged the children prior to a 3-week, 30-hour remediation program that included exercises in phonological segmentation, reading of science texts, and hearing lectures on science. This initial imaging showed a significantly higher lactate metabolism in dyslexics compared to normal control subjects when they performed a rhyme judgment task for printed words and nonwords. One year later and after the 3-week training program, the dyslexics' lactate metabolism was not significantly different from that of the normal controls during the rhyme judgment task. However, there was no appropriate statistical test for the interaction between brain scan times and reader group, and it is clear from the graphed results that this interaction would not have approached statistical significance. Thus, although the authors make strong claims that "phonological training" (there was no comparison to other types of training) changed the dyslexics' lactate metabolism in "language" areas of the brain, the dyslexics did not show a statistically significant change between scans. The next few years should see a number of new studies published on the effects of training on brain function, ideally with more appropriate statistical analyses, untreated or differently treated dyslexic control groups, and larger samples.

Conclusions and New Directions for Research

Genetic-linkage studies of reading disability and the assessment of brain activity related to reading are relatively new areas of research. Linkage studies have sometimes yielded conflicting results, possibly due to sample differences, different measures and criteria for reading disability, or inaccurate marker locations. For example, Field and Kaplan (1998) did not find evidence for linkage with reading disability on chromosome 6p that had been found in several other studies discussed in this chapter. Linkage studies with larger samples, more thorough reading assessments, and more closely spaced genetic markers are needed to resolve differences in results across studies and measures. In neuroimaging research, differences in image analysis, baseline subtraction conditions, subject samples, and reading-related tasks may be responsible for the varied and often conflicting results across studies (Pennington, 1999; Rumsey, 1996). Nevertheless, we believe that in the 21st century, genetic analyses and neurobiological research will provide valuable converging evidence on normal reading and on the etiology and remediation of reading disabilities.

One area of reading development that has received relatively little attention from a genetic and neurobiological perspective is reading comprehension. Accuracy and fluency in word reading are certainly important for reading comprehension (cf. Shankweiler et al., 1999). However, there is also evidence for some independence in the development of word recognition and reading comprehension. For example, remedial programs for word-decoding problems in children with reading disability show greater trained gains in word recognition and phonological skills in comparison to control groups, but they typically do not show similar advantages in reading comprehension (cf. Olson, Wise, Ring, & Johnson, 1997; Torgesen et al., 1999; Wise, Ring, & Olson, 2000). Preliminary analyses of twin data from the CLDRC have shown that the genetic and environmental etiologies for individual differences in word recognition are partly shared with, but also partly independent from, the genetic and environmental etiologies for higher-level language skills reflected in verbal IQ, listening comprehension, and reading comprehension. As noted in a recent request for proposals from the National Institutes of Health, more studies are needed to understand genetic and environmental influences on reading comprehension and their relations to brain function. This will pose some major challenges for researchers in the 21st century.

Finally, we must acknowledge the current paucity of direct evidence on genetic influences and brain function in *early* literacy development. We do know that there are significant correlations between preschool language deficits and later reading problems (cf. Catts, Fey, Zahng, & Tomblin, in press; see Scarborough, 1998, for review). There have been a few important family studies of preschool children at potential genetic risk for reading disability because of reading disability in older relatives (Pennington & Lefly, in press; Scarborough, 1990). These studies show that at-risk preschoolers have significantly lower levels of performance in several language measures compared to control children with no family history for reading disability. When the at-risk children with poor language skills have been followed through the early school years, they tend to show difficulty in learning to read.

The results from at-risk family studies suggest the possibility but do not prove that there is a shared genetic etiology between preschool language deficits and later reading deficits, as the familiality of reading disability could be due to family environment. A preschool longitudinal twin study would provide the necessary direct evidence for genetic, shared environment, and nonshared environment influences on preliteracy skills and later reading development. This type of study is currently under way in Colorado and at the University of New England in Australia under the direction of Brian Byrne. Along with common measures of important language skills, the studies are explicitly training preschool twins in phoneme awareness to assess individual differences in learning rate. We chose this "dynamic assessment" procedure because Byrne's previous preschool training studies had shown a strong correlation between learning rate for phoneme awareness and later reading ability (Byrne, Fielding-Barnsley, & Ashley, 2000).

To our knowledge, there have been no neuroimaging studies of preschool children. Such studies are needed before we can answer an important developmental question: To what extent do the patterns of brain activation in an 8-year-old struggling reader, for example, look like patterns of brain activation in 4- and 5-year-olds who will latter have difficulty learning to read (B. Blachman, personal communication, May 2000)? It would be interesting to learn whether language deficits that predict later reading deficits are associated with abnormal patterns of brain activation, and whether these patterns are related to later differences in brain activation when the children are learning to read.

There have been two interesting studies of event-related potentials (ERPs) during phoneme discrimination in infants that have shown relations to subsequent reading ability (Molfese, Molfese, & Espy, 1999), or differences between infants with and without a family history for reading disability (Leppaenen, Pihko, Eklund, & Lyytinen, 1999). If these results can be replicated, it might be appropriate to use this relatively inexpensive method to screen infants for early remedial treatment studies. It would also be interesting to explore the genetic and environmental etiology of these early individual differences in ERPs.

In conclusion, there is strong evidence for genetic influences on literacy development in older children, and there are differences in patterns of brain activity that are associated with differences in their reading ability. Soon we will learn whether genetic and environmental influences on reading disability overlap with those for preschoolers' language-learning deficits. Later we hope to learn more about the specific genes and their influences on brain development that are responsible for the behavioral genetic and linkage results, and we hope to better understand environmental influences on brain development as well as gene–environment interactions. We believe that this new knowledge will soon support early interventions in young children's environments to compensate for identified genetic and environmental risks. We hope that more direct biological interventions for reading and other learning disabilities are possible in the more distant future.

Acknowledgment

The research reported from the Colorado Learning Disabilities Research Center and computer-remediation projects was supported by NICHD Grant Nos. HD 11683 and HD 22223.

References

Byrne, B., Fielding-Barnsley, R., & Ashley, L. (2000). Effects of preschool phoneme identity training after six years: Outcome level distinguished from rate of response. *Journal of Educational Psychology, 92*, 659–667.

Cardon, L. R., Smith, S., Fulker, D., Kimberling, W., Pennington, B., & DeFries, J. (1994). Quantitative trait locus for reading disability on chromosome 6. *Science, 266*, 276–279.

Catts, H., Fey, M. E., Zahng, X., & Tomblin, J. B. (in press). Language basis of reading disabilities: Evidence from a longitudinal investigation. *Scientific Studies of Reading.*

Coles, G. (1987). *The learning mystique: A critical look at learning disabilities.* New York: Pantheon.

Defries, J. C., Filipek, P. A., Fulker, D. W., Olson, R. K., Pennington, B. F., Smith, S. D., & Wise, B. W. (1997). Colorado Learning Disabilities Research Center. *Learning Disability Quarterly, 8*, 7–19.

DeFries, J. C., & Fulker, D. W. (1985). Multiple regression analysis of twin data. *Behavior Genetics, 15*, 467–478.

DeFries, J. C., Fulker, D. W., & LaBuda, M. C. (1987). Evidence of a genetic aetiology in reading disability of twins. *Nature, 329*, 537–539.

Dunn, L. M., & Markwardt, F. C. (1970). *Examiner's manual: Peabody Individual Achievement Test.* Circle Pines, MN: American Guidance Service.

Field, L. L., & Kaplan, B. J. (1998). Absence of linkage of phonological coding dyslexia to chromosome 6p23–21. 3 in a large family data set. *American Journal of Human Genetics, 63*, 1448–1456.

Fisher, S. E., Marlow, A. J., Lamb, J., Maestrini, E., Williams, D. F., Richardson, A. J., Weeks, D. E., Stein, J. F., & Monaco, A. P. (1999). A quantitative trait locus on chromosome 6p influences different aspects of developmental dyslexia. *American Journal of Human Genetics, 64*, 146–156.

Galaburda, A. M. (1988). The pathogenesis of childhood dyslexia. *Research in Nervous Mental Disorders, 66*, 127–138.

Gayan, J., & Olson, R. K. (1999). Reading disability: Evidence for a genetic etiology. *European Child & Adolescent Psychiatry, 8*(Suppl. 3), 52–55.

Gayan, J., Smith, S. D., Cherny, S. S., Cardon, L. R.,

Fulker, D. W., Kimberling, W. J., Olson, R. K., Pennington, B., & DeFries, J. C. (1999). Large quantitative trait locus for specific language and reading deficits in chromosome 6p. *American Journal of Human Genetics, 64*, 157–164.

Grigorenko, E., Meyer, M. S., Hart, L. A., Speed, W. C., Shuster, A., & Pauls, D. L. (1997). Susceptibility loci for distinct components of developmental dyslexia on chromosomes 6 and 15. *American Journal of Human Genetics, 60*, 27–39.

Grigorenko, E. L., Wood, F. B., Meyer, M. S., & Pauls, D. L. (2000). Chromosome 6p influences on different dyslexia related cognitive processes: Further confirmation. *American Journal of Human Genetics, 66*, 715–723.

Grigorenko, E. L., Wood, F. B., Meyer, M. S., Pauls, J. E. D., Hart, L. A., & Pauls, D. L. (1998). Linkage studies suggest a possible locus for dyslexia near the Rh region on chromosome 1 [Abstract]. *Behavior Genetics, 28*, 470.

Harm, M. W., & Seidenberg, M. S. (1999). Phonology, reading acquisition, and dyslexia: Insights from connectionist models. *Psychological Review, 106*, 491–528.

Larsen, J. P., Hoien, T., & Odegaard, H. (1990). MRI evaluation of the size and symmetry of the planum temporale in adolescents with developmental dyslexia. *Brain and Language, 39*, 289–301.

Leppaenen, P. H. T., Pihko, E., Eklund, K. M., & Lyytinen, H. (1999). Cortical responses of infants with and without a genetic risk for dyslexia: II. Group effects. *Neuroreport: For Rapid Communication of Neuroscience Research, 10*, 969–973.

Liberman, I. Y., Shankweiler, D., Fisher, F. W., & Carter, B. (1974). Explicit syllable and phoneme segmentation in the young child. *Journal of Experimental Child Psychology, 18*, 201–212.

Manis, F. R., Seidenberg, M. S., Poi, L. M., McBride-Chang, C., & Peterson, P. (1996). On the bases of two subtypes of developmental dyslexia. *Cognition, 58*, 157–195.

Marshal, J. C., & Newcomb, F. (1966). Syntactic and semantic errors in paralexia. *Neuropsychologia, 4*, 169–176.

Molfese, D. L., Molfese, V. J., & Espy, K. A. (1999). The predictive use of event-related potentials in language development and the treatment of language disorders. *Developmental Neuropsychology, 16*, 373–377.

Morais, J., Cary, L., Alegria, J., & Bertelson, P. (1979). Does awareness of speech as a sequence of phonemes arise spontaneously? *Cognition, 7*, 323–321.

Morris, D. W., Robinson, L., Turic, D., Duke, M., Webb, V., Milham, C., Hopkin, E., Pound, K., Ferrnando, S., Easton, M., Hamshere, M., Williams, N., McGuffin, P., Owen, M. J., O'-Donovan, M. C., & Williams, J. (2000). Family-based association mapping provides evidence for reading disability on chromosome 15q. *Human Molecular Genetics, 9*, 843–848.

Neale, M. C. (1997). *Mx: Statistical modeling* (4th

ed.). Richmond, VA: Department of Psychiatry, University of Virginia.

Olson, R. K. (1985). Disabled reading processes and cognitive profiles. In D. Gray & J. Kavanagh (Eds.), *Biobehavioral measures of dyslexia* (pp. 215–244). Parkton, MD: York Press.

Olson, R. K., Datta, H., Gayan, J., & DeFries, J. C. (1999). A behavioral–genetic analysis of reading disabilities and component processes. In R. M. Klein & P. A. McMullen (Eds.), *Converging methods for understanding reading and dyslexia* (pp. 133–153). Cambridge MA: MIT Press.

Olson, R. K., Forsberg, H., & Wise, B. (1994). Genes, environment, and the development of orthographic skills. In V. W. Berninger (Ed.), *The varieties of orthographic knowledge I: Theoretical and developmental issues* (pp. 27–71). Dordrecht, The Netherlands: Kluwer Academic.

Olson, R. K., Wise, B., Conners, F., Rack, J., & Fulker, D. (1989). Specific deficits in component reading and language skills: Genetic and environmental influences. *Journal of Learning Disabilities, 22*(6), 339–348.

Olson, R. K., Wise, B. W., Ring, J., & Johnson, M. (1997). Computer-based remedial training in phoneme awareness and phonological decoding: Effects on the post-training development on word recognition. *Scientific Studies of Reading, 1,* 235–253.

Paulesu,, E., Frith, U., Snowling, M., Gallagher, A., Morton, J., Frackowiak, R. S. J., & Frith, C. D. (1996). Is developmental dyslexia a disconnection syndrome? Evidence from PET scanning. *Brian, 119,* 27–47.

Patterson, K. E., Marshal, J. C., & Coltheart, M. (1985). *Surface dyslexia.* Hillsdale, NJ: Erlbaum.

Pennington, B. F. (1999). Toward an integrated understanding of dyslexia: Genetic, neurological, and cognitive mechanisms. *Development and Psychopathology, 11,* 629–654.

Pennington, B. F., Filipek, P. A., Churchwell, J., Kennedy, D. N., Lefly, D., Simon, J. H., Filley, C. M., Galaburda, A., Alarcon, M., & DeFries, J. C. (1999). Brain morphometry in reading-disabled twins. *Neurology, 53,* 723–729.

Pennington, B. J., Filipek, P. A., Lefly, D. L., Chhabildas, N., Kennedy, D. N., Simon, J. H., Filley, C. M., Galaburda, A., & DeFries, J. C. (2000). A twin study of size variations in human brain. *Journal of Cognitive Neuroscience, 12,* 223–232.

Pennington, B. F., & Lefly, D. L. (in press). Early reading development in children at family risk for dyslexia. *Child Development.*

Plaut, D., McClelland, J. L., Seidenberg, M. S., & Patterson, K. E. (1996). Visual word recognition: Are two routes really necessary? *Psychological Review, 103,* 56–115.

Plomin, R., DeFries, J. C., & Loehlin, J. I. (1977). Genotype–environment interaction and correlation in the analysis of human variation. *Psychological Bulletin, 84,* 309–322.

Plomin, R., DeFries, J. C., & McClearn, G. E. (1990). *Behavior genetics: A primer.* San Francisco: Freeman.

Pugh, K. R., Mencl, W. E., Jenner, A. R., Katz, L., Frost, S. J., Lee, J. R., Shaywitz, S. E., & Shaywitz, B. A. (in press). Functional neuroimaging studies of reading and reading disability (developmental dyslexia). *Mental Retardation and Developmental Disabilities Research Reviews.*

Rabin, M., Wen, X. L., Hepburn, M., Lubs, H. A., Feldman, E., & Duara, R. (1993). Suggestive linkage of developmental dyslexia to chromosome 1p34-p36. *The Lancet, 342,* 178.

Rack, J. P., Snowling, M. J., & Olson, R. K. (1992). The nonword reading deficit in developmental dyslexia: a review. *Reading Research Quarterly, 27*(1), 28–53.

Richards, T. L., Corina, D., Serafini, S., Steury, K., Echelard, D. R., Dager, S. R., Marro, K., Abbott, R. D., Maravilla, K. R., & Berninger, V. W. (2000). The effects of a phonologically-driven treatment for dyslexia on Lactate levels as measures by Proton MRSI. *American Journal of Neuroradiology, 21,* 916–922.

Rodgers, B. (1983). The identification and prevalence of specific reading retardation. *British Journal of Educational Psychology, 53,* 369–373.

Rumsey, J. M. (1996). Neuroimaging in developmental dyslexia: A review and conceptualization. In G. R. Lyon & J. M. Rumsey (Eds.), *Neuroimaging* (pp. 57–77). Baltimore: Brookes.

Rumsey, J. M., Donohue, B. C., Brady, D. R., Nace, K., Giedd, J. N., & Andreason, P. (1997). A magnetic resonance imaging study of planum temporale asymmetry in men with developmental dyslexia. *Archives of Neurology, 54,* 1481–1489.

Scarborough, H. (1990). Very early language deficits in dyslexic children. *Child Development, 61,* 1728–1743.

Scarborough, H. (1998). Early identification of children at risk for reading disabilities. In B. K. Shapiro, P. J. Accardo, & A. J. Capute (Eds.), *Specific reading disability: A view of the spectrum* (pp. 75–119). Timonium, MD: York Press.

Scarr, S., & McCartney, K. (1983). How people make their own environments: A theory of genotype-environment effects. *Child Development, 54,* 424–435.

Seidenberg, M. S., & McClelland, J. L. (1989). A distributed developmental model of word recognition and naming. *Psychological Review, 96,* 447–452.

Shankweiler, D., Lundquist, E., Katz, L., Stuebing, K. K., Fletcher, J., Brady, S., Fowler, A., Dreyer, L. G., Marchione, K. E., Shaywitz, S. E., & Shaywitz, B. A. (1999). Comprehension and decoding: Patterns of association in children with reading difficulties. *Scientific Studies of Reading, 3,* 69–64.

Shaywitz, S. E., Escobar, M. D., Shaywitz, B. A., Fletcher, J. M., & Makuch, R. (1992). Evidence that dyslexia may represent the lower tail of a normal distribution of reading ability. *New England Journal of Medicine, 326,* 145–150.

Smith, S. D., Kimberling, W. J., & Pennington, B. F. (1991). Screening for multiple genes influencing dyslexia. *Reading and Writing: An Interdisciplinary Journal, 3,* 285–298.

Siegel, L. S. (1989). IQ is irrelevant to the definition of learning disabilities. *Journal of Learning Disabilities, 22,* 469–478.

Stanovich, K. E., & Siegel, L. S. (1994). Phenotypic performance profile of children with reading disabilities: A regression-based test of the phonological-core variable-difference model. *Journal of Educational Psychology, 86,* 24–53.

Torgesen, J. K., Wagner, R. K., Rashotte, C. A., Rose, E., Lindamood, P., & Conway, T. (1999). Preventing reading failure in young children with phonological processing disabilities: Group and individual responses to instruction. *Journal of Educational Psychology, 91,* 579–593.

VanOrden, G., Pennington, B., & Stone, G. (1990). Word identification in reading and the promise of subsymbolic psycholinguistics. *Psychological Review, 97,* 488–522.

Vellutino, F. R., Scanlon, D. M., & Lyon, R. (2000). IQ scores do not differentiate between difficult to remediate and readily remediated poor readers: More evidence against the IQ achievement discrepancy definition of reading disability. *Journal of Learning Disabilities, 33,* 223–238.

Wadsworth, S. J., Olson, R. K., Pennington, B. F., & DeFries, J. C. (2000). Differential genetic etiology of reading disability as a function of IQ. *Journal of Learning Disabilities, 33,* 192–199.

Wechsler, D. (1974). *Manual for the Wechsler Intelligence Scale for Children—revised.* Cleveland, OH: Psychological Corporation.

Wise, B. W., Ring, J., & Olson, R. K. (2000). Individual differences in gains from computer-assisted remedial reading with more emphasis on phonological analysis or accurate reading in context. *Journal of Experimental Child Psychology, 77,* 197–235.

II

STRANDS OF EARLY
LITERACY DEVELOPMENT

8

Connecting Early Language and Literacy to Later Reading (Dis)Abilities: Evidence, Theory, and Practice

❖

HOLLIS S. SCARBOROUGH

As recently as 20 years ago, learning to read was not thought to commence until formal instruction was provided in school. Accordingly, reading disabilities were largely considered to be an educational problem with no known antecedents at earlier ages. It is now abundantly clear that reading acquisition is a process that begins early in the preschool period, such that children arrive at school having acquired vastly differing degrees of knowledge and skill pertaining to literacy. Attention has thus turned to whether preschool differences in language and literacy development are reliable prognostic indicators, and perhaps direct causes, of later reading (dis)abilities. I review and discuss the available evidence from longitudinal research that has examined such issues, with particular attention to at-risk populations such as offspring of parents with reading disability and preschoolers diagnosed with early language impairments.

The Multifaceted Nature of Reading and Its Acquisition

Skilled readers are able to derive meaning from printed text accurately and efficiently. Research has shown that in doing so, they fluidly coordinate many component skills, each of which has been sharpened through instruction and experience over many years. Figure 8.1 illustrates the major "strands" that are woven together during the course of becoming a skilled reader. It is customary to consider separately the strands involved in recognizing individual printed words from those involved in comprehending the meaning of the string of words that have been identified, even though those two processes operate (and develop) interactively rather than independently. (For a fuller review of this material, see the recent report of the Committee on the Prevention of Reading Difficulties in Young Children, 1998.)

Most children who have trouble learning to read in the early school years stumble in mastering the "word recognition" strands. In English orthography, the spellings of spoken words are governed largely by the "alphabetic principle," the notion that our written symbols (letters or graphemes) systematically represent the smallest meaningful speech elements (phonemes) that make up the pronunciation of a word. (See Adams, Chapter 6.) It stands to reason that grasping the alphabetic principle will be difficult if a child does not yet appreciate that spoken words consist of phonemes, because without this "phonemic awareness" the

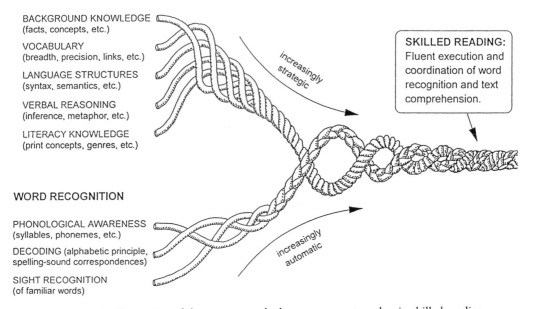

FIGURE 8.1. Illustration of the many strands that are woven together in skilled reading.

child cannot truly understand what letters stand for (Liberman, 1973).

Recognizing printed words further requires that one learn and apply the many correspondences between particular letters and phonemes, so that the pronunciation of a printed word can be figured out ("decoded"); matching the derived pronunciation to stored information about spoken words in one's mental lexicon enables the identity of the printed word to be recognized. Phonological decoding is the most reliable guide to word recognition, but there are also plenty of exceptions (words such as "of," "two," "choir," and "yacht") whose spellings must, wholly or in part, be memorized outright. Finally, skilled reading requires that the processes involved in word recognition become so well practiced that they can proceed extremely quickly and almost effortlessly, freeing up the reader's cognitive resources for comprehension processes.

Although most reading disabilities are associated with deficits in phonemic awareness, decoding, and sight recognition of printed words, reading skill can also be seriously impeded by weaknesses in the "comprehension" strands, particularly beyond second grade when reading materials become more complex. Even if the pronunciations of all the letter strings in a passage are correctly decoded, the text will not be well comprehended if the child (1) does not know the words in their spoken form, (2) cannot parse the syntactic and semantic relationships among the words, or (3) lacks critical background knowledge or inferential skills to interpret the text appropriately and "read between the lines." Note that in such instances, "reading comprehension" deficits are essentially *oral* language limitations.

A daunting fact about reading (dis)abilities is that differences among schoolchildren in their levels of reading achievement show strong stability over time, despite remedial efforts that are usually made to strengthen the skills of lower achievers. (For a review, see Scarborough, 1998). Only about 5–10% of children who read satisfactorily in the primary grades ever stumble later, and 65–75% of children designated as reading disabled early on continue to read poorly throughout their school careers (and beyond). In light of this continuity, there has been increasing interest in whether children at risk for reading disabilities might be identifiable at early ages, so that steps could be taken to prevent or ameliorate their difficulties in learning to read in school. Of course, early intervention requires that we know what early signs to look for in order to identify which preschoolers are most likely to develop reading disabilities. That topic is reviewed next.

Predicting Reading Achievement from Kindergarten Measures

Most research on the prediction of future reading abilities has involved samples who were first tested just prior to the start of schooling (in the United States, usually in the kindergarten year) and who were then followed up after having received 1 or 2 years of reading instruction. In a recent meta-analysis (Scarborough, 1998), I examined the findings from 61 samples, in which a wide variety of predictors had been used by the researchers. Table 8.1 summarizes those results for three sets of skill variables: those involving the processing of print itself, assessments of various facets of oral language proficiency, and measures of nonverbal skills.

It is reassuring that the results from prediction studies dovetail nicely with what has been learned from research on the cognitive requirements of skilled reading and the acquisition of its various "strands." That is, although visual and motor skills of entering students have been a traditional focus of readiness testing, performance on

TABLE 8.1. Average Correlations between Kindergarten Predictor Variables and Later Reading Scores, Based on a Meta-Analysis of Findings from 61 Research Samples

Predictor variable	No. of samples	Mean r	Median r
Measures requiring the processing of print			
Rudimentary reading: letter–sound knowledge or entire "readiness" battery	21	.57	.56
Letter identification: naming of upper- and lower-case letters	24	.52	.52
Print concepts: familiarity with the mechanics and purposes of book reading	7	.46	.49
Measures of oral language proficiency			
General language index: expressive and receptive skills	4	.46	.47
Phonological awareness	27	.46	.42
Expressive ("naming") vocabulary	5	.45	.49
Sentence or story recall	11	.45	.49
Rapid serial naming speed	14	.38	.40
Verbal IQ	12	.37	.38
Receptive language (syntactic)	9	$\leq$.37	.40
Receptive vocabulary	20	.33	.38
Expressive language skills	11	.32	.37
Verbal memory (digit or word list recall)	18	.33	.33
Receptive language (semantic)	11	.24	.25
Speech production (pronunciation accuracy)	4	—	.25
Speech perception (phoneme discrimination)	11	.22	.23
Measures of nonverbal abilities			
Visual memory	8	.31	.28
Nonverbal IQ	8	.26	.25
Motor skills	5	.25	.26
Visual discrimination	5	.22	.26
Visual–motor integration	6	.16	.13

Note. Data from Scarborough (1998).

such nonverbal tasks actually provides little prognostic information about future reading difficulties. On the other hand, rudimentary skills that tie in to the "word recognition" strands—especially letter identification and phonological awareness—are among the best predictor measures. Likewise, early differences in the sorts of verbal abilities that make up the "comprehension" strands—most notably vocabulary, sentence/story recall, and concepts of print—have also been reliable predictors of later reading.

On average, however, the correlations of individual kindergarten predictor measures with future reading achievement are not nearly as strong ($r \leq .57$) as the correlations between first- or second-grade reading scores and those earned 1 to 4 years later ($r = .75$). In efforts to improve predictive accuracy, some researchers have combined kindergarten predictor variables to compute a multiple correlation with reading outcome scores in their samples. When this has been done, the results (mean $R = .75$) suggest that the predictability of future reading ability is about as strong from kindergarten onward as it is from grade to grade once formal reading instruction has commenced.

In short, the results of kindergarten prediction studies suggest that the important cognitive–linguistic strands that must be coordinated in learning to read are rather securely in place before formal school instruction begins, such that children who arrive at school with weaker verbal abilities and literacy knowledge are much more likely than their classmates to experience difficulties in learning to read during the primary grades. This raises the next question: How far back in development can the roots of the various strands be traced?

Predicting Reading from Infant and Preschool Measures

Developmental relationships between language and literacy abilities have been studied from early ages in three kinds of samples: preschoolers with early language impairments, offspring of adults with reading disabilities, and unselected samples of infants or preschoolers. These studies of younger children are particularly valuable

because, unlike most kindergarten prediction research, the children's progress has typically been observed over several years prior to the start of schooling. Such longitudinal research makes it possible to discern developmental patterns in the acquisition of reading-related skills that may both shed light on theoretical questions and provide a foundation for designing early diagnostic and preventive programs. Very briefly, the highlights of each body of work are as follows.

Early Language Impairment

Several dozen follow-up studies have been conducted to look at the short- and long-range outcomes of preschoolers who were diagnosed (and, in most cases, treated) at speech–language clinics (e.g., Aram & Hall, 1989; Bishop & Adams, 1990; Catts, Fey, & Tomblin, 1997; Rescorla, 1999; Stothard, Snowling, Bishop, Chipchase, & Kaplan, 1998). Virtually every such study has confirmed that preschoolers with language impairments are indeed at considerable risk for developing reading disabilities (as well as for continued oral language difficulties) at older ages.

Family Incidence of Reading Disability

The fact that reading disabilities tend to "run in families" has been established for nearly a century, with higher incidence noted among the relatives of affected schoolchildren than in the families of their normally achieving classmates. Although family aggregation had not previously been examined in a prospective way, I reasoned that having a parent or older sibling with a reading disability should place a preschooler at risk for experiencing similar difficulties, and that if there are some early antecedents to reading disabilities, these could be discovered by following such at-risk youngsters from an early age. Accordingly, I undertook such a study in 1979 and showed that offspring of parents with reading problems were indeed at much higher risk for difficulty in learning to read, and that these children differed on language measures from otherwise-similar peers at ages as young as 30 months (Scarborough, 1989, 1990, 1991; Scarborough, Dobrich, & Hager, 1991). Recently, outcome results for several similar studies have been reported that tend to converge with these findings (Byrne et al., 1998; Elbro, 1999; Gallagher, Frith & Snowling, 1999); Lyytinen et al., 1999; Pennington, Lefly, & Boada, 1999). Risk estimates depend, of course, on the criteria used to diagnose reading disabilities in adults and children; averaging across studies, approximately 40% of offspring of affected parents, but less than 10% of other children (of otherwise similar backgrounds), develop a reading disability (Scarborough, 1998).

Unselected Infant/Preschool Samples

Rather than looking at particular at-risk populations, some researchers have sought to examine preschool differences in relation to future prereading and reading skills in entire groups of children from the same preschools or birth cohorts (e.g., Bryant, Maclean, & Bradley, 1990; Bryant, Maclean, Bradley, & Crossland, 1990; Maclean, Bryant, & Bradley, 1987; Molfese, 1999; Shapiro et al., 1990; Walker, Greenwood, Hart, & Carta, 1994; Whitehurst, 1999). As in the research on selected at-risk preschool samples, these studies have found reliable associations between early abilities and later prereading skills and/or reading achievement.

Findings in Common

Although it is customary to review these three bodies of literature separately, here I want to focus on the commonalities among their findings. In reading these various literatures over the years, I have been struck by the fact that the relationship between early language and literacy development and later reading achievement has appeared to be similar in many respects and not contradictory in any major way, despite the differing goals and sampling procedures of the three kinds of studies. What follows is a list of some empirical results that have been observed in at least two of the three kinds of research samples. (There is a wealth of additional detail to be found in each individual investigation, but a comprehensive review of that material is beyond the scope of this chapter.)

1. In these studies of younger children, as in the kindergarten prediction research summarized earlier, nonverbal skills generally have been unrelated to concurrent or future language and literacy levels, whereas verbal skills have been much better predictors. Even in infancy (birth to age 2 years), pediatric ratings of language milestones predict later reading achievement better than do perceptual–motor indices (Shapiro et al., 1990). Similarly, recent studies have found that electrophysiological responses of infants' brains to language—but not nonverbal—stimuli are correlated with language and reading abilities in subsequent years (Lyytinen et al., 1999; Molfese, 1999).

2. Somewhat surprisingly, in most cases the magnitudes of the longer-term correlations between preschool language abilities (at ages 2 to 4 years) and school-age outcomes have been about as large as the corresponding shorter-term associations (in Table 8.1) between kindergarten scores and subsequent achievement.

3. During the preschool period, most verbal skills have tended to be well correlated with each other, both concurrently and predictively (e.g., Anthony, Lonigan, Dyer, & Bloomfield, 1997; Chaney, 1992; Rescorla, 1999; Scarborough, 1990, 1991) and have been good prospective predictors of kindergarten-age differences in phonological awareness, letter knowledge, print concepts, and other relevant skills (e.g., Bryant et al., 1989, 1990; Byrne et al., 1998; Lonigan, Burgess, Anthony, & Barker, 1998; Scarborough, 1990; Whitehurst, 1999) as well as with subsequent reading achievement. These predictive correlations have often tended to be weaker for measures of speech than for other aspects of language production and for measures of receptive rather than expressive language (e.g., Bryant et al., 1989, 1990; Chaney, 1992; Gallagher et al., 1999; Lonigan et al., 1998; Pennington et al., 1999; Shapiro et al., 1990).

4. When several domains of developing language (phonological, syntactic, lexical, etc.) have been examined within a sample, the successful predictors of future reading abilities usually have not been confined to a single linguistic domain (e.g., Catts, Fey, Zhan, & Tomblin, 1999; Rescorla, 1999; Scarborough, 1989, 1990; Walker et al., 1994). It is often the case, furthermore, that

reading outcomes have been best predicted by different sets of language variables at different ages within longitudinal samples (e.g., Gallagher, Frith, & Snowling, 1999; Lyytinen et al., 1999). Figure 8.2, which shows some findings from my longitudinal sample, illustrates this phenomenon. At the youngest ages, syntactic and speech production abilities were most deficient, relative to those of the comparison group, in the group of youngsters who subsequently developed reading disabilities. Later in the preschool period, however, the groups differed instead in vocabulary and phonological awareness skills.

5. Similarly, when longitudinal data have been examined for individual children with weak early language skills, deficit profiles have actually been observed to change over time within individuals during the preschool years (e.g., Bishop & Edmundson, 1987;

Scarborough & Dobrich, 1990). For example, a 3-year-old with across-the-board weaknesses in syntactic, lexical, and phonological skills might show a narrower range of deficits (e.g., in just one domain) a year later.

6. Even when their early language deficits have lessened considerably in severity (or have disappeared entirely) by the time of school entry, children with a family history of reading disability and/or a history of early language impairment nonetheless remain at high risk for developing reading problems at a later age (Fey, Catts, & Larrivee, 1995; Rescorla, 1999; Scarborough & Dobrich, 1990; Stothard et al., 1998).

7. Despite the relationship that has been found between preschool language problems and school-age reading problems, exceptions to this trend have been seen in

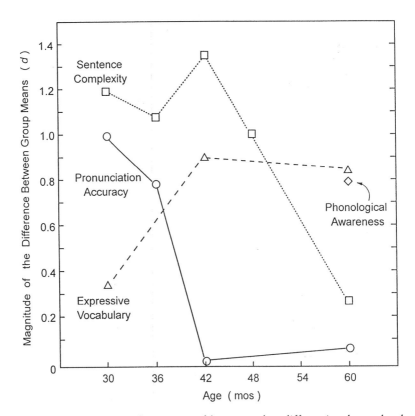

FIGURE 8.2. Changes over time in the aspects of language that differentiated preschoolers who became disabled readers from those who did not (Scarborough, 1990, 1991a). Effect sizes for the differences between the group means are shown for sentence complexity (Index of Productive Syntax), expressive vocabulary (Boston Naming Test), pronunciation accuracy (percentage of consonants correctly produced) and phonological awareness (matching of rhymes and initial phonemes).

every sample. That is, some children with early language deficits did not develop reading disabilities, and some children who became poor readers had not appeared to be behind in their preschool language development.

Taken all together, these results suggest that there is a great deal of continuity between early developmental differences and later ones. On the other hand, the data also suggest that the pattern of across-age continuities is not entirely simple or straightforward but, instead, presents some complexities that might be overlooked were it not for the fact that these phenomena have been observed by different researchers in various kinds of samples. Some implications of these common findings for theory and practice are discussed next.

Theoretical Issues: Present and Future

All the research reviewed previously has concerned the issue of how language development is related to the acquisition of literacy. Various researchers have recast and narrowed this broad question in different ways, such as: What are the consequences of early language impairment? Are preschool language disorders and later reading disabilities two manifestations (differing, perhaps, in severity) of the same clinical condition at different ages? What are the preschool antecedents of reading disability, and which ones play a causal role in its development? What preschool developments are necessary and sufficient for successful reading acquisition? And so forth. Although these differences in emphasis have guided the selection of research subjects by various investigators, the data from all such studies are pertinent to explaining language–literacy connections of all sorts. For that reason, I feel that looking at the commonalities among findings is helpful in addressing theoretical issues.

Given the wealth of evidence now available from longitudinal studies of early language and literacy, one would think that clear answers to the questions of interest would be rather easy to derive. This is not the case, however. Why has it been so difficult to answer these questions? There are

undoubtedly a host of reasons. Here, I want to focus on a few factors that, in my opinion, may have impeded the derivation of firm conclusions from the extant data.

Correlation versus Causality

We all have been taught that the existence of a relationship between two variables does not mean that one variable necessarily causes the other. Establishing causation requires experimental research in which it is demonstrated that manipulating the presumed cause (X) does indeed lead to changes in the presumed effect (Y). Such an experimental result, moreover, does not rule out the possibility of reciprocal, rather than just unidirectional, causation (i.e., that Y simultaneously exerts a causal influence on X).

With regard to reading disabilities, experimental training studies with beginning students have shown that there is a reciprocal causal relationship between attaining phonological awareness and learning to decode print (Ehri & Wilce, 1980; Perfetti, Beck, Bell, & Hughes, 1987). For the other verbal abilities that are good predictors of future reading achievement from kindergarten age (Table 8.1) or earlier, however, little evidence is available yet to determine their causal status. Some language skills may indeed play a causal role in the development of reading, but some may only be "correlates" or "markers" that are characteristic of children who will have trouble learning to read but that are not the reason those children have difficulty. In fact, there are indications that preschool training that successfully ameliorates early speech/language impairments is not effective in reducing such children's risk for later reading problems, as it ought to be if those language weaknesses are a causal impediment to learning to read (Fey et al., 1995; Stark et al., 1984).

At present, the most widely held view as to the cause of reading disabilities is that affected children have a core phonological deficit (often of constitutional, usually genetic, origin) that impedes the development of phonemic awareness and hence interferes with discovering the alphabetic principle and with learning to decode (e.g., Liberman, Shankweiler, & Liberman, 1989; Stanovich

& Siegel, 1994). Powerful and parsimonious though this theory is, it has been challenged for failing to account readily for several empirical trends. For example, training programs designed in accordance with the phonological deficit hypothesis have not been completely effective in preventing and treating reading disabilities (e.g., Torgesen, Wagner, & Rashotte, 1997). Also, some children who successfully overcome their initial difficulties in learning to decode in response to such instruction nevertheless start to fall behind again in reading at a later point (Slavin et al., 1996). Of greater relevance to the preschool focus of this handbook are the correlational data reviewed earlier. That is, several facets of verbal ability other than phonological awareness have been shown to be equally strong predictors of later reading, not just from kindergarten age but also at much younger ages. Similarly, phonological awareness itself seems to be predicted as well by previous lexical and syntactic abilities as by phonological ones. Findings such as these suggest that the phonological core deficit hypothesis may not account fully for the development of reading disabilities.

In response, proponents of the phonological deficit hypothesis have argued cogently that deficits in other aspects of developing language all stem from more fundamental weaknesses in the phonological domain. That is, even though other sorts of language deficits are predictive of future reading difficulties, they are just correlates (or secondary symptoms) rather than true causes of reading disability (Shankweiler & Crain, 1986). The developmental patterns and relative strengths of the correlations, however, do not readily accord with this explanation. (Consider, for example, the data in Figure 8.2.) Also, results of a recent genetic analysis of the heritability of phonological awareness, general language abilities, and reading skills were inconsistent with this account (Hohnen & Stevenson, 1999).

An alternative approach has been to propose moving from a single-deficit to a double-deficit (or, in principle, a multiple-deficit) model of reading disability. These are subtyping hypotheses, according to which some children's reading difficulties stem from phonological deficits, whereas others' have their roots in different language weaknesses, solely or in conjunction with phonological deficits (e.g., Bowers & Wolf, 1993; Manis et al., 1999). There is no consensus as to the nature of the additional deficit(s), however, and empirical support for the hypothesized subtypes is fairly limited. Moreover, proposed qualitative differences have tended to be confounded with severity of impairment. Although the notion of subtyping is appealing, research spanning several decades has been rather unsuccessful in revealing consistent subgroupings of disabled readers, and I am not sure that the latest subtyping hypotheses will stand the test of time.

It is possible, however, to imagine a single-deficit model of reading disabilities that incorporates the strengths of the phonological-deficit hypothesis and also accounts for the preschool correlational data reviewed in this chapter. To do so requires, however, that we stop thinking about causality only in terms of a "chain" of events that influence each other in turn (e.g., successive deficits in phonological processing, attaining phonological awareness, grasping the alphabetic principle, and, finally, learning to read). As illustrated in Figure 8.3, although some disorders progress in this manner (e.g., the disease glaucoma), others do not. The observable symptoms of syphilis, for instance, do not constitute a causal chain. Instead, the root cause is a persisting bacterial infection, which produces different symptoms at different stages of the disease. Note that knowing which type of causal model accounts for a disorder has important implications not just for theory but also for its treatment. For a causal chain, successive treatment of any symptom along the way will prevent the emergence of all successive stages of the disease. In contrast, for a syphilis-like disorder, effective treatment of a symptom will not halt the progression of the disorder; instead, it is necessary to identify and treat the underlying condition.

It is possible also to entertain a hybrid model that incorporates both an underlying condition (e.g., a genetic predisposition to have difficulty learning certain kinds of linguistic patterns) that is the root cause of a series of different symptoms *and* some causal influences between symptoms. With regard to reading disabilities, for instance,

A. CAUSAL CHAIN (e.g., GLAUCOMA)

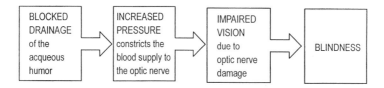

B. UNDERLYING CONDITION (e.g., SYPHILIS)

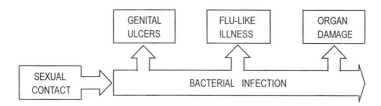

C. HYBRID MODEL

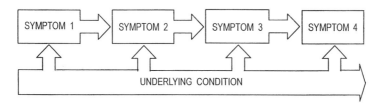

FIGURE 8.3. Models of possible causal relationships in the developmental progression of a condition or disorder. (In variations of the hybrid model, some horizontal arrows could be absent.)

suppose that successive "symptoms" include deficits in early syntactic proficiency, phonological awareness, and decoding of print, respectively. Although there are sizable correlations among all three measures, the syntactic deficit might have no causal influence on the subsequent development of the other two deficits, but the weakness in phonological awareness would indeed be an important ("proximal") cause of difficulty in learning to decode. If so, if a child is affected by the underlying condition, treatment of an early syntactic impairment would not reduce the child's risk for reading disability, but training in phonological awareness would be of benefit in eliminating or ameliorating the child's difficulty in learning to decode. It would still be possible, however, that the underlying condition would continue to exert its influence on

other strands during later stages of reading acquisition, leaving the child at risk for future difficulties despite having attained adequate skill in decoding. All these predictions from the model are consistent with the research that I have reviewed earlier.

Differences in severity of the underlying impairment, furthermore, would lead to differences in the number and severity of symptoms that are exhibited. Extrinsic factors (especially the quality of reading instruction) are sure to play a causal role too. Hence, anomalous cases (successful reading achievement by a child who had previously been diagnosed with a language impairment, and conversely, only subclinical weaknesses in early language in a child who later exhibited a reading disability) can be accommodated by the model, albeit not without costs in terms of parsimony.

Nonlinear Growth and an
"Ascendancy" Hypothesis

To explain the changing preschool deficit profiles that have been observed may require another break from traditionally linear ways of thinking about developmental disorders. It is fairly well established that growth in some (perhaps all) components of language consists of spurts and plateaus at particular times rather than steady incremental advances. If so, then a delay in acquisition will mean that spurts and plateaus will occur at a somewhat older age than usual, as illustrated by the dashed growth curve in Figure 8.4. In such a case (depending, of course, on the durations of plateaus and the degree of delay), there may be ages at which the performance levels of delayed and nondelayed cases will be virtually identical, a phenomenon that Scarborough and Dobrich (1990) termed "illusory recovery." It provides a simple explanation for the otherwise puzzling fact, noted earlier, that language and reading problems often (re)emerge at older ages in children who had appeared to have overcome their preschool language impairments by the time they entered school.

In more general terms, when growth of a skill is nonlinear, deficits in that skill will be most readily detectable during periods when normal development undergoes a spurt (e.g., when rapidly developing children are reaching the postspurt plateau, and growth of the slower developing children may just be starting to accelerate). Spurts in particular language skills occur at different ages, on average (e.g., the well-known vocabulary spurt, typically occurring at about 18 months, precedes the period of rapid acquisition of morphology and syntax from age 2 to 4 years). Therefore, at any given time, conditions for detecting individual or group differences in a skill will be best when that skill is normally "ascendant." According to this ascendancy hypothesis, furthermore, the milder the language delay (i.e., the smaller the horizontal distance between the dashed and solid curves in Figure 8.4), the more transient and domain-specific the pattern of observed deficits will be. A severe delay, in contrast, will be characterized by a more persistent

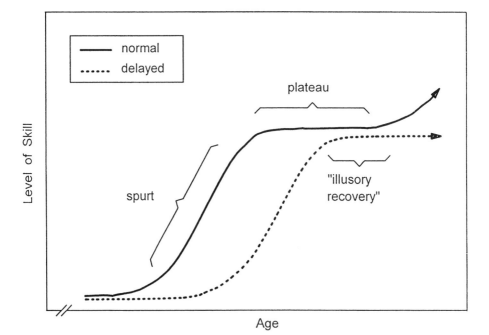

FIGURE 8.4. Illustration of how nonlinear development of language skills might lead to periods of "illusory recovery" by children who had previously appeared to be delayed. Data from Scarborough and Dobrich (1990).

and across-the-board deficit profile. (Note that what looks like a qualitative difference, or subtype, would really be a quantitative severity difference.) If this ascendancy hypothesis correctly captures the measurement situation for early language skills, then the notion that a single underlying language disorder could manifest itself as a series of deficits in different aspects of language, each correlated with the next, is precisely what would be expected for mild-to-moderate severity levels.

In sum, I believe that greater power and flexibility in theorizing about the relationships between language and literacy development can be obtained by considering alternatives to causal chains and linear growth assumptions. I have not tried to construct a full theory but, rather, to illustrate how some interesting phenomena seen in the available literature can perhaps be explained more satisfactorily than at present.

Practical Implications: Present and Future

With regard to diagnosis, the risk factors that have been identified by the correlational research on preschoolers and kindergartners provide the best current guidelines for designing screening batteries to identify those young children who are most likely to develop reading disabilities. As noted earlier, researchers who have assessed kindergartners on various subsets of such variables have attained high multiple correlations with subsequent reading scores. Figure 8.5 shows how well such screening batteries have succeeded in the typical study of this sort, in which 89% prediction accuracy has been obtained in samples of about 200 children. For most purposes, this is a reasonably satisfactory level of success. Note, however, that virtually every study has obtained few "miss" errors (i.e., children not identified as at risk by the screen but who

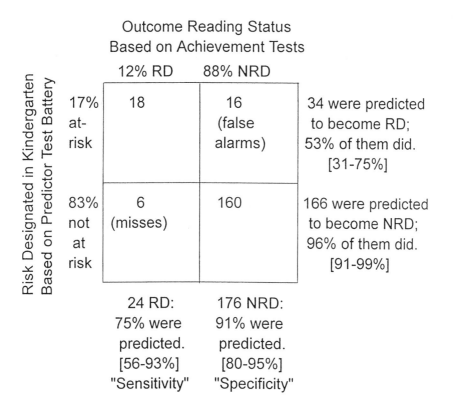

FIGURE 8.5. Typical results obtained by combining kindergarten-age measures to predict later reading in samples of about 200 children. The ranges of values across studies are shown in brackets. RD, reading disabled; NRD, not reading disabled. Based on data from Scarborough (1998, Table A–7).

became disabled readers) but a sizable proportion of "false alarms" (children identified by the screen as being at risk, but who later achieved adequately on the reading measure). If early intervention is targeted at all children designated as at risk, this means that about half of those receiving it might not actually be in need of it. At present, this is the most serious concern associated with using such screens, not just because the costs of intervention are substantially raised but also because the possible negative educational and psychological consequences of mislabeling "false alarms" are not known. If this issue is handled sensibly, though, I think a good case can be made that early identification and intervention are warranted.

The available data also indicate that diagnosing risk is more problematic at younger ages. The observations that language deficit profiles change over time within individual preschoolers (as well as between groups, as in Figure 8.2) means that assessment at a single time point may be misleading as to how broad a child's language impairment might be. In the future, I believe that diagnostic improvements can be achieved by giving increased consideration to the possibility of nonlinear growth in skills, to the ascendancy hypothesis (stronger detectibility of individual differences during expected growth spurts), and to the occurrence of "illusory recovery."

With regard to intervention, the data also provide some guidance as to what developing skills should be fostered in at-risk youngsters. First, although equating correlation with causality is a false inference, the opposite—that a lack of correlation implies a lack of causal influence—is usually a reasonable conclusion. Hence, for the purpose of preventing later reading problems, there is no reason to provide training in skills that poorly predict future reading achievement.

Second, among the stronger predictors, only phonological awareness has yet been demonstrated to play a causal role in learning to read. A successful intervention program would thus certainly include training in this skill. And, because connecting phonological awareness with letter knowledge has been shown to enhance the acquisition of the alphabetic principle, this too

should be a focus. The best candidates for additional components of an intervention program are those suggested by the correlational research, namely, print concepts, retention of verbal material, and oral language skills (especially expressive vocabulary). Although there is no guarantee that training in these skills will facilitate reading acquisition, this important causal question can be investigated through follow-up studies of the efficacy of intervention programs.

Finally, especially with regard to younger at-risk preschoolers (especially those with a diagnosis of language impairment and those with a family history of reading disability), interventions based on an accurate causal model are likely to be most effective in reducing risk for later reading problems. Simply addressing these children's current "symptoms" through conventional speech–language therapy apparently does not reduce such risk, probably because weaknesses in speech and language do not causally impede reading acquisition, at least over the short term. Hence, as Fey (1999) has urged, proactive training of known "proximal" causal factors (such as phonological awareness) may be required. If and when evidence accrues for the existence of an underlying "root" cause of reading ability differences, strengthening that factor would clearly be an important facet of any early intervention program.

Acknowledgments

Support for the preparation of this review was provided by Grant No. HD-01994 to Haskins Laboratories. I would also like to thank Susan Brady and Leslie Rescorla for their helpful comments during the preparation of this chapter.

References

Anthony, J. L., Lonigan, C. J., Dyer, S. M., & Bloomfield, B. (1997, April). *The development of phonological processing in preschool-aged children: Preliminary evidence from confirmatory factor analysis.* Paper presented at the meeting of the Society for Research in Child Development, Washington, DC.

Aram, D. M., & Hall, N. E. (1989). Longitudinal follow-up of children with preschool communication disorders: Treatment implications. *School Psychology Review, 18,* 487–501.

Bishop, D. V. M., & Adams, C. (1990). A prospective study of the relationship between specific language impairment, phonological disorders and reading retardation. *Journal of Child Psychology and Psychiatry, 31,* 1027–1050.

Bishop, D. V. M., & Edmundson, A. (1987). Specific language impairment as a maturational lag: Evidence from longitudinal data on language and motor development. *Developmental Medicine and Child Neurology, 29,* 442–459.

Bowers, P. G., & Wolf, M. (1993, March). *A double-deficit hypothesis for developmental reading disorders.* Paper presented at the meeting of the Society for Research in Child Development, New Orleans.

Bryant, P. E., Bradley, L., Maclean, M., & Crossland, J. (1989). Nursery rhymes, phonological skills and reading. *Journal of Child Language, 16,* 407–428.

Byrne, B., Fielding-Barnsley, R., Hindson, B., Mackay, C., Newman, C., & Shankweiler, D. (1998, April). *Early intervention with children at risk for reading disability: A mid-term report.* Paper presented at the conference of the Society for the Scientific Study of Reading, San Diego, CA.

Catts, H. W., Fey, M., & Tomblin, B. (1997, April). *The language basis for reading disabilities.* Paper presented at the meeting of the Society for the Scientific Study of Reading, Chicago.

Catts, H. W., Fey, M., Zhang, X., & Tomblin, B. (1999). Language bases of reading and reading disabilities: Evidence from a longitudinal investigation. *Scientific Studies of Reading, 3,* 331–361.

Chaney, C. (1992). Language development, metalinguistic skills, and print awareness in 3-year-old children. *Applied Psycholinguistics, 13,* 485–514.

Committee on the Prevention of Reading Difficulties in Young Children (1998). *Preventing reading difficulties in young children.* Washington, DC: National Academy Press.

Ehri, L., & Wilce, L. S. (1980). The influence of orthography on readers' conceptualization of the phonemic structure of words. *Applied Psycholinguistics, 1,* 371–385.

Elbro, C. (1999, April). How quality of phonological representations of lexical items predicts phonological processing of spoken and written language. In B. F. Pennington (Chair), *Longitudinal studies of children at family risk for dyslexia: Results from four countries.* Symposium conducted at the meeting of the Society for Research in Child Development, Albuquerque, NM.

Fey, M. E. (1999). Speech–language pathology and the early identification and prevention of reading disabilities. *Perspectives, 25,* 13–17.

Fey, M. E., Catts, H. W., & Larrivee, L. S. (1995). Preparing preschoolers for the academic and social challenges of school. In M. E. Fey, J. Windson, & S. F. Warrent (Eds.), *Language intervention: Preschool through the elementary years* (pp. 3–37). Baltimore: Brookes.

Gallagher, A., Frith, U., & Snowling, M. (1999, April). Early literacy development in children at genetic risk of dyslexia. In B. F. Pennington (Chair), *Longitudinal studies of children at family risk for dyslexia: Results from four countries.* Symposium conducted at the meeting of the Society for Research in Child Development, Albuquerque, NM.

Hohnen, B., & Stevenson, J. (1999). The structure of genetic influences on general cognitive, language, phonological, and reading abilities. *Developmental Psychology, 35,* 590–603.

Liberman, I. Y. (1973). Segmentation of the spoken word and reading acquisition. *Bulletin of the Orton Society, 23,* 65–77.

Liberman, I. Y., Shankweiler, D., & Liberman, A. M. (1989). The alphabetic principle and learning to read. In D. Shankweiler & I. Y Liberman (Eds.), *Phonology and reading disability: Solving the reading puzzle.* Ann Arbor: University of Michigan Press.

Lonigan, C., Burgess, S. R., Anthony, J. L., & Barker, T. A. (1998). Development of phonological sensitivity in 2- to 5-year-old children. *Journal of Educational Psychology, 90,* 294–311.

Lyytinen, H., Hietala, A., Leinonen, S., Leppanen, P., Richardson, U., & Lyytinen, P. (1999, April). Early language development among children with familial risk for dyslexia. In B. F. Pennington (Chair), *Longitudinal studies of children at family risk for dyslexia: Results from four countries.* Symposium conducted at the meeting of the Society for Research in Child Development, Albuquerque, NM.

Manis, F., Seidenberg, M. S., Stallings, L., Joanisse, M., Bailey, C., Freedman, L., Curtin, S., & Keafing, P. (1999). Development of dyslexic subtypes: A one-year follow up. *Annals of Dyslexia, 49,* 105–134.

Molfese, D. L. (1999, April). Predicting reading performance at eight years of age from auditory brain potentials recorded at birth. In V. J. Molfese (Chair), *Longitudinal studies of reading abilities: Biological and educational influences on development and persistence.* Symposium conducted at the meeting of the Society for Research in Child Development, Albuquerque, NM.

Pennington, B. F., Lefly, D. L., & Boada, R. (1999, April). Phonological development and reading outcomes in children at family risk for dyslexia. In B. F. Pennington (Chair), *Longitudinal studies of children at family risk for dyslexia: Results from four countries.* Symposium conducted at the meeting of the Society for Research in Child Development, Albuquerque, NM.

Perfetti, C. A., Beck, L., Bell, L., & Highes, C. (1987). Phonemic knowledge and learning to read are reciprocal: A longitudinal study of first grade children. *Merrill-Palmer Quarterly, 33,* 283–319.

Rescorla, L. R. (1999, July). *Outcomes of late talkers: Academic and language skills at age 13.* Paper presented at the meeting of International Association for the Study of Child Language, San Sebastian, Spain.

Scarborough, H. S. (1989). Prediction of reading disability from familial and individual differences. *Journal of Educational Psychology, 81,* 101–108

Scarborough, H. S. (1990). Very early language deficits in dyslexic children. *Child Development, 61,* 1728–1734.

Scarborough, H. S. (1991a). Early syntactic development of dyslexic children. *Annals of Dyslexia, 41,* 207–220.

Scarborough, H. S. (1991b). Antecedents to reading disability: Preschool language development and literacy experiences of children from dyslexic families. *Reading and Writing, 3,* 219–233.

Scarborough, H. S. (1998). Early identification of children at risk for reading disabilities: Phonological awareness and some other promising predictors. In B. K. Shapiro, P. J. Accardo, & A. J. Capute (Eds.), *Specific reading disability: A view of the spectrum* (pp. 75–119). Timonium, MD: York Press.

Scarborough, H. S., & Dobrich, W. (1990). Development of children with early language delays. *Journal of Speech and Hearing Research, 33,* 70–83.

Scarborough, H. S., & Dobrich, W. (1994). On the efficacy of reading to preschoolers. *Developmental Review, 14,* 245–302.

Scarborough, H. S., Dobrich, W., & Hager, M. (1991). Literacy experience and reading disability: Reading habits and abilities of parents and young children. *Journal of Learning Disabilities, 24,* 508–511.

Shankweiler, D., & Crain, S. (1986). Language mechanisms and reading disorders: A modular approach. *Cognition, 24,* 136–168.

Shapiro, B. K., Palmer, F. B., Antell, S., Bilker, S., Ross, A., & Capute, A. J. (1990). Precursors of reading delay: Neurodevelopmental milestones. *Pediatrics,* 416–420.

Slavin, R. E., Madden, N. A., Dolan, L .J., Wasik, B. A., Ross, S., Smith, L., & Dianda, M. (1996). Success For All: A summary of research. *Journal of Education for Students Placed at Risk, 1,* 41–76.

Stanovich, K. E., & Siegel, L. S. (1994). Phenotypic performance profiles of children with reading disabilities: A regression-based test of the phonological-core variable-difference model. *Journal of Educational Psychology, 86,* 24–53.

Stark, R., Bernstein, L., Condino, R., Bender, M., Tallal, P., & Catts, H. (1984). Four year follow-up study of language-impaired children. *Annals of Dyslexia, 34,* 49–68.

Torgesen, J. K., Wagner, R. K., & Rashotte, C. A. (1999). Prevention and remediation of severe reading disabilities: Keeping the end in mind. *Scientific Studies of Reading, 1,* 217–234.

Walker, D., Greenwood, C., Hart, B., & Carta, J. (1994). Prediction of school outcomes based on early language production and socioeconomic factors. *Child Development, 65,* 606–621.

Whitehurst, G. J. (1999, April). The role of inside-out skills in reading readiness of children from low-income families. In C. J. Lonigan (Chair), *From prereaders to readers: The role of phonological processing skills in at risk and typically developing children.* Symposium conducted at the meeting of the Society for Research in Child Development, Albuquerque, NM.

9

Early Phonological Development and the Acquisition of Literacy

❖

USHA GOSWAMI

The links between the child's development of spoken language and the child's subsequent development of literacy are becoming increasingly well understood. In particular, the child's phonological development—the progression in representing in the brain the speech units that make up different words—is now recognized to play a causal role in the acquisition of literacy. In this chapter, I describe the development of children's abilities to recognize and categorize different phonological units in spoken words, relating this to the development of their spoken vocabularies. These recognition and categorization skills are thought to be acquired informally, as growing vocabulary creates an implicit need for making comparisons between similar-sounding words ("lexical restructuring theory"). This theoretical approach can help us to understand the developmental importance of language games and nursery rhymes in helping the child to specify key aspects of the sound patterns of English more explicitly.

Moving to the early phase of reading, I then review some of the evidence that the child's awareness of the phonology of his or her language is one of the most important predictors of that child's progress in learning to read and to spell, noting that crosslinguistic research is increasingly showing that the phonological units that are high-

lighted by different languages may vary. I argue that we need to understand more about the relative weight that needs to be given to the different phonological units of syllable, rhyme, and phoneme and their connections with sequences of letters in different orthographies. For example, analogies based on rhymes may be particularly important for reading acquisition in English. Further, reading instruction can make important contributions to children's phonological development, particularly at the phonemic level. Using the theoretical understanding of development proposed, I consider possible contributions of varied factors to children's phonological development including their home environments and methods of classroom reading instruction.

Phonological Skills and Learning to Read: Research Background

Phonological awareness is measured by tasks that require a child to reflect on or to manipulate the component sounds of spoken words. A wide variety of such tasks has been designed, including asking children to monitor and correct speech errors (e.g., "sie" to "pie"), to select the "odd word out" in terms of sound (e.g., which word does not rhyme from "fit, pat, cat"), to make a judgment about similarity of sound (e.g., do these two words share a syllable: "repeat-compete"?), to segment words by tapping with a stick (e.g., tap out the component sounds in "book" = three taps), and to blend sounds into words (e.g., "d-ish," or "d-i-sh" to make "dish"; see, e.g., Bradley & Bryant, 1983; Chaney, 1992; Liberman, Shankweiler, Fischer, & Carter, 1974; Metsala, 1999, Treiman & Zukowski, 1991). Performance in all these phonological awareness tasks (and many others) has been related to literacy. However, it is important to point out that the cognitive demands made by these different tasks vary, so that performance will reflect not just phonological awareness per se but also extraneous task demands (e.g., McBride-Chang, 1995; Yopp, 1988). One recent way of conceptualizing task demands in phonological awareness, derived from work on linguistic development, is to distinguish "epilinguistic" processing from "metalinguistic" processing (see Gombert, 1992). Gombert argues that one approach is to consider whether a given phonological awareness task requires the recognition of shared phonological segments (such tasks can be performed using "epilinguistic" processing, which is an automatic part of speech processing and does not normally require conscious awareness) or the identification and production of shared phonological segments (such tasks require metalinguistic processing, meaning that the child must make implicit or "epilinguistic" knowledge explicit in order to perform the task). Either or both representational processes might entail the development of an abstract store of information about phonological segments (e.g., Butterworth, 1992), which might form the basis of responding in phonological awareness and other phonological tasks based on nonsense word stimuli (see Goswami & East, 2000, for more discussion).

Studies suggest that there is a developmental progression from phonological awareness of "large" segments or units of phonology (syllables, onsets, and rimes; the onset in a spoken syllable refers to the consonant phonemes before the vowel, and the rime is the vowel phonemes and any subse-

quent consonants [the coda], e.g., str-eet, spr-ing) to phonological awareness of "small" segments or units (phonemes, a phoneme is the smallest unit of sound that changes the meaning of a word, e.g., "cot" and "cat" differ in their medial phoneme; for reviews, see Goswami & Bryant, 1990; Goswami, in press a). Further, the developmental process of making phonological knowledge explicit seems to be much easier for syllables, onsets, and rimes than it is for phonemes. Phonemic awareness does not seem to develop automatically with age (e.g., adult illiterates generally lack phonemic awareness; e.g., Morais, Cary, Alegria, & Bertelson, 1979). Instead, it appears to largely depend on direct instruction in reading and spelling (e.g., Liberman et al., 1974) or on the receipt of training at the phonemic level (e.g., Byrne & Fielding-Barnsley, 1995; Content, Kolinsky, Morais, & Bertelson, 1986). Although some preliterate children can demonstrate some phonemic awareness in some phonemic awareness tasks (e.g., Stuart & Coltheart, 1988; Thomas & Senechal, 1998), in general phonemic awareness develops via direct instruction in an alphabetic orthography. Phonemic development can be rapid once this instruction commences, particularly in transparent orthographies such as German (e.g., Wimmer, 1990).

As this chapter is mainly concerned with early phonological development, it focuses on the processes underlying the development of segmented representations of words as part of the development of speech processing. In general, this does not include the development of phonemic awareness. Early phonological development centers on the phonological units of syllable, onset, and rime, and these are the phonological units highlighted in early linguistic routines such as nursery rhymes. Interestingly, the phonological correspondences established early in development seem to be less vulnerable to neurological accident than those established later. For example, onset–rime correspondences are still available to adult acquired dyslexics and alexics even when phonemic correspondences are not (e.g., Patterson & Marcel, 1992; Shallice, Warrington & McCarthy, 1983), and syllabic correspondences may still be available to adult phonological dyslexics even when onset, rime, and phoneme correspondences are not (Lesch & Martin, 1998).

The Development of Phonological Awareness: The Lexical Restructuring Hypothesis

Given its importance for literacy, surprisingly little work has been done on the linguistic and lexical factors that might determine the development of phonological awareness in all children. In thinking about what these factors might be, I have found the recent proposal that phonological awareness may emerge as a result of "lexical restructuring" processes that are an intrinsic part of language acquisition useful ("lexical restructuring theory"; Metsala, 1999; Metsala & Walley, 1998). Lexical restructuring theory is based on the premise that in the normal course of development, children's phonological representations become increasingly segmental and distinctly specified in terms of phonetic features with age (e.g., Fowler, 1991; Metsala, 1999; Walley, 1993).

The basic ideas behind this theory can be explained by thinking about early language acquisition. When children first begin to acquire spoken language, in infancy, their spoken vocabularies consist of rather few words. Each word, however, is represented in terms of certain semantic features ("Daddy" may refer to a person of a certain sex and size) and also in terms of certain phonological features (the child can recognize that "Daddy" is a different word from "doggy"). At this developmental time point, the motor program for producing the word "Daddy" is probably quite sketchy, and the child may say "Dada" or "Da" when intending to name "Daddy." Small vocabulary size at this time may also lead toddlers to "overextend" the words that they do know, and the child may use his or her word for "Daddy" to refer to such visitors as the milkman and the postman, and to uncles and other adult males as well.

Most children go through a dramatic burst in naming activity between the ages of 1 and 2 years. Spoken vocabulary suddenly grows exponentially (by the age of 6, the average child comprehends 14,000 words; see Dollaghan, 1994). Although phonological output typically remains imprecise initially (sometimes only a regular caretaker can decode the child's intended meaning), children at this point in development are rapidly acquiring more and more words which, of course, sound more and more similar to each other. There is considerable developmental pressure to represent these words in the brain in a way that will distinguish them from other words and allow the child to recognize them accurately and quickly during speech comprehension. For example, a 2-year-old probably knows the words "cot," "cat" and "cut," "hot," "not" and "lot," and "cough." All these words differ from "cot" by a single phoneme. To distinguish between these similar-sounding words both quickly and accurately, child linguists argue that children must begin to represent the sequences of sounds that constitute each known word in their brains. They must represent the "segmental phonology" of the words they know.

Metsala and Walley (1998) have suggested that segmental phonology is represented at an increasingly fine-grained level as development proceeds. They argue that children's first words represent fairly global phonological characteristics. Early in language development, the child needs to discriminate relatively few unique words, and so quite holistic representations of phonological forms will suffice (e.g., Ferguson, 1986; Juscyk, 1993). However, as more and more words are acquired, children are thought to begin to represent smaller segments in words. From the phonological awareness data discussed earlier, it seems likely that children will first represent the number of syllables in a word and the "onsets" and "rimes" in each syllable. This process may begin as early as age 1 or 2 (e.g., Swingley, Pinto & Fernald, 1999).

The syllable is thought to be the primary linguistic processing unit for English, as it is distinguished by a number of auditory cues including rhythm and stress. Within the syllable, the most prominent phonological segments are the onset and the rime. Linguistically, the rime is a salient phonological unit and seems to have an organizing function for English phonology. Many of the language games, linguistic routines, and nursery rhymes of early childhood emphasize segmental phonology by increasing the salience of syllables, onsets, and rimes. For example, popular nursery rhymes have strong rhythms that emphasize syllabification (think of Humpty Dumpty), and many contrast rhyming words in ways that distinguish the onset from the rime (e.g., "Twinkle Twinkle Little Star" rhymes "star" with "are," and "Incy Wincy Spider" rhymes "spout" with "out").

Metsala and Walley (1998) argue that the process of re-representing the segmental phonology of individual words is relatively *word-specific*. It will depend on the child's overall vocabulary size and also on the rate of expansion of that vocabulary. Children with large vocabularies who are rapidly acquiring lots of new words would be expected to have lexicons that are experiencing greater pressure for restructuring, and consequently to have represented the syllables, onsets, and rimes in many of the words in their vocabularies. Lexical restructuring also depends on word frequency or familiarity. Words that are encountered many times or that were acquired early are more likely to have been restructured, because the child needs to access these words rapidly and accurately on so many occasions. Finally, lexical restructuring depends on the number of similar-sounding words in the lexicon ("neighborhood density"). Words in "dense" neighborhoods (words such as "cot," with many similar-sounding neighbors) should experience most pressure for restructuring, as they must be distinguished from a large number of other extremely similar words. Words in "sparse" neighborhoods, which must only be distinguished from a small number of other extremely similar words, should experience less pressure for restructuring. Metsala and Walley propose that the degree to which segmental representation has taken place will determine how easily the child will become phonologically aware and will learn to read and write.

According to lexical restructuring theory, therefore, segmental representations emerge primarily as the result of spoken vocabulary growth and associated changes in the familiarity of individual lexical items and interitem phonological similarity relations ("phonological neighborhoods"). Accord-

ing to this "emergent" view of segmental representation, the phoneme is not an integral aspect of speech representation and processing from infancy onwards (e.g., Eimas, Siqueland, Jusczyk, & Vigorito, 1971) but, rather, emerges as a representational unit *via spoken language experience*. However, an important aspect of early language experience that is missing from the current version of lexical restructuring theory is the nature of the interitem phonological similarity relations that characterize different languages. A number of sources of evidence suggest that, for English, a salient phonological similarity relation is that of the rime.

Phonological Neighborhoods in English and the Importance of Rimes

As lexical restructuring theory proposes that implicit comparisons between similar-sounding words constitute the basis for the emergence of phonological awareness, it seems logical that the nature of the phonological neighbors in the child's lexicon in different languages will influence this developmental process. The traditional linguistic similarity metric for defining a phonological neighborhood considers neighbors to be words that differ by the addition, deletion and substitution of a single phoneme. According to this metric, rime neighbors such as "pot," onset-vowel or "lead" neighbors such as "cough," and "consonant" neighbors such as "kit," are all considered to be equal neighbors of a target word such as "cot." However, given the psychological salience of the rime to young children, it seems possible that many phonological neighbors in English might be rime neighbors. For example, a word such as "cot" (dense neighborhood) has been estimated to have 49 phonological neighbors (Luce & Pisoni, 1998), 24 of which are rime neighbors (49%). A word such as "crib" (sparse neighborhood) has been estimated to have 15 phonological neighbors, 7 of which are rime neighbors (47%). If it can be demonstrated that there is a prevalence of rime neighbors in the English phonological lexicon, this might help to explain the salience and utility of onset–rime representations in English.

To examine this possibility, we recently

TABLE 9.1. **Phonological Neighborhoods in English Monosyllabic Words (Ncvc Metric)**

	All monosyllabic words (n = 3,072)				High N (Ncvc ≥ 32) (n = 570)				Low N (1 ≤ Ncvc ≤ 13) (n = 619)			
	Ncvc	RN	CN	OVN	Ncvc	RN	CN	OVN	Ncvc	RN	CN	OVN
M	22.5	12.2	3.8	6.5	38.1	22.1	7.2	8.7	9.4	3.9	1.5	4.0
SD	10.1	7.8	3.2	4.4	5.3	6.5	3.0	4.6	2.9	2.9	1.8	2.9
%	100	54	17	29	100	58	19	23	100	41	16	43

Note. Ncvc represents all phonological neighbors that differ from a target word by one *onset, vowel, or coda* substitution, deletion, or addition. RN, rime neighbor ; CN, consonant phoneme neighbor; OVN, onset-vowel neighbor.

analyzed the corpus of single-syllable words in the Luce and Pisoni (1998) database of spoken-English forms in terms of rime neighbors (RN), onset-vowel neighbors (OVN), and consonant neighbors (CN) in dense versus sparse neighborhoods, respectively. We used two measures of phonological neighborhood; the traditional speech-processing definition (addition, deletion, or substitution of one phoneme, called here N ± 1), and a definition based on a linguistic analysis according to which monosyllables can be coded in terms of the phonological units onset, nucleus, coda (see Treiman, 1988, for review). This second measure, here Ncvc, was derived on the basis of the phonological awareness literature, which has demonstrated the psychological salience of onsets and rimes for young children. The chief difference psychologically would be that whereas words such as "spot" and "trot" would count as rime neighbors of "cot" in the Ncvc database, they would not count as rime neighbors of cot in the N ± 1 database. Tables 9.1 and 9.2 show our analyses (De Cara & Goswami, 1999).

It is clear from the tables that rime neigh-bors predominate in English phonological neighborhoods, particularly in dense neighborhoods. Thus words in dense neighborhoods might experience more pressure for early lexical restructuring to the rime level than words in sparse neighborhoods.

Because the similarity indices shown in Tables 9.1 and 9.2 were derived from an adult lexical database, it is not clear how applicable these indices are to young children. Children's lexical neighborhoods are smaller than those of adults and are constantly being updated, meaning that neighborhood statistics are much more dynamic. From this perspective, estimates of neighborhood similarity based on adult data can only approximate the developmental picture (e.g., Charles-Luce & Luce, 1990, 1995; Dollaghan, 1994; Logan, 1992). Nevertheless, there is no reason to suppose that rime neighbors are under-represented in the child's similarity neighborhoods. Indeed, one developmental function of language play such as nursery rhymes may be to highlight the salience of rime neighbors in English, and nursery rhymes certainly do not restrict their rhyming patterns to N ± 1

TABLE 9.2. **Phonological Neighborhoods in English Monosyllabic Words (N ± 1 Metric)**

	All monosyllabic words (n = 3,072)				High N (Ncvc ≥ 32) (n = 570)				Low N (1 ≤ Ncvc ≤ 13) (n = 619)			
	N ± 1	RN	CN	OVN	N ± 1	RN	CN	OVN	N ± 1	RN	CN	OVN
M	13.4	5.7	3.8	3.9	24.9	11.5	7.2	6.2	5.0	1.7	1.5	1.8
SD	8.7	4.6	3.2	3.1	7.6	4.7	3.0	4.6	3.2	1.7	1.8	2.0
%	100	43	28	29	100	46	29	25	100	34	30	36

Note. N ± 1 represents all phonological neighbors that differ from a target word by one *phoneme* substitution, deletion, or addition. RN, rime neighbor; CN, consonant phoneme neighbor; OVN, onset-vowel neighbor.

neighbors (e.g., Hickory Dickory Dock rhymes *dock* with *clock*, and Jack and Jill rhymes *down* with *crown;* see also Goswami, 1995).

It is not a priori clear whether more similarities or differences would be expected between the broad characteristics of the phonological neighborhoods of adults and children. We therefore also calculated the number of rime, onset-vowel and consonant neighbors for two different estimates of early-acquired words, those given by Gilhooly and Logie (1980) and those given by Morrison, Chappell, and Ellis (1997) (see De Cara & Goswami, 1999). Table 9.3 shows these results for monosyllables only. Although these analyses did not attempt to provide estimates of absolute lexicon size, they illustrate that rime neighbors are *not* likely to be underrepresented in children's phonological neighborhoods.

Phonological Neighborhoods and Phonological Awareness

The next step in testing the proposal that the basis for the emergence of phonological awareness is the child's implicit comparisons between similar-sounding words is to see whether there is any evidence that children are more accurate at processing rimes in dense phonological neighborhoods. If the statistical patterns demonstrated previously actually affect the development of phonological awareness, then children should find it easier to decide that "cot" and "pot" rhyme than to decide that "thud" and "mud" rhyme. Given that these are all highly familiar and early-acquired words, it may seem counterintuitive to propose that children will show better phonological aware-

TABLE 9.3. Percentage of Rime Neighbors among English Monosyllables as a Function of Age of Acquisition, Based on Published Norms

Database	Age of acquisition	% rime neighbors	No. of words
Gilhooly & Logie (1980)	3 years	51.6	183
	4 years	54.1	376
	5 years	53.4	482
Morrison et al. (1997)	3 years	43.3	41
	5 years	57.3	84

ness of one rime compared to another. However, if such an effect could be demonstrated, it would help us to understand the basis of phonological awareness. In essence, phonological awareness must be a consequence of how the brain processes language. If implicit comparisons between similar-sounding words are an important part of the emergence of phonological awareness, as suggested by lexical restructuring theory, then effects of neighborhood density should emerge in phonological awareness tasks, even when the child is recognizing a salient phonological unit in very familiar words.

In recent work (De Cara & Goswami, 1999), we used two different phonological awareness tasks to test this hypothesis. One was the oddity task pioneered by Bradley and Bryant (1983), in which children must select the "odd word out" from a triple of words, one of which has a different rime (e.g., pit, hit, and *got*). In our experiments, 4-, 5-, and 6-year-old children were asked to make judgments about triples of words from dense neighborhoods, such as "hot, lot, wait," and triples of words from sparse neighborhoods, such as "mud, thud, good." The second task was the same–different judgment task developed by Treiman and Zukowski (1991), in which children must decide whether or not two spoken words share a target sound. In our experiments, children were asked to make judgments about pairs of words from dense neighborhoods, such as "lick, sick" and pairs of words from sparse neighborhoods, such as "soot, foot." Both tasks were chosen because they should be measures of "epilinguistic" processing. By using epilinguistic tasks, we hoped to tap the level of phonological processing that might be expected to result primarily from spoken vocabulary growth and associated changes in the familiarity of individual lexical items and interitem phonological similarity relations.

We found significant effects of neighborhood density at every age that we studied (De Cara & Goswami, 1999). Children were significantly more accurate at making judgments about rhyme for words from dense neighborhoods than for words from sparse neighborhoods. Overall, therefore, neighborhood density effects do emerge in simple phonological awareness tasks. Our findings are consistent with recent data reported by Metsala (1999) using a blending task. In her task, the child had to choose, for example, the picture of a "bush" when the experimenter said /b/-/u/-/sh/. She found that 3- and 4-year-old children performed significantly better in this simple phoneme blending task when the target words were from dense neighborhoods rather than from sparse neighborhoods. This version of the blending task may also be an "epilinguistic" task, as the children basically had to recognize words spoken very slowly by the experimenter. The young age of the participating children makes Metsala's demonstration of neighborhood density effects particularly important.

Phonological Neighborhoods and Reading Development

Once reading level was taken into account in our experiments, it was clear that the effects of neighborhood density on rime processing were much stronger in the nonreaders. This is not surprising, because learning to read and spell is known to affect phonological awareness. Although most research has demonstrated this reciprocal relationship at the phonemic level (Goswami & Bryant, 1990, for review), effects at the rime level would also be expected (Goswami & East, 2000). For example, some of the rimes from the densest phonological neighborhoods of English monosyllables vary markedly in their orthographic transcription. The rime /Ir/ is one of the most frequent rimes in English monosyllabic words, but can be written as in "year," "here," "cheer" and "tier." As soon as children begin learning to read and to spell, their phonological categories are likely to be affected by their orthographic knowledge. Other very dense neighborhoods showing this inconsistency of rime spelling include the neighborhoods for /el/ (sail, whale, gaol), /Er/ (share, hair, where, their, swear) and /or/ (shore, for, roar, war).

The possibility that the experience of learning to read and spell an alphabetic orthography will have an important role to play in the lexical restructuring process is not specifically discussed by Metsala and Walley (1998). However, it is plausible to propose that the act of becoming literate will *in itself* affect the lexical restructuring

process. The ways in which this might operate in different languages and for different phonological units (e.g., onset, rime, and phoneme) create important questions for future research. For example, as discussed earlier, the representation of phoneme-level information might be expected to be largely dependent on the acquisition of literacy, because the feedback provided by graphemic information will help the child to represent segmental information at the phonemic level (see Morais, Alegria, & Content, 1987; Goswami, in press a; Goswami & Bryant, 1990, for reviews). The effects of literacy on lexical restructuring would also be expected to vary depending on the transparency of the language being acquired (see Goswami, 2000, for discussion). For example, some languages use only one spelling pattern to represent a given rime (e.g., Greek and German), whereas others use a variety of spelling patterns (e.g., English and French). We know that this variability across languages affects children's use of rime correspondences in reading acquisition (e.g., Goswami, Gombert, & De Barrera, 1998; Goswami, Porpodas, & Wheelwright, 1997). However, we do not yet know how this variability represents or interacts with the phonological characteristics of different languages.

The Developmental Pathway to Reading

So far, we have seen that there is some evidence in support of the proposal that one important basis for the emergence of phonological awareness is the child's implicit comparisons between similar-sounding words, which are a natural part of language processing. Metsala and Walley (1998) also proposed that the degree to which segmental representation had taken place would determine how easily the child would learn to read and write. In a trivial sense we already know this to be true, because there is an extensive literature documenting connections between children's phonological awareness and their reading and spelling development. We do not yet know whether specific predictions made by the lexical restructuring hypothesis would be supported for literacy acquisition, however. According to the hypothesis, the factors that govern the degree of lexical restructuring that has occurred for certain words should also govern early literacy acquisition. For example, early-acquired words should be easier to learn to read and to spell, and words in dense phonological neighborhoods should be easier to learn to read and to spell. This is because these are the words that are more likely to have segmented representations. In theory, it should be easier for children to connect these words to letters, because some of the sound segments that the letters represent have already been distinguished.

Rhyme and Reading in English:
Specific Connections

As argued previously, the phonological segments that should a priori be most affected by spoken vocabulary growth and associated changes in the familiarity of individual lexical items and interitem phonological similarity relations should be the syllable, the onset, and the rime. Although we do not yet know whether, for example, words in dense phonological neighborhoods are easier to learn to read and to spell, it has been shown that beginning readers are more likely to read words with large orthographic "rime neighborhoods" correctly than words with moderate or small orthographic rime neighborhoods (Leslie & Calhoon, 1995). Orthographic neighborhood is not directly comparable to phonological neighborhood because of the variability in rime spellings noted earlier (e.g., "year," "here," "cheer," and "tier" would all be in the same phonological rime neighborhood but different orthographic rime neighborhoods). The orthographic rime neighborhood is a measure of how many other words in the lexicon are spelled with the same rime. Thus a word such as "ship" has a large orthographic rime neighborhood (dip, hip, chip, lip, nip, skip, rip, slip.. etc.) as well as a large phonological rime neighborhood, whereas a word such as "seem" has a small orthographic rime neighborhood (deem, teem), even though the phonological rime neighborhood is much larger (13 rime neighbors, e.g., cream, dream, theme). Leslie and Calhoon (1995) found significant orthographic "rime neighbor-

hood" effects in both list-reading and story-reading tasks. The less skilled readers in their sample were also sensitive to rime neighborhood size when followed up 1 year later.

These data are at least consistent with the lexical restructuring hypothesis in regard to rime processing. What is required now is a systematic study of both phonological and orthographic neighborhood density in order to disentangle phonological and orthographic rime effects in reading acquisition.

Rhyme and Reading in English:
General Connections

There is, however, a great deal of general evidence that early awareness of rhyme facilitates literacy acquisition. Almost two decades ago, Bradley and Bryant (1978, 1983) demonstrated the importance of rhyme awareness for reading development in English in a series of studies using the oddity task described earlier. Bradley and Bryant found that rhyme awareness measured in preschoolers was a significant predictor of later progress in reading and spelling, even when other factors such as IQ and memory were controlled in multiple-regression equations. They also reported that backward readers had poorer rhyming skills than did younger children reading at the same level as them. MacLean, Bryant, and Bradley (1987) found a significant connection between rhyming skills at age 3 and single word reading at 4 years and 6 months. Following up MacLean et al.'s sample 2 years later, Bryant, MacLean, Bradley, and Crossland (1990) reported a significant relationship between nursery rhyme knowledge at age 3 and success in reading and spelling at ages 5 and 6, even after factors such as social background and IQ were controlled.

More recently, Chaney (1992) reported that 3-year-olds showed some success in rhyming tasks, and she found relationships between this early rhyme awareness and later phonological skills predictive of literacy. Chaney's rhyme measure (rhyme production) was the best correlate of the other metalinguistic skills in her study. Burgess and Lonigan (1998) found that "phonological sensitivity" measured in a large sample of 115 4- and 5-year-old children (comprising onset and rime oddity task performance and tasks of blending and segmenting compound words into words or syllables) predicted performance in both letter-name and letter-sound knowledge tasks 1 year later. The latter were argued to be rudimentary reading skills. Cronin and Carver (1998) used an onset oddity task and a rhyme matching task to measure phonological sensitivity in a group of 57 5-year-olds, and found that phonological sensitivity significantly discriminated the three different achievement levels used to group the children in terms of reading ability at the end of first grade, even when vocabulary levels were controlled. Baker, Fernandez-Fein, Scher, and Williams (1998) showed that kindergarten nursery rhyme knowledge was the strongest predictor of word attack and word identification skills measured in grade 2, accounting for 36% and 48% of the variance, respectively. The second strongest predictor was letter knowledge, which accounted for an additional 11% and 18% of the variance, respectively.

This selection of studies showing a connection between early rhyme awareness and the subsequent acquisition of literacy or literacy-related skills demonstrates that the developmental pathway to reading acquisition in English critically involves rhyme. However, the connection with rhyme might work in more than one way. For example, in Bryant et al.'s (1990) study, a path analysis showed a route from nursery rhymes to rhyme awareness to reading and an independent route from nursery rhymes to phoneme awareness to reading. This is shown in Figure 9.1. On the basis of this kind of evidence, we have previously argued (Goswami & Bryant, 1990) that rhyme awareness might contribute to reading development in at least two ways. First, rhyme might contribute to reading because rhyme awareness is a predictor of which children will find it easier to develop phoneme awareness. In terms of lexical restructuring theory, children who have already represented the onsets and rimes in single-syllable words will go on to segment the onset and the rime to represent individual phonemes. Second, rhyme might contribute to reading because in English rhymes are often represented by consistent spelling sequences (e.g., light, fight, and night; tail, nail, and mail). Children's awareness of rhyme might thus allow them to form implicit phonological categories of words that share onsets or rimes. By associating their phonological categories with strings of letters, children could learn spelling sequences for onsets and rimes, which are important spelling categories in English (see later). Children might thus be able to use analogies between words

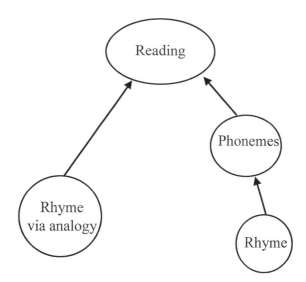

FIGURE 9.1. Rhyme and reading.

sharing spelling patterns for rimes as one mechanism of acquiring a reading vocabulary.

Analogies in Reading and the Spelling System of English

Research has shown that both children and adults can use analogies to decode unfamiliar words (Glushko, 1979; Goswami, 1986). Although it was initially thought that only older children could use analogies spontaneously in reading (after about 10 years of age, see Marsh, Desberg, & Cooper, 1977; Marsh, Friedman, Welch, & Desberg, 1981), it is now known that analogies are used much earlier. Even *beginning* readers can make analogies between shared spelling patterns in words (see Goswami, 1999, for a recent overview). Younger readers make fewer analogies than do older readers. This was thought to be because they have smaller reading vocabularies (Goswami, 1986). Analogies are also used when children are reading stories (Goswami, 1988). This suggested that analogy is a largely implicit process, driven by the child's phonological skills and the orthographic–phonological relations operating in the orthography that they are learning to read. The fact that analogy can be an implicit process does not mean that we do not need to teach children to use analogies. The use of an analogy strategy should develop faster if it is explicitly "taught to."

One reason why orthographic analogies may be useful in reading English is suggested by a statistical analysis conducted by Treiman, Mullennix, Bijeljac-Babic, and Richmond-Welty (1995). They calculated how many times individual letters mapped to the same sounds when they occurred in the same positions across different words for all the monosyllabic words of English with a consonant–vowel–consonant (CVC) phonological structure (e.g., "c" in *cat, cup, cone,* etc., "p" in *cup, top, cheap,* etc.). The CVC words in this analysis included words spelled with vowel digraphs, such as "rain" and "beak," and words with "rule of e" spellings, such as "cake" and "lane." Treiman et al. (1995) found that whereas the pronunciation of initial and final consonants was reasonably consistent ($C_1 = 96\%$, $C_2 = 91\%$), the pronunciation of vowels was very inconsistent across different words (51%). An analysis of the spelling–sound consistency of larger spelling units in the words, namely the onset-vowel (C_1V) and rime (VC_2) units, showed a clear advantage for the rime. Whereas only 52% of CVC words sharing a C_1V spelling had a consistent pronunciation (e.g., *bea* in *beak* and *bean*), 77% of CVC words sharing a VC_2 spelling had a consistent pronunciation (e.g., *eak* in *peak* and *weak*).

This statistical analysis of the spelling system of English shows that the spelling–sound consistency of the written language is greatest for initial consonants (onsets), final consonants, and rimes. It indicates that the context of the final consonant or consonants can disambiguate the pronunciation of the vowel (e.g., "a" makes a different sound in *cat, ball, car, day, saw, cake,* and *care,* but these different phonemic correspondences are consistent within rhyming groups: cat, mat, bat . . . ; ball, fall, wall . . . ; care, dare, stare . . . ; and so on). These statistical relationships may help us to understand the developmental pathway between rhyme awareness and reading. Treiman et al.'s (1995) analysis shows that many of the alternative pronunciations for vowel graphemes become highly predictable if the rime is considered as a unit. A child with good onset–rime awareness is thus in a better position to discover the stability of vowel phonemes within rimes, suggesting another possible reason for the link between rhyme awareness and phoneme awareness demonstrated in Bryant et al.'s (1990) study. For example, the vowel digraph "ou" is always used to represent one sound in the rimes sh*out* and h*ouse*. It is used to represent a different sound in s*oup* and gr*oup*, but this is predictable. The sound /u/ is spelled differently in rimes such as t*ooth* and sp*oon* but is again predictable given the rime. In truly "alphabetic" languages, reading instruction based on teaching children a fixed sequence of grapheme–phoneme correspondences is commonplace (e.g., Wimmer, 1993). However, for a language such as English, a joint focus on grapheme–phoneme correspondences and rimes may be more appropriate (Goswami & East, 2000).

Supporting the Developmental Pathway: Environment and Intervention

If one important basis for the emergence of phonological awareness is the implicit comparisons between similar-sounding words that are a natural part of language processing, then children whose environment encourages them to make such implicit comparisons should be at an advantage when it comes to learning to read and to spell. Similarly, children who have experienced intervention designed to teach them to compare similar-sounding words explicitly should be at an advantage when it comes to learning to read and to spell. At present, there is rather little evidence available with which to examine these hypotheses. Nevertheless, the studies that have been done suggest that direct instructional influences can have an important effect on the development of phonological awareness. For enhanced phonological awareness to, in turn, affect the acquisition of literacy, further direct instruction in how phonological categories are reflected in the orthography appears to be necessary, at least for children at risk of underachievement in reading. For these children, direct instruction in sound–letter correspondences seems to be very important.

Environment

At present, we can only speculate how the child's environment might encourage the implicit comparisons between similar-sounding words that are a natural part of language processing and thereby stimulate the developmental pathway to phonological awareness. However, it seems likely that children who experience a rich linguistic environment in early life will acquire a larger vocabulary at a faster rate than do children who experience a poorer linguistic environment. Vocabulary size and rate of vocabulary acquisition are both hypothesized to be important for lexical restructuring to occur. Similarly, it seems likely that children whose caretakers promote linguistic activities such as language games and nursery rhymes will spend more time implicitly comparing and contrasting the sounds of words than do children whose caretakers do not promote

these activities. Nursery rhymes and similar linguistic routines would be expected to facilitate and extend the implicit organization of spoken words in terms of rime neighborhoods, for example.

There is at least piecemeal evidence that is consistent with these possibilities. For example, the study by Burgess and Lonigan (1998) noted earlier found that receptive and expressive oral language skills measured in their sample of 4- and 5-year-olds at time 1 predicted performance in the oddity task measured 1 year later (onset and rime versions). This is consistent with the idea that there should be a general relationship between vocabulary skills and the development of phonological awareness. In fact, a recent Finnish study found that there was a connection between lexical development at age 1 (measured by the number of mappings of meanings to speech units that each child had at 1 year) and phonological awareness at age 4 (measured by the oddity task, see Silven, Niemi, & Voeten, 1998). Metsala (1999) reported that 4- to 5-year-olds performed an onset–rime blending task significantly more accurately with early-acquired words than with later-acquired words. Although not directly relevant to the hypothesis that a richer language environment will promote phonological awareness, this finding does suggest that early vocabulary acquisition and early phonological skills are directly connected. Avons, Wragg, Cupples, and Lovegrove (1998) have shown that rhyme detection measured at 4 years 11 months is also a significant predictor of vocabulary development (measured at age 6). This could reflect the fact that children who have restructured more words to the onset–rime level at time 1 (consequently performing better in a rhyme-detection task) are those same children who are actively acquiring more words, and who thus have larger vocabularies at time 2.

It has also been shown that children from lower socioeconomic status homes tend to perform less well on measures of phonological sensitivity than children from higher SES homes. The reasons for this are not well understood. For example, Dickinson and Snow (1987) measured phonological sensitivity in U.S. kindergarten children who were all attending high-quality daycare programs, and found that those from high-SES backgrounds performed at a significantly higher level than those from low-SES backgrounds. Raz and Bryant (1990) gave two phonological awareness tasks to high- and low-SES English children (initial phoneme identification and rime oddity), and found that those from lower-SES backgrounds had lower levels of phonological awareness at school entry. These children were not significantly worse than their high-SES counterparts at this stage, but after a year in school the gap had widened dramatically, and the low-SES children showed a significant deficit in phonological awareness. Bowey (1995) has reported similar SES findings in a sample of Australian children. She compared high- and low-SES children in early word reading achievement, and found significant differences by SES status. She also reported that these differences were mediated by preexisting differences in phonological awareness and not by underlying differences in general cognitive ability.

Intervention

A number of studies have used direct intervention to improve children's phonological awareness and measured consequent effects on literacy. For example, as part of the longitudinal study discussed earlier, Bradley and Bryant (1983) took the 60 children in their cohort of 400 who had performed most poorly in the oddity task at 4 and 5 years of age and gave some of them 2 years of training in grouping words on the basis of sounds. Training was based on a picture-sorting task in which the children were taught to group words by onset, rime and vowel and coda phonemes (e.g., placing pictures of a *hat*, a *rat*, a *mat*, and a *bat* together for grouping by rime). A control group learned to sort the same pictures by semantic category (e.g., placing pictures of a *rat*, a *pig*, and a *cow* together for "farmyard animals").

Half of the experimental group then spent the second year of the study learning how the shared phonological segments in words such as "hat," "rat," and "mat" were reflected in shared spelling. The children were given plastic letters for this task, and were taught, for example, that a word such as

"hat" could be changed into a word such as "rat" by discarding the onset and retaining the rime. The other half of the experimental group continued to receive phonological training only. At the end of the second year of the study, the children in the experimental group who had had plastic letters training were 8 months further on in reading than the children in the semantic control group and a year further on in spelling. Compared to children who had spent the intervening period in an additional unseen control group, they were an astonishing 2 years further on in spelling, and 12 months in reading. The gains made by the children who had continued to receive phonological training only were not significant but still notable. This study suggests that there is a clear connection between training children how the alphabet is used to represent sounds and reading and spelling development.

Similar results were found in a large study of 235 Danish preschool children conducted by Lundberg, Frost, and Petersen (1988). They gave the children 8 months of daily training in metalinguistic games and exercises such as clapping out the syllables in words and attending to the first sounds in the childrens' names. The aim of the program was "to guide the children to discover and attend to the phonological structure of language" (p. 268). The effectiveness of the program in attaining this aim was measured by comparing the children's performance in various metalinguistic tasks after training to that of 155 children in an unseen control group. The trained children were found to be significantly ahead of the control children in a variety of metalinguistic skills including rhyming, syllable manipulation, and phoneme segmentation. The long-term effect of the training on the children's reading and spelling progress in grades 1 and 2 was also assessed. The impact of the training was found to be significant at both grades for both reading and spelling, although effects were stronger for spelling.

A recent German study of the effects of providing training in phonological awareness in kindergarten found a similar pattern of results to that reported by Lundberg et al. (1988). Schneider, Kuespert, Roth, Vise, and Marx (1997) developed a 6-month metalinguistic training program covering syllables, rhymes, and phonemes and gave it to a sample of 180 kindergarten children in Germany. Reading and spelling progress were then monitored in grades 1 and 2. Schneider et al. (1997) found significant effects of the metalinguistic training program on metalinguistic skills in comparison to an unseen control group, as would be expected from Lundberg et al.'s (1988) results. They also found significant long-term effects of metalinguistic training on reading and spelling progress, with stronger effects for spelling. Recently, the same research group has reported significant effects of the same training program on the reading and spelling progress of German kindergarten children assessed as being at risk for dyslexia (Schneider, Roth, & Ennemoser, in press). The at-risk study showed that greatest progress in reading and spelling was made when the metalinguistic program was combined with direct training in letter–sound relations. This mirrors the findings reported by Bradley and Bryant (1983) for an at-risk sample. Whereas children who are not at risk for later literacy difficulties may benefit from phonological awareness training alone (cf. Lundberg et al., 1988; Schneider et al., 1997), those who are likely to have specific problems in acquiring literacy seem to need a combination of metalinguistic and letter–sound training. Interestingly, the Schneider et al. (in press) study included an at-risk group that received letter–sound training alone, without metalinguistic training. This group either performed at comparable levels in later reading and spelling progress to the metalinguistic training alone group or performed at lower levels than this group. This suggests that "guiding children to discover and attend to the phonological structure of language" may be as important for literacy acquisition as direct tuition in letter–sound correspondences.

Conclusion

This chapter has reviewed evidence for the proposal that vocabulary acquisition produces developmental pressure for the child to make implicit comparisons between similar-sounding words in the mental lexicon, and that such comparisons are one of the bases for the emergence of phonological awareness. It was argued that the nature of phonological neighbors in different languages will influence this developmental process, and it was then shown that phonological neighborhood characteristics in English support the emergence of the linguistic units of the onset and the rime. As syllables, onsets, and rimes are also emphasized in early linguistic routines such as nursery rhymes, it was suggested that informal environmental experiences can promote the organization of the mental lexicon around the syllable and rhyme. Direct training in phonological categories can also promote such an organization. It was argued that the acquisition of literacy will influence the further development of phonological categories, particularly at the phonemic level, and might possibly lead to the reorganization of existing categories (e.g., when a frequent rime has multiple spellings, as in share/hair/where/their). It was argued that future important directions for research on phonology and reading acquisition include research designed to help us to understand which aspects of phonological processing are due to basic brain function and which are culturally influenced and to help us to understand the relative weight that needs to be given to the different phonological units of syllable, rhyme, and phoneme and their connections with sequences of letters in different orthographies. A better understanding of the factors that affect the transfer of phonological awareness across different languages is a third important goal for future work.

References

Avons, S. E., Wragg, C. A., Cupples, L., & Lovegrove, W. J. (1998). Measures of phonological short-term memory and their relationship to vocabulary development. *Applied Psycholinguistics, 19,* 583–602.

Baker, L., Fernandez-Fein, S., Scher, D., & Williams, H. (1998). Home experiences related to the development of word recognition. In J. L. Metsala & L. C. Ehri (Eds.), *Word recognition in beginning literacy* (pp. 263–287). Hillsdale, NJ: Erlbaum.

Bowey, J. A. (1995). Socioeconomic status differences in preschool phonological sensitivity and first-grade reading achievement. *Journal of Educational Psychology, 87,* 476–487.

Bradley, L., & Bryant, P. E. (1978). Difficulties in

auditory organisation as a possible cause of reading backwardness. *Nature, 271,* 746–747.

Bradley, L., & Bryant, P. E. (1983). Categorising sounds and learning to read: A causal connection. *Nature, 310,* 419–421.

Bryant, P. E., MacLean, M., Bradley, L., & Crossland, J. (1990). Rhyme, alliteration, phoneme detection, and learning to read. *Developmental Psychology, 26,* 429–438.

Burgess, S. R., & Lonigan, C. J. (1998). Bidirectional relations of phonological sensitivity and prereading abilities: Evidence from a preschool sample. *Journal of Experimental Child Psychology, 70,* 117–142.

Butterworth, B. (1992). Disorders of phonological encoding. *Cognition, 42,* 261–286.

Byrne, B., & Fielding-Barnsley, R. (1995). Evaluation of a programme to teach phonemic awareness to young children: A 2- and 3-year follow-up and a new preschool trial. *Journal of Educational Psychology, 87,* 488–503.

Chaney, C. (1992). Language development, metalinguistic skills and print awareness in 3-year-old children. *Applied Psycholinguistics, 13,* 485–514.

Charles-Luce, J., & Luce, P. A. (1990). Similarity neighbourhoods of words in young children's lexicons. *Journal of Child Language, 17,* 205–215.

Charles-Luce, J., & Luce, P. A. (1995). An examination of similarity neighbourhoods in young children's receptive vocabularies. *Journal of Child Language, 22,* 727–735.

Content, A., Kolinsky, R., Morais, J., & Bertelson, P. (1986). Phonetic segmentation in prereaders: Effect of corrective information. *Journal of Experimental Child Psychology, 42,* 49–72.

Cronin, V., & Carver, P. (1998). Phonological sensitivity, rapid naming and beginning reading. *Applied Psycholinguistics, 19,* 447–461.

De Cara, B., & Goswami, U. (1999). *Phonological neighbourhood density, sonority profile and the development of rime processing.* Manuscript submitted for publication.

Dickinson, D. K., & Snow, C. E. (1987). Interrelationships among prereading and oral language skills in kindergartners from two social classes. *Early Childhood Research Quarterly, 2,* 1–25.

Dollaghan, C. A. (1994). Children's phonological neighbourhoods: Half empty or half full? *Journal of Child Language, 21,* 257–271.

Eimas, P. D., Siqueland, E. R., Jusczyk, P. W., & Vigorito, J. (1971). Speech perception in early infancy. *Science, 171,* 304–306.

Ferguson, C. A. (1986). Discovering sound units and constructing sound systems: It's child's play. In J. S. Perkell & D. H. Klatt (Eds.), *Invariance and variability in speech processes* (pp. 36–51). Hillsdale, NJ: Erlbaum.

Fowler, A. (1991). How early phonological development might set the stage for phoneme awareness. In S. Brady & D. Shankweiler (Eds.), *Phonological processes in literacy* (pp. 97–117). Hillsdale, NJ: Erlbaum.

Gilhooly, K. J., & Logie, R. H. (1980). Age of acquisition, imagery, concreteness, familiarity and

ambiguity measures for 1,944 words. *Behaviour Research Methods and Instrumentation, 12,* 395–427.

Glushko, R. (1979). The organisation and activation of orthographic knowledge in reading aloud. *Journal of Experimental Psychology: Human Perception and Performance, 5,* 674–691.

Gombert, J. E. (1992). *Metalinguistic development.* Hemel Hempstead, Herts, United Kingdom: Havester Wheatsheaf.

Goswami, U. (1986). Children's use of analogy in learning to read: A developmental study. *Journal of Experimental Child Psychology, 42,* 73–83.

Goswami, U. (1988). Orthographic analogies and reading development. *Quarterly Journal of Experimental Psychology, 40A,* 239–268.

Goswami, U. (1995). Rhyme in children's early reading. In R. Beard (Ed.), *Rhyme, reading and writing* (pp. 62–79). London: Hodder & Stroughton.

Goswami, U. (1999). Causal connections in beginning reading: The importance of rhyme. *Journal of Research in Reading, 22,* 217–240.

Goswami, U. (in press-a). Phonological and lexical processes. In M. L. Kamil, P. B. Mosenthal, P. D. Pearson & R. Barr (Eds.), *Handbook of reading research* (vol. 3, pp. 251–267). Hillsdale, NJ: Lea.

Goswami, U. (2000). Phonological representations, reading development and dyslexia: Towards a cross-linguistic theoretical framework. *Dyslexia, 6,* 133–151.

Goswami, U., & Bryant, P. E. (1990). *Phonological skills and learning to read.* Hillsdale, NJ: Erlbaum.

Goswami, U., & East, M. (2000). Rhyme and analogy in beginning reading: Conceptual and methodological issues. *Applied Psycholinguistics, 21,* 63–93.

Goswami, U., Gombert, J., & De Barrera, F. (1998). Children's orthographic representations and linguistic transparency: Nonsense word reading in English, French and Spanish. *Applied Psycholinguistics, 19,* 19–52.

Goswami, U., Porpodas, C., & Wheelwright, S. (1997). Children's orthographic representations in English and Greek. *European Journal of Psychology of Education, 12(3),* 273–292.

Jusczyk, P. W. (1993). From general to language-specific capacities: The WRAPSA model of how speech perception develops. *Journal of Phonetics, 21,* 3–28.

Lesch, M. F., & Martin, R. C. (1998). The representation of sublexical orthographic–phonologic correspondences: Evidence from phonological dyslexia. *Quarterly Journal of Experimental Psychology, 51A,* 905–938.

Leslie, L., & Calhoon, A. (1995). Factors affecting children's reading of rimes: Reading ability, word frequency and rime neighbourhood size. *Journal of Educational Psychology, 87,* 576–586.

Liberman, I. Y., Shankweiler, D., Fischer, F. W., & Carter, B. (1974). Explicit syllable and phoneme segmentation in the young child. *Journal of Experimental Child Psychology, 18,* 201–212.

Logan, J. S. (1992). A computational analysis of young children's lexicons. *Research on Speech Perception Technical Report 8*, Indiana University.

Luce, P. A., & Pisoni, D. B. (1998). Recognising spoken words: The neighbourhood activation model. *Ear and Hearing, 19*, 1–36.

Lundberg, I., Frost, J., & Petersen, O. (1988). Effects of an extensive programme for stimulating phonological awareness in pre-school children. *Reading Research Quarterly, 23*, 163–284.

MacLean, M., Bryant, P. E., & Bradley, L. (1987). Rhymes, nursery rhymes and reading in early childhood. *Merrill-Palmer Quarterly, 33*, 255–282.

Marsh, G., Desberg, P., & Cooper, J. (1977). Developmental strategies in reading. *Journal of Reading Behaviour, 9*, 391–394.

Marsh, G., Friedman, M. P., Welch, V., & Desberg, P. (1981). A cognitive-developmental approach to reading acquisition. In G. E. Mackinnon & T. G. Waller (Eds.), *Reading research: Advances in theory and practice* (vol. 3, pp. 199–221). New York: Academic Press.

McBride-Chang, C. (1995). What is phonological awareness? *Journal of Educational Psychology, 87*, 179–192.

Metsala, J. L. (1999). Young children's phonological awareness and nonword repetition as a function of vocabulary development. *Journal of Educational Psychology, 91*, 3–19.

Metsala, J. L., & Walley, A. C. (1998). Spoken vocabulary growth and the segmental restructuring of lexical representations: Precursors to phonemic awareness and early reading ability. In J. L. Metsala & L. C. Ehri (Eds.), *Word recognition in beginning literacy* (pp. 89–120). Hillsdale, NJ: Erlbaum.

Morais, J., Alegria, J., & Content, A. (1987). The relationship between segmental analysis and literacy: An interactive view. *Cahiers de Psychologie Cognitive, 7*, 415–438.

Morais, J., Cary, L., Alegria, J., & Bertelson, P. (1979). Does awareness of speech as a sequence of phones arise spontaneously? *Cognition, 7*, 323–331.

Morrison, C. M., Chappell, T. D., & Ellis, A. W. (1997). Age of acquisition norms for a large set of object names and their relation to adult estimates and other variables. *Quarterly Journal of Experimental Psychology, 50A*, 528–559.

Patterson, K. E., & Marcel, A. J. (1992). Phonological ALEXIA or PHONOLOGICAL alexia? In J. Alegria, D. Holender, J. J. de Morais, & M. Radeau (Eds.), *Analytic approaches to human cognition* (pp. 259–274). Amsterdam: N. Holland.

Raz, I. S., & Bryant, P. E. (1990). Social background, phonological awareness, and children's reading. *British Journal of Developmental Psychology, 8*, 209–226.

Schneider, W., Kuespert, P., Roth, E., Vise, M., & Marx, H. (1997). Short- and long-term effects of training phonological awareness in kindergarten: Evidence from two German studies. *Journal of Experimental Child Psychology, 66*, 311–340.

Schneider, W., Roth, E., & Ennemoser, M. (2000). Training phonological skills and letter knowledge in children at risk for dyslexia: A comparison of three kindergarten intervention programs. *Journal of Educational Psychology, 92*, 284–295.

Shallice, T., Warrington, E. K., & McCarthy, R. (1983). Reading without semantics. *Quarterly Journal of Experimental Psychology, 35A*, 111–138.

Silven, M., Niemi, P., & Voeten, M. (1998). *Do early interaction and language predict phonological awareness of 3- to 4-year-olds?* Manuscript submitted for publication.

Stuart, M., & Coltheart, M. (1988). Does reading develop in a sequence of stages? *Cognition, 30*, 139–181.

Swingley, D., Pinto, J. P., & Fernald, A. (1999). Continuous processing in word recognition at 24 months. *Cognition, 71*, 73–108.

Thomas, E. M., & Senechal, M. (1998). Articulation and phoneme awareness of 3-year-old children. *Applied Psycholinguistics, 19*, 363–391.

Treiman, R. (1988). The internal structure of the syllable. In G. Carlson & M. Tanenhaus (Eds.), *Linguistic structure in language processing* (pp. 27–52). Dordrecht, The Netherlands: Kluger.

Treiman, R., Mullennix, J., Bijeljac-Babic, R., & Richmond-Welty, E. D. (1995). The special role of rimes in the description, use and acquisition of English orthography. *Journal of Experimental Psychology, General, 124*, 107–136.

Treiman, R., & Zukowski, A. (1991). Levels of phonological awareness. In S. Brady & D. Shankweiler (Eds.), *Phonological processes in literacy* (pp. 67–83). Hillsdale, NJ: Erlbaum.

Walley, A. (1993). The role of vocabulary development in children's spoken word recognition and segmentation ability. *Developmental Review, 13*, 286–350.

Wimmer, H. (1990). How German-speaking first-graders read and spell: Doubts on the importance of the logographic stage. *Applied Psycholinguistics, 11*, 349–368.

Wimmer, H. (1993). Characteristics of developmental dyslexia in a regular writing system. *Applied Psycholinguistics, 14*, 1–33.

Yopp, H. K. (1988). The validity and reliability of phonemic awareness tests. *Reading Research Quarterly, 21*, 253–266.

10

Writing and Children's Symbolic Repertoires: Development Unhinged

❖

ANNE HAAS DYSON

In childhood literacy development, the basic questions are: What is "it" that develops? What is its developmental course? Where and how would one look to glimpse the forces energizing and organizing a child's control of it?

To answer these questions, researchers interested in writing development have tended to equate "it" with children's ways of encoding messages. The forces shaping literacy growth may be variously named—children's cognitive construction, teacher's instruction, or social coconstruction, but, typically, the developmental pathway is imagined as a linear road: Children's productions move straightforwardly from letter-like strings to orthographically sensible (if not conventionally spelled) words and sentences. That is, more sophisticated writing (or encoding) evolves from less sophisticated writing.

In this chapter, I envision "it" differently. I am not focusing on written language as a kind of code but as a kind of symbolic tool that mediates human experience and interaction. From this vantage point, the process of becoming literate is an inherently social one; it entails learning to differentiate and manipulate the elements of the written system (e.g., letters and words) in order to engage with, and manipulate, the social world. To study written language, then, one looks for change, not simply in organized print but in the nature of participation in communicative events. Thus studied, writing no longer seems to emerge unilaterally from

previous writing, nor is its development reducible to encoding (cf. Vygotsky, 1978).

Consider, for example, Noah, a small boy with a big grin, sitting with tablemates in his first grade. His official task is to write, and so, influenced by peers, he decides "to write *Space Jam*" (Reitman & Pytka, 1996), a film featuring basket ball star Michael Jordan and Looney Tune cartoon characters. The movie itself was a multidimensional experience, shared originally in a moviegoing event with his family and, since then, recontextualized and transformed in symbolic and social play with peers. Noah now recontextualizes this material once again, making much use of familiar practices and symbolic tools—of story making through narrative talk and drawing—even as he engages in the new communicative practice of writing workshop.

Noah draws an evolving scene in which Michael and Bugs Bunny make many baskets and accumulate many points. Noah records points (primarily ones followed by an increasing number of zeros) and provides oral narrative commentary on how "much points" the team is accumulating. He then writes a variant of his writing workshop standard—a personal experience text, reporting that he "woth [watch] Space Jam" with his cousins.

Noah participated quite differently in this communicative event through his multimodal story than he did through his written text. Through his multimodal retelling, Noah engaged with pretend characters in an imagined world, participated in peer dialogue about a media sensation and, more broadly, in the popular culture. His drawn and told story did not simply represent a pregiven world but, rather, mediated an interactive space. In contrast, his written graphics were of little immediate interest to his tablemates. Those graphics comprised a supplement, an adjunct, to his narrative fiction making and an acknowledgment of his status as a good student who does "his work" and, thus, his writing.

The essence of the developmental challenge of interest is revealed not by Noah's print in isolation but by the relationship of that print to the entire communicative event. That interest is in how written language itself assumes a substantive role within children's symbolic repertoires and social worlds. In other words, how do strings of (or pages of scattered) letters become mediators of interactional spaces?

In this chapter, I provide a discursive answer to this question. My ongoing research aim is to unhinge writing development from its narrow linear path and to portray its developmental links to the whole of children's symbolic repertoires and to the breadth of their textual landscapes. These developmental links foreground our key human strengths—social and symbolic flexibility and adaptiveness (Gould, 1998; Sutton-Smith, 1997; Vygotsky, 1978)—as key also to children's growth as skillful users of written symbols.

Theoretically, this research agenda has been influenced by Vygotsky (1978), who, early in the 20th century, urged that researchers locate writing within the "entire history of sign development in the child" (p. 106), and by Bakhtin (1981), who argued that individual language users build their "own" texts by borrowing signs from other people's texts, that is, from their landscape of textual possibilities. The work has also been shaped by pedagogical aspirations: given the diversity of literacy's enactment as a cultural and social tool and, thus, the diversity of experiences children bring to the classroom in a complex society, preexistent narrow pathways all children must tread would be usefully replaced with negotiable pathways all children may enter (cf. Clay, 1998). (For another discussion that uses a Vygotskian historical approach see Watson, Chapter 4; for an alternative discussion of writing development, see Richgels, Chapter 11.)

In the sections that follow, I work to unhinge writing development from a narrow pathway, illustrating my successive actions with vignettes drawn from qualitative research projects on child writing, ending with a recent project involving Noah and his peers. All the studied classrooms have been, for me, local public schools, all racially integrated ones in which African American children have been a dominant group; many of the focal children have been African American and from low-income and working-class neighborhoods, as were Noah and other children featured herein. These studies have yielded detailed, analytic narratives about specific children in specific settings, narratives that may be compared to equally detailed accounts of other children in other settings. Study conclusions have not been about any one population of children but about this phenomenon of interest—the symbolic and social dynamics that help explain the changing nature of young children's use of written language in their lives together as children as well as students.

Unhinging Development

Mapping Complications

The first step in this process of unhinging literacy development is to consider a central issue in the development of any symbol system: the mapping issue. Linear developmental trajectories have, at their core, a concern with this issue, that is, with how children map spoken messages onto written graphics and vice versa (e.g., Read, 1971; Vernon & Ferreiro, 1999).

To investigate the changing role of writing in children's symbolic repertoires, however, it is not possible to focus exclusively on the mapping issue. Young children, after all, do not necessarily attempt to encode messages when they write, particularly if they are "exploring with a pencil" (Clay, 1977, p. 334). Further, sometimes they write simply to take stock of the conventions they know, for example, lines of letters or lists of known words (Clay, 1975).

More important for this chapter, as a symbolic tool, oral language itself has multiple functions in early writing development beyond serving as raw material for analysis and encoding. As I discuss in the sections that follow, within a communicative event, the relationship between oral and written language—and between a child's constructed meaning and a written message—is not initially, or ever exclusively, a direct one.

THE MULTIPLE FUNCTIONS OF ORAL LANGUAGE

Speech organizes and guides children's use of symbolic tools well before alphabetic writing emerges (Vygotsky, 1978). Indeed, it is difficult to see how children could learn to compose with written graphics unless they already could use comfortably a natural language (oral or sign; Ramsey, 1997) as a tool to plan, narrate, make queries, and even reflect on, and analytically examine, speech itself.

Consider, for example, Ashley, a focal child in a study of early writing processes (Dyson, 1983). I observed Ashley and his peers when they chose to visit the classroom writing center, which was, in truth, a researcher concoction, a space for writing in a mandated curriculum with no such space. The mandated literacy curriculum focused exclusively on basic concepts (shapes, colors) and letter names and sounds.

At the writing center, Ashley typically wrote by telling an elaborate story, blending experiences from the television, the movies, and everyday life to create dramatic, imaginative narratives for anyone who would listen. Within those narratives, a drawing would evolve, often an action-packed story about danger, rescue, and superheroes. Speech was integral to Ashley's drawing. He used speech to label drawn figures and narrate unfolding action inside the imagined world; with speech, he also moved outside that world to plan and evaluate his efforts and monitor analytic attention to fine details (like drawing enough fingers); finally, he used speech to engage with others both within and outside his world, dramatizing his characters' actions or more directly calling others' attention to his efforts.

In contrast, speech was much less integral to Ashley's writing, which was often accompanied by silence. A string of letters, including those from his name, would take shape on top, under, or to the side of his drawing—except for the letter S, which was ap-

propriately placed on the superhero's shirt. The other printed graphics were indecipherable and simply the "letters of it"—of his story. Other than his name, Ashley did not read letters: "I just write 'em. I don't read 'em." Ashley's behaviors are exemplified in the illustration that follows; his behaviors accompanied the production of Figure 10.1.

Ashley has just drawn Superman, and now uses speech as a regulator to guide and monitor his actions as he adds the right number of fingers (later colored over):

> 1, 2, 3, 4, 5

Ashley then labels his figure and, then, plans and reports his writing of S:

> This right here is Superman.
> . . . [omitted talk]
> Then you write under (*pause*) S.

As he later says, "Superman always have a S on his shirt." Ashley expresses pride that S was also "some a' the stuff" that belongs to his name. He and Superman share the letter S. Ashley now plans, monitors, and reports his next actions.

> And now here goes the cape. (*Ashley draws Superman's cape.*)
> That's his cape, right here.
> . . .
> And here go that lady. . . .

Ashley next narrates and dramatizes characters' dialogue:

> Superman said, "Don't worry. I gotcha'." And the lady said. "I know you got me. But who's got you?"

Through a similarly talk-governed process, Ashley draws Spiderman and Spiderman's friend and, then, decides to write on the bottom of his page. Unusually for him, he plans his text:

> I'm gonna write the Superfriends right here. . . . Here go Spiderman. I'm writing both of 'em in real life."

Ashley is making vertical lines on the bottom of his page; in this way he writes Spiderman and plans to write "both of 'em." But his graphics are quite different from his usual mock writing, which incorporates letters and letter-like forms and cursive-like script. Perhaps for this reason, when he is done silently drawing his lines, he evaluates his efforts negatively:

> I'm not doing nothing but scribble scrabble.

FIGURE 10.1. Ashley's Superfriends.

As Ashley illustrates, young children's speech helps them orchestrate cultural and experiential resources and translate them into symbolic form for, and with the support of, others. In the foregoing event, Ashley's language use reveals his orchestration of diverse kinds of knowledge to construct an imaginative story space—knowledge of superhero characters, actions, and themes (i.e., danger and rescue), along with traditional gender roles and appropriate (and appropriated) utterances, presented with the stylistic edge of a cartoon.

CHILDREN'S MEANING MAKING
AS SYMBOL WEAVING

Ashley also illustrates another potential quality of young children's participation in open-ended composing activities which complicates the mapping issue: their use of multiple media.

The act of composing—the deliberate manipulation of meaning—occurs first in more directly representative media, among them gesture, play, and drawing. When contextual circumstances allow, just beginning writers may act on communicative intentions by relying on these earlier controlled symbolic tools (Dyson, 1983, 1989a, 1991). That is, children tend to rely on available symbolic media they more easily control to mediate symbolic, evaluative, and social ends during literacy events. As a result, their products (like all those featured in this chapter) may be woven from multiple symbolic media.

Although Ashley used drawing as a key resource in enacting a symbolic world, other young children may depend on different available media in classroom practices (e.g., dramatic play, as in Paley, 1980, or Dyson, 1997; for discussion of a breadth of constructive tools, see Clay, 1998, who cites Richardson, 1964; for a description of symbol weaving in an early childhood curriculum, see Genishi, Stires, & Yung-San, in press). Children's meanings, then, are not necessarily in linear oral form ready for encoding. Nelson's (1996) comments on oral language development are relevant to written language development as well:

Experience is multidimensional, often with many different things displayed and many different actions taking place at the same time. Speech, on the other hand, is one-dimensional, linearly ordered through time. To express experience in language requires recomposing it into linear form, conforming to the syntax of one's own language. This means that there is no one-to-one mapping of experience on language; the adult's intuition that there is arises, no doubt, from their being fully inducted into the uses of language. (p. 388)

In written language, as in oral, then, there is a tension between the expected linearity of the product and the multidimensional nature of experience, real or imagined. Initially, what is written may consist heavily of names and labels.

Finally, Ashley illustrates that very young children do not necessarily conceive of writing as speech written down (an idea developed most elaborately by Ferreiro & Teberosky, 1982; also Clay, 1975; Dyson, 1982; Luria, 1983; vivid examples are provided by Ballenger, 1999). Initially, oral language functions as a medium for investing meaning in written graphics by naming them or otherwise connecting them to important people or things (Dyson, 1983). In this way, written development mirrors the development of other symbolic forms in which children use their own actions and talk to invest a form (a graphic mark, a clay shape) with meaning before they differentiate the systemic features that allow a form, on its own, to mediate meaning (Vygotsky, 1978).

Even for children with an initial grasp of the alphabetic system (like Noah), letter graphics may only index people and things already represented in other media forms. In a sense, for many children, writing, relative to play and drawing, is much less embedded in their social and intellectual lives. Given children's existent experience with, and engagement as, orchestrators of symbolic worlds, how do written graphics themselves become central to children's orchestrations? How do they become the focus of children's interactive and self-regulatory talk? Most basically, how do written graphics become mediators of social and intellectual spaces where children explore human experiences with and for others?

Analyzing Shifts of Functions and Forms

"The developmental history of written language . . . does not follow a single direct line in which something like a clear continuity of forms is maintained"—this was a fundamental insight of Vygotsky (1978, p. 106), but it is compatible with the research on the development of all symbolic media (Werner & Kaplan, 1963). Children learn to "mean"—to fulfill certain kinds of intentions or functions—through particular forms that are later served by other media (Halliday, 1977). For example, gestures are used for some of the functions later fulfilled by words, and pictures may be used in ways that foreshadow the use of written language.

Moreover, developmental research has emphasized the role of communicative, interactive events in guiding children's understandings of the nature and use of symbolic tools (Nelson, 1996; Vygotsky, 1978). Thus, children's forms evolve new functions in social situations as they are seen to serve new human ends, and those functional ends in turn drive the evolution of forms themselves.

In early writing research in particular, a number of authors have written clear descriptions of teachers entering into children's composing events, helping them grasp the specific nature of the representational function of print (e.g., Clay, 1998; Watson, 1999). These descriptions feature instructional conversations, through which teachers help children focus on brief labels or messages as objects of analytic talk (e.g., Ashley's making letters for the Superfriends could have become writing "The Superfriends"). Teachers guide children to listen to their speech and build on nascent written knowledge (e.g., "S" for "Superman" and "Spiderman").

However, as Noah already illustrated, grasping the alphabetic nature of written language does not lead automatically to children's use of written language as a mediator of social interaction and individual reflection. In furthering this use, children's relationships with other children can play a central role.

Within the communicative activities teachers organize and guide, children's actions and interactions are inevitably influenced by the social concerns, relationships, and energy among the children themselves. Indeed the importance even young children place on relationships with other children has been discussed by many skilled teachers and researchers working in a variety of sociocultural contexts (Ashton-Warner, 1963; Corsaro, 1997; D'Amato, 1987; Philips,

1972; Sahni, 1994). Peer relationships are not necessarily always positive or productive (and, as experienced teachers attest, they too require active monitoring and guidance [Dyson, with Bennett et al., 1997]). Nonetheless, these relationships do have the potential—even when conflict-ridden—to invest children's writing with social meanings.

These meanings, established and organized in unofficial peer worlds, contribute to children's expectations for, and sense of the functional potential of, writing and, thus, they contribute to children's differentiation of the features and powers of the written system. This developmental dynamic is audible in children's talk as well as in the shifting functions and forms of their texts.

To provide a brief clarifying example, I turn to 6-year-old Jake. Jake was a case study child in a longitudinal study of the changing role of writing in 4- to 8-year-old children's symbol making and interacting during a daily composing period in an urban magnet school (Dyson, 1989a). Within the children's small school, the K–2 children had the same language arts teacher, Margaret, and participated in the same basic composing activities for 2 to 3 years. Thus, it was a school with a strong sense of textual practices—all K–3 children had a daily journal time, similar sharing time rituals, and sections of the school library for sharing finished products, as well as regular experiences with the visual and dramatic arts. Moreover, the children had the same friends, indeed, often the same chosen tablemates, for 2 to 3 years.

Within the official context of the daily writing time, first-grader Jake, like most children, situated his composing activity within his unofficial social relationships with other children. These relationships entailed much storytelling and play, as well as many evaluations of self and others. Also like most children, within these familiar relations, and these familiar ways with words, Jake's writing events entailed much drawing and talking. This symbol making was easily accessible to and interpretable by peers, and it came to play a key mediational role in peer life. Through these media, Jake and other children represented their ideas, connected with friends, and, at times, engaged in critical discussions about whether or not

a drawing was accurate, truthful, or sensible.

In the following example, Jake's ways of participating in school composing are well illustrated, as is his playful relationship with his close friend Manuel. Jake's narrative adventures were usually lively and wildly adventurous; Manuel, with his quieter temperament, seemed to be a very effective straight man for these adventures.

Jake is drawing the picture in Figure 10.2. He has just completed the ground and the sky and—

JAKE: Now I'm gonna make a mechanical man.

Manuel, sitting beside him, seeks some clarification:

MANUEL: A mechanical man? You mean a robot man?
JAKE: Yeah, I'm gonna make a robot man. You got it, Manuel.
              . . . [omitted data]
JAKE: Here's a bomb head. It's gonna explode. It hasn't even exploded yet. When it does—
MANUEL: I hope it explodes in the next century.
JAKE: . . . There is the fire, a little smoke. (*Makes quick back-and-forth motions with his marker.*)
              . . .
              It's gonna explode in the next few days.
MANUEL: I hope it happens on the weekend and then I won't be around.
JAKE: Not for long this school will be around.
              . . .
              (*Adds another figure.*) I'm gonna make a flying earthling!

For his robot man story, Jake writes:

Once upon a time there were two men. One was flying up in to the clouds. The other man was staying on the ground. The and [end]

As was typically the case with all Margaret's children, Jake's drawing, dramatic play, and social talk were neither homologous nor synonymous with his eventual writing. As Jake also illustrates, there were clear symbolic tensions between drawing, talking, and writing, tensions created, for example, by differences in the space and time conventions of these diverse media, as well as by the unidimensional nature of

FIGURE 10.2. Jake's mechanical men.

written language, which demands words for dramatized gestures and qualities of voice.

Jake in particular struggled with encoding, and, for support, he "copied offa" his pictures, in his words. Although his written content was appropriated from the static, flat surface of his picture, it was translated and transformed into familiar written forms used in school, that is, into descriptive statements. Indeed, the majority of kindergartners in this school began writing by dictating descriptive statements about their pictures. First-grader Jake did not use "This is" (ubiquitous among the kindergartners, despite the discouragement of Margaret); still the basic text form remained the same. (Dyson, 1989b, discusses the sociolinguistic complexities of "once upon a time.")

As children are drawn into the textual culture of the school, its practices and values, their composing time practices may become increasingly hybrid, reflecting both their own frameworks of symbolizing and socializing, as well as official frameworks. In the project featuring Jake, over time, chil-

dren began to attend to each other's evolving texts, and thus their playful and critical talk engulfed their writing and helped it become a legitimate object of attention, separate from their pictures.

Discrepancies between drawings, writings, and oral retellings—or restatements of the pictorially obvious—could therefore be commented on. Moreover, written texts, like drawn or dramatized ones, could be subject to children's objections to sense or truth value and to considerations of whether the story is meant to be like "real life" or just "pretend." Further, writing too could lead to judgments that the author was funny, mean, or a good friend who gave one a good part in his or her story. Oral objections to or evaluations of another's picture or text could be responded to with a decision to write a mitigating or elaborating next line.

Through such talk, children were supported in learning that a written text is a mediator of a social and textual event—children's manipulations of words had consequences in their social world. Their social and symbolic tensions could lead to new ways of using both other symbol systems and peer relations themselves. For example, children began to sequence drawings to capture narrative movement or to use drawings as points of illustration; they incorporated talk as dialogue in their written texts and began to transform friends into characters in their written worlds.

In the following example from Jake's case, which took place a year after the preceding one, Jake leans for support during writing not on singular pictures but on interactive play with others, especially Manuel:

Jake begins writing—he has not yet drawn his picture:

JAKE: (*to Manuel*) I'm deadly. I am deadly. I'm gonna put your name in this story and you are gonna be dead too. I'm gonna make sure you get blown to pieces. (*Laughs.*)
MANUEL: Blown to pieces. (*softly and a bit awed*)
JAKE: Yes, sir. You won't be able to see your mommy ever again.

Manuel playfully retaliates:

MANUEL: In my story you're going to meet a magician who's going to turn you into a snowman.
JAKE: Well, actually, guess wha—
MANUEL: And melt you flat.

Jake seems to back down.

JAKE: Actually, um, I I'm, I—we're gonna, I'm writing about um us flying the fastest jet in the world.
. . . [omitted data]
None of us—both of us are—isn't gonna get blown to pieces because it's the fastest jet—it can outrun any bullet.
MANUEL: Oh, WOW! I like that.
JAKE: And it's as bulletproof as it can get.

But later:

JAKE: Watch out Manuel! (*Writes blow up*)
MANUEL: Just at the very end when they're [the other children] just so happy, it's almost—they're just so happy and they read the entire story and they loved it, I get blown up.
JAKE: Yeah.
MANUEL: And they cry and cry and cry and cry—it's so dramatic.

When he finishes his story, Jake reads it to Manuel, grinning with Manuel's every grimace:

Once there was a boy that is named Manuel. Manuel is going to fly the fastest jet and I am going to fly the jet too. But Manuel's headquarters is going to blow up But I am OK. But I don't know about Manuel but I am going to find Manuel. . . . But I think I see him. He is in the jet. Manuel are you OK? Yes I am OK. You are being attacked. I will shoot the bad guys out of the universe. OK yet shoot them now. The end.

In the foregoing event, Jake's talk during writing is no longer focused primarily on encoding, as it was in the first grade; rather it serves multiple functions, including interactive and self-regulatory ones (i.e., planning and oral revising of those plans). Further, although the interaction is between the two boys, Manuel's talk in particular indexes the wider classroom world, and the classroom social practice of sharing time, in which the piece would eventually be read. Through written words, Jake and Manuel would play with others without talking or acting at all.

Although all children will need to differentiate a functional place for writing in their symbolic repertoire, the exact nature of their social and symbolic challenges will depend on the sociocultural frames of reference they bring to school, as well as the kind of communicative events and symbolic tools available to them in school. In the project involving Noah, who began this piece, I aimed to untangle the trajectories of converging practices undergirding children's early writing; that is, the way in which it was situated within, and reflected the cultural and textual materials of, diverse social worlds.

Recontextualizing across Frames

In an effort to unhinge literacy development from a linear path, in the preceding sections I have linked children's use of written language to their use of multiple symbol systems and, moreover, to their relationships with other people: Children must learn how to fulfill through writing the representational, social, and evaluative functions they already fulfill through other media, and it is social interaction that drives these shifts of functions and forms. The last step in unhinging literacy development entails linking children's relations in the moment to the broader social and ideological worlds in which they participate.

This last aspect of the unhinging process has, in fact, been ongoing, if unstressed, in the preceding sections as well. Although the cases stretch over a period of 20 years, Ashley and Jake, like Noah, were using cultural materials—words—that indexed or situated their actions in the classroom moment in worlds beyond the classroom walls. They wrote superhero stories, with themes, characters, plots and ideologies (e.g., gender and power) that indexed cultural and textual practices that were part of the breadth of children's social lives. Moreover, through the use of those materials in their local contexts, the children were constructing identities as small boys in contemporary, media-saturated times.

As Bakhtin argued, these links between the present utterance (the present turn at speaking or writing) and larger socioideological worlds are rooted in individuals' reliance on the public communication systems. Children, for example, learn words from other people in varied kinds of interactive events. For this reason, children's (like adults') words are always "used" words (Bakhtin, 1986); they are part of the social hierarchies and dynamics of the society. Any present utterance (any present turn at speaking or writing) has meaning because it echoes utterances that have come before— and anticipates those that will come after.

Given the diversity of children's textual and knowledge resources, though, the meanings of their words may be open to widely differing responses. Children are apt to offer words to peers and teachers who do not share their own tastes, interests, and values—for Looney Tunes or basketball, for instance. This is particularly true for materials appropriated from popular culture, which is complexly interrelated with social class, ethnicity, and gender (Bourdieu, 1984). Children may be surprised by the unintended interpretations and unanticipated responses their words may bring (Dyson, 1997), which is why a deliberateness about crafting words may be linked to a deliberateness (i.e., a sophistication) about social worlds (Bakhtin, 1981; Volosinov, 1973).

The interweaving of the breadth of children's social and communication experiences in their responses to school literacy is inevitable. Like all learners, children must use familiar frames of reference to recontextualize salient aspects of new activities (new concepts, new symbolic tools, and new social practices) (Miller & Goodnow, 1995; Nelson, 1996). This recontextualization allows children a sense of competence and agency—indeed, this allows them sense. In a dialectic fashion, children also recontextualize aspects of their familiar world within the frameworks of new activities and thus potentially gain new reflective angles on experiences—on, for example, the functional nature of drawing relative to writing, the expectations for storytelling in official contexts relative to unofficial or home ones, and the pleasures condoned by teachers relative to diverse significant others.

Thus, reframing processes—process of differentiation and translation of cultural material across social and symbolic borders (Bauman & Briggs, 1990)—are at the heart of developing a functional place for written language in a symbolic repertoire. In addition, these practices situate literacy learning within a diversity of developmental pathways, because children bring to school strikingly varied symbolic and communicative experiences. As Rockwell (1999) argues, the larger social processes of children's lives always "penetrate the space of schooling" (p. 122), although, I would add, they are not always recognized, acknowledged or responded to.

In the project involving Noah, I focused on children's appropriations of diverse cultural material for school composing. I was interested not just in children's symbol making and social interactions but also in the nature of their appropriations from out-of-school cultural and textual practices. Analysis of ethnographic data revealed that children drew deeply on nonacademic social worlds to negotiate their entry into school literacy; those worlds provided them with agency and meaningful symbols, including those from popular music, films, animated shows, and sports media. The children's use of this material was developmentally useful, in part because it provided them with conceptual content, functional genres, models of textual structures and elements, and a pool of potential characters, plots, and themes.

Moreover, the use of media material also posed useful developmental challenges in differentiating symbol systems and social practices. For example, information about games results is arranged differently on a television screen during a sports news show than it would be in a prose report (see Dyson, 1999), popular music themes are "too fast" for children and may best be written surreptitiously (see Dyson, in press b), and, as Noah will illustrate, animated characters' interactive style is more visual, more physical than the dialogue that provides the substance of young children's early reading books. Thus, at the same time that children were differentiating the elements of the written symbol system, they were also differentiating the new social practices of school and their underlying ideological values.

As already suggested, Noah made abundant use of animated media, especially cartoon and video characters, in his oral and drawn narratives. At the same time, he was committed to doing well in school. He relied on official school forms to frame his writing efforts. In a particularly rich composing event, Noah's talk made use of characters and plot elements from a video game, *Donkey Kong Country* (Stamper, 1986), but his writing made use of characters, plot elements, text structure, and even particular utterances from a classroom early reader, *Little Bear* (Minarik, 1957).

Little Bear is a sweet bear cub who lives in the woods. He progresses through his written narratives primarily through participating in dialogues comprised of short declarative sentences, often enacting a mild conflict. For example, in the excerpt that follows, Little Bear announces his desire to fly, which will figure into Noah's own story production:

"I'm going to fly to the moon," said Little Bear.
"Fly!" said Mother Bear. "You can't fly."
"Birds fly," said Little Bear.
"Oh yes," said Mother Bear. "Birds fly, but they don't fly to the moon. And you are not a bird." (Minarik, 1957, pp. 37–39)

In the last chapter in the cited book, Little Bear explicitly says, "'I wish that I could sit on a cloud and fly all around,'" and his mother explicitly says "'You can't have that wish'" (p. 52). Little Bear does receive one wish—a "surprise" birthday cake (p. 35).

In contrast to Little Bear, Donkey Kong is a big, uncouth gorilla who lives in the jungle and enjoys bananas. In the context of a Nintendo video game, he has a buddy named Diddy, a small chimp. Diddy has a girlfriend named Dixie, a chimpette with a prehensile ponytail. The Donkey Kong characters engage in melodramatic quest stories, as they aim to retrieve stolen items, rescue kidnaped persons, or just jump up and get a banana. The emphasis is on action, unlike the character emphasis of the Little Bear stories. Moreover, Donkey Kong characters do not talk. As Noah himself confirmed: "They just play. . . . They run and be happy."

Nonetheless, there *are* written graphics in the video experience: In game materials, the initials *D.K.* (plus a star) appear on a wooden sign (indicating Donkey Kong Country), and words containing Os typically sport a star inside those Os. During the game, the initials *D.K.* appear on barrels, which often hide one of the Donkey Kong characters; and each of the letter icons *K, O, N,* and *G* appears in a floating box, which the monkeys try to jump up and bump.

Despite their semiotic differences, the Donkey Kong creatures and Little Bear were all furry animals drawn in an iconic, rather than more realistic, style, and all were embedded in narratives (i.e., in sequenced events situated in imagined worlds). Their similarities seemed to strike Noah, who interrupted his reading group's engagement with *Little Bear* to announce that "I'm gonna get a little tiny baby gorilla. My mommy said Friday I would get one. I gotta get some bananas. . . ."

Although Donkey Kong and Little Bear seemed to come together in Noah's welcoming imagination, their symbolic and social incompatibility became evident in his composing efforts. After having met Little Bear and after having decided to get a little gorilla, Noah wrote a story that, orally and iconically, was about Donkey Kong but, orthographically, was about Little Bear, as illustrated next:

Noah is sitting by Denise and Vanessa, who are writing about their families. He talks mainly to himself, planning, rereading, monitoring his written efforts. (See Figure 10.3.)

NOAH: (*writing and rereading* "I Klo"), "call, I call, I call"
(*writing* "I waw to waw fly") "I, wish, wish"

Noah now pauses in his writing and draws a tiny flying monkey, commenting to no one in particular:

NOAH: This is Donkey Kong.
ANNE: Donkey Kong?

Sitting slightly behind Noah, I recognized "I wish to fly" from the Little Bear books. I expected the sweet cub himself, not Donkey Kong. Noah proceeds silently to write *OK*, accompanying those letters with stars and containing them in a box. He turns to me:

NOAH: And that says, "OK." It's a Donkey Kong monkey. . . . The monkey says he wants to fly. . . . Donkey Kong Country, deep in the jungle. (said in a deep voice)

Zephenia, a peer writing nearby, tells Noah that he knows *Donkey Kong Country 2*. After Zephenia and Noah discuss the video game for a while, Noah turns back to his writing. Now Little Bear himself appears:

Litt Barair I HavoA [Little Bear I have]
A soep fro you [a surprise for you]

ANNE: That's not about Donkey Kong, is it?

NOAH: (*working to explain his text to me and, seemingly, to himself too*) Oh, he he— bears live in some—no. They don't live in the jungle. It [the text] got both of them inside it. (*big breath*) Donkey Kong was in the video game. The monkey and the little monkey was in the video game. The little bear was playing with me and my brother. . . .

Noah continues writing, adding sentences about "suddenly" the lights going off (apparently because of the impending "surprise") and, then, someone saying, "I can't see." Noah's intense concentration is interrupted by Denise, who has a story to tell:

DENISE: Last night I spilled some Skitters [a food] on my homework. I was crying.
NOAH: I was too! I was too!
DENISE: I messed up my homework all up.
NOAH: I was crying too because my mommy yelled at ME:: because I, DID IT, WRONG:: And my daddy came mad at me. And I said, "O K::, Daddy, O K::, Daddy." My Daddy is so crazy sometimes.

Noah returns to his writing. He continues the generic structure of a Little Bear story, but his evaluative tone is strikingly different. He includes another boxed and starred "OK," but he does not silently write it, as before. This "OK" is not primarily iconic but orally expressive, like the "OKs" of his homework story.

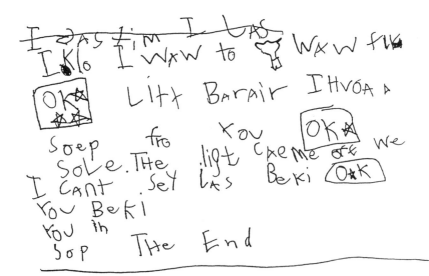

FIGURE 10.3. Noah's "Donkey Kong" text.

NOAH: "Jus' be quiet, O K::?" (*writing* "Jas BeKi O*K*")

When I ask who is talking, Noah says that the little girl monkey is telling the little boy monkey to "Just be quiet, O K::?" (*with exasperated tone*). He then returns to his story dialogue:

NOAH: "YOU be quiet." (*writing* "You Be Ki") "You, YOU in, shut up!" (*writing* "you in sop")

Noah's unfolding and enacted story seemed to consist of two related but not completely integrated utterances: one rooted in visual animation and oral play; the other in written form. His written text contains indices of its hybridity: the starred and boxed "OKs," the small drawn figure, and the blunt "Shut up." The original Little Bear conveys his irritation primarily visually, in gently disgruntled faces. Neither he nor his mother or friends say, "Be quiet," or, heaven forbid, "Shut up" . . . but Little Noah may have wanted to in the encounter he recalled over homework. He seemed to recontextualize the expressive element of his own homework story ("O K::, Daddy") along with the visual icon from Donkey Kong. In any case, Noah attributed the rude words to two little monkeys.

Despite these symbolic and social complexities, within the official world's sharing time, Noah's orally read words filtered the unruly Donkey Kong characters from public consideration. The instructional practice was about *reading* one's *writing*. His writing, as his teacher Rita explicitly commented, was about Little Bear. Still, Noah's peers did react to the most audible of his unruly symbols, as illustrated below:

Noah is standing in front of his class, which is sitting on a large, rectangular rug. He reads his piece. A few children gasp after Noah's last sentence. Rita does not allow children to say "Shut up." After the gasps, there is general amusement and laughing. Rita does not attend to this laughing but comments:

RITA: He didn't have any time for a picture because he was so busy writing a Little Bear story, right? (*apparently not noticing the tiny drawing*)

But Vanessa wants to comment on something different:

VANESSA: I love the end.

There is much child mumbling, and Lakeisha's strong voice:

LAKEISHA: Can you read that end again?

And Noah rereads the whole story.

As discussed in the larger case (Dyson, in press a), throughout the remainder of the school year, Noah used the Little Bear genre form to produce stories and, moreover, he continued to explore a variety of written voices. He also more conventionally coordinated the visual conventions and icons of animated media with print media. For example, Noah wrote a personal experience text about playing a Goosebumps video game after school with his brother. He used squiggly letters to write the name "Goosebumps," conveying spookiness, and placed a picture of the Goosebumps game underneath the text. Noah, like all the children discussed herein, was not just moving forward in the official school world; he was negotiating complex social worlds by adapting, stretching, and transforming his resources.

Resituating Development

> As educators focus on early literacy they tend to look backward from desirable literacy outcomes and ask, What are the precursors of success in school literacy learning, and how can we ensure that they are a part of children's preschool experiences? Such a backward look must etch a narrow view of a limited set of activities. . . . (Clay, 1998, p. 1)

In the lives of young children, school exists in a configuration of other social worlds, other relationships. Those relationships are enacted through the mediational powers of varied symbolic media. Children bring their experiences with social worlds and symbolic tools to school, and, more particularly, they bring textual frames and fragments to school composing. As illustrated herein, children's earliest composing events may draw on a diversity of materials and media, which themselves index a complex of overlapping social worlds. I have emphasized the symbolic resources and tensions inherent in this complexity, aiming to articulate a developmental framework that normalizes variations in (as well as broadens conceptions of) children's literacy resources and learning pathways.

Key to this framework are the dialectic processes of appropriating and recontextualizing cultural material across symbolic media (e.g., audiovisual sources and printed pages), social activities (e.g., watching videos and writing stories), and ideologies (e.g., the different values governing how time is spent at home and at school). Through these processes, children differentiate and expand their written language knowledge even as they orchestrate that knowledge in new, more deliberate ways. The pedagogical goal implied by these processes is not the mastery of a particular text type but a disciplining of discourse flexibility and adaptability (i.e., of recontextualization); that disciplining involves learning about "options, limits, and blends" of symbol use across practices (building on the nonliteracy work of Miller & Goodnow, 1995, p. 12).

Learning about written language is thus not just about learning a new code for representing meanings. It is about entering new social dialogues in an expanding life world. As such, written language learning is inevitably a part of learning about social and ideological worlds and about the place of a child's own relationships and experiences in those worlds.

This vision of literacy development—as entailing social and symbolic flexibility and adaptability—has not been a major one in the literacy development research, despite the area's dependence on the formal recognition of children's literacy's experiences in homes and communities. The implications of that recognition, though, have been narrowly contained within traditional school curricula: children may already grasp sound–letter relationships and, thus, invent spellings (Read, 1971); perhaps they have been read to and thus are "literate at two" (Scollon & Scollon, 1981, p. 57).

As McNaughton (1999) recently discussed, a large body of research supports conventional conceptions of resources for early literacy success (see, e.g., Snow, Burns, & Griffin, 1998):

These are relationships of *actuality* [sic], in which conventional literacy and instruction are assumed to be relatively fixed. But what if

we radically changed some of the features of early reading and writing instruction? . . . Or imagine that expert teachers could pick wonderful varieties of knowledge children brought with them. Then correlates might reduce, if not disappear. . . . (McNaughton, 1999, p. 4)

The possibility of alternative "pathways to literacy" (Clay, 1998) in no way deemphasizes educators' responsibility to introduce children to texts and text types not easily accessible outside of school. But it does emphasize educators' need to access more fully children's symbolic and social resources. Educators might consider, first, the need for "open-ended" composing periods, as well as more structured occasions for learning specific new writing practices. In those open-ended times, educators learn about children's cultural landscapes, and the particular voices and kinds of voices that appeal to them.

Second, official classroom sharing and discussion is centrally important as well. Such discussions provide children opportunities to explain their multimedia texts, including their words, and they provide teachers opportunities to provide an analytic language for genre and text features. In this way teachers help children differentiate and coordinate their multimedia efforts. Official sharing also allows opportunities for analytic attention to child audience responses to children's composed utterances. Children's giggles, laughs, scrunched up faces, and rolled eyes are often not polite. And yet, as child responses to Noah's rude Bear suggested, in these potential disruptions are potential reflections on textual qualities and on judgments of social appropriateness and ideological worthiness. How do texts—by other children, by adult authors of the school literary canon, by media writers and producers—appeal or not? How is our pleasure, or discomfort, linked to particulars of text (plot, characters, theme, discourse features, visual images)? How is it linked to our own current location (in school) or our broader positions and histories?

Most generally, for literacy to find a place in communiticative repertoires, children need opportunities not only to read and write but to play, draw, and sing. These diverse symbolic media provide an enabling loom for children's early symbol weaving and, moreover, feed the formation of classroom textual communities. "Oh," I imagine a teacher saying to a young child, "you've written/drawn/made an adventure story, a song, a script, a bit of fiction or fact. It reminds me of something we've heard, read, something someone else has written or read, something in our library, a movie we saw, something we saw here or there on a trip." In this way, composing texts—literacy—may acquire a social place and a social history in children's lives.

Such general implications will be differentially enacted in local circumstances, and so doing would be well supported by research which examines how variation in children's symbolic and communicative resources might influence the nature of their responses to varied instructional contexts. Nonetheless, I do not think that curricular or research efforts pose the greatest challenges to implementing these notions of recontextualization, of literacy situated within the stuff of children's experiential histories. I think critical and political efforts do.

This past week, as I worked on the conclusion to this chapter, the California State Department of Education released its Academic Performance Index. This index ranks schools on a 10-point scale. One familiar with the Bay Area would not need to consult the index to know the names of schools ranked low (1's or 2's) and those ranked high. Despite California's ostentatious swings to varied sides of pedagogical debates, at the school level, the official outcomes for children are related to the socioeconomic status of their neighborhoods, which themselves are related to race.

There are, of course, complex reasons for these links, including, for example, that here, in the Bay Area, as in other urban areas, the distribution of qualified teachers, stable school populations, and material resources reflect these same trends (Costantinou, 2000). However, there are also longstanding and much discussed relationships between the ideologies of schools as social and institutional contexts and child learning. Bourdieu (1977), for example, argues that "the school demands of everyone alike that they have what it does not give" (p. 494). What it does not give are certain kinds of cultural capital, certain predispositions to

use linguistic and symbolic material in particular ways; these linguistic and other cultural practices underlay how children appropriate—the frames within which they situate—school material. Within conventional frames, much of the discourse knowledge and symbolic skill displayed by Ashley, Jake, and Noah might be deemed irrelevant.

Learning, especially learning an expressive system like written language, is not divorced from one's identity and history but, of necessity, embedded within it. Children's present symbolic resources are not only reflective of their pasts but constitutive of the foundation from which they might move forward. Thus, it is only by embracing the complexity of children's social and symbolic lives that the fullness of their futures can be supported.

Acknowledgments

The research reported herein was supported by the Spender Foundation and the Faculty Grants program of the University of California at Berkeley. The findings and opinions expressed herein are my own and do not reflect the position or policies of any institution or agency. I would like to thank my hard-working project research assistant, Soyoung Lee.

References

Ashton-Warner, S. (1963). *Teacher*. New York: Simon & Schuster.

Bakhtin, M. (1981). Discourse in the novel. In C. Emerson & M. Holquist (Eds.), *The dialogic imagination: Four essays by M. Bakhtin* (pp. 259–422). Austin: University of Texas Press.

Bakhtin, M. (1986). *Speech genres and other late essays*. Austin: University of Texas Press.

Ballenger, C. (1999). *Teaching other people's children*. New York: Teachers College Press.

Bauman, R., & Briggs, C. C. (1990). Poetics and performance as critical perspectives on language and social life. *Anthropological Review, 19,* 59–88.

Bourdieu, P. (1977). Cultural reproduction and social reproduction. In J. Karabel & A. H. Halsey (Eds.), *Power and ideology in education* (pp. 487–510). New York: Oxford University Press.

Bourdieu, P. (1984). *Distinction: A social critique of the judgment of taste* (R. Nice, Trans.). Cambridge, MA: Harvard University Press. (Original work published 1979)

Clay, M. (1975). *What did I write?* Auckland, New Zealand: Heinemann.

Clay, M. (1977). Exploring with a pencil. *Theory into practice, 16,* 334–341.

Clay, M. (1998). *By different paths to common outcomes.* York, ME: Stenhouse.

Costantinou, M. (2000, February 1). Dismal Oakland school report no surprise. *The Examiner,* p. A–6.

Corsaro, W. (1997). *The sociology of childhood.* Thousand Oaks, CA: Pine Forge Press.

D'Amato, J. D. (1987). The belly of the beast: On cultural difference, castelike status, and the politics of school. *Anthropology and Education Quarterly, 18,* 357–360.

Dyson, A. H. (1982). The emergence of visible language: Interrelationships between drawing and early writing. *Visible Language, 16,* 360–381.

Dyson, A. H. (1983). The role of oral language in early writing processes. *Research in the Teaching of English, 17,* 1–30.

Dyson, A. H. (1989a). *Multiple worlds of child writers: Friends learning to write.* New York: Teachers College Press.

Dyson, A. H. (1989b). "Once upon a time" reconsidered: The developmental dialectic between function and form. *Written Communication, 6,* 436–462.

Dyson, A. H. (1991). Viewpoints: The word and the world: Reconceptualizing written language development, or, Do rainbows mean a lot to little girls? *Research in the Teaching of English, 25,* 97–123.

Dyson, A. H. (1997). *Writing superheroes: Contemporary childhood, popular culture, and classroom literacy.* New York: Teachers College Press.

Dyson, A. H. (1999). Coach Bombay's kids learn to write: Children's appropriation of media material for school literacy. *Research in the Teaching of English, 33,* 367–402.

Dyson, A. H. (in press b). The stolen lipstick of overheard song: Composing voices in child song, verse, and written text. In M. Nystrand & J. Duffy (Eds.), *The rhetoric of everyday life.* Madison, WI: University of Wisconsin Press.

Dyson, A. H. (in press a). Donkey Kong in Little Bear Country: Examining composing development in the media spotlight. *Elementary School Journal* (Special Issue on Writing).

Dyson, A. H. (with A. Bennett, W. Brooks, J. Garcia, C. Howard-McBride, J. Malekzaden, C. Pancho, L. Rogers, L. Rosenkrantz, E. Scarboro, K. Stringfield, J. Walker, & E. Yee). (1997). *What differences does difference make?: Teacher perspectives on diversity, literacy, and the urban primary school.* Urbana, IL: National Council of Teachers of English.

Ferreiro, E., & Teberosky, A. (1982). *Literacy before schooling.* Exeter, NH: Heinemann.

Genishi, C., Stires, S., & Yung-Chan, D. (in press). Writing in an integrated curriculum: pre-kindergarten English language learners as symbol makers. *Elementary School Journal: Special Issue on Writing.*

Gould, S. (1998). *Leonardo's mountain of clams and the diet of worms: Essays on natural history.* New York: Three Rivers Press.

Halliday, M. (1977). *Explorations in the functions of language.* New York: Elsevier North-Holland.

Luria, A. (1983). The development of writing in the child. In M. Martlew (Ed.), *The psychology of written language* (pp. 237–277). New York: Wiley.

McNaughton, S. (1999). Developmental diversity and beginning literacy instruction at school. In J. S. Gaffney & B. J. Askew (Eds.), *Stirring the waters: The influence of Marie Clay* (pp. 3–16). Portsmouth, NH: Heinemann.

Miller, P., & Goodnow, J. J. (1995). Cultural practices: Toward an integration of culture and development. In J. J. Goodnow, P. J. Miller, & F. Kessel (Eds.), *Cultural practices as contexts for development, No. 67. New Directions in Child Development.* San Francisco: Jossey Bass.

Minarik, E. H. (1957). *Little Bear, an I can read book.* New York: HarperCollins.

Nelson, K. (1996). *Language in cognitive development: The emergence of the mediated mind.* Cambridge, UK: Cambridge University Press.

Paley, V. (1980). *Wally's stories.* Cambridge, MA: Harvard University Press.

Philips, S. U. (1972). Participant structure and communicative competence: Warm Springs children in community and classroom. In C. B. Cazden, V. John, & D. Hymes (Eds.), *Functions of language in the classroom* (pp. 370–394). New York: Teachers College Press.

Ramsey, C. (1997). *Deaf children in public schools.* Washington, DC: Gallaudet University Press.

Read, C. (1971). Pre-school children's knowledge of English phonology. *Harvard Educational Review, 41,* 1–34.

Reitman, I. (Producer), & Pytka, J. (Director). (1996). *Space Jam* [film]. Burbank, CA: Warner Brothers.

Richardson, E. S. (1964). *In the early world.* Wellington: New Zealand Council of Educational Research.

Rockwell, E. (1999). Recovering history in the study of schooling: From the longue duree to everyday co-construction. *Human Development, 42,* 113–128.

Sahni, U. M. (1994). *Building circles of mutuality: A sociocultural analysis of literacy in a rural classroom in India.* Unpublished doctoral dissertation, University of California, Berkeley.

Scollon, R., & Scollon, S. B. K. (1981). *Narrative, literacy, and face in interethnic communication.* Norwood, NJ: Ablex.

Snow, C., Burns, S., & Griffin, P. (Eds.). (1998). *Preventing reading difficulties in young children.* Washington, DC: National Academy Press.

Stamper, T. (Creator). (1986). *Donkey Kong Country* [video game]. Super Nintendo Entertainment System.

Sutton-Smith, B. (1997). *The ambiguity of play.* Cambridge, MA: Harvard University Press.

Vernon, S., & Ferreiro, E. (1999). Writing development: A neglected variable in the consideration of phonological awareness. *Harvard Educational Review, 69,* 395–415.

Volosinov, V. N. (1973). *Marxism and the philosophy of language* (L. Matejka & I. R. Titunik, Trans.). New York: Seminar Press.

Vygotsky, L. S. (1978). *Mind in society.* Cambridge, MA: Harvard University Press.

Watson, B. (1999). Creating independent learners. In J. S. Gaffney & B. J. Askew (Eds.), *Stirring the waters: The influence of Marie Clay* (pp. 47–74). Portsmouth, NH: Heinemann.

Werner, H., & Kaplan, B. (1963). *Symbol formation: An organismic–developmental approach to language and the expression of thought.* New York: John Wiley.

11

Invented Spelling, Phonemic Awareness, and Reading and Writing Instruction

❖

DONALD J. RICHGELS

Any discussion of children's emergent writing must include an appraisal of the legacy in research and practice of Read's (1971, 1975) work with invented spelling. It has been 30 years since Read discovered invented spelling; it is no coincidence that those three decades have seen a revolution in what and how preschoolers and primary-grade children write. Read's work, especially as it was quickly interpreted and elaborated by others (e.g., Beers & Henderson, 1977; Chomsky, 1971; Gentry, 1978; Paul, 1976), awakened teachers and other researchers to the possibility of purposeful and prolific writing by children long before they master the conventions of penmanship, spelling, and reading. Unlike the failed experiment of the initial teaching alphabet (Downing, 1965), which earlier had similarly empowered young writers but had proven too impractical in its implementation and especially in its transition to conventional writing, invented spelling was found to be easily supported and encouraged in young writers and to be developmentally sound (it evolves in recognizable stages, culminating in conventional spelling). (For an alternative approach to considering writing development, see Dyson, Chapter 10; for related reviews of phonemic awareness, see Goswami, Chapter 8, and Adams, Chapter 9).

Charles Read's Legacy

No change in preschool and primary-grade practice in the last 30 years is more significant than the prolific writing by not yet conventionally literate children that is made possible by teachers' accepting and encouraging invented spelling. Before invented spelling, there was little or no writing in preschool, and primary-grade writing was largely a wasteland of penmanship drill, assigned copying, and fill-in-the-blanks work. Read's role in all this often has been obscured, perhaps due to his being a linguist, not a reading specialist. He immediately recognized the instructional implications of his findings, but the purpose of his original study (Read, 1971) was to document phonological knowledge in young children.

Read's discovery of invented spelling reminds me of a story I read as a young boy about Charles Goodyear's discovery of vulcanized rubber. Goodyear accidentally discovered the vulcanization process that enabled the widespread use of rubber when he spilled a raw rubber-and-sulfur mixture on a hot stove, where it remained long enough for the heating to change its properties (or so the story went in my elementary school basal reader); Read discovered the invented spelling process that enabled widespread early writing when he encouraged literacy-naive preschoolers to spell as a research task that would demonstrate what they knew or did not know about phonemes.

The many instructional methodologies that have followed from Read's discovery have been important to the emergent literacy revolution of the past 30 years. Equally, if not more important, however, are Read's and others' linguistic insights (i.e., findings about the nature of young children's phonological awareness), for there is no more basic research in literacy than that which illuminates what children know, how they know it, and when they know it about phonemes and their roles in spoken and written language.

If I have been sketching a picture of the last 30 years as the age of invented spelling, or the emergent literacy era, I would be remiss if I did not also acknowledge that those same years have been a time of significant research about the cognitive processes involved in early reading and writing and a time of redefinition of instructional practice in light of such research. Word identification, for example, has been demonstrated to depend on the process of phonemic awareness. Adams's (1990) comprehensive review of research establishing that dependence has had a major impact on subsequent research and especially on classroom practice. It would not be too much of an exaggeration to call the last 10 years in early literacy research and practice the decade of phonmeic awareness.

This trend is often characterized as a backlash against holistic or emergent literacy views and methodologies, as if concern for phonemic awareness requires direct instruction with isolated word sounds. I argue in this chapter that such a characterization is not necessary, that in fact, Read's study that launched the age of invented spelling or the emergent literacy era was as much about phonemic awareness as about invented spelling, that the two are inseparably entwined, and that invented spelling offers a holistic way for teachers and others who are interested in emergent literacy to assess and facilitate children's phonemic awareness.

To make my case, it will be necessary to examine in some detail Read's 1971 study and to clarify what really is meant by the words "phoneme" and "awareness."

What Phonemic Awareness Is

Phonemes are the units of sound from which words are built. In English, for example, the phonemes /p/, /i/, and /g/ are combined to make the word "pig," and the /g/ and /k/ phonemes are contrasted when distinguishing the words "pig" and "pick" (letters between slashes should be read as sounds, not as letter names). The difference in the pronunciations of /g/ and /k/ is slight. It is only that for /g/ we use our voices and for /k/ we do not (in linguistic terminology, /g/ has the feature of being voiced and /k/ lacks that feature); everything else—how we use our tongues and throats, how we shape our lips, how we part our teeth—is identical. Yet speakers and listeners rely on that very small difference, that contrast; it is what signals two very different English meanings, a farm animal that says "Oink" versus a small piece of plastic used for plucking guitar strings.

In speech, this combining and contrasting of phonemes is unconscious. Speakers and listeners need to be able to make and use the phonemic combinations and contrasts in these "pig" and "pick" examples, and thousands of others like them, quickly and automatically in order to construct and make sense of the stream of sounds that constitutes the utterances of everyday conversation, theatrical performances, news reports, political speeches, and classroom lectures.

Interestingly, humans never have to learn how to do this; they are born with the ability to perceive phonemes. Even 4-week-old infants have categorical perception of phonemes; they respond, for example, to the /g/ versus /k/ difference but ignore variations in pronunciation of /g/ and variations in pronunciation of /k/ (Eimas, Siqueland, Jusczyk, & Vigorito, 1971).

There are different kinds of /g/ and different kinds of /k/; each phoneme is a category that includes variation. Consider, for example, how /k/ is pronounced differently in "booklet" and "book sale"; in "booklet" it is not as fully pronounced, not as complete, as in "book sale" because of what the tongue and teeth have to do when pronouncing /k/ in "booklet" in order to be ready to pronounce the following /l/. Just as important as distinguishing between /g/ and /k/ is ignoring the variations within the categories of sounds that make up the phonemes /g/ and /k/.

This unconscious perception of phonemes is not awareness. Awareness implies consciousness. Rather, it is a special kind of knowing that often is involved in language competence and performance; it is knowing-without-knowing-that-you-know. Most phonological knowledge is of this unconscious variety. Speakers and listeners, as we have seen, unconsciously know one phoneme from another, but that is not all that is included in phonology. Phonology includes anything to do with the sounds of language. For example, speakers and listeners also unconsciously use the pitch and stress patterns of their language to distinguish stating as fact from asking in dismay ("George is class president." vs. "GEORGE is class president!?"). (Similarly, other kinds of linguistic knowledge are unconscious. Most of your syntactic knowledge is unconscious; for example, you know-without-knowing-that-you-know what you have to do with word order to construct and comprehend statements and questions: "George is class president." vs. "Is George class president?")

Phonemic awareness is conscious attention to phonemes. As we have seen, it is not needed in spoken language. What, then, is it good for? Not for accomplished writing and reading, the sort of automatic spelling and decoding that mature writers and readers do (as you have been doing if you are still with me, for, presumably, you have not been sounding out each word of this chapter, phoneme by phoneme). Phonemic awareness *is* good for learning how to read and write (Adams, 1990). Emergent readers and writers—not accomplished, mature readers and writers—need it. When first dealing with the extra layer of symbolization involved in written language, where letters stand for phonemes, children must be able consciously to attend to the phonemes of which the stream of speech is composed.

What Read Demonstrated about Phonemic Awareness

Read (1971) demonstrated that preschoolers, though untutored in reading and writing, were capable of the conscious attention to phonemes which cognitive psychologists were demonstrating is essential to learning to read and write. His serendipitous use of a writing task to entice his subjects (who knew most letters of the alphabet) to demonstrate this involved him in the "discovery" of invented spelling, and teachers and teacher educators quickly seized on this discovery in one of the most direct theory-to-practice transfers in the history of educational research.

UNCONSCIOUS KNOWLEDGE

Read (1971) requires a careful reading, keeping in mind the distinction I have made between *awareness* and *knowledge*. To begin, there is Read's use of the word "knowledge" in the title of his article, "Pre-School Children's Knowledge of English Phonology." Then, in the abstract, he mentions "unconscious knowledge" (p. 1). And in his conclusion, Read writes, "Evidently a child may come to school with a *knowledge* of some phonological categories and relations; *without conscious awareness,* he may seek to relate English spelling to these in some generally systematic way" (pp. 32–33, emphasis added).

Where is the conscious awareness in this? Isn't Read dealing only with the kind of linguistic knowledge that I have called "knowing-without-knowing-that-you-know" and that he and other linguists sometimes call "tacit knowledge?" The answer is that yes, he is dealing with this unconscious knowledge, but, no, he is not dealing *only* with it.

Yes, Read's primary purpose was to demonstrate that children have at their disposal the ability, without conscious analysis, to perceive and distinguish among features of pronunciations. It is this ability that enables our creating the categories known as phonemes (which, recall, include variations that we can and must ignore) and our contrasting phonemes in such pairs of words as "pig" and "pick." His article is organized around types of such phonological knowledge that he documents in his preschool subjects, for example, their knowledge of (read this as their ability to perceive and use, though without-knowing-that-they-know) affrication, alveolar flaps, and nasals.

At the same time Read was doing this work, Eimas was demonstrating that even infants have categorical perception of speech sounds; they know-without-know-ing-that-they-know one phoneme from another, and they ignore differences within phoneme categories. Read was being scooped—and with a much younger population; Eimas used 4-month-olds, not 4-year-olds!

CONSCIOUS AWARENESS

Luckily for Read, who would become famous in the literacy education community as the discoverer of invented spelling, his study was not only about unconscious knowing; it was also about awareness. This is because his experimental task was a spelling task that by its very nature requires conscious work—the choice of letters to represent sounds. (In contrast, Eimas used his infant subjects' instinctive sucking behavior and an ingenious dishabituation paradigm, so that even in their experimental behavior they did not have to act consciously.) Thus, although Read's subjects lacked conscious knowledge of affrications and alveolar flaps and nasals (most adults who are not trained linguists lack *conscious* knowledge of such features of sound), they did have the ability consciously to segment strings of phonemes in words and decide which phonemes to represent with which letters.

The fact that Read's subjects' decisions were consistent with such concepts as affrication, which they could not have defined, does not detract from the fact that they were conscious decisions. They were, in fact, decisions compelled by phonemic awareness.

And this is why, besides containing the previously cited uses of "unconscious" and "knowledge," Read's (1971) article is also replete with such terms as "analyze" (p. 6), "recognize" (p. 8), "organize" (p. 8), "choose" (p. 14), "become conscious of this distinction and exploit it" (p. 24), and "[make] phonological judgments" (p. 33). The agency implied in these terms is what ultimately justifies Read's coining the terms "created spellings" (p. 13) and "invented spelling" (p. 13).

Legitimizing Invented Spelling

What, then, did Read (1971) show us about preschool children's invented spelling? Be-

sides demonstrating that preschoolers untutored in literacy were capable of invented spelling, he gave their spellings legitimacy by demonstrating that they share with conventional spellings the characteristics of systematicity and abstractness, and he hinted at instructional implications.

All spelling is systematic, that is, nonrandom. Invented spelling, though not systematic in the same way as conventional spelling (it does not follow the same rules as conventional spelling), is nonetheless systematic. Inventive spellers have their own rules. Read documented such rules and repeatedly gave his subjects credit for having found a system, albeit not the same system that adults use. "What the children do not know is the set of lexical representations and the system of phonological rules that account for much of standard spelling; what they do know is a system of phonetic relationships that they have not been taught by their parents and teachers" (p. 30).

One way that any spelling system is non-random is that it must have a way of being abstract. "Being abstract" means ignoring some sounds and encoding others. This simplification provides an efficiency (the popular lament that English spelling fails to be a perfect sound-by-sound, sound-to-letter matching bespeaks an ignorance of the cumbersomeness such a method would entail) and is based on the assumption that the ignored sounds take care of themselves when the written word is read.

One of the ways Read demonstrated that this is so even with invented spelling was with affrication. Affrication is a sound feature, that is, a possible characteristic of a sound (recall another feature, voicing, in the earlier examples where /g/ has voicing and /k/ lacks it). A sound is affricated when it involves a harsh burst of air, such as is especially evident in the English phonemes usually spelled with *C-H* and *J*. When you pay close attention to your pronunciation of "tr" and "dr," you will hear such affrication. It is as if there are not just two sounds in "tr" or in "dr," but rather, squeezed between /t/ and /r/ and between /d/ and /r/ is an affrication.

Now it happens that conventional English spelling ignores this affrication. It abstracts away from it and represents only the /t/ and /r/ as in "try" and the /d/ and /r/ as in "dragon." Read found, however, that young inventive spellers consistently represented the affrication and abstracted away from the /t/ and the /d/, spelling "try," for example, as CHRIE and "dragon" as JRAGIN (p. 13).

Again, this systematicity earns for invented spelling the distinction of being true spelling, different in only a minor, not an essential, way from conventional spelling. Read wrote the following:

> [Inventive spellers] are spontaneously employing one of the basic devices of spelling systems. . . . The nature of this accomplishment is theoretically more important than the fact that they choose the wrong dimension, from the adult point of view. . . . The fact that children's spontaneous spelling is already systematically abstract suggests that it is chiefly the facts of English, rather than the principle of spelling, that they have yet to learn. (p. 16)

This suggests that teachers ought to build on, not seek to replace, children's invented spelling. Read pointed this out, and in so doing led the way for the many others who would soon articulate the theory-to-practice connection regarding invented spelling. I must quote at some length from Read's concluding remarks in order to reemphasize two important points that I have made about phonemes and invented spelling and to anticipate two themes in what others would do with Read's work.

> The educational importance of this [study's] conclusion seems clear enough, at least in general. We can no longer assume that a child must approach reading and writing as an untrained animal approaches a maze—with no discernible prior conception of its structure. . . . Evidently, a child may come to school with a knowledge of some phonological categories and relations. . . .
>
> In the classroom, an informed teacher should expect that seemingly bizarre spellings may represent a system of abstract phonological relations of which adults are quite unaware. Until we understand this system better, we can at least respect it and attempt to work with it, if only intuitively. . . . Drill and memorization of words with *tr-* and *dr-* may help the child to learn such cases, but these techniques suggest that spelling is arbitrarily related to speech and can only be memorized. This suggestion is not true of either standard spelling or the child's own invention. . . . Such a child needs to be

told, in effect, that his phonological judgments are not wrong (though they may seem so to most adults), and that it is reasonable, indeed necessary, to categorize abstractly what he hears. . . . He is on his way [to the adult system] when he begins to abstract from phonetic variations, as the spontaneous spellers did in their pre-school development. It may be particularly important [for a teacher] to recognize when [a student's] . . . efforts are too abstract, or abstract in the wrong direction, and to suggest, at least implicitly, that he is using the right principle, even if in the wrong place. We cannot teach him this principle if we ourselves continue to believe that to learn to spell is to get in the "habit" of associating sounds with letters, or phonemes with graphemes. For at least some children, to learn standard spelling is to learn to broaden and deepen their pre-school phonological analysis, which may already be abstract enough that phoneme–grapheme correspondences are indirect outcomes of an intricate system. (pp. 32–34)

What are the two ways this quotation looks back to what I have emphasized from the article? First, it is now abundantly clear that what Read is describing in inventive spellers is conscious work with phonemes. Invented spelling involves phonemic awareness. In the quoted paragraphs, Read writes about inventive spellers' making phonological judgments, categorizing, using principles, and performing phonological analysis.

Second, though his preschool subjects have it, phonemic awareness is not simple, for phonemes are not simple. They are not discrete items; they are categories within which is some variation that must be ignored. Nor are they the ultimate, the smallest, units of sound; rather, they are describable in terms of their component features (e.g., voicing and affrication). Inventive spellers reveal their tacit knowledge of these features through the decisions they make about which letters to use or not to use in the deceptively simple sounding process of sound–letter matching. These two characteristics of phonemes, that they are categories and are describable in terms of features, mean that spelling based on phonemic awareness must be systematic and abstract. Read repeatedly uses those words in the foregoing quotation from his concluding statement.

What are the two ways that the quotation looks forward to what others would soon make of Read's work? First, there is Read's emphasis on development. Invented spelling is not an isolated phase; it is a long-term, developmental sequence during which children can move from their own system to the standard system. Read's concluding remarks include mention of spelling development and children's being on their way to a more standard system by broadening and deepening their invented system. Much of others' invented spelling research in the first decade after this article would involve defining the stages of such development (e.g., Beers & Henderson, 1977).

I said in the previous paragraph that children *can move* along a sequence of development. The second way that Read's concluding remarks look forward is in his predicating such progress on teachers' being understanding and supportive. He writes about informed teachers' changing their notions about the nature of spelling; it is an abstract system built on children's existing phonological knowledge, not an arbitrary list of representations to be inscribed on a blank slate by drill and memorization. With this change, the bizarre becomes the expected and teachers recognize and respectfully respond to what their phonologically knowledgeable students bring to the writing process. This would be the theme of what would be written for teachers about invented spelling in the decades following Read (1971) (e.g., Paul, 1976).

Stages of Invented Spelling

By the end of the 1970s, researchers had documented the developmental nature of invented spelling by identifying stages through which inventive spellers move (e.g., Beers and Henderson, 1977; Gentry, 1978; Paul, 1976; Zutell, 1976). Beers and Henderson (1977) described first-graders' passage through a first stage marked by reliance on letter names; a second stage marked by greater awareness of vowels, so that, for example, spellers attempt to represent a vowel sound in every syllable even when it is difficult to find a letter name that reproduces that sound; and a third stage marked by attention to other than phonetic data, as when spellers use silent letters. Letter names make first-stage spelling of long

vowels easy, because the long vowel sound *is* the letter's name, for example, FET for "feet" (p. 140). An example of a second-stage invented spelling is MES for "miss" (p. 137), where spellers choose E for the short I sound because they know they must represent that vowel sound, and because, although the name of the letter E does not include the short "I" sound, it comes close (you do almost the same things with your throat and mouth when saying the name of the letter E and pronouncing the short I sound). You have already seen, in the earlier discussion of affrication, an example of third-stage invented spelling: CHRIE for "try" (Read, 1971, p. 13), where the speller is still being abstract in a nonconventional way, abstracting away from the /t/ and toward the affrication, but has learned—probably from seeing them in print—the C-H spelling for the "ch" sound and the "I-silent E" spelling for the long I sound. In contrast, invented spelling data frequently show that children still at the second stage represent the affrication in "tr" with only the letter H (because its name includes the "ch" sound), for example, HRAN for "train."

Gentry (1978) named these three stages the semiphonetic, the phonetic, and the transitional stages of invented spelling. And, further emphasizing the developmental nature of invented spelling, he added two others that are not invented spelling at all, an earlier deviant stage (later called precommunicative), which is marked by letter strings that are random and therefore cannot be considered spelling, and a later correct stage, which is marked by spellers' arriving at conventional spelling. These five stages became canonical; they have been cited, adapted, and applied in most references to invented spelling in the last 20 years, including in Gentry's (1982) own analysis of a thorough and intriguing case study of one boy's writing and reading development from 5 to 9 years of age, Bissex's (1980) *GNYS AT WRK: A child learns to write and read*.

Instructional Implications of Invented Spelling

As quick on the heels of Read (1971) as this stage-defining research were several articles that addressed the instructional implications of the discovery of invented spelling (Chomsky, 1971; Paul, 1976; Zutell, 1978). Paul (1976) encouraged kindergartners to label their pictures by asking them "to listen very carefully to the sounds they heard in the words they wanted, so they could figure out what letters they needed to write" (p. 196). Eventually many of her students took up other kinds of writing, including story writing. Paul's kindergartners' invented spellings were consistent with what Read had documented, with one exception. "Read had predicted that children would use consistent, though nonstandard, spellings for short vowel sounds. But my observations indicate that when the children wanted to spell a short vowel sound, they seemed to give the vowels that were formed similarly in the mouth equal value and to use them interchangeably as a sort of marker" (p. 199).

Paul identified stages of invented spelling similar to those that Beers and Henderson and Gentry were finding. She presented them as potential guidelines that "other teachers might find helpful when looking at their own students' spelling" (p. 198).

Other ways that Paul's article anticipated much of the next decade's practitioner-oriented writing about invented spelling were in her starting with a base of alphabet knowledge ("Most of the children recognized many letters and were familiar with most consistent consonant sounds" [p. 195]); her reassuring students that their way was okay ("It was explained that their spellings would probably be different from other people's, but that the spellings would represent the way those words sounded to the children now" [p. 196]); her addressing the "bad habit" concern ("I was concerned that wrong spelling might develop into a bad habit . . . [but t]he product—the way they actually decide to spell the word—appears to be greatly subordinate to the thinking process that leads to the decision. I also observed that as soon as children learned the standard spelling for a word, they would substitute it for their own" [pp. 199–200]); and her identifying a burst of writing enabled by children's being freed to spell in their own ways ("Several [children] have picked up on the idea and keenly enjoy being able to write whatever they like without a teacher's help. The greatest advantage

of the technique seems to be that it gives children the opportunity to write independently long before they are ready for a formal reading or spelling program" [p. 200]).

In the 1980s, numerous studies further documented the burst of writing made possible by invented spelling (e.g., Bissex, 1980; Clarke, 1988; Newman, 1984; Temple, Nathan, & Burris, 1982). Clarke (1988) found that first-graders who were encouraged to use invented spelling wrote more on their own and wrote longer pieces than first-graders who were encouraged to use standard spelling. Also, by the 1980s no textbook treatment of literacy development and pedagogy was complete without a discussion of invented spelling, usually using Gentry's (1978) stages and echoing the instructional implications that Paul (1976) had addressed.

Finally, Paul confirmed inventive spellers' conscious work with phonemes (i.e., their phonemic awareness, although she did not call it that), and she recognized the connection between their writing and reading development: "[Invented spelling] involves children in listening carefully and thinking about sounds in a very purposeful way. . . . [A]llowing children to write on their own in the early stages encourages active involvement and careful thinking about spelling which they spontaneously refine as their reading knowledge grows" (p. 200).

Adams and the Decade of Phonemic Awareness

Paul (1976) was typical of early writing about invented spelling in this describing phonemic awareness without identifying it as such. The era of fixation on phonemic awareness in nearly all things to do with early literacy would not be until after Adams's (1990) thorough and authoritative review of research pertaining to early reading. That review opened everyone's eyes to the link between phonemic awareness and learning to read. Adams wrote:

Faced with an alphabetic script, the child's level of phonemic awareness on entering school may be the single most powerful determinant of the success she or he will experience in learning to read and of the likelihood that she or he will fail. Measures of preschoolers' level of phonemic awareness strongly predict their future success in learning to read, and this has been demonstrated not only for English, but also for Swedish, Spanish, French, Italian, and Russian. . . . [Phonemic awareness] may be the most important core and causal factor separating normal and disabled readers. (pp. 304–305)

It is no wonder that Adams's book initiated the decade of phonemic awareness! But Adams had not overlooked the connection between phonemic awareness and invented spelling. What is important, she wrote, is "conscious, analytic knowledge . . . the awareness that [phonemes] exist as abstractable and manipulable components of the language" (p. 65). "The development of phonemic awareness seems to depend on finding oneself in a situation in which phonemic awareness is inescapably required" (p. 305). Everyday use of spoken language provides no such situations, but invented spelling does:

[T]he process of inventing spellings is essentially a process of phonics. Not surprisingly, then, the phonetic appropriateness of prereaders' invented spellings is found to be predicted by their level of phonemic awareness and to predict their later success in learning to read words.
The evidence that invented spelling activity simultaneously develops phonemic awareness and promotes understanding of the alphabetic principle is extremely promising, especially in view of the difficulty with which children are found to acquire these insights through other methods of teaching. (p. 387)

Adams relied on several studies (e.g., Clarke, 1988; Ehri, 1989; Mann, Tobin, & Wilson, 1987; Treiman, 1985, 1987) from the 1980s that confirmed what Read (1971) had demonstrated, that "the practice of inventing spellings was coupled with impressive awareness of and attention to the phonemic structure of words" (Adams, 1990, p. 387).

Invented Spelling as Assessment

Mann et al. (1987) is indicative of two trends in the 1980s: (1) the reaffirming of invented spelling's instantiation of the connections between spoken language and writ-

ten language and between writing and reading; (2) the bringing of invented spelling into the assessment arena. Mann et al. (1987) found relations between kindergartners' invented spelling ability and both their recognizing common initial phonemes in spoken word pairs and their first-grade word reading achievement as measured by the word identification and word attack subtests of the Woodcock Reading Mastery Tests (Woodcock, 1973). They measured invented spelling ability with a 14-item test scored for phonological accuracy.

Other invented spelling tests appearing at this time were used for similar purposes (e.g., Liberman, Rubin, Duques, & Carlisle, 1985; Morris & Perney, 1984; Richgels, 1986). Invented spelling measures began to be included in early literacy batteries and in kindergarten screenings. Ferroli and Shanahan (1987) wrote that an invented spelling test administered in March and May of kindergarten and then in May of first grade "offers reading prediction that is comparable to that of standardized reading readiness tests . . . [and] is an informal measure that can be used frequently to monitor progress" (p. 97). This represented a playing out of earlier assumptions that invented spelling would be a useful indicator to teachers of children's literacy development. Both Read (1971) and Paul (1976) had intimated as much, and Gentry (1978) had made it explicit: "It is essential for teachers to recognize the various stages that are a part of early development. A primary teacher should be able to identify five strategies that are frequently observed in the spelling of kindergartners, first-, and second-graders" (p. 90). In addition to invented spelling and word reading tests, Ferroli and Shanahan (1987) had administered concept of word, letter production, and phonemic awareness measures. Phonemic awareness explained 44% of the variance in invented spelling scores in May of kindergarten.

The Reading–Writing Connection

Invented spelling's connection to phonemic awareness is a connection between spoken language and written language that is fundamental to the constructs of both whole language (Goodman, 1986) and emergent literacy (Teale, 1987). Mann et al. (1987) and Ferroli and Shanahan (1987) are representative of studies that point to another connection involving invented spelling, that between writing and reading. Tierney and Pearson's (1983) description of a reading–writing connection revolutionized literacy curricula at all grade levels. Their work and others' since (e.g., McGinley & Tierney, 1989), however, emphasized processes used by mature readers and writers. Read's (1971) earlier discovery of invented spelling had already grounded the reading–writing connection in children's early, preconventional literacy work.

Shanahan (1980) addressed the potential of this connection when he speculated that "allowing students to invent spelling patterns does not reduce spelling achievement . . . but it might stimulate word recognition development" (p. 364). Ferroli and Shanahan (1987) demonstrated that the relation works in two directions. By May of first grade, after 1 year of formal reading instruction, reading achievement for the first time appeared in a regression equation, so that 50% of the variance in their subjects' invented spelling scores was explained by a combination of word-reading performance (beta weight of .52) and phonemic awareness (beta weight of .32). This is not surprising, considering that the movement from phonetic to transitional spelling (Gentry's, 1978, third and fourth stages) involves the appearance of nonphonetic, visual strategies, such as using silent letters and double consonants. These strategies are most likely a result of increased experience reading conventionally spelled text, such as the text in books.

Thus, by the late 1980s and early 1990s, invented spelling was in the thick of research about both writing and word reading. In a series of experimental studies, Ehri and her colleagues established some causal links in the early reading–writing connection (Ehri, 1987, 1989; Ehri & Robbins, 1992; Ehri & Wilce, 1985, 1987; Scott & Ehri, 1990).

Ehri and Wilce (1987) trained alphabet-knowledgeable nonspellers to spell phonetically simplified words and word parts. These subjects then learned to read similar-sounding phonetically simplified words more easily than did control subjects. Ehri and Wilce demonstrated that the success of spelling-trained subjects was due to their having acquired an understanding of the role of phonetic cues in written language. Earlier, Ehri and Wilce (1985) had explained, "If beginners can do this [spell inventively], then they ought to be able to use their letter knowledge to recognize and remember relations between boundary letters in spelling and sounds in pronunciations and in this way commence learning to read words" (p. 165).

Ehri's and her colleagues' experiments involved direct, outside-the-classroom training. Nevertheless, recognizing the different demands of controlled experiments and real-life classrooms, they cited Shanahan's (1980) and my (Richgels, 1987) recommendations for using invented spelling in classroom literacy instruction (Ehri & Wilce, 1987; Scott & Ehri, 1990).

Direct or Holistic Instruction?

The issue of direct instruction versus holistic classroom practices heated up as the decade of phonemic awareness (post-Adams, 1990) wore on. The question was whether or not ensuring phonemic awareness for all children requires that phonemic awareness training occur in isolation. Or, to pose the question more positively, does encouraging and supporting invented spelling in the contextualized, holistic ways that its proponents have advocated since Paul (1976) constitute in itself the best phonemic awareness training?

The Matthew Effect Argument

In-classroom phonemic awareness training described in the professional literature of the 1990s frequently involves direct instruction, even when it sometimes is part of a larger program or research design involving invented spelling (e.g., Ball & Blachman, 1991; Griffith & Olson, 1992; Tangel & Blachman, 1992; Yopp, 1992). Tangel and Blachman (1992) trained kindergartners in their classrooms in phonemic awareness using say-it-and-move-it phoneme segmentation activities in which children moved small tokens (at first blank and later inscribed with letters) as they pronounced the phonemes in one-, two-, and three-phoneme words, and segmentation-related games in which they categorized pictured words using rhyme or alliteration. These children performed better on a five-item invented spelling test designed by the researchers than did control subjects.

Ball and Blachman (1991) and Tangel and Blachman (1992, 1995) emphasize that their populations of kindergartners differ from those in many other invented spelling studies in that they come from low-income, inner-city schools and they have very little or no alphabet knowledge. These researchers suggest that their subjects lack the luxury of picking up alphabet knowledge and phonemic awareness from more indirect instruction before being caught in what Stanovich (1986)—in his describing the Matthew effect—calls "a causal chain of escalating negative side effects" (p. 364, quoted in Ball & Blachman, 1991). Still, Tangel and Blachman (1992) acknowledge that "[a]lthough in this study we have explored the influence of phoneme awareness on invented spelling, it is also likely that children who have repeated opportunities to invent spellings will enhance their phonemic awareness in the process" (p. 255).

It seems that as the 1990s have come and gone, many who recommend classroom practice have come to believe that concern for phonemic awareness requires direct instruction with isolated word sounds, at least for a large portion of the preschool and primary-grade population (e.g., Busink, 1997; Eldredge & Baird, 1996; Herrera, Logan, Cooker, Morris, & Lyman, 1997; Honig, 1997; Spector, 1995). This is so despite contrary recommendations concerning developmentally appropriate practice from the International Reading Association and the National Association for the Education of Young Children (1998).

A one-size-fits-all, direct-instruction approach to teaching phonemic awareness may reflect what has happened in phonemic awareness research. McGee (McGee & Purcell-Gates, 1997) observed, "Despite our intuitive and even research-based knowledge that adjusting instruction to children's understandings works best, one large body of research in emergent literacy, that which examines the effects of phonemic awareness instruction on literacy acquisition, for the most part does not vary instruction to meet the differing knowledges of individual children" (p. 312).

An Argument for Contextualized and Functional Literacy Instruction

McGee cited, as an exception to this observation, my (Richgels, 1995) replication of Ehri and Wilce's (1987) study of the invented-spelling–word-reading connection. Where Ehri and Wilce had trained inventive spellers with direct, outside-the-classroom instruction, I used non-word-reading inventive spellers who had emerged in holistic classroom settings. Good inventive spellers learned to read phonetically simplified words better than did poor inventive spellers. I argued the following:

Phoneme awareness, invented spelling, and word reading comprise only a single, albeit a very significant, piece of the larger picture of children's developing literacy knowledge and competence. . . . Fostering insights in all [areas of written language knowledge] is an important consideration when planning the best instruction for young readers and writers, including the best mix of direct and incidental instruction. . . .

Children need opportunities to discover phoneme–grapheme correspondences on their own *and* to see teachers demonstrate and highlight them (as teachers in this study's classrooms did). This does not mean, however, that every child will respond in the same way to such opportunities. Even the best planned support will be received differently by different children. . . .

If a teacher's demonstrating and highlighting are sufficiently holistic, that is, embedded in meaningful, social-communicative contexts, then it is possible for children to apply a single teaching event to varying individual problems they are on the verge of solving. (Richgels, 1995, pp. 107–108)

My current work is with a large data set acquired as a participant–observer for one school year in an exemplary kindergarten classroom. My goal is to provide rich descriptions of the contextualized, purposeful "demonstrating and highlighting" about which I speculated in the paragraphs just quoted. One such description (Richgels, Poremba, & McGee, 1996) is of a literacy routine involving holistic phoneme awareness instruction in which invented spelling is one part, for some children, of their clipboard writing in response to shared reading and shared writing (Fountas & Pinnell, 1996; Holdaway, 1979; Pinnell & Fountas, 1998).

I have emphasized the value of functional and contextualized experiences with written language. Functional experiences serve real purposes in children's everyday home and classroom lives. Contextualized experiences involve whole texts. Teachers and children may focus for a short time on words and letters and sounds, but the words are chosen during a class's reading of a big book, their preparing to do a choral reading of a displayed poem, or their composing together a fact list during a science or social studies discussion.

> The fact that some [children] may need additional help in the form of direct instruction does not justify depriving them of functional, contextualized literacy experiences. Those experiences benefit all children in ways besides their promoting phonemic awareness. They also, for example, demonstrate the functions of written language, foster the message concept, and provide enjoyment of literature. And functional, contextualized literacy experiences provide a context for practice, application, and strengthening of phonemic awareness skills that some children may need to acquire in other, direct-instruction activities.
>
> Nor does the fact that some kindergartners need additional help in the form of scripted, direct instruction justify subjecting all children to such instruction. Much of direct instruction is so divorced from actual reading and writing of authentic texts for real purposes as to be counterproductive for those students who already have phonemic awareness, or are on their way to acquiring it in other, more functional and contextualized ways. (McGee & Richgels, 2000, p. 212)

In October and April, Winsor and Pearson (1992) measured phonemic awareness and reading and writing abilities of first-grade children identified as at risk. They found that instruction that included invented spelling and repeated readings of predictable texts contributed to their at-risk students' acquiring phonemic awareness.

Dahl, Scharer, Lawson, and Grogan (1999) documented phonics instruction, including what I would call contextualized and functional phonemic awareness instruction, and what I believe McGee (McGee & Purcell-Gates, 1997) would call instruction varied to meet the different literacy-knowledge profiles of individual children, in eight first-grade classrooms whose whole language designation was independently verified. Among their findings were that "[w]riting experiences served as an essential context for developing phonics knowledge" (p. 328); that "[i]nstruction was tailor-made developmentally for learners in individual reading and writing conferences, and a substantial portion of phonics instruction was conducted one at a time" (p. 330); but, at the same time, that "[d]ifferentiated teacher actions supported individual children's participation in whole-group reading and writing activities" (p. 330).

Especially significant was a finding by Dahl et al. (1999) that, to my mind, begins to address the Matthew effect concern that less literacy-experienced and literacy-knowledgeable students not be allowed to fall farther behind their more experienced, more knowledgeable classmates. That did not happen in the first grades Dahl et al. studied, though phonemic awareness instruction and other phonics instruction was not direct, one-size-fits-all.

For data analysis, Dahl et al. (1999) divided their 178 first-grade subjects into three groups. The 123 students in group 1 had high October pretest scores (27 or more out of a possible 37) on a encoding-in-context measure (Clay's [1993] Hearing and Recording Sounds in Words, a kind of invented spelling test in which the subject writes two dictated sentences and is given credit for correct spellings of phonemes even when the whole word in which a phoneme occurs is not correctly spelled); the 42 students in group 2 had scores ranging from 15 to 26; and the 13 students in group 3 had scores below 15. Students also took this test in May, and they took pre- and posttests of decoding in context (Clay's (1993), Text Reading Level), encoding in isolation (Ganske's (1993), Developmental Spelling Analysis), and decoding in isolation (Leslie & Caldwell's (1995), Qualitative Reading Inventory—II Word List). Scores representing composites of the four measures yielded statistically equivalent pre- to posttest gains for Groups 1 and 3; Group 2's gain score was statistically significantly higher than those of Groups 1 and 3. Progress from pre- to posttest in Text Reading Level was from grade 1 to grade 5 for group 1, from preprimer 1 to grade 1 for group 2, and from below preprimer to preprimer 1 for group 3.

Future Directions

In this chapter, I have attempted to tell the story of Read's (1971) long-lasting, substantive, positive influence on literacy research and instruction. It is my hope that Dahl et al. (1999), by their findings and by the example of their methodology, will have the same influence. Future invented spelling research and pedagogy will be most productive when it strives to honor the legacy of Read's (1971, 1975) original work. A goal of future early literacy research should be to continue exploring both the invented-spelling–phonemic-awareness connection and the invented-spelling–word-reading connection but, more often than has been the case so far, in existing classroom contexts, such as those that Dahl et al. (1999) found. Proposed instructional methodologies should show teachers not just how to tolerate invented spelling as a cute trick but rather how to encourage it as a significant indicator of children's conscious experimentation with the very fundamentals of how written language works.

References

Adams, M. J. (1990). *Beginning to read: Thinking and learning about print.* Cambridge, MA: MIT Press.

Ball, E. W., & Blachman, B. A. (1991). Does phoneme segmentation training in kindergarten make a difference in early word recognition and developmental spelling? *Reading Research Quarterly, 26,* 49–66.

Beers, J. W., & Henderson, E. H. (1977). A study of developing orthographic concepts among first grade children. *Research in the Teaching of English, 11,* 133–148.

Bissex, G. L. (1980). *GNYS AT WRK: A child learns to write and read.* Cambridge, MA: Harvard University Press.

Busink, R. (1997). Reading and phonological awareness: What we have learned and how we can use it. *Reading Research and Instruction, 36,* 199–215.

Chomsky, C. (1971). Invented spelling in the open classroom. *Word, 27,* 499–518.

Clarke, L. K. (1988). Invented versus traditional spelling in first graders' writings: Effects on learning to spell and read. *Research in the Teaching of English, 22,* 281–309.

Clay, M. (1993). *An observation survey of early literacy achievement.* Portsmouth, NH: Heinemann.

Dahl, K. L., Scharer, P. L., Lawson, L. L., & Grogan, P. R. (1999). Phonics instruction and student achievement in whole language first-grade classrooms. *Reading Research Quarterly, 34,* 312–341.

Downing, J. (1965). *The initial teaching alphabet: Explained and illustrated.* New York: Macmillan.

Ehri, L. C. (1987). Learning to spell and read words. *Journal of Reading Behavior, 19,* 5–31.

Ehri, L. C. (1989). Movement into word reading and spelling: How spelling contributes to reading. In J. M. Mason (Ed.), *Reading and writing connections* (pp. 65–81). Boston: Allyn & Bacon.

Ehri, L. C., & Robbins, C. (1992). Beginners need some decoding skill to read words by analogy. *Reading Research Quarterly, 27,* 12–26.

Ehri, L. C., & Wilce, L. S. (1985). Movement into reading: Is the first stage of printed word learning visual or phonetic? *Reading Research Quarterly, 20,* 163–179.

Ehri, L. C., & Wilce, L. S. (1987). Does learning to spell help beginners learn to read words? *Reading Research Quarterly, 22,* 47–65.

Eimas, P. D., Siqueland, E. R., Jusczyk, P., & Vigorito, J. (1971). Speech perception in infants. *Science, 171,* 303–306.

Eldredge, J. L., & Baird, J. E. (1996). Phonemic awareness training works better than whole language instruction for teaching first graders how to write. *Reading Research and Instruction, 35,* 193–208.

Ferroli, L., & Shanahan, T. (1987). Kindergarten spelling: Explaining its relationship to first-grade reading. In J. E. Readence & R. S. Baldwin (Eds.), *Research in literacy: Merging perspectives, Thirty-sixth yearbook of the National Reading Conference* (pp. 93–99). Rochester, NY: National Reading Conference.

Fountas, I. C., & Pinnell, G. S. (1996). *Guided reading: Good first teaching for all children.* Portsmouth, NH: Heinemann.

Ganske, K. (1993). *Developmental spelling analysis: A qualitative measure for assessment and instructional planning.* Charlottesville: University of Virginia.

Gentry, J. R. (1978). Early spelling strategies. *Elementary School Journal, 79,* 88–92.

Gentry, J. R. (1982). An analysis of developmental spelling in *GNYS AT WRK. The Reading Teacher, 36,* 192–200.

Goodman, K. (1986). *What's whole in whole language?* Portsmouth, NH: Heinemann.

Griffith, P. L., & Olson, M. W. (1992). Phonemic awareness helps beginning readers break the code. *The Reading Teacher, 45,* 516–523.

Herrera, J. A., Logan, C. H., Cooker, P. G., Morris, D. P., & Lyman, D. E. (1997). Phonological awareness and phonetic-graphic conversion: A study of the effects of two intervention paradigms with learning disabled children. Learning disability or learning difference? *Reading Improvement, 34,* 71–89.

Holdaway, D. (1979). *The foundations of literacy.* New York: Ashton Scholastic.

Honig, B. (1997). Reading the right way. *School Administrator, 54*(6), 6–15.

International Reading Association and National Association for the Education of Young Children (1998). Learning to read and write: Developmentally appropriate practices for young children. *The Reading Teacher, 52,* 193–216.

Leslie, L., & Caldwell, J. (1995). *Qualitative reading inventory—II.* New York: HarperCollins.

Liberman, I. Y., Rubin, H., Duques, S., & Carlisle, J. (1985). Linguistic abilities and spelling proficiency in kindergartners and adult poor readers. In D. Gray & J. Kavanagh (Eds.), *Biobehavioral measures of dyslexia* (pp. 163–176). Parkton, MD: York Press.

Mann, V., Tobin, P., & Wilson, R. (1987). Measuring phonological awareness through the invented spellings of kindergarten children. *Merrill-Palmer Quarterly, 33,* 365–391.

McGee, L. M., & Purcell-Gates, V. (1997). Conversations: So what's going on in research in emergent literacy? *Reading Research Quarterly, 32,* 310–318.

McGee, L. M., & Richgels, D. J. (2000). *Literacy's beginnings: Supporting young readers and writers, 3rd ed.* Needham Heights, MA: Allyn & Bacon.

McGinley, W., & Tierney, R. J. (1989). Traversing the topical landscape: Reading and writing as ways of knowing. *Written Communication, 6,* 243–269.

Morris, D., & Perney, J. (1984). Developmental spelling as a predictor of first-grade reading achievement. *The Elementary School Journal, 84,* 441–457.

Newman, J. (1984). *The craft of children's writing.* Portsmouth, NH: Heinemann.

Paul, R. (1976). Invented spelling in kindergarten. *Young Children, 31,* 195–200.

Pinnell, G. S., & Fountas, I. C. (1998). *Word matters: Teaching phonics and spelling in the reading/writing classroom.* Portsmouth, NH: Heinemann.

Read, C. (1971). Pre-school children's knowledge of English phonology. *Harvard Educational Review, 41,* 1–34.

Read, C. (1975). *Children's categorization of speech sounds in English.* Urbana, IL: National Council of Teachers of English.

Richgels, D. J. (1986). Beginning first graders' "invented spelling" ability and their performance in functional classroom writing activities. *Early Childhood Research Quarterly, 1,* 85–97.

Richgels, D. J. (1987). Experimental reading with invented spelling (ERIS): A preschool and kindergarten method. *The Reading Teacher, 40,* 522–529.

Richgels, D. J. (1995). Invented spelling ability and printed word learning in kindergarten. *Reading Research Quarterly, 30,* 96–109.

Richgels, D. J., Poremba, K. J., & McGee, L. M. (1996). Kindergartners talk about print: Phonemic awareness in meaningful contexts. *The Reading Teacher, 49,* 632–642.

Scott, J. A., & Ehri, L. C. (1990). Sight word reading in prereaders: Use of logographic vs. alphabetic access routes. *Journal of Reading Behavior, 22,* 149–166.

Shanahan, T. (1980). The impact of writing instruction on learning to read. *Reading World, 19,* 357–368.

Spector, J. E. (1995). Phonemic awareness training: Application of principles of direct instruction. *Reading and Writing Quarterly: Overcoming Learning Difficulties, 11,* 37–51.

Stanovich, K. E. (1986). Matthew effects in reading: Some consequences of individual differences in the acquisition of literacy. *Reading Research Quarterly, 21,* 360–407.

Tangel, D. M., & Blachman, B. A. (1992). Effect of phoneme awareness instruction on kindergarten children's invented spelling. *Journal of Reading Behavior, 24,* 233–261.

Tangel, D. M., & Blachman, B. A. (1995). Effect of phoneme awareness instruction on the invented spelling of first-grade children: A one-year follow-up study. *Journal of Reading Behavior, 27,* 153–185.

Teale, W. H. (1987). Emergent literacy: Reading and writing development in early childhood. In J. E. Readence & R. S. Baldwin (Eds.), *Research in literacy: Merging perspectives, Thirty-sixth yearbook of the National Reading Conference* (pp. 45–74). Rochester, NY: The National Reading Conference.

Temple, C. A., Nathan, R. G., & Burris, N. A. (1982). *The beginnings of writing.* Boston, MA: Allyn & Bacon.

Tierney, R. J., & Pearson, P. D. (1983). Toward a composing model of reading. *Language Arts, 60,* 568–580.

Treiman, R. (1985). Phonemic analysis, spelling, and reading. In T. H. Carr (Ed.), *New directions for child development: The development of reading skills* (pp. 5–18). San Francisco: Jossey-Bass.

Treiman, R. (1987). *Spelling in first grade children.* Paper presented at Midwestern Psychological Association, Chicago.

Winsor, P. J., & Pearson, P. D. (1992). *Children at risk: Their phonemic awareness development in holistic instruction.* Urbana, IL: Center for the

Study of Reading. (ERIC Document Reproduction Service No. ED 345 209)

Woodcock, R. W. (1973). *Woodcock reading mastery tests*. Circle Pines, MN: American Guidance Services.

Yopp, H. K. (1992). Developing phonemic awareness in young children. *The Reading Teacher, 45,* 696–703.

Zutell, J. (1976). Spelling strategies of preschool children and their relationships to the Piagetian concept of decentration. *Dissertation Abstracts International, 36,* 5030-A. (Doctoral dissertation, University of Virginia, 1975)

Zutell, J. (1978). Some psycholinguistic perspectives on children's spelling. *Language Arts, 55,* 844–850.

III

HOME AND
COMMUNITY INFLUENCES

12

Young Bilingual Children and Early Literacy Development

❖

PATTON O. TABORS
CATHERINE E. SNOW

Our goal in this chapter is to summarize what we know about the early literacy development of young bilingual[1] children in the United States. This is an extensive and complicated topic, and a field of investigation that has generated remarkably little systematic research. Although there has been considerable research on second-language acquisition among young children, there is much less research on early literacy acquisition of bilingual children. Clearly, however, this is an important topic, not only as a theoretical area of inquiry that can illuminate comparative processes of literacy acquisition but also as a topic of compelling practical urgency, as more and more bilingual children are entering school in the United States.[2] And their prospects for literacy achievement, based on the scores of bilingual children in U.S. schools today, are not as good as those of their monolingual English-speaking peers.[3] Knowledge about how young children acquire more than one language and about what effect bilingualism has when these children begin the learning-to-read process is critical for all educators in the present circumstances. A better understanding of the process of literacy acquisition for such children may lead to recommendations for parents about language use in the home, to expanded programmatic options in early childhood and early elementary school programs, and to improved practices to ensure optimal learning in each of these settings.

To arrive at some understandings of the important influences on the literacy acquisition process of young bilingual children, we think it is critical to examine their learning experiences, not only confronting formal reading instruction in the early grades but also prior to their entrance into kindergarten. We know from research on monolingual English speakers that the early childhood period constitutes a critical opportunity for young children to develop language and emergent literacy skills that constitute the foundation for more sophisticated literacy skills (Snow & Tabors, 1993). In longitudinal analyses with a low-income, English-speaking population, the Home–School Study of Language and Literacy Development, for example, has shown that language input and support for literacy in the prekindergarten time period, at home and in preschool, is predictive of early literacy abilities in kindergarten, which in turn are highly predictive of skill in fourth-grade reading comprehension (Snow, Roach, Tabors, & Dickinson, 2001). Furthermore, we know that skills such as alphabet knowledge (Adams, 1990; Bruck, Genesee, & Caravolas, 1997; Ehri, 1997), phonological awareness (Adams & Bruck, 1993; Juel,

1988; Perfetti & Zhang, 1996), and understanding concepts of print (Clay, 1993; Downing, 1986) predict later literacy outcomes.

What happens to the development of these preliteracy and literacy-related language skills if a child is exposed to a second language during the early childhood period? Are young children capable of developing the full array of language skills in two languages simultaneously? How much exposure is required to ensure that their English level is comparable to that of monolingual speakers at school entry? Does the time needed to acquire English detract from attention to preliteracy skills for such children?

And what happens to the home language? When young children start to acquire a high-prestige societal language—as English is in this society—there is a real threat that they will, at the same time, suspend development in, or even begin to lose use of, their first language (Wong Fillmore, 1991a). Parents and children receive somewhat conflicting messages from educators and the media alike; one is that their home language is without value, irrelevant, or an impediment to learning English and, therefore, to school success, whereas another is that the home language, having been learned first, is robust, so all available learning efforts need to be directed to English. The sociopolitical context in the United States may result in the marginalization of the group to which the bilingual child belongs, leading to low expectations for learner success and failure to attend to maintenance of the first language. What impact does losing a first language have on literacy acquisition in that or another language?

In this chapter we discuss bilingual development in three periods: 0 to 3 years old, 3 to 5 years old, and 5 to 8 years old. We have selected a particular focus for each period in order to pinpoint major themes and organize the available research. Throughout the chapter we raise questions that still need to be addressed in the future by research on the literacy development of young bilingual children. To simplify an already complex topic, we concentrate on discussing the possible range of experiences that bilingual children born in or brought to the United States at a young age might have. Of course,

we recognize that bilingual children can and do, in fact, arrive in a second-language community at any time in their lives and start the second-language learning process at any age, inevitably making their experiences different in many ways from the children who will be the focus of this chapter (see Collier & Thomas, 1989, for achievement based on age of arrival; see Valdés, 1998, for a study of middle-school students; see Faltis & Wolfe, 1999, for studies of secondary school students).

Zero to Three: Family and Community Language Environments for Bilingual Children

All normally developing children learn a first language in the context of social interaction within their family structure, beginning with the production of babbled syllables at about 6 months, moving on to stable sound sequences used somewhat predictably for communication around 1 year of age, and continuing with the rapid acquisition of words and grammar throughout the early childhood period. For children to be considered native speakers of a particular language, they must have age-appropriate control over all aspects of the language system, including phonology, grammar, vocabulary, discourse, and pragmatics. Developing control of the linguistic system of their native language is a major undertaking of the early childhood period for all children.

Children who develop these skills in a second language as well as a first can be considered bilingual from the time they are exposed to a second language—even before they begin to use the language themselves. For some children this exposure to two languages begins at birth or occurs in infancy or toddlerhood (ages 0–3). Table 12.1 outlines the complexities of the types of language environments that very young bilingual children may be exposed to and the possible results of that exposure.

Table 12.1 details four different bilingual environments. The first column refers to an environment in which the home language is used, but the home is situated in the English-language society of the United States. Reading down this column, we see that the

TABLE 12.1. Family and Community Language Environments for Bilingual Children 0–3 Years Old

Bilingual exposure	I: Home language in English-language society	II: Home language in English-language community	III: Bilingual home in bilingual community	IV: Bilingual home in English-language community
Family members/ caretakers language use	L1	L1	L1 and English	L1 and English
Community language use	L1 (English)	English	L1 and English	English
What happens?	Child acquires L1; (may acquire some English)	Child acquires L1; may acquire some English	Child acquires L1 and English	Child acquires L1 and English; may begin to lose L1
Language outcomes in L1	Strong development of L1	Strong development of L1	Range of development in L1	Range of development in L1
Bilingual status	Monolingual in L1; (incipient bilingual)	Incipient bilingual	Emergent bilingual	At-risk bilingual

Note. L1, any first language other than English.

defining features of this environment are that family members use the home language exclusively with the child in the context of a community which also uses that language. However, English (as indicated by its parenthetical inclusion under community) is a powerful influence in the United States, particularly through the medium of television and other aspects of the popular culture of the country. It cannot, therefore, be assumed that the child's language exposure excludes English.[4] Although the language outcomes and bilingual status of a child raised in this environment point to the child being *monolingual* in the home language, the societal influence of English continues to be taken into account in the parenthetical comments under "what happens?" and "bilingual status."

In the second column, the environment at home is similar to that in the first column, but community context is more predominantly English speaking. This situation pertains to families that immigrate to neighborhoods in which there is no established community of speakers of their home language, or families that choose to live in English-speaking communities. In this case, the child can be considered an *incipient bilingual* at this time, with grounding in the linguistic system used at home but a good chance of some knowledge of English

phonology and even vocabulary from community sources by the age of 3.

In neither of the cases just outlined, however, would the child be considered an active bilingual, and, not surprisingly, there is no specific research that targets this early period for children who are being raised as non-English monolinguals or incipient bilinguals in the United States. The assumption would be that their development would parallel and vary in much the same way that any monolingual child's would. The research that has been done at this age has focused, instead, on very young children who are being raised as active bilinguals.

Early bilingual exposure may occur for young children because different members of the household use different languages with the child (see Fantini, 1985; Saunders, 1988; and Taeschner, 1983, for case studies of children raised in the "one-parent, one-language" model), because one language is used by members of the household and another is used by caretakers inside or outside the home (see Hatch, 1978, for case studies of children raised in these circumstances), or because some or all the members of the household are themselves bilingual, using two languages regularly (see Zentella, 1997). In columns three and four in Table 12.1, we can see how these different bilingual environments may vary for very young children and the differences such variations may generate.

In column three, the environment outlined is one in which a child is being raised bilingually in a bilingual community and, therefore, can be expected to be an *emergent bilingual* with a range of abilities in the two languages. Research with this group of children has focused on questions related to the types of input that they receive and the effect of that input on their emergent bilingualism.

For children growing up in a bilingual household and neighborhood the possible combinations of exposure to and use of two (or more) languages (or dialects) are numerous. In looking at language use at home in a Puerto Rican neighborhood in New York City, for example, Zentella (1997) characterizes six major patterns of language use among the 20 families in her ethnographic study. These patterns consisted of different combinations of who spoke what language to whom, including families in which adults spoke Spanish with other adults but used both Spanish and English with their children; families in which adults used both Spanish and English with each other and their children but children answered in English; families in which adults used only Spanish in the household but children were too young to use any language yet; families in which adults used English with each other but the males used English and the mothers used Spanish and English with the children; and single mothers who were Spanish dominant, one of whom chose to speak Spanish to her children and another who used both Spanish and English. To add to the complications for the children in these homes, many of the adults in this community spoke what Zentella calls "Hispanized English," in which the phonology of Spanish has been transferred to English. In this situation, a young child's first task might well be to figure out that there are actually two languages present in the household, before beginning the process of differentiating and acquiring those two languages.

What do these different types of language use and exposure mean for very young bilingual children? In a study of children being raised bilingually in Miami, Pearson and her colleagues (Pearson & Fernández, 1994; Pearson, Fernández, Lewedeg, & Oller, 1997) not only accounted for the words the children knew in each of their languages but also tracked the amount of exposure the children had in their two languages between 8 and 30 months of age. Given the fluidity of the social aspects of bilingual exposure, it is not surprising that the children in this study experienced various amounts of input in their two languages at different times across this time span. Although all 24 families intended to use equal amounts of each language with their children, the exposure of almost all of the children was unbalanced (i.e., more in one language than the other) and/or varied (i.e., one that changed over time). The exposure patterns were related to numbers of words learned in each language at different times during the study, with a lag of about 2 months between a change in the amounts of exposure and a change in vocabulary composition.

Figure 12.1 graphically displays the effect of the change in one child's language environment. In this case the child experienced a Spanish-dominant (70%) environment until 20 months of age, at which time Spanish input fell to between 40 and 50% for the remainder of the study. At the time of the change, the child's vocabulary in Spanish (SV) was well advanced over English vocabulary (EV). However, when the language environment changed, the child's Spanish word learning plateaued and the child's English vocabulary surged. It would appear that the child was acquiring English words for already known words in Spanish; the total vocabulary (TV; Spanish and English words added together) showed a marked increase after the environmental change, but total conceptual vocabulary (TCV; the number of concepts for which the child had a lexical representation) increased more slowly. Of course, this exposure pattern is only one of many that any one child being raised bilingually might experience before the age of 3.

Returning to Table 12.1, the final column represents a bilingual home situation similar to that of the child in column three but embedded in a community, including any out-of-home care for the toddler and educational settings of older siblings, which is predominantly English speaking. In this situation the child may be an *at-risk bilingual*. In these circumstances children often choose

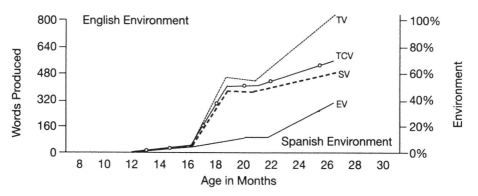

FIGURE 12.1. The effect of change in a young bilingual child's language environment. From Pearson and Fernández (1994). Copyright 1994 by Blackwell Publishers. Reprinted by permission.

to maintain receptive abilities in the non-English language but to develop productive use of only one language—English. Once children discover that most significant others in their life also understand or speak the societal language, they often shift rapidly, even at this young age, to operating in a single language. Wong Fillmore (1991b) writes about Mei-Mei, a young Chinese girl who arrived in the United States from Beijing when she was 3 years old. She and her mother had come to join her father who was already in the United States as a student. Over the period of a year, during which Mei-Mei attended an English-language preschool, she began answering in English when addressed in Chinese and then began not to understand what was being said to her in Chinese. When her father asked her to speak Chinese, she would say, "Papa, I can't say it in Chinese. Can I say it in English? English is easier." Sometimes this shift occurs not because the children have made the decision to use only English but because the adults in the family have decided that they need to speak English, even if it is not their stronger language, in order to "help" their children be successful in school (Evans, 1994; Rodriguez, 1983).

By age 3, then, young bilingual children can have already been exposed to a number of home and community factors that will have had an effect on their bilingual language proficiency. A child's bilingual status may fall anywhere along the spectrum from monolingualism in the home language to at risk for becoming monolingual in English. How does any of this relate to literacy development?

Given the link that research has established between language skills and literacy accomplishments (Snow, Burns, & Griffin, 1998), it is certainly of interest to know what linguistic capacity a child has developed, and in what language, by the age of 3. Children with a strong foundation in their home language and continuing support for that language through home activities such as book reading are developing skills that will transfer to English later. Children who are at-risk bilinguals, however, may also be at risk in acquiring English literacy; their parents may have insufficient proficiency in English to support high-level conversations and preliteracy activities in English but at the same time they may be so focused on English as the language of literacy that they fail to engage in such activities in the home language. This set of decisions leaves these children without the home support for language and literacy development that seems to be crucial in this early period as well as in the preschool period to follow (Dickinson & De Temple, 1998; Dickinson & Tabors, 2001). This means that the early language environment of young bilingual children, whether intentionally constructed by families or merely happenstance, will have an important impact on children's later language and literacy development.

Three to Five: Early Care and Education Settings

During the preschool period (ages 3–5), bilingual children may continue to be exposed to any combination of first language and/or bilingual environments at home and first language, bilingual, and/or English language environments outside the home. If they remain in at-home care, their language development will be most strongly influenced by the home-language environment and the language use patterns of caretakers, as it was in the 0–3 period. In this case, their development will most likely continue as outlined in Table 12.1.

However, this is often the time that children enter some type of out-of-home care for the first time; for bilingual children in the United States, this frequently means their first extensive exposure to an English-language environment. As there is no mandate for bilingual children to be served by bilingual programs at the prekindergarten level in the United States, it is unusual for them to be in a first-language or a bilingual classroom, although these types of settings do exist in some communities. Table 12.2 details the three main types of early childhood education classrooms that serve bilingual children, the defining features of each,

and the expected language outcomes for the children.

In a first-language classroom, as outlined in the first column, all interactions are conducted in the first (other-than-English) language, supporting the development of that language while developing conceptual knowledge in the first language of the children. Children who attend this type of classroom may be monolingual in the first language, or they may already be incipient or emergent bilinguals in the first language and English. In fact, some parents might seek out such a classroom because of concern about their children losing their home language. In this type of classroom, bilingual children will continue to develop their linguistic and, therefore, their preliteracy skills in their home language, maintaining the match between home support and the activities in the classroom.

An ethnographic study of a Spanish-language Head Start classroom serving 3-year-old monolingual and bilingual Spanish-speaking children (Tabors, Aceves,

TABLE 12.2. Early-Childhood-Education Settings for Bilingual Children 3–5 Years Old

Type of classroom	I: First-language classroom	II: Bilingual classroom	III: English-language classroom
Teachers	Native speakers of L1 (likely bilingual in L1 and English)	Bilingual in L1 and English *or* Native speaker of L1 paired with native speaker of English	Native speakers of English
Children	All native speakers of L1 *or* All bilingual speakers of L1 and English *or* Any combination of the above	All native speakers of L1 *or* All bilingual speakers of L1 and English *or* Any combination of L1 speakers, bilingual speakers, and English speakers	All native speakers of same L1 *or* All native speakers of different L1s *or* Any combination of native speakers of same or different L1s, bilingual speakers of same or different L1s and English, and English speakers
Language of interaction	All interaction in L1	Interaction split between L1 and English	All interaction in English (except between children with common L1s)
Language outcomes	Development of L1; no development of English	Maintenance or development of L1, while also developing English	Development of English; little or no maintenance or development of L1

Note. L1, any first language other than English.
From Tabors (1997, p. 4). Copyright 1997 by Brookes Publishing Co. Reprinted by permission.

Barttolomé, Páez, & Wolf, 2000) found that the teachers in the classroom felt strongly that they were in a position to work effectively with the children because they could use the language in which the children were most competent. Sara, the head teacher,

> explained that she had reached most of her social and language objectives for the children during the year precisely because she had been allowed to utilize Spanish. Sara reported that this group of bilingual children, in comparison to other groups she had worked with in the past, was much more verbal, confident, and independent. She attributed the children's quick progress to the use of Spanish in the classroom. (p. 431)

Alicia, the assistant teacher, similarly expressed her opinions about the benefits of Spanish-language use. She argued that second language learning would be greatly facilitated once the bilingual children had a strong home language foundation:

> [l]o importante es enseñar su primer idioma ... no van a tener problemas en aprender inglés—pero vamos a darle una buena base para que ellos sigan construyendo encima de su base. [*What is important is to teach them their native language ... they won't have problems learning English—but let's give them a good base on which to construct meaning.*] (p. 431)

What effect did this classroom have on the children's language proficiency? Unfortunately we do not have measures over time for these children. However, in receptive vocabulary testing at the end of the year in both languages (see Table 12.3), children who spoke only Spanish or Spanish and English at home scored better, on average, on the Spanish receptive vocabulary test (Test de Vocabulario en Imágenes Peabody [TVIP]; Dunn, Padilla, Lugo, & Dunn, 1986), than on the English receptive vocabulary test (Peabody Picture Vocabulary Test—Revised [PPVT-R]; Dunn & Dunn, 1981), indicating that Spanish was, indeed, the children's stronger language. Further, the children who were exposed to more English at home scored better, on average, on the English receptive vocabulary test than those whose families used Spanish alone, but the range of scores in English indicates widely differing abilities in English vocabulary among this group of children. A tentative conclusion from this study would be that the children's Spanish proficiency had been supported in this classroom, while their English proficiency depended on their exposure to English outside the classroom.

In a bilingual early education classroom, as outlined in column two of Table 12.2, children could be expected to have their home language supported at the same time that they are beginning to acquire English. The extent to which this happens may depend on the *actual* language use in the classroom setting, however. If the children's first language is used by the teachers only for management purposes rather than for curricular material, then they may well not increase either vocabulary or grammar skills in their first language in the classroom context. If the program has little curricular con-

TABLE 12.3. Standardized Scores for the Students in the Spanish-Language Classroom on the Spanish Receptive Vocabulary Test (TVIP) and the English Receptive Vocabulary Test (PPVT-R) by Language(s) Spoken at Home

	Number of children	Spanish vocabulary (TVIP) average score[a]	Spanish vocabulary (TVIP) range	English vocabulary (PPVT-R) average score[a]	English vocabulary (PPVT-R) range
Spanish	10	85.6	72–103	45.3	0–66
Spanish–English	5	93.2	86–102	61.2	0–91
English[b] (Spanish)	1	83	n.a.	85	n.a.

Note. A total of 16 children were tested. From Tabors, Aceves, Bartolomé, Páez, and Wolf (2000). Copyright 2000 by NHSA Dialog. Reprinted by permission.
[a]Standardized scores, normed on a population mean of 100.
[b]This child's mother spoke English and her father was bilingual in Spanish and English.
Source: Tabors, Aceves, Bartolomé, Páez, and Wolf (2000).

tent and if the children choose to spend most of their time within play groups where the first language is used, then their development in English may not be extensive. A well-balanced program that purposefully presents opportunities for children to be exposed to challenging levels in both languages is necessary if the maximum amount of language learning is to occur in both languages in a bilingual early care and education classroom.

In the comparative ethnographic study discussed previously (Tabors et al., 2000), children were also observed in a bilingual Spanish–English Head Start classroom, where Spanish was used by the teachers in communication with individual children or small groups but English was used as the language of circle time, book reading, and songs. In an interview Brenda, the head teacher, "stated that she strongly believed that children should have the choice of speaking their home language at school and that she supported the use of Spanish and English in her classroom. As she said in the interview, 'In my classroom everything is done in English and Spanish—this is how children learn' " (p. 422).

For analysis purposes it was useful to think of there being four groups of children in this classroom—a group of children from Spanish-speaking homes, a group of children from Spanish-dominant homes in which some English was spoken, a group of children from English-dominant homes in which some Spanish was spoken, and two

non-Spanish speakers, one from an English-speaking and one from a Vietnamese-speaking home. Table 12.4 displays the results of receptive vocabulary tests for the first three of these groups.[5]

The children who spoke Spanish at home and the children who were reported as using primarily Spanish with some English at home (Spanish–English) scored higher on the Spanish vocabulary test than did the children who were reported to speak mostly English at home with some Spanish (English–Spanish). The results of the English vocabulary test, not surprisingly, indicated that the children who were reported to speak mostly English at home with some Spanish did better than the other two groups. The fact that the children who were reported as speaking mostly English at home with some Spanish scored the lowest, as a group, on the Spanish receptive vocabulary test may reflect lack of focus on Spanish at home and/or insufficient support for development of Spanish in this particular bilingual preschool context.

In another study, Spanish-speaking children of Mexican descent who attended Spanish–English bilingual preschool classrooms were compared with a control group of similar children who did not attend preschool (Rodríguez, Díaz, Duran, & Espinosa, 1995). This study employed a repeated measures design, assessing receptive vocabulary, sentence comprehension, and story retelling in both languages at the beginning and end of the school year. The re-

TABLE 12.4. Standardized Scores for the Students in the Bilingual Classroom on the Spanish Receptive Vocabulary Test (TVIP) and the English Receptive Vocabulary Test (PPVT-R) by Language(s) Spoken at Home

Home language	Number of children	Spanish vocabulary (TVIP) average score[a]	Spanish vocabulary (TVIP) range	Number of children	English vocabulary (PPVT) average score[a]	English vocabulary (PPVT) range
Spanish	9[b]	85.1	59–98	8[c]	42.1	40–57
Spanish–English	3	86.3	77–98	2[d]	59.0	52–66
English–Spanish	3	70.7	63–77	3	66.3	63–73

Note. A total of 16 children were tested. From Tabors, Aceves, Bartolomé, Páez, and Wolf (2000). Copyright 2000 by *NHSA Dialog*. Reprinted by permission.
[a]Standardized scores, normed on a population mean of 100.
[b]One child did not pass the practice test.
[c]Two children did not pass the practice test.
[d]One child refused to be tested.

sults of this study indicated that the children in both groups (preschool and no preschool) increased their proficiency in Spanish, but the children in the bilingual preschool classrooms made greater gains in English. The authors of this study conclude that this faster rate of English development did not have a negative effect on the Spanish development of the children in the bilingual preschool classrooms. One reason for this conclusion might be that these children were growing up in a highly supportive Spanish-speaking community, so their language development in Spanish was being encouraged both inside and outside school at the same time that they were being exposed to greater amounts of English in the classroom.

The final type of early childhood classroom setting for bilingual children, presented in column three of Table 12.2, is an English-language classroom, by far the most typical experience for bilingual children in the United States. In this type of classroom the teachers communicate primarily in English, a practice that may be dictated by a number of factors: (1) it may be the only language that the teachers know, (2) the teachers may speak the first language of some or all of the children but feel it is more important for the children to begin to learn English, or (3) the teachers are working with children from a variety of first-language backgrounds and English is the "common" language for the classroom.

Research has shown that young children who are exposed to a second language in an out-of-home setting such as an English-language early-childhood classroom move through a specific developmental sequence that includes the following four phases (Tabors, 1997):

1. *Home language use.* Children who come from a monolingual other-than-English home may continue to speak their home language with those who speak that language, but they may also continue to speak their home language with others who do not speak that language. They have not yet discovered that a new language is being used in the new setting. These children may take time to realize that the language they are hearing is, in fact, a different language from the one they hear and use at home.

2. *Nonverbal period in the new language.* When children realize that their home language does not always work, they give up using it with those who do not understand it, but they do not stop communicating. Crying, whimpering, whining, pointing, and miming are all used as nonverbal requests during this period. These techniques are, of course, most effective with understanding adults. To become full members of the classroom, however, children need strategies for moving beyond the nonverbal period. Most children do this by using the nonverbal period to collect information: They watch and listen intently—spectating—and they talk to themselves—rehearsing—in preparation for using their new language. They also develop receptive understanding of the new language during this period.

3. *Telegraphic and formulaic language.* For most young bilingual children, breaking out of the nonverbal period means using a combination of telegraphic and formulaic language. Telegraphic language use includes naming people and objects, using the alphabet, and counting. Formulaic language use involves employing catch phrases for getting into and out of social situations (no, yes, uh oh, OK, hey!, mine, lookit, bye-bye, excuse me, I don't know). The use of these two types of language help children get into the flow of the activities in the classroom and begin to sound like members of the group.

4. *Productive use of the new language.* By combining formulaic phrases and the names of objects, young children begin the process of building their own unique sentences to describe their activities ("I do a ice cream"), their ideas ("I got a big"), or their needs ("I want a playdough"). Because they are no longer adopting whole phrases ("Hey, what's going on here?"), it may seem that their language ability has actually decreased; children make many more mistakes ("me's doctor") as they take on the process of figuring out how English works.

This developmental sequence is cumulative and there are individual differences in children's rate of acquisition. As children progress, they move into new phases without giving up earlier ones, except for giving up the use of their home language with those who do not speak it. Researchers have identified at least four factors—motivation, exposure, age, and personality—that may have an impact on how quickly young children acquire a second language. Older children, children with greater exposure to English, children who have higher motivation to communicate in English, and/or those with more outgoing personalities may move more quickly through the developmental sequence.

We present here a transcript (Figure 12.2) that demonstrates how volatile a young second-language-learning child's control over his new language can be, at times seeming very sophisticated, and at other times very fragile, so that the child needs to fall back on nonverbal communication. This interaction involved the first author and Leandro, a Portuguese-speaking, 5-year-old boy who had arrived from Brazil just before the start of school in the fall. This interaction occurred in the spring while we were working on building a house out of plastic blocks.

In this transcript we can see that Leandro has control over some aspects of English but that there are also areas that are still being developed. Perhaps the most advanced aspect of Leandro's English acquisition, and the one that can not be assessed by reading this transcript, is his phonological skill. Other than being a bit singsong, Leandro's English pronunciation at this time was close to native-like, indicating that he had already developed considerable competence in the English phonological system. His pragmatic abilities were also quite advanced. He certainly knew how to carry on a conversation, how to ask for help, and how to ask for further information. In each of these cases, the pragmatic skills that he had developed first in Portuguese combined with English vocabulary items, made it possible for Leandro to navigate the conversational context in an appropriate fashion.

In this interaction Leandro demonstrates a basic level of vocabulary in English, but there are times in the transcript when he is close but gets it wrong ("I make them apart") and he even acquires a new vocabulary item—"corner"—during the course of the interaction. At the end of the transcript, he needs to fall back on nonverbal communication when he does not know the required item in English—"roof."

English grammar is another area with which Leandro is struggling. Phrases such as "I need help . . . to building a house," "cuz to we can see outside," "how we going to put it?" show that he does not have complete control over more complex syntactic forms. In other interactions Leandro used overgeneralized past tenses and a negative insert strategy ("you no my mommy") as he worked hard at making sense of the English syntactic system. The use of these problematic forms, along with his rudimentary vocabulary knowledge, did not often impair Leandro's obvious desire to communicate. However, if Leandro had been in a kindergarten or first-grade classroom where the expectation was that he would be beginning to read in English, his inconsistent grasp of English could well have made that task quite challenging.

How much English do bilingual children learn in an English-language classroom? In the comparative ethnographic study presented earlier (Tabors et al., 2000), an English-language Head Start classroom was also studied. In this classroom, both teachers spoke English exclusively, although there were also children from Spanish-speaking and Haitian Kreyol-speaking homes, as well as English-speaking children. Robert, the lead teacher in this classroom, stated in an interview that he felt that children learn English more quickly and easily when they are immersed in the language in the classroom. However, he was also careful to use many supportive techniques in his work with the bilingual children, using lots of gesture and context-embedded speech.

Table 12.5 displays the receptive vocabulary scores for the children in the English-language classroom. The scores for the Spanish-speaking children who had been in this supportive English-language classroom for a school year are similar to the scores of children in the Spanish-language and bilingual classrooms who came from homes in which English was used at least some of the time (see Tables 12.3 and 12.4). The children from Haitian Kreyol homes scored higher in English receptive vocabulary, on average, than the Spanish-speaking children, but both groups scored well below the English-speaking children in the classroom. These findings indicate that young children do not miraculously make gains in English simply by being placed in an English-speak-

L: I need help.

P: OK. What do you need help with?

L: To, — to building a house.

P: Well, I have to start with a wall.

L: I make them apart.

P: You're making a what?

L: Part.

P: Apart? You're going to *take* them apart. OK. Let's see if we can get this door here.

L: How?

P: We have to go up to the top here . . . We need the . . . lintel (*pushing pieces around*).

L: And what is for that (*showing me a piece*)?

P: That's for the corners.

L: For the what?

P: Corner. To go around a corner.

L: Lot of windows . . .

P: You need a lot of windows?

L: The house has a lot of windows. (*pause*) I know what, why have windows.

P: Why?

L: Cuz to we can see outside.

P: That's true.

L: It's tru-u-u-e.

P: You couldn't see outside if you didn't have a window, right? (*pause*) Do you think it would be very dark inside, Leandro, without a window? I-it would be dark, wouldn't it?

L: Yeah . . . I think that window, window . . .

P: Is that one of these windows? One of these corner windows? Let me put it on the corner, huh?

L: Corner . . .

P: Can you get that one to go the right way?

L: Can you put it?

P: . . . There, you can do it. You just had to get those things lined up. (*pause*) Good. I think you got it . . .

L: The corner window.

P: Yeah . . .

L: Corner window. I didn't know it was a corner window. And we have to do it like that (*pointing to the picture*).

P: Really big?

L: Yeah.

P: We'll have the world's biggest house, huh?

L: Like—(*gesturing with his hands like a roof*).

P: You mean with a roof?

L: Yeah . . .

P: OK. That looks like it's going to be hard.

L: Yes. How we going to put it . . . ?

P: I don't know.

L: I think we're going to do it with windows.

P: OK. We'll have a solar roof.

FIGURE 12.2. "P" is Patton Tabors; "L" is Leandro, a 5-year-old Portuguese–English bilingual. From Tabors (1997). Copyright 1997 by Brookes Publishing Co. Reprinted by permission.

TABLE 12.5. Standardized Scores for the Students in the English-Language Classroom on the English Receptive Vocabulary Test (PPVT-R) by Language Spoken at Home

Home language	Number of children	English vocabulary (PPVT) average score[a]	English vocabulary (PPVT) range
Haitian Kreyol	4	75.5	50–100
Spanish	4	60.5	44–75
English	6	92.5	42–109

Note. At the time of the assessment, there were 17 children in the class. One child was absent and one refused to be tested. One child, a Haitian Kreyol speaker, was new to the classroom, spoke almost no English, and did not understand the test; therefore he could not be tested. From Tabors, Aceves, Bartolomé, Páez, and Wolf (2000). Copyright 2000 by *NHSA Dialog*. Reprinted by permission.
[a]Standardized scores, normed on a population mean of 100.

ing environment for part of each day. Once more, it would be important to know what other influences, at home and in the community, might be having an effect on these children's vocabulary acquisition.

What is the connection between the types of early care and education settings that bilingual children experience and their later literacy development? As foreshadowed in the discussion of the 0–3 period, the preschool period is important for the development, at home and in any out-of-home setting, of all the aspects of the linguistic system that will play a role in learning to read. It is during this period that monolingual children develop sound segmentation and rhyming abilities; expand their vocabularies by an estimated 6 to 10 new words a day; learn to use complex syntactic forms such as past, future, and conditional; and acquire discourse skills in such forms as narrative and explanations. What does all this mean for bilingual children?

If there has been continuity of language development in a child's first language throughout the early childhood period—either because the child has remained at home, has recently arrived in the United States, or has attended a first-language early-care setting—then we can predict that she will follow the course of acquisition outlined earlier for monolingual children with, perhaps, only minor modifications related to living in an English-speaking society. In fact, proponents of first language preschool classrooms (Wong Fillmore, 1991a) cite this as a major advantage for young children and advocate that these children then enter a bilingual program in which they will acquire literacy in their well-developed first

language, as they begin to acquire oral proficiency in English.

However, for children who have been in bilingual circumstances all along or for whom there has been a discontinuity—moving from a home language into a bilingual or monolingual English context—the 3–5 period may be more problematic in terms of developing precursor abilities for literacy. Let us take the example of vocabulary. Considerable evidence suggests that the size of a child's vocabulary—a good proxy for language knowledge in general—is heavily dependent on amount of total input for monolinguals (e.g., Hart & Risley, 1995; Huttenlocher, Haight, Bryk, Seltzer, & Lyons, 1991), and input per language for bilinguals (Pearson & Fernández, 1994; Pearson et al., 1997). For example, when the percentiles of vocabulary development of the 24 children in the Pearson study discussed earlier were collapsed across children over time and compared to a monolingual English-speaking sample (Pearson & Fernández, 1994), word learning *individually* in Spanish and English was well below the monolingual children's level in English, but the Total Vocabulary (Spanish and English added together) was greater than the monolinguals' word level. However, as Pearson (in press) cautions, "Practically speaking . . . the bilingual has a somewhat restricted vocabulary in each language, and this is something that educators of bilinguals need to take into consideration and work to expand for them."

The following conclusions can be drawn concerning vocabulary development of bilingual children: (1) variation in the amount of time devoted to each of a child's languages will be reflected in sophistication of knowledge of that language; (2) it is almost inevitable that a bilingual child for whom no planning of the language environment has occurred will be exposed to less input in a given language than a monolingual child, and thus will have a smaller vocabulary in each language during the preschool years; and (3) because vocabulary is an excellent predictor of reading skill, this limitation on a bilingual child's vocabulary skills, along with all the other linguistic skills the child will need, may well have implications for literacy outcomes once the child enters elementary school.

Further, there is certainly an assumption that some preliteracy skills, such as concepts of print, the alphabetic principle (if each language is alphabetic), rhyming, syntactic knowledge, and extended discourse abilities are transferable from one language to another (e.g., Nagy, McClure, & Mir, 1997). However, for these skills to be transferable, they must have been developed in the first place. And if there has been a discontinuity in language environment leading to truncated development of these aspects of preliteracy development in the child's first language, there may be nothing to transfer to the new language, requiring that teachers begin again building these under-

standings in a language that a child, like Leandro, may not yet have under sufficient control to use in the service of literacy acquisition.

Five to Eight: Bilingualism/Biliteracy in the Early Elementary Grades

When bilingual children enter elementary school programs, again a plethora of programmatic options exists, with an array of possible outcomes depending on the language status of the child and the type of program that the child experiences. It is, of course, during this period that these children will be expected to begin the formal process of learning to read and write. Further complexities are introduced at this time, because decisions are made concerning *in what language or languages* literacy instruction will occur.

Table 12.6 illustrates some of the programmatic options that may exist for bilingual children in the early elementary grades and the possible outcomes of these programs in terms of language and literacy development. Of course, not all these options will necessarily be available in the community in which a bilingual child resides and, even if they are all available, there may be a

TABLE 12.6. Elementary School Programs for Bilingual Children 5–8 Years Old

Program type	I: First language program	II: Transitional bilingual education	III: Two-way bilingual education	IV: Mainstream classrooms with or without ESL support
Language use	L1	L1 and English	L1 and English	English only
Language outcomes in L1	Strong development	Continued development, at risk	Strong development	No development
Literacy outcomes in L1	Strong development	Emergent, at risk	Emergent	None
English language development	Minimal	Continued development	Strong development	Range of proficiencies
English literacy development	Minimal	Emergent	Emergent	Range of proficiencies
Bilingual language development	Incipient	English-dominant, at-risk bilingual	Range of bilingual proficiencies	English dominant, highly at-risk bilingual
Bilingual literacy development	Incipient	English dominant, at-risk biliterate	Range of biliterate proficiencies	None

Note. L1, any first language other than English.

variety of constraints on the placement decisions that parents and/or school systems make on behalf of a particular child.

As with programming at the preschool level, a first-language program, as outlined in the first column, is an option that does not exist in many communities. However, there are programs (even transitional bilingual programs) that look very much like first-language programs in the early grades. In these programs, first-language and literacy development is strongly supported and second language and literacy development, in this case in English, is delayed or only enters the program informally from societal influences. For example, Éxito Para Todos, the Spanish-language version of Success for All, introduces English literacy only after children have achieved a criterial level, approximately end-of-second-grade reading level, in Spanish literacy skills (Slavin & Madden, 1999). The purpose of this type of program is to establish literacy in the child's first—and presumably still stronger—language, before exposing him or her to literacy in the second language. Children participating in this type of program become literate in their first language as a result of literacy instruction but are only incipient biliterates in the early grades because they have not yet received literacy instruction in English. The major question in this type of program is when and how to introduce oral English and English literacy, and whether or not to continue literacy instruction in the first language after introduction of literacy in English.

In traditional transitional bilingual programs, outlined in column two of Table 12.6, the emphasis is on beginning bilingual children's schooling experience in their first language but moving as quickly as possible to exit the children into mainstream English-only classrooms. In this situation, an initial effort is often made to instruct children in reading and writing in their first—and presumably still stronger—language, but English literacy instruction may be introduced simultaneously, while the children are still in the early stages of acquiring oral English-language skills. Alternately, English literacy instruction may be postponed until children are deemed to be proficient enough in English. In transitional programs, literacy and all other instruction in the children's

first language is discontinued as early as possible, placing the children at risk both as biliterates and as bilinguals.

The following narrative, written by the first author after a follow-up kindergarten visit for one of the Spanish-speaking children who was a participant in the research study of the New England Quality Research Center on Head Start,[6] illustrates this point:

Although Pamela was originally assigned to the bilingual Spanish kindergarten, she was mainstreamed in January into Ms. Logan's class. When we interviewed Ms. Logan she mentioned that she had the children organized in homogeneous groups and that Pamela was in the top group, despite the fact that she had only arrived in the classroom in January. I asked how the decision to move Pamela had been made. She said that, as part of the "expanded English program" at the school, all of the bilingual children spent time in the mainstream classrooms for specialist activities and that Pamela had been coming to her class since the fall. The decision to move her had been made in conjunction with the bilingual teacher because Pamela was "eager" and "ready" to join the mainstream class. The only concern that Ms. Logan had was that Pamela had some difficulty with vocabulary on occasion, but, according to Ms. Logan, she was already reading. During the visit there was no mention of any support for Spanish in the classroom and no attempt to make the classroom a venue for multilingualism or multiculturalism. Apparently, being mainstreamed into this classroom meant never having to speak or read Spanish in school again.

In this situation, first-language literacy skills are placed at risk because these skills are still developing and require opportunities to be practiced and consolidated if reading is to become fluent and pleasurable. The risk to first-language skills derives in part from the lack of literacy as an ongoing stimulus to language development. Much of the more sophisticated vocabulary and more complex syntax that adult speakers of a language know comes from exposure to literacy in that language; after about third grade, oral language development derives from and depends on literacy.

The contrasting model to transitional bilingual education is two-way bilingual education, as detailed in column three, a model that includes two groups of children in the same classroom: English-speaking children and children from the same other-than-English-speaking background. In this model, instruction is delivered alternately in the two languages, so that half the time the children are hearing their stronger language and the other half they are in a second-language learning situation. In this model, literacy is developed in both languages simultaneously, resulting ideally in bilingualism and biliteracy for both groups of children. This type of program requires a group of English-speaking parents who are interested in their children becoming bilingual and biliterate in the other language being offered. Spanish is the most popular of these languages, but there are also two-way programs in the United States in Chinese, French, Korean, Japanese, Navaho, Arabic, Portuguese, and Russian (Center for Applied Linguistics, 1999). A recent evaluation of one of the longest-established programs, the Amigos program, a Spanish–English two way program in Cambridge, Massachusetts, reported the following:

> [T]he data from these analyses of 8 years of the Amigos program suggest that both the English-Amigos and Spanish-Amigos are moving toward a balanced state of skill in reading both English and Spanish and in using the two languages to solve math problems. The Spanish-Amigos have achieved remarkable proficiency in both English and Spanish. The English-Amigos have maintained high proficiency in English, and although their Spanish achievement may occasionally fall behind that of Spanish speakers, they are clearly achieving a high degree of Spanish proficiency. (Cazabon, Nicoladis, & Lambert, 2000, p. 25).

The final type of classroom setting for bilingual children is a mainstream English classroom, as shown in column four of Table 12.6. Again, as in the preschool period, this is the most common experience for bilingual children. Although bilingual education is mandated for children who speak a language that is well represented in a given school district, there are a variety of reasons why a bilingual child might be placed in a mainstream classroom, including the fact that the child speaks a language that is not well represented in the school district, that the child is designated by the school system as sufficiently proficient in English to be

mainstreamed, or the child's parents have requested that the child be placed in such a classroom. Often bilingual children who are placed in a mainstream classroom are also designated as needing special services from an English as a Second Language (ESL) program (see Ernst, 1994, for a discussion of an exemplary ESL program).

Bilingual children in a mainstream English classroom are faced with the task of learning to understand and speak English, and beginning simultaneously to learn to read and write English, without the benefit of academic instruction in their first language. In this situation, there is no possibility of children becoming literate in their first language in the schooling context, and they are clearly placed at risk for loss of their first language.

Several ethnographic studies have been done to look specifically at how young English-language-learning children respond to literacy instruction in kindergarten and first grade when they are still only beginning the process of developing oral language proficiency in English (Fitzgerald & Noblit, 1999; Weber & Longhi-Chirlin, 2000; Xu, 1996). These studies indicate that young emergent bilingual children can and do engage in a wide variety of literacy-related activities in English, such as developing concepts about print, naming and writing letters of the alphabet, and, in some cases, developing impressive sight word vocabularies. Difficulties arise, however, when more sophisticated linguistic knowledge is required of the children (e.g., when they are asked to demonstrate rhyming abilities but know only a few words with any rhyme-pattern in English or are asked to predict what an unknown word might be from a context they only partially understand). All these case studies suggest that the early accomplishments of the children seem almost language free—centered around recognizing sight words and decoding regular words but not focused on integrating comprehension into early reading processes. Even the children who made the most progress in these case studies did not seem to be taking meaning from the texts they were reading.[7] As Weber cautions, "The risk is that learners' interests in literacy may subside without the meaning of the texts to support their engagement" (p. 35). Further, it does not appear that any of the children in these studies used literacy as an entry point for further development of their oral English abilities, which continued to develop slowly in parallel, drawing primarily from the social context of the classrooms rather than the texts in the reading program.

In the various programmatic models outlined in Table 12.6 the question of what language to use for initial reading instruction is answered in different ways. In first-language, transitional, and two-way bilingual programs, the assumption typically is made that it is more advantageous to begin literacy instruction in the child's first language (though some two-way programs choose to introduce literacy to all children in both languages simultaneously, and others start with non-English literacy for all students, including English speakers). In mainstream classrooms, the assumption is that young bilingual children can catch up with monolingual English speakers and learn to read in English. Which of these assumptions is correct?

Bilingual education has traditionally been justified on the grounds that children should be taught to read in the language that they know best (Collier & Thomas, 1989). This claim rests on two parallel arguments: (1) that reading is a meaning-construction process, and thus it is more difficult, less motivating, and less authentic to learn to read words one does not know; and (2) that literacy skills acquired in a first language transfer rapidly once oral proficiency in the second language has been established. Both these claims may well be true. Nonetheless, we have only a relatively shallow understanding both of how meaning supports literacy development and of how literacy transfer occurs. Can young children read words they do not understand? Can they learn decoding with unknown words? What skills are transferable from a first to a second language? Under what programmatic circumstances? Does the nature of transfer differ with different pairs of languages? Are there age limits on transfer? At what level of first-language literacy does transfer occur? At what level of second-language proficiency?

The National Research Council report *Preventing Reading Difficulties in Young Children* (Snow et al., 1998) concluded that

teaching a child to read initially in a second, not yet proficient, language carried with it additional risk of reading problems. Thus, that report did not claim that such instruction would never work; clearly many children in many parts of the world have been successfully taught to read in a second language. Rather, the report concluded that an increment of risk to reading success was introduced for children learning to read initially in a language they did not know reasonably well. If children are to understand that reading is about accessing and constructing meaning, then learning to read in a language in which they cannot yet access meaning is inherently risky. If children are meant to understand and become fluent in applying the alphabetic principle, they should have a grasp of the phonemic distinctions represented graphemically in the target language. If they are meant to be accessing lexical items through processing print, they need to have both stable phonological representations and meanings of those lexical items stored for accessing. If they need lots of practice to become good readers, they need access to texts which are comprehensible and pleasurable, as they are unlikely to persist in reading texts they do not understand.

This general conclusion leaves open, though, many questions about how and when to introduce second-language reading. How early in the process of first-language literacy development is it risk free to introduce second-language reading? Does reaching higher levels of first-language reading facilitate more rapid acquisition of second-language reading? Are there methods of reading instruction that protect children against the risk of being taught literacy initially in a language in which they have low proficiency? How much proficiency in a language is needed to safely introduce initial literacy instruction in that language? How long can one wait for children to develop oral proficiency without disrupting literacy development by having postponed its initiation too long?

Additional questions about initial literacy instruction arise if we consider not the largest subgroup of other language speakers in the U.S., namely, Spanish speakers, but the many speakers of other, lower-incidence first languages which may differ more dramatically from English in orthography and in vocabulary, and which may differ as well in not being world languages, richly supplied with literacy materials, as Spanish is. Does it make sense, for instance, to teach a child to read first in Hmong or Haitian Kreyol? There are few literacy materials available in those languages, because writing systems for them have only been developed recently. Furthermore, the parents of children who speak these languages themselves are more likely to be literate, if at all, in Vietnamese or French, respectively. Children's books and initial reading materials are unavailable. Thus, the likelihood that high levels of literacy will be achieved is very low. So how can one best introduce literacy to child speakers of languages such as these?

Conclusion

The purpose of this chapter has been to develop a framework for detailing the complexities of the circumstances of young bilingual children in the United States from birth to age 8 and to look at some of the research that has been developed to illuminate these complexities, particularly in the area of literacy acquisition. Clearly, one of the strongest conclusions that can be reached at this point is that there are multiple pathways available to young bilingual children, pathways that are susceptible to a variety of influences, many of which may not be under the child's control or that of his or her parents or educators, but others for which research can inform the decision-making process. As we have seen, some of these pathways involve consistent support for a child's bilingualism and support for literacy acquisition in two languages. Other pathways, however, while leading to acquisition of English-language and literacy skills are, nonetheless, dead ends for bilingualism or bilteracy. Further, some of these pathways, for example, ones that involve parents switching to English when it is not their stronger language or children attending an English language preschool before their first language is well developed, may even make it more difficult for bilingual children to develop high levels of achievement in literacy in English in the long run. However, many

questions remain in each of these areas, particularly related to the factors that may make a difference in each of these situations.

Given that there are many questions still remaining to be answered by research, what can educators do in the meantime in developing programs for young bilingual children?

First, it would clearly be useful if educators would encourage parents to maintain their first language at home and use it—if they are comfortable doing so—for literacy activities (see Nord, Lennon, Liu, & Chandler, 1999, for information about Hispanic and non-English speaking families' lower incidence of literacy activities at home) as well as everyday conversation throughout the early childhood period (see Tabors, 1997, Chapter 8, for suggestions for talking with parents). Educators know how important early-childhood interactions are but may not understand that it is the quality of the interaction, not the language that it is carried on in, that is the critical factor.

Second, educators need to find out much more about the language and literacy background of the bilingual children with whom they are working. Detailed language histories could reveal just what types of language exposure a child has had since birth. Asking some simple questions about home literacy experiences and the language associated with them (e.g., the Home Language and Literacy Exposure Index; Páez, De Temple, & Snow, 2000) could provide further critical information.

Finally, educators need to have creative ways of assessing young bilingual children's abilities. Knowing what a child knows—and in what language—is necessary before any informed placement or program decisions can be made. Often, however, assessment—if it occurs at all—only occurs in English, providing no information about possible early literacy strengths that have been developed in the child's first language. Unfortunately, assessment tools for young bilingual children that take into account their abilities in both languages are only just beginning to become available (Muñoz-Sandoval, Cummins, Alvarado, & Ruef, 1998) or are still being developed (Iglesias, Peña, Gutierrez-Clellen, Bedore, & Goldstein, 1999), but more informal methods can be used in lieu of normed tests. The crucial point is that young bilingual children, when confronted with the task of learning to read in either or both of the languages to which they have been exposed, will have skills to bring to the process. Educators need to know what those skills are and how to take advantage of them, so that the process of literacy acquisition can be optimized for all young bilingual children.

Acknowledgment

Some of the material in this chapter was presented by Parton O. Tabors in an invited address, "Becoming (and staying) bilingual in early childhood," for the Early Childhood Special Interest Group at the Meetings of the National Association of Bilingual Educators, Dallas, TX, February 26, 1998.

Notes

1. The term "bilingual" in this chapter is used in the most general sense possible, that is, to refer to individuals who have been exposed to at least two languages, no matter what their level of proficiency in the languages.
2. In the 1990 Census, about 14% of the total student population of the United States were reported to live in a home in which a language other than English was spoken. Clearly, not all these students could be considered limited English proficient (LEP), however, as estimates of the number of English-language learners in schools at this time ranged from 2.0 to 3.3 million depending on the estimation methods used (Hopstock & Bucaro, 1993). In the 1992–1993 school year, it was reported that around 8% of kindergarten, first-, and second-graders were LEP; the percentages declined throughout the grades to 3.2% in 12th grade (Fleischman & Hopstock, 1993). California had the largest percentage of LEP students (42%) followed by Texas and New York. Nearly three-quarters of these students came from Spanish-speaking backgrounds, but schools were given federal support in the form of Title VII funding for students from 198 different language groups in the early 1990s.
3. National Assessment of Educational Progress (NAEP) results suggest that Hispanic children (of whom some large, but undetermined, percentage are immigrants and/or LEP) score well below Anglo children in reading (Campbell, Hombo, & Hazzeo, 2000). For example, in the most recent NAEP, 64% of Hispanic students were reading below the basic level in fourth grade. States with higher than average numbers of immigrant children also perform poorly on the NAEP and schools with higher than average number of immigrant children, many of whom are bilingual, score poorly within their districts.
4. We focus here on English-language learners in the United States, but it is worth noting that precisely the same impact of the environmental language has been observed in countries with less "powerful" societal languages, such as The Netherlands (e.g., Vedder, Kook, & Muysken, 1996).
5. The English-speaking and Vietnamese-speaking child were not included in this testing.
6. The New England Quality Research Center on Head Start (NEQRC) is directed by David K. Dickinson of the Education Development Center, Newton, Massachusetts. The research consortium also includes the Harvard Graduate School of Education (Catherine E. Snow, Principal Investigator), Boston College (Martha Bronson, Principal Investigator), and the Massachusetts Society for the Prevention of Cruelty to Children (David Robinson, Principal Investigator). Head Start research partners include Community Teamwork, Inc. (CTI) Head Start in Lowell, MA, Cambridge Head Start (CHS) in Cambridge, MA, the Community Action Programs in the Inner City (CAPIC) Head Start in Chelsea, MA, Communities United, Inc. (CUI) Head Start in Waltham, MA, and Action for Boston Community Development, Inc. (ABCD) Head Start in Boston, Massachusetts.
7. These observational findings are echoed by results from large-scale quantitative analyses of bilingual children carried out in both Denmark and in The Netherlands, where initial literacy instruction for all children occurs entirely in Danish or Dutch, respectively. In the middle elementary grades, children of immigrant families scored very well on tests of word reading, but well below monolingual comparison groups on measures of comprehension and of vocabulary knowledge (Aarts & Verhoeven, 1999; Appel & Vermeer, 1998; Neilson, 1997, 1998; Verhoeven, 1987).

References

Aarts, R., & Verhoeven, L. (1999). Literacy attainment in a second language submersion context. *Applied Psycholinguistics, 20,* 377–394.

Adams, M. (1990). *Beginning to read: Thinking and learning about print.* Cambridge, MA: MIT Press.

Adams, M., & Bruck, M. (1993). Word recognition: The interface of educational policies and scientific research. *Reading and Writing, 5,* 113–139.

Appel, R., & Vermeer, A. (1998). Speeding up second language vocabulary acquisition of minority children. *Language and Education, 12,* 159–173.

Bruck, M., Genesee, F., & Caravolas, M. (1997). A cross-linguistic study of early literacy acquisition. In B. Blachman (Ed.), *Foundations of reading acquisition and dyslexia* (pp. 145–162). Mahwah, NJ: Erlbaum.

Campbell, J. R., Hombo, C. M., & Mazzeo, J. (2000). *NAEP 1999 trends in academic progress: Three decades of student performance* (NCES 2000–469). Washington, DC: U.S. Department of Education. Office of Educational Research and Improvement. National Center for Education Statistics. Available: http://nces.ed.gov/nationsreportcard/pubs/main1999/2000469.shtml (2000, August 29)

Cazabon, M. T., Nicoladis, E., & Lambert, W. E. (2000). *Becoming bilingual in the Amigos Two-Way Immersion Program.* Center for Research on Education, Diversity & Excellence. Available: http://www.cal.org/crede/pubs/research/rr3.htm (2000, August 24)

Center for Applied Linguistics. (1999). *Directory of two-way bilingual immersion programs in the U.S.* Available: http://www.cal.org/db/2way/tables.htm#table3 (2000, February 2)

Clay, M. (1993). *An observation survey of early literacy achievement.* Portsmouth, NH: Heinemann.

Collier, V., & Thomas, W. (1989). How quickly can immigrants become proficient in school English? *Journal of Educational Issues of Language Minority Students, 5,* 26–38.

Dickinson, D. K., & De Temple, J. M. (1998). Putting parents in the picture: Maternal reports of preschoolers' literacy as a predictor of early reading. *Early Childhood Research Quarterly, 13*(2), 241–261.

Dickinson, D. K., & Tabors, P. O. (Eds.). (2001). *Building literacy with language: Young children learning at home and school.* Baltimore: Brookes.

Downing, J. (1986). Cognitive clarity: A unifying and cross-cultural theory for language awareness phenomena in reading. In Y. Yaden, Jr., & S. Templeton (Eds.), *Metalinguistic awareness and beginning literacy* (pp. 13–29). Portsmouth, NH: Heinemann.

Dunn, L. M., & Dunn L. M. (1981). *Peabody Picture Vocabulary Test—Revised.* Circle Pines, MN: American Guidance Service

Dunn, L. M., Padilla, E. R., Lugo, D. E., & Dunn, L. M. (1986). *Test de Vocabulario en Imágenes Peabody.* Circle Pines, MN: American Guidance Service.

Ehri, L. (1997). Sight word learning in normal readers and dyslexics. In B. Blachman (Ed.), *Foundations of reading acquisition and dyslexia* (pp. 163–190). Mahwah, NJ: Erlbaum.

Ernst, G. (1994). Beyond language: The many dimensions of an ESL program. *Anthropology and Education Quarterly, 25*(3), 317–335.

Evans, C. A. (1994). English only children from bilingual homes: Considering the home–school connection. In C. K. Kinzer & D. J. Leu (Eds.), *Multidimensional aspects of literacy research, theory, and practice. Forty-third yearbook of the National Reading Conference* (pp. 172–179). Chicago, IL: National Reading Conference.

Faltis, C. J., & Wolfe, P. M. (Eds.). (1999). *So much to say: Adolescents, bilingualism, and ESL in the secondary school.* New York: Teachers College Press.

Fantini, A. (1985). *Language acquisition of a bilingual child.* San Diego, CA: College-Hill Press.

Fitzgerald, J., & Noblit, G. W. (1999). About hopes, aspirations, and uncertainty: First-grade English-language learners' emergent reading. *Journal of Literacy Research, 31*(2), 133–182.

Fleischman, H., & Hopstock, P. (1993). *Descriptive study of services to limited English proficient students.* Washington, DC: Development Associates.

Hart, B., & Risley, T. R. (1995). *Meaningful differences in the everyday experiences of young American children.* Baltimore: Brookes.

Hatch, E. M. (Ed.). (1978). *Second language acquisition: A book of readings.* Rowley, MA: Newbury House.

Hopstock, P., & Bucaro, B. (1993). *A review and analysis of estimates of the LEP student population.* Arlington, VA: Development Associates, Special Issues Analysis Center.

Huttenlocher, J., Haight, W., Bryk, A., Seltzer, M., & Lyons, T. (1991). Early vocabulary growth: Relation to language input and gender. *Developmental Psychology, 27,* 236–248.

Iglesias, A., Peña, E., Gutierrez-Clellen, V. F., Bedore, L., & Goldstein, B. (1999, November). *Development of a language test for bilingual Spanish-English speaking children.* Symposium presented at the annual meeting of the American Speech, Hearing, and Language Association, San Francisco.

Juel, C. (1988). Learning to read and write: A longitudinal study of 54 children from first through 4th grades. *Journal of Educational Psychology, 80,* 437–447.

Muñoz-Sandoval, A. F., Cummins, J., Alvarado, C. G., & Ruef, M. L. (1998). *Bilingual Verbal Ability Tests.* Itasca, IL: Riverside.

Nagy, W., McClure, E., & Mir, M. (1997). Linguistic transfer and the use of context by Spanish–English bilinguals. *Applied Psycholinguistics, 18,* 431–452.

Neilson, J. C. (1997). *Bilingual students' achievement in Danish at the uppermost levels of primary and lower secondary school.* Report from the Danish National Institute for Educational Research, Copenhagen.

Neilson, J. C. (1998). *Bilingual students' language and reading performance in their first and second languages—A study on Turkish-speaking students in Danish schools.* Report from the Danish National Institute for Educational Research, Copenhagen.

Nord, C. W., Lennon, J., Liu, B., & Chandler, K. (1999). *Home literacy activities and signs of children's emerging literacy, 1993 and 1999* (NCES

20000-026). Washington, DC: U.S. Department of Education. Office of Educational Research and Improvement, National Center for Education Statistics. Available: http://nces.ed.gov/pubs2000/2000026.pdf (2000, August 29)

Páez, M. M., De Temple, J. M., & Snow, C. E. (2000). *Home language and literacy exposure index.* Unpublished manuscript. Harvard Graduate School of Education, Cambridge, MA.

Pearson, B. Z. (in press). Bilingual infants: What we know, what we need to know. In M. M. Suárez-Orozco & M. M. Páez (Eds.), *Latinos in the 21st century: Mapping the research agenda.* Berkeley, CA and Cambridge, MA: University of California Press and Harvard University Press.

Pearson, B. Z., & Fernández, S. C. (1994). Patterns of interaction in the lexical growth in two languages of bilingual infants and toddlers. *Language Learning, 44*(4), 617–653.

Pearson, B. Z., Fernandez, S. C., Lewedeg, V., & Oller, D. K. (1997). The relation of input factors to lexical learning by bilingual infants. *Applied Psycholinguistics, 18,* 41–58.

Perfetti, C., & Zhang, S. (1996). What it means to learn to read. In M. F. Graves, P. Van Den Broek, & B. M. Taylor (Eds.), *The first R: Every child's right to read.* New York: Teachers College Press.

Rodríguez, J., Díaz, R., Duran, D., & Espinosa, L. (1995). The impact of bilingual preschool education on the language development of Spanish-speaking children. *Early Childhood Research Quarterly, 10,* 475–490.

Rodriguez, R. (1983). *Hunger of memory: The education of Richard Rodriguez.* New York: Bantam Books.

Saunders, G. (1988). *Bilingual children: From birth to teens.* Clevedon, UK and Philadelphia: Multilingual Matters.

Slavin, R. E., & Madden, N. A. (1999). *Success for All/Roots & Wings: Summary of research on achievement outcomes.* Center for Research on the Education of Students at Risk (CRESPAR), Report No. 41. Available: http://www.successforall.net/resource/research/report41entire.pdf (2000, August 24)

Snow, C., Burns, M., & Griffin, P. (Eds.). (1998). *Preventing reading difficulties in young children.* Washington, DC: National Academy Press.

Snow, C. E., Roach, K., Tabors, P. O., & Dickinson, D. K. (2001). *Predicting 4th grade reading comprehension: Home and school influences beginning at age three.*

Snow, C. E., & Tabors, P. O. (1993). Language skills that relate to literacy development. In B. Spodek & O. Saracho (Eds.), *Yearbook in early childhood education, 4.* New York: Teachers College Press.

Tabors, P. O. (1997). *One child, two languages: A guide for preschool educators of children learning English as a second language.* Baltimore: Brookes.

Tabors, P. O., Aceves, C., Bartolomé, L., Páez, M. M., & Wolf, A. (2000). Language development of linguistically diverse children in Head Start classrooms: Three ethnographic portraits. *NHSA Dialog 3*(3), 409–440.

Taeschner, T. (1983). *The sun is feminine: A study of language acquisition in bilingual children.* New York: Springer-Verlag.

Valdés, G. (1998). The world outside and inside schools: Language and immigrant children. *Educational Researcher, 27*(6), 4–18.

Vedder, P., Kook, H., & Muysken, P. (1996). Language choice and functional differentiation of languages in bilingual parent–child reading. *Applied Psycholinguistics, 17,* 461–484.

Verhoeven, L. (1987). *Ethnic minority children acquiring literacy.* Dordrecht, The Netherlands: Foris.

Weber, R.-M., & Longhi-Chirlin, T. (in press). Beginning in English: The growth of linguistic and literate abilities in two Spanish-speaking first graders. *Reading Research and Instruction.*

Wong Fillmore, L. (1991a). When learning a second language means losing the first. *Early Childhood Research Quarterly, 6,* 323–346.

Wong Fillmore, L. (1991b). Language and cultural issues in the early education of language minority children. In S. Kagan (Ed.), *The care and education of America's young children: Obstacles and opportunities. Ninetieth yearbook of the National Society for the Study of Education, Part I* (pp. 30–49). Chicago, IL: University of Chicago Press.

Xu, H. (1996). A Filipino ESL kindergartner's successful beginning literacy learning experience in a mainstream classroom. In D. J. Leu, C. K. Kinzer, & K. A. Hinchman (Eds.), *Literacies for the 21st century: Research and practice. Forty-fifth yearbook of the National Reading Conference* (pp. 219–231). Chicago, IL: National Reading Conference.

Zentella, A. C. (1997). *Growing up bilingual: Puerto Rican children in New York.* Malden, MA: Blackwell.

13

Joint Caregiver–Child Storybook Reading: A Route to Literacy Development

❖

ADRIANA G. BUS

Book reading has a long history as a family routine. At the age of 6 Rousseau (1712–1778) shared with his father the books that his mother had left after her premature death (Rousseau, 1832). The French philosopher Sartre describes his first reading experiences as shared events (Sartre, 1964). When he became eager to learn more about the content of the numerous books in his grandfather's library, Sartre's mother began to read to him. Sartre describes how he "reread" books such as *Alone on the World* by memorizing the content word for word. Book reading has become a daily routine in most modern Western literate families. Assuming that children acquire knowledge of reading and writing long before formal instruction starts, following suggestions of Sulzby (1985), I began to wonder how this prototypical and iconic aspect of home literacy may contribute to children's reading development. The relation between book reading and later language and literacy skills (e.g., Bus, van IJzendoorn, & Pellegrini, 1995; Scarborough & Dobrich, 1994) may be driven by the child's initial cognitive and language capacities. The child's interest in books and joint reading may be rooted in a biologically endowed trait for exploration of uncharted territories stimulating their development (e.g., Crain-Thoreson & Dale, 1992). According to this theory, book read-

ing is a by-product of children's natural interest in stories and other information. Measures of parent–child interaction reflect the child's interest in continuing the interaction as much or more than the parent's.

According to *the social-construction hypothesis,* book reading is a socially created, interactive activity (Sulzby & Teale, 1991). Children's interest is as much a prerequisite as a consequence of book reading. Children to whom parents have read books from an early age on display more interest in reading books than do children who lack this early experience (Arnold, Lonigan, Whitehurst, & Epstein, 1994). Stories in books including the wording of the story deviate in many respects from the child's world and the familiar interactive verbal language. Assuming a social-constructionist nature of book reading, books may not be enjoyable and comprehensible for young children without intensive help and support from adults. Consequently, children may almost never encounter solely an oral rendering of the text. Instead, in most cases the words of the author are surrounded by the social interaction between adult reader and child. The book-reading paradigm assumes that it depends on this social context whether or not children become interested in books and shared reading experiences become part of daily routines. It is in the interactional framework of the family that the child first learns to handle written language skills. The first part of this chapter explores the social-constructionist nature of book reading. Most of this research focuses on the emotional bond between parent and child. These studies test the hypothesis that the quality of the attachment relationship between primary caregivers and their children affects parent–child book reading. It then examines cross-cultural differences in the interactional framework of the family.

Exposure to books provides a rich source of linguistic stimulation for the child that may foster literacy development in a unique way. Book reading may stimulate text understanding because it supports children's knowledge of oral and written language in a contextual framework. Research in emergent literacy represents a step forward in recognizing the potential continuity of book-reading experiences with what children learn later; in each developmental phase they may use their whole repertoire of knowledge, including the knowledge acquired through joint book reading, to make sense of text (Sulzby, 1996). Notwithstanding our growing knowledge of early literacy development, book-reading as a predictor of reading difficulties is far from understood. This chapter concludes therefore with a discussion of research that includes special groups such as language-delayed (e.g., Kaderavek & Sulzby, 1998) and dyslexic children (Laakso, 1999). Social predictors may partly explain reading problems, in addition to other endogenous factors. A genetic disposition for reading difficulties may also include exogenous factors. Several researchers have argued that a genetic disposition for language or reading difficulties may also explain differences in environmental characteristics such as book-reading experiences. When caregivers have reading difficulties themselves, they may be less likely to expose children to a rich and stimulating linguistic environment.

Security of the Parent–Child Relationship: A Prerequisite for the Emergence of Book-Reading Routines in Families?

The social-construction hypothesis implies a central role for the caregiver who makes the book interesting and relevant to the child. It is assumed that the child's interest in books and shared reading may reflect early experiences with and joint engagement in books (DeBaryshe, 1993). Parents who start to read early may evoke children's interest toward books and literacy, which is sustained throughout the developing years. Indeed, there is evidence that children who are frequently read to by both parents begin at an early age to attend to books and to show initiative for reading (Lyytinen, Laakso, & Poikkeus, 1998). To further investigate how such processes originate, we initiated a research program that explored book reading of dyads differing in the emotional bond between caregivers and children. Related to the social-construction hypothesis, we expected that exogenous factors such as a negative history of parent–child interactive experiences might inhibit children's reading experiences and reading development. Therefore, we began to compare groups different in their early interactive experiences. Departing from the assumptions and findings of the attachment theory, the studies tested the hypothesis that the interactional framework was a major factor in family literacy.

Attachment theory assumes that children build a mental representation of their interactions with parents and that this model influences their expectations and responses. Basic to this model are the interactive experiences that children share with their parents. It is also assumed that parents differ in the extent to which they are able to help their child explore new domains and that the parents' sensitivity is rooted in their own attachment biography (Bus & van IJzendoorn, 1992; van IJzendoorn, 1995). Children anticipate parent's future behavior on the basis of their past interactions. Our major hypothesis was that prototypical aspects may depend on family characteristics such as the quality of the parent–child relationship (Bus, in press). We expected then that aspects of home literacy such as the frequency and quality of book reading relate strongly to the history of interactive experiences that children share with their parents. Assuming that insecurely attached children have negative expectations of parental assistance during reading, insecure children might show less interest in books because enjoyment depends strongly on parental help. Children with pleasant book-reading experiences might want to be read to more frequently, to spend more time pretending to read, and to look more frequently at books during free play than do their counterparts with less frequent and less pleasant reading experiences. Another question was the quality of the book reading. Less secure parents might be less supportive and adaptive to the child's needs.

Using a questionnaire to determine frequency of book reading, two groups of mother–child pairs were selected (Bus & van IJzendoorn, 1995). The frequently reading pair read at least once a day. The infrequent readers did not read everyday. Few mothers admitted that they did not read to their 3-year-old child at all. Comparing frequently reading pairs (reading at least once a day) with infrequently reading pairs (reading at most twice a week), we found some striking differences in the quality of the parent–child relationship and in the mother's own attachment model. Using Ainsworth's Strange Situation (Ainsworth, Blehar, Waters, & Wall, 1978), we observed how children responded to an unexpected and unpleasant separation from the parent. The child's response to the separation from the parent is assumed to be a valid indicator of the security of the parent–child relationship. The caregiver's security was derived through a semistructured interview (Main, Kaplan, & Cassidy, 1985). The results were in line with the assumption that book reading depends on contextual characteristics such as the parental ability to support their child during activities (e.g. book reading). In the group of infrequently reading pairs from a low socioeconomic status (SES), children with negative expectations of parental support (the insecure ones) were strongly overrepresented (73%) compared to the group of frequent readers from a low SES (33%) or frequent readers from a high SES (13%). The quality of the parent–child relationship correlated with the mother's mental representation of her own attachment history (Bus & van IJzendoorn, 1992).

The inexperienced group appeared to be most intensively involved in activities indirectly related to the reading of text suggesting that digressive tactics are more characteristic for the infrequently reading group.

However, the variety among mothers coincides with differences recorded from previous research on reading styles (Dickinson, 1991; Reese & Cox, 1999). Following a *comprehender* style of reading, some mothers mainly focus on story meaning and the meaning of illustrations, making inferences and predictions of story events whereas, according to the *performance-oriented* style, other mothers read the text nearly verbatim, only interrupting now and then with short comments (Reese & Cox, 1999). The latter style of reading also occurred in this young group of 3-year-olds. One boy, for example, was concentrated during the book reading session but hardly responded verbally to the book. During the whole session his mother quickly continued reading without making serious attempts to elicit comments from the child. It has been suggested that reading style might vary according to children's developing language abilities, reflecting their growing ability to understand book language on their own (Martin, 1998; Pellegrini, Brody, & Sigel, 1985). This explanation fits to the present data. The readings with the least experienced children were highly interactive similar to the comprehender style, whereas more advanced children mainly sat and listened like an audience. The differences in reading style seemed to reflect children's growing level of book understanding.

Insecure Parents Are Less Able to Make Text Understandable

To better understand the correlation between the parent–child relationship and the frequency of book sharing, we explored the process of scaffolding in a series of studies. It was our thesis that less secure caregivers might be less successful in creating engaging and enjoyable contexts for reading. Less secure relationships might relate to less supportive interactions surrounding the reading of the book. Our first studies focused on the interactions between parents and children. We hypothesized that successful engagement might vary among the securely and insecurely attached dyads. From a cross-sectional study of interactive reading with 18-, 32-, and 66-month-old children (Bus & van IJzendoorn, 1988), we found that the atmosphere surrounding the interaction of securely attached dyads was more positive than that of anxiously attached dyads. We examined conflicts between mother and child resulting from non-task-related behavior of the child. In response to this, parents engaged in disciplining behavior. Included here were all maternal verbal and nonverbal behaviors to reduce the child's distracted behavior, to bring attention back to the task, or to restore concentration on the written language or the content and illustrations of the story. The outcome suggested that a key element in book reading is a mutually enjoyable atmosphere. In securely attached dyads there was less need to discipline because the children were less distracted than in anxiously attached dyads. We also explored differences in the focus of the interactions between parents and children. As children were younger and less experienced, a narrative style dominated whereas in the older and more experienced group it was protoreading (i.e., naming letters and familiar words) that dominated. Positive correlations between this latter style of book reading and children's emergent reading skills, may suggest that parents adapt their reading style to their child's competence.

Assuming that infants, as well, are able to participate in affective responses to books and in the evocative powers of language, we designed a study with preverbal infants. Particularly at this early age, when children still have little understanding of the meaning of pictures and information communicated by pictures (DeLoache & Burns, 1994), we expected that mothers have to be active and supportive to keep the child focused on the task. From the very start of book reading, around children's first birthday, the insecure ones may be harder to engage in the reading sessions (Bus & van IJzendoorn, 1997). To test this hypothesis, we studied infants' understanding and participation in the construction of simple stories. Interactions indeed appeared to be less pleasant when children were insecurely attached to their mother. Consequently, the onset of joint reading may be delayed when children are insecurely attached to their main caregiver. Sharing a simple expository book with thematically ordered pictures, insecurely attached infants in the age range of 44–63 weeks were less attentive than the secure ones: They often looked at other objects in the environment or made attempts to escape from their mother's lap. Their mothers were more controlling during the whole session, putting an arm around the child or by keeping the book out of reach. Also, insecurely attached children were less inclined to respond to the content, to touch the pictures, or to make movements to represent an object on a picture. These children all seemed to be less acquainted with book content. The security of the parent–child relationship seemed to relate to lower levels of understanding.

In a more recent study involving 18-month-old white Caucasian American boys, all very similar in age, we explored the idea that insecure parents are less likely to foster children's engagement, leading to less rewarding and less informative book-reading sessions (Bus, Belsky, van IJzendoorn, & Crnik, 1997). The mothers in this study read from an expository book that includes a series of pictures with babies making faces, crawling, staying, walking, playing, eating, drinking, being dressed or bathed, and sleeping. Each page also contained a few sentences printed over two pages. We conducted a microanalysis of how the mother made the book understandable. Most children in this study mainly responded to the baby pictures by pointing and labeling, and their mothers initiated such actions by following predictable routines as described by Ninio and Bruner (1976). Typically, mothers initiated interactions by motivating ("look here"), pointing at pictures, questioning ("look, what's that?"), labeling ("see, his foot"), commenting ("it's the same color as your sock"), and positive feedback ("yes, it's a foot"). Children initiated interactions and responded to parental questions and comments by pointing, labeling, commenting, and responding nonverbally. In some insecure dyads (the anxious attached ones), mothers were indeed less successful in creating an age-appropriate interaction with their children. Instead of evoking the interactive routines around the pictures, these mothers often just read the verbal text, ignoring the child's limited ability to understand pictures and the accompanying language of the text. Their children were unresponsive to book content and more distracted than others, suggesting a limited interest and limited exposure to book reading experiences.

Other insecure dyads revealed different problems. Overstimulating and overcontrolling behaviors by mothers coincided with ambivalence toward books from children. Young children need opportunities for active participation (e.g., pointing, manipulating, and vocalizing), as is suggested by other studies (e.g., Cornell, Sénéchal, & Broda, 1988). In response to the restrictive maternal behavior, these insecurely attaached children were not obviously disengaged by showing distracted behavior, but they explored the book less than others. Parental behaviors, such as excessive directiveness combined with low interactional sensitivity, may hinder engagement in and learning from books.

Parental Strategies to Engage Young Children in Book Reading

Some researchers assume that book reading is most effective when parents place demands on the child for active and verbal participation when reading aloud (e.g., Whitehurst et al., 1988). From experimental research it can be derived that *dialogic* parent–child book reading stimulates children's vocabulary (Whitehurst et al., 1988). During typical shared reading the adult reads and the child listens, but in dialogic reading, the child learns to become the storyteller (Whitehurst et al., 1999). The adult assumes the role of active listener, asking questions, adding information, and prompting the child to increase the sophistication of descriptions of the material in the picture book. It is my impression (untested as yet) that children's active participation and learning strongly depend on the parental ability to bridge the discrepancy between the child's world and the world of the book through careful choice of pictorial images and language. A prerequisite for entering the world of the book is the mental and emotional capital of background knowledge and firsthand experience that younger readers often lack. To bridge the gap between the book and the child, the parent has to become both "reader" (of the original written) text, and "creator" (of the story as actually told).

It is to be expected that caregivers will "read" the pictorial contents of an illustrated story and its accompanying text more idiosyncratically as children are younger and/or less experienced. Jones's (1996) ethnographic study, for example, shows that parents are more successful in engaging infant readers in books when they find cues that give pleasure and that narrow the gap between book and child. More successful parents identify a large number of pictorial details, their visual content and linguistic coding both carrying a high emotional charge for the infant reader. Parents create a story not of the hero but of their own child. A disproportionate amount of adult speech time may be devoted to details of the pictures that often have little to do with the printed version of the story. The parent may adapt the story to include pictorial details more salient to the child. In Bruner's (1983) terms, the child (listener)–parent (narrator) axis is exceptionally strong, whereas the hero of the story occupies a relatively minor place. In this way, the illustrations give pleasure, but not necessarily because they have anything to do with the ongoing action of the story as written. Labeling and describing of the elements conveyed in the pictures may add to children's vocabulary (Laakso, Poikkeus, & Lyytinen, in press), but these strategies are not purposefully applied.

We are in the process of exploring how parents engage 30- to 38-month-old children in repeated readings of the same book (Bus & Sulzby, 2000). Sitting next to their child, mothers in this study read *Sam Vole and His Brothers* (Waddell & Firth, 1992) on four different occasions spread over a few weeks. One of the hypotheses was that as caregivers became more sensitive to children's knowledge, interest, and experience, they would develop abridged versions of stories to motivate their child. And, as children become more familiar with the book, they would interpret illustrations and content in accordance with the writer's original intention. Preliminary results indicated that similar to the younger age range described by Jones (1996), a disproportionate amount of time was devoted to aspects of the pictures having little to do with the text. The following fragment illustrates how this emphasis often had the effect of driving the 'official version' of the story into the background. The bumblebee in this fragment is not part of the official story, but it is part of the child's story. (M, mother; C, child.)

M: (*reads*) I am going voling for grass

M: (*reads*) sam told his mother

M: (*reads*) I am going voling all by myself

M: (*reads*) sam went voling out in the meadow

C: what is that (*points*)

C: what is he [means sam] looking at? (*points at a big bumblebee*)

M: that is a bumblebee

C: sam sees a bumblebee

M: yes he does

As the following fragment illustrates, the child hardly responds to the mother's attempts to explain the "official version" of the story. Consequently, the mother starts to make up new stories that have more appeal to the child. Thematically, the discussions apart from the official story may reflect closely the child's current real-life interest. These "moments of time out" seem to be highly motivating and engaging to the child. I speculate that insecure caregivers may show less empathy in what motivates their child and may be less inclined to create idiosyncratic stories.

M: (*reads*) sam went voling in the meadow

M: (*reads*) but arthur and henry went too

M: (*reads*) they carried home more grass than sam

M: (*reads*) enough for them all

M: (*reads*) sam gave his grass to mother

M: look sam has a few pieces of grass

M: his brothers have a lot more (*points*)

M: do you know why

M: because . . .

C: hungry

M: yes they may be hungry

M: but they are also bigger than sam isn't it

M: look many lady birds

C: what's that (*points*)

M: those are beetles

C: and this (*points*)

[Hereafter follows a long discussion about several details of the illustration.]

Increasing familiarity with the focal story's grammar and content may lead to fewer adaptations for the child. Parents may be less inclined to induce these moments of time out when this strategy is already applied in previous sessions in which the book was read. Consequently, during later readings of the same book the narrative may become less fragmented and flow more easily. Surprisingly, the discussion of details and irrelevant story extensions (moments of time out) did not decrease with familiarity. Similar to other studies (e.g., Panofsky, 1994; Philips & McNaughton, 1990), there was a shift from a predominance of parent initiatives to a predominance of child initiatives. Children exhibited more control of the discussions as they had more experience with the focal book. They did not initiate new topics but mostly repeated discussions initiated by parents in previous sessions. Parents did not initiate an alternative conversational pattern with which to replace the previous elaboration of pictures and/or text. There was, for example, not a growing amount of intellectually stimulating talk to make books more challenging, as some authors expect to occur (e.g., Dickinson, De Temple, Hirschler, & Smith, 1992). Parents may prefer other strategies to keep book reading challenging, such as the selection of more complex books.

**Book Reading
as a Literacy-Stimulating Tool
across Cultures**

Culturally disparate groups may differ in educational beliefs that result in different ways of responding to and supporting their children (Sonnenschein et al., 1996). From a study among Surinam–Dutch parents, for example, it appeared that these parents generally are more restrictive and discipline oriented than their Dutch counterparts during play and feeding interactions (van IJzendoorn, 1991). These parents seem to consider obedience and respect for adults as important characteristics for their children and instill these values already at an early age. Educational beliefs may influence the literacy learning potential of the home. These parents may show less empathy in their children's interests, knowledge, and conceptions when they mediate a text to their child, and, consequently, their children may have less book-reading experiences when they enter school. But there may be other relevant differences across cultures. Parents' personal reading experience may affect how they mediate books. When for parents themselves reading is not a source of amusement, activities such as storybook reading may not be firmly embedded in family practice and parents may not know how to engage children in reading sessions (Bus & Sulzby, 1996). De Groot and Bus (1995) found that immigrant parents in The Netherlands consider book reading an important preparation for school, but they obviously consider book reading different from games or singing songs. Statements such as "I don't read now because it is summer holiday" indicate that they assume book reading to be "work" instead of play. In a group of Dutch low-SES parents we assessed their knowledge of the reading domain (De Groot & Bus, 1995). We asked the mothers to recognize authors, book titles, or magazine titles from checklists that contained plausible foils (cf. Cunningham & Stanovich, 1990). As mothers scored higher on these scales, they were more inclined to consider book reading a source of pleasure for their children in preschool age. A U.S. study involving low-SES African American parents and children showed that ratings of maternal use of literacy (ranging from nonreader to "print worm") correlate significantly with word-recognition skills in school (Snow, Barnes, Chandler, Goodman, & Hemphill, 1991). Sénéchal, LeFevre, Hudson, and Lawson (1996) report that parent print exposure assessed with similar scales accounted for significant variance in children's vocabulary.

To study differences in how book reading proceeds across cultures, we composed groups of parents from different cultural backgrounds, strictly controlling for SES differences (Bus, Leseman, & Keultjes, 2000). The data were derived from a longitudinal study designed by Leseman and de Jong (1998). One of three groups included was composed of indigenous Dutch children and their families. The other two groups were first- and second-generation immigrants from Surinam (South America) and Turkey (Europe), respectively. All selected dyads were from low-SES families. According to interviews (Leseman & de Jong, 1998), the parents originating from Turkey, Surinam, and The Netherlands differed in how they use literacy for recreational and related instrumental goals (e.g., using the TV schedule in the newspaper). The Dutch parents read significantly more books and journals for pleasure than did the Turkish–Dutch with the Surinam–Dutch falling between these two groups. Ethnic background was more strongly related to recreational literacy than to informational literacy. Although illiteracy rates have decreased in the present groups, there seems to remain a division line between indigenous and immigrant groups concerning the everyday use of literacy for informational, entertaining, and instrumental functions.

Storybook reading may not hold a monopoly on the socialization of early literacy even at the level of a children's book (see also Serpell, 1997). According to my findings (Bus et al., 2000) the potential role of book reading as a stimulus for early literacy varies among culturally divergent groups. From indepth analyses of book-reading sessions, parents from different cultural backgrounds appeared to sustain children's curiosity and exploratory behavior in different ways. There were differences in the empathy of parents in children's interests, knowledge, motives, and conceptions, and these were related to the didactic aspects of the reading session. As parents were more helpful and supportive, the conversations accompanying the reading went beyond the text and included discussion of relevant background information or children's own experiences related to the story. As parents were less helpful and supportive, sessions generally resulted in cognitive low-demand conversations emphasizing naming and paraphrasing. Particularly the Surinam–Dutch parents tended to be more restrictive and discipline oriented than the Turkish–Dutch or Dutch parents. However, it is important not to generalize based on the present differences across cultural groups. In fact, many Surinam–Dutch dyads were more similar to their Dutch or Turkish–Dutch counterparts than to each other.

Parents' own literacy practices appeared to determine opportunities for young children to become involved in literacy-related interactions. Parents were more inclined to respond to their child's interest in books when they had a positive orientation toward literacy, which was manifested in mutually enjoyable book-reading sessions. Overall the study supported the hypothesis that when reading is less important for the parents personally, parents and children were less involved in meaning-related discussions that may make the book more understandable and enjoyable for young children. These parents did not intitiate themes that go beyond the text, and they did not discuss how text relates to pictures to the same extent as parents who did read for pleasure. They were also less inclined to change text in order to make it easier to comprehend. Probably in response to a lack of support from the parents, their children initiated more interactions than other children did, but low cognitive demand behaviors such as naming details or identifying pictures of characters were typical for these interactions. Thus for parents with little or no experience in reading for pleasure, the greatest difficulty may be the creation of a social routine (cf. Sulzby & Edwards, 1993).

Effects of Book Reading

Wells (1987) reported that a significant difference between children in school achievement at the end of the elementary years was already determined by differences before they came to school. Out of four types of activity (looking at a picture book, drawing and coloring, listening to a story, and writing or pretending to write), it was the difference in the frequency with which children had stories read to them that best explained the differences in their subsequent achievement. The emphasis on significance testing can often obscure consistent trends running through the research literature. We decided therefore to carry out a quantitative meta-analysis to test effects of book reading on children's language and literacy development in preschool and school age (Bus et al., 1995). In selecting the studies to be included in this meta-analysis, we focused on studies examining the frequency of parental book reading to preschoolers. We tested the hypothesis that the home literacy environment uniquely predicts literacy outcomes in kindergarten and primary school. Combining almost 30 studies from which pertinent data could be derived, we found that reading experiences not only related to language growth but also to outcome measures as emergent literacy and reading achievement. Early storybook reading predicts reading skills somewhat less strongly than experimentally mainipulated phonological awareness; combined r's for storybook reading and phonological awareness are .33 and .28, respectively (Bus & van IJzendoorn, 1999).

It could be that book reading predicts concepts about print, alphabet knowledge, word reading, and invented spelling (Sénéchal, LeFevre, Colton, & Smith, 1999). It could also be that the association between early home literacy experiences and later reading achievement is mediated through oral and written language skills. Through book reading children may become familiar with structures and cadences that are to be found in the sustained meaning making that is characteristic of writing (Sulzby, 1985, 1996). Reading books implies a new opportunity to go beyond the here and now of the immediate environment into other times and places, into the world of "maybe" and "might have been" (Dickinson, 1991). The structures are more closely packed with meaning than those more typical of conversational speech (Chafe, 1982). Therefore, texts have a range of features that are only rarely employed in speech addressed to young children: subordinate clauses, direct speech quoted as it occurs between two or more protagonists, passive constructions, unfamiliar expressions, colloquialisms, and idioms. One of my ongoing studies (Bus & Sulzby, 2000) focuses on children's ability to abstract written language features from the repeatedly read story *Sam Vole and His Brothers*. As parents have been successful in engaging their child during the preceding reading sessions the speech that children produce when they pretend to read the book may be more differentiated prosodically, syntactically, and topically from the child's conversation surrounding the reading event. It has been argued that subsequent emergent readings show evidence of children's abstractions of what the storybooks should contain (Purcell-Gates, 1988; Sulzby, 1985; Sulzby & Zecker, 1991). As

Pappas (1987) concluded, the internalizations that can be observed in reading-like behavior cannot be explained simply in terms of rote memory. The child is using conceptually driven behaviors that include overgeneralization of written-language-like patterns and self-corrections.

Some assume that knowledge of written-like language becomes most important for children around grade 4, hypothesizing that the nature of the reading task then shifts from decoding written words to reading for meaning (e.g., Chall, Jacobs, & Baldwin, 1990). To me it seems more plausible that knowledge of written-like language is just as important in the beginning stages of becoming a conventional reader than later on. Similar to more advanced readers, beginners read for meaning. Furthermore, written-like language makes text more transparent and predictable and in this way also contributes to beginning reading skills (Pearson, 1999). The context affects the phonological rendering of letters in words and sentences particularly as long as children's skills in phonological recoding are rudimentary (Vander Velden & Siegel, 1995).

The Role of Exogenous Variables in the Etiology of Dyslexia

Assuming a central role of book reading in becoming literate, it seems plausible that the absence of family environment factors such as shared book reading raise the risk that a child will develop reading problems. Dyslexic children differ from "normally" reading children in phonemic coding—a form of information processing which plays an important role in reading development (Snowling, 2000). Snowling developed a theory to explain how a delay in children's language development and the so-called non-word-reading deficit—main characteristics of dyslexia—result from individual differences in phonemic coding. In addition to such endogenous factors, exogenous factors such as book reading may affect the development of language and reading problems that are typical to this group. Children who have less advanced language skills to begin with may find it less appealing to interact with books (e.g., Scarborough & Dobrich, 1994). Parents who have reading

problems themselves are less likely to provide for their children a rich and stimulating linguistic environment (Lyytinen et al., 1998). An obvious hypothesis is therefore that in families with a genetic disposition for reading problems, the chance that reading problems indeed develop is raised by exogenous factors such as the frequency and quality of parent–child book reading that relate to the endogenous ones. Because learning the letter–sound rules appeared to be a stumbling block for dyslexic children, they may depend on textual redundancy during the stage of learning to read, more than do normally developing children. If knowledge of the written language register is underdeveloped, reading outcomes could be even more unfavorable (Kaderavek & Sulzby, 1998).

From an early meta-analysis we concluded that the "non-word-reading deficit" explains a substantial but restricted part of the differences between normally developing readers and dyslexic children (van IJzendoorn & Bus, 1994). To understand better which other variables may explain how a reading problem develops, researchers have begun to explore exogenous variables in groups of children with an elevated chance to develop reading problems. Dyslexia has been shown to be genetically related (DeFries, 1991). Infants of dyslexic parents as young as 6 months of age have been found to differ significantly from those infants with normal reading parents in phonemic awareness (Scarborough, 1989). Although certainly no causal connections can be made, findings from longitudinal research suggest that dyslexic children from dyslexic families had less frequent exposure to books than did those preschoolers who became normal readers (Scarborough, Dobrich, & Hager, 1991). The Jvaskyla Longitudinal Study of Dyslexia (Laakso, 1999) explored longitudinally parent–child book reading in a group of children with genetic risk for dyslexia and language skills. Children with an elevated risk to develop serious reading and writing problems were followed from birth on and compared to a normal control group. This Finnish study included 39 mothers who were diagnosed as reading disabled and had a familial background of reading difficulties and 89 normally reading mothers and their children. Analyses suggested joint storybook reading occurred less frequently in families with reading difficulties than in families with normally reading parents (Laakso, Poikkeus, & Lyytinen, 1997).

Further longitudinal observational research seems warranted to examine whether children from families with a genetic predisposition for reading problems lag behind in storybook reading. Combined with low interactional sensitivity, children may be at risk for reading failure.

Summary and Conclusions

The child's interest in book reading is not only a genetically mediated trait, it also reflects the child's early experiences and joint engagements with books. Cultural and social variables influence the frequency and quality of book reading. It is likely that parents who are readers themselves are better able to engage their children in book reading, to evoke their children's interest toward books and literacy, and to maintain this interest throughout the developing years. Talk surrounding the reading helps to bridge the gap between the child's interest and the book content. When reading is not a source of pleasure to parents themselves, they may not know how to make book reading enjoyable and meaningful to them. It may also depend on their ability to create a close and intimate atmosphere in which to share books together.

A key factor in high-quality storybook reading may be the way in which adults mediate the reading experience in response to children's interests, personal experiences, conceptions, and knowledge. Using intimate knowledge of their own child's personal world; the settings, possessions, and sensations which are familiar and meaningfu;, and the language with which these are associated, parents may bridge the world of the infant reader and that of the book. If the parent–child relationship is insecure, the parent may have more problems finding cues that give pleasure and that narrow the gap between book and child, resulting in less engagement and learning for children. Further exploration of such key strategies is warranted.

Concluding that book reading is a pro-foundly social process, embedded in the social–emotional and cultural context, it is clear that not each parent can easily adopt the "technique". Children's accumulated knowledge of uses of language is built up over several years of joint book-reading experiences. When parents are not used to reading storybooks and reading is not a source of amusement for them, they may need permanent support in selecting appropriate books and in scaffolding interactions. Initial effects of interventions (e.g., Neuman, 1997; Whitehurst et al., 1994) may fade away when parental support is discontinued after a short period of training. Whitehurst's (Whitehurst et al., 1999) intervention in preschool age involving children from Head Start centers and their parents indeed had a short-term but not a long-term effect. Studies of dyslexia may result in new forms of treatment and preventive measures. In remedial training processes based on and keyed to the elements of the word itself are often more emphasized than knowledge of the particular context in which the word occurs (e.g., Freppon & Dahl, 1998). However, assuming that our hypothesis concerning the role of exogenous variables is correct, an overemphasis on word identification may result in students being denied opportunities to acquire the full process of reading as meaning making that can be so well exemplified in joint book reading.

References

Ainsworth, M. D. S., Blehar, M. C., Waters, E., & Wall, S. (1978). *Patterns of attachment: A psychological study of the Strange Situation.* Hillsdale, NJ: Erlbaum.
Arnold, D. S., Lonigan, C. J., Whitehurst, G. J., & Epstein, J. N. (1994). Accelerating language development through picture-book reading: Replication and extension to a videotape training format. *Journal of Educational Psychology, 86,* 235–243.
Bruner, J. (1983). *Child's talk: Learning to use language.* Oxford, UK: Oxford University Press.
Bus, A. G. (1994). The role of social context in emergent literacy. In E. M. H. Assink (Ed.), *Literacy acquisition and social context* (pp. 9–24). New York: Harvester Wheathef.
Bus, A. G. (in press). Parent–child book reading through the lens of attachment theory. In L. Verhoeven & C. Snow (Eds.), *Literacy and motivation, chapter 2* (pp. 39–53). Hillsdale: Erlbaum.
Bus, A. G., Belsky, J., van IJzendoorn, M. H., &

Crnik, K. (1997). Attachment and bookreading patterns: A study of mothers, fathers, and their toddlers. *Early Childhood Research Quarterly, 12,* 81–98.

Bus, A. G., Leseman, P. M., & Keultjes, P. (2000). Joint book-reading across cultures: A comparison of Surinamese-Dutch, Turkish-Dutch, and Dutch parent–child dyads. *Journal of Literacy Research, 32,* 53–76.

Bus, A. G., & Sulzby, E. (1996). Becoming literate in a multicultural society. In: J. Shimron (Ed.), *Literacy and education: Essays in memory of Dina Feitelson* (pp. 31–45). Cresskill, NJ: Hampton Press.

Bus, A. G., & van IJzendoorn, M. H. (1988). Mother–child interactions, attachment, and emergent literacy: A cross-sectional study. *Child Development, 59,* 1262–1273.

Bus, A. G., & van IJzendoorn, M. H. (1992). Patterns of attachment in frequently and infrequently reading mother–child dyads. *Journal of Genetic Psychology, 153,* 395–403.

Bus, A. G., & van IJzendoorn, M. H. (1995). Mothers reading to their three-year-olds: The role of mother–child attachment security in becoming literate. *Reading Research Quarterly, 40,* 998–1015.

Bus, A. G., & van IJzendoorn, M. H. (1997). Affective dimension of mother–infant picturebook reading. *Journal of School Psychology, 35,* 47–60.

Bus, A. G., & van IJzendoorn, M. H. (1999). Phonological awareness and early reading: A meta-analysis of experimental training studies. *Journal of Educational Psychology, 91,* 403–414.

Bus, A. G., van IJzendoorn, M. H., & Pellegrini, A. D. (1995). Joint book reading makes for success in learning to read: A meta-analysis on intergenerational transmission of literacy. *Review of Educational Research, 65,* 1–21.

Bus, A. G., & Sulzby, E. (2000). *Connections between characteristics of parent–child readings and characteristics of subsequent emergent readings.* Unpublished manuscript, Leiden University, Leiden, The Netherlands.

Chafe, W. (1982). Integration and involvement in speaking, writing, and oral literature. In D. Tannen (Ed.), *Spoken and written language* (pp. 35–54). Norwood, NJ: Ablex.

Chall, J. S., Jacobs, V. A., & Baldwin, L. E. (1990). *The reading crisis. Why poor children fall behind.* Cambridge, MA: Harvard University Press.

Cornell, E. H., Senechal, M., & Broda, L. S. (1988). Recall of picture books by 3-year-old children: Testing and repetition effects in joint reading activities. *Journal of Educational Psychology, 80,* 537–542.

Crain-Thoreson, C., & Dale, P. S. (1992). Do early talkers become early readers? Linguistic precocity, preschool language, and emergent literacy. *Developmental Psychology, 28,* 421–429.

Cunningham, A. E., & Stanovich, K. E. (1990). Tracking the unique effects of print exposure in children: Associations with vocabulary, general knowledge, and spelling. *Journal of Educational Psychology, 83,* 264–274.

DeBaryshe, B. D. (1993). Joint picture-book reading correlates of early language skill. *Journal of Child Language, 20,* 455–461.

DeFries, J. C. (1991). Genetics and dyslexia: An overview. In M. J. Snowling & M. Thomson (Eds.), *Dyslexia: Integrating theory and practice* (pp. 3–20). London: Whurr.

De Groot, I. M., & Bus, A. G. (1995). *Boekenpret voor baby's.* [Book-fun for babies] (Final report on a project to stimulate emergent literacy). Leiden/The Hague: Leiden University/Sardes.

DeLoache, J. S., & Burns, N. M. (1994). Symbolic functioning in preschool children. *Journal of Applied Developmental Psychology, 15,* 513–527.

Dickinson, D. K. (1991). Teacher agenda and setting: Constraints on conversation in preschool. In A. McCabe & C. Peterson (Eds.), *Developing narrative structure* (pp. 255–301). Hillsdale, NJ: Erlbaum.

Dickinson, D., De Temple, J. M., Hirschler, J. A., & Smith, M. W. (1992). Book reading with preschoolers: Coconstruction of text at home and at school. *Early Childhood Research Quarterly, 7,* 323–346.

Freppon, P. A., & Dahl, K. L. (1998). Theory and research into practice: Balanced instruction: Insights and considerations. *Reading Research Quarterly, 33,* 240–251.

Jones, R. (1996). *Emerging patterns of literacy. A multi-disciplinary perspective.* London: Routledge.

Kaderavek, J. N., & Sulzby, E. (1998). Parent–child joint book reading: An observational protocol for young children. *American Journal of Speech–Language Pathology, 7,* 33–47.

Laakso, M.-L. (1999). *Prelinguistic skills and early interactional context as predictors of children's language development.* Unpublished doctoral dissertation, University of Jyväskylä, Finland.

Laakso, M.-L., Poikkeus, A.-M., & Lyytinen, P. (1997, April). *The role of parent–child interaction in the early development of children's cognitive and linguistic skills.* Paper presented at the biennial meeting of the Society for Research in Child Development, Washington, DC.

Laakso, M.-L., Poikkeus, A.-M., & Lyytinen, P. (in press). Shared reading interaction in families with and without genetic risk for dyslexia: Implications for toddlers' language development. *Infant and Child Development.*

Leseman, P. M., & de Jong, P. F. (1998). Home literacy: Opportunity, instruction, cooperation and social–emotional quality predicting early reading achievement. *Reading Research Quarterly, 33,* 294–318.

Lyytinen, P., Laakso, M.-L., & Poikkeus, A.-M. (1998). Parental contribution to child's early language and interest in books. *European Journal of Psychology of Education, 13,* 297–308.

Main, M., Kaplan, N., & Cassidy, J. (1985). Security in infancy, childhood, and adulthood: A move to the level of representation. In I. Bretherton &

E. Waters (Eds.), Growing points of attachment theory and research. *Monographs of the Society for Research in Child Development, 50* (1–1, Serial No. 209).

Martin, L. E. (1998). Early book reading: How mothers deviate from printed text for young children. *Reading Research and Instruction, 37,* 137–160.

Neuman, S. B. (1997). Children engaging in storybook reading: The influence of access to print resources, opportunity, and parental interaction. *Early Childhood Research Quarterly, 11,* 495–514.

Ninio, A., & Bruner, J. S. (1976). The achievement and antecedents of labelling. *Journal of Child Language, 5,* 1–15.

Panofsky, C. P. (1994). Developing the representational functions of language: The role of parent–child book-reading activity. In V. John-Steiner, C. P. Panofsky, & L. W. Smith (Eds.), *Sociocultural approaches to language and literacy* (pp. 223–242). Cambridge, MA: Cambridge University Press.

Pappas, C. C. (1987). Exploring the textual properties of "protoreading." In R. Steele & T. Threadgold (Eds.), *Language topics: Essays in honour of Michael Halliday* (pp. 137–162). Amsterdam: John Benjamins.

Pearson, P. D. (1999). A historically based review of Preventing Reading Difficulties in Young Children. *Reading Research Quarterly, 34,* 231–246.

Pellegrini, A. D., Brody, G. H., & Sigel, I. E. (1985). Parents' bookreading habits with their children. *Journal of Educational Psychology, 77,* 332–340.

Philips, G., & McNaughton, S. (1990). The practice of storybook reading to preschool children in mainstream New Zealand families. *Reading Research Quarterly, 25,* 196–212.

Purcell-Gates, V. (1988). Lexical and syntactic knowledge of written narrative held by well-read-to kindergartners and second graders. *Research in the Teaching of English, 22,* 128–160.

Reese, E., & Cox, A. (1999). Quality of adult book reading affects children's emergent literacy. *Developmental Psychology, 35,* 20–28.

Rousseau, J.-J. (1832). *Les confessions* [confessions]. Paris: Lebigre Frères.

Sartre, J. P. (1964). *Les Mots* [The words.]. Paris: Gallimard.

Scarborough, H. S. (1989). Prediction of reading disability from familial and individual differences. *Journal of Educational Psychology, 81,* 101–108.

Scarborough, H. S., & Dobrich, W. (1994). On the efficacy of reading to preschoolers. *Developmental Review, 14,* 245–230.

Scarborough, H. S., Dobrich, W., & Hager, M. (1991). Preschool literacy experience and later reading achievement. *Journal of Learning Disabilities, 24,* 508–511.

Sénéchal, M., LeFevre, J-A., Colton, K. V., & Smith, B. L. (1999, April). On the refinement of theoretical models to inform policy and practice. In K. Roskos, *Early literacy at the crossroad: Policy, practice and promise.* Paper presented at the annual meeting of the Aerican Educational Research Association, Montreal.

Sénéchal, M., LeFevre, J.-A., Hudson, E., & Lawson, E. P. (1996). Knowledge of storybooks as a predictor of young children's vocabulary. *Journal of Educational Psychology, 88,* 520–536.

Serpell, R. (1997). Literacy connections between school and home: How should we evaluate them? *Journal of Literacy Research, 29,* 587–616.

Snow, C. E., Barnes, W. S., Chandler, J., Goodman, I. F., & Hemphill, L. (1991). *Unfulfilled expectations. Home and school influences on literacy.* Cambridge, MA: Harvard University Press.

Snowling, M. (2000). *Dyslexia.* Second edition. New York: Blackwell.

Sonnenschein, S., Baker, L., Serpell, R., Scher, D., Fernandez-Fein, S., & Munsterman, K. (1996). *Strands of emergent literacy and their antecedents in the home: Urban preschoolers' early literacy development* (Reading Research Report No. 48). Athens, GA: National Reading Research Center.

Sulzby, E. (1985). Children's emergent reading of favorite storybooks: A developmental study. *Reading Research Quarterly, 20,* 458–481.

Sulzby, E. (1996). Roles of oral and written language as children approach conventional literacy. In C. Pontecorvo, M. Orsolini, B. Burge, & L. B. Resnick (Eds.), *Early text construction in children* (pp. 25–46). Hillsdale, NJ: Erlbaum.

Sulzby, E., & Edwards, P. A. (1993). The role of parents in supporting literacy development of young children. In B. Spodek & O. N. Saracho (Eds.), *Language and literacy in early childhood education: Volume 4, Yearbook in early childhood education* (pp. 156–177). New York: Teachers College Press.

Sulzby, E., & Teale, W. (1991). Emergent literacy. In R. Barr, M. Kamil, P. Mosenthal, & P. D. Pearson (Eds.), *Handbook of reading research* (vol. 2, pp. 727–758). New York: Longman.

Sulzby, E., & Zecker, L. B. (1991). The oral monologue as a form of emergent reading. In A. McCabe & C. Peterson (Eds.), *Developing narrative structure* (pp. 175–213). Hillsdale, NJ: Erlbaum.

van IJzendoorn, M. H. (1991). Attachment in Surinam–Dutch families: A contribution to the cross-cultural study of attachment. *International Journal of Behavioral Development, 13,* 333–344.

van IJzendoorn, M. H. (1995). Adult attachment representations, parental responsiveness, and infant attachment: A meta-analysis on the predictive validity of the adult attachment interview. *Psychological Bulletin, 117,* 387–403.

van IJzendoorn, M. H., & Bus, A. G. (1994). Meta-analytic confirmation of the nonword reading deficit in developmental dyslexia. *Reading Research Quarterly, 30,* 266–275.

VanderVelden, M. C., & Siegel, L. S. (1995). Phonological recoding and phoneme awareness in early literacy: A developmental approach. *Reading Research Quarterly, 30,* 854–875.

Waddell, M., & Firth, B. (1992). *Sam Vole and his brothers*. Cambridge, UK: Camblewick Press.

Wells, G. (1987). The learning of literacy. In B. Fillion, C. Hedley, & E. Dimartino (Eds.), *Home and school: Early language and reading* (pp. 27–46). Norwood, NJ: Ablex.

Whitehurst, G. J., Epstein, J. N., Angell, A. C., Payne, A. C., Crone, D. A., & Fischel, J. E. (1994). Outcomes of an emergent literacy intervention in Head Start. *Journal of Educational Psychology, 30*, 679–689.

Whitehurst, G. J., Falco, F. L., Lonigan, C., Fischel, J. E., DeBaryshe, B. D., Valdez-Menchaca, M. C., & Caulfiels, M. (1988). Accelerating language development through picture-book reading. *Developmental Psychology, 24*, 552–558.

Whitehurst, G. J., Zevenbergen, A. A., Crone, D. A., Schultz, M. D., Velting, O. N., & Fischel, J. E. (1999). Outcomes of emergent literacy intervention from Head Start through second grade. *Journal of Educational Psychology, 91*, 261–272.

14

Early Language and Literacy Skills in Low-Income African American and Hispanic Children

❖

LYNNE VERNON-FEAGANS
CAROL SCHEFFNER HAMMER
ADELE MICCIO
ELIZABETH MANLOVE

Children from diverse backgrounds, ethnicity, and culture begin public school in the United States at age 5 or 6 with the expectation of success in the school environment. Unfortunately, too many of our children who live in poverty have difficulty in the early years of schooling, primarily because of the failure to learn to read (Snow, Burns, & Griffin, 1998; Vernon-Feagans, 1996). Reading in the first few years of school is the major task children need to accomplish and the major thrust of teaching. If a child fails to learn to read well by that time, poor performance in school is almost assured (Alexander & Entwisle, 1988; Children's Defense Fund, 1994; Snow & Tabors, 1993). Understanding how and under what circumstances children of the poor fail to acquire literacy skills is critical for developing programs that will ensure the success of more of our children in the 21st century. This chapter focuses on describing the skills and experiences of children in poverty during the preschool years and how we might use their preschool experiences to more easily ensure the successful transition to literacy. Especially important is an emphasis on understanding the cultural and ethnic diver-sity issues within poverty and how these are related to the acquisition of literacy skills.

The largest group of children who are at risk for school failure in the United States are the children of the poor. Over the last 30 years, poverty rates for children have increased 50% while poverty rates for the elderly have decreased 50%. These poor children perform between 11% and 25% below their nonpoor peers on achievement tests (Children's Defense Fund, 1994). African American children are three times more likely to be poor than are Caucasian and Hispanic children (Children's Defense Fund, 1994) and are twice as likely to read below grade level (Kao & Tienda, 1995). Children of the poor are also at risk for learning disabilities and other special education services often because of failure in literacy. From a summary of 12 studies of long-term poor, poverty was a stronger predictor of school achievement than maternal schooling or family structure (Duncan & Brooks-Gunn, 1997). Because one in four preschool children live in poverty in the United States during the preschool period (Children's Defense Fund, 1994), a large number of children in this country are at risk for school failure, especially in reading. Although there are more poor white children than nonwhite children, a disproportionate percentage of poor children are from black and Hispanic families.

Because of our failure as a society to remedy the poorer performance of these poor and often minority children, scholars have sought to understand the possible causal mechanisms within and outside the child that lead to this poorer performance in school.

Why Are Poor Children at Risk?: The Causal Explanations

Any causal explanation of the poorer performance in reading of poor children must be multifaceted and multiply determined, but three main hypotheses have dominated the literature in an explanation of poor reading and school performance by the children of the poor. They include biological/health mechanisms, the environments in which poor children live, and finally the discrimination and poor fit for many of these children created by schools and the larger society. Each of these is described briefly in an effort to give a backdrop to the literature reviewed in the following sections.

First, families in poverty have poorer health and less access to good health care, not only because they have fewer financial resources but also because of the multiple risk factors associated with poverty (Carnegie Corporation, 1994; Children's Defense Fund, 1994). There is no doubt that poor children have higher rates of being born prematurely, poorer nutrition, lower immunization rates, greater exposure to lead, and a host of other health-related factors (Carnegie Corporation, 1994; Children's Defense Fund, 1994; Shaywitz et al., 1998). All these biological mechanisms can and do have an impact on the developing child. For instance, we know that iron deficiency in infancy and early childhood can lead to poorer cognitive performance in children throughout childhood (Lozoff, 1988, 1992). Children with chronic otitis media (ear infections) in early childhood have been found to be at risk for later school problems in language, reading, and attention (Vernon-Feagans, Hurley, & Yont, in press; see Roberts & Burchinal, Chapter

16). This is especially true for children who are in suboptimal environments such as low-quality child care (Feagans, Kipp, & Blood, 1994; Vernon-Feagans, Emanuel, & Blood, 1997). Children of the poor who are often in crowded living conditions and have poorer health care are even more at risk for the poorer outcomes associated with otitis media. We also know that overall general child health is related to later learning (Carnegie Corporation, 1994). Although not always measured carefully in most studies of literacy development, these factors should not be underestimated, especially in interaction with other risk factors in children's lives.

The environments in which children live have received the greatest attention in the research literature on the possible causes of school failure among the poor. This emphasis has probably been primary because we know that early stimulating environments are related to later performance. The early work of scholars in the field of child development (Bloom, 1964; Hunt, 1961) provided a framework within which to think about the influence of early environments of children. These authors argued that early stimulating environments could permanently alter the neural organization and development of the brain that could lead to better intellectual functioning later. Children not exposed to these stimulating environments may not develop these neurological connections. The early intervention movement and Head Start began with these arguments about children's development (Zigler & Muenchow, 1992) and assumed that the environments of most poor children were much less stimulating than the environments of middle-income families.

Poor families have not always been able to provide their children with the abundant language and especially literacy environments that middle-income families provide. These include the provision of preschool materials in the home, book reading, phonological awareness, and other preliteracy experiences. For instance, 90% of middle-income families reported visiting the library at least once a month, whereas only 43% of low-income families visited the library that often (Baker, Serpell, & Sonnenschein, 1995). Hart and Risley (1995) found that low-income mothers had a much poorer vocabulary in conversation with their young children. Examples such as this, in combination with other studies of the poor, have been used to argue for the powerful influence of early preliteracy and language skills on children's development. More will be said about these experiences in later parts of this chapter. Suffice it to say here that although we have documented many differences in experiences among poor and minority children compared to middle-class families, we still lack important information about specific causal mechanisms that could lead these children to have problems acquiring literacy.

The third explanation relates to the discrimination in the larger society that influences the way in which we think about school failure as well as how these children view themselves in the schooling situation. This also includes how teachers approach teaching these children (Delpit, 1995; Ogbu, 1982, 1988, 1990; Steele, 1992; Vernon-Feagans, 1996). Many authors have argued that institutional racism has affected the ways our schools are structured to teach poor/minority children, making cultural clashes between home and school and home and society so pervasive that failure by many poor children is inevitable without large changes in our teaching of literacy. Again, this explanation is elaborated further in this chapter.

Probably the truth in understanding all this is a combination of all these explanations that may interact in complex ways during the critical preschool years. One theoretical perspective that combines these approaches is a "cumulative risk model." Rutter (1987) and Sameroff, Seifer, Barocas, Zax, and Greenspan (1987) have argued that most individuals, including children, have compensatory mechanisms that buffer them against some of the risk factors that affect all of us. Yet, it is the accumulation of major risks that can make it much less possible that compensatory mechanisms within the individual or in the environment will be able to work. For instance, a child might live in poverty but have a large extended family that provides support and encouragement to the child and no other social/biological risks. This child might do quite well in school. On the other hand, a child who comes from an abusive home environ-

ment, is isolated from others, lives in poverty, and may have been born prematurely has multiple risk factors that put the child at much greater risk. Sameroff et al. (1987) found that children with these multiple risks can be four or five times more likely to have school problems than children with only one or two risk factors.

The problem with much of the literature on children in poverty is that studies have focused on measuring only a few of the risk factors. In fact, most studies of poverty have generally measured environmental factors in the home at the exclusion of measuring health and the larger discrimination in the larger society. In the next sections of this chapter we review the literature with respect to (1) general language and narrative skills in poor young children, (2) the specific experience of book reading and later literacy, and (3) early phonological awareness, especially with respect to dialect and bilingualism. These experiences and skills in early childhood can be attributed to the combination of hypotheses/explanations just discussed and will be refined as the literature is reviewed.

Language, Literacy, and Poverty

Although few large-scale studies specifically focus on language, literacy, and poverty, a variety of smaller studies have provided evidence for some of the critically important factors in early childhood that are related to literacy development. From a number of studies of young preschool children we know that some of the preliteracy skills that children develop over the first 5 or 6 years of life are related to later reading and school achievement in the elementary school years (Hart & Risley, 1995; Snow, Hamphill, & Barnes, 1991; Vernon-Feagans, 1996). Among middle-class white children there is good evidence that parental book reading, high-quality day care, oral narrative/storytelling skills, rhyming activities, parental sensitivity, and other home environment variables are important in predicting literacy outcomes for children (Snow et al., 1999; Sulzby & Teale, 1987, 1991; Taylor & Strickland, 1986; Teale & Sulzby, 1987). We know that some poor children may not be exposed to the same amount or quality of some of these important experiences such as adult elaborated vocabularies, book reading, exposure to libraries, and so on (Hart & Risley, 1995; Ninio, 1990; Snow, Barnes, Chandler, Goodman, & Hemphill, 1991), yet we need to understand more clearly how these skills and experiences that related to literacy in middle-class groups of children are similar or different from those factors in poor and minority children and whether these factors are indeed related to literacy in the same way.

It has been shown in numerous studies that children with early language impairments are more likely to have later significant problems in reading. Recent studies have estimated that between 40–75% of preschoolers with diagnosed language problems develop reading difficulties at school age (Bashir & Scavuzzo, 1992). Although children living in poverty do not all have language impairments their language development has been continually examined over the last 30 years as a source of their general greater rates of school failure (Bereiter & Engelmann, 1966; Bishop & Adams, 1990; Bernstein, 1971; Hart & Risley, 1995; Hess & Shipman, 1965; Ramey & Campbell, 1991). Although poor children enter school slightly behind their nonpoor peers they precipitously decline compared to their peers over the elementary school years (Puma et al., 1997), with one possible explanation that language deficits/differences could be implicated.

Recent evidence from a cultural and bilingual perspective have led us to reexamine early literacy skills and experiences for poor and minority children by trying to understand how their environments support or hinder literacy in different ways from the more mainstream culture (Heath, 1983; Ogbu, 1990; Vernon-Feagans, 1996). Recent studies of the relationship between language and literacy among poor and often minority children have created more complex explanations that integrate cultural and language differences coupled with the pervasive racism and classism within our society.

In an intensive reanalysis of language collected on 29 mostly African American children who were part of the Juniper Gardens project in Kansas City in comparison to 13 children from professional families, it was found that the vocabulary development of the children was vastly different than that of the middle-class children (Hart & Risely, 1995). These differences increased dramatically over the preschool period and were linked later to school achievement in reading and other subject areas. Although the sample size was small, the size of the effect was large. The authors argued that these poor children had been exposed to many fewer vocabulary items by parents as young children and that exposure was causally related to later outcomes. Further, they saw these differences in vocabulary widening with age so that the poor children were unlikely to be able to catch up to their middle-class peers. Greater vocabulary knowledge has been shown to be related to reading comprehension in school-age children (Snow, Burns, & Griffin, 1998; Stanovich, West, Cunningham, Cipielewski, & Siddiqui, 1996). Home literacy activities, such as reading with parents at home during elementary school, have been related to larger vocabularies by the children and more skilled reading comprehension in school (Cain, 1996). As reported in Snow et al. (1998), a review of five studies of expressive vocabulary in kindergarten indicated a consistent correlation of about .45 with reading scores later in elementary school.

The Abecedarian Project in the Piedmont area of North Carolina, a more rural African American sample of poor children, found that these black children had excellent oral language, including vocabulary and superior narrative skills in comparison to middle-class Caucasian children (Feagans & Haskins, 1986; Vernon-Feagans, 1996). These data were collected in the naturalistic neighborhood environment of the children when they were in kindergarten. Black boys were particularly facile at storytelling, with greater numbers of words and narratives than either middle-class white boys and girls or black girls. For many of the Abecedarian children these superior storytelling skills took place in the context of joint storytelling, with an older child helping a younger child create complex and lyrical scenarios of "witches brew with snakes and lizards." The middle-class children were more likely to relate a story they had been told or to talk about an event in their lives without the cooperation of other children or an adult. This replicated the ethnographic work of Heath (1983), who observed young boys from a more rural area of North Carolina learning to tell rich narratives at a very young age and being encouraged by adults to do so. These superior narrative skills in the neighborhood context by the poor black children were paradoxically negatively related to literacy and other school-related and teacher rating measures (Feagans & Haskins, 1986). On the other hand, the neighborhood narrative skills of the Caucasian children in the same classrooms as the Abecedarian children were positively related to school literacy and achievement. There appeared to be a cultural clash between neighborhood and classroom that prevented these black children from using their narrative skills to do well in school.

The Kansas City and North Carolina studies of poor black children highlight the importance of examining context in these developmental studies. It may be that the more rural context with a larger network of extended kin provided the rural poor children with a richer language input not available in the more urban Kansas City context. For instance, in the Abecedarian study it was reported that the poor black children saw on average 37 different relatives per month, whereas the middle-class children saw an average of less than 2 relatives a month (Vernon-Feagans, 1996).

Other data from the Abecedarian Project may also be important in understanding the cultural context of poverty and understanding why the superior language skills of the black children did not protect them from poorer literacy skills. In a structured oral storytelling task, given to the children at school entry and 2 years later, the children in poverty were less able to paraphrase a story they had just demonstrated they understood and they were also less able to answer abstract questions about the story in comparison to their middle-class classroom peers (Feagans & Farran, 1981, 1994; Feagans & Fendt, 1991). Even though the Abecedarian children who received the preschool intervention did better than the preschool control group, both groups of Abecedarian children did more poorly than their middle-class counterparts. It was argued (Feagans & Farran, 1981, 1994; Fea-

gans & Fendt, 1991) that the Abecedarian children may have been less able to paraphrase the stories because they embellished their stories during the paraphrase. That is, unlike their middle-class white peers, they produced elaborate stories but the stories were not generally the ones that had been told to them. They may have interpreted the task quite differently than did middle-class children as one that demanded more creativity and elaboration as we had seen them do in their neighborhood. Yet, this kind of elaborated language use would not be rewarded in school where teachers were trying to ascertain whether the child could parrot back a story as a way of assessing the child's understanding of a story or narrative. This might be construed by some as a kind of discrimination against a style of language. Schools may need to be much more sensitive about these differences, especially early in schooling when children are forming their view about themselves as competent or incompetent learners (Delpit, 1995; Ogbu, 1990).

When both groups of children were asked questions about the story narratives there were no group differences in the number of correct responses but there were differences in the kinds of errors, especially in answer to abstract questions such as "why," "when," and "how." The Abecedarian children more often gave answers that could not be possible answers to these questions by answering a "why" question with a "where" response. These category mistakes have been called unteachable answers (Blank, 1975) because it was found that teachers did not know how to respond constructively to such errors by children. On the other hand, the middle-class white children made a different kind of error by being silent or saying, "I don't know." On the face of it, these two kinds of errors are probably culturally learned as a way to deal with a question when you do not know how to answer it. It should make no difference for the learning of the children in school, but we have evidence to the contrary. In the Abecedarian study, children who made the most category mistake errors were the ones who did the most poorly on reading tests in first and second grade (Feagans & Fendt, 1991), thus indicating that this error type was implicated in literacy failure.

In a follow-up of the group differences in error types by the Abecedarian and mainstream children to understand why this relationship between category mistakes and literacy measures might exist, the actual elementary classroom teachers of the Abecedarian children in kindergarten and second grade were asked to go through a wordless picture book with the Abecedarian child and ask concrete and abstract questions about the picture-book story. The teachers also did this task with the mainstream middle-class same-sex peers chosen as a classroom comparison child for the Abecedarian child in the classroom (Vernon-Feagans, 1996). The teachers were told to try to help each child get the right answer if the child answered incorrectly. Again, there were no differences in the number of correct answers between the middle-class white children and the Abecedarian children, but like the previous finding, the Abecedarian children made more category mistakes while the middle-class white children made more "I don't know" errors. Teachers were very good at following up an incorrect response with a good strategy to help the child get the right answer when the child made an "I don't know" or no-response answer, but they were not at all good in helping children who made category mistakes (Vernon-Feagans, 1996). This gave us some evidence for the possible reason that the Abecedarian children's errors could lead to less learning. Teachers had a difficult time dealing with this cultural difference in error types, which may have resulted in the Abecedarian children receiving less effective feedback in teacher–child dialogues. The Abecedarian children were the children who most needed good corrective feedback, and they were just the ones not receiving it. This kind of poorer interaction between child and teacher may have been at least one of the reasons that these poor children and others were not doing as well in school.

Although few studies of language, literacy, and poverty have examined biological/health data, the Abecedarian project collected excellent health data on a monthly basis from infancy through 5 years of age for those children who were in the intervention day-care group. It was found that children with early nutritional deficits within this group were at much greater risk for later development (Zeskind & Ramey, 1981). In addition, otitis media (middle ear effusion) was carefully documented. Although chronic experience with otitis media in the first 3 years of life did not appear to affect basic language skills such as syntax and vocabulary (Feagans, Sanyal, Henderson, Collier, & Appelbaum, 1987; Roberts, Burchinal, Koch, Footo, & Henderson, 1988), chronic otitis media did predict poorer narrative skills at 5 and 7 years of age. Children with nine or more episodes of otitis media were twice as often observed to be off task in their kindergarten classrooms compared to the children who had fewer episodes (Feagans et al., 1987). This same off-task behavior was also found throughout the elementary school years as assessed by their teachers who found them to be less task oriented (Roberts, Burchinal, Collier, Ramey, Koch, & Henderson, 1989). Although there are many more health-related issues that might influence language and literacy, few other studies have carefully documented these after the preschool years. (See Roberts & Burchinal, Chapter 16, for a more recent analysis.)

More studies need to be conducted that measure the full range of risks that children in poverty face, be it biological/health risks, discrimination, poor teaching, or a poor home environment. These studies support the need to probe more deeply into the use of language in different cultural contexts and to help teachers understand and respond to language use differences more appropriately.

Book-Reading Experiences of African American and Hispanic Children

Although general narrative and language skills appear to be important for good literacy development, the context for that learning that has received the most recent attention is book reading. Although many of these studies are not large, they do provide insight into the possible processes that promote literacy skills in young children. (See Bus, Chapter 13.) Children's early book-reading experiences have been studied extensively because of the benefits they are thought to provide to children's language and literacy development. Researchers have demonstrated that book-reading interactions enhance children's vocabularies (Ninio, 1983; Senechal, LeFevre, Hudson, & Lawson, 1996), provide children with knowledge of language in and talk about books, expose children to print and literacy conventions (Dickinson, De Temple, Hirschler, & Smith, 1992; Snow & Ninio, 1986), and stimulate metalinguistic awareness (Bus, van IJzendorn, & Pelligrini, 1995).

With regard to how parents structure book-reading interactions, investigators have found that when reading to their young children, parents set up joint routines (Ninio & Bruner, 1978). Within these routines, parents ask a high percentage of questions (Anderson-Yockel & Haynes, 1994), adjust their teaching strategies as their children become more proficient in participating in the interactions (Ninio & Bruner, 1978; van Kleeck, Gillam, Hamilton, & McGrath, 1997), and produce more abstract utterances and questions when their children become preschool age (Pellegrini, Perlmutter, Galda, & Brody, 1990; van Kleeck et al., 1997). Although this research provides us with insights about early literacy activities, it is limited in that it has focused on the styles and behaviors of the mothers and children from the white middle class, which may or may not describe what occurs in families from other socioeconomic and cultural groups. The work that has been conducted on families from diverse backgrounds has focused on low-income families. This research, however, has primarily employed samples that consisted of (1) white, low-income children; (2) white and black children combined; or (3) children whose race/culture was not specified. Relatively few investigations have examined the practices of specific minority groups. Research on specific cultural groups, however, is essential, because we cannot assume that cultural differences do not occur between low-income families. In the following section, we review the literature on the book-reading practices of families from African American and Hispanic cultures. Specifically, we discuss how children's experiences differ from the white, middle-class children's experiences, experiences that complement interactions that take place in children's classrooms and address the impact these differences may have on children's learning in school.

The Quantity of Children's Book-Reading Experiences

Research on the quantity of children's book-reading experiences generally supports the conclusion that children from low-income homes and multicultural families are read to less frequently than white, middle-class children (cf. Anderson-Yockel & Haynes, 1994; Hammer, 2001). The Federal Interagency Forum on Child and Family Statistics (1999) found that 41% of families living below the poverty level read to their preschoolers on a daily basis as opposed to 61% of the families whose incomes were at or above the poverty level. Forty-four percent and 39% of African American and Hispanic families, respectively, read daily to their preschoolers as compared with 64% of the white families, demonstrating a clear difference between the mainstream culture and minority cultures.

The Quality of Children's Book-Reading Experiences

Book-Reading Experiences of African American Children

Like their white, middle-class counterparts, African American mothers provide a general interactional structure when looking at books with their children; however, variations in their styles were observed. Three studies have been identified in the literature that have investigated this area. The first study was conducted by Heath (1983), who demonstrated that children's preschool home experiences may differ greatly from the white, middle-class culture. Unlike the nearby mainstream community, the rural, African American families studied by Heath treated literacy activities as a group event. Texts were typically read out loud by adults to others in their group. The meanings of the texts were then jointly constructed as the group members discussed what was read. Children typically had no books, nor were they read to or taught how to read by adults. Rather, they were embedded in a world of environmental print. Adults exposed children to and expected them to tell oral narratives that were "fictionalized" truths or stories that were based on a real event but which emphasized the strengths of the storyteller. This also was found in the narratives told by African American 5-year-old children in a more recent study of African American children in the South (Vernon-Feagans, 1996). She also found sophisticated stories that were jointly created by children of different age levels and skills.

The next studies discussed demonstrate more subtle differences in the book-reading styles of African American mothers. Hammer (2001) described four book-reading styles used by mothers of low and middle socioeconomic status mothers with their infants. These families were living in an urban environment. The first style identified was a "modeling style," a style that one-third of the mothers in the low-SES group exhibited. Mothers who employed this style typically labeled the pictures in the book that served as a model for their children to imitate. The majority of mothers in the middle-SES group and one mother in the low-SES group used a second style, referred to as "different styles for different texts." In general, when looking at picture books with labels or minimal text, the mothers used a modeling style. When looking at books with text, however, they combined reading the text with providing their children models. The third style identified was "reading from the text." One mother in the middle-SES group read straight from the text and deviated from the printed word only when her child's attention to the text waned. The fourth style was labeled "limited periods of joint attention," which two low-SES and one middle-SES mother exhibited. Although all three of these mothers attempted to talk about the books with their children by labeling the pictures, their children did not display interest in the activity. It was hypothesized that the low-SES dyads engaged in book reading for short periods because, as the mothers reported, they were not accustomed to looking at books together. The middle-SES mother reported reading books to her child on a daily basis, but her child did not demonstrate an interest in them. It is important to note, however, that none of the mothers who participated in the study engaged in question-asking routines, a style that is commonly employed by white, middle-class mothers.

Pellegrini et al. (1990) studied an older group of children than Hammer (1999). These researchers investigated how mothers of preschoolers in Head Start provided a general structure to their interactions surrounding narrative and expository texts. In general, Pellegrini et al. (1990) found that mothers produced more low-, medium-, and high-demand strategies when reading expository texts (texts that they read more frequently at home) as opposed to narrative books, and that their children participated to a greater extent when looking at expository texts. In addition, when examining the cognitive demands that mothers placed on the children when looking at familiar and less familiar types of expository texts, these authors determined that the mothers produced more cognitive demands and used more metalinguistic verbs when reading familiar expository texts. Pellegrini et al. (1990) concluded that the mothers were adjusting their language according to their children's abilities and familiarity with the format of the text, a behavior, the authors argue, that white, middle-class mothers engage in with their children.

African American mothers' use of specific communicative acts during book reading have also been investigated to some extent, with the reference group varying in these studies. Hammer (1999) examined the communicative behaviors of low- and middle-SES African American mothers with 12- to 18-month-old infants. The two groups of mothers were similar in that they produced statements, questions, and responses with the same frequency. Low-SES mothers produced significantly more directives than did the middle-SES mothers. This may have been due to the fact that the low-SES mothers reported reading less frequently to their children, and, thus, they needed to use their language to structure their children's attention to the task at hand. Unlike white mothers of infants who set up question-asking routines, both the low- and middle-SES mothers produced relatively few questions.

Anderson-Yockel and Haynes (1994) compared the communicative acts produced by working-class African American and working-class white mothers when reading books to their toddlers. The two groups were similar with respect to frequency with which they produced the various types of communicative acts, with one exception. The African American mothers produced significantly fewer questions than did their white counterparts. This difference in the question-asking behaviors of the mothers had an impact on the children's verbalizations. Not surprisingly, Anderson-Yockel and Haynes (1994) discovered that the white children produced more question-related communications whereas the African American children produced more spontaneous vocalizations.

Thus, the few studies that have been conducted on African American mothers indicate that mothers from this cultural group employ a variety of styles when looking at books with their children, styles that differ from the book-reading routines that white, middle-class mothers display. The studies illustrate that African American mothers resemble white, middle-class mothers in that they adjust their communication (i.e., to involve more abstract language and thought) according to their children's abilities and familiarity with the text genre.

Book-Reading Experiences
of Hispanic Children

Our understanding of the book-reading experiences of Hispanic children from low-income homes is severely limited, even in comparison to our knowledge about African American families. Few studies have examined the home literacy experiences of Hispanic preschoolers. The investigations that have been conducted either explored the general aspects of the children's environment or studied the effects of a home literacy program. Specifically, two studies examined the contexts in which literacy events occurred in children's lives. When studying preschoolers from low-income Hispanic, African American, and white homes, Teale (1986) found, contrary to a commonly held belief that children from low-income homes had little exposure to literacy, that children from all three cultural groups were exposed to literacy experiences throughout their daily routines. However, within all three groups, the children were exposed to a range of and varying amounts of literacy

events in their respective homes. Similarly, Delgado-Gaitan (1990) studied the home literacy opportunities of school-age, Mexican American children (the SES level of the children was not specified). She too found a variety of opportunities available to the children that ranged from the parents providing emotional support for the children's efforts in school to the parents reading books to their children.

Goldenberg, Reese, and Gallimore (1992) investigated Hispanic kindergartners' literacy experiences by studying the effects of a home literacy program which involved sending photocopied storybooks and worksheets home with the children. The results indicated that use of the worksheets but not use of the storybooks was related to children's literacy achievement. The authors suggested that the reason the worksheets were effective was that the worksheets were "more consistent with parents' views of how children learn to read and, therefore, were used in a way that was more meaningful both to parents and children" (Goldenberg et al., 1992, p. 525; see also Chapter 15).

Although these studies on the home environments of Hispanic children are important, the role of bilingualism is an essential aspect of children's development that needs to be understood in relationship to children book-reading and other literacy experiences. However, no studies were found in the literature that specifically examined this issue. Studies have been conducted that examined the children's acquisition of two languages in the home and in school as well as that have studied how to support children's development of both Spanish and English in schools (e.g., Genesee, 1994; Tabors 1997; Vasquez, Pease-Alvarez, & Shannon, 1994; Zentella, 1997), indicating a critical gap in the research base.

The Potential Impact of These Differences on Children's Language Development and School Success

The literacy styles employed by families from the mainstream culture complement the practices used in preschool and elementary classrooms. Thus, children from these families are at an advantage at school because of the similarity between interactional styles, life experiences, and uses of literacy in the home and school environment (Heath & Branscombe, 1986; Panofsky, 1994). Specifically, parents from the mainstream culture employ story grammars and question-asking routines that resemble those used in the schools. As a result, children who do not have such experiences are at risk for school failure for several reasons (Vogt, Jordan, & Tharp, 1987).

First, if book reading is not a common occurrence at home, children may not have gained the abilities that are thought to come from exposure to books at home, which includes vocabulary development, knowledge of print conventions, and emerging metalinguistic awareness. Second, children from different cultures may not have experienced the events the characters encounter in the stories used in school (Bloome, Harris, & Ludlum, 1991). Children who have experienced a particular event or script and are familiar with the vocabulary associated with that event are at an advantage over children who cannot relate to the story due to a lack of knowledge about the topic. Third, children may have different expectations for how meaning is derived and what constitutes a story. The research reviewed illustrates this point well. Heath (1983), for example, found that in the homes of the families she studied, the meaning of the text was jointly constructed and what constituted a "story" differed from what occurred in school, which Heath argued contributed to the children's difficulties in succeeding in school. Finally, and more specifically, children may experience different styles of interaction surrounding books. None of the studies discussed found that African American or Hispanic parents engaged their children in question-asking routines, unlike in white, middle class families where children are asked questions to which adults know the answer. As a result, children from other cultures may experience difficulty attempting to answer the types of questions asked by their teachers. As demonstrated by Heath (1983) and Vernon-Feagans (1996), children may think that they are being tricked or may not understand why they are being asked a question with a known answer and may respond incorrectly.

The question remains what to do about these differences between the home practices of families from nonmainstream cultures and those employed in the school. One solution is to provide parents with training, so that their styles and literacy practices more closely resemble the educational system of this country. The problem with this solution is that literacy is more than a decoding skill. It is an activity that is embedded in a social and cultural context (Bloome et al., 1991; Heath & Branscombe, 1986; McLane & McNamee, 1990; Westby, 1995). Thus, literacy experiences vary between cultures because parents from these cultures provide their children with opportunities to acquire literacy abilities that are pertinent to their lives, abilities that may or may not be the same as those stressed by in school (Heath, 1983; Rogoff, Mistry, Goncu, & Mosier, 1993). Because literacy events are inextricably tied to a family's cultural belief system, making changes in the home environment may be difficult. In addition, asking a family to change its culture by changing its literacy practices may be inappropriate. The problem with this argument, of course, is that literacy skills are needed in order to be successful in the United States. The solution we propose is that instead of asking the family to make all the changes, we ask that school systems meet parents halfway. We suggest that school systems strive to (1) learn about the literacy practices of the children they serve, (2) become sensitive to how these differences between home and school practices may impact children's performance in the classroom, and (3) incorporate the children's home styles into the classroom to help bridge the children's experiences between home and school. (See prevention and intervention strategies, in Strickland, Chapter 22.)

We still need to understand whether these differences can be better used as children enter school. For instance, if African American children have less experience with the question–answer paradigm but do have experience and skill in elaborated storytelling that is often jointly initiated with others, it would seem important that teachers use this knowledge in developing effective literacy strategies. Too often this does not happen and too often the children are found to be "deficient" and not "different" as they enter school.

Phonological Skills and Literacy

Because it is important to understand the general literature on phonological skills independent of the specific issues related to literacy and poverty, this section reviews more generally the importance of phonological skills in the acquisition of literacy and then specifically discusses issues related to dialect and Hispanic bilingualism.

Young children need to acquire a progression of skills to become good readers. They must recognize the relationship between alphabetic symbols and spoken language. This is not an easy task because the printed symbols that make up a word are discrete letters but the units of speech to which they refer (i.e., phonemes) are not (Liberman & Shankweiler, 1985). When a word is spoken, the phonemes overlap to form larger syllabic units (Liberman, Cooper, Shankweiler, & Studdert-Kennedy, 1967). The basic task of the beginning reader is to learn that graphemes represent phonemes (see Adams, Chapter 6). To do this, a child must be aware that the spoken word is composed of individual sounds. This conscious awareness of the sound structure of language and the ability to manipulate phonological segments is called "phonological awareness" (Blachman, 1994; see Goswami, Chapter 9). The relationship between reading and phonological understanding appears to be a reciprocal one. Improved phonology fosters improved reading and vice versa (Bradley & Bryant, 1983; Bryant, MacLean, Bradley, & Crossland, 1990; Byrne, Freebody, & Gates, 1992; Catts, 1991; Ehri & Wilce, 1987; Mann, 1993; Perfetti, Beck, Bell, & Hughes, 1997; Spector, 1992; Torgesen, Wagner, & Rashotte, 1994; Vellutino & Scanlon, 1987). Even when cognitive ability is held constant, phonological awareness tasks account for a large proportion of the variance in reading achievement (Wagner & Torgesen, 1987).

Early problems with phonological awareness have cumulative adverse effects and can lead to reading disability (MacDonald & Cornwall, 1995; Mann, 1993; Stanovich, 1986). Prereaders with the poorest phoneme segmentation skills are most likely to become the poorest readers (Ball & Blachman, 1988). Beginning readers need to have knowledge both of phonological seg-

ments and of letters in order to develop word-recognition abilities; neither alone is sufficient (Byrne & Fielding-Barnsley, 1991). Many beginning readers, unfortunately, do not have this knowledge and children from homes with lower incomes may be most at risk (Adams, 1990). Children who start out behind in phonemic awareness tend to fall further behind (Stanovich, 1987).

Children easily gain access to larger units such as words. Once this is accomplished, a child must become aware that words can be segmented into syllables. Preschoolers are likely to have a general awareness that two words rhyme or that one word is longer than another, but young children generally do not recognize that spoken syllables are composed of phonemes (Treiman, & Baron, 1981). The ability to detect onsets and rhymes is a midway point between awareness of syllables and awareness of phonemes. The onset and rhyme is a linguistic unit that falls between the syllable and the phoneme (Treiman, 1985). An onset is the initial consonant or consonant cluster of a word or syllable and the rhyme is the remainder of the word or syllable (the vowel and any consonant(s) that follow it). In the word "pot," /p/ is the onset and "ot" is the rhyme.

Dialect

Language is used differently by different social groups as well as groups that are separated geographically. The prestige associated with a particular dialect, social pressure, and identity all are important factors in how a child speaks (Labov, 1972). As children become competent communicators, they will use language the way their social group uses language. Dialectal differences affect all aspects of language, including vocabulary and phonology. Unfortunately, there are few good data on the phonological awareness of poor African American children, but we will review a few representative studies.

In an effort to develop methods for teaching reading that take into account home language and culture, Labov, Baker, Bullock, Ross, and Brown (1998) addressed the specific limitations in the reading ability of children who speak African American English (AAE). In the United States, minority status and poverty are highly correlated, and socioeconomic status is highly correlated with reading performance (Labov, Cohen, Robins, & Lewis, 1968). Labov et al. (1998) found that second- and third-grade children suffered a high level of frustration when attempting to read books at their grade levels. In addition to phonological problems, errors appeared to be due to lack of familiarity with the vocabulary and poor strategies for deducing the meanings of unfamiliar words from context. They found specific weaknesses in children's grapheme-to-phoneme processing.

The children in the Labov study (Labov et al., 1968) accurately detected the first letter of a word; however, they did not apply rules of sound–letter correspondences; for example, the word "ceiling" was read as "killing," showing a failure to apply the rule that "c" is pronounced as /s/ before front vowels "e" or "i." It was, however, recognized as "c." This situation changed, however, when onsets had more than a single consonant. Digraphs were read as single graphemes (*their* as *her*) and as other digraphs (*that* as *what*). Locational errors also occurred (*strong* as *short*, *settling* as *stealing*). Labov's data showed that when words were read incorrectly, a lone initial consonant was rarely involved, but if a complex onset was present, it was likely responsible for the error. In addition, errors for the vowel nucleus showed a much higher level of errors than did onsets. Spoken patterns of West Philadelphia English that are not stable (e.g., production of postvocalic /r/) were obstacles in the reading patterns of the children.

Differences between written language and spoken language are greater for AAE than for other dialects, primarily because the reduction of final consonants is more extensive. Among young children, this tendency can lead to an extreme use of homonymy and a greater difficulty in recognizing distinctions that are obvious in more standard dialects. These phonological patterns appeared to obstruct the step from orthographic representation to phonemic interpretation. The success of the children in Labov's study in identifying initial consonants may be attributed to phonics instruction. It is clear from the children's reading

problems, however, that time needs to be devoted to teaching the rhyme of the syllable with emphasis on the ends of words. If there is a high correlation between frequency of reading errors and the complexity of the word and syllable, a lot may be gained by introducing these relationships in early literacy activities.

Bilingualism

In recent years, the growth of diverse ethnic groups in the United States has been explosive. In 1990, it was estimated that 6.3 million school-age children in the United States spoke a language other than English at home. By the turn of the century over 30% of the U.S. population will be from a racial/ethnic minority group (U.S. Bureau of the Census, 1990; see Tabors & Snow, Chapter 12).

There are wide discrepancies between the literacy achievement of minority children from diverse language backgrounds in comparison to that of their majority culture peers. Children from Hispanic backgrounds (the largest language minority in the United States) lag behind their non-Hispanic peers in the acquisition of school-related skills during the preschool years and continue to do so throughout elementary and middle school. To serve these children, differences in language experience that may affect literacy development must be addressed and strategies that meet the particular needs of second-language (L2) learners must be addressed (Gutierrez-Clellan, 1999). Developmental processes that affect children's first-language (L1) phonology are similar across languages. Children from all language backgrounds, for example, tend to produce sounds in the front of the mouth for those in the back (e.g., *key* is produced as *tea*). All language learners, when confronted with syllable structures that are far too complex for their phonetic ability, will modify those structures to make them conform to their phonetic ability (i.e., omit final consonants or reduce clusters to one phoneme).

There is some evidence that the phonological systems of bilingual speakers develop somewhat differently from monolingual speakers of either language because the L1 affects the learning of L2 (Gildersleeve, Davis, & Stubbe, 1996). Existing evidence points to an overall lower intelligibility rating, more errors on consonants and vowels, more distorted sounds, and more uncommon error patterns among bilingual children. Errors may be common to both languages or common to only one (Yavas & Goldstein, 1998). Children in bilingual environments may initially show a greater number of errors but are likely to demonstrate more rapid improvement, closing the gap with monolingual speakers.

Bilingual preschool children initially demonstrate more errors in their spoken phonologies than do their monolingual peers. Some errors are due to transfer from one language to another, but other differences in learners' productions cannot be explained in this way. L2 learners appear to use their own interlanguage, a system that is separate from both the native and target languages (Selinker, 1972). Spanish speakers of English, for example, often produce all final stops as voiceless. Because English has both voiced and voiceless final stops, this phenomena cannot be explained by English input. Spanish does not allow "b," "d," or "g" in final position. Consequently there is nothing for a final consonant devoicing rule to apply to. Thus, it appears that L2 learners internalize their own version of the target language.

The bilingual experience leads to an early awareness of language (Bialystok, 1997; Clyne, 1987; Levy, 1985). Because bilingualism induces an early separation of word and referent, bilingual children develop an early capacity to focus on and analyze the structural properties of language (Hakuta & Diaz, 1985). Despite these findings, many bilingual families encounter prejudices against early bilingualism. Well-intended, but uninformed, educational professionals may view normal language mixing as harmful and ask parents to speak only English. Bilingual families have been known to give up being bilingual, much to their social, cultural, and emotional detriment, because of worries caused by misinformation (Romaine, 1989). Competent bilinguals may be a select group of children with advantaged language learning situations.

Relatively little is known about the influences of bilingualism on early literacy because of the varying definitions of bilingualism stretching from dual exposure at birth

to the introduction of a second language sometime later in childhood. In addition, the learning situation is affected by the languages the parents speak with their children, the parents' native language, and the extent to which the parents' language reflects the dominant language of the community at large (Bialystok, 1997; de Houwer, 1995). One may find that a child goes to a bilingual Spanish–English Head Start program, the child's grandparents speak only in Spanish, the parents mix Spanish and English, and older siblings speak only English. The child may, however, see the grandparents only once a week or, on the other hand, if the grandparent is the babysitter, they may spend most of their waking moments exposed to Spanish. Television programs using English may be watched, but the family may go to Puerto Rico for holidays. Even if a child's larger community is English-speaking, the actual day-to-day reality for the child may be Spanish dominant. It is the language use within the child's individual social network that determines input patterns. Current research findings do not, as a rule, report details of how much time a child spends exposed to a particular language or dialect.

It appears that L2 learners have more difficulty with sounds that are similar to those in their L1 than with sounds that are different (Wode, 1980; Young-Scholten, 1985). The type of errors children produce in L2 will also vary depending on the particular dialect of L1 that is spoken in the child's community. Data on bilingual Spanish–English children indicate different error patterns in English in children who speak Mexican versus Puerto Rican Spanish (Yavas & Goldstein, 1998). Children who speak Puerto Rican Spanish tend to delete word-final /s/ and /n/ as a dialect feature. Speakers of Mexican Spanish are more likely to produce final consonants.

L2 learners may have different reading and spelling skills depending on their familiarity with the written code in their native language. Children across languages use analogies to determine the pronunciation of irregular words (Gombert, Bryant, & Warrick, 1997). Children who are learning to read orthographies in transparent languages, such as Spanish, need less ability to process analogies. Learning opaque languages such as English (more discrepancies in sound–letter relations) requires analogical processing to be used more often. Children with the more transparent language may decode with greater accuracy than those with opaque orthographies (Goswami, Gombert, & Fraca de Barrera, 1998). Ability to use lexical strategies that depend on familiarity with target words may be more difficult for Spanish-speaking children. Consequently, it is important that L2 learners learn several different strategies for decoding and spelling new words, including increased experiences with reading, increased phonological knowledge, and explicit teaching of analogy strategies (Jimenez, Garcia, & Pearson, 1996).

Word decoding or spelling of unfamiliar words can be accomplished by memory, invention, or analogy (Ehri, 1997). Children's previous experiences with the target words are crucial to the retrieval of their memorized representation. Using invention, children assemble pronunciations from letters to decode unfamiliar words. In analogy, knowledge about the pronunciations or spellings of similar words is used to decode the new word. Readers with limited English proficiency have difficulty applying any of these strategies to reading English due to a restricted store of lexical representations for English words and limited phonological knowledge about the pronunciations of different words. Reading comprehension is significantly related to both knowledge of vocabulary and ability to identify cognates (Nagy, Garcia, Durgunoglu, & Hancin-Bhatt, 1993).

Many bilingual children experience some kind of language loss (Kessler, 1984). The degree of competence in both languages before a changed input condition and age play a role in the extent to which productive control over language continues. Parents who are discouraged from speaking naturally to their children, either by mixing or by using one language at a time, are not likely to provide a rich language input to their children. A rich language environment, either monolingual or bilingual, is the most important aspect of early literacy.

Young bilingual children are adept at code switching, hinting at increased metalinguistic awareness. Most studies, however, have paid little attention to the sociolinguistic context in which the child's speech productions occurred. Expectations of the communication partner's language capabilities play a major part in a child's language selection. Like monolingual children, bilingual children attempt to talk like the people around them. Adjusting to the listener's language as well as to what the child senses is expected or approved of may result in less than optimal language performance. Studying bilingual children is an immensely complex problem and the baseline of normal bilingual development is not yet established. Thus, it is difficult to know when bilingual children are experiencing problems.

Traditional family literacy programs focus on having the family read to the child. For families with limited literacy skills or limited school support, this expectation may increase feelings of incompetence as parents. Ruiz (1995) suggests the performance of bilingual children may be maximized if the child is allowed to choose the code (English vs. Spanish), the topic, and the genre of the book. Topics that represent the child's experiences can be incorporated into learning activities (border stories, folktales, etc.).

Although phonological awareness has been shown to be linked to later better reading ability in mainstream children, it is still not clear how dialect and bilingualism affect specific aspects of literacy acquisition. It will be especially important to understand in future studies how the multiple factors associated with minority status and poverty can be separated from such skills as phonological awareness. Further, educators need to be sensitive to those aspects of the dialect or first language that might be especially problematic in acquiring good reading skills.

Future Research

Clearly, given the limited research conducted on both African American and Hispanic children, additional investigations are warranted. Given the piecemeal nature of the research, there needs to be a greater emphasis on measuring the full range of risk and protective factors for poor children, including the importance of health and access to good health care in early childhood, the complex home environment, teaching strategies as children enter school, discrimination, cultural values, and so on. This means investment in large-scale studies that focus on the child and the child's home environment as well as a greater focus on these children's transition to school. Our schools have not always been prepared to teach these children or to deal with the discrimination in the larger society against poor and minority children. Trying to understand the insidious way in which discrimination plays out in the microcosm of the classroom is as important as assessing the developing skills of these children.

A critical area of need relates to the emerging literacy skills of Hispanic children. Studies that document the home, literacy environment, and book-reading interactions between children and caregivers in particular, are greatly lacking. Future studies, however, should focus on families from specific Hispanic subgroups (Puerto Rican American, Mexican American, Cuban American, etc.), as "Hispanic" individuals do not represent a homogeneous group. In addition, studies are needed that examine children's literacy development in both Spanish and English. Specifically, information is needed about (1) children's development of literacy in both languages, (2) children's oral language development in both languages, (3) children's language use and production as a function of the language(s) their communicative partners speak (e.g., monolingual English and Spanish interactants and bilingual interactants), and (4) the relationship between children's home-literacy experiences, oral language abilities, reading, and written language competencies.

Additional studies are needed that examine the home and neighborhood environments of urban versus rural children from both African American and Hispanic families to determine similarities and differences that exist cross-culturally and between socioeconomic groups with respect to preliteracy language experiences and skills. There may be more important differences between urban and rural children than between some SES groups, but currently we have few data especially on rural children. There is a real need to understand the early literacy and language skills of these groups of children so they can be used by teachers in the class-room to promote literacy. Although not discussed at length in this chapter, but found in other chapters in this book (e.g., Goldenburg, Chapter 15; Vellutino & Scanlon, Chapter 20; Strickland, Chapter 21), there is a real need to develop better prevention strategies that teachers can use as poor children enter school. Many programs are being implemented, but not many are individuated for the background multiple risk factors presented by the child. The 21st century presents a number of challenges for understanding literacy development in poor children and especially designing ways to ensure that all our children will be successful in school.

Acknowledgment

The preparation of this chapter was supported in part by Grant No. HD131540 from the National Institutes of Health.

References

Adams, M. J. (1990). *Beginning to read: Thinking and learning about print.* Cambridge, MA: MIT Press.

Alexander, L. K., & Entwisle, D. R. (1988). Achievement in the first 2 years of school: Patterns and processes. *Monographs of the Society for Research in Child Development, 53* (2, Serial No. 218).

Anderson-Yockel, J., & Haynes, W. (1994). Joint picture-book reading strategies in working-class African American and white mother–toddler dyads. *Journal of Speech, Language, and Hearing Research, 37,* 583–593.

Baker, L., Serpell, R., & Sonnenschein, S. (1995). Opportunities for literacy learning in the homes of urban preschoolers. In L. M. Morrow (Ed.), *Family literacy: Connections in schools and communities* (pp. 236–252). Newark, DE: International Reading Association.

Ball, E., & Blachman, B. (1988). Phoneme segmentation training: Effect on reading readiness. *Annals of Dyslexia, 38,* 208–225.

Bashir, A. S., & Scavuzzo, A. (1992). Childern with language disorders: Natural history and academic success. *Journal of Learning Disabilities, 25,* 53–65.

Bereiter, C., & Engelmann, S. (1966). *Teaching disadvantaged children in the preschool.* Englewood Cliffs, NJ: Prentice-Hall.

Bernstein, B. (1971). Language and socialization. In N. Minnis (Ed.), *Linguistics at large* (pp. 227–245). New York: Viking.

Bialystok, E. (1997). Effects of bilingualism and

biliteracy on children's emerging concepts of print. *Developmental Psychology, 33,* 429–440.

Bishop, D. V. M., & Adams, C. (1990). A prospective study of the relationship between specific language impairment, phonological disorders and reading retardation. *Journal of Child Psychology and Psychiatry, 31,* 1027–1050.

Blachman, B. (1994). Early literacy acquisition: The role of phonological awareness. In G. P. Wallach & K. G. Butler (Eds.), *Language learning disabilities in school-age children and adolescents* (pp. 253–274). New York: Merrill.

Blank, M. (1975). Mastering the intangible through language. In I. D. Aaronson & R. W. Rieber (Eds.), *Developmental psycholinguistics and communication of sciences* (pp. 44–58). New York: New York Academy of Sciences.

Bloom, B. (1964). *Stability and change in human characteristics.* New York: Wiley.

Bloome, D., Harris, O., & Ludlum, D. (1991). Reading and writing as sociocultural activities: Politics and pedagogy in the classroom. *Topics in Language Disorders, 11,* 14–27.

Bradley, L., & Bryant, B. (1983). Categorizing sounds and learning to read—A causal connection. *Nature, 301,* 419–421.

Bryant, MacLean, M., Bradley, L., & Crossland, J. (1990). Rhyme and alliteration, phoneme detection, and learning to read. *Developmental Psychology, 26,* 429–438.

Bus, A. G., van IJzendoorn, & Pellegrini, A. D. (1995). Joint book reading makes for success in learning to read: A meta-analysis on intergenerational transmission of literacy. *Review of Educational Research, 65,* 1–21.

Byrne, B., & Fielding-Barnsley, R. (1991). Evaluation of a program to teach phonemic awareness to young children. *Journal of Educational Psychology, 83,* 451–455.

Byrne, B., Freebody, P., & Gates, A. (1992). Longitudinal data on the relations of word-reading strategies to comprehension, reading time, and phonemic awareness. *Reading Research Quarterly, 27,* 140–151.

Cain, K. (1996). Story knowledge and comprehension skills. In C. Cornoldi & J. Oakhill (Eds.), *Reading comprehension difficulties: Processes and intervention* (pp. 167–192). Mahwah, NJ: Erlbaum.

Carnegie Corporation of New York. (1994). *Starting points: Meeting the needs of our youngest children.* New York: Author.

Catts, H. (1991). Early identification of dyslexia: Evidence from a follow-up study of speech-language impaired children. *Annals of Dyslexia, 41,* 163–177.

Children's Defense Fund. (1994). *Wasting America's future: The Children's Defense Fund report on the costs of child poverty.* Boston: Beacon Press.

Clyne, M. (1987). "Don't you get bored speaking only English?" Expressions of metalinguistic awareness in a bilingual child. In R. Steele & T. Threadgold (Eds.), *Language topics: Essays in honour of Michael Halliday* (pp. 85–103). Amsterdam: John Benjamins.

de Houwer, A. (1995). Bilingual language acquisition. In P. Fletcher & B. MacWhinney (Eds.), *The handbook of child language* (pp. 219–250). Cambridge, MA: Blackwell.

Delgado-Gaitan, C. (1990). *Literacy for empowerment: The role of parents in children's education.* New York: Falmer Press.

Delpit, L. (1995). *Other people's children: Cultural conflict in the classroom.* New York: New Press.

Dickinson, D. C., De Temple, J. M., Hirschler, J. A., & Smith, M. W. (1992). Book reading with preschoolers: Coconstruction of text at home and at school. *Early Childhood Research Quarterly, 7,* 323–346.

Duncan, G., & Brooks-Gunn, J. (1997). *Consequences of growing up poor.* New York: Russell Sage.

Ehri, L. C. (1997). Learning to read and learning to spell are one and the same, almost. In C. A. Perfetti, L. Rieben, & M. Fayol (Eds.), *Learning to spell: Research, theory, and practice across languages* (pp. 237–269). Mahwah, NJ: Erlbaum.

Ehri, L. C., & Wilce, L. (1987). Does learning to spell help beginners learn to read words. *Reading Research Quarterly, 12,* 47–64.

Feagans, L., & Farran, D. C. (1981). How demonstrated comprehension can get muddled in production. *Developmental Psychology, 17,* 718–727.

Feagans, L. V., & Farran, D. C. (1994). The effects of daycare intervention in the preschool years on the narrative skills of poverty children in kindergarten. *International Journal of Behavioral Development, 17,* 503–523.

Feagans, L., & Fendt, K. (1991). The effects of intervention and social class on children's answers to concrete and abstract questions. *Journal of Applied Developmental Psychology, 12,* 115–130.

Feagans, L., & Haskins, R. (1986). Neighborhood dialogues of black and white 5-year-olds. *Journal of Applied Developmental Psychology, 7,* 181–200.

Feagans, L. V., Kipp, E. K., & Blood, I. (1994). The effects of otitis media on the language and attention skills of daycare attending toddlers. *Developmental Psychology, 30,* 701–708.

Feagans, L., Sanyal, M., Henderson, F., Collier, A., & Appelbaum, M. (1987). Relationship of middle ear disease in early childhood to later narrative and attention skills. *Journal of Pediatric Psychology, 12,* 581–594.

Federal Interagency Forum on Child and Family Statistics. (1999). *America's children: Key national indicators of well-being, 1999.* Washington, DC: U. S. Government Printing Office.

Genesee, F. (1994). *Educating second language children.* New York: Cambridge University Press.

Gildersleeve, C., Davis, B., & Stubbe, E. (1996). *When monolingual rules don't apply: Speech development in a bilingual environment.* Paper presented at the annual meeting of the American

Speech–Language–Hearing Association, Seattle, WA.

Goldenberg, C., Reese, L., & Gallimore, R. (1992). Effects of literacy materials from school on Latino children's home experiences and early reading achievement. *American Journal of Education, 100,* 497–536.

Gombert, J. E., Bryant, P., & Warrick, N. (1997). Children's use of analogy in learning to read and to spell. In C. A. Perfetti, L. Rieben, & M. Fayol (Eds.), *Learning to spell: Research, theory, and practice across languages* (pp. 221–235). Mahwah, NJ: Erlbaum.

Goswami, U., Gombert, J. E., & Fraca de Barrera, L. (1998). Children's orthographic representations and linguistic transparency: Nonsense word reading in English, French, and Spanish. *Applied Psycholinguistics, 19,* 19–52.

Gutierrez-Clellan, V. F. (1999). Mediating literacy skills in Spanish-speaking children with special needs. *Language, Speech, and Hearing Services in Schools, 30,* 285–292.

Hakuta, K., & Diaz, R. (1985). The relationship between degree of bilingualism and cognitive ability. In K. Nelson (Ed.), *Children's language* (vol. 5, pp. 319–344). Hillsdale, NJ: Erlbaum.

Hammer, C. S. (2001). Come sit down and let mama read: Book reading interactions between African American mothers and their infants (pp. 21–44). In J. Harris, A. Kamhi, & K. Pollock (Eds.), *Literacy in African American communities.* Hillsdale, NJ: Erlbaum.

Hammer, C. S. (1999). Guiding language development: How African American Mothers and their infants structure play. *Journal of Speech and Hearing Research, 42,* 1219–1233.

Hart, B., & Risley, T. R. (1995). *Meaningful differences in the everyday experience of young American children.* Baltimore: Brookes.

Heath, S. B. (1983). *Ways with words.* New York: Cambridge University Press.

Heath, S. B., & Branscombe, A. (1986). The book as narrative prop in language acquisition. In B. Schieffelin & P. Gilmore (Eds.), *The acquisition of literacy: Ethnographic perspectives* (pp. 16–34). Norwood, NJ: Ablex.

Hess, R. D., & Shipman, V. C. (1965). Early experience and the socialization of cognitive modes in children. *Child Development, 36,* 869–886.

Hunt, J. (1961). *Intelligence and experience.* New York: Ronald Press.

Jimenez, R. T., Garcia, G. E., & Pearson, P. D. (1996). The reading strategies of bilingual Latino/o students who are successful English readers: Opportunities and obstacles. *Reading Research Quarterly, 3,* 90–112.

Kao, G., & Tienda, M. (1995). Optimism and achievement: The educational performance of immigrant youth. *Social Science Quarterly, 76,* 1–19.

Kessler, C. (1984). Language acquisition in bilingual children. In N. Miller (Ed.), *Bilingualism and language disability: Assessment and remediation* (pp. 26–54). London: Croom Helm.

Labov, W. (1972). *Sociolinguistic patterns.* Philadelphia: University of Pennsylvania Press.

Labov, W., Baker, B., Bullock, S., Ross, L., & Brown, M. (1998). *A graphemic–phonemic analysis of the reading errors of inner city children.* Unpublished manuscript, University of Pennsylvania. Available: http://www. Ling. upenn. edu/~labov/Papers/GAREC/GAREC. html

Labov, W., Cohen, P., Robins, C., & Lewis, J. (1968). A study of the nonstandard English of Negro and Puerto Rican speakers in New York City. *Cooperative Research Report 3288. Vols I and II.* Philadelphia: U. S. Regional Survey (Linguistics laboratory, University of Pennsylvania).

Levy, Y. (1985). Theoretical gains from the study of bilingualism: A case report. *Language Learning, 35,* 541–54.

Liberman, I. Y., Cooper, F. S., Shankweiler, D., & Studdert-Kennedy, M. (1967). Perception of the speech code. *Psychological Review, 74,* 431–461.

Liberman, I. Y., & Shankweiler, D. (1985). Phonology and the problems of learning to read and write. *Remedial and Special Education, 6,* 8–17.

Lozoff, B. (1988). Behavioral alterations in iron deficiency. *Advances in Pediatrics, 35,* 331–360.

Lozoff, B. (1992). Iron deficiency anemia and infant behavior. In E. J. Susman, L. V. Feagans, & W. J. Ray (Eds.), *Emotion, cognition, health, and development in children and adolescents* (pp. 111–120). Hillsdale, NJ: Erlbaum.

MacDonald, G. W., & Cornwall, A. (1995). The relationship between phonological awareness and reading and spelling achievement eleven years later. *Journal of Learning Disability, 28,* 523–527.

Mann, V. (1993). Phoneme awareness and future reading ability. *Journal of Learning Disabilities, 26,* 259–269.

McLane, J., & McNamee, G. (1990). The beginnings of literacy. *Zero to Three, 12,* 1–8.

Nagy, W. E., Garcia, G. E., Durgunoglu, A. Y., & Hancin, Bhatt, B. (1993). Spanish–English bilingual students' use of cognates in English reading. *Journal of Reading Behavior, 25,* 241–259.

Ninio, A. (1983). Joint book reading as a multiple vocabulary acquisition device. *Developmental Psychology, 19,* 445–451.

Ninio, A. (1990). Early environmental experiences and school achievement in the second grade: An Israeli study. *International Journal of Behavioral Development, 13,* 11–22.

Ninio, A., & Bruner, J. (1978). The achievement and antecedents of labeling. *Journal of Child Language, 5,* 1–15.

Ogbu, J. U. (1982). Societal forces as a context of ghetto children's school failure. In L. Feagans & D. C. Farran (Eds.), *The language of children reared in poverty* (pp. 117–138). New York: Academic Press.

Ogbu, J. (1988). Cultural diversity and human development. *New Directions for Child Development, 42,* 11.

Ogbu, J. U. (1990). Minority status and literacy in comparative perspective. *Daedalus, 119,* 141–168.

Panofsky, C. (1994). Developing the representational functions of language. In V. John-Steiner, C. Panofsky, & L. Smith (Eds.), *Sociocultural approaches to language and literacy* (pp. 223–242). New York: Cambridge University Press.

Pellegrini, A., Perlmutter, J., Galda, L., & Brody, G. (1990). Joint reading between black Head Start children and their mothers. *Child Development, 61,* 443–453.

Perfetti, C. C., Beck, I., Bell, L. C., & Hughes, C. (1997). Phonemic knowledge and learning to read are reciprocal: A longitudinal study of first grade children. *Merrill-Palmer Quarterly, 33,* 283–319.

Puma, M. N., Karweit, N., Price, C., Ricciuti, A., Thompson, W., & Vanden-Kiernan, M. (1997). *Prospects: Final report on student outcomes.* Washington, DC: U. S. Department of Education, Planning and Evaluation Services.

Ramey, C. T., & Campbell, F. A. (1991). Poverty, early-childhood education, and academic competence: The Abecedarian experiment. In A. Huston (Ed.), *Children reared in poverty* (pp. 190–221). New York: Cambridge University Press.

Roberts, J. E., Burchinal, M. R., Collier, A. M., Ramey, C. T., Koch, M. A., & Henderson, F. W. (1989). Otitis media in early childhood and cognitive, academic and classroom performance of the school-aged child. *Pediatrics, 83,* 477–485.

Roberts, J. E., Burchinal, M. R., Koch, M. A., Footo, M. M., & Henderson, F. W. (1988). Otitis media in early childhood and its relationship to later phonological development. *Journal of Speech and Hearing Disabilities, 53,* 416–424.

Rogoff, B., Mistry, J., Goncu, A., & Mosier, C. (1993). Guided participation in cultural activity by toddlers and caregivers. *Monographs of the Society for Research in Child Development, 58*(8).

Romaine, S. (1989). *Bilingualism.* Oxford: Blackwell.

Ruiz, N. T. (1995). The social construction of ability and disability: I. Profile types of Latino children identified as language learning disabled. *Journal of Learning Disabilities. 28,* 476–490.

Rutter, M. (1987). Psychosocial resilience and protective mechanisms. *American Journal of Orthopsychiatry, 57,* 316–331.

Sameroff, A. J., Seifer, R., Barocas, R., Zax, M., & Greenspan, S. (1987). Intelligence quotient scores of 4-year-old children: Social environmental risk factors. *Pediatrics, 79,* 343–350.

Selinker, L. (1972). Interlanguage. *International Review of Applied Linguistics, 10,* 209–2321.

Senechal, M., LeFevre, J., Hudson, E., & Lawson, E. P. (1996). Knowledge of storybooks as a predictor of young children's vocabulary. *Journal of Educational Psychology, 88,* 520–536.

Shaywitz, S. E., Shaywitz, B. A., Pugh, K. R., Fulbright, R. K., Constable, R. T., Mencl, W. E., Shankweiler, D. P., Liberman, A. M., Skudlarski, P., Fletcher, J. M., Katz, L., Marchione, K. E., Lacadie, C., Gatenby, C., & Gore, J. C. (1998). Functional disruption in the organization of the brain for reading in dyslexia. *Proceedings of the National Academy of Sciences, 95,* 2636–2641.

Snow, C. E., Barnes, W. S., Chandler, J., Goodman, I. F., & Hemphill, L. (1991). *Unfulfilled expectations: Home and school influences on literacy.* New York: Cambridge University Press.

Snow, C., Burns, S., & Griffin, M.. (1998). *Preventing reading difficulties in young children.* Washington, DC: National Academy Press.

Snow, C. E., Hamphill, L., & Barnes, W. S. (Eds.). (1991). *Unfulfilled expectations: Home and school influences on literacy.* Cambridge, MA: Harvard University Press.

Snow, C. E., & Tabors, P. O. (1993). Language skills that relate to literacy development. In B. Spodek & O. N. Saracho (Eds.), *Language and literacy in early childhood education* (pp. 1–20). New York: Teachers College Press.

Spector, J. (1992). Predicting progress in beginning reading: Dynamic assessment of phonemic awareness. *Journal of Educational Psychology, 84,* 353–363.

Stanovich, K. E. (1986). Matthew effects in reading: Some consequences of individual differences in the acquisition of literacy. *Reading Research Quarterly, 21,* 360–407.

Stanovich, K. E. (Ed.). (1987). Introduction. Children's reading and the development of phonological awareness [Special issue]. *Merrill–Palmer Quarterly, 33*(3).

Stanovich, K. E., West, R. F., Cunningham, A. E., Cipielewski, J., & Siddiqui, S. (1996). The role of inadequate print exposure as a determinant of reading comprehension problems. In C. Cornoldi & J. Oakhill (Eds.), *Reading comprehension difficulties: Processes and intervention.* Mahwah, NJ: Erlbaum.

Steele, C. M. (1992). Race and the schooling of black Americans. *Atlantic Monthly, 269,* 67–78.

Sulzby, E., & Teale, W. H. (1987). *Young children's storybook reading: Longitudinal study of parent–child interaction and children's independent functioning* (Final report to the Spencer Foundation). Ann Arbor: University of Michigan Press.

Sulzby, E., & Teale, W. (1991). Emergent literacy. In R. Barr, M. Kamil, P. Mosenthal, & P. D. Pearson (Eds.), *Handbook of reading research* (vol. II, pp. 727–758). New York: Longman.

Tabors, P. (1997). *One child, two languages.* Baltimore: Brookes.

Taylor, D., & Strickland, D. (1986). *Family storybook reading.* Portsmouth, NH: Heinemann.

Teale, W. (1986). Home background and young children's literacy development. In W. Teale & E. Sulzby (Eds.), *Emergent literacy: Writing and research* (pp. 173–206). Norwood, NJ: Ablex.

Teale, W. H., & Sulzby, E. (1987). Literacy acquisition in early childhood: The roles of access and mediation in storybook reading. In D. Wagner (Ed.), *The future of literacy in a changing world* (pp. 111–130). New York: Pergamon Press.

Torgesen, J., Wagner, R., & Rashotte, C. (1994). Longitudinal studies of phonological processing and reading. *Journal of Learning Disabilities, 27,* 276–286.

Treiman, R. A. (1985). Onsets and rimes as units of spoken syllables: Evidence from children. *Journal of Experimental Child Psychology, 39,* 161–181.

Treiman, R., & Baron, J. (1981). Segmental analysis ability: Development and relation to reading ability. *Reading Research: Advances in Theory and Practice, 3,* 159–198.

U. S. Bureau of the Census. (1990). *Statistical abstract of the United States (11th ed.).* Washington, DC: U. S. Department of Commerce.

Van Kleeck, A., Gillam, R. B., Hamilton, L., & McGrath, C. (1997). The relationship between middle-class parents' book-sharing discussion and their preschoolers' abstract language development. *Journal of Speech and Hearing Research, 40,* 1261–1271.

Vasquez, O., Pease-Alvarez, L., & Shannon, S. (1994). *Pushing boundaries: Language and culture in a Mexicano community.* New York: Cambridge University Press.

Vellutino, F., & Scanlon, D. (1987). Phonological coding, phonological awareness, and reading ability: Evidence from a longitudinal and experimental study. *Merrill–Palmer Quarterly, 33,* 321–363.

Vernon-Feagans, L. (1996). *Children's talk in communities and classrooms.* Cambridge, MA: Blackwell.

Vernon-Feagans, L., Emanuel, D. C., & Blood, I. (1997). The effect of otitis media and quality of daycare on children's language development. *Journal of Applied Developmental Psychology, 18,* 395–409.

Vernon-Feagans, L., Hurley, M., & Yont, K. (in press). The effect of daycare quality and otitis media on mother/child bookreading and other language measures. In D. J. Lim, C. D. Bluestone, & M. L. Casselbrant (Eds.), *Proceedings of recent advances in otitis media.* Ontario: Decker Periodicals.

Vogt, L., Jordan, C., & Tharp, R. (1987). Explaining school failure, producing school success: Two cases. *Anthropology and Education Quarterly, 18,* 276–286.

Wagner, R. K., & Torgesen, J. K. (1987). The nature of phonological processing and its causal role in the acquisition of reading skills. *Psychological Bulletin, 101,* 192–212.

Westby, C. (1995). Culture and literacy: Frameworks for understanding. *Topics in Language Disorders, 16,* 50–66.

Wode, H. (1980). Phonology in L2 acquisition. In S. Felix. (Ed.), *Second language development* (pp. 123–136). Tubingen: Narr.

Yavas, M., & Goldstein, B. (1998). Phonological assessment and treatment of bilingual speakers. *American Journal of Speech–Language Pathology, 7,* 49–60.

Young-Scholten, M. (1985). Interference reconsidered: The role of similarity in second language acquisition. *Selecta, 6,* 6–12.

Zentella, A. (1997). *Growing up bilingual.* Malden, MA: Blackwell.

Zeskind, P. S., & Ramey, C. T. (1981). Preventing intellectual and interactional sequelae of fetal malnutrition: A longitudinal, transactional and synergistic approach to development. *Child Development, 52,* 213–218.

Zigler, E., & Muenchow, S. (1992). *Head Start: The inside story of America's most successful educational experiment.* New York: Basic Books.

15

Making Schools Work for Low-Income Families in the 21st Century

❖

CLAUDE GOLDENBERG

In the final decade of the last century, the United States committed itself to eight education goals for the year 2000 (National Education Goals Panel, 1997a). Three of these goals are at the heart of this chapter: All children will begin school "ready to learn" (Goal 1); all students will leave grade 4 (as well as grades 8 and 12) demonstrating "competency over challenging subject matter" (Goal 3); and every school will promote parent involvement to support "the social, emotional, and academic growth of children" (Goal 8).

These goals are highly interrelated. School readiness predicts school success, and parent involvement is deeply implicated in both. More to the point of this volume, the literacy experiences, skills, and knowledge with which a child begins school will influence literacy development, and parents are an important influence at all points in this development. Parents influence how much experience children have with books and other reading materials, their familiarity with letters and sounds, the vocabulary they develop, and the reading and writing habits, opportunities, and experiences they have, in and out of school, once they begin school. All these influence literacy development. I do not mean to suggest that factors intrinsic to the child (e.g., motivation and interest, intelligence, phonemic sensitivity)

are irrelevant. The focus of this chapter, however, is on environmental factors, that is, the sorts of experiences schools and families can provide that will enhance literacy development, either independent of these intrinsic factors or working through them.

The three goals—school readiness, school success (academic competence), and parent involvement—are of a piece, each one shining a light on a distinct facet of children's academic and literacy development (see Figure 15.1). All children must start school ready to benefit from the learning experiences they will have there; all children, once they begin school, must develop academic competencies required for later success in school and in life, and every school must engage parents as partners in an educational process that will help advance the goals of school readiness and school success.

These are tall orders. "All" children and "every" school mean a lot of children and many schools. As the 20th century came to an end, there were nearly 23 million children between the ages of 0 and 5 in the United States.; by 2020 there will be more than 26 million. There were another 24 million between the ages of 6 and 11; by 2020 there will be nearly 26 million (Federal Interagency Forum on Child and Family Statistics, 1999). More than 46 million children in all attend nearly 88,000 pre-K–12

211

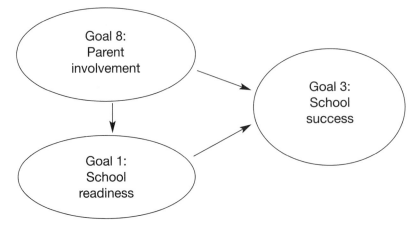

FIGURE 15.1. Three national educational goals.

public schools (U.S. Deptartment of Education, 1999a), and the numbers continue growing (U.S. Deptartment of Education, 1999b).

Now that the year 21st century is here, how close are we to reaching these national goals? The short answer is we have a way to go. And for some children—especially those who are poor and members of certain ethnic/cultural and linguistic groups—we have an even longer way to go (see Table 15.1).

Despite nearly universal agreement on the importance of these national goals, we were far from attaining them as the 20th century drew to a close. The goals were even more distant for low-income and culturally diverse students. The challenge of making these goals a reality is likely to increase as we see not only increases in the actual numbers of children and schools but also increases in the social, economic, and linguistic diversity of our populace (Federal Interagency Forum on Child and Family Statistics, 1999).

Attaining these goals is essential if we are to make schools work for all students. What do we need to do to accomplish our national education goals for children from low-income families? Not surprisingly, there are no simple answers. They depend on a wide range of considerations having to do with the nature of early literacy and how best to promote it; the influence of socioeconomic status, language, and culture on children's formal schooling; and what parent involvement (sometimes referred to as home–school

connections or partnerships) can and should be. Each of these topics is discussed in turn.

The Challenges We Face

The challenge of making schools work for all children, regardless of income level, is formidable for many reasons. One is the nature of learning to read itself and the many uncertainties and controversies surrounding this critical accomplishment. Another is the issue of poverty and cultural and linguistic diversity. I review these issues in this section.

Learning to Read: Controversies and Emerging Consensus

One of the most controversial topics in education centers on questions of what early literacy is and how children learn to read. These questions are central to the three national goals of school readiness, parent involvement, and high levels of academic competence. Other chapters in this volume (see Chapters 1–5 in Part I) address what literacy is directly, so I do not go into great detail here. But readers must be aware of how fundamentally these issues color our thinking about how to accomplish the education goals our nation has set for *all* children. Children from low-income families are more dependent on school experiences for their academic literacy development than are middle-class children (Alexander & En-

TABLE 15.1. National Education Goals for All: The Rhetoric-to-Reality Gap

Goal 1: All students will begin school ready to learn	
% 3- and 4-yr-olds attending preschool[a]	48
• % children from homes earning more than $75K/yr who attend preschool[a]	79
• % children from homes earning less than $10K/yr who attend preschool[a]	43
• % Hispanic children who attend preschool[b]	31
• % black children who attend preschool[b]	55
% 3- to 5-yr-olds read to every day[c]	57
• % read to 3+/wk whose parents have graduate/professional degrees[c]	96
• % read to 3+/wk whose parents have less than high school diploma[c]	59
• % white, non-Hispanic children read to every day[b]	64
• % Hispanic children read to every day[b]	39
• % black children read to every day[b]	44

Goal 3: All students will demonstrate competency over challenging subject matter	
% 4th-graders reading at least at "basic" level[d]	62
% 4th-graders writing at least at "basic" level[e]	84
% 4th-graders reading at "proficient" level[d]	31
% 4th-graders writing at "proficient" level[e]	23
• % non-low-income 4th-graders who are "proficient" readers[d]	40
• % low-income 4th-graders who are "proficient" readers[d]	13
• % 4th-graders with college graduate parent who are "proficient" writers[e]	27
• % 4th-graders with non-high school graduate parent who are "proficient" writers[e]	12
• % white 4th-graders who are "proficient" readers[d]/writers[e]	39/29
• % Asian 4th-graders who are "proficient" readers[d]/writers[e]	37/36
• % Hispanic 4th-graders who are "proficient" readers[d]/writers[e]	13/10
• % black 4th-graders who are "proficient" readers[d]/writers[e]	10/8
• % American Indian 4th-graders who are "proficient" readers[d]/writers[e]	14/11

Goal 8: All schools will promote parent involvement to support children's social, emotional, and academic growth	
% elementary schools having these parent involvement activities	
• Parent conferences, arts events, open houses, or back-to-school nights[f]	92–97
• Providing information about school test performance, student progress, or school goals/objectives[g]	83–85
• Providing information about how to promote learning at home (e.g., helping with homework and study skills) and how to inform parents about child-rearing issues (e.g., discipline) [g]	82–89
• Parent advisory group or policy council[f]	79
• Providing information about improvements in children's performance[g]	72
• Providing examples of student work meeting high standards[g]	60
% elementary schools reporting most or all parents attend	
• Open house or back-to-school night[f]	49
• Parent–teacher conferences[f]	57
• Performing arts events[f]	36
• Science fairs or academic events[f]	19
• % schools with <25 % high-poverty students reporting high parent turnout[f]	72
• % schools with >50% high-poverty students reporting high parent turnout[f]	28
• % schools with <20% minority enrollment reporting high parent turnout[f]	60
• % schools with >50% minority enrollment reporting high parent turnout[f]	30

[a]National Education Goals Panel (1997b); [b]Federal Interagency Forum on Child and Family Statistics (1999); [c]U.S. Department of Education (1998a); [d]U.S. Department of Education (1999c); [e]U.S. Department of Education (1999d); [f]U.S. Department of Education (1996); [g]U.S. Department of Education (1998b).

twisle, 1996; Snow, Barnes, Chandler, Goodman, & Hemphill, 1991). It is not that low-income children have no literacy experiences at home; this is a harmful misconception. And it is flatly untrue (see, e.g., Anderson & Stokes, 1984; Clark, 1983; Goldenberg & Gallimore, 1995; Goldenberg, Reese, & Gallimore, 1992; Paratore, Melzi, & Krol-Sinclair, 1999; Taylor & Dorsey-Gaines, 1988; Teale, 1986). Nonetheless, low-income children come to school with fewer literacy experiences than their more affluent peers. Disagreements over how best to promote early and continued literacy growth, therefore, take on added significance for children who face greater risk for underachievement.

A key dimension in this controversy is the classic question of how much to emphasize letters and sounds and how they combine to form words, usually referred to as phonics. The historic significance of this controversy (see Chall, 1983) was acknowledged once again when the *Reading Research Quarterly* reprinted the classic "First Grade Studies," along with commentaries and personal reflections from reading educators (*Reading Research Quarterly*, 1997). Over the past two decades, an analogous controversy during the preschool years has emerged and become an important component in discussions of what it means to be "ready" to start school. Researchers in the 1980s discovered that "phonological awareness" is an important precursor of learning to read ("Children's reading," 1987) (see also Adams, Chapter 6; Vellutino & Scanlon, Chapter 20; and Stahl, Chapter 22, for example).

Although there is fairly wide agreement that phonological awareness is an important aspect of being ready to learn to read (e.g., Ralph, Ellis, & Medina, 1998; Snow, Burns, & Griffith, 1998; Troia, 1999; Yopp, Yopp, Harris, & Stapleton, 1998), there is less agreement about what this means practically. Should children receive direct instruction and training (e.g., Ball & Blachman, 1988, 1991)? Or should teachers promote phonological awareness by using "natural language" activities, such as poems, chants, and songs (Ralph et al., 1998)? How do teachers attain the right "balance between authentic tasks and skill practice" (Schickedanz, 1998, p. 34) when helping

children develop phonological awareness? Not surprisingly, the disagreements over the place and nature of appropriate phonological awareness instruction mirror those over phonics instruction.

Practical recommendations for what should be done to help all children, particularly those at risk for poor outcomes, begin school "ready to learn" differ, depending on what we view as critical components of learning to read and what needs to be emphasized to promote early reading success. Proponents of strong phonics and phonological awareness training recommend a different set of practices than do those who emphasize more contextualized uses of literacy. A "sociocultural, developmentalist perspective" on literacy (Neuman, 1998) emphasizes the importance of meaningful and functional literacy experiences. Neuman and Roskos (1993, 1997), for example, have shown that low-income preschoolers can learn important information about print (e.g., identifying a calendar or a telephone book and pretending to take an order at a restaurant by scribbling on a pad) when classroom environments are structured so that they engage with these kinds of literacy activities and materials. In contrast, a "cognitive–linguistic" perspective emphasizes the critical role of phonological knowledge in learning to read. Brady, Fowler, Stone, and Winbury (1991) have shown that inner-city preschoolers can be taught important phonologically related skills, such as generating rhymes and segmenting phonemes.

These perspectives appear to be sharply contrasting. But reading educators are attempting to forge a broad consensus about what literacy is and how best to promote it that incorporates different emphases on literacy development (e.g., Pressley, 1998; Snow et al., 1998). The broad outlines of this consensus suggest that productive early literacy experiences and effective literacy instruction must address comprehensively several distinguishable, yet ultimately interrelated, aspects of literacy:

- Understanding and using print functionally (reading and writing for communication, expression, etc.).
- Understanding and using the "alphabetic principle" (phonological awareness, let-

ter names and sounds, efficient and automatic decoding, i.e., reading, and encoding, i.e., writing).

- Motivation and interest in using print for a variety of purposes.
- Language, cognitive skills, and knowledge necessary for comprehension and communication.

Although there is no widespread agreement about how much of each aspect should be stressed, a successful literacy program addresses each of these in sufficient depth and breadth to promote literacy growth in the earliest and later years. "Optimal" will probably vary by learner and stage of literacy development, but the basic ingredients of a healthy literacy diet are probably the same for all children (and adults) learning to read an alphabetic language. At the prereading ("emergent"), early, and beginning stages of reading, phonological processes (e.g., hearing the sounds in words) and insight into the alphabetic principle (letters represent sounds in a predictable system, and words comprise patterns of letters and corresponding sounds) are especially critical for learning to read. Effective literacy practices and programs, particularly for children who do not enjoy a wide range of literacy experiences outside school, must include adequate amounts of instruction and other learning opportunities specifically targeted at helping them acquire these understandings and skills. But children must also have literacy and oral language experiences that promote vocabulary and language development, build background knowledge and familiarity with stories, and provide opportunities to see and engage in meaningful literacy activities. Such experiences, both early and later on, become increasingly important as children advance in their literacy development.

Effective instructional practices to promote emergent and beginning literacy, for all children, include the following:

1. Literate environments in which print is used for diverse and interesting purposes, including opportunities for student choice and ample time for looking at books and reading or "pretend reading."
2. Direct, explicit, systematic instruction in specific skills (e.g., phonological aware-

ness, letter names/sounds, decoding, and comprehension strategies), with sufficient practice in successful use of skills in order to promote transfer and automaticity.
3. Discussions and conversations about materials children read or that are read to them.
4. Focus on word-recognition skills and strategies (direct instruction, but also use of techniques such as word walls and making words).
5. Strategically sequenced instruction and curriculum materials to maintain optimal challenge (instructional or independent, as appropriate).
6. Organizational and classroom management strategies to maximize academic engagement and appropriate use of materials.
7. An explicit focus on language (including vocabulary) development.
8. Valid and frequent assessments, using multiple measures as needed and appropriate, to allow teachers to gauge developing skills and target instruction appropriately.
9. A home–school connection component that links the school's efforts with children's home experieces and enlists parents in supporting their children's academic development.

This emerging consensus (see also IRA/NAEYC Position Statement, 1998) might provide a foundation for national efforts to make schools work for all children. Later in this chapter I describe programs that embody one or more these practices and have been successful in helping improve literacy development among low-income children.

The Influence of Socioeconomic Status, Language, and Culture on Learning to Read

Matters become further complicated when we factor in socioeconomic status (SES) and issues of language and culture. Low-income children and children from some cultural and linguistic groups have traditionally done poorly in U.S. schools (Natriello, McDill, & Pallas, 1990). As we have seen, we are further from accomplishing our education goals with poor and minority children than we are with nonpoor, nonminority children. There is a high correlation among socioeconomic status and cultural and linguistic group membership in the United States; thus as a practical matter, it is extremely difficult to talk about one without the other. The picture becomes highly complex, with several interrelated factors bearing on children's literacy development.

SOCIOECONOMIC FACTORS

Socioeconomic issues are obviously central to discussions of how schools can meet the needs of low-income students and their families. There is an association between SES and kinds and amount of home literacy experiences and literacy skills and knowledge a child brings to school, although it is untrue that there are no literacy activities in low-income children's homes, as many educators assume. Baker, Serpell, and Sonnenschein (1995), for example, found that compared to children from middle-income homes, low-income children had fewer opportunities for interactions involving literacy (e.g., food preparation, shopping, storybook reading, pretend play, and educational toys). Middle-income parents reported significantly more play with print and more independent reading by children, although only slightly more joint book reading, than did low-income families. Ninety percent of the middle-class families in this study reported that their child visited the library at least once a month, whereas only 43% of the low-income families reported this to be so. Once children entered kindergarten, low-income parents (particularly African Americans) reported more reading-skills practice and homework (e.g., flash cards and letter practice) than did middle-income parents.

Upon school entrance, not surprisingly, low-income children appear to be "less ready," as Whitehurst and Lonigan (1998) point out. They have had less experience with books, writing, hearing stories, learning and reciting rhymes, and many other types of experiences that promote literacy learning. Goldenberg and Gallimore (1995) found that on average low-income Spanish-speaking children (tested in Spanish, so language was not an issue) had relatively few

"emergent" literacy skills. Presented with 10 of the most frequently used letters, the average number recognized was 1 lower case and 1.5 upper case. Two-thirds of the children could not name or recognize a single letter. More than three-fifths could write no letters at all. The majority also could write no words, either correctly or attempted. Fewer than half pointed somewhere in the print when asked where the tester should read; one-fourth indicated that print was read from left to right; fewer than one-fourth could point to the "first" and "last" parts of text on a page.

In contrast, children from higher-income families have more text-based literacy experiences and opportunities at home. They arrive in kindergarten able to recognize more letters; they can write letters, words, even phrases. They have more invented spelling and engage in more scribble writing. They have more "concepts about print," such as where in the page the printed text is and that text is read from left to right. Some of these children are even readers in a more conventional sense, although this is less common (Adams, 1990; Chall, 1983; Clay, 1993; Mason, 1977). There is clearly wide variability within any social group or economic level, yet in general, low-income children begin school with fewer literacy experiences and less literacy knowledge. Once they begin first grade, they tend to fall further behind more affluent peers. During school months the rate of low-income children's academic progress is equivalent to that of higher-income children. But during summers the academic gap widens (Alexander & Entwisle, 1996).

There are two important qualifications to the economic status–achievement connection, however: (1) family socioeconomic effects on achievement are in fact quite modest; and (2) effective school programs will help more children achieve, regardless of their economic class.

The association between socioeconomic status and early reading achievement is quite weak when measured at the individual family level. Socioeconomic "influence" on achievement is much stronger when measured at the school or community level. In other words, the effects of economic status on achievement are largely the result of living in communities and attending school with large numbers of children from a particular social class, not the result of a single family's socioeconomic characteristics. Average correlations between family socioeconomic status and measures of academic achievement are a modest .2–.3 (Walberg & Tsai, 1985; White, 1982). In contrast, when socioeconomic status is measured at the level of the school or community, the correlation with achievement is nearly .7 (White, 1982). So, for example, a low-SES child attending a low-income school and living in a low-income community is at far greater risk for reading difficulties than is the same child attending and living in a middle- or high-income school and community.

One reason for the weak link between family economic status and learning to read is that there is a great deal of variability in family practices and student achievement within any economic stratum. We must therefore avoid deterministic assumptions about the "effects" of economic status on literacy development. Children's preliteracy skills and knowledge (e.g., phonological awareness, letter knowledge, and concepts of print) are far better predictors of reading achievement than is family SES (Scarborough, 1998). What children know and can do are variable within economic class and more closely related to literacy outcomes than is economic class. We also know that there is great variability in children's experiences within any social group or economic stratum. Among low-income families, there are those where children experience relatively high levels of literacy, academic learning, and encouragement (Anderson & Stokes, 1984; Clark, 1983; Goldenberg & Gallimore, 1995; Goldenberg et al., 1992; Heath, 1983; Paratore et al., 1999; Taylor & Dorsey-Gaines, 1988; Teale, 1986). Taylor and Dorsey-Gaines (1988), for example, described how families living below the poverty line and in the inner city engage in a wide range of literacy activities, including writing letters, making lists and schedules, reading the newspaper and magazines, and reading textbooks and manuals. One of the most pernicious and persistent assumptions among many educators is that low-income families, particularly those from cultural groups that typically have done poorly in U.S. schools, barely survive in a "culture of poverty" and have little time, inclination, or

ability to provide their children with learning opportunities to benefit academic achievement (e.g., Grossman, 1984).

Furthermore, as Baker et al. (1995) and Goldenberg et al. (1992) have shown, once children begin school, the amount of literacy in the homes of low-income children increases, suggesting that families are responsive to children's school experiences and support changes in children's home activities to reflect a more academic focus. Indeed, perhaps in part due to families' responsiveness, effective school and classroom practices have been shown to improve the attainment of students from diverse socioeconomic, cultural, and linguistic backgrounds. This is the second qualification we must bear in mind: Effective school and classroom programs will make a difference, despite SES. I will return to this point later.

LANGUAGE

In the United States, socioeconomic factors are often conflated with language and culture, because disproportionate numbers of children from certain ethnolinguistic groups are low income. August and Hakuta (1997) report that 77% of English learners qualify for free or reduced-price lunches in contrast to only 38% of the overall student population in the same schools. Latino immigrants, who constitute by far the largest immigrant group and whose children constitute the largest group of English learners in California and the United States, come to this country with low levels of education and few material resources (Goldenberg, 1996). Mexican and Central American immigrants tend to have relatively little formal education and are more likely than native-born U.S. residents or immigrants from other countries to be living in poverty. African American, native Hawaiian, and American Indian students are among those groups with disproportionately high numbers of low-SES families (Federal Interagency Forum on Child and Family Statistics, 1999; Tharp, 1989; Tharp & Gallimore, 1988).

Language is perhaps the most controversial of the three demographic dimensions considered in this chapter, particularly whether children for whom English is not the primary language should be taught to read first in their home language or instead be "immersed" in English from the outset of their school careers. The language-of-instruction question has almost completely dominated research and discussions about the education of limited-English-proficient students, now commonly referred to as English-language learners (August & Hakuta, 1997). Yet cognitive, affective, instructional, curricular, and school-based factors that are important for English speakers learning to read in English, as outlined previously, are also important for English learners learning to read. Indeed, there is considerable evidence that reading and learning to read in one's native language is in many ways like reading and learning to read in a second language (Chiappe & Siegel, 1999; Fitzgerald, 1995). Nonetheless, there are differences that teachers must take into account, such as the more limited vocabulary of English learners and the different experiential base from which English learners can draw in order to make sense of academic instruction. All these considerations are relevant to discussions of how best to promote high levels of academic literacy attainment in early elementary school.

What is the proper role of the primary language in the academic instruction of limited English-speaking children? Primary language advocates on one extreme say that the longer, more intensively, and more effectively students learn literacy and academic skills in their home language, the better their eventual academic attainment will be *in English* (Thomas & Collier, 1997). The theoretical rationale is that we learn best in the language we know best, and that once basic concepts and skills are learned in the primary language, they transfer readily to a second language. In diametric opposition, advocates of English-only instruction say that early, sustained, and effective use of English in the classroom leads to superior attainment in English (Rossell & Baker, 1996). They cite a different rationale: The more time spent learning and practicing a language, the greater the eventual attainment in that language.

Studies point policy in opposite directions. Rossell and Baker's (1996) review of research concludes that students should be immersed in English as soon as possible and as intensively as possible. But two quantitative syntheses have concluded precisely the opposite: Use of students' primary language produces superior achievement results—in English—when compared to immersion in English (Greene, 1997; Willig, 1985). One prominent demonstration of the superiority of primary language instruction in the early stages of reading was provided in a nationwide study by Ramírez, Yuen, and Ramey (1991). Ramírez et al. found that kindergarten and first-grade students who received academic instruction *in Spanish* had higher achievement in beginning reading *in English* than did comparable students who received academic instruction in English (there were no significant differences in language and mathematics). At the preschool level, some studies have shown that Spanish-language classrooms for Spanish speakers are also associated with higher levels of language and early literacy attainment in both Spanish and English (e.g., Campos & Keatinge, 1988).

A different rationale for using the primary language as an instructional vehicle has to do with the intrinsic advantages of knowing two languages. Whatever the controversy over the role of primary language (e.g., Spanish) in second-language (e.g., English) attainment, there is no controversy over the facts that (1) primary-language instruction leads to primary-language maintenance without blocking second-language acquisition, in other words, a greater chance of bilingualism; and (2) bilingualism confers cognitive, cultural, and economic benefits (August & Hakuta, 1997; Crawford, 1991; Rossell & Baker, 1996). Of course, a key question is whether school programs that promote primary-language maintenance and bilingual development sacrifice some degree of English acquisition. The answer would appear to be no, but this is part of the complex debate over the role of the home language in the education of English learners. Unfortunately, knowing two languages has attracted little attention in our great national debate over improving schools; certainly it is not among our national education goals. Consequently, the advantages of bilingualism—which are beyond dispute—have played virtually no role in informing research and policy discussions. This is indeed unfortunate and can only serve to heighten the perception of U.S. cultural and linguistic insularity (Simon, 1980).

We must also keep the language issue in perspective and understand that language of instruction per se is only one of several issues educators face in teaching English learners (National Educational Research Policy and Priorities Board, 1999; see also Tabors & Snow, Chapter 12; Vernon-Feagans, Hammer, Miccio, & Manlove, Chapter 14). Other important issues have to do with the sorts and quality of literacy experiences and instruction children receive, as discussed in the previous section.

CULTURE

Culture and cultural differences have also played a role in discussions and research on the education of historically disadvantaged groups. By definition, the single most distinguishing characteristic of English learners is their lack of English proficiency. However, English learners are also members of diverse ethnocultural groups, which itself might have implications for learning to become literate (Tharp, 1989). Socioeconomic and sociopolitical issues might also be relevant, particularly for Spanish-origin English learners in the United States, who historically have been victims of discrimination and economic disadvantage.

As with language, the issue is complex and difficult to disentangle from ideological or philosophical considerations that go far beyond empirical questions and matters of curriculum and instruction. Cultural diversity is increasingly a fact of life in U.S. schools, particularly in states along the border, such as California, Arizona, and Texas, and states that traditionally or more recently have been destinations of successive waves of immigrants (e.g., New York, Illinois, and Washington). Yet "culture" means different things to different people. Even among anthropologists there is no universal, agreed-on definition. Is culture defined by how people dress? The food they eat? The language they speak? How they think? Behave? Are some more important to "cultural identity" than others? Culture has many dimensions and no one dimension can be said to define any group of people. Moreover, there is considerable disagreement over whether and how different peoples' distinct cultural experiences should inform school programs (Schlesinger, 1991).

Why does "culture" matter in the early reading development of culturally diverse students, and therefore what is its relevance to a discussion of national education goals? There are several possibilities. One is that members of different cultural groups might socialize their children differently and have different behavioral expectations for children, and that some of these differences might have a negative impact on children's schooling experiences. Valdés (1996) provides an illustration. She shows how children of Mexican immigrants are socialized not to be assertive around adults; nor do children learn to engage in displays of information. Yet teachers often expect a certain amount of assertiveness, even aggressiveness, from students. They expect students to be eager to "show off" what they know. Children in the kindergarten and first-grade class she studied "had to be ready to perform and indeed outperform their peers" (p. 147). Otherwise, teachers assumed that things hadn't yet "clicked" (p. 146). In the case of the Mexican-origin children who did not display expected behaviors, teachers lowered their academic expectations for them and placed them in lower reading groups. Valdés suggests this was the beginning of a downward spiral of failure for these students.

Research indeed suggests that certain types of cultural accommodations to behavioral or interactional styles improve students' academic engagement and participation. The most well-known example comes from the Kamehameha Early Education Project (KEEP; see Tharp & Gallimore, 1988, and later) and reported in Au and Mason (1981–1982). Au and Mason found that when a teacher engaged Hawaiian children in small-group discussions that were similar to the sorts of free-flowing interactions children were used to at home, children were more engaged and participated at a higher cognitive level. When the teacher employed a more controlled turn-taking discussion style, which was very dissimilar to what students were used to, children participated less and their contributions to the discussion were at a lower academic level. As important as this and other studies of cultural accommodation are (see Tharp, 1989), however, there is actually very little evidence that cultural accommodation per se produces measured gains *in achievement* (Fueyo & Bechtol, 1999; Goldenberg & Gallimore, 1989). Even when teachers and students are matched by race/ethnicity, there is no difference in student achievement in comparison to students with teachers who are dissimilar racially or ethnically (Vierra, 1984). The most compelling argument to be made that cultural accommodation produces improvements in student learning and other outcomes has been provided by Allen and Boykin (1992) in their review of laboratory and classroom studies involving African American children (see also Vernon-Feagans, Hammer, Miccio, & Manlove, Chapter 14). The hypothesis that cultural accommodation can lead to improved student outcomes is important; however, teachers must realize that the evidence for its effects—and therefore, its significance to classroom practice—is not a strong as might be assumed.

The outstanding example of a culturally based intervention that demonstrated important effects on beginning and early reading development is KEEP, begun in the 1960s as an effort to improve the early (K–3) reading attainment of native Hawaiian children (Tharp & Gallimore, 1988). KEEP students at the original demonstration site and at remote sites when the program was exported to other schools demonstrated significant improvement in early reading achievement compared to control and comparison groups (Tharp, 1982). Hawaiian children received literacy instruction and classroom experiences that contained elements compatible with their natal culture. For example, they worked in small, peer-oriented collaborative groups in which children were free to interact around academic tasks, compatible with the peer-oriented child culture Hawaiian children experience, with relatively little adult supervision. KEEP teachers also used a more free-flowing discussion style during reading comprehension lessons, which paralleled the overlapping discourse patterns (dubbed "talk–story"; see Au & Mason, 1981–1982, discussed previously) that native Hawaiian children and adults engage in naturally.

KEEP is widely cited as a illustrating the power of culturally accommodated instruction to improve early literacy attainment, particularly for children who are both from low-income and cultural-minority families. But the KEEP instructional program also contained many elements found to be effective universally, that is, not necessarily accommodated to any particular group (Goldenberg & Gallimore, 1989). For example, KEEP employed active, direct teaching of reading comprehension, collaborative learning, well-run and organized classrooms, a good balance of word-recognition (including phonics) skills instruction and comprehension instruction, and ongoing and substantive professional development for teachers. It is impossible to disentangle the effects of culturally accommodated instruction from the effects of more general or "universal" principles of effective curriculum and teaching (Goldenberg & Gallimore, 1989). A plausible hypothesis is that both sets of factors—universal principals and culturally accommodated instruction—made contributions to the improvements in achievement.

There are other compelling reasons for teachers to know about cultural facets of children's learning, aside from their possible direct (or indirect) influence on measured outcomes and accomplishing national education goals. If nothing else, different cultural groups have different norms of behaving and interacting; teachers should understand and be sensitive to these, as doing so can only help students and families feel more comfortable and welcomed in what might seem a very foreign institution. Moreover, educated professionals—particularly those who work with children—must know about the varieties of human experiences, even if that knowledge does not translate neatly into educational prescriptions. But teachers should also understand that there are no consistent set of factors that have yet been discovered that take cultural understandings and turn them into effective educational interventions.

It is also worthwhile to note, particularly in light of the following section on home–school connections, that parents are skeptical of the idea that their children's teachers must come from similar backgrounds in order to be effective. A *Los Angeles Times* poll asked residents in the Los Angeles Unified School District whether they thought students learned better when teachers and administrators were the same race/ethnicity as theirs. An overwhelming majority of parents—85%—responded that race/ethnicity did not matter. Latino and black respondents felt just as strongly that race/ethnicity did not matter as did white respondents (*Los Angeles Times* Poll, 1999).

What Parent Involvement Can and Should Be

Since the 1960s, a vast literature has emerged documenting the relationship between children's homes and their school achievement. This literature provides the empirical and conceptual basis for the nation's eighth education goal, that every school will promote parent involvement to support "the social, emotional, and academic growth of children." And to the extent that parent involvement has implications for children's school readiness and continued school achievement, the literature is also relevant to these other two goals. Researchers have investigated scores of links between home and school, and a clear consensus has emerged: Children's experiences at home profoundly influence their chances for success at school. Homes and schools are inextricably linked (see, e.g., Epstein, 1992, 1996; Goldenberg, 1993; Hess & Holloway, 1984). Advocates of parent involvement argue that schools should actively seek ways to collaborate with parents for children's academic benefit. Epstein (1996), for example, has outlined different forms of parent involvement. She writes that along with more traditional dimensions of school improvement, such as curriculum, instruction, and staff development, "school–family–community connections [are] now viewed as one of the components of school organization that may help to promote student learning and success" (p. 209).

Yet parent involvement in children's school learning has always been surprisingly controversial. Seventy years ago Waller (1932) wrote of the inevitable "distrust and enmity" that exists between teachers and parents. Although both want what is best for the child, Waller wrote, each has a different conception of what constitutes "best," leading Waller (1932) to conclude that "parents and teachers are natural enemies, predestined each for the discomfiture of the other" (p. 68). Waller's pronouncements, with different sociopolitical variations, have been repeated regularly in the ensuing years. Most recently, parent involvement has become especially controversial for precisely those children who are the subjects of this chapter. Schlossman (1978) and Fine (1993), for example, suggest that parent involvement and training, particularly for low-income parents, will lead to shifting the blame for failure onto parents. Lightfoot (1978) argues that low-income parents and teachers are "worlds apart." Heath and McLaughlin (1987) charge that schools are insensitive to the changing realities of U.S. family life and that parent involvement is at best dubious. Lareau (1996) writes that "the emphasis on family involvement in education [is] shrouded in sentimental enthusiasm. . . . [M]any working-class and lower-class parents do not accept, nor comply, with crucial aspects of the model of family-school involvement . . ." (pp. 57–58).

ENHANCING PARENT INVOLVEMENT IN CHILDREN'S LEARNING

But considerable research suggests that skeptics are probably mistaken. Parent involvement seems to hold considerable promise for helping improve the achievement of children who our schools have traditionally not served well. Even among low-income, minority families—often assumed to be unable or unwilling to respond to school efforts to involve them in their children's education—parents are willing and able to play a role to help children succeed in school (Chavkin, 1989; Epstein, 1992, 1996; Goldenberg, 1987, 1993; Moles, 1996; Neuman, Hagedorn, Celano, & Daly, 1995). Instead of home–school connections producing conflict, blame, and dysfunction, schools and families can work together to help children succeed academically. This proposition is perhaps especially true in the area of early literacy, where most parents—even low-income and culturally and linguistically diverse parents—possess the attitudes and at least sufficient early literacy skills and knowledge to help their children get on the road to literacy. Our national goal of widespread parent involvement to support children's academic growth is neither fantasy nor "sentimental enthusiasm." It is a reasonable, if ambitious, aim that could have a substantial impact on early literacy development and beyond.

For example, a study of Spanish-speaking kindergartners found that teachers' parent involvement efforts were related both to parents' satisfaction with the child's school experience and to children's early literacy attainment (Goldenberg & Arzubiaga, 1994). The more teachers attempted to involve parents in children's academic learning—by sending home activities or through messages or phone calls home—the more satisfied parents were with both the academic content of their child's classroom and the extent to which they felt involved in their children's learning. Similarly, Campbell and Ramey (1995) report that low-income African American parents were very positive about a home–school academic contact program. Over 90% of the parents reported completing home activities with their children. Parents gave 83% of the activities positive ratings, 16% neutral, and 2% negative (Campbell & Ramey, 1995).

In the Goldenberg and Arzubiaga (1994) study, the more teachers attempted to involve parents in children's learning, the higher were children's end-of-year kindergarten literacy scores. There was no relationship between teachers' parent-involvement efforts and beginning-of-year achievement; thus we can rule out the explanation that teachers were more likely to reach out to the parents of higher-achieving students. Furthermore, there was a striking relationship between teachers' parent-involvement attempts and changes in children's early literacy attainment in relation to other kindergartners across the year. Students whose teachers took the initiative to involve parents in children's learning gained ground in comparison to peers; students whose teachers did not take the initiative to involve parents, slipped back in their relative achievement standing. Additional evidence from successful programs and interventions (including Campbell & Ramey, 1995) is discussed later in the chapter.

PARENTS' VIEWS OF HOW CHILDREN
BECOME LITERATE

Another issue has to do with parents' views of how children learn to become literate

and, moreover, what their own roles can and should be in this process. We might expect that if parents' and educators' understandings are consistent with or complement each other, parent involvement is more likely to have the intended effects. If they do not, this might not be a productive route to enhancing literacy. A study I conducted with Leslie Reese and Ronald Gallimore showed that parents will use materials and interact with their children in ways that are consistent with their understandings of what it means to learn to read and how best to help children learn to read (Goldenberg et al., 1992). Thus the effects of parent involvement might not be what was intended.

Parents in one set of classrooms received photocopied storybooks in Spanish (*Libros*) that teachers had read with children at school then sent home. Teachers suggested to parents during the fall conference that they read the books with the children as they would any other children's book. Parents were told to engage children in repeated readings, accompanied by conversation focusing on the meaning of the texts. Teachers in the comparison classrooms sent home packets comprising phonic and syllable worksheets borrowed from two kindergarten teachers who were extraordinarily successful in helping their young students begin to read and write conventionally (Goldenberg, 1994). We observed use of the materials (storybooks or phonic packets) over many hours of home observations throughout the kindergarten year. As expected, children in classrooms using the storybooks were more advanced in their literacy development than were children in classrooms using the district's basal "readiness" program, supplemented by the phonics-oriented worksheets we provided (Goldenberg, 1990). However, use of the storybooks at home was *unrelated* to children's literacy development; children's attainment was the same regardless of how much they used the storybooks at home. In contrast, use of the phonics worksheets was *strongly related* to children's literacy development—the more they used them the higher their attainment.

How can we explain these paradoxical findings? One possibility is that letter sounds and syllables are precisely what children need to practice in the early stages of reading. The more children and parents worked on these worksheets, the greater children's early literacy attainment. But why wouldn't reading the storybooks bear any relationship to our early literacy measures, which included comprehension, listening, and print concepts—not just letters, sounds, and syllables? A plausible explanation has to do with parents' own understandings of how children learn to read, and therefore how they used the materials provided by the school. The Latino parents with whom we work equate learning to read with learning to decode and not with learning to construct meaning from written texts (Goldenberg, 1988). Far from having an "emergent literacy" perspective, parents see reading in more categorical terms—one can either read or one can not (although they recognize that one can read well or poorly). They attach less importance to children hearing books or having opportunities to "pretend read" or talk about books and more importance on children remembering the sounds of letters and how to read words conventionally.

When the matter at hand was helping children learn to read, regardless of the materials used, they engaged children in repetitive, drill-like activities *para que se les grabe,* as parents say ("so that they [letters or words] become 'recorded' or 'engraved' [in their minds]"). Whether working with the *Libros* or the worksheets, parents constructed literacy events heavy with repetition and largely devoid of attention to meaning. (This description of the parents' reading behavior with their children is consistent with the baseline readings in Delgado-Gaitan's, 1994, study and with other studies of low-income parents' beliefs about how young children learn; e.g., Stipek, Milburn, Clements, & Daniels, 1992). The storybooks' use at home was therefore unrelated to children's kindergarten literacy attainment. In contrast, there was a congruence between the worksheets and parents' beliefs about learning to read, which led to their more effective use in the homes. The more children used the worksheets at home, the higher their literacy attainment (on a broad spectrum of measures) at the end of the school year.

These results do not suggest that teachers ought not send home books and other "real" reading materials. But they do underscore the importance of considering the family context that will receive materials from school or receive some other form of intervention. Parents' beliefs about literacy will influence how they use materials and engage in literacy interactions with children. Moreover, because learning letters, sounds, and how they combine to form words is most assuredly part of learning to read, engaging parents in the sorts of activities that make most sense to them would seem to be a natural connection for family literacy activities.

PARENT TRAINING

Parent training is another possibility for enhancing parent involvement in children's learning and for dealing with parents conceptions about how children learn to read (Stipek et al., 1992) (see Wasik, Dobbins, & Hermann, Chapter 29, for a discussion of different programs). But although training parents how to read to their children can produce at least short-term changes (Delgado-Gaitan, 1994; Edwards, 1989; Henderson & Garcia, 1973), we must be concerned about whether training programs will tend to exclude substantial numbers of parents who are unable or unwilling to participate. Parent involvement and family literacy programs that involve considerable meeting time for on-site parent activities necessarily deal with a select group of parents. In one well-known effort in northern California, Ada (1988) met with parents monthly to discuss children's literature and to show them how to read with their elementary-age children. Ada reports that the monthly meetings drew 60–100 parents. This is from a total district student population of 14,500. It is not difficult to believe, as Ada reports, that participating parents and children found the experience extremely beneficial (although she reports no data indicating effects on reading development). But clearly the vast majority of parents were excluded.

Parent training programs are also more likely to draw from the portion of the population already involved in their children's literacy development. In another well-regarded and successful parent education program with immigrant Latino parents (Rodriguez-Brown, Li, & Albom, 1999), all participants at the beginning of the program—that is, before training—reported reading to their preschool children; 56% reported reading to their child more than three times per week. Over half reported having and using a library card. These figures contrast with much lower figures reported elsewhere for Latino parents (Ramirez, Yuen, Ramey, & Merino, 1986; Teale, 1986). In my own studies, I've gotten lower figures still, with only 27% of parents of entering kindergartners reporting they read to their child and only 23% reporting having taken their kindergarten-age child to the library during the preceding year.

Given that parent training programs will necessarily include a relatively select group of parents, what happens with the other families? If parent involvement efforts are open only to those parents who can or will go to training sessions, we invariably exclude substantial numbers of families, those perhaps with the greatest need. We might expect that parent involvement programs that build on what parents already know and can do—in addition to introducing those parents who can participate to new ideas, knowledge, and skills—will include larger numbers of families in potentially productive activities to promote children's literacy development.

Examples of Effective Programs: Prospects and Limitations

Over the past few years a number of programs and demonstration projects have emerged that hold promise for helping attain the national education goals set forth at the beginning of this chapter. Several examples illustrate both the prospects and the limitations of the programs (see Strickland, Chapter 22, for additional examples).

Three themes in these programs stand out. One is that there is indeed an emerging consensus on what constitutes effective literacy practices and experiences for young children (Snow et al., 1998). Unanimity eludes us, but certain elements appear with regularity, for example, direct, explicit, and systematic instruction; a focus on the

sounds of language and how they are represented by letters; opportunities for meaningful interactions around reading materials; basic skills instruction balanced with higher level, comprehension-oriented activities; frequent and systematic assessment; productive, focused classroom environments; and productive home–school communication and collaboration. A second theme is that comprehensive frameworks for intervention are more likely to yield meaningful results. "Incrementalism," as Schorr (1994) has written, is insufficient when social, educational, and economic challenges compound one another. A third theme is that we have made progress and more is possible, but we still have a long way to go. Even the most successful programs fail to eliminate the gap that exists between high- and low-income students in terms of both opportunities and attainment.

A prime example of a comprehensive, schoolwide reading program components is Success for All (SFA; Slavin, Madden, Dolan, & Wasik, 1996). The original program was intended for low-income English-speaking students and has since been adapted for English learners. There is also a Spanish version (*Exito para todos*) and an English version that uses instructional strategies specifically suited for English learners learning to read and write in English (Slavin & Madden, 20001). SFA is more than simply a reading program; it has comprehensive organizational, management, and home–school connection components. Indeed, it is among the most successful and effective "whole school" reform models to emerge in the 1990s (Bodilly, 1998). SFA uses a structured and explicit program of reading and writing skill development, beginning in kindergarten and continuing through third grade. Students are in heterogenous classrooms but are regrouped homogenously (across classrooms) for 90 minutes of daily reading instruction. The program uses well-known instructional strategies such as direct instruction, cooperative learning, writing as a process, and frequent assessment. Regular home–school contacts are a key feature, particularly for children experiencing difficulty.

Despite its admirable record of success, however, "Sucess for All" (SFA) is not literally successful with all students. Slavin,

Madden, Karweit, Dolan, and Wasik (1994) report that only 46% of third-grade children in SFA schools were on or above grade level in reading, in contrast to 26% of children in control schools. Although clearly a meaningful effect, it is still far short of success for *all*. Nonetheless, it constitutes success for many more students than would otherwise be successful.

Another well-known and important effort to promote early literacy development for low-income children is the Carolina Abecedarian Project (Campbell & Ramey, 1995; Ramey & Campbell, 1984; Vernon-Feagans, Hammer, Miccio, & Manlove, Chapter 14, for a more detailed account). Ramey and Campbell report short- and long-term intervention effects on cognitive (reading and math tests) and school-based (special education placement, grade retention) measures. One of the reasons this study is so important is because it used a fully randomized design to examine the combined and separate effects of two interventions on low-income African American children's early academic performance. The preschool intervention comprised a number of curricular and instructional programs, including preliteracy and prephonics curricula emphasizing "phoneme identification" (Campbell & Ramey, 1995). A school-age follow-up consisted of a home–school resource teacher providing parents with activities designed to "reinforce the basic reading and mathematics concepts being taught at school" (Campbell & Ramey, 1995, p. 751).

In third grade, the group of children who received both the preschool and school-age intervention substantially outperformed other groups (no intervention or only the preschool or only the school-age intervention). The mean third-grade standard score of this group of children on the Woodcock–Johnson reading cluster (letter–word identification, word attack, passage comprehension) was 96, still below the national mean, but substantially higher than the no-intervention controls (83). The effects of the school-age intervention alone, which consisted of the "home–school resource teacher," was negligible. The preschool intervention alone had a substantial effect, although not as great as that of the combined preschool and school-age interventions.

These programs demonstrate that we have the wherewithal to get closer to accomplishing our national education goals for all students. One indication of this comes from a study by Baron (1999). She sought to find the state and local policy explanations for Connecticut's reading achievement, which, according to the National Assessment of Educational Progress, was the highest in the nation in 1998 and the most improved since 1992. Students across all ethnic and socioeconomic groups improved, and they outperform their counterparts in other states. Baron studied the 10 most improved districts in Connecticut and noted several common characteristics. Many of these had to do with curriculum, instruction, assessment, and professional development consistent with the principles set forth in this chapter. Particularly noteworthy were Baron's findings with respect to parent involvement in one of the poorest districts in the state. New Britain is one of a group of districts that has by far the highest percentage of children in single-parent families (51.4%), receiving AFDC; Aid to Families with Dependent Children (42.6%), and speaking a language other than English in the home (37.4%). Yet it engaged in a number of successful parent involvement practices, such as hiring a parent organizer in each school to encourage parents to volunteer and keep track of monthly parent involvement. Parents also receive training in "First Steps," a prereading and reading-skills program. Parents volunteer in the schools, and 100% of elementary school parents attend parent conferences. Between 1993 and 1998, New Britain's scores on the state reading test increased at a faster rate than the state average.

An as-yet-unanswered question is whether effective school and classroom practices developed to date can completely overcome the effects of low SES. Miller (1995) concludes that "there is little evidence that any existing strategy can close more than a fraction of the overall achievement gap between high- and low-SES children" (p. 334). Using SFA as a telling example—as it is the most successful of the current school reform models designed to improve reading achievement in Title 1 schools—Miller points out that the program can raise overall achievement levels from approximately the 30th to the 46th percentile.

These are noteworthy gains to be sure. But the level of attainment is still "below middle-class and upper-middle-class performance norms," typically well above the 50th percentile on nationally normed tests (Miller, 1995, p. 331).

Many argue that even this is a gross underestimate of what educators could truly accomplish. In any case, a strong, effective academic program will produce better results on student outcomes than will a weak and ineffective program. *This is so whether students are of low or high SES and despite their cultural and linguistic background.* Low SES cannot be used as an excuse for failing to increase substantially the number of low-income and culturally and linguistically diverse students meeting national education goals.

Implications and Future Directions

Our country's commitment to high levels of student achievement are on display in the form of national education goals. But at the moment, the goals remain distant visions. What must we do if they are ever to be within our reach?

First, and most obviously, we must work to put into practice as much as possible that we have good reason to believe "works." Despite gaps in our knowledge, there are many effective practices for which we have good research evidence but which are not necessarily finding their way into schools and classrooms (e.g., phonological awareness instruction for children who need it, explicit and systematic instruction, other language and literacy experiences to promote familiarity and knowledge about literacy, early identification and intervention for children at risk for reading difficulties, and parent involvement to promote school readiness and beginning literacy). Moreover, there are programs that operationalize these and other approaches to improving opportunities and outcomes for low-income children. Despite uncertainties and ongoing controversies, we can make substantial progress toward our stated national goals if we can make these practices much more widespread than they now are. One avenue is through professional development for teachers. Another avenue is through program implementation at schools and in districts throughout the country. But we must have a realistic view of what it takes to implement findings from research. The implementation challenge is all too familiar to whomever attempts to make changes in schools or other social institutions (Fullan, 1991, 1993, 1999). Some programs, such as SFA, have a well-developed technology for effective implementation, which takes a very comprehensive view of professional development and schoolwide change (Bodilly, 1998). SFA is not the norm, however.

Unquestionably we have made progress in our understanding of what contributes to early literacy development, what puts children at risk for reading problems, and what schools and families can do to promote literacy growth and minimize literacy difficulties. But many challenges still lie ahead. Preeminent among them is how to nurture (perhaps "accelerate" is a better word) the literacy growth of far more low-income children than we are now succeeding in helping to achieve high levels of literacy. Successful implementation of effective programs will undoubtedly take us in this direction; but clearly this is not sufficient. Even in these programs, as I have pointed out, there are still too many children who do not do well enough. A clear challenge for the 21st century, therefore, is to find even more effective ways to help all children—regardless of socioeconomic level or linguistic and cultural background—achieve at reasonable literacy levels.

The problem goes far beyond learning to read and write, of course. Many of these children come to school and attend school under circumstances likely to influence adversely academic processes and outcomes. As a group, low-income children are more likely to have to endure a wide range of disadvantages associated with poverty—single-parent families, poor access to quality health care, poor diets, dangerous neighborhoods, and behavioral and social–adaptational challenges (Federal Interagency Forum on Child and Family Statistics, 1999). Although we can find examples of children who have succeeded in the face of formidable environmental challenges, and therefore we know that poor outcomes for children at risk are not a foregone conclusion (Werner & Smith, 1982), why should children have to struggle against the odds? The issue is one of social justice, not simply improving reading scores. Ultimately, our solutions must go beyond educational interventions, as important as they might be. They must focus on integration of programs, policies, and services, the school being but one of many agencies implicated. As Schorr (1994) has argued, "We need bold and comprehensive strategies. Incrementalism will not do it. There are chasms you cannot cross one small step at a time" (p. 237). Efforts to improve educational outcomes for disadvantaged children must be part of a broader social and political agenda.

If we take seriously the challenge of implementing well those things we have reason to believe make a difference in children's literacy, while vigorously pursuing research and political agendas aimed at further breaking down barriers to access for large numbers of low-income and culturally diverse children, there is a chance we will not peer out from the first year of the next century and once again report that we have failed to reach our national educational goals. Or, in the year 2100, will we—again—have to confront the chasm Kameenui (1998) has identified: the rhetoric of all, but the reality of some?

Acknowledgments

This chapter was made possible by grants from The Spencer Foundation and the U.S. Department of Education (Education Research and Development Program, PR/Award No. R306A60001, Center for Research on Education, Diversity & Excellence, or CREDE). The contents, findings, and opinions expressed here are those of the author and do not necessarily represent the positions or policies of any funding agency.

References

Ada, A. F. (1988). The Pajaro Valley experience: Working with Spanish-speaking parents to develop children's reading and writing skills through the use of children's literature. In T. Skutnabb-Kangas & J. Cummins (Eds.), *Minority education: From shame to struggle* (pp. 223–238). Clevedon, UK: Multilingual Matters.

Adams, M. (1990). *Beginning to read: Thinking and learning about print.* Cambridge, MA: MIT Press.

Alexander, K., & Entwisle, D. (1996). Schools and children at risk. In A. Booth & J. Dunn (Eds.), *Family and school links: How do they affect educational outcomes?* (pp. 67–88). Mahwah, NJ: Erlbaum.

Allen, B., & Boykin, A. (1992). African-American children and the educational process: Alleviating cultural discontinuity through prescriptive pedagogy. *School Psychology Review, 21,* 586–596.

Anderson, A. B., & Stokes, S. J. (1984). Social and institutional influences on the development and practice of literacy. In H. Goelman, A. Oberg, & F. Smith (Eds.), *Awakening to literacy* (pp. 24–37). Portsmouth, NJ: Heinemann.

Au, K., & Mason, J. (1981–1982). Social organizational factors in learning to read: The balance of rights hypothesis. *Reading Research Quarterly, 17,* 115–152.

August, D., & Hakuta, K. (Eds.). (1997). *Improving schooling for language-minority children: A research agenda.* Washington, DC: National Academy Press.

Baker, L., Serpell, R., & Sonnenschein, S. (1995). Opportunities for literacy learning in the homes of urban preschoolers. In L. Morrow (Ed.), *Family literacy: Connections in schools and communities* (pp. 236–252). Newark, DE: International Reading Association.

Ball, E., & Blachman, B. (1988). Phoneme segmentation training: Effects of reading readiness. *Annals of Dyslexia, 38,* 208–225.

Ball, E., & Blachman, B. (1991). Does phoneme awareness training in kindergarten make a difference in early word recognition and developmental spelling? *Reading Research Quarterly, 26,* 49–66.

Baron, J. (1999). *Exploring high and improving reading achievement in Connecticut.* Paper commissioned by the National Education Goals Panel.

Bodilly, S. (1998). *Lessons from New American Schools' scale-up phase: Prospects for bringing designs to multiple schools.* Santa Monica, CA: RAND.

Brady, S., Fowler, A., Stone, B., & Winbury, N. (1991). Training phonological awareness: A study with inner-city kindergarten children. *Annals of Dyslexia, 44,* 27–59.

Campbell, F., & Ramey, C. (1995). Cognitive and school outcomes for high-risk African-American students at middle adolescence: Positive effects of early intervention. *American Educational Research Journal, 32,* 743–772.

Campos, J., & Keatinge, H. (1988). The Carpinteria language minority student experience: From theory, to practice, to success. In T. Skutnabb-Kangas & J. Cummins (Eds.), *Minority education: From shame to struggle* (pp. 299–308). Clevedon, UK: Multilingual Matters.

Chall, J. (1983). *Learning to read: The great debate* (updated ed.). New York: McGraw-Hill.

Chavkin, (1989). Debunking the myth about minority parents. *Educational Horizons, 67,* 119–123.

Chiappe, P., & Siegel, L. (1999). Phonological awareness and reading acquisition in English- and

Punjabi-speaking Canadian children. *Journal of Educational Psychology, 91,* 20–28.

Children's reading and the development of phonological awareness [Special issue]. (1987). *Merrill–Palmer Quarterly, 33*(3).

Clark, R. (1983). *Family life and school achievement: Why poor black children succeed or fail.* Chicago: University of Chicago Press.

Clay, M. (1993). *An observation survey of early literacy achievement.* Portsmouth, NH: Heinemann.

Comer, J. (1980). *School power: Implications of an intervention project.* New York: Free Press.

Crawford, J. (1991). *Bilingual education: History, politics, theory, and practice* (2nd ed.). Los Angeles: Bilingual Education Services.

Delgado-Gaitan, C. (1994). Sociocultural change through literacy: Toward the empowerment of families. In B. Ferdman, R. M. Weber, & A. Ramirez (Eds.), *Literacy across languages and cultures.* New York: SUNY Press.

Edwards, P. (1989). Supporting lower SES mothers' attempts to provide scaffolding for book reading. In J. Allen & J. M. Mason (Eds.), *Risk makers, risk takers, risk breakers: Reducing the risks for young literacy learners* (pp. 222–250). Portsmouth, NH: Heinemann.

Epstein, J. (1992). School and family partnerships. In M. Alkin (Ed.), *Encyclopedia of educational research* (6th ed., pp. 1139–1152). New York: MacMillan.

Epstein, J. (1996). Perspectives and previews on research and policy for school, family, and community partnerships. In A. Booth & J. Dunn (Eds.), *Family and school links: How do they affect educational outcomes?* (pp. 209–246). Mahwah, NJ: Erlbaum.

Federal Interagency Forum on Child and Family Statistics (1999). *America's children: Key national indicators of well-being, 1999* (NCES 1999-019). Washington, DC: Superintendent of Documents. Availabl: http://www. childstats. gov

Fine, M. (1993). [Ap]parent involvement: Reflections on parents, power, and urban public schools. *Teachers College Record, 94,* 682–710.

Fitzgerald, J. (1995). English-as-a-second-language learners' cognitive reading processes: A review of research in the United States. *Review of Educational Research, 65,* 145–190.

Fueyo, V., & Bechtol, S. (1999). Those who can, teach: Reflections on teaching diverse populations. *Teacher Education Quarterly, 26*(3), 25–36.

Fullan, M. (1991). *The new meaning of educational change.* New York: Teachers College Press.

Fullan, M. (1993). *Change forces.* London: Falmer.

Fullan, M. (1999). *Change forces: The sequel.* London: Falmer.

Goldenberg, C. (1987). Low-income Hispanic parents' contributions to their first-grade children's word-recognition skills. *Anthropology and Education Quarterly, 18,* 149–179.

Goldenberg, C. (1988). Methods, early literacy, and home–school compatibilities: A response to Sledge et al. *Anthropology and Education Quarterly, 19,* 425–432.

Goldenberg, C. (1993). The home–school connection in bilingual education. In B. Arias & U. Casanova (Eds.), *Ninety-second yearbook of the National Society for the Study of Education. Bilingual education: Politics, research, and practice* (pp. 225–250). Chicago: University of Chicago Press.

Goldenberg, C. (1994). Promoting early literacy achievement among Spanish-speaking children: Lessons from two studies. E. Hiebert (Ed.), *Getting reading right from the start: Effective early literacy interventions* (pp. 171–199). Boston: Allyn & Bacon.

Goldenberg, C. (1996). Latin American immigration and U. S. schools. *Social Policy Reports, 10*(1).

Goldenberg, C., & Arzubiaga, A. (1994, April). *The effects of teachers' attempts to involve Latino parents in children's early reading development.* Paper presented at the annual meeting of the American Educational Research Association, New Orleans.

Goldenberg, C., & Gallimore, R. (1989, Autumn). Teaching California's diverse student population: The common ground between educational and cultural research. *California Public Schools Forum, 3,* 41–56.

Goldenberg, C., & Gallimore, R. (1995). Immigrant Latino parents' values and beliefs about their children's education: Continuities and discontinuities across cultures and generations. In P. R. Pintrich & M. Maehr (Eds.), *Advances in motivation and achievement: Culture, ethnicity, and motivation* (vol 9, pp. 183–228). Greenwich, CT: JAI Press.

Goldenberg, C., Reese, L., & Gallimore, R. (1992). Effects of school literacy materials on Latino children's home experiences and early reading achievement. *American Journal of Education, 100,* 497–536.

Greene, J. (1997). A meta-analysis of the Rossell and Baker review of bilingual education research. *Bilingual Research Journal, 21,* 103–122.

Grossman, H. (1997). *Educating Hispanic students: Cultural implications for instruction, classroom management, counseling and assessment.* Springfield, IL: Charles C. Thomas.

Heath, S. B. (1983). *Ways with words: Language, life, and work in communities and classrooms.* Cambridge, UK.: Cambridge University Press.

Heath, S. B., & McLaughlin, M. W. (1987, April). A child resource policy: Moving beyond dependence on school and family. *Phi Delta Kappan, 68,* 576–580.

Henderson, R., & Garcia, A. (1973). The effects of parent training program on the question-asking behavior of Mexican-American children. *American Educational Research Journal, 10,* 193–201.

Hess, R. D., & Holloway, S. (1984). Family and school as educational institutions. In R. D. Parke

(Ed.), *Review of child development research, 7: The family* (pp. 179–222). Chicago: University of Chicago Press.

Hispanic Policy Development Project (1984). *"Make something happen": Hispanics and urban high school reform* (vol. I). New York: Author.

IRA/NAEYC Position Statement. (1998). Learning to read and write: Developmentally appropriate practice. *The Reading Teacher, 52,* 193–216.

Kameenui, E. (1998). The rhetoric of all, the reality of some, and the unmistakable smell of mortality. In J. Osborn & F. Lehr (Eds.), *Literacy for all: Issues in teaching and learning* (pp. 319–338). New York: Guilford Press.

Lareau, A. (1996). Assessing parent involvement in schooling: A critical analysis. In A. Booth & J. Dunn (Eds.), *Family and school links: How do they affect educational outcomes?* (pp. 57–64). Mahwah, NJ: Erlbaum.

Lightfoot, S. L. (1978). *Worlds apart.* New York: Basic Books.

Los Angeles Times Poll. (1999, March 20–27). Study #424. Available: http://www. latimes. com (April 3)

Mason, J. M. (1977). *Reading readiness: A definition and skills hierarchy from preschoolers' developing conceptions of print* (T. R. No. 59). University of Illinois at Urbana-Champaign: Center of the Study of Reading.

Miller, L. (1995). *An American imperative: Accelerating minority educational advancement.* New Haven: Yale University Press.

Moles, O. (1996). New national directions in research and policy. In A. Booth & J. Dunn (Eds.), *Family and school links: How do they affect educational outcomes?* (pp. 247–254). Mahwah, NJ: Erlbaum.

National Education Goals Panel. (1997a). *The National Education Goals report: Building a nation of learners, 1997.* Washington, DC: Superintendent of Documents. Available: http://www. negp. gov

National Education Goals Panel. (1997b). *Special early childhood education report, 1997.* Washington, DC: Superintendent of Documents. Available: http://www. negp. gov

National Educational Research Policy and Priorities Board. (1999). *Improving the education of English language learners: Best practices.* Washington, DC: Office of Educational Research and Improvement.

Natriello, G., McDill, E., & Pallas, A. (1990). *Schooling disadvantaged students: Racing against catastrophe.* New York: Teachers College Press.

Neuman, S. (1998). How can we enable all children to achieve? In S. Neuman & K. Roskos (Eds.), *Children achieving: Best practices in early literacy* (pp. 5–10). Newark, DE: International Reading Association.

Neuman, S., Hagedorn, T., Celano, D., & Daly, P. (1995). Toward a collaborative approach to parent involvement in early education: A study of teenage mothers in an African-American community. *American Educational Research Journal, 32,* 801–827.

Neuman, S. B., & Roskos, K. (1993). Access to print for children of poverty: Differential effects of adult mediation and literacy-enriched play settings on environmental and functional print tasks. *American Educational Research Journal, 30,* 95–122.

Neuman, S. B., & Roskos, K. (1997). Literacy knowledge in practice: Contexts of participation for young writers and readers. *Reading Research Quarterly, 32,* 10–32.

Owen, V., Li, R., Rodriguez-Brown, F., & Shanahan, T. (1993, April). *Parent attitudes: Critical perspectives of the changing nature of parents' pedagogical theories.* Paper presented at the annual meeting of the American Educational Research Association, Atlanta.

Paratore, J., Melzi, G., & Krol-Sinclair, B. (1999). *What should we expect of family literacy? Experiences of Latino children who parents participate in an intergenerational literacy project.* Newark, DE: International Reading Association.

Pressley, M. (1998). *Reading instruction that works: The case for balanced teaching.* New York: Guilford Press.

Ralph, K., Ellis, J., & Medina, T. (1998). Developing phonemic awareness through poetry, song, word play, and literature. In C. Cox (Ed.), *Research and practice: "a-m+" reading requirements* (pp. 31–40). Los Angeles: Los Angeles County Office of Education.

Ramey, C., & Campbell, F. (1984). Preventive education for high-risk children: Cognitive consequences of the Carolina Abecedarian Project. *American Journal of Mental Deficiency, 88,* 515–523.

Ramirez, D., Yuen, S., & Ramey, D. (1991). *Final report: Longitudinal study of structured English immersion strategy, early-exit and late-exit transitional bilingual education programs for language-minority children* (Executive summary). San Mateo, CA: Aguirre International.

Ramirez, D., Yuen, S., Ramey, D., & Merino, B. (1986). First year report: Longitudinal study of immersion programs for language-minority children. San Mateo, CA: Aguirre International.

Reading Research Quarterly. (1997). [Entire issue.] *32*(4).

Rodriguez, R. (1982). *Hunger of memory: The education of Richard Rodriguez.* Toronto: Bantam.

Rodriguez-Brown, F., Li, R., & Albom, J. (1999). Hispanic parents' awareness and use of literacy-rich environments at home and in the community. *Education and Urban Society, 32,* 41–58.

Rossell, C., & Baker, K. (1996). The educational effectiveness of bilingual education. *Research in the teaching of English, 30,* 1–68.

Scarborough, H. (1998). Early identification of children at risk for reading disabilities: Phonological awareness and some other promising predictors. In B. Shapiro, P. Accardo, & A. Capute (Eds.),

Specific reading disability: A view of the spectrum (pp. 75–119). Timonium, MD: York Press.

Schickedanz, J. (1998). What is developmentally appropriate practice in early literacy? Considering the alphabet. In S. Neuman & K. Roskos (Eds.), *Children achieving: Best practices in early literacy.* Newark, DE: International Reading Association.

Schlesinger, A., Jr. (1991). *The disuniting of America.* New York: Norton.

Schlossman, S. (1978). The parent education game: The politics of child psychology. *Teachers College Record, 79,* 788–808.

Schorr, L. (1994). Looking ahead: Integrating urban policies to meet educational demands. In K. Wong & M. Want (Eds.), *Rethinking policy for at-risk students* (pp. 221–238). Berkeley, CA : McCutchan.

Simon, P. (1980). *The tongue-tied American: Confronting the foreign-language crisis.* New York: Continuum.

Slavin, R., & Madden, N. (2001). Effects of bilingual and English as a second language adaptations of Success for All on the reading achievement of students acquiring English. In R. Slavin & M. Calderón (Eds.), *Effective programs for Latino students* (pp. 207–230). Mahwah, NJ: Erlbaum.

Slavin, R., Madden, N., Dolan, L., & Wasik, B. (1996). *Every child, every school: Success for All.* Thousand Oaks, CA: Corwin Press.

Slavin, R., Madden, N., Karweit, N., Dolan, L., & Wasik, B. (1994). Success for All: A comprehensive approach to prevention and early intervention. In R. Slavin, N. Karweit, & B. Wasik (Eds.), *Preventing early school failure: Research, policy, and practice* (pp. 175–205). Needham Heights, MA: Allyn & Bacon.

Snow, C., Barnes, W., Chandler, J., Goodman, I., & Hemphill, L. (1991). *Unfulfilled expectations: Home and school influences on literacy.* Cambridge, MA: Harvard University Press.

Snow, C., Burns, M., & Griffin, P. (1998). *Preventing reading difficulties in young children.* Washington, DC: National Academy Press.

Stipek, D., Milburn, S., Clements, D., & Daniels, D. (1992). Parents' beliefs about appropriate education for young children. *Journal of Applied Developmental Psychology, 13,* 293–310.

Taylor, D., & Dorsey-Gaines, C. (1988). *Growing up literate: Learning from inner-city families.* Portsmouth, NH: Heinemann.

Teale, W. (1986). Home background and young children's literacy development. In W. H. Teale & E. Sulzby (Eds.), *Emergent literacy: Writing and reading* (pp. 173–206). Norwood, NJ: Ablex.

Tharp, R. (1982). The effective instruction of comprehension: Results and description of the Kamehameha Early Education Program. *Reading Research Quarterly, 17,* 503–527.

Tharp, R. (1989). Psychocultural variables and constants: Effects on teaching and learning in schools. *American Psychologist, 44,* 349–359.

Tharp, R., & Gallimore, R. (1988). *Rousing minds to life: Teaching, learning and schooling in social context.* Cambridge, UK: Cambridge University Press.

Thomas, W., & Collier, V. (1997). *School effectiveness for language minority students.* Washington, DC: National Clearinghouse for Bilingual Education. Available: http://www. ncbe. gwu. edu/ncbepubs/resource/effectiveness/

Troia, G. (1999). Phonological awareness intervention research: A critical review of the experimental methodology. *Reading Research Quarterly, 34,* 28–52.

U.S. Department of Education. (1996). *Parents and schools: Partners in student learning* (NCES 96–913). Washington, DC: Superintendent of Documents

U.S. Department of Education. (1998a). *Early literacy experiences in the home* (NCES 1999-003). Washington, DC: Superintendent of Documents. Available: http://nces. ed. gov/pubs99/quarterlyapr/3-early/3-esq11-b. html

U.S. Department of Education. (1998b). *Parent involvement in children's education: Efforts by public elementary schools* (NCES 98-032). Washington, DC: Superintendent of Documents. Available: http://nces. ed. gov/pubs98/98032. html

U.S. Department of Education. (1999a). *Overview of public elementary an secondary schools and districts: School year 1997–98* (NCES 99–322). Washington, DC: Superintendent of Documents. Available: http://nces. ed. gov/pubs99/1999322. pdf

U.S. Department of Education. (1999b). *Projections of education statistics to 2009* (NCES 1999-038). Washington, DC: Superintendent of Documents. Available: http://nces. ed. gov/pubs99/1999038. pdf

U.S. Department of Education. (1999c). *NAEP 1998 reading report card for the nation and states* (NCES 1999–500). Washington, DC: Superintendent of Documents. Available: http://nces. ed. gov/nationsreportcard/pubs/main1998/1999500. pdf

U.S. Department of Education. (1999d). *NAEP 1998 writing report card for the nation and states* (NCES 1999–462). Washington, DC: Superintendent of Documents. Available: http://nces. ed. gov/nationsreportcard/pubs/main1998/1999462. pdf

Valdés, G. (1996). *Con respeto: Bridging the distances between culturally diverse families and schools.* New York: Teacher College Press.

Vierra, A. (1984). The relationship between Chicano children's achievement and their teachers' ethnicity. *Hispanic Journal of Behavioral Sciences, 6,* 285–290.

Walberg, H., & Tsai, S. (1985). Correlates of reading achievement and attitude: A national assessment study. *Journal of Educational Research, 78,* 159–167.

Waller, W. (1932). *The sociology of teaching.* New York: Russell & Russell.

Werner, E., & Smith, R. (1982). *Vulnerable but invincible.* New York: McGraw-Hill.

White, K. (1982). The relation between socioeconomic status and academic achievement. *Psychological Bulletin, 91,* 461–481.

Whitehurst, G., & Lonigan, C. (1998). Child development and emergent literacy. *Child Development, 69,* 848–872.

Willig, A. (1985). A meta-analysis of selected studies on the effectiveness of bilingual education. *Review of Educational Research, 55,* 269–317.

Yopp, H., Yopp, R., Harris, P., & Stapleton, L. (1998). Phonemic awareness. In C. Cox (Ed.), *Research and practice: "a-m+" reading requirements* (pp. 41–54). Los Angeles: Los Angeles County Office of Education.

16

The Complex Interplay between Biology and Environment: Otitis Media and Mediating Effects on Early Literacy Development

❖

JOANNE E. ROBERTS
MARGARET R. BURCHINAL

Emergent literacy is the behaviors, knowledge, and attitudes that are acquired in the early years and the environments that affect this process (Sulzby, 1989; Teale & Sulzby, 1986; Whitehurst & Lonigan, 1998). The multiple determinants of children's success in reading and writing have been of considerable interest in the research literature for the past 25 years. Children's early literacy skills build on their cognitive and linguistic capabilities. Emergence of these skills results from a sound, functioning biological system, a supportive environment, and the interplay between them. Study of disruption of any of these systems can help shed light on factors that support children's normal development, just as the study of the impact of interventions can help reveal the capacity of supportive environments to counteract the negative effects of some environments. One variable hypothesized to affect children's early language and literacy skills and possibly cause learning disabilities is a child's experience with otitis media. Otitis media with effusion (OME), or middle ear fluid, is prevalent in early childhood (Stool et al., 1994). OME generally causes a mild to moderate fluctuating hearing loss which persists until the fluid goes away. Whether recurrent or persistent

OME and the associated hearing loss during the first few years of life, a critical period for learning language, increases a child's risk for later language, reading, and learning difficulties continues to be debated (Paradise, 1998; Roberts & Wallace, 1997; Ruben et al., 1998; Stool et al., 1994). The study of otitis media can help reveal the complex interplay between biology and the environment in affecting children's acquisition of early literacy skills, while the study of factors such as the quality of child care can help reveal the capacity of supportive environments to counteract the negative effects of other environments. This chapter describes the role of OME in affecting children's early language and literacy skills, how children's home environment and child-care environment can interact or independently affect children's early language and literacy acquisition, and the implications of this literature for future research directions.

Influence of Otitis Media

Otitis media, after the common cold, is the most frequent illness of early childhood and the most common diagnosis made by physicians (Lanphear, Byrd, Auinger, & Hall, 1997; Schappert, 1992; Stool et al., 1994). By their third birthday, greater than 80% of children have had at least one episode of otitis media and more than 40% have experienced three or more episodes (Teele, Klein, & Rosner, 1989). The middle ear transmits sounds from the outer ear to the inner ear, from which information is carried by the acoustic nerve to the brain. When a child has OME, the middle ear is inflamed, the tympanic membrane between the outer and middle ear is thickened, and fluid is present in the middle ear cavity. Fluid present in the middle ear cavity during OME can persist for several weeks or even months after the onset of an episode. These conditions impair the normal transmission of acoustic information, generally resulting in a mild to moderate conductive hearing loss (Bess, 1983; Bluestone, Beery, & Paradise, 1973). The hearing loss associated with OME is conductive, because of the buildup of fluid in the middle ear, and prevents sound from being transmitted normally from the middle ear to the inner ear. The degree of hearing loss is typically around 26 dB (equivalent to plugging one's ears with a finger) but can range from no loss to a moderate loss, making it hard to hear conversational speech. It can be extremely difficult to detect this hearing loss by observing or interacting with a child, because symptoms are often absent or subtle and may be mistaken for developmental problems or changes. However, a health care provider can reliably test hearing in children as young as infants.

A child who has a mild to moderate fluctuating hearing loss due to an episode of OME will receive a partial or inconsistent auditory signal, which may result in misperceiving or not hearing words. It has been hypothesized that a child who experiences repeated and persistent episodes of OME and hearing loss may build up an inaccurate catalogue of words, and be left with an incomplete representation of the linguistic system. As a result, a child with frequent OME may then be at a disadvantage for learning the rules of language, affecting the development of speech sounds, vocabulary, grammar, and use of language. This may in turn lead to difficulties in emerging literacy skills such as phoneme–grapheme correspondence and phonemic awareness and at-

tention problems which ultimately affect children's ability to learn to read. It is also hypothesized that children who experience frequent changes in the intensity of signals, due to mild hearing loss, may be particularly susceptible to the effects of noise. They can "tune out" when an environment is noisy (e.g., television on, other children talking, and open classroom) and therefore develop attention difficulties for auditory information. This inattention to language may persist beyond the episode of OME and be manifested in a classroom as distractibility and difficulty working independently.

Developmental Models

Several general developmental models have been discussed in the research linking early OME and later developmental outcomes (Feldman & Gelman, 1986). Early models of the link between early OME and later development have been from a behavioral or reductionistic model of development which is currently not widely accepted by developmentalists (Feldman & Gelman, 1986). Advocates of this model believe that learning is proportionally associated with the amount and diversity of sensory input. Based on this model, developmental delays should be directly related to the amount of the sensory loss associated with the OME episodes and these delays may be evidenced in any or all types of cognitive activities. A second model, the "critical period" developmental model, is also implicitly or explicitly invoked in OME research and is not widely accepted by developmentalists. It has been argued that normal speech, language, and intellectual development is contingent upon the child's being exposed to the requisite stimulation at particular points in the lifecycle (critical periods) and that hearing loss resulting from OME during these critical periods could impede these developmental processes. Both the behavioral and critical period theories have been criticized for their lack of theoretical attention to developmental resiliency (self-righting tendencies) and the potential of the child or the child's environment to compensate for these temporary deficits (Feldman & Gelman, 1986; Paradise, 1980).

More recently, OME investigators (Roberts et al., 1995, 1998; Roberts & Wallace, 1997; Vernon-Feagans, 1999; Vernon-Feagans, Emanuel, & Blood, 1997) have based their research on models of early language and literacy acquisition using a general systems and ecological view of developmental change (Bronfrenbrenner & Crouter, 1983; Sameroff, 1983). This model emphasizes the contributions of the child, the environment, and the dynamic transactions between the child and environment. The child's development is embedded in a number of hierarchically organized, interrelated systems (e.g., the home environment and child-care environment) where changes that occur at one level of the hierarchy (e.g., child has chronic OME) may have influences both within that level and across systems (e.g., child not attentive in child care). Such a model also describes a multitude of risk (e.g., child-poor phonemic awareness skills, mother less than a high school education, and noisy environment) and protective (e.g., literacy-rich home and responsive child-care environment) factors that can affect children's development. It can also identify different developmental patterns for those who have higher language and literacy skills than those who do not and determine the etiology of these differences (Burchinal & Appelbaum, 1991).

According to a transactional model of development, hearing losses can be indirectly related, due to early OME, to later language and literacy problems. From this viewpoint, the child has a biological endowment toward selecting and processing sensory input, even young children play an active role in seeking out such experiences, and the manner in which the child interacts with his or her environment affects the types of stimulation received. Early OME may have indirect long-term consequences if the manner in which caregivers interact with the child becomes less responsive as a consequence of the hearing loss associated with OME. For example, negative feedback loops could begin when the child appears unresponsive due to the mild hearing loss. A caregiver, in turn, may become less inclined to initiate interactions or behave responsively to the child and may view the child as less skilled in language or willfully ignoring him or her.

The route by which recurrent OME could affect a child's development of language is not clear. It is likely that the many factors affecting children's development operate singly, synergistically, or in a protective fashion. For example, a child could have language difficulties, because of auditory discrimination difficulties, secondary to a fluctuating hearing loss due to OME. However, if that child spent time in a supportive listening environment (i.e., responsive home and child-care environment, low signal-to-noise ratio in environments), the child may acquire normal language skills. Each child who has recurrent or persistent OME is affected by the variable conditions of their age, frequency, and degree of OME-associated hearing loss, listening environment, and interactions with caregivers and others in the child's environment.

The Data Examining OME Language/Literacy Links

The relationship between early OME and later developmental outcomes remains inconclusive despite extensive research. Several studies have found a relationship between a history of otitis media in early childhood and later speech, language, and auditory processing skills during the preschool years and reading skills during the early elementary school years (Gravel & Wallace, 1992; Roberts, Burchinal, Koch, Footo, & Henderson, 1988; Teele et al., 1990). Specifically, in comparison to children who infrequently experienced otitis media, infants and preschoolers with a history of OME scored lower on standardized assessments of receptive and expressive language (Friel-Patti, & Finitzo-Hieber, 1990; Teele, Klein, Rosner, & Greater Boston Otitis Media Study Group, 1984; Wallace et al., 1988) in specific language areas including phonology (Teele et al., 1990; Roberts et al., 1988), morphology (Teele et al., 1990) and paraphrasing (Feagans, Sanyal, Henderson, Collier, & Applebaum, 1987), listening in demanding environments (Gravel & Wallace, 1992), academic achievement (Gravel & Wallace, 1992; Teele et al., 1990), and classroom behavior (Roberts, Burchinal, & Campbell, 1994; Roberts et al., 1989). However, many studies failed to find associations between early history of OME and later measures of speech, language, attention, academic achievement, and classroom behavior (Fischler, Todd, & Feldman, 1985; Peters, Grievink, van Bon, & Schilder, 1994; Roberts et al., 1986; 1989; Teele et al., 1990). Further, two recent studies of more than 200 children reported that OME was not related to language skills at 1 year of age, a weak correlation for expressive vocabulary (using parent report) at 2 years of age, and at 3 years of age a weak correlation (explaining 1–3% of the variance) for middle-income but not low-income children on measures of vocabulary and aspects of cognition, but not measures of speech or other aspects of language (Feldman et al., 1999; Paradise et al., 2000).

Our work at the Frank Porter Graham Child Development Center illustrates the types of research that have been conducted to study whether a history of OME in early childhood relates to children's later language and learning. In 1990, the Carolina Otitis Media Project began studying 80 African American children attending nine community child care programs whose age at study entry was between 6 and 12 months. Between study entry and 5 years of age, children's ears were examined every other week and their hearing sensitivity was examined every 3 months, as well as during episodes of OME. Children's speech, language, and cognitive skills were assessed annually during the first 5 years of life. School readiness was assessed at kindergarten entry and achievement in reading and math in the early elementary school years. Children are now in second through fourth grade and the study continues to document children's academic skills. Measures of the interactions of the child and his or her mother and of child-care quality were also made annually.

Children in this study frequently experienced OME, particularly when children were under the age of 2 years (Zeisel et al., 1995). Despite the frequent OME, we did not find a direct relationship between OME history and children's language skills between 1 and 5 years of age (Roberts et al., 1995; 1998, 2000). We found that the caregiving environment mediated the relationship between children's history of OME and associated hearing loss and later communication development at 1 and 2 years of age (Roberts et al., 1995, 1998). That is, children with more OME and associated hearing loss tended to live in less responsive

caregiving environments, and these environments were linked to lower performance in receptive and expressive language. Furthermore, we also found a mild association between the amount of OME and associated hearing loss and school-readiness measures (applied math problems and an auditory closure task) at entry into kindergarten, even after partialing out the effects of gender, quality of child care, home environment, and income (Roberts et al., 2000).

Support for this transactional model of OME developmental effects can be found in several other studies. Wallace, Gravel, Schwartz, and Ruben (1996) found that children with recurrent OME whose mothers provided a rich language environment displayed communication skills equivalent to children without OME. Feagans, Kipp, and Blood (1994) found that quality of child care (as defined by the caregiver–child ratio) interacted with OME experience, affecting children's attention skills but not their language skills. Black et al. (1988) also reported with a sample of low-socioeconomic-status mothers and 1–2-year-old children that mothers of the OME-prone children were less warm and sociable in interactions with their children than were mothers of children with little or no OME. In a study of 79 middle-class, white children, mothers of 2-year-olds who experienced recurrent OME have also described themselves as more depressed and less competent and their children as more demanding than mothers of 2-year-olds without an OME history (Forgays, Hasazi, & Wasserman, 1992). However, Paradise et al. (1999), in a study of over 2,000 children, found no relationship between parenting stress and children's OME history.

In summary, the controversy surrounding the issue of whether recurrent OME affects the acquisition of language and subsequent academic skills is unresolved due to the conflicting findings of investigations that have examined this issue. The results of the prospective studies are inconclusive regarding the extent and nature of the language and learning sequelae of OME. There is some suggestion of a mild association between OME and expressive rather than receptive language skills during infancy rather than in the later school years. However, for studies that reported significant findings, the effect size is generally small, accounting for only about 1–8% of the variance. The clinical significance of this effect for language and learning is not clear. Furthermore, the caregiving environment at home and in child care may play a much more important role than OME in affecting later language and literacy skills. Thus, these data suggest that a history of OME in early childhood may be one of many variables that can affect children's language development, and this link needs to be studied further.

Two areas that have an important impact on children's early literacy and language development must be considered when examining the OME language/literacy links: the influence of both the home and the child-care environments. Both the child's home and his or her child-care environments have been shown to have a much stronger impact on language and literacy skills than a history of OME or associated hearing loss. The child's home and child-care environment may also have the potential capacity to counteract the negative effects of some environments, if a child were to experience particular developmental difficulties due to OME histories.

Influence of Home and Child-Care Environments

Home Environment

Home environmental factors important to children's emergent literacy acquisition include the interactions of caregivers during joint book reading, exposure to literacy-related activities, and the responsiveness of caregivers in the environment. (See Bus, Chapter 13, and Roskos & Neuman, Chapter 20.) Shared book reading is the most widely studied and believed to be the most important activity for supporting children's emergent literacy skills (Bus, IJzenedoorn, & Pelligrini, 1995; Scarborough & Dobrich, 1994). Shared book reading advances a child's language—increasing understanding and use of vocabulary and concepts, structure of story narratives, and decontextualized language, as well as the conventions of print, letter–sound correspondences, and linguistic awareness. During

book reading, the adult scaffolds and supports the child's interactions, allowing him or her to acquire higher levels of skills. Certain styles of interactions (describing, labeling, and focusing on meanings and inferences) during book reading may be particularly facilitative of literacy skills and this may depend on the child's level of literacy skills (Haden, Reese, & Fivush, 1996; Reese & Cox, 1999; Whitehurst et al., 1994). In addition to joint book reading, the number of books in the home, access to literacy artifacts (e.g., crayons and paper), and literacy interactions (e.g., visits to the library and child and adult making shopping list) also are important for learning about the purpose and value of print and ultimately for learning to read (Payne, Whitehurst, & Angell, 1994; Purcell-Gates, 1996; Teale & Sulzby, 1986). In addition, a large body of research supports the influence of the amount of talk and style of parents' conversational interactions (e.g., responsive and elaborative) in facilitating children's vocabulary and other aspects of language development (Bornstein, Haynes, & Painter, 1998; Hart & Risley, 1992, 1995; Hoff-Ginsberg, 1990; Huttenlocher, Haight, Bryk, Seltzer, & Lyons, 1991). Overall measures of the responsiveness, organization, and support of the home environment have also been shown to predict children's language development during the early preschool years (Bradley, 1994; Bradley et al., 1989; Elardo, Bradley, & Caldwell, 1977; Siegel, 1982). Thus, there is considerable research support for the importance of both the home language and literacy environments in developing children's emergent literacy skills, although the crucial aspects of these experiences continue to be debated.

We have examined the relationship between patterns of mother–infant interaction and developmental outcomes at 1 year of age in 92 African American dyads (Wallace, Roberts, & Lodder, 1998). The elaborativeness of the mothers' language independently related to children's receptive language after controlling for background measures. Roberts, Burchinal, and Durham (1999) examined how child and family factors affect individual differences in the language development of African American children between 18 and 30 months using a standardized parent report tool to assess language.

Children from more stimulating and responsive homes were reported to have larger vocabularies, use more irregular nouns and verbs, and use longer utterances, in addition to having more rapid rates of acquisition of irregular forms and longer utterances over time. These results support the role of the responsiveness of the home environment in the language development of African American infants.

Child-Care Environment

Child-care environmental factors, which we believe are important in influencing children's emergent literacy, involve many of the same factors as in the home environment. Language development is believed to be enhanced in child-care settings in which caregivers speak frequently to children, ask open-ended questions, use decontextualized language, and scaffold interactions to match the developmental level of the child. Lamb (1997) concludes in his review of the child-care literature that children in high-quality child care have modestly larger vocabularies and more preliteracy skills than children in lower quality care, even after adjusting for differences among families related to the selection of child care of a particular type and quality. Most studies have shown that child outcomes are related to global measures of child-care quality, including the extent to which caregivers are sensitive and responsive toward children and the kinds of activities available in the child-care environment. These global measures modestly predicted child outcomes in all large multisite studies (Howes, Phillips, & Whitebrook, 1992; NICHD Early Child Care Research Network, 2000; Peisner-Feinberg & Burchinal, 1997) and many smaller studies (Dunn, 1993; Phillips, McCartney, & Scarr, 1987; Schliecker, White, & Jacobs, 1991). Two recent studies have examined specific aspects of the environment. They found that children's language and preliteracy development are enhanced when they attend child care settings in which caregivers frequently talked with children (NICHD Early Childhood Care Research Network, 2000; Zill, 1999).

The relations between quality of center-based child care and early cognitive and language development were examined longitudinally from 6 to 36 months in a sample of 89 African American children (Burchinal, Roberts, Nabors, & Bryant, 1996; Burchinal et al., in press). Results indicated that higher-quality child care was related to higher measures of cognitive development, language development, and communication skills across time, even after adjusting for selected child and family characteristics. In addition, classrooms that met professional recommendations regarding (1) child–adult ratios tended to have children with better language skills, and (2) teacher education tended to have girls with better cognitive and receptive language skills.

Implications and Future Directions

There is currently a lack of consensus whether a history of OME in early childhood affects children's language and emergent literacy development. Some children experiencing recurrent and persistent OME during the first few years of life may be at increased risk for later language and learning difficulties. However, it is clear that that the home and child-care environments are much more important factors than a child's history of OME in affecting children's early language and literacy development. Thus, these results highlight the importance of the interaction patterns of caregivers in children's homes and in their child-care settings in affecting the early language and literacy skills. Therefore, all children regardless of their OME history should receive a responsive and stimulating language- and literacy-rich family environment to best facilitate their language and emergent literacy development. Until further research can resolve whether such a relationship exists and can determine what aspects of language are affected, children's hearing status and language skills need to be considered in the management of young children with histories of OME.

There are several specific strategies when working with young children who are experiencing chronic OME that have been detailed in our previous publications (Roberts & Medley, 1995; Roberts & Wallace, 1997). First, the hearing of a child with 3 months of bilateral OME should be tested (Stool et al., 1994). In addition, speech and language should be screened for children who have had 3 months of persistent OME, four to six episodes of otitis media in a 6-month period, whenever hearing loss is present and/or when families or caregivers express concerns regarding a child's development. Second, families and other caregivers (e.g., child-care providers) of young children who have recurrent or persistent OME need current, clear, and accurate information to make decisions about their child's medical and educational management. Third, children who experience recurrent or persistent OME will benefit from a highly responsive language environment using strategies that have been shown to facilitate language in young children. Caregivers should respond to communication attempts, provide frequent opportunities for children to participate in conversations, and elaborate on conversational topics. Fourth, children with chronic OME will also benefit from an environment that increases children's attention to language. Activities that increase children's attention to sounds, words, and phrases can be very helpful. Finally, some children with a history of OME may exhibit language and other developmental difficulties and may benefit from early intervention.

There are currently many ongoing prospective studies of the links between OME and later language and early literacy skills using correlational designs in North Carolina (Roberts et al., 1995, 1998), New York (Gravel & Wallace, 2000; Wallace et al., 1996), Pittsburgh (Feldman et al., 1999; Paradise, et al., 1999, 2000), and Pennsylvania (Feagans et al., 1994). There is also an ongoing experimental study being conducted in Pittsburgh (Paradise et al., 1999) in which children are randomly assigned to early versus late tubes and thus the amount of OME is manipulated and its effect on development examined. These studies use prospective designs to monitor children's OME and developmental histories from infancy using models of child development that consider the many variables that may affect this relationship. They are using measures of the child's home and child-care environment. Most are documenting hearing loss to determine the degree of hearing loss that may be accounting for any associations between OME and later development.

These studies are also looking at specific aspects of children's language and emergent literacy skills during the preschool years and later literacy and language skills into the school years. The results will help us understand in the 21st century whether history of OME plays a role in children's language and literacy development and the role of the home and child-care environment in affecting these links.

Acknowledgments

This research was supported by grants from National Institute on Deafness and Other Communication Disorders (No. 1 R01 CD03817-01A1), Maternal and Child Health Bureau (No. MCJ-370599, 370649, Title V, Social Security Act), Health and Human Resources and Services Administration, Department of Health and Human Services, and the Spencer Foundation.

References

Bess, F. H. (1983). Workshop on effects of otitis media on the child: Hearing loss associated with middle ear effusion. *Pediatrics, 71,* 640–641.

Black, M. M., Gerson, L. F., Freeland, C. A. B., Nair, P., Rubin, J. S., & Hutcheson, J. J. (1988). Language screening for infants prone to otitis media. *Journal of Pediatric Psychology, 13*(3), 423–433.

Bluestone, C. D., Beery, O. C., & Paradise, J. L. (1973). Audiometry and tympanometry in relation to middle ear effusions in children. *Laryngoscope, 83,* 594–604.

Bornstein, M. H., Haynes, M. O., & Painter, K. M. (1998). Sources of child vocabulary competence: A multivariate model. *Journal of Child Language, 25,* 367–393.

Bradley, R. H. (1994). The HOME inventory: Review and reflections. *Advances in Child Development and Behavior, 25,* 241–288.

Bradley, R. H., Caldwell, B. M., Rock, S. L., Barnard, K. E., Gray, C., Hammond, M. A., Mitchell, S., Siegel, L., Ramey, C. T., Gottfried, A. W., & Johnson, D. L. (1989). Home environment and cognitive development in the first 3 years of life: A collaborative study involving six sites and three ethnic groups in North America. *Developmental Psychology, 28,* 217–235.

Bronfenbrenner, U., & Crouter, A. C. (1983). The evolution of environmental models in developmental research. In P. H. Mussen (Ed.), *Handbook of child psychology* (pp. 357–414). New York: Wiley.

Burchinal, M., & Appelbaum, M. I. (1991). Estimating individual developmental functions:

Methods and their assumptions. *Child Development, 62,* 23–43.

Burchinal, M. R., Roberts, J. E., Nabors, L., & Bryant, D. M. (1996). Quality of center infant care and infant cognitive and language development. *Child Development, 67,* 606–620.

Burchinal, M. R., Roberts, J. E., Riggins, R., Zeisel, S., Neebe, E., & Bryant, D. (2000). Relating quality of center child care to early cognitive and language development longitudinally. *Child Development, 71*(2), 339–357.

Bus, A. G., van IJzendoorn, M. H., & Pellegrini, A. (1995). Joint book reading makes for success in learning to read: A meta-analysis on intergenerational transmission of literacy. *Review of Educational Research, 65,* 1–21.

Dunn, L. (1993). Proximal and distal features of day care quality and children's development. *Early Childhood Research Quarterly, 8,* 167–192.

Elardo, R., Bradley, R., & Caldwell, B. M. (1977). A longitudinal study of the relation of infants home environments to language development at age three. *Child Development, 48,* 595–603.

Feagans, L. V., Kipp, E., & Blood, I. (1994). The effects of otitis media on the attention skills of day-care-attending toddlers. *Developmental Psychology, 30,* 701–708.

Feagans, L., Sanyal, M., Henderson, F., Collier, A., & Applebaum, M. (1987). Relationship of middle ear diseases in early childhood to later narrative and attentions skills. *Journal of Pediatric Psychology, 12,* 581–594.

Feldman, H. M., Dollaghan, C. A., Campbell, T. F., Colborn, D. K., Kurs-Lasky, M., Jaosky, J. E., & Paradise, J. L. (1999). Parent-reported language and communication skills of one and two years of age in relation to otitis media in the first two years of life. *Pediatrics, 104*(4), 52.

Feldman, H., & Gelman, R. (1986). Otitis media and cognitive development: Theoretical perspectives. In J. F. Kavanagh (Ed.), *Otitis media and child development* (pp. 27–41). Parkton, MD: York Press.

Fischler, R. S., Todd, N. W., & Feldman, C. M. (1985). Otitis media and language performance in a cohort of Apache Indian children. *American Journal of Diseases of Children, 139,* 355–360.

Forgays, D., Hasazi, J., & Wasserman, R. (1992). Recurrent otitis media and parenting stress in mothers of two year old children. *Developmental and Behavioral Pediatrics, 13,* 321–325.

Friel-Patti, S., & Finitzo-Hieber, T. (1990). Language learning in a prospective study of otitis media with effusion in the first two years of life. *Journal of Speech and Hearing Research, 33,* 188–194.

Gravel, J. S., & Wallace, I. F. (1992). Listening and language at 4 years of age: Effects of otitis media. *Journal of Speech and Hearing Research, 35,* 588–595.

Gravel, J. S., & Wallace, I. F. (2000). Effects of otitis media with effusion on hearing in the first three years of life. *Journal of Speech and Hearing Research, 43*(3), 631–644.

Haden, C. A., Reese, E., & Fivush, R. (1996). Mothers' extratextual comments during storybook reading: Stylistic differences over time and across texts. *Discourse Processes, 21,* 135–169.

Hart, B., & Risley, T. R. (1992). American parenting of language-learning children: Persisting differences in family-child interactions observed in natural home environments. *Developmental Psychology, 28*(6), 1096–1105.

Hart, B., & Risley, T. R. (Eds.). (1995). *Meaningful differences in the everyday experience of young American children.* Baltimore: Brookes.

Hoff-Ginsberg, E. (1990). Maternal speech and the child's development of syntax: A further look. *Journal of Child Language, 17,* 337–346.

Howes, C., Phillips, D. A., & Whitebrook, M. (1992). Thresholds of quality: Implications for the social development of children in center-based child care. *Child Development, 53,* 449–460.

Huttenlocher, J., Haight, W., Bryk, A., Seltzer, M., & Lyons, T. (1991). Early vocabulary growth: Relation to language input and gender. *Developmental Psychology, 27*(2), 236–248.

Lamb, M. E. (1997). Nonparental child care: Context, quality, correlates, and consequences. In W. Damon (Gen. Ed.), I. E. Sigel, & K. A. Renniger (Vol. Eds.), *Handbook of child psychology* (5th ed.). *Vol. 4. Child psychology in practice* (pp. 73–134). New York: Wiley.

Lanphear, B. P., Byrd, R. S., Auinger, P., & Hall, C. B. (1997). Increasing prevalence of recurrent otitis media among children in the United States. *Pediatrics, 99*(3), e1.

NICHD Early Child Care Research Network. (2000). The relation of child care to cognitive and language development. *Child Development, 71*(4), 960–980.

Paradise, J. L. (1980). Otitis media in infants and children. *Pediatrics, 65,* 917–943.

Paradise, J. L. (1998). Otitis media and child development: Should we worry? *Pediatric Infectious Disease Journal, 17*(11), 1076–1083.

Paradise, J. L., Dollaghan, C. A., Campbell, T. F., Feldman, H. M., Bernard, B. S., Colborn, D. K., Rockette, H. E., Janosky, J. E., Pitcairn, D. L., Sabo, D. L., Kurs-Lasky, M., & Smith, C. G. (2000). Language, speech sound production, and cognition in three-year-old children in relation to otitis media in their first three years of life. *Pediatrics, 105*(5), 1119–1130.

Paradise, J. L., Feldman, H. M., Colborn, K., Campbell, T. F., Dollaghan, C. A., Rockette, H. E., Janosky, J. E., Kurs-Lasky, M., Bernard, B. S., & Smith, C. G. (1999). Parental stress and parent-rated child behavior in relation to otitis media in the first three years of life. *Pediatrics, 104*(6), 1264–1273.

Payne, A. C., Whitehurst, G. J., & Angell, A. L. (1994). The role of literacy environment in the language development of children from low-income families. *Early Childhood Research Quarterly, 9,* 427–440.

Peisner-Feinburg, E. S., & Burchinal, M. R. (1997). Relations between preschool children's child-care experiences and concurrent development: The Cost, Quality, and Outcomes Study. *Merrill–Palmer Quarterly, 43,* 451–477.

Peters, S. A. F., Grievink, E. H., van Bon, W. H. J., & Schilder, A. G. M. (1994). The effects of early bilateral otitis media with effusion on educational attainment: A prospective cohort study. *Journal of Learning Disabilities, 27,* 111–121.

Phillips, D. A., McCartney, K., & Scarr, S. (1987). Child care quality and children's social development. *Developmental Psychology, 23,* 537–543.

Purcell-Gates, V. (1996). Stories, coupons, and the TV Guide: Relationships between home literacy experiences and emergent literacy knowledge. *Reading Research Quarterly, 31*(4), 406–428.

Reese, E., & Cox, A. (1999). Quality of adult book reading affects children's emergent literacy. *Developmental Psychology, 35*(1), 20–28.

Roberts, J. E., Burchinal, M. R., & Campbell, F. (1994). Otitis media in early childhood and patterns of intellectual development and later academic performance. *Journal of Pediatric Psychology, 19*(3), 347–366.

Roberts, J. E., Burchinal, M. R., Collier, A. M., Ramey, C. T., Koch, M. A., & Henderson, F. W. (1989). Otitis media in early childhood and cognitive, academic, and classroom performance of the school-aged child. *Pediatrics, 83,* 477–485.

Roberts, J. E., Burchinal, M., & Durham, M. (1999). Parents' report of vocabulary and grammatical development of African American preschoolers: Child and environmental associations. *Child Development, 70*(1), 92–106.

Roberts, J. E., Burchinal, M. R., Jackson, S. C., Hooper, S. R., Roush, J., Mundy, M., Neebe, E. C., & Zeisel, S. A. (2000). Otitis media in early childhood in relation to preschool language and school readiness skills among African American children. *Pediatrics, 106*(4), 1–11.

Roberts, J. E., Burchinal, M. R., Koch, M. A., Footo, M. M., & Henderson, F. W. (1988). Otitis media in early childhood and its relationship to later phonological development. *Journal of Speech and Hearing Disorders, 53,* 424–432.

Roberts, J. E., Burchinal, M. R., Medley, L. P., Zeisel, S. A., Mundy, M., Roush, J., Hooper, S., Bryant, D., & Henderson, F. W. (1995). Otitis media, hearing sensitivity, and maternal responsiveness in relation to language during infancy. *Journal of Pediatrics, 126*(3), 481–489.

Roberts, J. E., Burchinal, M. R., Zeisel, S. A., Neebe, E. C., Hooper, S. R., Roush, J., Bryant, D., Mundy, M., & Henderson, F. W. (1998). Otitis media, the caregiving environment, and language and cognitive outcomes at two years. *Pediatrics, 102*(2), 346–352.

Roberts, J. E., & Medley, L. (1995). Otitis media and speech–language sequelae in young children: Current issues in management. *American Journal of Speech-Language Pathology, 4*(1), 15–24.

Roberts, J. E., Sanyal, M. A., Burchinal, M. R., Collier, A. M., Ramey, C. T., & Henderson, F. (1986). Otitis media in early childhood and its re-

lationship to later verbal and academic performance. *Pediatrics, 78,* 423–430.

Roberts, J. E., & Wallace, I. F. (1997). Language and otitis media. In J. E. Roberts, I. F. Wallace, & F. Henderson (Eds.), *Otitis media in young children: Medical, developmental and educational considerations* (pp. 133–161). Baltimore: Brookes.

Ruben, R. J., Haggard, M. P., Bagger-Sjoback, D., Gravel, J. S., Morizono, T., Paparella, M. M., Roberts, J. E., & van Cauwenberge, P. B. (1998). Complications and sequelae. In D J. Lim, C. D. Bluestone, & M. L. Casselbrant (Eds.), *Recent advances in otitis media: Report of the sixth research conference. Annals of Otology, Rhinology, and Laryngology, Suppl. 174, 107*(10, pt. 2), 81–94.

Sameroff, A. J. (1983). Developmental systems: Contexts and evolution. In W. Kennen (Ed.), *History, theories, and methods* (vol. 1, pp. 237–254). New York: Wiley.

Scarborough, H. S., & Dobrich, W. (1994). On the efficacy of reading to preschoolers. *Developmental Review, 14,* 245–230.

Schappert, S. M. (1992). *Office visits for otitis media: United States, 1975–90* (Advance Data from Vital and Health Statistics of the National Center for Health Statistics, No. 214). Hyattsville, MD: National Center for Health Statistics.

Schliecker, E., White, D. R., & Jacobs, E. (1991). The role of day care quality in the prediction of children's vocabulary. *Canadian Journal of Behavioral Science, 23,* 12–24.

Siegel, L. S. (1982). Early cognitive and environmental correlates of language development at 4 years. *International Journal of Behavioral Development, 5,* 433–444.

Stool, S. E., Berg, A. O., Berman, S., Caryney, C. J., Cooley, J. R., Culpepper, L., Eavey, R. D., Feagans, L. V., Finitzo, T., Friedman, E. M., Goertz, J. A., Goldstein, A. J., Grundfest, K. M., Long, D. C., Macconi, L. L. Melta, L. L., Roberts, J., Skerrod, J. L., & Sisk, J. E. (1994). *Otitis media with effusion in young children. Clinical Practice Guideline, Number 12* (AHCPR Publication No. 94-0622). Rockville, MD: Agency for Health Care Policy and Research, Public Health Service, U.S. Department of Health and Human Services.

Sulzby, E. (1989). Assessment of writing and of children's language while writing. In L. Morrow & J. Smith (Eds.), *The role of assessment and measurement in early literacy instruction* (pp. 83–109). Englewood Cliffs, NJ: Prentice-Hall.

Teale, W., & Sulzby, E. (1986). *Emergent literacy: Writing and reading.* Norwood, NJ: Ablex.

Teele, D. W., Klein, J. O., & Rosner, B. (1989). Epidemiology of otitis media during the first seven years of life in children in greater Boston: A prospective cohort study. *Journal of Infectious Diseases, 160,* 83–94.

Teele, D. W., Klein, J. O., Rosner, B. A., & Greater Boston Otitis Media Study Group. (1984). Otitis media with effusion during the first three years of life and development of speech and language. *Pediatrics, 74,* 282–287.

Teele, D. W., Klein, J. O., Chase, C., Menyuk, P., Rosner, B. A., & the Greater Boston Otitis Media Group. (1990). Otitis media in infancy and intellectual ability, school achievement, speech, and language at age 7 years. *Journal of Infectious Diseases, 162,* 685–694.

Vernon-Feagans, L. (1999). Impact of otitis media on speech, language, cognition, and behavior. In R. M. Rosenfeld & C. D. Bluestone (Eds.), *Evidence-based otitis media* (pp. 353–398). St. Louis, MO: Decker.

Vernon-Feagans, L., Emanuel, D. C., & Blood, I. (1997). The effect of otitis media on the language and attention skills of daycare attending toddlers. *Developmental Psychology, 30,* 701–708.

Wallace, I. F., Gravel, J. S., McCarton, C. M., Stapelis, D. R., Bernstein, R. S., & Ruben, R. J. (1988). Otitis media, auditory sensitivity, and language outcomes at one year. *Laryngoscope, 98,* 64–70.

Wallace, I. F., Gravel, J. S., Schwartz, R. G., & Ruben, R. J. (1996). Otitis media, communication style of primary caregivers, and language skills of 2 year olds: A preliminary report. *Journal of Developmental Behavioral Pediatrics, 17,* 27–35.

Wallace, I. F., Roberts, J. E., & Lodder, D. E. (1998). Interactions of African American infants and their mothers: Relations with development at 1-year of age. *Journal of Speech, Language, and Hearing Research, 41,* 900–912.

Whitehurst, G. J., Arnold, D. H., Epstein, J. N., Angell, A. L., Smith, M., & Fischel, J. E. (1994). A picture book reading intervention in daycare and home for children from low-income families. *Developmental Psychology, 30,* 679–689.

Whitehurst, G. J., & Lonigan, C. J. (1998). Child development and emergent literacy. *Child Development, 69*(3), 848–872.

Zeisel, S. A., Roberts, J. E., Gunn, E. G., Riggins, R., Evans, G. A., Roush, J., & Henderson, F. W. (1995). Prospective surveillance for otitis media with effusion among African-American infants in group child care. *Journal of Pediatrics, 127,* 875–880.

Zill, N. (1999). Enhancing school readiness for low-income children: A national study of Head Start quality and outcomes. In M. Lopez & L. Turillo (Chairs), *The fragile crucible: developmental and policy dilemmas in defining and assessing the school readiness of preschool children.* Symposium presented at the biennial meeting of the Society for Research in Child Development, Albuquerque, NM.

IV

SCHOOLING INFLUENCES:
THE PRESCHOOL YEARS

17

Early Literacy and Developmentally Appropriate Practice: Rethinking the Paradigm

❖

REBECCA S. NEW

I walked into the Early Head Start center with some doughnuts for the staff, the cardboard container tucked under my arm along with some books and my briefcase. An 18-month-old headed my way, eyes on the box with the hot pink and orange letters. "Doughnut?" he asked? "Yes," I confessed, chagrined that I hadn't thought to disguise the familiar trademark container. "They're for the teachers. And your lunch is coming soon!" I hurried on to the staff room, where we continued our conversations about how we might best contribute to the development and learning potentials of this very young group of infants and toddlers. As coffee was poured and the contents of the telltale box were shared, I was again reminded of the extent to which children's early literacy, no less than any other early learning, results not only from teachers' purposeful efforts but also children's actual lives—in their homes, their schools, and the larger community.

This chapter builds on the notion of children's embeddedness in particular sociocultural contexts as the platform from which to consider current issues in early childhood education. The chapter embraces a broad and similarly context-specific interpretation of literacy—as an individual competence, a social act, and a cultural tool. From such a perspective of "situatedness" (of children's learning in general, and literacy in particular), questions of priorities and privilege

come to mind. In this light, discussions of developmentally appropriate practice move beyond an exclusive focus on pedagogy (the *how* of children's learning) to include the political and the personal (*what? why?* and *says who?*). These views contribute to an underlying premise of this chapter, which is that educational responses to children's early literacy potentials serve both as metaphor and means by which we educate (or fail to educate) for a democratic society.

The purpose of this chapter is to take up the challenge inherent in this premise and to propose an approach to early literacy as one among many topics of study, negotiation, and collaboration between parents and teachers regarding the rights, needs, and potentials of young children. The discussion begins with a brief review of the sociocultural context of children's learning and development. Particular attention is paid to competing interpretations of literacy as a natural developmental process and/or a formal educational goal for young children. The evolving concept of developmentally appropriate practices is described as it pertains to current understandings and controversies regarding children's early care and education, including their early literacy experiences. Against this backdrop, research conducted in Italian early childhood programs is used to support a view of early childhood and early literacy as socially constructed, with educational decisions shared among stakeholders of children's early learning and development. The chapter concludes with a dynamic conceptualization of literacy practices as a catalyst for teacher development, reciprocal home–school relations, and civic engagement regarding the purposes of schooling.

Culture and Child Development

The relationship between human development and participation in particular cultural contexts is well established. Once considered little more than an explanation for difference, culture is now understood as a composite of norms, social relationships, material conditions, and a language with which to negotiate these features. From this perspective, culture can be regarded as both the means and the target of children's learning (Trevarthen, 1999). Among the many implications of this line of thinking is that culture and human development serve as mutual sources of reflection—each has something to say about how well the other is doing. Two bodies of research in diverse cultural contexts are relevant to this discussion as it pertains to early literacy: studies on (1) adult ideologies or belief systems and (2) the social and interpretative processes through which knowledge is constructed.

Culture and Parental Belief Systems

The anthropological literature is replete with ethnographic accounts describing the relationship between subsistence patterns, geographic features of the environment, and strategies of child care. Within the last quarter of the 20th century, some anthropologists widened their focus to include the powerful role of adult ideologies in mediating these environmental conditions. Robert LeVine's (1974) parental goals theory articulated a functional relationship among cultural values, environmental features, biological characteristics of the child, and patterns of childrearing. Within this framework, physical and then economic survival would reasonably be associated with a press for child obedience; such a developmental aim would necessarily take precedence over

more luxurious hopes such as the development of creativity and self-expression. By the 1980s cross-cultural studies of child development were sufficient to call into question universal assumptions of parental behavior as well as traditional research paradigms characterized by monocultural views of optimal child development. The critical role of ideologies in guiding parental behavior was further supported in studies of how parents manage the universal issues of feeding, sleeping, and physical safety (LeVine, Miller, & West, 1988), as well as in how they talk to and play with their infants (Snow, DeBlauw, & van Roosmalen, 1979). Parental beliefs are now understood to play an instrumental role in children's development (Goodnow & Collins, 1990). More recently described as "ethnotheories," caregiver beliefs are a key feature of the child's developmental niche—a conceptualization that describes place, processes, and rationale by which children's learning and behavior is guided, nurtured, and interpreted (Harkness & Super, 1995; Super & Harkness, 1986). As is discussed later in this chapter, parental beliefs also play a powerful role in mediating children's literacy experiences.

Culture and the Social Construction of Knowledge

Children's development is influenced by more than the decisions adults make in the form of rational responses to environmental conditions. The social features (including relationships and activities) of cultural settings also contribute directly to children's knowledge construction in culturally specific ways. The dynamics of this relationship between culture and child development are described in recent syntheses of research on the complex relationship between culture, social activity, and cognition. This work builds on contemporary interpretations of sociocultural (or social constructivist) theory, as articulated by Lev Vygotsky (1978) and expanded on by Jerome Bruner, Barbara Rogoff, and others. More recent studies also incorporate interpretive approaches to understanding children's socialization within sociocultural contexts. On the basis of this work, the relationship between cultural contexts and social activities is now recognized as dynamic, negotiated, and transactional rather than fixed and unilateral (Goodnow, Miller, & Kessel, 1995). Research aligned with this perspective has contributed to increasingly sophisticated theoretical constructs regarding the various sociocultural dynamics in children's learning and development, including concepts of scaffolding, apprenticeship, and guided participation (Rogoff, 1995).

These two bodies of research—on adult ideologies and the social dynamics of cognition—have contributed to increasing interest in the sociocultural construction of parental priorities and strategies of promoting children's development. Such a research orientation also characterizes recent efforts to understand how and to what ends adults in various sociocultural contexts conceptualize the nature and purposes of early education. What is clear at this point is that adults have multiple images of children, images that vary as a function of the viewer's lens (Hwang, Lamb, & Sigel, 1996). That lens is ground in (and by) diverse sociocultural, political, and economic conditions. Images and expectations converge in the structuring of children's early educational experiences and accomplishments.

Culture, Diversity, and Early Childhood Education

For most of the 20th century, industrialized societies have attempted to support children's development through the institutionalization of developmental goals and learning experiences. Within the United States, as societal views of childhood have changed—from an early emphasis on domestication and physical nurturance to the increased significance assigned to peer relations and cognitive stimulation—early schooling has assumed a growing importance in the life of the child and the routines of the family (Beatty, 1995). And yet the concept of schooling, although generally distinct from more informal learning environments, is also variable as a function of the cultural context in which it takes place. Several decades of comparative educational research reveal the powerful consequences of belief systems and images of childhood on interpretations of early care and education. Reviews of educational policies and programs in European and Asian contexts, for example, reveal divergent beliefs about the nature and purposes of early education (Cochran, 1993; Tobin, Wu, & Davidson, 1989) as well as diversity in the structural supports necessary to translate such beliefs into practices (OECD, 1999). Included within these belief and practice systems are "contrasting ideas about the forms of human learning" (Pepin & Moon, 1999, p. 12). Such studies support the hypothesis that educational responses to and expectations of young children reflect deeply held cultural values and beliefs, including assumptions about what is normative, necessary, and developmentally appropriate (New, 1999b).

Challenges of Diversity in a Pluralistic Society

Differences in interpretations of the goals of early schooling are not limited to those found through international comparisons. In spite of the growing number of studies that point to the cultural situatedness of curriculum and pedagogy (Gordon, 1995), research conducted within the United States demonstrates that there is no one particular U.S. curriculum (Cornbleth, 1998). Conceptions of the *how* and the *what* of U.S. early-childhood education have historically varied as a function of which children are being served and for what purposes. On the one hand, efforts throughout the 20th century to establish the field of early childhood as a profession have led to an increasingly standardized, decontextualized, and age-graded curriculum in public elementary and kindergarten settings (Bloch, 1987). On the other hand, U.S. children of preschool age (3 to 5 years) continue to be the recipients of diverse and competing interpretations of curriculum and pedagogy, ranging from programs described as play based and child centered to those characterized by various forms of direct instruction and behavior modification. This eclectic approach to early education not only represents contrasting and changing theoretical interpretations of children's learning. Such program diversity is also directly linked to the pluralistic nature of U.S. society and associated judgments about children's needs as a function of race, income, language, and ability.

Within the last decade, questions regarding the relationship between diverse and sometimes competing interpretations of children's developmental and educational needs have increased in frequency and tone. In the field of early childhood, controversy has centered on the defining features of developmentally appropriate practices (Bredekamp, 1987) as they contribute to curriculum decisions and teaching strategies for diverse populations of young children (Kessler & Swadener, 1992; Mallory & New, 1994). Within this context, growing and competing concerns have been expressed regarding the role of preschool as it supports concepts of inclusion and equity in children's academic readiness (New, 1998, 1999a). In spite of continuing efforts to better articulate principles for educational practice that acknowledge children's individual and cultural differences (Bredekamp & Copple, 1997), teachers continue to experience difficulties in translating such principles into classroom practice (Dunn & Kontos, 1997). Of potentially greater significance than the lack of congruity between teachers' beliefs and classroom practices is the continued controversy around the concept of developmental appropriateness itself.

Prevailing interpretations of young children's diverse needs and potentials as they might best be served have been subject to criticism from postmodern, theoretical, and political perspectives. At the more general level, the debate has focused on the practical and political challenges of multiculturalism and the risks of imposing a common culture vis-à-vis a uniform and standardized pedagogy in a pluralistic democratic society. In early childhood, any singular interpretation of educational quality is now subject to critique for failing to acknowledge the legitimacy of alternative perspectives on children's current and future lives (Dahlberg, Moss, & Pence, 1999). Diverse but targeted approaches to differences among children are also critiqued in that they, too, deny multiple forms of child and family competence, fail to represent contemporary understandings of children's learning potentials, and limit the role of schooling in a democratic society (New & Mallory, 1996). Given that a significant majority of funded targeted programs have historically served minority populations, they have also been subject to accusations that they represent a form of institutional racism (Baratz & Baratz, 1970), reify social class distinctions (Lubeck, 1994), and deny an ethic of inclusion (New & Mallory, 1994).

Concurrent with the raising of these concerns, research on the dynamics of teaching and learning continues to demonstrate the extent to which children's diverse ways of knowing develop within the course of social interactions which are, themselves, culturally situated and reinforcing (Tharp & Gallimore, 1988). Among the implications of such studies, in combination with the previously described critical analyses, is the likelihood that children learn more or less useful ways of negotiating the world in their various educational settings (Tharp, 1989). They also learn about themselves—as they are viewed and esteemed by others. The negative valence of some children's diversity is sorely felt in pluralistic educational settings where teachers convey a "deference to difference" (New, 1999a, p. 143) that denies children equitable and challenging learning opportunities. Diversity can also be perceived as a liability when prevailing norms and expectations are contrary to those experienced in other aspects of their lives (New & Mallory, 1996). When parents perceive, through their "own eyes," a mismatch between their dreams for their children and the aims of educational institutions, they also lose trust in the ability of early schooling to make a positive difference (Holloway, Fuller, Rambaud, & Eggers-Pierola, 1997). Each of these concerns is well represented in contemporary discussions of early literacy.

Developmentally Appropriate Practices and Early Literacy: The "Great Debate" Writ Large

One might think, given the wealth of research cited in this volume and conducted over the past several decades, that we are well beyond "the great debate" described by the late Jeanne Chall in her classic text, *Learning to Read* (Chall, 1967). Far from it. The quest to identify the most appropriate and effective means by which to promote children's literacy development has remained elusive for the last half century. Even as scholars become increasingly articulate about the processes associated with the acquisition of literacy skills and knowledge within children's "social spheres," teachers remain unclear about the nature of developmentally appropriate literacy practices (Mcgill-Franzen, 1992). Controversy also remains regarding the extent to which literacy instruction is necessary or even appropriate for young children. These disagreements reflect theoretical, political, and cultural interpretations of the purposes of literacy and early childhood education in the lives of children and their families.

Changing Views of Early Literacy Development

Differences in the *what*, the *how*, and the *why* of children's early learning are well represented among competing interpretations of literacy as a natural developmental process or as a formal educational goal. At first glance, historical differences are most apparent in how literacy is now understood and valued. For much of the 20th century, definitions of literacy within the United States focused on basic reading and writing competencies, otherwise described as "active autonomous engagement with print." Throughout most of this period, the *how* of literacy entailed formal reading instruction beginning at age 6. This practice was associated with the age of compulsory schooling and based on the belief—supported by the 1930s child study and testing movements—that a mental age of 6.5 years is associated with better reading progress than what occurs when instruction is initiated at younger ages. Challenges to this notion were first initiated when researchers began to suspect that the onset of reading is more a function of instructional strategy than child age. Research on early readers—young children learning to read without any type of formal instruction (Durkin, 1966)—eventually shifted the discussion from identification of the precise instructional strategy or time when children are "ready" to read to an interest in the processes by which children's literacy skills emerge.

As researchers began to focus on literacy as a "social foundation of discourse" in all of its attendant complexities (Daiute, 1993,

p. 124), literacy studies were increasingly characterized by attention to children's social lives. Literacy's dependency on oral discourse led some to propose that children "who explain, explore, argue, and play with language and ideas" were more likely to "grow as writers and readers" than would children who did not use language in those ways (Daiute, 1993, p. 122). Interest also grew in children's development of literacy skills in particular "activity settings" (Gallimore & Goldenberg, 1993) such as those found in families (Snow, 1993) and as supported by their social relationships and emotional experiences (Dyson, 1996). Ethnographic studies supported these interpretations (Schieffelin & Gilmore, 1986) and researchers gained valuable understandings of "what no bedtime story means" (Heath, 1986). The premises of emergent literacy ultimately centered on the idea that literacy competencies are developed by "people in relation" who use and produce literate acts in particular sociocultural and historical contexts (Whitehead, 1997). Most recently, as scholars have moved away from the notion that literacy competencies come from within the child, the term "emergent literacy" has been replaced by "early literacy." From this perspective, literacy begins at birth, is ongoing, and is influenced and interpreted by the surrounding sociocultural context (Neuman & Roskos, 1998).

Multiple Forms and Meanings of Literacy

Cultural interpretations of the *what* of literacy merge with and expand on these findings. Researchers in the loosely connected field of literacy studies point to the numerous ways in which literacy is understood, practiced, and valued in diverse cultural settings. As a result of such studies, literacy is now broadly defined as *any number* of standard practices used by people during literacy "events," which are themselves "situated in broader social contexts and social relations" (Barton, 1994, p. 35). Literate acts, in turn, are now understood to serve as part of a "symbolic system for communicating and representing the world" (Barton, 1994, p. 35). This interpretation of literacy blurs the distinction between formal and informal literacy instruction (Hawkins, 1990). It also places the acquisition of literacy understandings and skills under the influence of cultural values as well as social processes.

These new understandings of early literacy are consistent with the premises of sociocultural and constructivist theories previously outlined, such that children are guided to participate in practices that vary according to cultural values and developmental aims and that support them in the acquisition of culturally distinct intellectual tools. This theoretical premise goes a long way toward explaining the successes of some children (e.g., those in U.S. middle-class homes) to easily acquire the literacy skills, attitudes, and understandings associated with school achievement. In such settings, children as young as 1 and 2 years have been observed to develop literacy "contracts" in which they learn how to interact with books, to understand that "books are for reading" and to grasp the relationship between picture and story, sound and text (Snow & Ninio, 1986). When children are embedded "in a way of life in which reading and writing are integral to communication, recreation, and livelihood" (Rogoff, Mosier, Mistry, & Goncu, 1993, p. 232), learning to read might even be regarded as something that comes naturally.

A problem arises when only *some* children, but not others, have the types of linguistic and literacy experiences that would prepare them for the standard discourse of the classroom. Researchers acknowledge that it is "not a question of households being literate or not" (Barton, 1994, p. 152). Rather, it is a matter of having different orientations to communication and social relations, styles of living and relating that are linked to the fundamental dynamics of households. Such dynamics may include oral literacy traditions but little or no experience with the tools of formal schooling such as pencils or books. Shirley Brice Heath's (1983) work in three Appalachian communities aptly illustrates the extent to which some children's literacies count for more than others when measured within the public school setting. And yet it is not just teachers who are making such judgments. In spite of the fact that learning how to read remains a primary goal of U.S. public education, significant differences of opinion exist among families regarding the value of early literacy activities for young children

(Fuller, Holloway, & Liang, 1996). Such differences are especially prevalent among some minority populations within the United States, many of whose children are eligible for yet not enrolled in publicly funded early childhood programs. Parents of such children question the need for prescholastic activities; they are also concerned about the lack of linguistic and emotional continuity between home and school settings (Fuller, Eggers-Pierola, Holloway, Liang, & Rambaud, 1996). These research findings provide essential new understandings about some of the causes of the cycle of illiteracy that occurs when culturally diverse families are expected to value "other people's words" more than their own (Purcell-Gates, 1995). Amidst these controversies, the press for children to acquire specific literacy skills and concepts at increasingly earlier ages has reached an all-time high. Head Start performance standards now include discrete literacy objectives, and presidential candidates compete for the claim of having the strongest record of support and accountability expectations for a nation of readers. These varying interpretations of children's learning in and outside the school setting place early childhood educators at the center of a growing debate—not only about literacy but also about the purposes of schooling in a pluralistic democratic society.

In the discussion to follow, I use lessons from the Italian culture to suggest limitations of the current literacy debates within the U.S. early childhood community, including the associated quest for "best practices" that currently engages professional associations, scholars, parents, classroom teachers, and national research institutes. I also draw on Italian experiences to suggest new ways of responding to the diverse needs and capabilities of children and families within our pluralistic society.

Italian Perspectives on Early Learning and Literacy

The Italian culture provides a fascinating context within which to explore this expanded set of theoretical premises, among them children's remarkable abilities to live up to a wide range of adult expectations as informed by cultural values, beliefs, and goals. Italian cultural values and beliefs are reflected in the 1968 law that proclaims the *scuola materna* [preprimary school] as a right of all children. This same law also acknowledges the legitimacy of diverse interpretations of an early childhood education as well as the critical role of parents in children's early educational experiences (New, 1993). That is, the content and nature of children's early educational experiences are among many broadly construed decisions to be discussed, debated, and negotiated by the stakeholders—parents, teachers, community members, and policymakers. By definition and design, results of these deliberations will vary from place to place. Particularly in programs funded locally, teachers and parents are expected to work together to identify strategies by which children will be fed, cared for, and educated, drawing less on national standards than on their own careful and prolonged deliberations.

Two decades of observation and study in several Italian communities support a view of early literacy and developmentally appropriate practices that is consistent with these characteristics. Of particular relevance are the diversity of interpretations regarding the actual content and developmental appropriateness of children's early educational experiences *and* the essential nature of shared decision making in determining program aims and characteristics. Common and diverse features of an Italian early childhood education—including curriculum goals, interpretations of early literacy, the role of teachers as researchers, and parental participation—will be briefly highlighted in the following descriptions. Examples are drawn from cities as diverse as Milan, Trento, Parma, Reggio Emilia, San Miniato,[1] Pistoia, Naples, and Palermo.

Curriculum Goals and Concepts of Competence

In both casual and formal settings, when asked to prioritize goals for children's development, Italian parents and teachers talk about social, emotional, and physical concerns, *not* about preparing children for academic careers. These developmental goals also pertain to children's early learning experiences. What appears to be most important for Italian parents as well as early

childhood educators is that children learn how to get along with one another and to feel comfortable in the multiple social worlds represented by home, school, and community. The conviction of this belief was recently evidenced when the Minister of Education proposed to relocate programs for 5-year-olds from the *scuola dell'infanzia* to become a part of the elementary school setting. This initiative was met with such fierce public resistance by parents, grandparents, teachers, and university researchers that the debate was covered in the national news. Representatives of the state school system argued for beginning compulsory school at age 5 as a means of ensuring that all children take advantage of the availability to experience what we (in the United States) might consider a "kindergarten" year. Opponents to the proposal successfully defended the critical importance of a flexible *scuola dell'infanzia* model as one of separate and distinct educational functions, and they warned of the dangers of a too early emphasis on scholastic achievement. After a year of public debate, the initiative failed to become law.

The resistance to joining 5-year-olds with elementary-age children and classes illustrates two widely shared Italian beliefs: (1) that early childhood programs should reflect local as well as state interests and efforts and (2) that the primary purpose of such programs is to invite children and their families into a social community. Such aims reflect a cultural valuing of social relations beyond those of the family as well as a cultural image of children that assumes they are capable of developing such relations during the period of infancy and early childhood (New, 1998). In response to Italy's rapidly decreasing birthrate (currently one of the lowest in the world) and the declining role of extended family members in the care of young children, the *asilo nido* [infant–toddler center] and *scuola dell'infanzia* [preprimary school] are considered ideal places for children to develop such meaningful relationships with peers and nonfamilial adults in the first 5 years of life.

COMMON GROUND, DIVERSE STRATEGIES

The cultural emphasis on children's and adults' relationships appears widespread, and many of Italy's municipal *asili nido* and *scuola dell'infanzia* have developed diverse staffing patterns and curriculum strategies to promote children's learning and to ensure continuity and stability of children's and parents' social relations. For example, within the context of discussions of the role of early education in children's lives, parents and teachers in the small hilltown of San Miniato hypothesized that mixed-age grouping might serve as a strategic means by which to create a classroom community for children in the first 3 years (Fortunati, 1986). This strategy was responsive to the adults' shared desire to promote prosocial behaviors and affiliative relationships in children without older or younger siblings and afforded parents the opportunity to serve as supports for one another, giving and receiving advice on their children's developmental crises and accomplishments. In response to the diverse needs of immigrant and working families in the large industrial city of Milan, family–child centers [*Tempo per la famiglie*] were established for families not using full-time child care but interested in opportunities to meet other adults and children in a setting staffed by professionals.

In addition to program structures, curriculum strategies also vary as a function of local interests and resources. The most well-known is surely Reggio Emilia's interpretation of curriculum as long-term *progettazione* (Edwards, Gandini, & Forman, 1998), but other communities have developed their own interpretations of developmentally appropriate curriculum aims and strategies. In Milan, for example, teachers use observations of children to identify a theme that can be elaborated upon and sustained throughout the 3 years that the child attends preschool. Such an approach is valued for its contributions to a source of identity within each small group of children, families, and teachers. This pedagogical strategy also provides children the opportunity to explore in greater depth those aspects of the social environment or physical world that they find particularly compelling. The city of Pistoia takes this notion of a collaborative and thematic approach to curriculum by reaching beyond the school walls. Each of the city's municipal preschools has an area of special focus as it corresponds to the interests and expertise of

adults in the surrounding neighborhood. Drawing on the tradition of apprenticeship, preschool curricular projects range from needlework and sewing to carpentry. Teachers explained that the actual curriculum topic is less critical than its attributes: multiple avenues of exploration and application, with opportunities for creative thinking and skill development that require some form of collaboration between children and adults, schools and the community. A preschool in the city of Naples was also concerned with community relations; there, teachers invited grandparents to assist in the production of local "wine" by showing children how to crush grapes and filter the juice using traditional tools and methods. This project was based as much on the desire to convince the larger community of the value of out-of-home preschool experiences as it was to provide children with a rich learning opportunity. In each city, educational aims and objectives include the fostering and utilization of relationships among and between adults as well as children (New, 1999b). And yet this emphasis on social relations does not mean that Italians are disinterested in promoting children's early literacy skills and understandings.

CONCEPTS OF EARLY LANGUAGE AND
LITERACY DEVELOPMENT

Italian researchers have contributed to contemporary understandings of children's early communicative competencies, including conversational competence as it develops during infancy (Camioni, Volterra, & Bates, 1986), toddlerhood (Camioni, Gerbino, & Hvastja-Stefani, 1978), and preschool (Orsolini, 1988); and the notion of shared contributions to knowledge construction (Pontecorvo, 1993). Work focused specifically on the concept of early literacy has addressed symbolic communication in the infant–toddler center (Catarsi, 1993), the value of book sharing by children and adults in the *asilo nido* (Mantovani, 1988), and what it means to *leggere prima di leggere* [to read before reading] (Cardarello & Chiantera,1989). Although such work is consistent in many respects with that conducted within the United States on the role of social relations and symbolic communications in early literacy development, Italian educators have resisted, for the most part, any single-minded interpretation that regards literacy activities as little more than the means to promote successful readers and writers. Rather, the expectation that children should and *will* eventually learn to read and write is mediated by encouragement of other forms of literacy acts, as evidenced, for example, by Reggio Emilia's support of children's multiple symbolic languages.

Reggio Emilia educators believe that children's learning is facilitated when they have the need and the opportunity to communicate their understandings through a variety of representational forms (New, 2000). Thus an *atelierista* [art educator] works closely with teachers to ensure that children have opportunities to experiment with a variety of materials and media, including clay, pencil and fine-tipped graphic drawings; painting; shadow play; and large and small constructive activities. These and other forms of symbolic representation are among the numerous opportunities available to children as they explore and express their ideas and understandings of the world around them. Curriculum activities are designed so children can work together in small groups on projects over long periods. In this context, the emphasis on symbolic representation becomes central to the ongoing processes of knowledge construction. With support from the atelierista, children represent their developing understandings around a common theme as a source of hypothesis generating, ongoing reflection and, finally, a means of sharing their ideas, plans, or discoveries with classmates. Although all Italian early childhood programs do not employ art educators, most share another distinguishing feature—one that builds on the importance of knowledge construction and representation as it informs *adult* learning.

Expectations for Adults in Early Educational Programs

TEACHERS AS RESEARCHERS

Until recently, preservice teacher education in Italy has been limited to a high school diploma for early childhood and elementary teachers. While some bemoaned this lack of professional preparation, many Italian early childhood educators have steadfastly maintained the belief that things about children and for children are best learned *from* children and their families (Malaguzzi, 1998). The study of children's learning and development thus serves as a necessary meeting place from which to consider relevant educational goals as they might be addressed within the context of highly meaningful explorations. In north-central Italian settings such as Reggio Emilia, Pistoia, San Miniato and, more recently, in southern Italian cities such as Palermo, teachers have fine-tuned the art of careful documentation of children's behaviors and ideas, the significance of which is debated during lengthy staff meetings. These collaborative discussions are often followed by the development of research hypotheses regarding children's existing understandings as well as the processes associated with their meaning making (Fortunati, 1991). The process of documenting and discussing children's learning and development provides teachers with many of the same types of opportunities that they provide the children: creative thinking, collaborative problem solving, articulation of collective understandings, and new hypotheses through multiple representational forms. In each of these settings, the relationship between curriculum activities and teacher research on children's learning and development is articulated and visible. Such documentation also provides concrete and compelling means by which to engage parents in discussions about children's early educational experiences.

HOME–SCHOOL RELATIONS AND THE CONCEPT OF *PARTECIPAZIONE*

It is difficult to describe the essential nature of the parent–teacher relationship in Italian early childhood education programs other than to say that the two appear inextricable. The evolution of close ties between home and school has both political and psychological roots, the former growing out of the labor movement of the late 1960s. The national principle of *gestione sociale* [social management], initially developed for civic functions and industrial management processes but first legislated in the 1971 law for infant–toddler centers, affirmed that they *"devono essere gestiti con la partecipazione delle famiglie e delle rappresentanze delle formazioni sociali organizzate nel territorio"* [should be managed with the participation of families and representatives of social organizations within the region] (Spaggiari, 1991, p. 114). Extended, in 1974, to preschools through secondary schools, the goal of the mandate is to encourage parents to actively contribute to their children's education rather than delegating their potentials and their responsibility to others (New, Mallory, & Mantovani, 2000).

This partnership between Italian parents and their children's schools begins early, during the time of the child's initial enrollment in an early childhood program. Each of the Italian early childhood programs previously mentioned has developed strategies associated with a period of *inserimento,* many of which go beyond the initial aim of supporting the child during the transition period. Both teachers and parents talk about the need to (1) support the parent in the emotionally loaded process of leaving the child in a new and nonfamilial setting, and (2) begin developing a reciprocal and collaborative relationship between parents and caregivers (Bove, 1999). As parents subsequently become more aware of and interested in other aspects of their child's school experience—due not only to specific strategies associated with l'inserimento but also to the seductive invitation conveyed by extensive documentation displays that cover the walls of these centers—they move to a level of partnership that few U.S. parents or teachers have experienced.

This Italian interpretation of home–school relationships expands on the common value assigned to parental involvement as it supports children's learning. In Italy, the adults also develop relationships with each other. Although there is no expectation that such adult relations will always be harmonious, there is the widely shared belief in their essential nature as parents and teachers negotiate structural and organizational decisions associated with the management of the early childhood programs. Given the quality and quantity of encounters, the adults also become more knowledgeable of each other's children. This knowledge serves them well as parents and teachers engage in challenging questions associated with an early childhood curriculum as it might reflect both professional and personal knowledge and priorities. Such adult relations influence far more than pedagogical decisions; they also contribute to national debates on early care and education, local program development, and the richness and diversity of children's educational experiences in their respective communities.

Implications

Given Italy's continued insistence on protecting the preschool period from becoming "a period of school learning" (OECD, 1998, p. 38) and the nation's general lack of anxiety about children's literacy as defined by U.S. standards, the implications of this research for understanding and supporting early literacy within the United States are not immediately apparent. And yet, specific features of Italian early education remind us of alternative interpretations of child development, early schooling, and the roles and responsibilities of the adults in children's lives. These interpretations have direct implications for discussions on the concepts of developmentally appropriate practices and early literacy in the United States.

The Social Construction of Early Childhood

Italian adults want children to become well-educated *Italians,* even as they also ascribe to more global expectations associated with public schooling. In discussions of early childhood, Italian parents and teachers add their own interpretations to research that has repeatedly demonstrated the role of interpersonal relationships in emotional well-being, social competence, and cognitive development. In their emphasis on children's language development (described most often in terms of the ability to communicate with others and to express one's self), parents and teachers are also providing support for the burgeoning body of research on the role of linguistic competencies in the subsequent acquisition of reading skills. And yet, as Italian parents seek experiences for children that promote social and language development, they do so for their immediate and intrinsic value, not because these competencies will contribute to the acquisition of some other educational goal. This interpretation of early childhood conveys respect for children's *present* lives even as it also acknowledges their futures.

Strongly held opinions about appropriate structuring and aims of children's early school experiences are not limited to the Italian society. While early childhood programs in England are moving to a form of "narrow curriculum control" characterized by increasing academic expectations for children (Whitehead, 1997, p. xi.), most other European nations share Italy's practice of postponing formal academic instruction, including that associated with literacy, until the elementary grades (OECD, 1999). In Sweden, for example, children are not exposed to formal academic instruction until age 7. Such differences in educational aims correspond to more than different opportunities and expectations for children. They also contribute to images of children as successes or failures as a function of how their learning has been conceptualized and structured, rather than any inherent difficulty of the task or deficiency within the child. When we consider that an approach such as Reading Recovery is based on identifying reading "failures" before children have reached the age for formal instruction in another cultural context, we are reminded of the extent to which the at-risk child is a social construction (Lubeck & Garrett, 1990).

The discussion of Italian early education also illustrates the role of educational settings as particular "developmental niches," each with its own social, physical, organizational and ideological features (Super & Harkness, 1986). As noted previously, Italian parents and professionals share the belief that the time for academic instruction is after age 6. Within that context, however, *time* itself takes on a new meaning. In Italian preschool as well as elementary school settings, children can look forward to a continuity of relationships that is unheard of in most U.S. educational settings, staying with the same teacher(s) and group of children throughout their years in a particular program or building. Such an organizational characteristic is consistent with the previously described value of enduring and high-quality relations; it also allows for greater flexibility in teacher responses to the in-evitable variability in children's developmental and academic milestones. Only recently have U.S. teachers begun to experiment with contemporary interpretations of the one-room schoolhouse of prior generations in the forms of mixed-age groupings and "looping" (when teachers follow children to the next grade level and then "loop" back to the earlier grade for another 2-year cycle). Such reconfigurations of the early childhood classroom resonate with contemporary theories that emphasize the value of emotional well-being, social relations, and mixed-ability interactions for children's learning and development. Longer continuity within the classroom also provides greater cause and occasion to develop reciprocal relations with parents. Extended time together in classrooms might also allow for more sustained and useful professional study of such aspects of children's learning as their literacy attitudes and practices.

Cultural Interpretations of Early Childhood Education and Literacy

The continuity of relations among Italian classmates, teachers, and parents provides a challenging alternative to the observation that schools still have "one expected tempo as 'normal'" (Hawkins, 1990, p. 5). The Italian example also illustrates the possibility that common values and societal aims can be addressed in myriad ways as a function of local knowledge and support. The case of Reggio Emilia, as well as examples from other cities, reminds us of other ways in which our own cultural "blinders" inhibit our ability to more closely and creatively examine U.S. educational priorities and practices.

With respect to early literacy, the work being done by 3-, 4- and 5-year-old Italian children in clay, painting, drawing, and collaborative constructions makes clear that children have the capacity and the desire to use more than just a few of their "hundred" symbolic languages, if only such variations in expression and exploration were imagined and valued. While Reggio Emilia's exploration of children's symbolic languages is likely the most sustained, many Italian educators seem to understand the principle that "the educational quality of literacy is a continuation of its experiential roots"

(Hawkins, 1990, p. 12). The felt necessity of children's representational efforts as they correspond to the children's engagement in long-term projects is strikingly similar to Hawkin's (1990) description of "conditions for reading and writing with commitment and quality," in which one's performance is likely to be "in proportion to the opportunity to engage with matters of importance and about which one would wish to learn and communicate" (p. 6). When children work together with teachers and *atelieriste* as in Reggio Emilia, or members of the neighborhood community as in Pistoia, they are experiencing the sort of apprenticeships for which literacy scholars advocate (Resnick, 1990). When children are encouraged to alternate between sequences of representation and exploration, such experiences resonate with Eisner's (1994) interpretation of literacy as "the ability to encode or decode meaning in any of the forms of representation used in the culture to convey or express meaning" (p. x).

Italian approaches to early literacy in all of its various manifestations (De Vecchi, 1999) moves beyond the methods fetish that has characterized much of the current debate. Rather, they speak to the necessity for learning environments that create occasions and incentives for children to figure out the meaningfulness of their own and others' literacies (Cazden, 1992). Examples of children's work from Reggio Emilia do more than challenge conventional interpretations of children's symbolic languages. We can only hypothesize the potential contributions of learning how to communicate through various forms of symbolic representation on children's subsequent cognitive development and literacy skills. It seems reasonable to imagine that when children have such an array of languages to choose from, early literacy efforts are more likely to capitalize on "the role of the imagination in the construction of possible worlds" (Eisner, 1994, p. x). Among the other contributions that such a pedagogy of multiple literacies (Cazden, 1996) invites us to imagine is children's increasing ability to more fully participate in life within a complex and pluralistic society, whether Italy or the United States. Indeed, within the Italian early childhood programs just described, parents and teachers seem determined to chart the course of their children's development as it might reflect *and contribute to* the larger cultural context.

New Roles and Responsibilities of Parents and Teachers

Italian teachers in high-quality municipal programs in cities such as Pistoia, San Miniato, Milan, and Reggio Emilia have taken on the challenges of teacher observation and documentation to generate a new image of teachers as reflective practitioners who routinely engage in collaborative forms of inquiry. This image of teaching as "epistemic inquiry" (Wood, 1999, p. 174) moves the quest for the elusive nature of good teaching beyond the identification of particular instructional strategies to a commitment to and competence in learning about children—who they are, where they are coming from, what and how they might want to learn (Drummond, 1994).

Such an interpretation of teacher as researcher is especially useful to the promotion of early literacy, because one of the problems with teaching something that seems, to some, to be so natural (Goodman & Goodman, 1979) is in translating teacher expertise into an awareness of how such expertise is learned (Holt-Reynolds, 1999). Responses to children in the Italian classrooms just described contribute to such an awareness, as teachers study real rather than "straw" children as found in laboratory settings (Wood, 1999, p. 158). Within a multicultural society, such an approach to teacher research would also help teachers appreciate the value and necessity of teaching children that they do not always understand; and of changing their own understandings of what they are trying to teach (Ballenger, 1999, p. 9). When combined with developing relations with children's families (Snow, Barnes, Chandler, Goodman, & Hemphill, 1991), this interpretation of teacher research goes outside the classroom to include efforts to understand children's cultures, including what counts as knowledge in their homes and neighborhoods (New, 1994).

And yet it is not always easy for teachers to develop functional relationships with parents that are respectful of their diverse circumstances and solicitous of their points of view. Even in settings such as Head Start, where parental involvement has been a cornerstone for decades, teachers and program directors cite numerous difficulties of shared decision making with parents (Ceglowski, 1998). Research on early intervention suggests that what is often missing from the discourse is the meaning of key constructs to families themselves (Bernheimer, 1999). A recent study of cross-national differences in academic achievement (Bempechat & Drago-Severson, 1999) argues for the importance of understanding the "deeper" meanings that children and parents attach to school experience, including explanations for success and failure as well as interpretations of how children might best be socialized for school achievement. Many have described the importance of making literacy skills and concepts more useful and meaningful to children. Early literacy learning must also be made more relevant, necessary, and meaningful to the life experiences of *adults*—in this case, the parents and other family members of young children. When parents and teachers construct shared understandings of children's development and appropriate educational goals, they move beyond the cultural conflicts that silence some and privilege others (Delpit, 1995). They may even begin to approach the liberating possibilities of education that progressive educators have long imagined (Dewey, 1926; Friere, 1990, Beane, 1997).

Conclusion

As a nation and a profession, we continue to debate how best to teach diverse populations of children to become productive citizens of the 21st century. Many have acknowledged the powerful influence of schooling and its attendant emphasis on formal literacy instruction on the very nature of human knowledge. And yet gains in school achievement have not been evenly distributed across populations within or between diverse cultural settings. Even as some bemoan "the inability of the formal schooling system to guarantee sufficient literacy for all children . . ." (Wagner & Venezky, 1999, p. 22), educators are inundated with increasingly conflicting recommendations as to what, in fact, they ought

to be doing differently. A recently released report from the Center for the Future of Teaching and Learning (1996) placed renewed emphasis on a basic skills approach to literacy. Based on a spate of studies on children with severe reading disabilities and financed by the National Institute of Child Health and Human Development (NICHD), this report was heralded by policymakers and legislative bodies. More recently, the National Research Council released its own report on *Preventing Reading Difficulties in Young Children* (Burns, Snow, & Griffin, 1998), emphasizing the critical importance of diverse forms of support for children's early literacy, including not only phonemic awareness but also meaningful literacy events. While the latest report seemed to resolve the polemics between skills-based versus whole-language advocates, the hoped-for "end of the Reading Wars" (Neuman, Copple, & Bredekamp, 1999, p. vii) has not yet occurred. The battle for who knows best is far from over.

Differing responses to the two reports reveal the political capital of "scientific" evidence and the politics of literacy teaching (Allington & Woodside-Jiron, 1999). As we begin a new century in which literacy demands have never been higher, some scholars have responded to the controversy by attacking the "bad science that hurts children" (Coles, 2000). Others cite the continued lack of a critical stance regarding the extent to which the unquestioned goal of universal literacy competence precludes consideration of other aspects of contemporary society that work against optimal development and social participation (Lankshear & O'Connor, 1999). In the meantime, significant numbers of families from minority populations keep their children out of professionally esteemed early childhood programs because they reflect neither shared understandings of the problems nor the solutions to children's learning (Garcia, 1997). As a nation, we are far from a common ground on which to consider the meanings, means, or purposes of early literacy.

So What Do We Do?

John Dewey (1899) spoke of schooling as an experiment in the possibilities of human development in carefully arranged environments. In his treatise, he envisioned an educational setting characterized by utopian conditions within which the epistemological and political ideals of a democratic society might be best learned and practiced. His ideas for society, in turn, were expressed in the classroom as desirable norms of growth for each individual child. And yet Dewey missed one of the most essential components of a democratic society—that a school's character, including those "desirable norms," must reflect more than one person's ideas and ideals. Rather, the concept of norms must be turned somehow on its head to encompass multiple and even competing points of view. The basic premise of this chapter is that "developmental appropriateness" is a socially constructed concept whose very subjectivity is what makes the term meaningful even as it necessitates constant reevaluation. Examples drawn from the Italian culture have been used to illustrate some of the means and the possibilities for locally constructed definitions of educational goals and strategies that are informed but not dictated by a professional knowledge base. Such a collaborative and negotiated process is essential to determining the goals and roles of early literacy within a pluralistic democratic society such as the United States.

All this is not to say that reading and writing do not matter for children. Few educators question the critical importance of traditional literacy skills and understandings to children's subsequent school achievement and equal employment opportunities. Increasingly, however, some have begun to encourage children to consider the possibilities of "literacy with an attitude" as it might better support their own self-interests (Finn, 1999). Still others use literacy experiences to promote parental empowerment (Delgado-Gaitan, 1990). Parents gain new understandings of the power of literacy when teachers point to the prejudice and exclusion conveyed by peer cultures for children who cannot read as well as others think they should (Gallas, 1998). Work by early childhood special educators (Koppenhaver, Spadorcia, & Erickson, 1998) makes clear that we have only begun to imagine the instructional strategies that can and should be successfully adapted to promote literacy in children with special needs. Such understandings heighten the importance of what is already regarded as a central educational concern.

Henry Giroux (1993) was likely not thinking about the field of early childhood education when he wrote of the growing conflict over "the relationship between democracy and culture, on the one hand, and identity and the politics of representation on the other" (p. 90). And yet his challenge to educators to "live dangerously" by questioning the status quo is based on a goal consistent with that expressed in this chapter—to approach teaching in a way that nurtures and celebrates the multiple possibilities in children's lives. To consider multiple possibilities, however, requires giving attention to new perspectives, all of which requires that teachers learn how to "teach on the edge" (New, 1998). I have written elsewhere of an interpretation of DAP as an acronym for documentation, advocacy, and parent participation as means to determining educational goals and practices (New, 1997). The relationship between parents and teachers implied in this acronym might well lead to more rather than less conflict in the classroom. And yet conflict can also be understood as something potentially worthwhile, particularly as it contributes to social development and cultural change (Turiel, 1999).

The image of an early childhood education presented in this chapter is consistent with the Italian belief of schooling as a system of relations—a system in which multiple and minority voices count, where teachers use their observations and parents' understandings of young children as a basis from which to consider individual and societal educational goals. In such a context, discussions of early literacy could serve as the catalyst for conversations among diverse groups of children and adults. Discussions of literacy's political and social capital are not beyond the concerns of parents and teachers, some of whom are now successfully demonstrating their abilities to find common ground among diverse interpretations of children's needs and abilities (Meier, 1999). Many Americans understand that just because literacy is necessary to a good education does not mean that it is sufficient (Hawkins, 1990). In at least a few classrooms with minority populations of children, literacy development is now regarded not as an end in itself but, rather, as a starting point to talk about racism, resistance, and the politics of cultural texts (Wilson, 2000). These interpretations of developmentally appropriate literacy practices are consistent with the observation that there is no simple solution to teaching other people's children (Ballenger, 1999). Recent successful experiences with diverse populations of children challenge the notion that "the school system cannot move far ahead of the general culture" (Resnick, 1990, p. 183).

The goal in this chapter has been to describe a dynamic interpretation of literacy practices that requires classroom-based research to inform teacher practice, parental participation in establishing educational goals, and alternative interpretations of literacy as a means of expression, exploration, and representation. Such an approach to early literacy seems likely to contribute to an education of the sort that Dewey imagined—one that enhances the development of children, teachers, families, and the communities in which they live. Damon (1995) wrote of the need for greater expectations for children. Some of those expectations will remain unfulfilled, however, until schools and communities, families and teachers, learn to work together more effectively on behalf of children. This chapter echoes the plea for greater expectations, although the focus of these heightened expectations is on us—the adults, not the children.

Note

1. The first five cities named are participants in a two-phase collaborative research project on home-school relations funded by the Spencer Foundation (R. New, B. Mallory, and S. Mantovani, co-principal investigators).

References

Allington, R. L., & Woodside-Jiron, H. (1999). The politics of literacy teaching: How "research" shaped educational policy. *Educational Researcher, 28*(8), 4–12.

Ballenger, C. (1999). *Teaching other people's children: Literacy and learning in a bilingual classroom.* New York: Teachers College Press.

Baratz, S. S., & Baratz, J. C. (1970). Early childhood intervention: The social science base of institutional racism. *Harvard Educational Review, 40,* 29–50.

Barton, D. (1994). *Literacy: An introduction to the ecology of written language.* Oxford, UK: Blackwell.

Beane, J. (1997). *Curriculum integration: Designing the core of democratic education.* New York: Teachers College Press.

Beatty, B. (1995). *Preschool education in America: The culture of young children from the colonial era to the present.* New Haven: Yale University Press.

Bempechat, J., & Drago-Severson, E. (1999). Cross-national differences in academic achievement: Beyond etic conceptions of children's understandings. *Review of Educational Research, 69*(3), 287–314.

Bernheimer, L. P. (1999). Through a new looking glass: Cultural models and early intervention research. *Journal of Early Intervention, 22*(4), 286–299.

Bloch, M. (1987). Becoming scientific and professional: An historical perspective on the aims and effects of early education. In T. S. Popkewitz (Ed.), *The formation of the school subjects* (pp. 25–62). Basingstoke, UK: Falmer.

Bove, C. (1999). *L'inserimento del bambino al nido* [Welcoming the child into childcare]. *Young Children, 54*(2), 32–33.

Bredekamp, S. (1987). *Developmentally appropriate practice guidelines for programs serving children from birth through age eight.* Washington, DC: National Association for the Education of Young Children.

Bredekamp, S., & Copple, C. (Eds.). (1997). *Developmentally appropriate practice in early childhood programs. Revised edition.* Washington, DC: National Association for the Education of Young Children.

Burns, S., Snow, C., & Griffin, P. (1998). *Preventing reading difficulties in young children.* Washington, DC: National Academy Press.

Camioni, L., Gerbino, W., & Hvastja-Stefani, L. (1978). *L'interazione sociale tra bambini coetanei e tra bambini e adulto: Una ricerca sullo sviluppo dell'interazione sociale da due a tre anni* [Social interaction among peers and between children and adults: Research on the development of social interaction from two to three years. Giornale Italiano di Psicologia [*Italian Journal of Psychology*], *V*(2), 291–321.

Camioni, L., Volterra, V., & Bates, E. (1986). *La comunicazione nel primo anno di vita* [Communication in the first year of life]. Torino: Boringhieri.

Cardarello, R., & Chiantera, A. (Eds.). (1989). *Leggere prima di leggere: Infanzia e cultura scritta* [To read before reading: Early childhood and cultural text]. Florence: La Nuova Italia.

Catarsi, E. (1993). *Leggere e capire nell'asilo nido* [To read and understand in the daycare center]. *Infanzia, 6,* 19–26.

Cazden, C. (1992). *Whole language plus: Essays on literacy in the United States & New Zealand.* New York: Teachers College Press.

Cazden, C. (1996). A pedagogy of multiliteracies: Designing social futures. *Harvard Educational Review, 66,* 60–92.

Ceglowski, D. (1998). *Inside a Head Start center: Developing policies from practice.* New York: Teachers College Press.

Center for the Future of Teaching and Learning (1996). Thirty years of NICHD research: What we now know about how children learn to read. *Effective School Practices (15),* 33–46.

Chall, J. (1967). *Learning to read: The great debate.* New York: McGraw-Hill.

Cochran, M. (Ed.). (1993). *International handbook of child care policies and programs.* Westport, CT: Greenwood Press.

Cole, M. (1995). Culture in development. In M. Woodhead, D. Faulkner, & K. Littleton (Eds.), *Cultural worlds of early childhood* (pp. 11–33). London: Routledge.

Coles, G. (2000). *Misreading reading: The bad science that hurts children.* Westport, CT: Heinemann.

Cornbleth, C. (1998). An American curriculum? *Teachers College Record, 99*(4), 622–646.

Dahlberg, G., Moss, P., & Pence, A. (1999). *Beyond quality in early childhood education and care: Postmodern perspectives.* London: Falmer Press.

Daiute, C. (Ed.). (1993). *The development of literacy through social interaction: New directions for child development* (No. 61). San Francisco: Jossey-Bass.

Damon, W. (1995). *Greater expectations: Overcoming the culture of indulgence in our homes and schools.* New York: Free Press.

Delgado-Gaitan, C. (1990). *Literacy for empowerment: The role of parents in children's education.* New York: Falmer Press.

Delpit, L. (1995). *Other people's children: Cultural conflict in the classroom.* New York: The New Press.

De Vecchi, E. (1999). *Guardare, parlare e capire: Il libro al nido* [To watch, to speak, and to understand: The book at daycare]. In M. Poropat & L. Stefani (Eds.), *La ricerca-axione tra programmazione e progetto educativo: Un itinerario formativo al nido* [Action research between planning and the educational project: An itinerary for development in the daycare center] (pp. 54–72). San Paolo (Bergamo), Italy: Edizioni Junior.

Dewey, J. (1976). *The school and society.* In J. A. Boyolston (Ed.), *The middle works of John Dewey, 1899–1924.* Carbondale: Southern Illinois University Press. (Original work published 1899)

Dewey, J. (1926). *Democracy and education: An introduction to the philosophy of education.* New York: Macmillan.

Drummond, M. (1994). *Learning to see: Assessment through observation.* York, ME: Stenhouse.

Dunn, L., & Kontos, S. (1997). What have we learned about developmentally appropriate practices? *Young Children, 52*(5), 4–13.

Durkin, D. (1966). *Children who read early.* New York: Teachers College Press.

Dyson, A. H. (1996). Cultural constellations and childhood identities: On Greek gods, cartoon heroes, and the social lives of schoolchildren. *Harvard Educational Review, 66,* 471–495.

Edwards, C., Gandini, L., & Forman, G. (1998). *The hundred languages of children: The Reggio Emilia approach—Advanced reflections.* Revised second edition. Greenwich, CT: Ablex.

Eisner, E. W. (1994). *Cognition and curriculum reconsidered* (2nd ed.). New York: Teachers College Press.

Finn, P. J. (1999). *Literacy with an attitude: Educating working-class children in their own self-interest.* Albany, NY: State University of New York Press.

Fortunati, A. (1986). *Il gruppo misto nell'asilo nido* [Mixed age group in the infant–toddler center]. Milano: Franco Angeli.

Fortunati, A. (1991). *Progettare e documentare le esperienze al nido: Metodi, esperienze, strumenti* [To plan and document experiences at the infant-toddler center: Methods, experiences, and instruments]. Bergamo, Italy: Juvenilia.

Friere, P. (1990). *Pedagogy of the oppressed.* New York: Continuum. (Original work published 1970)

Fuller, B., Eggers-Pierola, C., Holloway, S., Liang, X., & Rambaud, M. (1996). Rich culture, poor markets: Why do Latino parents forgo preschooling? *Teachers College Record, 97*(3), 400–418.

Fuller, B., Holloway, S., & Liang, X. (1996). Family selection of child-care centers: The influence of household support, ethnicity, and parental practices. *Child Development, 67*(6), 3320–3337.

Gallas, K. (1998). *"Sometimes I can be anything." Power, gender, and identity in a primary classroom.* New York: Teachers College Press.

Gallimore, R., & Goldenberg, C. (1993). Activity settings of early literacy: Home and school factors in children's emergent literacy. In E. Forman, N. Minick, & A. Stone (Eds.), *Contexts for learning: Sociocultural dynamics in children's development* (pp. 315–335). New York: Oxford University Press.

Garcia, E. (1997). The education of Hispanics in early childhood: Of roots and wings. *Young Children, 52*(3), 5–14.

Giroux, H. (1993). *Living dangerously: Multiculturalism and the politics of difference.* New York: Peter Lang.

Goodman, K. S., & Goodman, Y. M. (1979). Learning to read is natural. In L. B. Resnick & P. A. Weaver (Eds.), *Theory and practice of early reading* (Vol. 1, pp. 137–154). Hillsdale, NJ: Erlbaum.

Goodnow, J. J., & Collins, W. A. (1990). *Development according to parents: The nature, sources, and consequences of parents' ideas.* Hillsdale, NJ: Erlbaum.

Goodnow, J. J., Miller, P. J., & Kessel, F. (Eds.). (1995). *Cultural practices as contexts for development. New directions for child development* (No. 67). San Francisco: Jossey-Bass.

Gordon, E. W. (1995). Culture and the sciences of pedagogy. *Teachers College Record, 97*(1), 32–46.

Harkness, S., & Super, C. (Eds.). (1995). *Parents' cultural belief systems: Their origins, expressions, and consequences.* New York: Guilford Press.

Hawkins, D. (1990). The roots of literacy. *Daedalus: Literacy in America, 119*(2), 1–14.

Heath, S. B. (1983). *Ways with words: Language, life, and work in communities and classrooms.* New York: Cambridge University Press.

Heath, S. B. (1986). What no bedtime story means: Narrative skills at home and at school. In B B. Schieffelin & E. Ochs (Eds.), *Language socialization across cultures* (pp. 97–126). Cambridge: Cambridge University Press.

Holloway, S., Fuller, B., Rambaud, M., & Eggers-Pierola, C. (1997). *Through my own eyes.* Cambridge, MA: Harvard University Press.

Holt-Reynolds, D. (1999). Good readers, good teachers? Subject matter expertise as a challenge in learning to teach. *Harvard Educational Review, 69*(1), 29–50.

Hwang, C. P., Lamb, M. E., & Sigel, I. E. (Eds.). (1996). *Images of childhood.* Mahwah, NJ: Erlbaum.

Kessler, S., & Swadener, B. (1992). *Reconceptualizing the early childhood curriculum: Beginning the dialogue.* New York: Teachers College Press.

Koppenhaver, D., Spadorcia, S., & Erickson, K. (1998). How do we provide inclusive early literacy instruction for children with disabilities? In S. Neuman & K. Roskos (Eds.), *Children achieving: Best practices in early literacy* (pp. 77–97). Newark, DE: International Reading Association.

Lankshear, C., & O'Connor, P. (1999). Response to "Adult Literacy: The Next Generation." *Educational Researcher, 28*(1), 30–36.

LeVine, R. A. (1974). Parental goals: A cross-cultural view. *Teachers College Record, 76*(2), 226–239.

LeVine, R. A., Miller, P. M., & West, M. M. (Eds.). (1988). *Parental behavior in diverse societies. New directions for child development* (No. 40). San Francisco: Jossey-Bass.

Lubeck, S. (1994). The politics of developmentally appropriate practice: Exploring issues of culture, class and curriculum. In B. Mallory & R. New (Eds.), *Diversity and developmentally appropriate practices: Challenges for early childhood education* (pp. 17–43). New York: Teachers College Press.

Lubeck, S., & Garrett, P. (1990). The social construction of the "at risk" child. *British Journal of Sociology of Education, 11*(3), 327–340.

Malaguzzi, L. (1998). History, ideas, and basic philosophy: An interview with Lella Gandini. In C. Edwards, L. Gandini, & G. Forman (Eds.), *The hundred languages of children: The Reggio Emilia approach—Advanced reflections* (2nd ed., pp. 49–97). Greenwich, CT: Ablex.

Mallory, B., & New, R. (Eds.). (1994). *Diversity and developmentally appropriate practices: Challenges for early childhood education.* New York: Teachers College Press.

Mantovani, S. (1988). *Incoraggiare a leggere al nido* [To encourage reading at in daycare]. In L. Lumbelli (Ed.), *Incoraggiare a leggere* [To encourage reading]. Florence: La Nuova Italia.

Mcgill-Franzen, A. (1992). Early literacy: What does "developmentally appropriate" mean? *The Reading Teacher, 46*(1), 56–58.

Meier, D. R. (1999). *Scribble scrabble: Learning to read and write: Success with diverse teachers, children and families.* New York: Teachers College Press.

Neuman, S., Copple, C., & Bredekamp, S. (1999). *Learning to read and write: Developmentally appropriate practices for young children.* Washington, DC: National Association for the Education of Young Children.

Neuman, S., & Roskos, K. (Eds.). (1998). *Children achieving: Best practices in early literacy.* Newark, DE: International Reading Association.

New, R. (1993). Italy. In M. Cochran (Ed.), *International handbook of child care policies and programs* (pp. 291–311). Westport, CT: Greenwood Press.

New, R. (1994). Culture, child development, and developmentally appropriate practices: An expanded role of teachers as collaborative researchers. In B. Mallory & R. New (Eds.), *Diversity and developmentally appropriate practices: Challenges for early childhood education* (pp. 65–83). New York: Teachers College Press.

New, R. (1997). Reggio Emilia's commitment to children and community: A reconceptualization of quality and DAP. *Canadian Children, 22*(1), 7–12.

New, R. (1998). Diversity and early childhood education: Making room for everyone. In C. Seefeldt & A. Galper (Eds.), *Continuing issues in early childhood education* (2nd ed., pp. 238–267). Columbus, OH: Merrill.

New, R. (1999a). Playing fair and square: Issues of equity in preschool mathematics, science, and technology. In *Dialogue on early childhood science, mathematics, and technology education* (pp. 138–156). Washington, DC: American Association for the Advancement of Science, Project 2061.

New, R. (1999b). What should (preschool) children learn? Making choices and taking chances. *Early Childhood Research and Practice, 1*(2), 1–25.

New, R. (2000). Reggio Emilia: An approach or an attitude? In J. Roopnarine & J. Johnson (Eds.), *Approaches to early childhood education* (3rd ed., rev.). Columbus, OH: Merrill.

New, R., & Mallory, B. (1994). Introduction: The ethic of inclusion. In B. Mallory & R. New (Eds.), *Diversity and developmentally appropriate practices: Challenges for early childhood education* (pp. 1–13). New York: Teachers College Press.

New, R., & Mallory, B. (1996). The paradox of diversity. In E. Erwin (Ed.), *Visions for a brighter future* (pp. 143–167). Baltimore: Brookes.

New, R., Mallory, B., & Mantovani, S. (2000). Cultural images of children, parents and professionals: Italian interpretations of home–school relationships. *Early Education and Development. [Special issue on Families and Early Childhood Education], 11*(5), 599–616.

OECD. (1998). *Reviews of national policies for education: Italy.* Paris: Centre for Educational Research and Innovation.

OECD. (1999). *Education policy analysis 1999.* Paris: Centre for Educational Research and Innovation.

Pepin, B., & Moon, B. (1999). *Curriculum, cultural traditions and pedagogy: Understanding the work of teachers in England, France, and Germany.* Paper presented to American Educational Research Association Conference, Montreal, Canada.

Pontecorvo, C. (Ed.) (1993). *La condivisione della conoscenza* [The sharing of knowledge]. Florence: *La Nuova Italia.*

Purcell-Gates, V. (1995). *Other people's words: The cycle of illiteracy.* Cambridge, MA: Harvard University Press.

Resnik, L. (1990). Literacy in school and out. *Daedalus: Literacy in America, 119*(2), 169–185.

Rogoff, B. (1995). Observing sociocultural activity on three planes: Participatory appropriation, guided participation, and apprenticeship. In J. Wertsch, P. del Rio, & A. Alvarez (Eds.), *Sociocultural studies of mind* (pp. 139–164). Cambridge: Cambridge University Press.

Rogoff, B., Mosier, C., Mistry, J., & Goncu, A. (1993). Toddlers' guided participation with their caregivers in cultural activity. In E. Forman, C. Minick, & A. Stone (Eds.), *Contexts for learning: Sociocultural dynamics in children's development* (pp. 230–253). New York: Oxford University Press.

Schieffelin, B. B., & Gilmore, P. (Eds.). (1986). *The acquisition of literacy: Ethnographic perspectives.* Norwood, NJ: Ablex.

Snow, C. (1993). Families as social contexts for literacy development. In C. Daiute (Ed.), *The development of literacy through social interaction: New directions for child development* (No. 61, pp. 11–24). San Francisco: Jossey-Bass

Snow, C. E., Barnes, W. S., Chandler, J., Goodman, I. R., & Hemphill, L. (1991). *Unfulfilled expectations: Home and school influences on literacy.* Cambridge, MA: Harvard University Press.

Snow, C., DeBlauw, A., & van Roosmalen, G. (1979). Talking and playing with babies: The role of ideologies of child-rearing. In M. Bullowa

(Ed.), *Before speech: The beginning of interpersonal communication* (pp. 123–146). Cambridge, UK: Cambridge University Press.

Snow, C., & Ninio, A. (1986). The contracts of literacy: What children learn from learning to read books. In W. H. Teale & E. Sulzby (Eds.), *Emergent literacy: Writing and reading* (pp. 116–138). Norwood, NJ: Ablex.

Spaggiari, S. (1991). *Considerazione critiche ed esperienze di gestione sociale* [Critical reflections and the experience of social management]. In A. Bondioli & S. Mantovani (Eds.), (1991), *Manuale critico dell'asilo nido* [Critical manual on infant-toddler care] (pp. 111–139). Milan, Italy: Franco Angeli.

Super, C., & Harkness, S. (1986). The developmental niche: A conceptualization at the interface of child and culture. *International Journal of Behavioral Development, 9,* 545–569.

Tharp, R. G. (1989). Psychocultural variables and constants: Effects on teaching and learning in schools. *American Psychologist, 44*(2), 349–359.

Tharp, R. G., & Gallimore, R. (1988). *Rousing minds to life: Teaching, learning, and schooling in social context.* New York: Cambridge University Press.

Tobin, J., Wu, D., & Davidson, D. (1989). *Preschool in three cultures: Japan, China, and the United States.* New Haven: Yale University Press.

Trevarthen, C. (1999). The child's need to learn a culture. In M. Woodhead, D. Faulkner, & K. Littleton (Eds.), *Cultural worlds of early childhood* (pp. 87–100). London: Routledge.

Turiel, E. (1999). Conflict, social development, and cultural change. In E. Turiel (Ed.), *Development and cultural change: Reciprocal processes* (No. 83, pp. 77–92). San Francisco: Jossey-Bass.

Vygotsky, L. S. (1978). *Mind in society: The development of higher psychological processes.* Cambridge, MA: Harvard University Press.

Wagner, D. A., & Venezky, R. L. (1999). Adult literacy: The next generation. *Educational Researcher, 28*(1), 21–29.

Whitehead, M. (1997). *Language and literacy in the early years* (2nd ed.). London: Chapman.

Wood, D. (1999). Aspects of teaching and learning. In M. Woodhead, D. Faulkner, & K. Littleton (Eds.), *Cultural worlds of early childhood* (pp. 157–177). London: Routledge.

Wilson, C. (2000). *Telling a different story: Teaching and literacy in an urban preschool.* New York: Teachers College Press.

18

The Nature and Impact of Early Childhood Care Environments on the Language and Early Literacy Development of Children from Low-Income Families

❖

DAVID K. DICKINSON
KIMBERLEY E. SPRAGUE

The majority of children in the United States are regularly cared for by someone other than their parents (Children's Defense Fund, 2000; Schulman, Blank, & Ewen, 1999). Indeed, in 1995, the National Center for Education Statistics reported that 80% of all children in families surveyed were in some type of formal care before they entered first grade (National Association of the Education of Young Children, 2000).[1] The prevalence of out-of-home care is linked to major societal shifts such as woman's increasing participation in the work force, the rising cost of living, and the recent effect of welfare reform. Given the power of these societal shifts, we must anticipate that the need for nonparental child care in the preschool years will continue to increase. As the demand for child care continues to grow, studies of literacy development have begun to focus on children's language and literacy status in kindergarten, and researchers have begun to call attention to the role of the preschool era in children's long-term literacy success.

In this chapter we first examine the nature of care children receive in the preschool years, considering the quality of care provid-ed and the impact quality has on children's development, with a special emphasis on the needs of children from low-income families. Next we review data pointing to the critical importance of the early years in children's literacy development and then discuss the line of research on early literacy development that we have been pursuing. After sketching the theoretical assumptions that govern our work, we draw on recently analyzed data from multiple studies that examine children's experiences in preschool classrooms and identify factors that affect children's later language and literacy development. We describe an effective professional development intervention for preschool teachers designed to support children's language and literacy development. We then conclude with a discussion of implications for theory and policy.

Child Care[2] in the United States

There is considerable variability in child-care arrangements available for young children and the patterns of utilization and funding mechanisms. Arrangements by which children are cared for are broadly categorized into formal and informal care. Formal care occurs in the home (nanny, babysitter: 6%) and outside the home (family day care: 16%; center-based care: 32%). Informal care is provided primarily by parents (23%) and relatives (in-home: 9%; in relative's home: 14%) (Capizzano, Adams, & Sonenstein, 2000; Children's Defense Fund, 2000).[3] The use of a particular care arrangement varies with the age of the child. Younger children are more often cared for within the home, or by relatives, and older children are more often cared for outside the home in formal care arrangements: 54% of infants and toddlers are in relative or parent care and 59% of children 3 years old and older are in center-based care (45%) and family day care (14%). When children are over four years of age they are even more likely to be in center-based care—three of every four children not yet attending kindergarten are regularly in center care (National Association for the Education of Young Children, 2000). The complexity of child care is increased by the fact that families often require multiple child-care arrangements, especially for older preschoolers. When parents combine two types of care arrangements, typically less formal care situations are used for after-hours and after-school care (Capizzano & Adams, 2000).

Family income has an important impact on the child-care settings that families use. Children from low-income families are more likely to be in the care of a relative (28% vs. 20%, respectively) than other forms of care (Capizzano et al., 2000; NICHD, 1997b) and less likely to be in centers than children from high-income families (26% vs. 35%, respectively).[4] Among children 3 to 5 years of age, the income differential in child-care arrangements is especially noteworthy. In 1998, enrollment in prekindergarten[5] for families that earned less than $15,000 was 42%, but for families that earned $50,000 the enrollment was 65% (Children's Defense Fund, 2000, p. 47). This association between cost and family income is not surprising, because full-day child care is estimated to cost between $4,000 and $10,000 per year, an amount that the Children's Defense Fund (2000) ob-

serves is basically equivalent to public university or college tuition. In addition, the Children's Defense Fund notes that parents pay the majority of the cost of this care, whereas the majority of higher education costs are the burden of the public and private sector.[6]

Considerable variability exists in patterns of state funding, subsidies, and other supports that affect the utilization of care for low-income families (Capizzano et al., 2000).[7] In general, child-care policies are heavily determined by state-level policies, yet not all states have developed systems for effectively using the doubling in federal funds that has occurred since 1991. The challenge to state systems is indicated by the fact that of the 42 states with prekindergarten funding in 1998–1999, the majority of the available money was spent in only 10. In addition, despite the availability of additional funds, states do not provide child-care assistance to all families eligible to receive it (Children's Defense Fund, 2000; Schulman et al., 1999).[8]

With the increase in the demand for child care, state and local efforts have concentrated on increasing the number of child-care slots without emphasizing the need for providing quality care. This lack of focus on improving quality is not surprising given the urgency of providing spaces needed to keep pace with demand and the fact that higher-quality child care is generally more expensive than lower-quality child care (Burchinal et al., 2000; Cost, Quality, and Outcomes Team, 1995; NICHD, 1997b).[9] States typically provide far less in subsidies than is necessary to purchase quality care (Children's Defense Fund, 2000), making it difficult for low-income families to purchase high quality care for their children. In addition, state and local efforts have focused only sporadically on improving the quality of care. The nation's largest provider of child care for low-income children, Head Start, now emphasizes the importance of program quality. Initially conceptualized in 1995, the performance standards were created to address children's academic needs. In addition, the standards create a system of "outcome-oriented" accountability by requiring the measurement of children's progress toward the goals outlined (Administration for Children and Families, 1998).

Quality of Child Care and Its Impact on Child Development

The effort by Head Start to ensure that children are provided high-quality care reflects an awareness of converging research findings that suggest that program quality is important to children's development. (See Barnett, Chapter 27, for a more extended discussion of program quality and its impact on children.) Although the consideration of the impact of the quality of care on children's development might seem self-evident, it has not been to those who have seen the primary role of child care as custodial in nature—purely a way of enabling parents to work. In this section, we present the recent research on quality and the impact of quality.

DEFINING QUALITY OF CARE

Assessing the quality of child care is an extremely complex challenge because of the variability in the forms of child-care arrangements coupled with the major developmental changes of children during this era—infants have radically different needs than 4-year-olds. Much of the research to date has been conducted in classrooms, partly because the classrooms are relatively public and more accessible than family-care settings. The implication of potential bias is an imperfect understanding of child care. However, we must keep in mind that quality ratings tend to be higher for center-based care than for other forms of care. A major challenge to those conducting research in early-childhood settings is the fact that interpretations of what counts as "quality" vary from one study to the next. The absence of a widely accepted and fully articulated vision of quality forced the Cost, Quality, and Child Outcomes Study—one of the most comprehensive studies to date—to use a pragmatic definition: "that which is most likely to support children's positive development" (Cost, Quality, and Outcomes Team, 1995, p. 1).

Although definitions of program quality are varied, researchers and practitioners have drawn on standard ideas from the field of child development, and generally accepted notions of what constitutes good early-childhood practice, to create widely used classroom rating tools. General considerations across several standard measures of child-care quality include classroom environment (e.g., support for learning and health safety standards), teacher–child interaction, and curriculum/language and literacy support. Program and teacher/staff characteristics are also important factors that contribute to the level of quality of the early care environment.[10] Primarily, these instruments tend to focus on environments and interactions more so than on curriculum and language (U.S. Department of Education, 1993) and include few items dealing with early literacy (Dickinson, 1999).

VARIABILITY IN QUALITY OF CARE

Despite the variability in tools used to assess quality, there is considerable convergence across measures providing evidence of an impact of early classroom quality on child development. Although there is variation across states in quality of care, several studies indicate that the overall quality of child care in the United States is generally fairly low (Burchinal et al., 2000; Cost, Quality, and Outcomes Team, 1995; NICHD, 1999b; in press). Quality is especially low for infants and toddlers, but a recent study suggests the quality of care individual children receive generally increases as they grow older (Burchinal et al., 2000). This shift may reflect the general trend of children's movement from less formal care arrangements to center-based care as they grow older. Other studies indicate that many early-childhood programs do not meet professional guidelines for quality (NICHD, 1999b, in press). One study estimated that "positive caregiving" was somewhat uncharacteristic for most programs nationwide (NICHD, in press).

Child-care situations primarily used by low-income families (family day care or care by a relative) are generally of low quality except when these families used center-based child care (NICHD, 1997b). In the case of center-based care, the quality of care children received was similar to that of children from high-income families. In general, families with moderate incomes had lower-quality child care than did families with higher *and* lower incomes—the latter the likely result of the eligibility of low-income families to participate in subsidized programs such as Head Start and to afford center-based care (NICHD, 1997a, 1997b).

IMPACT OF CHILD CARE ON CHILDREN
OF LOW-INCOME FAMILIES

Recent research has highlighted the importance of quality in early childhood settings and indicated an impact of quality on children's social, cognitive, language, literacy, and communication skills (Burchinal et al., 2000; Cost, Quality, and Outcomes Team, 1995; NICHD, 1999b, in press; Peisner-Feinberg & Burchinal, 1997; see also Barnett, Chapter 27).

A recent and important longitudinal study conducted by Burchinal et al. (2000) identified an impact of quality over time for disadvantaged children in care from infancy through the preschool years. The researchers found a relationship between higher levels of child-care quality in the first 3 years of life and better performance on child outcomes (including cognitive, language, and communication measures) over time, even when the impact of individual and family characteristics were considered. In addition, Burchinal et al. (2000) found a significant effect of "regulatable aspects" of quality such as the teacher–child ratio and levels of teacher education and training on language outcomes. The study authors also suggest that the impact of classroom quality is underestimated because the children in the poorest quality care, with the poorest assessment performances, dropped out of care situations more often (Burchinal et al., 2000). Other studies have also found an impact of teacher–child ratio as well as class size on teacher–child interactions, teacher sensitivity, and higher global quality. One study found positive child outcomes associated with those programs that were meeting more standards for early childhood care (NICHD, 1999b). The conclusions from this recent wave of research are consistent with research on early-intervention programs. Researchers studying the impact of the Abecedarian and Care interventions found that high-quality intervention programs in infancy and early childhood can overcome early deficits and may have parent and child benefits that persist into early adulthood (Burchinal, Lee, & Ramey, 1989;

Burchinal et al., 2000; Wasik, Ramey, Bryant, & Sparling, 1991).

Several studies have identified a differential effect of quality for children of low-income families. Primarily, the relationship between quality and child outcomes has been stronger for disadvantaged children (Bryant, Burchinal, Lau, & Sparling, 1994; Burchinal, Campbell, Bryant, Wasik, & Ramey, 1997; Burchinal et al., 2000). Some studies suggest that family factors are potential moderators of quality (Peisner-Feinberg & Burchinal, 1997), though this relationship has not been demonstrated in other studies (Burchinal et al., 2000). A relationship between longer hours in child care and less maternal sensitivity and child engagement has been observed, but higher-quality child care positively predicted higher levels of maternal sensitivity (NICHD, 1999a). In addition, the number of hours in care does not appear to be associated with family income (NICHD, 1997b).

In summary, the broad picture presented for early-childhood practice is one of enormous growth and extreme variability, with differences linked to factors that include geographical location, age of the child, family income, nature of the early-child-care setting, and quality of care. As our society has begun to recognize the importance of the preschool years for children's long-term intellectual and emotional development, studies of the impact of quality are now drawing attention to the inescapable fact that higher-quality early-childhood programs, though often more costly, are more beneficial for children.

Why We Need to Attend to the Early Literacy Needs of Low-Income Children

As indicated previously, there is evidence of an impact of early-childhood classroom quality on children's development and a modest impact for language and literacy outcomes in particular. As we come to better understand the early roots of literacy, it is increasingly apparent that the preschool years are crucial to children's long-term literacy success. Cunningham and Stanovich (1997) found that 1st-grade reading status predicts 3rd-, 5th-, and 11th-grade reading.

Strong evidence of long-term stability between the early elementary school years and later schooling has also been found by Scarborough (Chapter 8) and Whitehurst (Chapter 2), as well as in earlier studies (Barrington & Hendricks, 1989; Lloyd, 1978; Morrison & Griffin, 1997).

Unfortunately, these patterns of long-term stability are paired with differential levels of early achievement that mirror the fault lines in our society, with children from lower-income and minority backgrounds showing signs of falling behind their more advantaged peers even before they enter school. In the preschool years and early primary grades, gaps between children from different economic, racial, and linguistic backgrounds begin to appear (Chaney, 1992; Dickinson & Snow, 1987; Hart & Risley, 1995; Fernandez-Fein & Baker, 1997; Laosa, 1983; Walker, Greenwood, Hart, & Carta, 1994; Zill, Collins, West, & Hausken, 1995). The magnitude of these differences is so great that one study estimated that, at entry into first grade, roughly half of all disadvantaged children are approximately 2 years behind their peers in literacy skills (Brizius & Foster, 1993). Given the weight of evidence pointing to the critical nature of the early years, it comes as no surprise that the National Research Council's report, *Preventing Reading Difficulties,* stressed the urgent need for more effective literacy support by preschool programs that serve low-income children (Snow, Burns, & Griffin, 1998).

With such powerful evidence of the importance of the early years combined with earlier research finding beneficial effects of program quality on children's development, one would hope to find clear evidence that preschool programs bolster early literacy, especially for children from lower-income families. Unfortunately, researchers repeatedly have found that the quality of program support for language and literacy often is rather low. Bryant et al. (1994) observed Head Start classrooms using the ECERS and found that mean scores for these classrooms were the lowest on the language and reasoning subscales (3.76), indicating that few opportunities occur for literacy learning. Additional studies have found similar limits in language and literacy support in curriculum and practices (U.S. Department of Education, 1993). Similarly, the High/Scope Educational Research Foundation's (1997) study of Michigan's School-Readiness Program also suggests a lack of support for language and literacy activities because less than half the classrooms observed failed to receive "high" ratings for adult encouragement of children's language. Finally, recent studies have continued to find that many classrooms serving low-income children still do not provide optimal support for their language and literacy learning (Burchinal et al., 2000; NICHD, 1999b, in press).

Despite the pattern of data indicating limitations in classroom quality with respect to language and literacy, several major studies have found evidence of an impact of classroom quality on children's language development. The first such study included all the center-based children in Bermuda and found relationships between children's language and several dimensions of program quality (McCartney, 1984). More recently, the Family and Child Experiences Survey (FACES), a nationally representative study of Head Start, found evidence of a relationship between program quality and receptive vocabulary (Administration on Children, Youth, and Families, 2000). Two recent studies provide evidence of an impact of quality on growth trajectories. Burchinal et al. (2000) found evidence of program quality on growth trajectories of language acquisition among children from low-income families. Also, the Quality Improvement Center from Georgia State used a random assignment approach to study the effects of Head Start on children and found an impact on children's receptive language growth trajectories and on phonemic awareness (Abbott-Shim, Lambert, & McCarty, 2001).

Whereas studies have found associations between program quality and language, the linkage to more print-related aspects of literacy has been less evident. The FACES study found no evidence of fall-to-spring growth in knowledge of letter names among Head Start children. Similarly, studies of Even Start, a program designed to improve literacy and promote school readiness, have found only a mixed or moderate impact of preschool on language and literacy development (Administration on Children, Youth, and Families, 2000; U.S. Department of Education, 1995). However, more encouraging results come from a study that compared the impact of high- verus low-quality Head Start classrooms on children's literacy and phonemic awareness. High-quality programs were found to have a significant effect on children from homes in which the parents themselves have low levels of literacy (Greenberg, Franze, McCarty, & Abbott-Shim, 2000).

The research that we have reviewed briefly indicates that program quality can affect children's language development and may be related to literacy development. These studies suggest that children's experiences in classrooms can have an effect on their early patterns of language and literacy development. In our work, we too have found associations between classroom quality and children's development and have provided additional details regarding specific features of children's classroom experiences that foster development.

Observing Classroom Quality and Children's Development

In the following pages we discuss findings from three related studies in which we have been involved since the late 1980s. Because these studies are closely related, we first discuss their general structure and then present our findings. The study that provided the starting point for our work is the Home–School Study of Language and Literacy Development (HSLLD), a longitudinal study of 85 children from low-income families launched in 1987 (Dickinson & Tabors, in press). When the children were 3 years old, we began collecting data about their home and classroom language experiences (for details, see Dickinson & Tabors, 2001). We began assessing children's language and literacy development in kindergarten and continued into middle school. Data included audiotaped home and classroom interactions, observations, interviews, and a battery of child assessments that included measures of receptive vocabulary (Peabody Picture Vocabulary Test—Revised), early literacy (print concepts, phonemic awareness, early writing), and productive language (storytelling, a word-definition task).

In 1995, we extended our study of the effect of home and early-care environments on Head Start children through work conducted by the New England Quality Research Center (NEQRC).[11] Using research tools and similar methods of data collection employed by the HSLLD study, we gathered data on the homes, classrooms, and fall-to-spring growth in language and literacy over a 2-year period on a large sample of 3- and 4-year-old children from English- and Spanish-speaking homes ($n = 393$).[12]

Also in the mid-1990s, we began to use our growing understanding of preschool classrooms and their impact on development as we worked with colleagues in EDC's Center for Children and Families to develop and evaluate a professional development program for preschool teachers that is intended to enable teachers to more effectively support children's language and literacy development. This approach is now a credit-bearing course that is being delivered by the project that provides technical assistance to Head Start programs throughout New England. During the first 2 years that this course was provided to New England programs, we collected data to examine its effectiveness. To evaluate the impact of this course, now called the Literacy Environment Enrichment Program (LEEP), we used a comparison group design and employed the same classroom quality tools and child assessment tools employed by the NEQRC. This data collection effort will continue through 2002, allowing us to track changes among staff and children and to determine how changes in children's classroom experiences affect patterns of growth in language and literacy.

Observations of Classroom Dynamics

In our studies we have collected considerable detailed information about aspects of early-childhood classrooms that are important to language and literacy development. In the following pages we review these findings about key aspects of classrooms.

BOOK READING

Given the extensive literature on the beneficial effects of book reading on children's development (e.g., Bus, van IJzendoorn, & Pellegrini, 1995), one would expect to find books and book reading to be ubiquitous in early-childhood classrooms. Our recent and ongoing studies of Head Start classrooms in New England have found that classrooms are reasonably well supplied with books, indicating the programs value books. In the 42 classrooms visited by NEQRC researchers, the majority had 26 or more books accessible to children in the room; only 10% had less than 15 books available. We also found distinct book areas (i.e., areas that did not also serve as meeting areas or block areas) in 57% of the classrooms.

With the importance of books suggested by their availability in the environment, one would expect to find use of books to be extensive, but this was not the case. For the HSLLD, we asked teachers how often they planned to read to children in groups. When the children in our study were 3 years of age (n = 61), about 15% of the teachers reported reading two or fewer times per week and 38% reported reading four or more times per week. Remarkably, when these children were 4 years of age, about 20% of the teachers reported reading two or fewer times a week while only 16% reported planning to read four or more times per week. Children spent more time in transition from one activity to another (age 3, 13%; 4, 11% of observed time) than they did reading books (age 3, 7%; age 4, 8%).

The pattern of book use observed in HSLLD is relatively consistent with what we have found as we extended our studies to classrooms throughout New England. In the fall of 1999, we visited 42 Head Start classrooms for 2 days of classroom quality data collection. In 26% of these rooms we did not observe book reading either day. In the spring we returned to these rooms. In the 26 that had not received our literacy intervention, we saw no reading across two days in 35% of the classrooms and on those days when full-group book reading occurred, the time spent on book reading was 2½ minutes, or less than 38% of the time. Patterns of reading to individuals or in small groups were equally depressing; in 58% of all the classrooms observed, this form of reading never occurred. These rates are especially low considering that teachers were aware they were being observed by researchers with an interest in the general quality of their classroom. Finally, it should be noted that nearly all our data come from Head Start classrooms, programs that have relatively strong accountability systems and support for professional development; use of books in community child care serving low-income children is likely to be even weaker. Indeed, data we collected in eight classrooms from three child-care centers revealed the overall quality as well as use of books to be lower than what we found in Head Start classrooms.

Book reading provides an ideal context for conversations that can develop children's language skills, but there are many ways to read and discuss books (Dickinson & Keebler, 1989; Dickinson & Smith, 1994). Earlier analyses of data about the book-reading experiences of the first cohort in HSLLD revealed that the quality of teacher–child conversations—when children were 4 years old—was related to children's end-of-kindergarten receptive vocabulary levels after controlling for basic home background demographic factors and features of classroom quality distinct from the nature of the book-reading conversations (Dickinson & Smith, 1994). Conversations that were linked to children's development were those that involved a back-and-forth exchange between the teacher and child that involved analysis of the story. Recent analyses of data from both cohorts again found this association between analytical conversations and subsequent vocabulary growth (Dickinson, in press-b). Furthermore, regression analyses that included the frequency of analytical conversations during book-reading conversations controlling for other classroom and home factors, indicate that such conversations make significant and independent contributions to children's vocabulary growth (Dickinson, 2001).

SUPPORT FOR WRITING

Writing has long been recognized as a valuable way for children to learn to focus on how sound maps onto print (Dickinson, 1986; see Richgels, Chapter 11). Results from our analyses of preschool data from the HSLLD support this finding; the quality of support for writing when children were 4 years of age was found to be related to their language and literacy growth at the end of kindergarten (Dickinson, in press-c; Smith, in press). Furthermore, analysis of data collected in the first grade revealed that the best classroom predictor of children's end-of-grade scores on our assessments was the use of writing across varied curriculum areas (Dickinson & DiGisi, 1998).

Our observations conducted in Head Start classrooms across New England provide some indication of the extent to which Head Start teachers have begun to support children's writing activities. We often observed a distinct area set aside to encourage writing (63% of the classrooms) and typically found a variety of environmental supports for writing (alphabet, 67%; word cards, 54%; three or more kinds of writing tools, 49%). What was less evident were efforts on the part of the teacher to support children's writing (not observed in 72% of the rooms) or to intentionally model writing (observed in only 34% of the classrooms). At least in Head Start centers in New England, it seems there is a reasonably broad realization of the value of writing, but teachers have not yet begun to include active support for writing among their standard classroom practices.

TEACHER–CHILD CONVERSATIONS

A major focus of the HSLLD was the creation of detailed descriptions of the patterns of conversation occurring throughout the day in preschool classrooms in order to examine the impact of these conversations on later reading development. We anticipated that children would benefit from teacher–child conversations that included varied vocabulary and dealt with topics that challenge children's thinking (Dickinson & Tabors, 2001). As our results have come in, certain findings have proven to be especially interesting because they provide a broad sense of the conversational environment in classrooms. One finding came as a surprise to us—the limited amount of conversation that an individual child actually engages in during a classroom day. We catalogued the amount of time children engaged in different kinds of conversations. (If 5 seconds or more elapsed without anything other than an isolated sound or word, we recorded "no talk" for that period.) We found that more than half of the 3- and 4-year-olds and approximately three-quarters of all kindergartners were not engaging in sustained au-

dible conversation. When preschool-age children were conversing, the majority of this time was spent talking with or listening to the teacher (Dickinson, 2001).

Correlational data suggest interesting patterns of association between children's language use in preschool classrooms and their subsequent literacy development. When children were 3 years old, the amount of time they spent conversing with other children and the amount of time spent in verbalized dramatic play were correlated with their end-of-kindergarten literacy, vocabulary, and storytelling skills. When children were 4 and 5 years old, trends suggested continued positive associations between free play conversation and our assessments (Dickinson, in press-a[13]). The relative strength of the correlational data from the 3-year-old children suggests that children bring into the classroom preestablished skills that they employ in pretend play. Thus, these long-term correlations likely reflect the interplay between classroom environments that foster dramatic play and children's preexisting language skills.

Given that children's language experiences are heavily influenced by their teachers, we expect to find patterns of teacher–child talk associated with children's later development if preschool classrooms have an enduring impact on children's language growth (Dickinson, Cote, & Smith, 1993; Smith, 1996). We used three basic approaches to describe children's language experiences: we coded the content of their conversations with peers and teachers, we coded the content of their teacher's conversations, and we analyzed the frequency of use of different words by teachers and children. Using both our coding and vocabulary tallying approaches to teacher–child conversations, we found a variety of first-order correlations between children's classroom experiences in mealtime and free play and end-of-kindergarten language and literacy development (Cote, 2001; Dickinson, 2001), with the associations more prevalent for 4-year-olds than for 3-year-olds.

During free play, our analysis of the content of the teacher's conversations revealed the importance of the frequency with which they extended children's comments and engaged children in cognitively challenging conversations (conversations about nonpresent topics that encouraged reflection on language or discussed things thought to be generally true about the social or physical world). We found two aspects of teacher's conversations to be associated with our end-of-kindergarten assessments: their use of rare words and their ability to limit how much they said and, hence, listen to what children were saying (Dickinson, 2001). Similar results emerged from our analysis of mealtime conversations when children were 4 years of age (Cote, 2001; Dickinson et al., 1993). Interestingly, the patterns of rare word use by children in the classroom as they spoke to teachers during free play were also related to our subsequent assessment of their language skills. This finding suggests that future research should consider the possibility that teachers may influence children's patterns of language use.

Given the evidence that teacher–child conversations play an important role in supporting children's long-term literacy development, and with the realization of the labor-intensive work of audiotaping, transcribing, and coding, we developed the Teacher–Child Verbal Interaction Profile (TCVI; Dickinson, Haine, & Howard, 1996). This tool allows observers to code multiple features of conversations that occur during 30-second intervals during free play and mealtimes. When we collapse categories that reflect the use of academic topics (literacy, math, world knowledge), we find that during those intervals when teachers were engaged with children, such topics accounted for 12% of free-play talk and 3% of the free-play intervals. Talk that dealt with nonpresent topics or pretending was observed during free play in 14% of the intervals and 22% of the mealtime intervals. Clearly, classroom context affects the content of teacher–child conversations. Teachers engaged more frequently in intentional, instructional conversations during free play as well as more relaxed talk about past and future events, topics that enable teachers to connect with children on a personal level. The frequency of teacher engagement in such conversations was comparable to that in the HSLLD data, suggesting that the dynamics that give rise to the ways in which teacher's talk with children may be quite stable across time and classroom settings.

Given the importance of vocabulary use by teachers, the TCVI includes codes to indicate when teachers make intentional efforts to draw children's attention to the meaning of words. Such intentional vocabulary teaching was very rare, appearing in less than 1% of the mealtime intervals and 1% of the free-play intervals. The intentional uses that we did see were often clustered among a limited number of teachers and were absent in 75% of the observed teacher's mealtimes and 50% of the free-play times. Although many teachers were never observed introducing new vocabulary, we did see much higher rates in some classrooms (i.e., mealtimes, 9%; free play, 13%). The presence of such rates of intentional new vocabulary use illustrates that such conversations can occur in preschool. We can only wonder what might occur with long-term exposure to such levels of intentional attention to vocabulary use.

LARGE-GROUP TIMES

Researchers have devoted little attention to the nature and impact of large-group time activities other than book reading. The failure to take seriously the possible role of large-group settings is striking given that a major study of preschools in Bermuda (McCartney, 1984) found the nature of teacher's talk during group times to be an important predictor of children's language growth. The HSLLD study data have again highlighted the importance of these settings for children's language and literacy development and have underscored the importance of taking activity setting into account when examining language data. When children were 3 and 4 years old, we found correlations between their large-group experiences and their subsequent kindergarten assessments. We found that children benefited from teachers' explicit efforts to hold the attention of the group and engage children in conversations with the intention of teaching information or exploring ideas. The amount of child participation in conversations was also positively associated with later child outcomes. These data are relevant because they indicate that even young children can benefit from participating in large-group conversations. The data also alert us to the danger of being lulled by our own assumptions about the forms of classroom experiences that foster growth. We did not expect to find that large-group time played a major role in supporting language growth; indeed, analyses conducted for the NEQRC and the LEEP evaluations do not specifically assess the quality of large-group times.

Effects of Experiences during the Preschool Years

Results from the HSLLD allow us to investigate the ways in which children's experiences at home and in preschool affect their end-of-kindergarten language and reading levels. Observations of children's experiences in the home help describe the contributions of low-income parents to their children's development. The aspects of children's home experiences were described by three composite variables: literacy support (parental reports of patterns of book reading and library use), density of rare words used in the home, and extended discourse (Roach & Snow, 2000; Tabors, Roach, & Snow, 2001). Likewise, three composite variables were created to capture children's classroom experiences when they were 4 years of age: classroom vocabulary environment, quality of teachers' talk, and curriculum quality (Dickinson, 2001). After controlling for demographic factors, both homes and classrooms accounted for significant variance in children's scores (Dickinson & Tabors, 2001). The home variables accounted for 17–18% of the variance in the Peabody Picture Vocabulary Test (PPVT)

and early literacy scores. When the three classroom composites were added to the models, we predicted 49% of the variance in PPVT and early literacy scores in kindergarten. When home and classroom factors are combined, we found overlap in the variance accounted for by the two models but still found that classroom predictors contribute significantly to our model, with our final models predicting slightly more than 50% of the variance in literacy and nearly 60% of the variance in vocabulary scores. These data indicate that the classroom experiences of children from low-income families play an important role in determining language and literacy status at the end of kindergarten.

Furthermore, growth trajectory analyses of receptive vocabulary, literacy, and academic language scores (a word-definition task) suggest that children's preschool experiences may affect their reading abilities at the end of fourth grade (Roach & Snow, 2000). Both home and classroom variables describing literacy support were related to fourth-grade reading comprehension and, when these forms of support are considered together, they play an important role in predicting the children's initial status in vocabulary and literacy (see Tables 18.1, 18.2). Children's initial status and rates of growth accounted for 67% of the variance in fourth-grade reading comprehension. Our interpretation of this analysis is that preschool experiences play an important role in determining later reading success by set-

TABLE 18.1. Home and School Preschool-Age Predictors of Academic Language, Vocabulary, and Word Recognition

	Controls only	Controls plus home and school preschool-age predictors
Kindergarten academic language		
Initial status	28%	57%
Rate of change	16%	36%
Kindergarten vocabulary		
Initial status	22%	55%
Rate of change	24%	31%
Grade 1 word recognition		
Initial status	21%	43%
Rate of change	12%	22%

Note. Data from Roach and Snow (2000).

TABLE 18.2. Growth Trajectories in Academic Language, Vocabulary, and Word Recognition as Predictors of Fourth-Grade Reading Comprehension

	Full model	Final model
Academic language		
Initial status	−0.07	
Rate	1.08	
Vocabulary		
Initial status	0.88**	0.85***
Rate	1.31~	1.31*
Word recognition		
Initial Status	1.13**	1.13***
Rate	2.90*	2.98**
R^2 statistic	0.67	0.67

Note. Data from Roach and Snow (2000).
~$p < 10$; *$p < .05$; **$p < .01$; ***$p < .001$.

ting the stage for children's subsequent literacy development.

In addition, data from the end of seventh grade also suggest that kindergarten status plays a role in predicting later reading comprehension (Dickinson & Tabors, 2001). The receptive vocabulary scores children received near the end of kindergarten were strongly related to end-of-seventh-grade vocabulary ($r = .64$, $n = 51$) and reading comprehension ($r = .68$, $n = 51$). Children's end-of-kindergarten literacy scores were also correlated with seventh-grade reading comprehension ($r = .61$, $n = 51$). The reported associations underscore the importance of determining how classroom and home experiences during the preschool years help to shape children's end-of-kindergarten language and literacy capacities.

The HSLLD data provide important evidence of the link between children's classroom experiences and their subsequent development, but the sample is necessarily small. The NEQRC study of the impact of variations in the quality of Head Start classrooms used a much larger sample and provides additional evidence that preschool classrooms can have an effect on the language and literacy development of children from low-income families. We assessed a sample of 393 children from 71 classrooms drawn from four Head Start programs in eastern Massachusetts and evaluated the quality of the classrooms using a battery of tools, one of which—the Early Language and Literacy Classroom Observation (ELLCO)—was designed for this study (Smith, Dickinson & Sangeorge, 2001).

Using hierarchical linear modeling, we analyzed the contributions of classroom quality to children's receptive vocabulary (PPVT-III) and early literacy scores (Early Literacy Profile; Dickinson & Chaney, 1997). Our level-one models took into account differences between children associated with their backgrounds, such as home language (English or Spanish speaking), gender, and age. The variance in scores that was not accounted for by the background factors (15% for vocabulary, 20% for literacy) was accounted for by classroom support for language and literacy as measured by the ELLCO: 80% of between-classroom variance in vocabulary and 67% of the between-classroom variance in early literacy (Dickinson et al., 2000). These analyses provide additional evidence that the quality of preschool classrooms attended by children from low-income families can play an important role in supporting their vocabulary growth and early literacy development.

Given the importance of classroom quality, it is sobering to recognize that the level of quality to which one would aspire is rarely present. As we noted earlier, patterns of support for literacy that we have observed throughout New England fall far short of the ideal. Results displayed in Table 18.3 illustrate that, while nearly half the classrooms were rated as high quality in provision of a positive overall climate, the levels of support for language and literacy were often below standard. As many classrooms were rated as being of "Low Quality" as were rated highly. In addition, few classrooms (14%) were rated as effectively supporting parental efforts to foster their children's linguistic, literacy, and intellectual growth.

These generally low levels of quality in the area of language and literacy reflect the low levels of global quality found in previously discussed research. Early-childhood teachers and administrators have long been concerned about the impact of inappropriate approaches to literacy instruction. Since the mid-1980s, statements of what constitutes

TABLE 18.3. Classroom Quality as Determined by Selected Items from ELLCO Ratings Based on Observations in 125 New England Classrooms

Selected items	Low quality	Basic support	High quality
Positive classroom climate	14%	38%	49%
Support for oral language	26%	45%	29%
Support for writing	35%	34%	31%
Strong curriculum	41%	32%	27%
Facilitating home support	52%	35%	14%

developmentally appropriate practice and standards for program accreditation and guidelines provided by the NAEYC (Bredekamp, 1987) have reflected a concern about the imposition of drill-and-practice and other high-pressure curricular approaches. A recent position statement, jointly issued by the NAEYC and the International Reading Association (IRA & NAEYC, 1998) reflects major progress in the promotion of literacy practices and curriculum, though program accreditation guidelines still lag behind the levels of quality established in this statement (Dickinson, 1999).

Interestingly, the ambivalence of early-childhood educators has been shared by researchers, as indicated by the limited attention given to literacy practices in widely used research tools employed to assess classroom quality (Dickinson, 1999). Given the historical ambivalence of the field toward the place of literacy in early-childhood classrooms, it is not surprising that our data indicate that classrooms tend to be strong along the dimension long valued by the early-childhood community, overall classroom climate, and relatively weak with respect to those aspects of classrooms that reflect a more academic orientation. Further, the low scores assigned to communication with parents indicate that, although preschool teachers tend do a better job of communicating with families than many kindergarten teachers (Porche, 2001), these communications often do not include consideration of a parental role in fostering children's literacy development. Many teachers have not been instructed in the current conceptions of literacy development, the critical importance of the preschool years, and the role that they and parents must play in fostering development.

As we indicated early in this chapter, we are not the first to report findings indicating that preschool classrooms fall short in their ability to provide optimal support for children's literacy development (Bryant et al., 1994; High/Scope Educational Research Foundation, 1997). Taken as a whole, all results point to the urgent need to develop strategies to raise the quality of literacy support provided children in preschool classrooms.

Intervening to Improve Classroom Quality

Based on the results from the HSLLD, a method to help preschool teachers adopt more effective classroom language and literacy practices was developed. This course, LEEP, is conducted with teams of teachers and their supervisors. This approach is consistent with the neo-Vygotskian theories (Minick, Stone, & Forman, 1993; Tharp & Gallimore, 1988), recent work on teacher development (Cochran-Smith & Lytle, 1990), and the assumption that the institutional context of a teacher's work must be altered if enduring changes in practice are to result (Miller, Lord, & Dorney, 1994). Through LEEP, teachers learn about early-language and literacy development and engage in activities designed to help them become more reflective and intentional about their practice. Therefore, class sessions and assignments are designed in ways that are intended to help teachers become more reflective about their classroom practices. For example, teachers audiotape, transcribe, and analyze their own conversations; assess children's literacy; and make changes based on what they learn.

Our quantitative LEEP data come from two waves of data collection during the years 1998–1999 and 1999–2000. Data were collected prior to the intervention and after the course from participating teachers (n = 30) and supervisors (n = 17) as well as comparison-group teachers (n = 35) and supervisors (n = 18). Teachers rated children's language, literacy, and social development. Multiple dimensions of the literacy environment were measured using research tools developed and used by the NEQRC. Analysis of data indicates comparable effects each year, and when the 2 years are combined, results indicate a significant and beneficial effect of LEEP on classroom environments, teachers' approach to curriculum, and general support for literacy (Dickinson, Miller, & Anastasopolous, 2000). Using ELLCO, we found that overall classroom quality, such as management and classroom climate, showed improvement. However, the strongest effect of LEEP was seen specifically in ELLCO items reflecting attention to children's language and literacy. Additional evidence of changes in classroom practices comes from our observations of book reading. As we noted previously, in the spring of 2000, across 2 days of classroom observation in 26 comparison-group classrooms, we saw no reading across 2 days in 35% of the time, and those readings that did occur lasted 2½ minutes, or less than 38% of the time. In the spring, in the 14 classrooms of teachers who attended LEEP, we never observed for 2 days without seeing at least one full-group book reading, and these sessions always lasted more than 2½ minutes.

To determine whether the changes in classroom practices were affecting children, we compared fall-to-spring change scores of teacher ratings of children's literacy and social development. These analyses revealed that children in classrooms of LEEP teachers were rated significantly higher in the fall than in the spring on reading and writing. In addition, teachers rated children as displaying fewer problem behaviors, possibly suggesting that, as the classroom curriculum becomes more lively, children become more engaged and less likely to amuse themselves in inappropriate ways (see Table 18.4). These results indicate that LEEP has a positive effect on teachers and that children benefit from the changes teachers have implemented.

Toward a Theory of Early Literacy Development

In the coming century, early childhood will continue to receive growing attention from researchers and policymakers. The need for services is pressing, the level of quality is uneven, and evidence of the long-term impact of this period on later literacy functioning is compelling. Our data provide evidence of the importance of the preschool years to children's later language and literacy development.

The three studies we discussed provide evidence that high-quality preschool classrooms can and do make substantial contributions to children's literacy success. Growth model analyses from the HSLLD indicate that children's language and literacy status at the end of kindergarten is related to their fourth-grade status. In addition, our

TABLE 18.4. Comparing LEEP and Comparison-Group Fall–Spring Change Scores

Variable	Mean LEEP change	Mean Comparison grp. change	t-statistic	Sig. level
ELLCO ratings[a] (n = 68)				
ELLCO total (minus technology)	.816	.197	4.480	.000
General environment	.507	.009	2.317	.024
Language literacy and curriculum	.850	−.001	5.602	.000
Literacy Checklist[b] (n = 66)				
Total literacy environment	7.75	1.61	5.00	.000
Books and book use	4.93	1.49	4.20	.000
Writing area and writing materials	2.98	.41	3.21	.002

[a]Early Language and Literacy Classroom Observation. This tool has 14 items, each having a 5-point scale.
[b]This tool rates classrooms for specific literacy-related areas and tools.

other data suggest that relationships between kindergarten and later functioning remain strong over time. We have made strides toward the identification of specific interactions that foster the acquisition of school-readiness abilities. The NEQRC data lend further support to the HSLLD results, using different methods and a much larger sample to demonstrate a link between the kinds of classroom experiences highlighted in HSLLD results and children's language and literacy development in the preschool years. Both HSLLD and NEQRC data are correlational; therefore, our intervention data provide corroboration for our correlational data, illustrating the impact on children's language resulting from enriched classroom language and literacy opportunities. Taken as a whole, our data support two conclusions: (1) language experiences in preschool classrooms affect the vocabulary and early literacy development of children from low-income families; and, (2) changes during the preschool years have effects that endure, with the duration of effects possibly remaining through the middle school years.

Our data also allow us to speculate about the very nature of literacy development and mechanisms underlying it. Our work has been based on the assumption that aspects of oral language enable children to use extended discourse to construct meaning apart from the immediate context of use, and the ability to do so is of particular relevance to literacy development (see Watson, Chapter 4, for similar discussion). The HSLLD was designed specifically to consider the hypothesis that decontextualized language skills are essential to later reading comprehension. Available data provide evidence that vocabulary is central to later literacy, that growth in vocabulary is related to broader discourse skills, and that engagement in extended discourse that requires decontextualized language skills fosters literacy development. Our analyses do not yet allow us to draw firm conclusions about the contribution of early extended discourse skills, but they suggest that considerable additional research in this area is warranted.

Our data also lend support to the idea that early-emerging oral language capacities and print-based knowledge are related and may mutually facilitate language and literacy development. The analyses of data from all of the studies we have conducted consistently demonstrate associations among language and print-based tasks and our longitudinal data indicate that these associations continue to be strong over time. In addition, our studies linking early experiences to literacy growth do not provide evidence of a simple mechanistic relationship between specific experiences and selected dimensions of literacy development. For example, HSLLD data on the nature of teachers' conversations with children are stronger predictors of later growth than are measures of classroom curriculum—including writing. Further, we find that homes and classrooms seem to have a relatively similar pattern of impact on children's language and literacy development even though they provide children with very different kinds of experiences. These data point toward a model of literacy development in which different kinds of knowledge that comprise early literacy (e.g., vocabulary, phonemic awareness, and print knowledge) are conceptualized as being part of a dynamic, mutually reinforcing system. The lexical restructuring hypothesis is one model that provides a way to understand how such mutually reinforcing cycles might work (see Whitehurst & Lonigan, Chapter 2; Goswami, Chapter 9). We anticipate that in coming years, further work will identify other mechanisms that help account for the early interdependencies among language and literacy and the long-term stability of these relationships once they are established.

Implications for Policymakers

The preliminary and promising results from our intervention, LEEP, suggest that relatively modest changes in the educational experiences of low-income children during the preschool years have long-lasting and significant effects. We anticipate that in the coming decades we will witness a proliferation in approaches to providing children from low-income backgrounds with needed enrichment. Our data demonstrate that providing high-quality professional development opportunities to classroom teachers is one of many possible avenues that deserves exploration. Although our data indicate the potential of professional development efforts, they also suggest that current approaches to preservice and in-service training around language and literacy support are not adequate. Much remains to be learned about the duration, intensity, and content of pedagogical interventions that will be required if we are to significantly boost children's language and literacy skills. Equally vexing questions will arise as we seek to tailor professional development opportunities to the diverse settings in which child care is delivered and to the diverse language and educational backgrounds of the staff who care for children. We are hopeful that current awareness of the importance of child care and its impact on children will translate into sustained research into the child-care and early-care environment's role in the nature of early literacy and multiple approaches to ensuring that all children make needed progress to enable them ultimately to master the high literacy levels required in our world today.

Acknowledgments

The research reported in the chapter was funded by two separate major program awards from the Spencer Foundation; and by awards from the Agency for Children, Youth and Families (Nos. 90YD0017 and 90CD0827); from the Office for Educational Research and Improvement, (No. R305T990312-00), and from the National Science Foundation (No. 9979948). We thank Margo Sweet for her assistance in the preparation of this chapter.

Notes

1. It is important to note that the numbers differ slightly based on the source as a result of different typologies of care.
2. In the field of early childhood and early care, there is a distinction between nursery school or preschool and child care. The former is considered to be primarily an educational program to prepare for primary school and is differentiated from general child care provided when a parent needs to work. For the purposes of this chapter, we refer to all care as child care to simplify the reference.
3. There is a great deal of complexity in the typology of these forms of care, which states often regulate or license. However, sources reporting the percentages or estimates of children in the United States in each form of care do not differ a great deal (see Children's Defense Fund, 2000).

4. The use of family day care is almost equally distributed by income background (14% and 17%, respectively).
5. It is unclear whether "prekindergarten" refers only to state programs or to all known child-care programs serving children in this age range. In other reports the authors use the term to refer to state-funded programs which may include Head Start.
6. In 1999, 30% of all working mothers with children younger than 6 years of age were single and bear an even larger burden of the cost of child care than other low-income, two-parent families (Children's Defense Fund, 2000).
7. For example, in Massachusetts, California, and Washington, more children are in parent care (over 30%) versus center-based care compared to less than one in five in Mississippi and Alabama where the use of center care is the highest (approximately 40%) (see Capizzano & Adams, 2000).
8. "Only 50 percent of children eligible for Head Start and only 10 percent of children eligible for federal child care assistance receive it . . ." (Children's Defense Fund, 2000, p. xviii).
9. The Head Start Program, federally subsidized, is an exception.
10. Widely used measures include the Early Childhood Environmental Rating Scale (ECERS-R; Harms, Clifford, & Cryer, 1998); Assessment Profile for Early Childhood Classrooms (Abbott-Shim & Sibley, 1998); Infant/Toddler Environmental Rating Scale (ITERS; Harms, Cryer, & Clifford, 1990); Family Day Care Rating Scale (FDCRS; Harms & Clifford, 1984); Arnett Scale of Caregiver Behavior (Arnett, 1989).
11. The NEQRC included researchers from the Education Development Center, Inc., Harvard Graduate School of Education, Boston College, and the Massachusetts Society for the Prevention of Cruelty to Children.
12. Children from Spanish-speaking homes were assessed in Spanish and English on selected measures (receptive vocabulary, phonemic awareness).
13. Note that we have not yet completed analyses of these data; therefore, we cannot at this time report results that control for other relevant variables (e.g., home background and dimensions of classroom quality).

References

Abbott-Shim, M., Lambert, R., & McCarty, F. (2001). *A study of Head Start effectiveness using a randomized design.*

Abbott-Shim, M., & Sibley, A. (1998). *Assessment*

Profile for Early Childhood Programs. Atlanta, GA: Quality Assist.

Administration on Children, Youth, and Families. (2000). *FACES Findings: New research on Head Start program quality and outcomes*. Washington, DC: U.S. Department of Health & Human Services, Head Start Family and Child Experiences Survey.

Administration for Children and Families. (1998). *Head Start program performance standards: Second progress report*. Washington, DC: US Department of Health and Human Services.

Arnett, J. (1989). Caregivers in day care centers: Does training matter? *Journal of Applied Developmental Psychology, 10*, 541–552.

Barrington, B. L., & Hendricks, B. (1989). Differentiating characteristics of high school graduates, dropouts, and nongraduates. *Journal of Educational Research, 82*(6), 309–319.

Bredekamp, S. (Ed.). (1987). *Developmentally appropriate practice in early childhood programs serving children from birth through age 8* (expanded ed.). Washington, DC: National Association for the Education of Young Children.

Brizius, J. A., & Foster, S. A. (1993). *Generation to generation: Realizing the promise of family literacy*. Ypsilanti, MI: High/Scope.

Bryant, D. M., Burchinal, M., Lau, L. S., & Sparling, J. J. (1994). Family and classroom correlates of Head Start children's developmental outcomes. *Early Childhood Research Quarterly, 9*, 289–310.

Burchinal, M. R., Lee, M. W., & Ramey, C. T. (1989). Type of day-care and preschool intellectual development in disadvantaged children. *Child Development, 60*, 128–137.

Burchinal, M. R., Campbell, F. A., Bryant, D. M., Wasik, B. A., & Ramey, C. T. (1997). Early intervention and mediating processes in cognitive performance of children of low-income African-American families. *Child Development, 68*(5), 935–954.

Burchinal, M. R., Roberts, J. E., Riggins, Jr., R., Zeisel, S. A., Neebe, E., & Bryant, D. (2000). Relating quality of center-based child care to early cognitive and language development longitudinally. *Child Development, 71*, 339–357.

Bus, A. G., van IJzendoorn, M. H., & Pellegrini, A. D. (1995). Joint book reading makes for success in learning to read: A meta-analysis on intergenerational transmission of literacy. *Review of Educational Research, 65*(1), 1–21.

Capizzano, J., & Adams, G. (2000). *The number of child care arrangements used by children under five: Variation across states*. Washington, DC: The Urban Institute.

Capizzano, J., Adams, G., & Sonenstein, F. (2000). *Child care arrangements for children under five: Variation across states*. Washington, DC: The Urban Institute.

Chaney, C. (1992). Language development, metalinguistic skills, and print awareness in 3-year old children. *Applied Psycholinguistics, 13*(4), 485–514.

Children's Defense Fund. (2000). *The state of America's children: Yearbook 2000*. Washington, DC: Author.

Cost, Quality, and Outcomes Team. (1995). *Cost, quality, and child outcomes in child care centers: Executive summary*. Denver: University of Colorado Press.

Cote, L. R. (2001). Language opportunities in preschool classrooms: Mealtime. In D. K. Dickinson & P. O. Tabors (Eds.), *Preparing for literacy at home and school: The criticial role of language development in the preschool years*. Baltimore: Brookes.

Cunningham, A. E., & Stanovich, K. E. (1997). Early reading acquisition and its relation to reading experience and ability 10 years later. *Developmental Psychology, 33*(6), 934–945.

Dickinson, D. K. (1986). Cooperation, collaboration and a computer: Integrating a computer into a first-second grade writing program. *Research in the Teaching of English, 20*, 357–378.

Dickinson, D. K. (1999, April). *Shifting images of DAP as seen through different lenses*. Paper presented at the annual meeting of the American Educational Research Association, Montreal, Canada.

Dickinson, D. K. (2001-a). Large group and free play times as conversational settings. In D. K. Dickinson & P. O. Tabors (Eds.), *Preparing for literacy at home and school: The critical role of language development in the preschool years*. Baltimore: Brookes.

Dickinson, D. K. (2001). Patterns of book reading in preschool classrooms. In D. K. Dickinson & P. O. Tabors (Eds.), *Preparing for literacy at home and school: The critical role of language development in the preschool years*. Baltimore: Brookes.

Dickinson, D. K. (2001). Putting the pieces together: The impact of preschool on children's language and literacy development in kindergarten. In D. K. Dickinson & P. O. Tabors (Eds.), *Preparing for literacy at home and school: The critical role of language development in the preschool years*. Baltimore: Brookes.

Dickinson, D. K., & Chaney, C. (1997). *Profile of early literacy development*. Newton, MA: Education Development Center, Center for Children and Families.

Dickinson, D. K., Cote, L., & Smith, M. W. (1993). Learning vocabulary in preschool: Social and discourse contexts affecting vocabulary growth. In C. Daiute (Ed.), *The development of literacy through social interaction: New directions in child development* (pp. 67–78). San Francisco: Jossey-Bass.

Dickinson, D. K., & Digisi, L. (1998). The many rewards of a literacy-rich classroom. *Educational Leadership, 55*(6) 23–26.

Dickinson, D. K., Haine, R. A., & Howard, C. (1996). *Teacher–Child Verbal Interaction Profile*. Newton, MA: Education Development Center, Center for Children and Families.

Dickinson, D. K., & Keebler, R. (1989). Variation in preschool teacher's style of reading books. *Discourse Processes, 12*(3), 353–376.

Dickinson, D. K., Miller, C. M., & Anastaspoulos, L. P. (2000, June). *The impact of the Literacy Enrichment Environment Program on teachers, supervisors, and children.* Poster session presented at the annual conference of National Association for the Education of Young Children's National Institute for Early Childhood Professional Development, San Francisco.

Dickinson, D. K., & Smith, M. W. (1994). Long-term effects of preschool teachers' book readings on low-income children's vocabulary and story comprehension. *Reading Research Quarterly, 29*(2), 104–122.

Dickinson, D. K., & Snow, C. E. (1987). Interrelationships among prereading and oral language skills in kindergartners from two social classes. *Early Childhood Research Quarterly, 2,* 1–25.

Dickinson, D. K., Sprague, K., Sayer, A., Miller, C., Clark, N., & Wolf, A. (2000, June). Classroom factors that foster literacy and social development of children from different language backgrounds. In M. Hopmann (Chair), *Dimensions of program quality that foster child development: Reports from 5 years of the Head Start Quality Research Centers.* Poster symposium presented at the biannual National Head Start Research Conference, Washington, DC.

Dickinson, D. K., & Tabors, P. O. (Eds.). (2001). *Beginning literacy with language: Young children learning at home and in school.* Baltimore: Brookes.

Fernandez-Fein, S., & Baker, L. (1997). Rhyme and alliteration sensitivity and relevant experiences among preschoolers from diverse backgrounds. *Journal of Literacy Research, 29,* 433–459.

Greenberg, D., Franze, S., McCarty, F., & Abbott-Shim, M. (2000). *The role of Head Start classroom quality and the development of preliteracy skills of children of low literate parents.* Unpublished manuscript, Georgia State University, Atlanta, GA.

Harms, T., & Clifford, R. M. (1984). *Family Day Care Rating Scale.* New York: Teachers College Press.

Harms, T., Clifford, R. M., & Cryer, D. (1998). *Early Childhood Environment Rating Scale.* (rev. ed.) New York: Teachers College Press.

Harms, T., Cryer, D., & Clifford, R. M. (1990). *Infant/Toddler Environment Rating Scale.* New York: Teachers College Press.

Hart, B., & Risley, T. R. (1995). *Meaningful differences in the everyday experience of young American children.* Baltimore: Brookes.

High/Scope Educational Research Foundation. (1997). *Early returns: First year report of the Michigan School-Readiness Program Evaluation.* Ypsilianti, MI: Author.

International Reading Association and National Association of Young Children. (1998). Learning to read and write: Developmentally appropriate practices for young children. A joint position statement of the International Reading Association (IRA) and the National Association for the Education of Young Children (National Association for the Education of Young Children), Adopted 1998. *Young Children, 53*(4), 3–46.

Laosa, L. M. (1983). Families as facilitators of children's intellectual development at 3 years of age. In L. M. Laosa & I. E. Spiegal (Eds.), *Families as learning environments for children* (pp. 1–45). New York: Plenum.

Lloyd, D. N. (1978). Prediction of school failure from third grade data. *Educational and Psychological Measurement, 38,* 1193–1200.

McCartney, K. (1984). Effect of quality of day care environment on children's language development. *Developmental Psychology, 20*(2), 244–260.

Miller, B., Lord, B., & Dorney, J. (1994). *Staff development for teachers: A study of configurations and costs in four districts.* Newton, MA: Education Development Center.

Minick, N., Stone, C. A., & Forman, E. A. (1993). Introduction: Integration of individual, social, and institutional processes in accounts of children's learning and development. In E. A. Forman, N. Minick, & C. Addison Stone (Eds.), *Contexts for learning: Sociocultural dynamics in children's development* (pp. 3–16). New York: Oxford University Press.

Morrison, F. J., & Griffin, E. A. (1997, April). Early literacy: The nature and sources of individual differences. In F. J. Morrison (chair), *Individual differences in the transition to school: Language literacy, and context.* Symposium conducted at the biennial meeting of the Society for Research in Child Development, Washington, DC.

National Association for the Education of Young Children. (2000). *National Center for Education Statistics: Survey* [on-line]. Available: http://www.parenthoodweb.com.

NICHD Early Child Care Research Network. (1997a). Familial factors associated with the characteristics of nonmaternal care for infants. *Journal of Marriage and the Family, 59*(2), 389–408.

NICHD Early Child Care Research Network. (1997b). Poverty and patterns of child care. In G. J Duncan, & J. Brooks-Gunn (Eds.), *Consequences of growing up poor* (pp. 100–131). New York: Russell Sage.

NICHD Early Child Care Research Network. (1999a). Child care and mother–child interaction in the first 3 years of life. *Developmental Psychology, 36*(6), 1399–1413.

NICHD Early Child Care Research Network. (1999b). Child outcomes when child care center classes meet recommended standards for quality. *American Journal of Public Health, 89,* 1072–1077.

NICHD Early Child Care Research Network. (in press). Characteristics and quality of child care for toddlers and preschoolers. *Journal of Applied Developmental Science.*

Peisner-Feinberg, E. S., & Burchinal, M. R. (1997). Relations between preschool children's child-care experiences and concurrent development: The Cost, Quality, and Outcomes Study. *Merrill-Palmer Quarterly, 43,* 451–477.

Porche, M. (in press). Parent involvement as a link between home and school. In D. K. Dickinson & P. O. Tabors (Eds.), *Beginning literacy with language: Young children learning at home and in school.* Baltimore: Brookes.

Roach, K. A., & Snow, C. E. (2000, April). *What predicts 4th grade reading comprehension?* Paper presented at the annual conference of the American Education Research Association, New Orleans.

Schulman, K., Blank, H., & Ewen, D. (1999). *Seeds of Success: State prekindergarten initiatives 1998–1999.* Washington, DC: Children's Defense Fund.

Smith, M. W. (1996). *Teacher–child interaction in preschool classrooms: Theoretical and practical perspectives.* Doctoral dissertation, Clark University School of Education, Worcester, MA.

Smith, M. W. (2001). Preschool experiences of children in the Home–School Study of Language and Literacy Development. In D. K. Dickinson & P. O. Tabors (Eds.), *Beginning literacy with language: Young children learning at home and in school.* Baltimore: Brookes.

Smith, M. W., Dickinson, D. K., & Sangeorge, A. (in press). *The Early Language and Literacy Classroom Observation.* Baltimore: Brookes.

Snow, C. E., Burns, S. M., & Griffin, P. (Eds.). (1998). *Preventing reading difficulties.* Washington DC: National Academy Press.

Tabors, P. O., Roach, K. A., & Snow, C. E. (2001).

Home language and literacy environment. In D. K. Dickinson & P. O. Tabors (Eds.), *Beginning literacy with language: Young children learning at home and in school.* Baltimore: Brookes.

Tharp, R., & Gallimore, R. (1988). *Rousing minds to life: Teaching, learning, and schooling in social context.* New York: Cambridge University Press.

U.S. Department of Education. (1993). *Life in Preschool: Volume One of an observational study of early childhood programs for disadvantaged four-year-olds: Final report* (1993). Cambridge, MA: Abt Associates.

U.S. Department of Education. (1995). *National evaluation of the Even Start Family Literacy Program.* Washington, DC: Planning and Evaluation Service.

Walker, D., Greenwood, C., Hart, B., & Carta, J. (1994). Prediction of school outcomes based on early language production and socioeconomic factors. *Child Development, 65,* 606–621.

Wasik, B. H., Ramey, C. T., Bryant, D. M., & Sparling, J. J. (1991). A longitudinal study of two early intervention strategies: Project CARE. *Child Development, 61,* 1682–1696.

Zill, N., Collins, M., West, J., & Hausken, E. G. (1995). *Approaching kindergarten: A look at preschoolers in the United States.* Washington, DC: Office of Educational Research and Improvement, National Center for Education Statistics, National Household Education Survey.

19

Environment and Its Influences for Early Literacy Teaching and Learning

❖

KATHLEEN ROSKOS
SUSAN B. NEUMAN

Environments are not passive wrappings but, rather, active processes, which are invisible. The ground rules, pervasive structure, and overall patterns of environments elude easy perception.

—MARSHALL MCLUHAN

That the environment influences children's behavior is a well-established maxim in early childhood education. Pedagogies of such renowned scholars as Montessori, Piaget, Dewey, and Malaguzzi, are based on the understanding that children play an active role in exploring their environments, creating solutions to problems within its supports and constraints. As children engage in their environment, they adapt their intellectual tools to meet new situations or challenges, integrating thought and action. Both their mental and their physical processes are the means by which children achieve new understandings and developing skills.

Consequently, the environment plays a central role in learning. Its features, organizational structures, props, and materials influence the types, quality, and complexity of activity for children. Yet, studies of environment (e.g., Weinstein, 1977; Weinstein & David, 1987) have been conducted only intermittently throughout the years; in fact, the environment has served more often as a backdrop for intervention studies rather than as a subject of analysis. In contrast, this chapter is designed to focus on the central features of environment, highlighting aspects of context with importance for cognition. It begins by a brief history of ecological research. It then examines how environments may be restructured to improve access to print. This research argues for the importance of environment and its potential to enhance children's understanding of the functions and forms of literacy in the early years.

A Brief History

Ecological psychology is largely anchored in the research tradition established first by Barker and his colleagues (Barker, 1968; Barker & Wright, 1955). In an attempt to define representative samples of environments in their investigations, they operationalized the term "environment" as *behavior settings*—common contexts of everyday life. Behavior settings were described as shops, offices, classrooms, meetings, and festivals—places that mark our day-to-day lives. Within each behavior setting, they argued, exists routine patterns of goal-directed behavior that seem to endure despite the comings and goings of participants. A grocery store, for example, seems to encourage certain patterns of behavior that are linked to time, place, and material things. Its aisles, counters, foodstuffs, and time frame create a set of behaviors and expectations. In this setting, individuals are likely to make choices between items, calculate price differentials between products, and engage freely in conversations with others over products. These patterns of behavior contrast sharply with those expected in a church or a library, which offers a different set of constraints, and choices.

As conceptualized, behavior settings provided an analytic tool for observing environment for researchers (e.g., Gibson, 1979), increasing the ability to predict and perceive common patterns of activity in settings. The concept also revealed the *coercive power* (Gump, 1978) of the organization, structure, and complexity of behavior settings. And it was this potential power of the environment and its attendant attributes that intrigued a number of early childhood researchers interested in how environment might influence children's behaviors. Examining typical preschool activity settings, such as art, blocks, and housekeeping, for example, Rosenthal (1974) studied children's attention and involvement in activities. He found that certain activities (e.g., blocks) seemed to attract children more than others (how many children appeared) and some activities seemed to have greater holding power (how long children remained in a setting) than others. Both blocks and art held a strong attraction for children, but the art area exhibited greater holding power. Other activities (e.g., individual construction projects) were likely to elicit higher levels of on-task behavior than others. From this research, a science of activity and its concomitant behaviors within the environment began to emerge: Size and density of space in which to interact, degree of child choice in activity selection, and the goal-directed nature of the activity all seemed to influence children's persistence, and attention. In combination, these variables began to form a set of design principles and guidelines for creating early-childhood classroom environments (Weinstein & David, 1987).

The Literacy Environment and the Early-Childhood Classroom

Although highly relevant, these design principles were not initially applied to specific content learning. Designing environments for content learning was not the original intent of ecological researchers in early childhood. This was to change, however, as a result of a somewhat serendipitous finding from an ethnographic study by Jacob (1984). In her observations of Puerto Rican kindergartners, she described multiple instances of spontaneous literacy activity (e.g., list making and reading enactments) among the kindergartners as they pretended to shop and play house. Similarly, Roskos (1987), in her extensive observations of eight 4-year-old children, reported ongoing activities of children, acting "as if" they were already reading and writing. Children, on their own and with others, engaged in reading recipes, checking out books, writing, and organizing literacy activities during their free play. Recognizing children's natural interest in literacy-like activity, it made sense to consider how environments might be constructed to support and extend literacy activity.

In one of the first intervention studies of this type, Morrow and Weinstein (1986) examined the impact of creating library corners in early-childhood classrooms. These library corners were specially constructed to be in (1) a clear location in space with well-defined borders and sufficient surface area to accommodate five to seven children; (2) comfortable, child-scaled seating, and cozy spots for privacy; (3) organized materials that are accessible and cue behavior (regular open-faced book shelves, color coding of books); and (4) provision for related activities that extended the activities, including puppets, writing materials and listening posts. Morrow and Weinstein (1986) found that the frequency of use rose significantly when library corners were made more visible, accessible, and attractive.

Hall (1987) reported greater activity in a play center as a result of design changes. They created a print-rich environment in a home corner at nursery school with the intent of relating it to the real world of print outside the school. Their print flood included cookbooks, recipe pads, writing tools, telephone directories, note pads, newspapers, and other literacy materials often found in home environments. Over days of observation, the researchers witnessed numerous literacy events from fleeting interactions to more sustained literacy-related play episodes. Ready access to literacy resources, they surmised, helped children use their general knowledge of literacy to support their play. And, in a preliminary study examining the impact of literacy-enriched play areas on children's literacy behaviors, Neuman and Roskos (1989) found that preschool children spontaneously used almost twice as much print in their play than they did prior to the environmental changes.

Thus, given the potential of environmental factors for learning about literacy, Neuman and Roskos (1989, 1990) began to develop classroom design principles to include what was known about children's emerging conceptions of literacy. The goal was to create literacy environments within specific play settings that appealed to young children's play preferences and could meet their developmental needs as emerging writers and readers. Following extensive observations of preschoolers' (ages 3–5 years) spontaneous literacy in free play, a typology was developed to indicate how children used literacy. They seemed to engage in literacy play for the following purposes: (1) exploratory (what is it?), (2) interactional (between you and me), (3) personal (for me), (4) authenticating (legitimating), and (5) transactional (between text) and me. Children demonstrating the exploratory function used reading and writing to manipulate and investigate various objects in their environment. Examples included playing with envelopes, using a computer, and handling paper and pencils. The interactional functions focused on literacy for communication and social purposes. Here, children used reading and writing to spend time with others, to play games, and to record information in play. The transactional function emphasized the uses of literacy as a means to negotiate meaning between print and the user. Children used reading and writing to label or name items and to make events more meaningful in play. The uses of literacy for personal reasons included more egocentric behaviors such as expressing oneself or claiming ownership, "That's mine." And

finally, the authenticating function involved literacy actions such as verifying information or taking the role of an adult in daily literacy-related activities. Understanding how children were likely to use literacy in play provided clues as to potential play settings, literacy objects, and spatial arrangements that might be particularly appealing and familiar from the children's point of view.

Design Principles

Synthesizing research from ecological psychology, and the extensive observations of children's free play, Neuman and Roskos (1992) established a set of design principles for early-childhood classrooms.

SPACE INFLUENCES CHILDREN'S
INTERACTIONS AND LEARNING

Sufficient space (at least 25 square feet per child) is critical to quality interactions and activity. Studies indicate that children are more cooperative and interactive in these settings. Limited space and crowding tend to lead to increased quarreling, teasing, and aggression (Smith & Connolly, 1977). Further, the way in which space is allocated also sends a message. Open-space classrooms tend to suggest a freedom of movement and to imply the learner's centrality in the instructional processes. Large expanses, in contrast, invite young children to run and roughhouse.

Organizing the physical space in ways that are clearly visible to young children appears to support their learning (Phyfe-Perkins, 1980). Whether there is a big space for play or a small one, children use the boundaries to regulate and guide their own responses. For example, smaller, well-defined niches and nooks seem to encourage greater language and collaboration with peers and adults. Children are likely to use these more intimate settings to engage in longer and richer conversations with peers and adults.

However, play spaces that are too private are difficult to monitor and supervise. Semi-fixed structures such as cupboards, screens, tables, and directional signs provide definition and yet allow for adequate adult presence and supervision. Further, definitional print (i.e., environmental signs, lists, and charts) serves as a reference point for locations, enhancing the spatial organization of a room using print and picture.

COMPLEXITY OF MATERIALS ENHANCES CHILDREN'S INVOLVEMENT

Numerous studies of materials—amount, types, variety, display—indicate that their presence has behavioral consequences for young children. Some materials, as Rosenthal's (1974) research indicated, demonstrate more sustained activity than others do and engage children's attention at different ages. Toddlers seem to be enamored with "pull" toys, while preschoolers may become glued to small, manipulative toys (McCall, 1974; Rubin, 1977). Some materials tend to elicit social interaction and cooperation, such as the doll corner, whereas others encourage solitary and parallel play, such as play with puzzles and small blocks (Rubin & Seibel, 1979). Children's easy access to richly varied and sufficiently abundant materials appears to increase their behavioral repertoire, which in turn creates more opportunities to learn through interaction with objects.

Language and print awareness is enhanced when objects are clustered together to create a schema—or meaning network—for children to discover and explore. As children play with objects, they are guided to the print resources associated with them, linking objects to their oral and written names. These experiences provide a semantic network of connected, well-organized, and in-depth information, which facilitates and supports literacy learning. Further, literacy objects should consider three additional criteria (Neuman & Roskos, 1990): appropriateness (item is naturally and safely used by young children), authenticity (a real item in the child's general environment), and utility (item useful to children in their imitative literacy attempts). These criteria help children to connect what is already known to new understandings. For example, props associated with mailing letters, envelopes, writing instruments, stamps, and stationery that are placed in close proximity encourage children to embellish on common literacy-related routines they observe in their community—visiting the post office, checking

out books at the library, making grocery lists. Clusters of items that might be regarded as functional to daily activity (reading a map, copying a recipe) engage children in activities that have purpose, place, and combined play related to their lives.

VARIATION AND OWNERSHIP ENHANCES ENGAGEMENT

Although studies of children's participation in planning their environment are quite rare in the United States, evidence from British nursery schools and Reggio Emilia demonstrate that children are highly capable of designing their own learning environments. Studies (Edwards, Gandini, & Forman, 1998; Proshansky & Fabian, 1987) suggest children's active participation in environmental design and participation in making decisions helps to create a feeling of identity and belongingness with school. In child-centered settings (Kantor, Miller, & Fernie, 1992) there are a variety of large and small group activities that encourage creativity and problem solving, which provide children with ample opportunities and time to think, talk, cooperate, and do. The fundamental assumption is that children's participation in creating environments that are spatially well defined and functionally complex (e.g., art, blocks and dramatic play) enhances cognitive activity and, at the same time, builds logical connections between what is learned at home and at school.

Play settings that promote great language development are more attractive to children when they represent authentic literacy contexts in the children's real-world environment and are natural adaptations of existing play areas (Neuman & Roskos, 1990, 1992). Because children seem to play best at what they know, literacy-enriched play settings should reflect real-life problem-solving situations for children. For example, children may have considerable background knowledge about grocery stores but much less experience, interest, and language about a bank. The comfort of familiar surroundings that contain known objects is important to children. Under these circumstances, children engage in more complex interactions and are eager to try new things. Familiarity within settings and objects also frees children to go beyond physically exploring them to using them as springboards for language interactions and routines.

Intervention Studies

A number of studies (Morrow, 1990; Neuman & Roskos, 1992; Vukelich, 1991, 1994) have been developed to test these design principles in early-childhood classrooms, recognizing their potential benefit for literacy learning. Given that previous surveys had indicated the paucity of literacy props and materials in most child-care settings (e.g., Dunn, Beach, & Kontos, 1994), a number of intervention studies attempted to examine the influence of enriching classrooms with literacy materials. Vukelich (1991), for example, transformed two play centers into a flower shop with sales forms and receipts and a bank with literacy materials including withdrawal slips, instructions on how to use a cash machine, and loan application forms. Morrow (1990) cre-

ated a veterinary corner, with forms and books to accompany play. Neuman and Roskos (1992) created multiple play settings in classrooms—including an office, library, and post office—transforming two typical classrooms into literacy-enriched contexts for play with accompanying related objects for each setting. (See Figures 19.1 and 19.2.)

These studies used a similar methodology. They examined the frequency of children's interactions with print before intervention and the influx of additional literacy props after intervention (see Figures 19.1 and 19.2). The results of these studies indicated several converging themes: In settings in which there were more literacy artifacts, children engaged in more literacy acts. These literacy activities tended to become more complex over time, as children began to move from exploratory play to mastery of concepts. There was also an increase in language routines as children became famil-

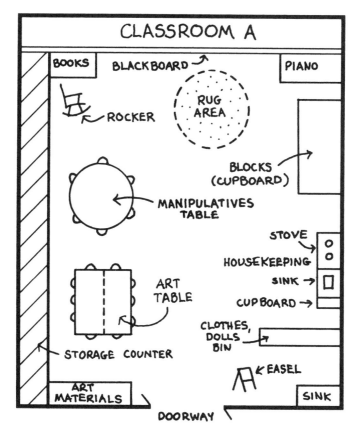

FIGURE 19.1. Design of the play environment prior to the literacy enrichment.

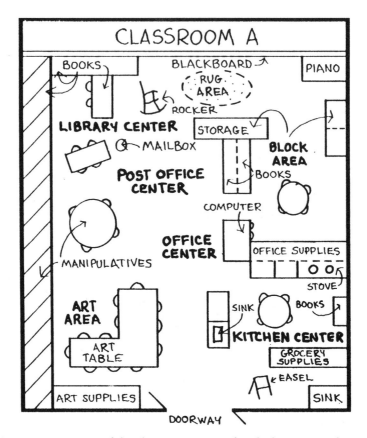

FIGURE 19.2. Design of the play environment after the literacy enrichment.

iar with language used in these settings. Enriched environments seemed to stimulate more challenging activity, with a greater repertoire of behaviors—questions, responses, and complexity of language interactions. Consequently, these studies indicated that a more deliberate approach to the selection and arrangement of materials according to specific design criteria could enhance children's uses of literacy. It also provided further evidence of the environment's influence on behavior.

**From Behavior Setting
to Activity Setting**

Behavior settings, defined as physical environments alone, however, have their limitations. Contexts in which collaborative interaction and shared understandings are formed are more than just behavior settings. Rather, contexts include environments and

participants that interact to establish goals and goal-directed activity (Rogoff, 1982). It is the interaction between context and interaction among people that creates opportunities (and unfortunately, in some cases, constraints) for learning. In varying contexts, people engage in narrative scripts—regular interactions used routinely in the course of everyday activities. In play, for example, children engage in many different scripts according to setting, pretending to order food from a fast-food restaurant by asking, "Whatya want?" followed by the response, "burger, cheese, and fries." And, according to research by Nelson (1978, 1981), children's involvement in these day-to-day scripts have a direct relation to their developing a sense of narrative and storytelling and recalling. Activity settings (Tharp & Gallimore, 1988), sometimes described as ecological niches, produce different scripts and roles to play according to the participants present, their background experiences, and their values. Consequently, activity setting acknowledges the integration of place, people, and occasion—children engage in goal-directed behavior within a setting, which has a set of assumptions and expectations.

These distinctions are important in considering environmental influences in children's early literacy development and learning. They distinguish between what children can learn on their own and what they are able to learn through assisted performance. In Vygotskian (1987) terms, activity settings emphasize that learning requires teaching, whether it is in formal or informal settings. Further, as Tharp and Gallimore (1988) suggest, it is less important who is offering the assistance or teaching to perform at higher levels of achievement than whether or not it is being offered at all. To the extent that peers, parents, and teachers can work on the edge of children's current competencies, learning will occur through that assistance.

A large corpus of research provides substantial evidence for the influence of activity settings on children's learning. In one study, for example, McGill-Franzen, Allington, Yokoi, and Brooks (1999) compared the benefits of two interventions compared to a control group. They established classroom libraries in several kindergartens by providing a large supply of high-quality, multicultural children's books, along with open-face bookshelves to display them. In several other classrooms, they provided books and training to teachers to enhance interactivity and high-level thinking skills with children. These classrooms were compared with a control group that received neither intervention. Results indicated that supplies alone were insufficient to enhance children's literacy development. However, classrooms that were restructured to include resources and quality teaching showed significant improvement over control groups. Having books in close proximity and coaching teachers to use books with children for verbal problem solving and creative thinking created an activity setting that promoted literacy development.

A study of literacy-related play and learning to recognize words in context demonstrates the effects of teaching even more specifically. In this study, Neuman and

Roskos (1992) designed a literacy-related office setting in eight Head Start classrooms. These office play settings included environmental print signs, such as the words "office, open time in, time out, sorry we're closed, EXIT, hello," and functional print objects, such as "message pads, occupant mail, catalogues, brochures, and stationery" along with a desk, post-office box, and other items such as a telephone and calculator that one might see in an office. Then, each classroom was assigned to one of three conditions. In one condition, parent volunteers were asked to actively engage in children's play in the setting. Following children's leads, they helped to define literacy objects (in the context of the play) and execute and extend their meaning when appropriate. For example, two children and a parent are in the office setting:

PARENT: Oh, look, Johanna, these are stamps. You put them on envelopes so that you can mail things.

JOHANNA: (*Puts a stamp on the envelope.*)

PARENT: That's great. But next time, you put the stamp on the front of the envelope, over here, not on the back. OK.

JOHANNA: This is the back?

PARENT: That's the front—here let me show you.

JOHANNA: (*Takes another envelope and puts the stamp on the front.*)

In the second condition, parents were asked to monitor children's activity, to observe and write anecdotal notes, but to try not to directly interact in their play. And the third condition included the office play settings without parent involvement. The results of the study provided powerful evidence for the influence of teaching as a key environmental factor in learning. In settings in which parents explicitly made reference to labels, signs, and language routines directly associated with the setting, children learned significantly more words than they did in others. The setting gave parents and children specific purposes and occasions for using literacy, creating goal-directed activity that supported literacy development. A study by Vukelich (1994) on the effects of adult mediation in redesigned play settings reported similar findings for young children's knowledge of the functions of writing.

As children begin to become familiar with language routines and specific skills, the responsibility for task performance is shifted eventually from the environment to the individual child. But in the process of transference, children need opportunities to take increasing responsibility in learning, as the assistance from the adult steadily declines. It is during this stage, from assistance provided by parents, teachers, and more capable peers, to collaboration and consultation with peers and eventual internalization that children need time to practice without such direct intervention. For example, Sulzby and Teale (1989) reported that children gain a wide understanding of the purposes and processes of reading through their pretend reenactments of storybooks that have been read to them. Similarly, Paley (1994), and Rowe (1999) found that reenactments of storybooks in contexts that supported such activity helped to instantiate mental models of stories, which led to improved understandings and flexibility of responses.

Thus, in activity settings with peers or on their own, children are likely to demonstrate increasing self-regulation. They are likely to self-instruct, self-praise, self-question—showing signs of metacognitive and strategic behavior. Until recently, it had been assumed that children younger than age 5 were incapable of such intentional behavior. Nevertheless, recent studies (Salomon, 1996) have revealed that even preschoolers show signs of being intentional at the level of demonstrating an awareness of a goal and show an understanding that something should be done to reach that goal. Neuman and Roskos (1997), for example, examined children's metacognitive activity in three literacy-enriched play settings (doctor's office, restaurant, and post office) in a preschool center over a 7-month period. Unlike the previous research, teachers and aides were requested to observe the children at play but not to mediate the activity in any substantive way. The built literacy environment supported a repertoire of literacy performances that may not appear in other contexts, such as formal literacy instruction. Observations indicated that children used a variety of strategies to monitor

their understandings of events. They would seek information and attempt to check their understandings against existing hypotheses, like in the following example:

CHILD 1: (*To everyone*) Hey, come here, the post office is open.

CHILD 2: No, its closed.

CHILD 1: It's not closed, right?

CHILD 2: Yes, because this is closed. (*Points to the "closed" sign.*)

CHILD 1: Yes, it says, "I am closed."

CHILD 2: Yeah.

CHILD 1: You read it? (*Checking*)

CHILD 2: Closed. C-L-O-S-E-D.

CHILD 1: I'll put an "open" sign up and then you read it. When it gets dark, we'll put up the "closed" one. (*Pauses, looks at the sign.*) P-O-N. Open. It says "open."

Moreover, the specific strategies used by children varied according to activity setting. For example, children tended to organize, arrange, and allocate materials in the post-office center and make transactions and use literacy as a memory device in the restaurant setting. These differences in strategy use indicated that children's responses were related to the purposes of the activity, the physical environment, materials, and the occasion, which emerged from the interplay between peers.

Activity settings, therefore, can have multiple purposes and multiple goals. They include the physical setting, which creates organizational opportunities or constraints for behavior, and the participants, who bring their cultural values, background experiences and knowledge to the situation. Unlike behavior settings, activity settings assume that the children, especially at the initial stages of learning, receive assistance from adults or more capable peers to enhance and extend what they can already do. These individuals act as social resources who provide information and feedback through demonstrations and interactions. For Vygotsky (1987), it was the contrast between assisted performance (what children can do with help) with the support of the environment and unassisted performance (the environment alone) that differentiates learning from development.

Conclusions

Research from an ecological and neo-Vygotskian perspective (Rogoff, 1982; Tharp & Gallimore, 1988) highlights the interaction between context and literacy acquisition and development. These studies (Barker, 1968; Barker & Wright, 1955) first began with a focus on behavior settings, emphasizing objective features of the environment. Studies of literacy environments (Neuman & Roskos, 1990, 1992) created design features that supported important principles for literacy practice. First, even in preschool, classrooms need to provide a widespread *presence* of print and literacy activity in the environment in ways that are accessible to children. Placing print at children's eye level (Neuman, 1999), using print in functional ways, directing children's attention to print, and extending their knowledge and uses of it in meaningful ways enhance children's use and desire to become literate. Second, print needs to be in close *proximity* (Neuman, 1999) to children's activity and daily experiences. Books need to be available to children in areas that are close to activity. It is also critically important to take into account children's culture, experience, language, and interests in provisioning settings (Neuman & Roskos, 1998), preparing literacy activities, and creating links between settings. Placing items of cultural meaning in specific areas in classrooms builds coherence, continuity, and communication between home and school. And third, the *portability* of resources among and between classroom spaces and activities to facilitate children's growing understanding of objects and concepts must be supported. Props used in multiple contexts build children's vocabulary and language usage. Specific design features include networks of literacy props around the environment and flexibility in activity formats and related extensions (e.g., materials for multimodal representations). Incorporating such design features in early-childhood classrooms increases the viability of the environment as place for literacy activity.

Still, much about what makes the best possible spaces for children's early literacy experiences remains invisible to the mind's eye. Patterns, structures, and processes that are the infrastructure of environments, as McLuhan observed, easily elude our perception. At this juncture in the study of literacy environments at school, a new synthesis among them is required if we are to more completely understand the significance of environment in early literacy development and learning. Traditionally the scientific lens has focused primarily on the physical components and objective features of the literacy environment (i.e., its structure) and less so on the patterns and processes that give it form, order, quality, and meaning. However, for a full understanding of the literacy environment as an activity system, research information about structure, although critically important, is not enough. We also need to illuminate "the web of relationships" that creates the environment's pattern of organization, because it is this pattern that becomes absorbed as literacy activity and process. Pattern, however, is embodied in structure and to "see" it calls for an integrative stance—a binocular view—that searches for networks of relationships that give shape and form to an environment. A search for "networks of relationships" sets a new course for literacy researchers in at least two directions.

In the direction of basic and applied research, we need to know more about the design of place–object–action configurations that are authentic and productive in terms of literacy development. At issue is creating environmental networks of literacy information that scaffold young children's thinking and language all along the developmental continuum. In the early years, such networks may need to be especially physical and flexible in their composition, as Rowe's (1999) observations of 2–3-year-olds' book-related play suggests, allowing for ample gesturing, movement, inventing, and active physical manipulation of literacy ideas and skills in the company of toys and others (also see Fein, 1995). Physical opportunity, in fact, may be the signature architecture of the very early literacy environment in terms of both structure and pedagogical process. For preschoolers, busily exploring and testing language, scripts, and roles, pretend play may serve as an important proximal environment of developmental change that helps children move literacy ideas and interactions from hand to mind. Converging streams of literacy-oriented play research point to play transformations and negotiations as pivots that turn physically situated understandings toward new cognitive levels (e.g., narrative, Branscombe & Taylor, 2000; emergent writing, Pellegrini, Galda, Dresden, & Cox, 1991; oral language, McCune, 1995). For primary-grade children faced with the challenge of mastering reading and writing as tools for academic learning, sufficient opportunities to manipulate literacy as an object of knowledge may distinguish the most effective literacy environment. Children in classrooms in which they are required to talk, read, and write a lot experience variety and challenge in consistent instruction and are expected to be successful readers and writers who outperform their peers in classrooms in which these environmental features are less prevalent (Allington & Cunningham, 1996; Newman and Associates, 1996; Postlethwaite & Ross, 1992).

Lacking, however, is a developmental grasp of the design of literacy environments for young children in educational settings that is integrative and research based. Although often described, much information remains piecemeal and fragmented about the organization and maintenance of literacy environments that are growth producing for young children in preschool and school. Too often the creation of literacy-rich settings for play and inquiry follows the tradition of "adding things to" the space, in this case literacy props and tools, and examining the influence of these things. The literacy environment, however, cannot be fully understood by the scrutiny of its parts. More effort needs to be directed to describing and explaining the relationships between environmental elements (physical and social) and how these combine to support or constrain children's literacy development in the school context. Such an analysis needs to go beyond structural features to environments as complex relational systems that both shape and respond to children's emerging and evolving understandings of literacy and its practices.

In the direction of everyday practice, we need to better articulate and explain the concept of the literacy environment as a "pattern of relations" for teachers and their professional work. Much emphasis of late has been placed on creating the "print-rich environment" and "flooding" classrooms with books and print. Yet this advice, although sound, does little to enlarge teachers' conceptualizations of what the environment includes. An essential understanding for teachers is how to *design the organization of activity* to create patterns that steadily enliven and invigorate children's literacy learning in the classroom. Such understanding entails a more deeply intellectual design process than traditionally applied in preparing the classroom environment for literacy instruction and experience (e.g., arranging space).

In closing, the progress of environmental research makes more visible the invisible patterns that also define the literacy environment beyond the material resources we can see and provide. It enlarges our appreciation of the tremendous power the literacy environment holds over young children's literacy development and achievement. And it stimulates further research in the design and implementation of high-quality literacy environments that support young writers and readers.

References

Allington, R., & Cunningham, R. (1996). *Schools that work: Where all children read and write.* New York: Harper Collins.

Barker, R. (1968). *Ecological psychology: Concepts and methods for studying the environment of human behavior.* Stanford, CA: Stanford University Press.

Barker, R., & Wright, H. (1955). *Midwest and its children.* New York: Harper & Row.

Branscombe, N. A., & Taylor, J. (2000). "It would be good as Snow White,": Play and prosody. In K. Roskos & J. Christie (Eds.), *Play and literacy in early childhood: Research from multiple perspectives* (pp. 169–188). Mahwah, NJ: Erlbaum.

Dunn, L., Beach, S. A., & Kontos, S. (1994). Quality of the literacy environment in day care and children's development. *Journal of Research in Childhood Education, 9*(1), 24–34.

Edwards, C., Gandini, L., & Forman, G. (1998). *The hundred languages of children* (2nd ed.). Greenwich, CT: Ablex.

Fein, G. (1995). Toys and stories. In A. D. Pellegrini (Ed.), *The future of play theory* (pp. 151–164). Albany, NY: SUNY Press.

Gibson, J. J. (1979). *The ecological approach to visual perception.* Boston: Houghton Mifflin.

Gump, P. (1978). School environments. In I. Altman & J. Wohlwill (Eds.), *Children and the environment* (pp. 131–169). New York: Plenum.

Hall, N. (1987). The literate home corner. In P. Smith (Ed.), *Parents and teachers together* (pp. 134–144). London: Macmillan.

Jacob, E. (1984). Learning literacy through play: Puerto Rican kindergarten children. In H. Goelman, A. Oberg, & F. Smith (Eds.), *Awakening to literacy* (pp. 73–86). Portsmouth, NH: Heinemann.

Kantor, R., Miller, S., & Fernie, D. (1992). Diverse paths to literacy in a preschool classroom: A sociocultural perspective. *Reading Research Quarterly, 27*(3), 184–201.

McCall, R. (1974). Exploratory manipulation and play in the human infant. *Monographs of the Society for Research in Child Development, 39*(2, Serial No. 155).

McCune, L. (1995). A normative study of representational play at the transition to language. *Developmental Psychology, 31*(2), 198–201.

McGill-Franzen, A., Allington, R., Yokoi, L., & Brooks, G. (1999). Putting books in the room seems necessary but not sufficient. *Journal of Educational Research, 93*, 67–74.

McLuhan, M. (1954). *Understanding media.* New York: Signet Books.

Morrow, L. M. (1990). Preparing the classroom environment to promote literacy during play. *Early Childhood Research Quarterly, 5*, 537–554.

Morrow, L. M., & Weinstein, C. S. (1986). Encouraging voluntary reading: The impact of literature programs on children's use of library corners. *Reading Research Quarterly, 21*, 330–346.

Nelson, K. (1978). How children represent knowledge of their world in and out of language: A preliminary report. In R. S. Siegler (Ed.), *Children's thinking, What develops?* (pp. 255–273). Hillsdale, NJ: Erlbaum.

Nelson, K. (1981). Social cognition in script framework. In J. Flavell & L. Ross (Eds.), *Social cognitive development: Frontiers and possible futures.* (pp. 97–118). New York: Cambridge University Press.

Neuman, S. B. (1999). Books make a difference: A study of access to literacy. *Reading Research Quarterly, 34*, 286–312.

Neuman, S. B., & Roskos, K. (1989). Preschoolers' conceptions of literacy as reflected in their spontaneous play. In S. McCormick & J. Zutell (Eds.), *Cognitive and social perspectives for literacy research and instruction* (pp. 87–94). Chicago: National Reading Conference.

Neuman, S. B., & Roskos, K. (1990). The influence of literacy-enriched play settings on preschoolers' engagement with written language. In J. Zutell & S. McCormick (Eds.), *Literacy theory and research: analyses from multiple perspectives* (pp. 179–187). Chicago: National Reading Conference.

Neuman, S. B., & Roskos, K. (1992). Literacy objects as cultural tools: Effects on children's literacy behaviors in play. *Reading Research Quarterly, 27*, 202–225.

Neuman, S. B., & Roskos, K. (1997). Literacy knowledge in practice: Contexts of participation for young writers and readers. *Reading Research Quarterly, 32*, 10–33.

Neuman, S. B., & Roskos, K. (1998). (Eds.). *Children achieving: Best practices in early literacy.* Newark, DE: International Reading Association.

Neuman, F. & Associates (1996). *Authentic achievement: Restructuring Schools for Intellectual Quality.* San Francisco, CA: Jossey-Bass.

Paley, V. (1994). *The boy who would be helicopter.* Cambridge MA: Harvard University Press.

Pellegrini, A. D., Galda, L., Dresden, J., & Cox, S. (1991). A longitudinal study of the predictive relations among symbolic play, linguistic verbs, and early literacy. *Research in the Teaching of English, 25*, 215–235.

Phyfe-Perkins, E. (1980). Children behaviors in preschool settings—A review of research concerning the influence of the physical environment. In L. Katz (Ed.), *Current topics in early childhood education* (pp. 91–123). Norwood, NJ: Ablex.

Postelthwaite, J. N., & Ross, K. N. (1992). *Effective schools in reading: Implications for educational planners.* The Hague: International Association for the Evaluation of Educational Achievement.

Proshansky, H. M., & Fabian, A. K. (1987). The development of place identity in the child. In C. S. Weinstein & T. G. David (Eds.), *Spaces for children: The built environment and child development* (pp. 21–40). New York: Plenum Press

Rogoff, B. (1982). Integrating context and cognitive development. In M. E. Lamb & A. L. Brown (Eds.), *Advances in developmental psychology* (pp. 125–169). New York: Erlbaum.

Rosenthal, B. A. (1974). An ecological study of free play in the nursery school. (Doctoral dissertation, Wayne State University). *Dissertation Abstracts International, 34*(7-A), 4004–4005.

Roskos, K. (1987). *The nature of children's literate behavior in pretend play episodes.* Unpublished doctoral dissertation, Kent State University, Kent, OH.

Rowe, D. W. (1999). The literate potentials of book-related dramatic play. *Reading Research Quarterly, 33*, 10–35.

Rubin, K. H. (1977). Play behaviors of young children. *Young Children, 32*(6), 16–24.

Rubin, K. H., & Seibel, G. (1979). *The effects of ecological setting on the cognitive and social play behaviors of preschoolers.* Paper presented at the annual meeting of the American Educational Research Association, San Francisco. (ERIC Document Reproduction Service No. ED 168 691)

Salomon, G. (1996). Studying novel learning environments as patterns of change. In S. Vosniadou, E. DeCorte, R. Glaser, & H. Mandl (Eds.), *International perspectives on the design of technology-supported learning environments* (pp. 363–378). Mahwah, NJ: Erlbaum.

Smith, P. K., & Connolly, K. J. (1977). Social and aggressive behaviour in preschool children as a factor of crowing. *Social Science Information, 16*(5), 601–620.

Sulzby, E., & Teale, W. (1989). Emergent literacy:

New perspectives. In D. Strickland & L. Morrow, *Emergent literacy* (pp. 1–15). Newark, DE: International Reading Association.

Tharp, R., & Gallimore, R. (1988). *Rousing minds to life-teaching, learning, and schooling in social context*. Port Chester, NY: Cambridge University Press.

Vukelich, C. (1991). Materials and modeling: promoting literacy during play. In J. F. Christie (Ed.), *Play and early literacy development* (pp. 215–231). Albany, NY: SUNY Press.

Vukelich, C. (1994). Effects of play intervention on children's reading of environmental print. *Early Childhood Research Quarterly, 9,* 153–170.

Vygotsky, L. (1987). *Collected works of L. S. Vygotsky: Vol. 1: Problems of general psychology.* Albany, NY: SUNY Press.

Weinstein, C. S. (1977). Modifying student behavior in an open classroom through changes in the physical design. *American Educational Research Journal, 14*(3), 249–262.

Weinstein, C. S., & David, T. G. (1987). *Spaces for children: The built environment and child development.* New York: Plenum.

V
INSTRUCTIONAL MATERIALS
AND CLASSROOM PRACTICES

❖

20

Emergent Literacy Skills, Early Instruction, and Individual Differences as Determinants of Difficulties in Learning to Read: The Case for Early Intervention

❖

FRANK R. VELLUTINO
DONNA M. SCANLON

Functional literacy is an achievement that eludes a significant proportion of children from all social strata, even those in our most affluent and successful schools. It has been well established that the highest proportion of children who have difficulty attaining functional literacy comes from disadvantaged populations being educated in inner-city and rural schools that have limited resources to allocate to education (Knapp, Shields, & Turnbull, 1992). Yet, it is also true that a shocking number of children from more advantaged populations being educated in suburban schools that have more adequate resources for education also have difficulty attaining functional literacy. Such children are generally assumed to be impaired by what has been called specific reading disability (often called dyslexia), in accord with the widespread belief that poor readers who come from at least middle-class backgrounds more than likely suffer from some type of neurodevelopmental disorder which has undermined their ability to learn to read, even if they are intellectually capable.

Specific reading disability has been conventionally defined as extraordinary difficulty in learning to identify printed letters and words in children who have average or better than average intelligence and who are not generally impaired academically. It is typically diagnosed using measures of intelligence, reading achievement, and reading-related cognitive abilities, along with measures designed to rule out alternative causes of reading difficulties such as uncorrected sensory deficits, emotional disorder, frequent absences from school, and/or socioeconomic disadvantage. However, in most school districts, the central defining criterion for classifying children of this description as "reading disabled" is the IQ–achievement discrepancy, or, more specifically, a statistically significant discrepancy between the score a child obtains on a standardized measure of intelligence and the score obtained on a standardized measure of reading achievement.

Current estimates suggest that the incidence of specific reading disability ranges anywhere from 10% to 20% of the population of school children (Harris & Sipay, 1990; Shaywitz, Escobar, Shaywitz, Fletcher, & Makuch, 1992), and as high as 30% in less formal inventories taken in local school districts. However, research we have conducted over the years evaluating factors contributing to early reading difficulties, along with our own clinical experience, suggested to us that these estimates are greatly inflated, and that most reading difficulties are caused by limitations in the child's early literacy experiences and/or less than adequate literacy instruction. This intuition was reinforced by a penetrating article written by Marie Clay (1987) questioning the psychological reality of specific reading disability as a distinct clinical entity.

In her article, Clay argued that studies evaluating the etiology of reading disability typically produce results that are inconclusive, given that they tend not to incorporate procedures which control for or evaluate the child's preliteracy experiences and educational history. She also stressed the need for caution in interpreting any given cognitive deficit as a significant cause of reading difficulties, given that such difficulties can, themselves, cause deficiencies in reading-related cognitive abilities such as phoneme awareness, vocabulary knowledge, and verbal memory. She pointed out further that deficiencies in one or more of these abilities are all too often misinterpreted as manifestations of specific reading disability, and that the probability of making this error in judgement would be especially high in the case of children suffering from long-standing reading difficulties (see Stanovich, 1986; Vellutino, Scanlon, & Spearing, 1995; Vellutino, Scanlon, & Tanzman, 1988, for confirming evidence). Finally, Clay stressed the need for longitudinal studies incorporating an intervention component as a potentially useful means for developing criteria and procedures that would assist educators in distinguishing between experiential/instructional and cognitive deficits as primary causes of reading difficulties.

Because our own experiences were quite in keeping with the concerns expressed in Clay's (1987) article, we were able to resonate to these concerns and felt that they were amply justified by early-intervention studies demonstrating that most impaired readers can achieve at least an average level of skill in reading if they receive early, intensive, and individualized remediation, specifically daily one-to-one tutoring (Clay, 1985; Iversen & Tunmer, 1993; Pinnell, 1989; Wasik & Slavin, 1993). At the same time, our own research, along with research conducted by other investigators, gave us reason to believe that some impaired readers may well be encumbered by basic cognitive deficits which make it difficult for them to learn to read. The evidence suggests that such deficits tend to be in the language domains, especially the phonological domain, and have their greatest impact on the child's ability to master the alphabetic code (Vellutino, 1979, 1987; see Vellutino et al., 1996, for a more recent review). Yet, difficulty in mastering the alphabetic code could also be a consequence of reading instruction that does not adequately attune the child to the alphabetic properties of written English, and it is difficult to be certain, in any given case, whether this or any other reading difficulty is caused by basic cognitive deficits or by experiential/instructional deficits. Thus, in line with Clay's (1987) suggested approach for distinguishing between these sources of reading difficulties, we designed a longitudinal study that incorporated both a classroom observation component and a first-grade intervention component which, together, allowed us to evaluate the contribution of emergent literacy skills, early literacy instruction, and individual differences in reading-related cognitive abilities as determinants of early reading achievement (Vellutino et al., 1996).

The general design of the study involved (1) evaluation of all entering kindergartners in participating schools ($N = 1407$) on a battery of measures used to assess both emergent literacy skills and cognitive abilities which had been hypothesized to be related to early reading achievement (Adams, 1990; Vellutino & Scanlon, 1987); (2) periodic observation of language arts instruction in kindergarten classrooms; (3) identification, in mid-first grade, of children having substantial difficulty learning to read along with a comparison group of normally developing readers; (4) provision of daily one-to-one tutoring in reading for a randomly selected subgroup of identified poor readers for purposes of comparison with a randomly selected subgroup of identified poor readers who received remedial reading provided by their home schools; (5) evaluation of reading achievement in all available participants toward the end of first grade; (6) evaluation of the cognitive profiles of the children in the poor and normal reader groups in first and third grades; and (7) periodic evaluation of reading achievement in the children in the poor and normal reader groups through the end of fourth grade.

Of primary interest in this study were the poor readers who received the daily one-to-one tutoring in reading. We anticipated that the reading achievement of children in this group, when compared with the reading achievement of children in the poor reader group that received the remediation provided by their home school, would allow us to evaluate the twofold assumption that (1) beginning reading difficulties in most impaired readers are caused by limitations in early reading experience and/or limitations in early reading instruction, and (2) beginning reading difficulties in (tutored) children who are found to be difficult to remediate would be more likely associated with basic cognitive deficits than would beginning reading difficulties in (tutored) children who are found to be readily remediated. Thus, of special interest were the cognitive profiles of the children in both the difficult to remediate and readily remediated groups, relative to the normally developing readers, in addition to the kindergarten entry-level literacy skills and the kindergarten instruction to which these children were exposed. We expected that the cognitive profiles of children who were found to be readily remediated would be more like those of the normal readers than would the cognitive profiles of children who were found to be difficult to remediate, and that most of the children identified as impaired readers in first grade would be found to be deficient in entry-level (kindergarten) literacy skills such as knowledge of letter names and phoneme awareness when compared with normally developing readers.

We also expected that the type of literacy instruction children received in kindergarten would be significantly correlated with their reading achievement in first grade. In previous longitudinal studies targeting emergent readers, it was found that children who had been exposed to phoneme-awareness training and other code-based activities subsequently performed better on measures of reading achievement than children who had not been exposed to such activities (e.g., Blachman, 1994; Bradley & Bryant, 1983; Foorman, Francis, Novy, & Liberman, 1991; Lundberg, Frost, & Petersen, 1988; Vellutino, 1991). Moreover, our own informal observations of kindergarten and other elementary school classroms suggested that teachers who spend a considerable portion of their daily lesson on language arts instruction and expose children to a full range of literacy and language-enrichment activities that include code-based as well as meaningful text-based components tend to produce more engaged and generally better emergent readers than do teachers whose language arts instruction tends to be more narrowly focused and/or constitutes a relatively small portion of their daily lesson. Thus, our kindergarten observation program was designed to estimate the percentage of each daily lesson that kindergarten teachers in participating schools devoted to language arts instruction, and within the language arts period of each daily lesson, the percentage of time devoted to various activities believed to be important for literacy development (phoneme analysis, letter identification, letter–sound learning, sight word learning, shared reading, writing, etc.).

Finally, the design of the study also allowed us to further evaluate the predictive value of kindergarten entry-level skills and abilities as precursors of success in beginning reading. On the basis of previous research conducted in our laboratory (Vellutino & Scanlon, 1987) and elsewhere (Adams, 1990), we anticipated that the strongest predictors of achievement in first-grade reading would be phonologically based skills such as letter naming, phoneme segmentation, name retrieval, and verbal memory.

A Brief Summary of the Prediction Component of the Study

A consistent finding in previous longitudinal studies is that measures of language and language-based skills administered to kindergarten children or preschoolers were among the best predictors of reading achievement in later grades (Badian, 1982; Butler, Marsh, Sheppard, & Sheppard, 1985; Catts, 1991; de Hirsch, Jansky, & Langford, 1966; Jansky & de Hirsch, 1972; Satz, Taylor, Friel, & Fletcher, 1978). However, in contrast to the present study, the children included in those studies came largely from deprived economic backgrounds and/or from families which did not use English as the primary language. Moreover, important language and language-based skills such as phonological awareness and verbal memory were not assessed in these studies. It therefore seemed important to conduct a kindergarten prediction study with the population of children evaluated in the present investigation using a test battery that was more comprehensive than any used in previous studies (Scanlon & Vellutino, 1997).

To be sure of obtaining a large enough sample to realize the various objectives of our study, two cohorts of kindergartners (N = 700 per cohort) were assessed in two consecutive years. The children were selected from 17 schools located in middle- to upper-middle-class neighborhoods in the Albany, New York, area. To evaluate entry-level skills and abilities, the children in each cohort were administered a large battery of tests evaluating rudimentary literacy skills, cognitive development, language and language-based skills, visual abilities, verbal memory, and attentional and organizational abilities (see Figure 20.1). For both cohorts, testing commenced at the beginning of the kindergarten year and was completed by late fall. In November of their first-grade year, the reading ability of all the children who participated in the study as kindergartners was rated by their first grade classroom teachers using a 5-point scale, with a rating of 1 indicating that the child was experiencing extreme difficulty with reading and a 5 indicating that the child was progressing well. The children's reading achievement was also evaluated using the Word Identification and Word Attack subtests of the Woodcock Reading Mastery Test—Revised (WRMT-R; Woodcock, 1987) during the spring of their first-grade year.

Table 20.1 presents correlations between each of the kindergarten measures and the three measures of first-grade reading

achievement: teacher ratings and the WRMT-R Word Identification and Word Attack subtests. It can be seen that the measures evaluating rudimentary reading and math skills produced the largest correlations with the first-grade reading measures, the largest being those involving letter and number identification. However, it is also evident that several of the other measures were found to be moderately correlated with the first-grade reading measures, and among these, the correlations involving the language-based measures tend to be higher than those involving the nonverbal measures. Thus, to obtain more precise estimates of the relative effectiveness with which the different types of kindergarten skills and abilities predicted first-grade reading achievement, stepwise regression analyses were conducted using the measures in each of the areas assessed as predictors and the WRMT-R Word Identification subtest as the dependent measure. Similar analyses were conducted using the other measures of reading achievement as the dependent measure, but because all three analyses produced essentially the same results, we focus only on the analysis involving the Word Identification subtest. Table 20.2 presents results from these analyses. Within a given set, only those measures that accounted for unique variance are included in the table.

First, note that the prereading and rudimentary reading measures were the best predictors of skill in first-grade word identification (in terms of explained variance) whereas the rudimentary math measures were the second best predictors. Note also that the Letter Identification subtest was the single best predictor among the rudimentary reading measures and the Number Identification subtest was the single best predictor among the math measures. Moreover, they accounted for comparable amounts of variance on the first-grade Word Identification test. When we consider that both tests evaluate the child's ability to discriminate and learn the names of graphic symbols, and that both, quite likely, reflect the influence of home environments which facilitate academic readiness, this pattern of results becomes coherent. More important is the fact that both of these tests directly or indirectly evaluate cognitive abilities that are prereq-

KINDERGARTEN BATTERY

A. **Conceptual Development** (estimated)—Wechsler Preschool and Primary Scale of Intelligence—Revised (WPPSI-R) and Concrete Operations.

  1. Information subtest: asks child questions evaluating general knowledge.

  2. Block Design subtest: requires that the child assemble blocks to reproduce abstract geometric designs under time constraints; evaluates visual–spatial analysis and reasoning ability.

  3. Concrete Operations: measures of conservation, seriation, and class inclusion were administered to determine whether the child had attained the concrete operational stage of conceptual development (Piaget, 1952).

B. **Concepts of Print**

  1. Print Awareness: assesses understanding of the communication value of print. For example, the child is asked to indicate which would be the best way to find out what is in a can: read the label or open the can.

  2. Print Conventions: assesses understanding of left/right sequencing of words, the concept of word and letter, etc.

C. **Achievement Measures**

  1. Rudimentary Reading Skills: measured by subtests of the Woodcock Reading Mastery Test—Revised (WRMT-R):
     a. Letter Identification.
     b. Word Identification (naming whole words on sight).
     c. Word Attack (pronouncing nonsense words).

  2. Arithmetic:
     a. WPPSI-R Arithmetic subtest: evaluates ability to solve "story problems" presented auditorily.
     b. Experimental test evaluating basic number concepts and simple arithmetic operations. Subtests included:
        (1) Counting by 1's.
        (2) Counting by 2's.
        (3) Number Identification (identifying numbers on sight).

D. **Language Measures**

  1. Phoneme Segmentation
     a. Initial Deletion: say the word that remains after deleting the initial sound of a word (e.g., cup–up).
     b. Final Deletion: say the word that remains after deleting the final sound of a word (e.g., plate–play).
     c. Articulation: vocalize the different sounds in minimally contrasted word pairs (/f/ and /c/ for fat and cat).

  2. Syntactic/Grammatical Processing. The Linguistic Concepts subtest of the Clinical Evaluation of Language Fundamentals—Revised: children hear sentences directing them to perform certain operations in order ("Point to the red line after you point to the blue one.").

  3. Semantic Development. Peabody Picture Vocabulary Test—Revised: evaluates recognition of vocabulary words depicted pictorially.

  4. Naming and Fluency:
     a. Rapid Automatized Naming: requires child to name simple objects presented in a 5 × 10 array as quickly as possible. Score reported is total amount of time taken (in seconds) to complete the array.
     b. Rapid Articulation: requires child to repeat word pairs as quickly as possible. Score reported is mean time (in seconds) to complete seven repetitions.

  5. Verbal Memory and Visual–Verbal Learning:
     a. Sentence Memory: child hears sentences and must repeat each verbatim.
     b. Word Memory: child hears strings of randomly ordered words and must repeat each verbatim.
     c. Visual–Auditory Learning subtest from the WRMT-R: child learns to associate novel symbols with words and learns to "read" sentences made up of these symbols.

E. **Visual Skills**

  1. Visual–Spatial Reasoning: The Block Design subtest from the WPPSI-R evaluates analysis and synthesis of spatial relations, visual–spatial reasoning, visual–motor coordination, etc. Child assembles blocks to reproduce geometric designs

  2. Visual Memory: child is asked to reproduce dot patterns from memory on a magnetic drawing board. Patterns are either labelable (e.g., dots form a "T") or nonlabelable (randomly arrayed).

F. **Executive Functions** (Attention, Concentration, Planning and Vigilance)

  1. Visual matching (Matching Familiar Figures Test—Modified): the child is asked to find the identical match for a line drawing in a group of four similar drawings.

  2. Visual Search (Target Search Test): the child is asked to look at a large group of geometric designs and put a line through all those that are identical to a target design.

FIGURE 20.1. Kindergarten and First-Grade Battery Administered to Target Children in First-Grade Intervention Study.

(continued)

FIRST-GRADE BATTERY

A. **Intellectual Ability:** The full Wechsler Intelligence Scale for Children—Revised (WISC-R) was administered to all target subjects.

B. **Achievement Measures:**

1. First-Grade Selection Measures:
   a. WRMT-R Word Identification: evaluates whole word naming.
   b. WRMT-R Word Attack: evaluates ability to decode nonsense syllables.

2. First-Grade Outcome Measures:
   a. WRMT-R Word Identification: see above.
   b. WRMT-R Word Attack: see above.
   c. Text reading: evaluates oral reading accuracy using narrative text presented in short paragraphs.

3. Math Achievement (Woodcock–Johnson Tests of Achievement):
   a. Calculation: assesses ability to perform written math calculations such as addition and subtraction.
   b. Applied Problems: assesses the ability to solve math "story problems."

C. **Language Measures**

1. Phonological Processing:
   a. Phonemic Segmentation: initial phoneme deletion, final phoneme deletion, phoneme articulation (see kindergarten measures for descriptions).
   b. Phonological Memory: memory for six nonsense syllables assessed over eight presentation/recall trials.

2. Syntactic/Grammatical Processing:
   a. Token Test (subtests IV and V): evaluates the ability to comprehend spoken directions.
   b. Test of Language Development—Primary:2 (TOLD-P:2) Grammatic Understanding subtest: evaluates sentence comprehension.
   c. Grammaticality Judgment: the child hears sentences, some of which contain grammatical errors; the child's task is to indicate whether sentences are grammatically well formed.
   d. Oral Cloze: the child listens to paragraphs containing sentences from which given words are deleted; as each sentence is presented, the child is asked to fill in missing words using sentence contexts and story themes to aid in doing so.

3. Semantic Processing:
   a. Vocabulary subtest of the WISC-R: the child is asked to define spoken words.
   b. Similarities subtest of the WISC-R: the child is asked to detect and characterize commonalities in verbally presented concepts.

4. Naming and Fluency:
   a. Rapid Naming of Letters, Numbers, Colors and Objects arrayed in a 5×10 matrix (see kindergarten battery for description).
   b. Boston Naming Test: evaluates the ability to retrieve the names of objects presented pictorially.

5. General Language Processing—Listening Comprehension component of the Spache Diagnostic Reading Scales: evaluates ability to answer main idea and factual questions about narrative text presented auditorily.

6. Verbal Memory:
   a. Digit Span subtest of the WISC-R: evaluates verbatim recall of randomly presented digits.
   b. Sentence Imitation subtest from the TOLD-P:2: evaluates verbatim recall of sentences.
   c. Memory for Words: evaluates recall of concrete and abstract words under immediate and delayed recall conditions.
   d. Syntactic Word Order: child hears sentences presented in scrambled order and must repeat each sentence in correct order.
   e. Phonological Memory: see kindergarten battery.

D. **Visual Processing Skills**

1. Performance Scale of the WISC-R: measures a variety of visual processing abilities (visual recognition, visual coding, visual–spatial analysis and synthesis, visual–spatial reasoning, visual–motor coordination, etc.).

2. Visual Memory: child reproduces a pattern of dots from memory. (see kindergarten battery for task description).

FIGURE 20.1. cont.

TABLE 20.1. Correlations between Kindergarten Measures and First-Grade Reading Measures and Correlations among First-Grade Outcome Measures

	Teacher rating	Word Identification	Word Attack
Kindergarten measures			
Age	.09	.02	−.01
Gender (0 = male, 1 = female)	.17	.13	.03
Prereading and rudimentary reading measures			
Letter Identification	.61	.59	.44
Word Identification	.38	.46	.42
Print Awareness	.25	.27	.20
Print Conventions	.24	.26	.17
Rudimentary math measures			
WPPSI-R Arithmetic	.44	.41	.39
Counting by 1's	.44	.41	.33
Counting by 2's	.27	.28	.26
Number Identification	.56	.56	.47
Addition	.34	.34	.32
Linguistic measures			
Phoneme Segmentation	.36	.42	.43
Rapid Naming (Time)	−.29	−.32	−.28
Rapid Naming (Error)	−.18	−.18	−.21
Rapid Articulation (Time)	−.14	−.16	−.15
Linguistic Concepts	.32	.30	.28
Peabody Picture Vocabulary	.31	.28	.25
Memory and new learning measures			
Sentence Memory	.31	.34	.31
Word Memory	.32	.33	.34
Visual Memory	.22	.23	.17
Visual–Auditory Learning	.38	.39	.31
Conceptual development			
WPPSI-R Information	.35	.38	.32
WPPSI-R Block Design	.31	.26	.24
Concrete Operations	.33	.31	.27
Executive function measures			
Matching Familiar Figures—Time	.13	.13	.09
Matching Familiar Figures—Error	−.26	−.26	−.21
Target Search Test—Time	−.15	−.16	−.06
Target Search Test—Correct	.14	.10	.07
First-grade outcome measures			
Teacher rating		.73	.59
Word Identification			.81

uisites to success in learning to read, most notably visual discrimination, phonological coding, name encoding and retrieval, and visual–verbal association learning.

Second, both the lingistic measures and the memory and new learning measures were found to be reasonably good predic-tors of performance on the first-grade Word Identification test, and among these mea-sures, it was the tests that depend heavily on phonological coding that were the best predictors, especially the tests evaluating phoneme segmentation and visual–verbal learning ability. The tests evaluating concep-

TABLE 20.2. Stepwise Regression Analyses for Predicting End of First Grade Word Identification Performance Based on Various Measures Administered at the Beginning of Kindergarten

Kindergarten measures	R^2	R^2 change	Significance levels
Prereading and rudimentary reading measures			
Letter Identification	.354	.354	.000
Word Identification	.410	.056	.000
Print Awareness	.416	.006	.003
Rudimentary math measures			
Number Identification	.314	.314	.000
WPPSI-R Arithmetic	.335	.021	.000
Addition	.341	.006	.002
Linguistic measures			
Phoneme Segmentation	.175	.175	.000
Rapid Naming (Time)	.235	.060	.000
Linguistic Concepts	.261	.026	.000
Peabody Picture Vocabulary	.267	.006	.005
Memory and new learning measures			
Visual–Auditory Learning	.149	.149	.000
Word Memory	.209	.060	.000
Sentence Memory	.235	.027	.000
Visual Memory	.246	.011	.000
Conceptual development			
WPPSI-R Information	.142	.142	.000
Concrete Operations	.164	.022	.000
WPPSI-R Block Design	.171	.007	.005
Executive function measures			
Matching Familiar Figures—Error	.069	.069	.000
Target Search Test—Time	.088	.019	.000
Target Search Test—Correct	.096	.008	.003
Matching Familiar Figures—Time	.100	.004	.038
All measures(which increase R^2 by .001 or more)			
Letter Identification	.354	.354	.000
Number Identification	.400	.047	.000
Phoneme Segmentation	.426	.026	.000

Note. Results reported in this table are based on between 950 and 1,000 children and with samples this large, even small amounts of variance tend to be statistically significant. Thus, contrasts between given measures in terms of explained variance will be more informative than examination of significance levels.

tual development accounted for lesser amounts of unique variance on first-grade word identification, and the tests evaluating executive functions accounted for even less unique variance.

Finally, a stepwise regression analysis that included all the kindergarten variables was conducted and the entire battery accounted for approximately 43% of the variance on the Word Identification test. And, as might be expected, most of the total variance was attributed to the measures of reading-readiness skills, particularly Letter Identification and Number Identification subtests. In fact, the other measures included in the test battery accounted for little additional variance once these measures were entered into the equation, although the test of phoneme segmentation accounted for a small but significant amount of unique variance.

In sum, in accord with results obtained in

previous prediction studies (e.g., Adams, 1990; Vellutino & Scanlon, 1987), kindergarten readiness skills such as letter identification, number identification, and phoneme segmentation were found to be the best predictors of first-grade reading achievement. However, of the measures evaluating cognitive abilities believed to underlie reading ability, it was the language and language-based measures that were the best predictors of first-grade reading achievement, in contrast to measures evaluating conceptual development or nonverbal abilities such as visual memory, attention, and concentration.

A Brief Summary of the Classroom Observation Component of the Study

As we indicated earlier, the purpose of the kindergarten observation component of our study was to document the type of literacy instruction to which kindergarten children in participating schools were exposed, in the interest of addressing whether or not variation in such instruction would be significantly related to reading achievement in first grade. Accordingly, we conducted naturalistic observations in the kindergarten classrooms of the 17 schools that participated in the study (Scanlon & Vellutino, 1996). Most of the kindergartens had half-day sessions, but four schools had full-day sessions. A total of 43 teachers provided kindergarten instruction for the 1,400 kindergartners involved in the study, and we conducted systematic observations in each of their classrooms. Research assistants visited each classroom five or six times during the course of the school year and remained in the classroom for the entire kindergarten session on each visit. Instruction provided by the teachers rather than the children's responses and behaviors was the focus of each observation, and the activities of each teacher were systematically coded using a time-sampling procedure. A computer program designed specifically for the study was used to assist in conducting the observations. Using laptop computers, the research assistants were prompted to observe the teacher's activities for 20-second periods and then to respond to a series of six questions:

1. Who is the teacher interacting with (individual child, small group, whole class, etc.)?
2. What is the general focus of the activity (direct reading, indirect reading, writing, language development, management, etc.)?[1]
3. What is the teacher's purpose in the interaction (modeling, answering or asking questions, providing feedback, etc.)?
4. What type of material is in use? (trade book, student journals, pictures, workbooks, etc.)?
5. What is the specific focus of the activity (listening to and discussing a story, working on letter names or letter sounds, phoneme-awareness activities, sight word identification, etc.)?
6. What is the expected response from the children (listening, answering questions, shared reading, writing, etc.)?

The amount of time for the typical kindergarten session was approximately 2 hours and 15 minutes. However, because no observations were conducted during special classes (art, music, physical education, etc.), the total amount of time for the typical observation session was approximately 1 hour and 45 minutes. The percentage of time spent on each of the activities was computed for each teacher, collapsing over the five or six observations. For questions 1 and 2, percentages for total time spent on given activities were based on the entire kindergarten session. For questions 3 through 6, percentages were based on the total amount of time devoted to language arts instruction.

Table 20.3 presents means, standard deviations, and ranges for the amount of time, in percentages, allocated by the kindergarten teachers to the various activities encompassed by the six questions included in our observation schedule. It can be seen that there is a great deal of variability in the time devoted by teachers to the various activities within each category. Especially striking is the fact that of all the possible activities included in the typical kindergarten session, almost half the time was spent in classroom management activities. Given that all but a few kindergartens involved in the study had half-day sessions, this finding indicates that only about 1 hour per day was devoted to direct instruction.

TABLE 20.3. Percentage of Time Allocated to Various Activities during Observations in Each Kindergarten Classroom

	M	SD	Range
Question 1: Instructional group[a]			
Whole class	45.9	8.6	13–60
Small group	13.1	5.8	5–31
Individual	31.2	7.1	21–57
Other adult	4.1	2.6	1–12
No contact	5.2	2.7	1–15
Question 2: General focus[a]			
Direct reading	5.7	2.7	1–13
Indirect reading	8.5	3.2	2–15
Composing (writing)	4.9	2.7	1–10
Language development	12.1	3.7	4–20
Other academic	9.3	4.1	2–17
Art and physical education	3.0	1.6	1–8
General management	46.1	4.5	36–60
Informal interaction	4.1	1.8	1–8
Question 3: Teacher purpose[a]			
Modeling	43.3	8.8	23–64
Tell information	5.4	2.3	1–12
Question and answer	22.4	5.7	11–39
Feedback	4.3	1.9	1–11
Listen and watch	21.1	7.5	6–38
Question 4: Materials[b]			
Trade book	36.3	10.9	7–57
Text other	5.4	3.7	0–16
Student composition	16.5	10.2	2–44
Sentence written	1.5	1.5	0–6
Word written	5.5	3.5	0–16
Letters written	5.4	5.0	0–24
Workbook	1.5	2.7	0–14
Oral text	6.7	5.8	0–23
Oral presentation	9.8	7.9	0–30
Words oral	6.1	5.2	1–20
Pictures	1.9	1.4	0–7
Video or film	2.0	3.9	0–19
Question 5: Specific focus[b]			
Read text	12.9	7.0	2–35
Word identification	3.8	2.1	0–8
Letter sounds	2.7	2.7	0–12
Phoneme awareness	8.1	4.7	0–20
Graphic features	2.7	2.8	0–12
Word meaning	2.4	1.8	0–7
Text meaning	40.4	9.1	16–60
Recitation	5.4	4.8	0–22
Letter names	1.5	1.6	0–7
General information	13.5	7.4	1–33

(continued)

TABLE 20.3. cont.

	M	SD	Range
Question 6: Expected response[b]			
Read silently	8.1	4.2	1–20
Read orally	11.8	5.3	1–24
Oral	35.9	10.2	13–65
Listen and look	35.1	9.2	17–54
Write	4.9	3.5	0–15
Other	3.9	3.2	0–17

Note. Five or six full-session observations were conducted in each classroom. Codes with a mean of less than 1.0 are not listed.
[a]Percentages are based on the entire observation period.
[b]Percentages are based on the time allocated to language arts instruction only.

However, in this component of the study, we were particularly interested in evaluating the relationship between the type of instruction the children received in kindergarten and reading achievement in first grade relative to their reading-readiness skills on entering kindergarten. Therefore, as the letter identification measure administered at the beginning of kindergarten proved to be the best predictor of success in first-grade reading, we used this measure to divide the kindergartners into two groups: one group operationally defined as being at increased risk for early reading difficulties and a second group defined as being at low risk for such difficulties. The at-risk group was defined by a score at or below the 40th percentile on the Letter Identification subtest of the WRMT-R and was designated the "low letter identification" group (LLID). The "not at risk" group was defined by a score above the 40th percentile on the WRMT-R Letter Identification subtest and was designated the "high letter identification" group (HLID). Each of these groups was further divided into five groups on the basis of teacher ratings of their reading achievement in November of first grade (the rating scale was a 5-point scale ranging from "very low" to "very high" achievement). We then evaluated the relationship between instructional focus in kindergarten and first-grade reading achievement in both the LLID and HLID groups. Of particular interest was whether observed relationships between the amount of time spent on given types of activities (defined by questions 5 and 6 in the observation system) and first-grade reading achievement would be similar or different in these two groups.

Although the total amount of time spent by the classroom teachers on language arts instruction did not distinguish the LLID and HLID groups, the percentage of time specifically focused on phoneme-awareness and shared-reading activities did distinguish these groups. First, we found that teachers of children in the LLID group tended to spend more time on phoneme-awareness activities than did teachers of children in the HLID group. However, the relationship between time spent on phoneme-awareness activities and first-grade reading achievement was quite different in these two groups. This difference is clearly evident in Figure 20.2, which shows that children in the LLID group who were judged by their teachers to be average or better than average readers in first grade tended to come from kindergarten classrooms in which teachers spent more time on phoneme-awareness activities. This relationship was not evident in the HLID group, suggesting, perhaps, that children in this group entered kindergarten with greater reading-readiness skills than did children in the LLID group and, as a result, may have required less explicit instruction in phoneme analysis to become at least average readers in first grade.

A converse finding emerged when we examined the relationship between teacher rating of first-grade reading achievement and the proportion of instructional time spent in kindergarten on shared-reading activities (e.g., the teacher reading aloud a large-print text such as a big book or language experi-

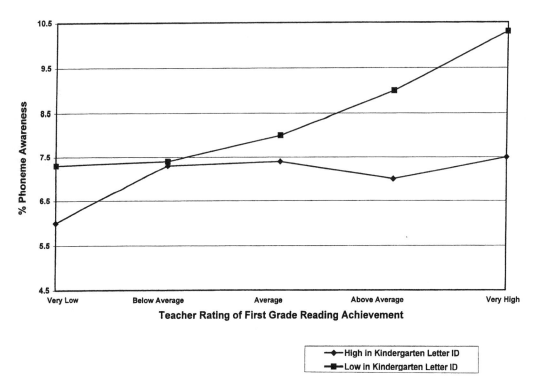

FIGURE 20.2. Relationship between percentage of language arts time spent on phoneme-awareness activities and teacher rating of first-grade reading achievement.

ence chart while drawing the children's attention to the printed text). As evident in Figure 20.3, the children in the HLID groups who were rated as average or better than average readers in first grade tended to come from kindergarten classes in which more time was spent on shared-reading activities. However, this pattern was not evident among children in the LLID groups, which suggests that the children in these latter groups may have entered kindergarten with inadequate reading-readiness skills and, thus, may not have been as well equipped to profit from shared-reading activities as were the children in the HLID groups.

Finally, we found that children who were rated by their teachers as average or better than average readers in first grade had more exposure to sight word activities when they were in kindergarten than did children who were rated as below average readers in first grade (data not shown). This relationship was observed among children in both the LLID and HLID groups, suggesting that limited time spent on word-recognition ac-

tivities in kindergarten may have contributed to reading difficulties in first grade, regardless of the child's entry-level risk status in kindergarten.

Taken together, these findings suggest that kindergarten literacy instruction may well be an influential determinant of first-grade reading achievement. The finding that amount of exposure to either code-based (phoneme awareness) or text-based (shared reading) activities differentially affected level of reading achievement in first grade, depending on entry-level skills, is of special interest because it suggests that both types of activities are important for success in beginning reading. More generally, it suggests that emergent readers can profit greatly from a comprehensive and even-keeled language arts program that takes into account a child's entry-level knowledge and abilities and tailors instruction to his or her strengths and weaknesses. Conversely, the failure to provide such a program may increase the probability that a child is identified as a "disabled reader" in first grade and

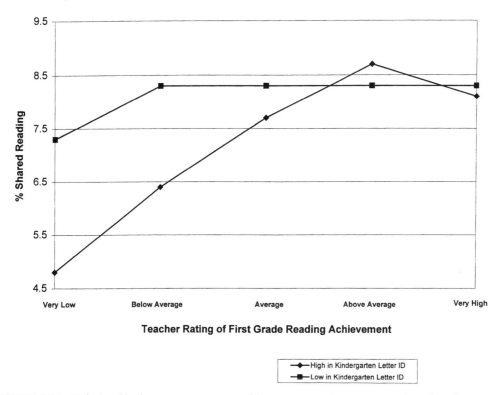

FIGURE 20.3. Relationship between percentage of language arts time spent on shared-reading activities and teacher rating of first-grade reading achievement.

beyond, even if that child has basically normal learning potential.

A Brief Summary of the Intervention Component of the Study

As indicated previously, a major objective of the present study was to assess the utility of using early and intensive remedial intervention as a "first-cut diagnostic" to aid in distinguishing between impaired readers whose reading difficulties are caused by basic deficits in reading-related cognitive abilities and impaired readers whose reading difficulties are caused by experiential and/or instructional deficits. We were especially interested in contrasts between children who were found to be readily remediated and children who were found to be difficult to remediate because we expected that the reading achievement and cognitive profiles of children who were found to be readily remediated would be more like

those of normal readers than would the reading achievement and cognitive profiles of children who were found to be difficult to remediate. Accordingly, children who were initially identified by their classroom teachers as severely impaired readers were further evaluated at approximately the midpoint of their first-grade year using the Word Identification and Word Attack subtests of the WRMT-R (Woodcock, 1987), and these measures, along with the Wechsler Intelligence Scale for Children—Revised (WISC-R; Wechsler, 1974), were used for final selection of the poor reader sample. To qualify for the severely impaired reader sample, a child had to score at or below the 15th percentile on either the Word Identification or the Word Attack subtests of the WRMT-R, and had to have an IQ of at least 90 on either the Verbal or the Performance subscales of the WISC-R. The final sample of impaired readers was selected using "exclusionary criteria" typically employed to define specific reading disability.

Thus, children whose reading difficulties could have come about because of uncorrected sensory deficits, physical disabilities, neurological disorder, emotional disorder, frequent absences from school, and/or socioeconomic disadvantage were excluded from the sample. Using these criteria, 118 children from the larger sample qualified for the severely impaired reader group. The number of impaired readers identified using these criteria represented approximately 9% of the population of (available) first-graders from the group of kindergartners originally evaluated.

For purposes of comparison, we also selected a group of normal readers consisting of children who were identified by their teachers as having average to above-average reading ability and who scored at or above the 45th percentile on both the Word Identification and the Word Attack subtests of the WRMT-R. To qualify for inclusion in this group, these children also had to have an IQ score of at least 90 on either the Verbal or the Performance subtests of the WISC-R. Because we were interested in the relationship between intelligence and early reading achievement, the normal readers were divided into an average IQ group (AvIQNorm, $N = 28$) and an above-average IQ group (AbAvIQNorm, $N = 37$) using the mean Full Scale IQ score on the WISC-R for the entire normal reader group as the cut point. Seventy-six of the 118 children in the impaired reader group were randomly selected and assigned to receive daily one-to-one tutoring by project tutors (half hour per day) beginning in January of their first-grade year. Tutoring continued at least through the end of the first-grade year for all children assigned to the tutoring condition. Tutored children who had not acquired average or better than average reading skills at the beginning of second grade continued to receive daily one-to-one tutoring during the fall of their second-grade year after which the intervention program was terminated. The impaired readers who were not assigned to the daily one-to-one tutoring condition ($N = 42$) received whatever form of remediation happened to be provided at their home school by school personnel. In the majority of cases ($N = 26$), school-based remdiation involved small-group instruction, but in some cases ($N = 16$), it involved one-to-one tutoring two or three times a week. Although it was not possible to obtain detailed information about the types of remedial activities to which children who received school-based remediation were exposed, we know that insructional approaches and philosophies varied from school to school. However, because the children included in our intervention program received a greater amount of remedial assistance than did the children who received school-based remediation, the children who received school-based remediation served as a contrast group that allowed us to evaluate the effectiveness of our intervention.

The daily one-to-one tutoring provided by our intervention program was carried out by certified teachers, many of whom had obtained certification in reading. All but one had 2 or more years of teaching experience. The tutors were trained by project staff. Initial training consisted of a week-long workshop during which the tutors were acquainted with the general approach to remediation we expected them to implement along with the theoretical foundations of this approach. To ensure fidelity of treatment, all tutoring sessions were audiotaped and project staff met with each tutor both individually and in group settings in bimonthly supervisory sessions that extended throughout the duration of the intervention program.

Our intervention program was essentially a "pull-out" program carried out at the child's home school and was tailored to the child's individual strengths and weaknesses and individual knowledge base. However, each lesson incorporated activities designed to strike a balance between word-level skills such as word identification and phonological decoding on the one hand and text-processing skills on the other. Because a major goal of remediation was to foster the use of complementary and interactive strategies for word identification and comprehension in reading connected text (use of context, picture clues, confirmation and self-monitoring, letter–sound analysis, etc.), and because we wanted to foster a sense of enjoyment for reading, fully half of each remedial session (15 minutes) was devoted to text reading that entailed both rereading of familiar texts for fluency and initial reading of new texts. The remaining half was divided among activities designed to facilitate (1) phoneme analysis and phoneme awareness, (2) letter identification and letter–sound decoding, (3) generative use of redundant spelling clusters (at, am, ch, sh, ing, tion, etc.), (4) accuracy and fluency in identifying high-frequency "sight" words, and (5) writing.

Progress in reading was periodically assessed in both the impaired and normal readers from the beginning of kindergarten through the end of fourth grade using measures of word identification and pseudoword decoding. Reading comprehension was also assessed periodically after the child had received one semester of remediation. To distinguish between cognitive deficits and experiential/instructional deficits as primary causes of reading difficulties, cognitive abilities similar to those assessed in kindergarten were assessed in both first and third grade (see Figure 20.1). In addition, the impaired readers who received the daily one-to-one tutoring implemented by project staff were divided into four roughly equal groups on the basis of the initial progress they made in one semester of tutoring (75 sessions on average). The groups were designated as follows: Very Limited Growth (VLG, $N = 19$); Limited Growth (LG, $N = 18$); Good Growth (GG, $N = 18$); and Very Good Growth (VGG, $N = 19$). (Two of the children were lost through attrition by the beginning of the second-grade year, leaving a total of 74 children on whom many of the subsequent analyses are based.)

As we pointed out in a previous section, the amount of daily one-to-one tutoring a child received depended on that child's progress. Thus, tutoring was discontinued for those children who received a score at or above the 45th percentile on both the Word Identification and Word Attack subtests of the WRMT-R when they were tested in the fall of second grade. Those children who scored below this cutoff on one or both of these measures received an additional semester of tutoring. All the children in the VGG group and approximately half the children in the GG group were discontinued after one semester of tutoring. All the children in both the LG and VLG groups were given daily one-to-one tutoring by project tutors for an additional semester. Many of the children in these latter groups had not achieved average-level reading skills at the termination of the intervention program, but it was not possible to obtain detailed information about the remediation provided by their home schools thereafter.

Summary of Major Findings

Reading Achievement

SELECTION MEASURES

Table 20.4 presents results for each of the reader groups on the reading achievement tests used as selection measures before the intervention program was initiated (winter of first grade). Also presented are the WISC-R IQs for each group. Note first that the children in the tutored groups performed well below the children in both of the normal reader groups on each of the reading measures. Note also that the children in each of the tutored groups had at least average intelligence. Thus, given that the children in these groups were selected on the basis of the exclusionary criteria typically used to diagnose "specific reading disability," they would have qualified as "disabled learners" at sample selection and some were already classified as such by their home schools. Of special importance, however, is that there were no statistically significant differences between and among the tutored groups on any of the IQ measures. Neither were there any statistically significant differences between any of the tutored groups and the AvIQNorm group on these measures. Moreover, there were no appreciable differences between the AvIQNorm and the AbAvIQNorm groups on either of the reading measures. These findings are important because they indicate that (1) IQ scores do not discriminate between poor and normal readers who have just begun to learn to read, (2) IQ scores do not predict a child's ability to profit from remediation, and (3) IQ scores do not predict level of reading ability in normally developing readers. The findings, therefore, add to the growing body of evidence undermining the use of IQ scores and the IQ–achievement discrepancy in particular as criteria for defining specific reading disability (Fletcher et al., 1994; Siegel, 1988,

TABLE 20.4. Scores Obtained by Tutored Poor Readers Grouped in Accord with Growth in Reading over Time and by Normal Readers on the Reading and Intelligence Measures Administered for Sample Selection Prior to Intervention

		Normal readers		Tutored groups			
		Average IQ (N = 28)	Above-average IQ (N = 37)	VLG (N = 19)	LG (N = 18)	GG (N = 18)	VGG (N = 19)
VIQ	M	106.14	121.51	100.89	101.11	104.11	105.42
	SD	6.70	8.57	14.47	10.19	10.46	12.01
PIQ	M	107.00	119.03	102.32	102.67	106.11	105.26
	SD	9.03	5.97	9.84	9.59	13.35	9.43
FSIQ	M	106.89	122.86	101.37	101.94	105.56	105.58
	SD	6.57	5.33	10.17	7.66	12.53	10.24
Word Identification	M	37.39	38.81	4.42	6.89	11.56	11.53
raw score	SD	12.91	10.83	3.34	4.59	4.62	5.51
Word Identification grade equivalent	M	2.20	2.22	.96	1.07	1.26	1.25
Word Attack raw score	M	12.79	13.73	.74	1.06	.78	1.32
	SD	8.36	7.46	2.28	1.86	.94	1.67
Word Attack grade equivalent	M	2.01	1.97	.60	.67	.65	.73

Note. Tutored children are grouped on the basis of initial growth after one semester of remediation.

1989; Stanovich & Siegel, 1994; Vellutino, Scanlon, & Lyon, 2000).

OUTCOME MEASURES

In regard to results from the intervention component of the study, we should initially point out that the intervention proved to be reasonably successful in reducing the number of children who would qualify as disabled readers. Of those impaired readers who received daily one-to-one tutoring by project teachers, 67% (51/76) were brought to within an average or above-average level of reading achievement (at or above 30th percentile on the Basic Skills Cluster)[2] after one semester of remediation. The number of impaired readers who were yet below average (N = 25) represents only 3% of the population of children available for tutoring (25/827), and the number who continued to be severely impaired (N = 12) represents only 1.5% of this population (12/827).[3] Both of these estimates constitute a significant reduction in the percentage of children from the population of those initially identified as impaired readers, which, it will be recalled, was approximately 9%.

Not surprisingly, the daily one-to-one tutoring provided by project teachers was found to be more effective than the small-group remediation provided by school personnel in that the former placed a larger percentage of children above the 45th percentile on the reading measures than did the latter (44.7% vs. 19.2%) and a smaller percentage below the 15th percentile on these measures (15.8% vs. 26.9%). And, although the 2- or 3-day-a-week (one-to-one) tuoring provided by school personnel placed about as many children above the 45th percentile on the reading measures (43.8%) as the daily (one-to-one) tutoring provided by project tutors, the former placed a larger percentage of children below the 15th percentile than did the latter (25%). However, the finding that some children who received either small-group remediation or lesser amounts of one-to-one tutoring were brought to at least an average level of reading achievement suggests that daily one-to-one tutoring may not be necessary for all impaired readers provided that they receive some form of early intervention. Yet, the finding that there was a small percentage of the tutored children who continued to function below this level, despite the fact that they received even two semesters of daily one-to-one tutoring, suggests that some impaired readers will require long-term remediation to correct their reading difficulties, perhaps even the type of individualized and intensive remediation provided by daily one-to-one tutoring.

As we indicated earlier, comparisons of both the reading achievement profiles and the cognitive profiles of the difficult to remediate and readily remediated tutored children were of special interest in this study. We expected that the reading achievement and cognitive profiles of children who were the most readily remediated would be closer to those of normal readers than would the reading achievement and cognitive profiles of children who were the most difficult to remediate. These expectations were confirmed.

Figures 20.4 and 20.5 present mean raw scores on the WRMT-R Word Identification and Word Attack subtests, respectively, for children in the four tutored groups partitioned on the basis of initial growth in reading. The same data are presented for the two normal reader groups. In both graphs, means are presented for the period encompassing the beginning of kindergarten through the end of fourth grade. As is apparent, the children in the normal reader groups performed well above the children in the tutored groups on both measures prior to the onset of remediation (winter of first grade). However, after only one semester of tutoring (spring of first grade), the children in the tutored group that made the greatest amount of initial progress—that is, those in the VGG group—performed at levels closer to those of the normal reader groups on both subtests and maintained these levels of performance throughout the period evaluated (long after tutoring had been discontinued). In contrast, children in the VLG group—the tutored group that made the least initial progress—performed well below children in the normal reader groups on

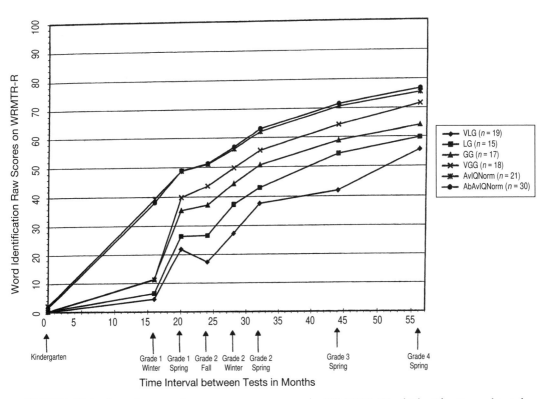

FIGURE 20.4. Growth curves for mean raw scores on the WRMT-R Word Identification subtest for normal and tutored poor readers.

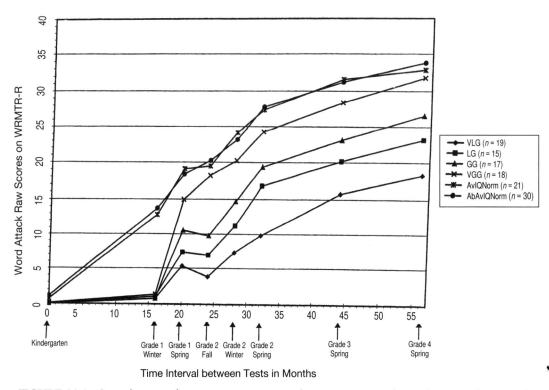

FIGURE 20.5. Growth curves for mean raw scores on the WRMT-R Word Attack subtest for normal and tutored poor readers.

these measures over the same period. They also fell well below children in the VGG group. Children in the LG and GG groups performed at levels intermediate between the children in the VLG and VGG groups, and the groups maintained their relative positions through the end of fourth grade when the study was terminated.

Finally, the two normal reader groups performed at virtually equivalent levels on both of the reading measures from the beginning of kindergarten through the end of fourth grade.

Because the data presented in Figures 20.4 and 20.5 are based on mean raw scores, they do not allow norm-referenced comparisons. Accordingly, Table 20.5 presents group mean percentile ranks for the Basic Skills Cluster (BSC) of the WRMT-R, which is a composite of the WRMT-R Word Identification and Word Attack subtests. Data are presented for the period encompassing the winter of first grade through the spring of fourth grade. Also presented are

the group mean percentile ranks on the Woodcock–Johnson Passage Comprehension Test (Woodcock & Johnson, 1989) for the spring of first grade and the spring of third grade. As would be expected, the pattern of results on the BSC parallel the pattern of results on the Word Identification and Word Attack subtests. However, it is of some significance that on the reading comprehension test, the children in each of the tutored groups were able to score at least within the average range (>30th percentile) by the end of third grade. Thus, it is clear that despite their continued difficulties in word identification and phonological decoding, most of the tutored children had acquired enough proficiency in extracting meaning from connected text to become functional readers, even those in the groups that were found to be the most difficult to remediate (i.e., the VLG and LG groups).

Note also that children in the above-average-IQ normal reader group (AbAvIQNorm) performed substantially better than children

TABLE 20.5. Percentile Ranks for Reading Achievement Measures Administered to Normal Readers and Children in Respective Tutored Groups from Winter of First Grade through Spring of Fourth Grade

		Normal readers		Tutored groups			
		Average IQ (N = 28)	Above-average IQ (N = 37)	VLG (N = 19)	LG (N = 18)	GG (N = 18)	VGG (N = 19)
First grade (winter)							
Basic Skills Cluster	X	72.21	72.65	8.58	13.56	18.72	22.26
	SD	16.68	16.99	9.99	8.15	6.99	10.92
First grade (spring)							
Basic Skills Cluster	X	74.21	76.11	19.84	29.11	47.83	62.63
	SD	22.19	19.13	12.47	8.31	9.78	11.99
Woodcock–Johnson	X	73.46	80.49	18.21	21.44	35.72	36.89
Passage Comprehension	SD	22.89	16.96	14.40	14.73	19.30	20.67
Second grade (fall)							
Basic Skills Cluster	X	70.35	73.69	5.47	17.11	35.72	60.16
	SD	24.04	23.38	3.29	5.75	8.15	13.49
Second grade (winter)							
Basic Skills Cluster	X	72.31	73.42	9.00	22.56	38.83	58.21
	SD	20.84	21.03	7.92	11.06	14.65	17.64
Second grade (spring)							
Basic Skills Cluster	X	74.62	79.11	14.37	27.56	43.50	63.79
	SD	20.57	15.96	16.66	12.12	16.83	15.08
Third grade (spring)							
Basic Skills Cluster	X	72.27	74.88	15.42	27.47	38.41	58.03
	SD	21.01	17.40	19.89	15.51	16.71	17.59
Woodcock–Johnson	X	70.22	89.13	33.74	38.32	52.53	70.11
Passage Comprehension	SD	21.44	8.50	21.40	21.28	23.07	18.05
Fourth grade (spring)							
Basic Skills Cluster	X	64.57	69.47	12.26	21.20	31.06	56.11
	SD	19.82	19.88	15.00	13.81	14.28	16.00

Note. Tutored children are grouped on the basis of initial growth after one semester of remediation.

in the average-IQ normal reader group (AvIQNorm) on the reading comprehension test, which is not surprising given that intelligence tests measure knowledge and abilities that are important for comprehending what one reads (vocabulary knowledge, general knowledge, inferencing, reasoning, etc.). This finding contrasts with the finding that these two groups did not differ on the measures of word identification and letter–sound decoding skills, from which it may be inferred that intelligence tests do not adequately measure the language-based abilities that

underlie one's ability to acquire these skills and the ability to learn to read in general.

In view of the results on the reading outcome measures, we think it is reasonable to suggest that the beginning reading difficulties of the children in the VLG and LG groups may well have been caused, in part, by basic cognitive deficits, given that the children in these groups continued to perform at below-average levels on the tests of basic reading subskills, despite the fact that all received two semesters of daily one-to-one remediation. Conversely, we can have some faith in the possibility that the reading difficulties of the children in the VGG and GG groups were caused primarily by experiential and instructional deficits rather than by basic cognitive deficits, especially because all the children in the VGG group and approximately half the children in the GG group received only one semester of one-to-one remediation. These impressions were given additional credibility by results from the cognitive batteries administered in kindergarten and first grades. (The data from the third grade battery are currently being analyzed.)

Group Contrasts on the Kindergarten and First-Grade Batteries

Table 20.6 presents results on kindergarten measures of entry-level literacy skills and reading-related cognitive abilities that distinguished between the tutored groups and the normal reader groups and, in several instances, between the most readily remediated and the most difficult to remediate tutored groups. Table 20.7 presents results on the first-grade measures that evaluated similar skills and abilities. Raw score means and standard deviations are presented for the

TABLE 20.6. Measures of Foundational Literacy Skills and Cognitive Abilities Evaluated in Kindergarten That Distinguished between Tutored Children and Normal Readers and between Tutored Children Who Were Difficult to Remediate and Tutored Children Who Were Readily Remediated

		Normal readers		Poor readers in tutored groups[a]			
		Average IQ (N = 28)	Above-average IQ (N = 37)	VLG (N = 19)	LG (N = 18)	GG (N = 18)	VGG (N = 19)
Letter Naming[b, c, d]	X	27.57	.11	−2.93	−2.17	−1.73	−1.52
	SD	5.69					
Word Naming[b, c]	X	1.71					
	SD	2.68	.62	−.62	−.52	−.58	−.60
Counting by 1s[b, d]	X	7.89					
	SD	2.28	.15	−1.20	−1.00	−1.00	−.45
Number Naming[c, d]	X	9.48					
	SD	1.65	−.06	−2.31	−1.67	−1.02	−1.24
Arithmetic[b, c]	X	15.61					
	SD	2.74	.48	−1.07	−.95	−.85	−.70
Phoneme Segmentation	X	5.08	.07	−.53	−.49	−.43	−.26
	SD	7.18					
RAN Objects Time[b]	X	68.98	−.15	.84	.69	.67	.53
	SD	16.69					
Rapid Articulation Time[b]	X	6.95	.19	1.34	.33	1.42	.57
	SD	1.35					
General Knowledge[b, d] (WISC-R Information)	X	9.39	.86	−1.34	−.83	−1.29	−.45
	SD	2.02					
Sentence Memory[b]	X	4.96	.71	−.88	−.50	−.61	−.27
	SD	1.04					
Word Memory[b, c]	X	1.50	.36	−1.03	−.56	−.77	−.76
	SD	.79					
Visual–Verbal Learning[b, c, d]	X	41.52	.17	−2.13	−1.22	−1.13	−1.04
	SD	4.44					

Note. RAN, Rapid Automatized Naming; time reported in seconds.
[a]Grouped by slopes for *W* scores obtained on the Basic Skills Cluster of the WRMT-R from kindergarten through fall of second grade.
[b]Significant differences between average IQ versus VLG.
[c]Significant differences between average IQ versus VGG.
[d]Significant differences between VGG versus VLG.

TABLE 20.7. Measures of Cognitive Abilities Evaluated in First Grade That Distinguished between Tutored Children and Normal Readers and between Tutored Children Who Were Difficult to Remediate and Tutored Children Who Were Readily Remediated

| | | Normal readers | | Poor readers in tutored groups[a] | | | |
		Average IQ (N = 28)	Above-average IQ (N = 37)	VLG (N = 19)	LG (N = 18)	GG (N = 18)	VGG (N = 19)
Phoneme Segmentation Winter[b, c, d]	X	9.63	.23	−1.59	−.86	−1.28	−1.08
	SD	4.88					
Spring[b, d]	X	21.64	.37	−1.36	−.57	−1.24	−.59
	SD	7.23					
RAN Objects Time[b]	X	55.38	−.14	.93	.40	.49	.64
	SD	12.04					
RAN Colors Time[b]	X	52.92	−.18	1.53	.15	.53	.87
	SD	8.60					
RAN Letters Time[b, d]	X	37.36	−.19	1.44	1.10	.90	.04
	SD	10.80					
RAN Numbers Time[b, d]	X	40.83	−.37	.79	.54	.39	−.19
	SD	12.25					
Boston Naming Text (Correct)[b, d]	X	35.39	.41	−1.35	−.80	−.82	−.54
	SD	5.79					
WISC-R Information[b, d]	X	9.39	.86	−1.34	−.83	−1.29	−.45
	SD	2.02					
Token Test IV[b, c]	X	8.00	.36	−1.94	−.81	−1.35	−1.39
	SD	1.44					
Token Test V[b, d]	X	16.07	.34	−1.13	−.41	−.14	−.23
	SD	2.85					
Oral Cloze[c]	X	17.14	.64	−.34	−.81	−.33	−.91
	SD	2.77					
WISC-R Digit Span[b, c]	X	8.22	.45	−1.70	−.93	−1.47	−1.65
	SD	1.44					
TOLD Sentence Imitation[b]	X	18.89	.61	−1.24	−.55	−.92	−.72
	SD	4.72					
Syntactic Word Order[b, c, d]	X	20.04	.09	−2.15	−1.71	−1.01	−1.00
	SD	2.04					
Phonological Memory[b]	X	14.50	.52	−.76	−.50	−.65	−.22
	SD	5.40					
Delayed Recall Concrete Words[d]	X	3.04	.10	−.39	−.11	.31	.45
	SD	1.32					
Immediate Recall Abstract Words[b, d]	X	14.32	.55	−.61	−.26	−.17	.17
	SD	5.16					
Delayed Recall Abstract Words[b, d]	X	1.96	.01	−.95	−.80	−.55	−.25
	SD	1.35					
Visual Memory Labelable[b, c]	X	5.39	.15	−1.38	−1.29	−.81	−1.60
	SD	1.17					
Target Search No. Correct[b, d]	X	12.54	.04	−1.31	−.59	−.83	−.06
	SD	1.92					

Note. RAN, Rapid Automatized Naming; time reported in seconds.
[a]Grouped by slopes for *W* scores obtained on the Basic Skills Cluster of the WRMT-R from kindergarten through fall of second grade.
[b]Significant differences between average versus VLG.
[c]Significant differences between average versus VGG.
[d]Significant differences between VGG versus VLG.

average-IQ normal readers. For all other groups, the data are presented as effect sizes computed relative to the performance of the average-IQ normal reader group. However, for the sake of brevity, we focus on contrasts involving the average-IQ normal readers (AvIQNorm group) and the tutored children found to be the most and least difficult to remediate (VLG and VGG groups). Thus, significance levels are presented only for these groups.

KINDERGARTEN BATTERY

It can be seen that on the kindergarten battery, the normal readers performed significantly better than children in the VLG group on measures that depend heavily on phonological coding ability, in particular, measures evaluating letter, word, and picture naming; counting and other rudimentary number skills; speed of naming objects; immediate recall of words and sentences; rapid articulation; and visual–verbal (associative) learning. The normal readers performed significantly better than children in the VGG group on the letter, word, and number-naming tasks; on the counting and rudimentary arithmetic tasks; and on the visual–verbal learning and word memory tasks as well. At the same time, children in the VGG group performed significantly better than children in the VLG group on the tests evaluating letter naming, counting, number naming, and visual–verbal learning. The only phonological task that did not distinguish these groups in kindergarten was the phoneme-segmentation task. However, there appeared to be a serious floor effect on this task in that most if not all the children in all the groups performed poorly on this measure.

In contrast to results on tests that evaluated phonologically based skills, there were no significant differences between and among respective reader groups on the kindergarten tests evaluating semantic, syntactic, and visual abilities, nor were there significant group differences on tests evaluating print awareness, knowledge of print conventions, conceptual development, and "executive functions" such as attention, concentration, and organizational ability (data not shown). The only exception was a significant difference between the AvIQNorm and the VLG groups and between the VGG and VLG groups, on the test of general knowledge (WISC-R Information). The AvIQNorm and VGG groups did not differ on this measure.

FIRST-GRADE BATTERY

On the first-grade battery (Table 20.7), children in the AvIQNorm group once again performed significantly better than children in the VLG group on tests that depend heavily on phonological and other language-based skills, in particular, tests evaluating phoneme segmentation; rapid naming of objects, colors, letters, and numbers; confrontational naming of pictures (Boston Naming); and memory for digits, sentences, concrete and abstract words, and nonsense syllables (Phonological Memory). These groups were also found to differ on tests that evaluated sentence comprehension (Token Test subtests IV and V), general language (listening) comprehension, auditory "cloze" (Oral Cloze), construction of sentences from scrambled words presented auditorily (Syntactic Word Order), and general knowledge (WISC-R Information).

At the same time, children in the VGG group performed better than children in the VLG group on tests evaluating phoneme segmentation, rapid naming of letters and numbers, confrontational naming of pictures, and memory for concrete and abstract words. They also performed better than children in the VLG group on the Syntactic Word Order test, on one of the sentence comprehension tests (Token Test V), and on the test of general knowledge. In contrast, the VGG and the AvIQNorm groups were not found to differ significantly on any of the naming tests, nor were they found to differ on the tests evaluating sentence memory, word memory, memory for nonsense syllables, and one of the sentence comprehension tests (Token Test V). Neither did they differ on the phoneme-segmentation test administered in spring of first grade, or the test of general knowledge (WISC-R Information).

As with the kindergarten battery, there were no significant differences between respective groups on the tests evaluating semantic and syntactic abilities (WISC-R Vocabulary, WISC-R Similarities, and Grammaticality Judgements), nor were there any significant group differences on the tests evaluating visual processing (including the WISC-R Performance Scale) and executive functions (administered in second grade). However, the AvIQNorm group performed better than the VLG and VGG groups on the test evaluating memory for labelable dot patterns, and both the AvIQNorm and VGG groups performed better than the VLG group on a visual scanning test evaluating accuracy in searching for pronounceable nonsense syllables. These differences are not surprising given that both tests entail verbal coding ability, and poor and normal readers have consistently been found to differ on processing tasks when the visual stimuli presented on such tasks can be assigned a verbal code (see Katz, Shankweiler, & Liberman, 1981).

We infer from these results that the reading difficulties experienced by beginning readers from populations such as those evaluated in the present study may well be caused by basic deficits in certain of the cognitive abilities underlying the ability to learn to read, especially phonological abilities such as phoneme analysis, letter–sound decoding, name encoding and retrieval, and verbal memory. However, our data suggest that the number of children impaired by basic cognitive deficits represents a relatively small percentage of beginning readers compared with the substantially larger percentage of those children whose reading difficulties are caused by experiential and instructional deficits.

Summary and Conclusions

Several conclusions can be drawn from the present findings. First, our data are quite in keeping with results from other intervention studies which have shown that the majority of children who experience early reading difficulties can become functional readers if they are provided with early and intensive remediation tailored to their individual strengths and weaknesses (Clay, 1985; Iversen & Tunmer, 1993; Pinnell, 1989; Santa & Hoien, 1999; Torgesen, Wagner, & Rashotte, 1997; Wasik & Slavin, 1993). They therefore provide confirmation of Clay's (1987) contention that reading difficulties in most beginning readers are caused

by experiential and instructional deficits rather than by neurodevelopmental deficits and lend support to the growing consensus that current estimates of the incidence of specific reading disability are greatly inflated. Indeed, using exclusionary criteria such as those typically employed in public school settings, we found that approximately 9% of the population of available children could have been diagnosed as "disabled readers," and some were already assigned this diagnosis. However, after one semester of daily one-to-one tutoring, only about one-third of the tutored children continued to perform below the average range (i.e., below the 30th percentile). This figure represents only 3% of the population from which these children were drawn. And if we applied the more stringent severity criterion we used to select our sample of impaired readers (at or below the 15th percentile), only 1.5% of this population would qualify as severely impaired readers.

These estimates are substantially below the 9% population estimate produced by the exclusionary criteria we used for sample selection, and they are well below the 10–20% estimates that have emerged from the reading disability literature. And when it is considered that it was primarily those children who continued to score below the 15th percentile on the reading measures who were consistently found to be deficient on tests of reading-related cognitive abilities, it seems reasonable to suggest that it is only children of this description who might be accurately classified as "disabled readers." Thus, there would seem to be ample justification for using early intervention as a first-cut approach to diagnosing specific reading disability, perhaps making use of relevant psychometric tests to aid in cross-validating the diagnosis in children who are not readily remediated. Yet, it should be apparent that such classification would be unnecessary if school systems were able to provide adequate remediation for all children who required it.

This latter assertion relates to a second conclusion that can be drawn from the present findings, which is that there are likely to be some impaired readers who will require protracted periods of intensive remediation, even with the most effective remediation. Despite the fact that most of the tutored children became average-level readers in two semesters (if not one semester) of one-to-one tutoring, almost 30% of these children continued to perform below average, and they all received two semesters of such tutoring. Because we did not collect the relevant data, we have no information as to the amount or type of remediation these children received following termination of the tutoring program. However, informal contact with school officials gives us reason to believe that a small percentage of these children did ultimately become average-level readers. Moreover, all the tutored children made significant progress during the period in which they participated in the tutoring program, and we infer from these outcomes that many, if not all, of the children who continued to perform below average in reading could have become functional readers had they been able to receive additional one-to-one remediation tailored to their individual needs.

This brings into focus a third conclusion that can be drawn from our findings, which is that many impaired readers can be successfully remediated with less intensive and less protracted remediation, provided that intervention is implemented at an early point in their reading development. Although a substantially larger percentage of children who received school-based small-group instruction for one semester continued to perform below average on the reading outcome measures, compared with the children in our intervention project who received daily one-to-one tutoring over the same period (46% vs. 30%, respectively), over half of the children in the former group (54%) performed within the average range on these measures, and approximately one-fifth (19%) performed above the 45th percentile. Thus, it is clear that one of the important objectives of future research is to develop the means for determining which children will require intensive one-to-one tutoring to be successfully remediated and which children can be successfully remediated with small-group instruction.

Still another conclusion that can be drawn from the present findings relates to the issue of when, in the struggling child's reading development, remedial intervention should be initiated. There is, as yet, no definitive answer, but conventional wisdom suggests that children should be exposed to

formal reading instruction before making any determination as to the need for remedial intervention. In fact, Clay (1985)—the architect of the well-known Reading Recovery (RR) program—suggests that children be given a full year of reading instruction before assessing their eligibility for the RR program. Yet, results from our prediction study suggest that it may be possible to identify children at risk for early reading difficulties even before they are exposed to formal reading instruction. It will be recalled that language-based measures such as letter identification, phoneme awareness, and rapid naming were reasonably good predictors of reading achievement in first grade. Moreover, results from our kindergarten observation study suggest that some children who entered kindergarten with reasonably well-developed reading-readiness skills were exposed to kindergarten language arts programs that did not adequately prepare them for first-grade reading instruction. Conversely, the data suggest that some children who entered kindergarten with poorly developed reading-readiness skills were exposed to kindergarten language arts instruction that compensated for their deficient reading-readiness skills. If we couple these findings with our observation that the severely impaired readers in our first-grade sample entered kindergarten with poor reading-readiness skills, we have reason to suggest that such deficiencies can be identified and corrected early in the child's kindergarten year as a means of better preparing that child for success in beginning reading. In fact, we are currently conducting another longitudinal study that was designed to evaluate this suggestion and the preliminary findings are encouraging (Scanlon, Vellutino, Small, & Fanuele, 2000).

Two other conclusions are warranted by our data. First, they add to the growing body of evidence documenting that intelligence test scores do not reliably predict reading achievement when the latter is defined as the ability to learn to decode print and is assessed using measures of basic reading skills such as word identification and letter–sound decoding (Fletcher et al., 1994; Siegel, 1988, 1989; Stanovich & Siegel, 1994; Vellutino et al., 2000). This, in turn, questions the validity of using the IQ–achievement discrepancy as a basic defining criterion for identifying and classifying children as "reading disabled." In the present instance, IQ scores neither distinguished between children who were found to be difficult to remediate and children who were found to be readily remediated nor distinguished between children who tentatively qualified for "disabled reader" status and normal readers having average intelligence. Moreover, with the exception of performance on measures of reading comprehension, measures of reading achievement did not distinguish between normal readers having average intelligence and normal readers having above-average intelligence. Because reading comprehension entails knowledge and abilities that are typically evaluated by intelligence tests (e.g., vocabulary knowledge, inferencing, and reasoning ability), observed differences between these two groups on the comprehension measures is not surprising. Thus, our data provide ample justification for abandoning the practice of using IQ scores to define specific reading disabity.

Finally, although results from our intervention study suggest that beginning reading difficulties in the large majority of impaired readers are not caused by basic cognitive deficits, the data also suggest that a relatively small percentage of these children may suffer from such deficits. This possibility is suggested in our findings that the children who proved to be the most difficult to remediate performed significantly below both the normal readers and the children who were readily remediated on measures of language-based skills, especially those measures evaluating phonological skills such as letter and number naming, phonological decoding, phoneme awareness, rapid naming, confrontational naming, and verbal memory. In contrast, there were no reliable differences between these groups on measures of visual, semantic, and syntactic abilities. Thus, we cautiously suggest that "specific reading disability" as a diagnostic category may have psychological reality in the case of some children who have difficulty learning to read.

Acknowledgments

The data for this study were collected as part of a project implemented under the auspices of a special center grant awarded to the Kennedy Krieger Institute of Johns Hopkins University by the National Institute of Child Health and Human Development (No. P50HD25806). Martha B. Denckla was the principal investigator overseeing the various projects initiated under the grant. The research reported in this chapter was part of Project IV (The Reading and Language Project) implemented under a subcontract directed by Dr. Frank R. Vellutino and Dr. Donna M. Scanlon of the Child Research and Study Center of the University at Albany. The authors wish to express their sincere gratitude to the teachers, students, and secretarial and administrative staff in participating schools. Many, many thanks also go to our colleagues Sheila Small and Diane Fanuele who devoted years of their lives to this project!

Notes

1. To amplify the definitions of the literacy and literacy-related subcategories subsumed under the *general focus* category, *direct reading* was coded when written materials were the focus of the lesson and the teacher expected the children to be looking at these materials while either she or they (or both) were reading. An activity was coded as *indirect reading* when the intention of the instruction was to develop skills and attitudes which promote reading but the children were not actually expected to read. Included under *indirect reading* were activities such as discussing a story or other text as well as word-level activities such as letter naming, letter–sound learning, sight word learning, and phoneme analysis. *Writing* was coded for activities wherein the children were encouraged to use their developing phoneme analysis and letter–sound (invented spelling) skills in writing words and simple sentences, as well as activities designed to assist them in learning to form letters of the alphabet. An activity was coded as *language development* if the (apparent) intent of the lesson was to facilitate vocabulary knowledge, understanding of a new idea, and/or expressive language.
2. On the Woodcock Reading Mastery Tests—Revised the standard score mean for all of the reading measures is 100 and the standard deviation is 15. Thus, given that the 30th percentile on all these measures corresponds with a standard score of 92, those who score at or above the 30th percentile are solidly within the average range.
3. Percentage estimates corresponding with the number of children who would have qualified for the diagnosis of "specific reading disability" were calculated as follows: To obtain the percentage estimate for the population of elementary school children from which our im-

paired readers were initially selected, we divided the number of children from our kindergarten sample who were identified as impaired readers in mid-first grade using only exclusionary criteria such as those typically employed in our schools (N = 118) by the total number of children from our kindergarten sample who were yet available in mid-first grade after attrition (N = 1284). This yielded approximately 9% (118/1284) as the estimate of the percent of children in the population who could have been classified as "disabled readers."

However, this figure was calculated before initiation of the remedial intervention program and was based on a total (N = 118) that included the number of impaired readers given daily one-to-one remediation by project staff (N = 76), as well as the number of impaired readers given school-based remediation (N = 42). To obtain a more accurate estimate of the population of available children, excluding the children given school-based remediation, we multiplied the number of children in the total population of available children (after attrition) by the percentage of identified poor readers who received daily one-to-one tutoring by project staff (76/118 = 64.4%; 1,284 × 64.4% = 827). Using this figure as the population base, the number of tutored children who scored below the 15th percentile on the Basic Skills Cluster (BSC) after one semester of remediation represents 1.5% (12/827) of the total population from which these children were drawn, while the total number of tutored children who scored below the 30th percentile on the BSC after the same amount of remediation represents 3% (25/827) of the population from which they were drawn. Both of these percentages represent significant reductions of the estimate of the percentage of children in the population who would have qualified for the diagnosis of "specific reading disability" compared with the 9% estimate obtained before remedial intervention, using only the exclusionary criteria typically employed in our schools.

References

Adams, M. J. (1990). *Beginning to read: Thinking and learning about print.* Cambridge, MA: MIT Press.

Badian, N. A. (1982). The prediction of good and poor reading before kindergarten entry: A 4-year follow-up. *Journal of Special Education, 16,* 309–318.

Blachman, B. (1994). Early literacy acquisition: The role of phonological awareness. In G. Wallach & K. Butler (Eds.), *Language learning disabilities in school age children and adolescents: Some underlying principles and applications* (pp. 253–274). Columbus, OH: Merrill.

Bradley, L. & Bryant, P. E. (1983). Categorizing sounds and learning to read: A causal connection. *Nature, 303,* 419–421.

Butler, S. R., Marsh, H. W., Sheppard, M. J., & Sheppard, J. L. (1985). Seven-year longitudinal study of the early prediction of reading achievement. *Journal of Educational Psychology, 77,* 349–361.

Catts, H. W. (1991). Early identification of dyslexia: Evidence from a follow-up study of speech-language impaired children. *Annals of Dyslexia, 41,* 163–177.

Chall, J. (1967). *Learning to read: The great debate.* New York: McGraw-Hill.

Clay, M. M. (1985). *The early detection of reading difficulties,* (3rd ed.). Auckland, New Zealand: Heinemann.

Clay, M. M. (1987). Learning to be learning disabled. *New Zealand Journal of Educational Studies, 22,* 155–173.

de Hirsch, K., Jansky, J., & Langford, W. (1966). *Predicting reading failure.* New York: Harper & Row.

Fletcher J. M., Shaywitz, S. E., Shankweiler, D. P., Katz, L., Liberman, I. Y., Steubing, K. K., Francis, D. J., Fowler, A. E., & Shaywitz, B. A. (1994). Cognitive profiles of reading disability: Comparisons of discrepancy and low achievement definitions. *Journal of Educational Psychology, 86,* 6–23.

Foorman, B. R., Francis, D. J., Novy, D. M., & Liberman, D. (1991). How letter–sound instruction mediates progress in first-grade reading and spelling. *Journal of Educational Psychology, 83,* 456–469.

Harris, A. S., & Sipay, E. R. (1990). *How to increase reading ability.* (9th ed.) New York: Longman.

Iversen, S., & Tunmer, W. (1993). Phonological processing skills and the Reading Recovery program. *Journal of Educational Psychology, 85,* 112–126.

Jansky, J., & de Hirsch, K. (1972). *Preventing reading failure: Prediction, diagnosis, intervention.* New York: Harper & Row.

Katz, R. B., Shankweiler, D., & Liberman, I. Y. (1981). Memory for item order and phonetic recoding in the beginning reader. *Journal of Experimental Child Psychology, 32,* 474–484.

Knapp, M. S., Shields, P. M., & Turnbull, B. J. (1992). *Academic challenge for the children of poverty.* Menlo Park, CA: SRI.

Lundberg, I., Frost, J., & Petersen, O. P. (1988). Effects of an extensive program for stimulating phonological awareness in preschool children. *Reading Research Quarterly, 23,* 263–285.

Pinnell, G. S. (1989). Reading recovery: Helping at risk children learn to read. *Elementary School Journal, 90,* 161–184.

Santa, C. M., & Hoien, T. (1999). An assessment of Early Steps: A program for early intervention of reading problems. *Reading Research Quarterly, 34,* 54–79.

Satz, P., Taylor, H. G., Friel, J., & Fletcher, J. (1978). Some developmental and predictive precursors of reading disabilities: A six year follow-up. In A. L. Benton & D. Pearl (Eds.), *Dyslexia: An appraisal of current knowledge* (pp. 313–348). New York: Oxford University Press.

Scanlon, D. M., & Vellutino, F. R. (1996). Prerequisite skills, early instruction, and success in first grade reading: Selected results from a longitudinal study. *Mental Retardation and Developmental Disabilities, 2,* 54–63.

Scanlon, D. M., & Vellutino, F. R. (1997). A comparison of the instructional backgrounds and cognitive profiles of poor, average, and good readers who were initially identified as at risk for reading failure. *Scientific Studies of Reading, 1*(3), 191–215.

Scanlon, D. M., Vellutino, F. R., Small, S. G., & Fanuele, D. P. (2000, April). *Severe reading difficulties: Can they be prevented? A comparison of prevention and intervention approaches.* Paper presented at the annual convention of the American Educational Research Association, New Orleans.

Shaywitz, S. E., Escobar, M. D., Shaywitz, B. A., Fletcher, J. M., & Makuch, R. W. (1992). Evidence that dyslexia may represent the lower tail of a normal distribution of reading ability. *New England Journal of Medicine, 326,* 145–150.

Siegel, L. S. (1988). Evidence that IQ scores are irrelevant to the definition and analysis of reading disability. *Canadian Journal of Psychology, 42*(2), 201–215.

Siegel, L. S. (1989). IQ is irrelevant to the definition of learning disabilities. *Journal of Learning Disabilities, 22,* 469–478.

Stanovich, K. E. (1986). Matthew effects in reading: Some consequences of individual differences in the acquisition of literacy. *Reading Research Quarterly, 21,* 360–407.

Stanovich, K. E., & Siegel, L. S. (1994). Phenotypic performance profile of children with reading disabilities: A regression-based test of the phonological-core variable-difference model. *Journal of Educational Psychology, 86*(1), 24–53.

Torgesen, J. K., Wagner, R. K., & Rashotte, C. A. (1997). Approaches to the prevention and remediation of phonologically based reading disabilities. In B. Blachman (Ed.), *Foundations of reading acquisition and dyslexia: Implications for early intervention* (pp. 287–304). Mahwah, NJ: Erlbaum.

Tunmer, W. E. (1989). The role of language related factors in reading disability. In D. Shankweiler &

I. Y. Liberman (Eds.), *Phonology and reading disability: Solving the reading puzzle* (pp. 91–131). Ann Arbor: University of Michigan Press.

Vellutino, F. R. (1979). *Dyslexia: Theory and research.* Cambridge: MIT Press.

Vellutino, F. R. (1987, March). Dyslexia. *Scientific American,* pp. 34–41.

Vellutino, F. R. (1991). Introduction to three studies on reading acquisition: Convergent findings on theoretical foundations of code-oriented versus whole language approaches to reading instruction. *Journal of Educational Psychology, 83,* 189–264.

Vellutino, F. R., & Scanlon, D. M. (1987). Phonological coding, phonological awareness, and reading ability: Evidence from a longitudinal and experimental study. *Merrill–Palmer Quarterly, 33,* 321–363.

Vellutino, F. R., Scanlon, D. M., & Lyon, G. R. (2000). Differentiating between difficult-to-remediate and readily remediated poor readers: More evidence against the IQ-achievement discrepancy definition of reading disability. *Journal of Learning Disabilities, 33*(3), 223–238.

Vellutino, F. R., Scanlon, D. M., Sipay, E. R., Small, S. G., Pratt, A., Chen, R., & Denckla, M. B. (1996). Cognitive profiles of difficult to remediate and readily remediated poor readers: Early intervention as a vehicle for distinguishing between cognitive and experiential deficits as basic causes of specific reading disability. *Journal of Educational Psychology, 88*(4), 601–638.

Vellutino, F. R., Scanlon, D. M., & Spearing, D. (1995). Semantic and phonological coding in poor and normal readers. *Journal of Experimental Child Psychology, 59,* 76–123.

Vellutino, F. R., Scanlon, D. M., & Tanzman, M. S. (1988). Lexical memory in poor and normal reader: Developmental differences in the use of category cues. *Canadian Journal of Psychology, 42,* 216–241.

Wasik, B. A., & Slavin, R. R. (1993). Preventing early reading failure with one-to-one tutoring: A review of five programs. *Reading Research Quarterly, 28,* 179–200.

Wechsler, D. (1974). *Wechsler Intelligence Scale for Children—Revised.* New York: Psychological Corporation.

Woodcock, R. W. (1987). *Woodcock Reading Mastery Tests—Revised.* Circle Pines, MN: American Guidance Services.

Woodcock, R. W., & Johnson, M. B. (1989). *Woodcock–Johnson Psychoeducational Battery-Revised.* Allen, TX: DLM Teaching Resources.

21

Early Intervention
for African American Children
Considered to Be at Risk

❖

DOROTHY S. STRICKLAND

Malik, age 4, enters his child-care center. It is warm and inviting. A series of Mother Goose cutouts line the walls and bright colored carpeting covers various areas of the floor. It is December and Malik's classroom has been decorated for the holidays. He looks across the room and notices some letters hung across one wall. They spell out "Merry Christmas." Suddenly Malik becomes very excited. He points to the word "Merry" and shouts, "That my name!" The caregiver, who is busily helping children take off their coats, notices what Malik is pointing to but fails (or is too busy) to acknowledge its significance. Instead, she urges him to start unbuttoning his coat. He persists several times, turning to the other children to announce what he has discovered. At this point he is told, "Quiet down now. We'll talk about the decorations later."

It is cooking time in an urban kindergarten. The children are excited because they have been told that they are going to make holiday cookies. It is a special occasion because several people from the nearby university are coming to observe what they do. Seventeen children are seated at two long tables. The instructional assistant positions herself on one side where the two tables meet, thus making it possible for all of the children to see her. She proceeds to measure and mix the ingredients. The teacher stands at the opposite side of the tables. She describes what her assistant is doing and monitors the children's behavior to see that they watch attentively. Children who sit nicely are allowed to stir the batter. The instructional assistant carefully drops small portions of batter on the cookie sheets and places them in the oven. The cooking "demonstration" ends.

Upon revisiting a child-care center to which she had recently given 50 picture books, a university professor is surprised to find that most of the books are nowhere to be seen. She does notice two of the sturdy board books in the classroom for 3-year-old children, but none of the others are visible. When she inquires about this, she is told that they have been placed safely in the closet out of reach of the children so that they will be kept clean and not be destroyed. She is assured that they are being used as read-aloud material, however.

Each of the foregoing is an actual incident. To be sure, these are only snapshots of total programs. However, they are highly representative of the types of learning experiences available to many children in early-education settings. Although no one incident in itself is alarming, a composite of these occurrences reveals a great deal about the application (or lack of application) of well-known principles of early literacy development. There is cause for concern.

322

Clearly, any one of these vignettes could have occurred in any early-childhood program anywhere. Research reveals, however, that occurrences such as these are more likely to occur in settings in which children are poor, teachers are inadequately trained, and quality early literacy learning experiences are rare (Barnett & Boocock, 1998). It is in settings such as these that large numbers of African American children often reside.

This chapter focuses on issues related to the support of literacy development among young children considered to be at risk for failure. A particular emphasis is placed on concerns associated with educating young African American children and the need to close the gap between their achievement and that of other children. Nevertheless, much of the information contained in this chapter may be applied to any child judged to be at high risk for academic difficulty. The following topics are covered:

- Causes of reading failure
- The shift from remediation to intervention
- A sampling of representative programs
- Lessons from intervention programs

Examining the Causes of Reading Failure

Researchers have spent considerable time and effort identifying the characteristics prevalent in children who have difficulty learning to read. This information is a useful resource for educational policymakers and practitioners as they make programmatic decisions for young children. Although these variables are useful in making general decisions for groups of children, it must be kept in mind that each child is a complex individual who fits no single prototype. Nevertheless, an awareness of some of the possible underlying causes of learning difficulties is useful and important information on which educators can build constructively. In so doing, it is important to resist the tendency to use that information as justification for placing blame on the child or the child's circumstances.

The factors that follow have been well documented in the literature as characteristics of many children for whom learning to

read is highly challenging. It should be noted that some of the risk factors refer to the child's personal development. Others refer to the group or situation in which the child resides. Factors that often accompany low achievement in reading include the following.

Preschool Language Impairment

Although children vary widely in their early language development, there are indicators outside the normal range, such as severe delay in pronunciation accuracy and use of complex sentences that signal language delay to parents, pediatricians, and caregivers (Scarborough, 1998). Language delay is often part of a broader condition such as general developmental disability, hearing impairment (Conrad, 1979), or a neurological condition. The occurrence of reading problems is most likely when the language impairment is severe, broad in scope, and persistent.

In the case of African American children, who speak a nonstandard dialect of English (often called Ebonics or Black English Vernacular), educators must be careful not to automatically characterize the child's language as impaired or delayed. As with all children, African American youngsters simply learn the language to which they are exposed. It would be extremely odd to do otherwise. These children may be facile and articulate in their home dialect or their language may indeed be delayed (Flores, Cousin, & Diaz, 1991).

Limited Proficiency in English

When a child's home language is other than English, the likelihood of reading difficulty increases. This is particularly true if reading instruction in English begins before the child has acquired oral proficiency in English (August & Hakuta, 1997).

Educators must be mindful that problems, arising when a child speaks a dialect or language other than the one predominant in the school, are not due to an inherent deficiency in the child or the language spoken by the child. Rather, the problems occur when the differences between the child's dialect or language and the language of instruction are not taken into consideration or when the child's language is viewed in a stereotypical way to make negative judgments about his or her learning capacity (Labov, 1995; Smitherman, 1977).

History of Reading Problems in the Family

If a child is diagnosed with a reading disability, there is a higher than normal chance that other family members have also had difficulties with reading (Gilger, Pennington, & DeFries, 1991; Volger, DeFries, & Decker, 1985).

Although researchers have determined that a history of reading difficulties often occurs in families, the exact cause or causes may vary. In the case of children who are members of poor families and living in impoverished neighborhoods, multiple environmental factors are apt to be implicated. In poor-performing urban schools, low achievement in reading and writing among large numbers of African American children is so common it may easily affect several children of the families that attend those schools.

Attention-Deficit/Hyperactivity Disorder

Long-term studies indicate that from the beginning of formal schooling, reading disability is relatively common in children with inattention problems (31% in first grade) and become even more frequent among these children as they mature (Shaywitz, Fletcher, & Shaywitz, 1995). It is probably safe to assume that this phenomenon is at least equally as prevalent among children living in African American communities.

Lack of Motivation to Learn to Read

Children who have never experienced purposeful and pleasurable experiences with books and literacy are apt to be unenthusiastic about learning to read and write. Those who experience continued failure tend to avoid reading and thus deny themselves the most important means to improve their reading abilities (Snow, Barnes, Chandler, Goodman, & Hemphill, 1991).

Both home and school are powerful influences on children's motivation to read. Even before they begin formal schooling, those

children who have access to books, choose to spend time looking at them independently (Baker, Scher, & Mackler, 1997). Their actions suggest that they value literacy as a source of entertainment. Though studies indicate more frequent independent experiences with books by middle-income preschoolers than low-income preschoolers, children from diverse income and ethnic groups are reported by their parents to engage regularly in this activity (Baker et al., 1997; Marvin & Mirenda, 1993; Raz & Bryant, 1990).

Providing access to reading materials, space, and encouragement to read all contribute to a child's motivation. The importance of establishing and maintaining reading habits from the early years is confirmed by a study of African American, inner-city students in the middle grades in which Thompson, Mixon, and Serpell (1996) found that other leisure-time pursuits were preferred to reading, such as watching television, listening to music, and playing games. Few of these students had personal book collections. Unfortunately, inner-city libraries often are plagued by budgetary problems and thus do not offer the appealing milieu of suburban libraries that are rich in books as well as multimedia technologies. Moreover, parents in the inner city may not take their young children to the library because of genuine concerns about safety (Britt & Baker, 1997).

Poor Neighborhoods

Children who attend schools and live in communities in which low socioeconomic status is widespread are more likely to be at risk for failure in reading. Families that lack sufficient resources to provide adequate housing, health care, and nutrition for their children are less likely to focus on their children's educational needs (Snow, Burns, & Griffin, 1998).

Lack of resources within the home and in early-education settings put many young African American children at severe risk for failure. Recent welfare reforms mandate that mothers of young children find employment to support their families. Many view this as an opportunity to provide children with quality early literacy experiences. Unfortunately, evidence suggests that many children in inner-city early-education programs receive care of quite poor quality. It is inadequate with regard to supervision, nurturance, and responsiveness of caregivers; health and safety practices; and the availability of stimulating toys and other learning materials and opportunities (Hernandez, 1998).

Long-standing poverty appears to have had a lasting effect on African American families, even after they have escaped poor neighborhoods. Ladson-Billings (1999) reports that middle-class, college-educated black parents are often the first generation of their families to have such success; thus the roots of their academic and economic accomplishments are shallower than those of many white families.

Ineffective Classroom Practices

Classroom practices in ineffective schools (regardless of community socioeconomic status) are characterized by significantly lower rates of student time-on-task, less teacher presentation of new material, lower rates of teacher communication of high academic expectations, fewer instances of positive reinforcement, more classroom interruptions, more discipline problems, and classroom ambiance generally rated as less friendly (Teddlie, Kirby, & Stringfield, 1989)

Although low-quality instruction can and does happen in any school, it becomes a major detriment in schools in low-income areas, where resources for children's out-of-school learning are limited (Puma et al., 1997; Natriello, McDill, & Pallas, 1990).

It should be noted that none of these factors is an automatic barrier to the attainment of literacy. Nor, do any of these factors usually function alone as a single causal determinant or predictor of an individual child's reading problems. For example, although low reading achievement is a widespread problem among Latino students, linguistic differences are not solely responsible for the high degree of risk faced by these children. Many children who have limited English proficiency come from homes in which the parents are poorly educated and the family income is low.

Similarly, African American students who speak a nonstandard dialect of English are apt to live in poor neighborhoods and attend schools in which achievement is chronically low. In such cases, co-occurring group risk factors such as the socioeconomic circumstances of the child's family, the child's home literacy background, the neighborhood where the child lives, and the quality of the instruction in the school the child attends must be taken into account to fully comprehend the problem. A low socioeconomic-status child in a generally moderate-to upper-status school or community is far less at risk than that same child in a whole school or community of low socioeconomic-status children (Snow et al., 1998). Simply put, the factors listed here are those often associated with reading difficulties and, thus, are among those that must be considered when decisions regarding policy and practice are made for children who are experiencing difficulty with reading and writing.

Clearly, many children overcome one or more of these negative factors and go on to become successful readers and learners. However, unfortunately, children who are poor and living in less than stable circumstances are less likely to possess the resources that would enable them to overcome multiple negative factors in their lives. It is in such cases that the school and community play a major role.

Children who are both poor and African American are likely to be subject to multiple negative factors. The need for quality early-intervention programs that focus on language development, cognitive stimulation and enjoyment of books and stories, and an attempt to improve and coordinate educational and social services for families is abundantly clear. Ironically, early intervention is a relatively new concept. Historically, educators focused their attention on remediation, allowing children to fail before help was given. The importance of intervening early and effectively is well established among educators and social service providers (as described in the previous chapter). Following is a rationale for this important shift in the thinking of educators and policymakers with brief descriptions of several representative prevention and early-intervention programs.

The Shift from Remediation to Prevention and Intervention

Several factors have caused educators to turn to early intervention to help students who are experiencing difficulty learning to read and write. Research indicates that the cycle of failure often starts early in a child's school career. Stanovich (1986) argues, with good evidence, that children who encounter problems in the beginning stages of learning to read fall further and further behind their peers. Longitudinal studies (Juel, 1988) reveal that there is a near 90% chance that a child who is a poor reader at the end of grade 1 will remain a poor reader at the end of grade 4. As they move through the grades, these youngsters are apt to experience continued failure and defeat, which may account for the tendency of low-achieving students to drop out of school.

Another compelling reason to promote early intervention is the realization that supplementary remedial programs such as Title 1 and "replacement" programs that substitute for regular, in-class instruction have had mixed results over the years (see McGill-Franzen & Goatley, Chapter 30). Some argue that such programs cause classroom teachers to overrely on special help and neglect their responsibility for less able students. Others suggest that where these programs exist, instruction within and outside the classroom is often at odds with one another. Even when such programs are considered highly successful, they appear to work best where there is a strong, compatible instructional program in the regular classroom. Regardless of the supplemental help offered, there is a growing recognition that more attention needs to be given to incorporating the best prevention and intervention procedures into regular classroom instructional practice (Allington & Walmsley, 1995).

Increased demands to make every child a reader by the end of the primary grades have also spurred early-intervention efforts. National, state, and local school reform movements have raised expectations for what young learners should know and be able to do, and they specify the grade levels at which they should be able to do it. Standards have been raised for all students regardless of who they are, where they live, their linguistic backgrounds, or whether or not they have been classified as having a learning disability. The gradual trend away from long-term remedial programs at all levels and the growing emphasis on early intervention, prevention, and good "first teaching" make the early years a key focus of reform.

Those who have turned their attention to early intervention state that it is ultimately less costly than years of remediation, less costly than retention, and less costly to students' self-esteem (Barnett, 1998). This final point may be the most compelling of all because the savings in human suffering and humiliation is incalculable. Teachers in remedial programs often observe that students who feel they are failures frequently give up and stop trying to learn despite adequate instructional opportunities.

Following is a description of several prevention and intervention programs. Although only a limited number can be included here, these are representative of current efforts designed to prevent reading failure in young children. Virtually all have reported some degree of success in settings in which African American children are considered to be at risk. Although the goals of these programs are similar, implementation varies widely.

A Sampling of Representative Programs

This section briefly describes a number of prevention and intervention programs currently in use across the country. Family-oriented prevention programs tend to focus on both parents and their young children. Such programs may be located in a variety of settings and often target a number of outcomes other than language and literacy alone. For example, the Even Start Family Literacy Program consists of a variety of family literacy projects established for the purpose of integrating early-childhood education and adult education for parents into a unified program. Four features have been found to be critical to the success of these programs:

(1) steps must be taken to ensure participation through such means as providing transportation and child care and attention to possible emotional barriers such as fear of school and low self-esteem; (2) the curriculum must be meaningful and useful to the participants; (3) the staff must be stable and highly capable; and (4) there must be ample funding to ensure that the program is sustained over time (DeBruin-Parecki, Paris, & Siedenburg, 1997).

The Home Instruction Program for Preschool Youngsters (HIPPY) is another example of a home-based instruction program designed to help parents provide their children with school-readiness skills. Parents and children engage in a variety of reading-related activities. Components of HIPPY have been adapted into many other family literacy programs (Baker & Piotrkowski, 1996).

As the focus shifts from prevention to intervention, most programs reside in school settings. Many employ small-group instruction; others restrict instruction to one-on-one tutoring models. Some take place in the regular classroom with instruction supplied by the regular classroom teacher or a reading specialist. Others occur outside the regular classroom and make use of reading specialists or well-supervised volunteers or paid tutors. Some programs are linked to classroom instruction, as is Success for All's tutoring component (Wasik & Slavin, 1993); others, such as Reading Recovery and Book Buddies, do not attempt to foster a tight curriculum link (Invernizzi, Juel, & Rosemary, 1997). Success has been demonstrated in a variety of settings: large urban districts, small suburban schools, and rural areas.

Head Start is the most widely known early-intervention program for economically disadvantaged children. Although Head Start programs vary widely, they all strive to provide a range of comprehensive services for children and families, including a "developmental" curriculum. Like many other programs designed for children in poverty, Head Start programs often produce immediate effects for reading achievement which tend to decline over time. Nevertheless, some programs have produced sizable gains that persist into the school years. The magnitude of initial effects appears to be related to a program's intensity, breadth, and atten-

tion to the involvement of the children's parents (Bryant, Lau, Burchinal, & Sparling, 1994).

Book Buddies and Early Reading Intervention involve small group or individualized tutorials in school settings. Book Buddies is a supplementary intervention in which selected children receive one-on-one tutorials twice a week in addition to classroom reading instruction, using community volunteers as tutors. Tutors receive continuous on-site training and supervision. The four-part lesson consists of repeated reading of familiar text, word study (phonics), writing for sounds, and reading a new book (Invernizzi, Juel, Rosemary, 1997).

Early Reading Intervention (ERI) is a small-group tutoring program that targets first- and second-graders at risk for failure to read. The program is organized to enable a small group of students to work with their teacher 15–20 minutes a day, 3 days a week. The children also read individually to an instructional aide, volunteers, or older students for 5 minutes a day. The program focuses on word-analysis strategies in the context of reading storybooks. Opportunities for rereading through choral reading or partner reading are offered (Taylor, Strait, & Medo, 1994).

Reading Recovery is perhaps the best known and researched beginning reading intervention program. Designed for first-graders, it involves one-on-one tutoring by teachers, who receive extensive training in theory and practical approaches to working with children experiencing difficulty learning to read. The lessons involve rereading previously read books, independent reading of a new book introduced in a previous lesson, word analysis and comprehension strategies, writing and reading of the child's own sentences, and the introduction and supported reading of a new book (Pinnell, Deford, & Lyons, 1988). First Steps is a one-to-one tutoring program based on many of the principles of Reading Recovery. The 30-minute tutoring session consists of book reading in which the child rereads a book from a series of leveled books; a word-study component in which the tutor takes the child through a series of letter/word sorts based on need and level of development; a writing activity; and the reading of a new story (Morris, 1995; Santa & Hoien, 1999).

Success for All is among the most well-known schoolwide programs. It is a comprehensive school restructuring program which serves students placed at risk for failure in grades 1 through 6. It includes Curiosity Corner, a prekindergarten and kindergarten program, a Beginning Reading or Reading Roots program, and a Beyond the Basics or Reading Wings Program. The program includes a mixture of phonics, direct instruction of comprehension strategies, and listening comprehension skills. Cooperative learning strategies are integrated heavily throughout the curriculum, as are one-to-one tutorials (Slavin et al., 1996). Another schoolwide program, The Kamehameha Early Education Program (KEEP) Whole Literacy Curriculum, was designed for native Hawaiian students in kindergarten through grade 6, this program addresses issues faced by any at-risk children facing similar challenges. It includes readers' and writers' workshops, portfolio assessment, word-reading strategies and spelling, voluntary reading, and established literacy benchmarks for student success. The ongoing staff development of teachers prior to and during implementation is heavily stressed (Au & Carroll, 1997).

Several researchers have analyzed the components of the programs described here and others like them that have research support. These analyses allow us to tease out common elements and provide a conceptual framework for the essential elements of sound intervention. These analyses are offered here as lessons learned with particular emphasis on the needs of African American children considered to be at risk for failure.

Lessons from Intervention Programs

An examination of the characteristics of successful prevention and intervention programs reveals a fair degree of agreement regarding essential elements or components that receive attention (Duffy-Hester, 1999; Pikulski, 1994; Snow et al., 1998; Wasik, 1998). Following is a list of principles based on consistent elements across these programs. Each principle is followed by recommendations that highlight the needs of African American children who are likely to be at risk.

1. *Early intervention is preferable to extended remediation.* Age-appropriate efforts aimed toward prevention and intervention should begin during the prekindergarten years and continue to receive special emphasis during the early primary grades.

In early-education programs, African American children's language and cognitive growth must become a major priority along with their health and safety. Carefully developed curricula that take advantage of what is known about young children's oral language development and their emerging interest and knowledge of literacy should become *institutionalized* as a major emphasis at the prekindergarten levels. Strengthening and extending the language and literacy foundation of young African American children must be a major focus in the primary grades, where lifelong habits and attitudes are established.

2. *A systematic program of home support is essential.* Strengthening the bond between home, school, and community is an important element of programs that seek to prevent or intervene when children are at risk. Collaboration with local agencies that support families and family literacy initiatives is common.

Early literacy programs targeting young African American children must make every attempt to involve the home and the community. Edwards (1992) suggests that a common misconception among many educators is that African American parents are simply not interested in helping their children. She asserts that nonmainstream parents who lack knowledge do not necessarily lack interest in their children's schools or in learning how to help their children. She successfully used local churches and businesses to help publicize her family literacy program. Many primary-grade intervention programs include built-in monitoring systems designed to provide instructional links to the home and feedback from the home.

3. *Children considered at risk require more time on task than do others.* Prevention and intervention programs must be ongoing and consistent and must offer opportunities for learning beyond the regular curriculum.

Support programs for African American children should supplement, not supplant, the regular curriculum. According to Allington and Walmsley (1995), the fact that many instructional support programs have not adequately met the needs of students assigned to them may be in part an unfortunate by-product of their existence. Once programs have been established to meet the needs of students with learning difficulties, regular classroom teachers may sometimes excuse themselves from the responsibility of the education of low-achieving students.

4. *Students must be given materials they can handle successfully.* Although materials vary widely among interventions, it is safe to say that in all such programs careful attention is given to their selection and use.

For teacher-led and independent reading experiences, African American children need exposure to a wide variety of materials, including those characterized as predictable and phonologically or linguistically regular and those that are leveled or sequenced from easy to more difficult. Teachers should be aware of the importance of reading aloud regularly to children from materials that strengthen their vocabulary and concept development and broaden their background knowledge. Programs should strive for an abundance of materials that are multicultural, interesting, and engaging and provide a fair degree of challenge without frustration. Materials must be made accessible to children so that they can "revisit" them as a source for independent learning, at their leisure (Strickland, 1998).

5. *Careful consideration must be given to the content and nature of the learning experiences offered.* Successful prevention and intervention programs are based on a well-formulated and consistent plan or approach.

At the prekindergarten level, African American children need early-education programs that have a thoughtfully planned and executed curriculum focusing on language development with an emphasis on vocabulary and concepts, understandings about the functions of print, print awareness and concepts about print, literacy as a source of enjoyment, understandings about the nature of stories and their structure, experiences with books and print of all types, knowledge of the alphabet, phonemic awareness, and opportunities to write. The curriculum should be clearly articulated in curriculum documents that serve as the basis for concerted planning and action on the part of all members of the staff. This stated curriculum should be in evidence as an integral part of the day in ways that are developmentally appropriate for the children involved.

At the kindergarten and primary-grade levels, African American children need early-intervention-oriented programs that exist both as a regular part of the curriculum and carried out by the regular classroom teachers as well as special programs aimed at intervention that go beyond the regular curriculum. Both efforts should take inventory of the components listed previously for younger children and address those areas needing attention. In addition, special emphasis is placed on reading comprehension strategies, word-recognition strategies including phonics and structural analysis, fluency, writing, and extensive amounts of independent reading and book discussion. Emphasis should be placed on skillful application of strategies *in use* in small-group and one-to-one instructional formats.

6. *Individual progress monitored on a regular, ongoing basis.* Intervention programs generally have well-developed monitoring systems. Students are evaluated in relationship to a set of predetermined program goals, benchmarks, or levels.

Schools in which large numbers of African American children have a history of poor achievement are required to take into account the standards and benchmarks set forth for all children in a district or state. However, the primary goal in these schools must be focused on the amount of growth made within a given period. Thus teachers and schools should be held accountable for the growth or lack of growth among their students and not whether or not they meet a fixed criterion. During the early-childhood years, growth may be determined by informal (but rigorous and valid) classroom assessments that are ongoing, efficient, and used to inform the instructional plan (see Johnston & Rogers, Chapter 25).

7. *The professional development of teachers, aides, and volunteers is a key component for success.* Although intervention programs vary widely in their training and use of personnel, the professional development of teachers, aides, and volunteers is considered a critical component of the success of all intervention models.

All children considered at risk need the best teachers available. In the case of African American children, living in poor neighborhoods, extraordinary efforts must be taken to attract and keep professionals who are well trained, experienced, and committed to working with these children (Strickland, 1994, 1995).

Some Conclusions and Lingering Questions

As educators, we have learned a great deal about what must be done to prevent reading failure in the classroom. Though the application of what is known is highly uneven and lacking in many ways, there is optimism that we are gradually moving forward. Many are concerned that the changes are too slow. Given what is known about early literacy development, scenes such as those that opened this chapter should not occur even in today's less than ideal circumstances. Even with a minimum amount of training in early literacy development, Malik's teacher might have briefly acknowledged the associations he was making between his name and the word Merry. Children who are told that they are going to make cookies should be allowed to truly engage in the process. They should participate as adults read and refer to the recipe written on a chart. They should work in small, hands-on groups where their exuberance can be better tolerated and where they are allowed to stir and drop the cookie batter themselves. In the process, they should be encouraged to use the language of cooking such as "batter," "stir," and "measure." Even with limited resources, teachers must make books accessible to children, especially those they had read aloud, as those are the books to which children naturally gravitate to revisit on their own.

Taub (2000) asserted that education may not be able to conquer the disadvantages impoverished children bring with them to school and return to at home. The gains made by current intervention programs are described as only moderately hopeful and extremely limited. Black psychologist Edmund Gordon, a highly respected and long-time figure in intervention efforts, is quoted

in the article as saying, "School works for people who have the [cultural] capital to invest in it. And if they don't, then schooling is going to be greatly handicapped." Taub (2000) sees hope in totally changing the environment of very young children. Describing Impact, a school in Vineland, New Jersey, he reported that "not so much a preschool as a multi-purpose social-service agency" (p. 90). Taub describes the teachers as well-spoken professionals, the classes small and richly stocked with books and art materials and computers, and the children as moving purposefully among activities. Even in the child-care center each group of children has a teacher who is certified in early-childhood education. Though some will take issue with specific points in Taub's message, his appeal to nurture the child's total well being and thus change the "neighborhood" is well made.

Changing the "neighborhood" will require full-blown national, state, and local initiatives that include active attention to opportunity-to-learn standards for early literacy that speak to a range of factors such as class size, condition and maintenance of physical environments, the coordination of social services, and the quality of the learning experiences offered in the classroom. Key to this initiative is the establishment of clear and focused guidelines and action plans for dramatically upgrading the quality of the preparation, certification, and ongoing professional development of those who work with young children.

We approach the new millennium as the wealthiest nation in the world. True wealth must be measured in both material and human capital. Surely, one of the most important measures of our success will be our ability to advance the human capital represented in *all* our nation's children.

References

Allington, R. L., & Walmsley, S. A. (1995). *No quick fix*. New York: Teachers College Press.
Au, K. H., & Carroll, J. H. (1997). Improving literacy achievement through a constructivist approach: The KEEP demonstration classroom project. *Elementary School Journal, 97,* 203–221.
August, D. A., & Hakuta, K. (Eds.). (1997). *Improving schooling for language-minority children:*

A research agenda. Washington, DC: National Academy Press.

Baker, A. J., & Piotrkowski, C. S. (1996). *Parents and children through the school years: The effects of the home instruction program for preschool youngsters*. Final Report to the David and Lucile Packard Foundation. Los Altos, CA.

Baker, L., Scher, D., & Mackler, K. (1997). Home and family influences on motivations for literacy. *Educational Psychologist, 32,* 69–82.

Barnett, S. W. (1998). Long-term effects on cognitive development an school success. In S. W. Barnett & S. Boocock (1998). *Early care and education for children in poverty* (pp. 11–44). Albany, NY: State University of New York.

Britt, G., & Baker, L. (1997). *Engaging parents and kindergartners in reading through class lending library* (Instructional Resource No. 41). Athens GA: Universities of Georgia and Maryland, National Reading Research Center.

Bryant, D. M., Lau, L. B., Burchinal, M., & Sparling, J. J. (1994). Family and classroom correlates of Head Start children's developmental outcomes. *Early Childhood Research Quarterly, 9*(3–4), 289–309.

Conrad, R. (1979). *The deaf school child*. London: Harper & Row.

DeBruin-Parecki, A., Paris, S., & Siedenburg, J. (1997). Family literacy: Examining practice and issues of effectiveness (in Michigan). *Journal of Adolescent and Adult Literacy, 40,* 596–605.

Duffy-Hester, A. (1999). Teaching struggling readers in elementary school classrooms: A review of classroom reading programs and principles for instruction. *The Reading Teacher, 52,* 480–495.

Edwards, P. (1992). Involving parents in building reading instruction for African-American Children. *Theory into Practice, 31,* 350–359.

Flores, B., Cousin, P. T., & Diaz, E. (1991). Transforming deficit myths about learning, language, and culture. *Language Arts, 68,* 369–379.

Gilger, J. W., Pennington, B. F., & DeFries, J. C. (1991). Risk for reading disability as a function of family history in three family studies. *Reading and Writing: An Interdisciplinary Journal, 3,* 205–217.

Hernandez, D. J. (1998). Economic and social disadvantages of young children: Alternative policy responses. In W. S. Barnett & S. S. Boocock (Eds.), *Early care and education: Promises, programs, and long-term results*. Albany, NY: State University of New York Press.

Invernizzi, M., Juel, C., & Rosemary, C. A. (1997). A community volunteer tutorial that works. *The Reading Teacher, 50,* 304–311.

Johnston, P. A., & Allington, R. L., & Aflerbach, P. (1985). The congruence of classroom and remedial reading instruction. *Elementary School Journal, 85,* 465–478.

Juel, C. (1988, April). *Learning to read and write: A longitudinal study of fifty-four children from first through fourth grade*. Paper presented at the annual meeting of the American Educational Research Association, New Orleans.

Ladson-Billings, G. (1999, July 4). *New York Times,* p. 15.

Labov, W. (1995). Can reading failure be reversed: A linguistic approach to the question. In V. Gadsden & D. Wagner (Eds.), *Literacy among African-American Youth: Issues in learning teaching and schooling* (pp. 39–68). Cresskill, NJ: Hampton Press.

Marvin, C., & Mirenda, P. (1993). Home literacy experiences of preschoolers enrolled in Head Start and special education programs. *Journal of Early Intervention, 17,* 351–367.

Morris, D. (1995). *First steps: An early reading intervention program*. (ERIC Documentation Reproduction Service No. ED 388956)

Natriello, G. E., McDill, E., & Pallas, A. (1990). *Schooling disadvantaged children: Racing against catastrophe*. New York: Teachers College.

Pikulski, J. (1994). Preventing reading failure: A review of five effective programs. *Reading Teacher, 48,* 30–39.

Pinnell, G. S., Deford, D. E., & Lyons, C. A. (1988). *Reading recovery: Early intervention for at-risk students*. Arlington, VA: Education Research Services.

Puma, M., Karweit, N., Price, C., Ricciuti, A., Thompson, W., & Vaden-Kiernan, M. (1997). *Prospects: Final report on student outcomes*. Washington, DC: U. S. Department of Education, Planning and Evaluation Services.

Raz, I. T., & Bryant, P. (1990). Social background, phonological awareness and children's reading. *British Journal of Developmental Psychology, 8,* 209–225.

Santa, C., & Hoien, T. (1999). An assessment of Early Steps: A program for early intervention of reading problems. *Reading Research Quarterly, 4,* 54–79.

Scarborough, H. H. (1998). Early identification of children at risk for reading disabilities: Phonological awareness and some other promising predictors. In K. Shapiro, P. J. Accardo, & A. J. Capute (Eds.), *Specific reading disability: A view of the spectrum* (pp. 77–121). Timonium, MD: York Press.

Shaywitz, B. A., Fletcher, J. M., & Shaywitz, S. E. (1995). Defining and classifying learning disabilities and attention-deficit/hyperactivity disorder. *Journal of Child Neurology, 10*(Suppl.), S50–S57.

Slavin, R. E., Madden, N. A., Dolan, L. J., Wasik, B. A., Ross, S. M., & Smith, L., Dianda, M. (1996). Success for All: A summary of research. *Journal of Education for Students Placed At Risk, 1,* 41–76.

Smitherman, G. (1977). Black English and the education of Black children and youth. *Proceedings of the National Invitational Symposium on the KING Decision*. Detroit: Center for Black Studies, Wayne State University.

Snow, C. E., Barnes, W. S., Chandler, J., Goodman, I. F., & Hemphill, L. (1991). *Unfulfilled expectations: Home and school influences on literacy*. Cambridge, MA: Harvard University Press.

Snow, C. E., Burns, S., & Griffin, P. (Eds.). (1998). *Preventing reading difficulties in young children.* Washington, DC: National Academy Press.

Stanovich, K. E. (1986). Matthew effects in reading: Some consequences of individual differences in the acquisition of literacy. *Reading Research Quarterly, 21,* 360–407.

Strickland, D. S. (1994). Educating African American learners at risk: Finding a better way. *Language Arts, 17,* 328–336.

Strickland, D. S. (1995). Pre-elementary programs: A model for professional development. In S. Wepner, J. Feeley, & D. Strickland (Eds.), *The administration and supervision of reading programs* (pp. 41–58). New York: Teachers College Press.

Strickland, D. S. (1998). Differentiating instruction in the classroom: Tapping into the intelligence of every learner. In B. Presseisen (Ed.), *Teaching for intelligence* (pp. 244–260). Arlington Heights, IL: Skylight Training.

Taylor, B., Strait, J., & Medo, M. A. (1994). An early intervention in reading: Supplemented instruction for groups of low-achieving students provided by first grade teachers. In E. Hiebert & B. Taylor (Eds.), *Getting reading right from the start* (pp. 107–121). Boston: Allyn & Bacon.

Teddlie, C., Kirby, P., & Stringfield, S. (1989). Effective vs. ineffective schools: Observable differences in the classroom. *American Journal of Education, 97,* 221–236.

Thompson, R., Mixon, G., & Serpell, R. (1996). Engaging minority students in reading: Focus on the urban learner. In L. Baker, P. Afflerback, & D. Reinking (Eds.), *Developing engaged readers in school and home communities* (pp. 43–63). Mahwah, NJ: Erlbaum.

Traub, J. (2000, January 16). What no schools can do. *New York Times Magazine,* pp. 53–57, 68, 81, 82.

Volger, G. P., DeFries, J. C., & Decker, S. N. (1985). Family history as an indicator of risk for reading disability. *Journal of Learning Disabilities, 18,* 419–421.

Wasik, B. A. (1998). Early literacy: Prevention and intervention. In P. D. Pearson (Eds.), *Report of New York State Reading Symposium* (pp. 59–82). Albany, NY: The State Education Department.

Wasik, B. A., & Slavin, R. E. (1993). Preventing early reading failure with one-to-one tutoring: A review of five programs. *Reading Research Quarterly, 28,* 178–200.

22

Teaching Phonics and
Phonological Awareness

❖

STEVEN A. STAHL

In 1967, Jeanne Chall published her landmark review of beginning reading instruction, *Learning to Read: The Great Debate.* At that time, there were many questions about the role of phonics in beginning reading. These questions about beginning reading were not just confined to the educational community but were very much in public discourse. Flesch (1955), in a best-selling book *Why Johnny Can't Read,* argued that children were being abused by the then-current whole-word methodology. If children were only taught the 44 letter–sound correspondences, he argued, they could read any word they encountered, and there would be no reading problems. Spurred on partially by Flesch and partially by advances in linguistics, new phonics programs had been developed and were gaining a beachhead against the then-dominant whole-word method of beginning reading instruction (see Aukerman, 1981; Popp, 1975).

Chall's (1967) review was only one of many projects attempting to "solve" the problems of beginning reading. The Cooperative Research Program in First Grade Reading (First Grade studies; Bond & Dykstra, 1967/1998) was one of the first federally funded research projects. It consisted of 29 coordinated studies examining everything from the role of phonics to the effects of different types of instruction on children of different ethnic groups. The sheer complexity of 29 separate studies, which exam-

ined everything from synthetic phonics instruction to the initial teaching alphabet to language experience to gender differences to time on task, made it difficult to draw conclusions. Dykstra (1968), one of the project coordinators, suggested that the First Grade studies basically confirmed Chall's findings about the superiority of code-based instruction but, as Chall also found, did not suggest that any one method was superior to any other. At the same time, Project Literacy (Levin & Williams, 1970) was another federally funded project, this one intended to develop a theoretical base for beginning reading based on advances in psychology and linguistics.

Chall's review is full of insight, but one basic finding continues to be cited to this day—Early and systematic instruction in phonics seems to lead to better achievement in reading than later and less systematic instruction. In addition, she felt the research could not distinguish between different methods of phonics instruction, that phonics instruction benefited from a strong base in kindergarten, and that phonics instruction should be confined to the early grades. She did not find that a "phonics-first" or "phonics-only" approach; instead she cautioned that reading should be meaningful, even as children are taught to decode.

These results have been supported in nearly every review since (e.g., Adams, 1990; Anderson, Hiebert, Wilkinson, & Scott, 1985;

Balmuth, 1982; National Reading Panel, 2000), although not without continued controversy (Grundin, 1994; Smith, 1999; Taylor, 1998). Her basic findings were also supported by the First Grade studies (Dykstra, 1968), although the findings of the First Grade studies have been interpreted in a number of ways. Indeed, there is nothing in this chapter to contradict Chall's basic finding. The purpose of this chapter is to update the research on both phonics and the somewhat newer notion of phonological awareness as a precursor to phonics instruction.

Research on Phonics Instruction

Two studies, one a large-scale experimental study and one a review of research, illustrate how little has changed in research in this area since 1967.

The experimental study, Foorman, Francis, Fletcher, Schatschneider, and Mehta (1998), contrasted the effects of four different beginning reading programs with first- and second-grade struggling readers eligible for Title 1 services. The first treatment, *direct code,* involved direct synthetic phonics instruction combined with practice in decodable texts. Instruction involved direct teaching of letter sounds, blending instruction, and practice using small storybooks containing a high percentage of decodable words (but often not a structured story). The second treatment, *embedded code,* was based on Hiebert, Colt, Catto, and Gary's (1992) program involving teaching of a set of phonograms matched to practice in predictable trade books containing those patterns. Activities included shared writing, shared reading, choral reading, and guided reading. The code instruction involved substituting initial consonants to create new words with the same phonogram, "making and breaking" activities using magnetic letters (see Clay, 1993), and various writing activities. The code practice was embedded into the reading, thus supporting the reading. In contrast, in the direct code treatment, the reading supported the instruction. The two other treatments were variants of the whole-language instruction used in the district.

The study involved 285 children in 65 classrooms in 8 urban elementary schools. Students were pretested on a variety of phonological awareness, alphabet knowledge, and language measures. Classrooms were visited periodically to ensure compliance. Similar to the First Grade studies (Bond & Dykstra, 1967/1998), this study was touted by some as providing the "final" solution to the phonics debate. The study has also received severe criticism, not only through the various listservs that discuss reading education but also in books (e.g., Coles, 1999; Taylor, 1998) and articles in peer-reviewed journals (e.g., Taylor, Anderson, Au, & Raphael, 2000).

They found that the direct code approach was clearly superior to the other approaches in measures of phonological awareness and decoding. The embedded code approach appeared to be the next most successful approach. The majority of posttest measures assessed isolated word reading, either regular or irregular words or phonological awareness. On measures of comprehension, the results were less distinct. The direct code approach had a slight advantage over the other approaches on one comprehension measure, but, given the number of comparisons, this difference did not exceed the Bonferroni-adjusted alpha level. There were no significant differences on the other measure. Chall (1967) found that the effects of code-emphasis instruction on comprehension measures were weaker and may not reach significance until second grade.

On a measure of attitude toward reading, the control conditions had an advantage over the direct code condition. This mirrors the finding of Stahl, Suttles, and Pagnucco (1996), who found that although children in traditional classes outperformed children in whole-language–oriented classes on measures of reading achievement, there were indications that children in the whole-language classes had higher motivation and better attitudes about reading. This, in turn, echoes the study of Agnew (1939), reviewed by Chall (1967), who found that children in phonics classes achieved at higher levels on measures of achievement but did not differ in terms of interest. Agnew, unlike Foorman et al. (1998) and Stahl et al. (1996) did not directly test children's relative interest but inferred it from his observations.

These two studies, together or separately, conform closely to Chall's (1967) and Bond and Dykstra's (1967/1998) findings. What is striking is how little change there has been in research in this area in 40 years. Although the designs have gotten more sophisticated, the basic question asked is similar—Is phonics instruction effective?—and the answers, as one might expect, are equally similar.

The Foorman et al. (1998) study was not the only large-scale study during this period supporting the importance of early and systematic phonics instruction. Studies in the United States (Vellutino & Scanlon, 1988; Vellutino, Scanlon, Sipay, & Small, 1996), in Great Britain (Johnston & Watson, 1997), and in Ontario (Sumbler & Willows, 1998) have all examined the effects of synthetic phonics instruction with large numbers of children.

The review of research was conducted for the National Reading Panel (2000). The panel reviewed a large corpus of studies using meta-analytic techniques. Studies were selected by a carefully conscribed set of criteria, limiting review to research that was quantitative and published in peer-reviewed journals. They found the following:

- Phonics instruction produced significant effects on measures of achievement. These effects were most pronounced on measures of decoding and reading nonsense words, and less so on measures of oral reading and reading comprehension. However, significant effects were found on measures of comprehension as well as isolated word reading.
- Phonics instruction was more effective in kindergarten and first grade than in the upper grades.
- Phonics instruction was effective for struggling readers in the early grades, but did not produce significant effects for older children with reading problems.
- There were no significant differences between different approaches to teaching phonics—synthetic, phonogram-based, or eclectic.

Defining "Phonics"

But what do we mean by "phonics"? Phonics has been called one among many cues used in reading (e.g., Dahl, Sharer, Lawson, & Grogran, 1999). By this definition, phonics instruction is found in many different types of reading programs, including whole language (Routman, 1998). Phonics has also been used to refer to only one particular type of phonics program, such as synthetic phonics (Sweet, 1997). By this definition, code-emphasis programs that were not synthetic phonics would not be considered "true" phonics approaches. Both definitions are too restrictive. Instead, I will define phonics instruction as "any approach in which the teacher does/says something to help children learn how to decode words" (after Durkin, 1978–1979). This may involve teaching sound–symbol correspondences directly, having children manipulate sounds in written words through spelling tasks, pointing out patterns in similarly spelled words, or anything else which helps children learn about orthographic patterns in written language.

It is important to note that Chall (1967) did not recommend any particular type of phonics instruction. Common forms of phonics instruction in the 1960s included synthetic phonics instruction, analytic instruction, and "linguistic" readers (see Aukerman, 1981). By the 1990s, there were new approaches to phonics instruction, based on constructivist principles. These approaches —spelling-based approaches such as Making Words (Cunningham & Cunningham, 1992) or Word Study (Bear, Templeton, Invernizzi, & Johnston, 2000), embedded phonics approaches (Hiebert et al., 1992), and compare/contrast or analogy-based approaches (e.g., Gaskins, 1995; Gaskins, Gaskins, & Gaskins, 1992; Gaskins, Ehri, Cress, O'Hara, & Donnelly, 1996)—all involved children in active construction of knowledge about orthographic patterns.

Traditional Approaches

Of the traditional approaches, analytic approaches begin with words the children already know and analyze them into sounds; synthetic approaches begin by teaching letter–sound relationships and blending letters into words.

Analytic Approaches

Although analytic approaches had dominated basal reading programs through the

1980s (e.g., Popp, 1975), they have fallen out of favor by the 1990s. A typical analytic lesson may begin with a word already known by the students, such as "cat." The students are told that the sound of "short a" is the sound heard in the middle of "cat." Then, a list of words is read aloud. Students are to indicate whether each word has the target sound. Next students may read words containing the target sound, but the majority of time seems to be devoted to workbook practice. Time spent on workbook practice does not seem to correlate to gains in achievement (e.g., Leinhardt, Zigmond, & Cooley, 1981). At least partially because of their reliance on workbook practice, these approaches are rarely seen now.

Synthetic Approaches

In a synthetic phonics approach, children are taught individual letter–sound relations and then taught explicitly to blend these letters into words. Synthetic phonics programs can include Direct Instruction elements (Englemann & Bereiter, 1969) or integrate spelling and/or tracing (Gillingham, 1956). They usually include practice in connected text, although these texts are rarely structured as stories and are usually practice for decoding patterns rather than truly comprehensible texts.

Many of the programs used in home reading programs or as supplemental programs in schools were based on either the Gillingham or Direct Instruction approaches (Osborn, Stahl, & Stein, 1997), but without the extensive training required to successfully use either approach.

ORTON–GILLINGHAM APPROACHES

Orton–Gillingham approaches begin with direct teaching of individual letters paired with their sounds using a visual–auditory–kinesthetic–tactile (VAKT) procedure that involves tracing the letter while saying its name and sound, blending letters together to read words and sentences, and finally reading short stories constructed to contain only taught sounds. Among those approaches based on Orton and Gillingham's work are the Slingerland approach (Lovitt & DeMier, 1984), the Spaulding approach, Recipe for Reading, and Alphabetic Phonics

(Ogden, Hindman, & Turner, 1989). There are differences among these approaches, largely in sequencing or materials, but they all have the general characteristics discussed. Spelling the words from dictation is also part of an Orton–Gillingham lesson. Each letter sound is mastered through repetition. More advanced lessons involve teaching learners to blend syllables together and to read more complex texts.

The Orton–Gillingham approach has been around since the 1920s. In spite of its longevity, there is relatively little research on the method. There have been case studies attesting to the approach's effectiveness, beginning with Monroe (1932), but these have been little more than testimonials. Stahl, Duffy-Hester, and Stahl (1998) note that when Gillingham was compared to conventional instruction with children with reading problems (e.g., Kline & Kline, 1975), it seemed to be more effective, but when introduced along with other approaches that were new to the student, the Orton–Gillingham approach did not seem any more effective than any other approach. However, there is little information available to support or to disprove its use.

DIRECT INSTRUCTION APPROACHES

Direct Instruction approaches, such as Distar (later Reading Mastery), are based on a behavioral analysis of decoding (Kameenui, Simmons, Chard, & Dickson, 1997). Students are taught letter sounds (not letter names, at least in the beginning stages of the program) through highly structured instruction using cuing and reinforcement procedures derived from behavioral analyses of instruction. The task of decoding is broken down into its component parts and each of these parts is separate, from letter sounds to blending to reading words in context. Instruction is scripted and the lessons are fast paced, with high student involvement. The text for the first-year program is written in a script that although it preserves English spelling, cues the reader to silent letters and different vowel sounds. Children practice in specially constructed books containing taught sounds, although children may be encouraged to read widely in children's literature as well (e.g., Meyer, 1983).

Stahl et al. (1998) found that although early research with Direct Instruction reported strong effects, it differs from other programs on many dimensions. The major study of the effects of Distar is Project Follow Through classes (Abt-Associates, 1977). This was a national project involving hundreds of classes. Distar was the only program which produced achievement in poor children that was near the national average. In this study, and in many of the early studies, Distar was compared to approaches which had radically different goals than it did and did not stress phonics as strongly as it did. Although Distar produced the strongest effects on achievement tests, many of the other programs had different goals and did not stress the same academic content.

Adams and Englemann (1996) performed a meta-analysis on the effects of Direct Instruction on student achievement, and found that Direct Instruction approaches produced large effect sizes on achievement measures. Although these results are impressive, they need to be viewed critically. First, both Adams and Englemann are associated with Reading Mastery, and this review has not been peer-reviewed. Second, Stahl et al. (1998) easily found a number of relevant studies not included in the Adams and Englemann review, including some studies that did not find positive effects for Distar in beginning reading. They conclude that further research investigating the success of Reading Mastery seems warranted.

META-PHONICS

This approach lies somewhere between traditional and contemporary approaches. In meta-phonics, reading and spelling are taught simultaneously through social interaction and group problem solving, as in contemporary approaches. But the content is traditional, based largely on the development of the English language. Sounds are introduced through phonemic-awareness instruction. This instruction stresses articulation as a key to learning sounds (Calfee, 1998). Thus, /p/ /t/ and /k/ are "popping sounds." Vowels are taught as "glue letters." After these are established, students are given letters and sounds and asked to make a make a word by adding consonants to vowels. Students begin with short consonant–vowel–consonant (CVC) words but progress to longer words such as "discombobulate" or "sassafras."

This component has been embedded into a larger program, Project READ. Preliminary results suggest that the program has been successful in three school settings (Calfee, 1998). Students who have used this program were at or above district and/or national averages in reading comprehension, fluency, word recognition, spelling, and writing. These evaluations were informal, without a true control group, and, also were evaluated as part of a redesign of reading instruction, making it difficult to ascertain how important this component was to overall achievement gains. This approach awaits a fuller, more controlled evaluation.

Constructivist Approaches

Constructivist approaches view the learner not as a passive receiver of instruction but as actively constructing knowledge (Stanovich, 1994). Most often, whole-language authors have cited constructivism as support for a natural method of learning to read, but other authors have used constructivist principles to develop programs for teaching children to decode. Arguments for a constructivist approach to teaching decoding stem from the importance of children's learning of the alphabetic principle, or that letters stand for sounds. We have large bodies of research in both word recognition (Ehri, 1997, 1998) and spelling (Bear & Barone, 1989; Bear et al., 2000; Henderson, 1981; Zutell & Rasinkski, 1989) that indicate that children gradually develop in their construction of alphabetic knowledge.

In word recognition, Ehri (1998) suggests that children go through a series of phases of word learning. Initially, children are in a pre-alphabetic phase in which they rely on visual cues, such as the "tail" in "monkey." As children develop phonological awareness (see Stahl & Murray, 1998), they begin to use phonetic cues, first the initial sound and later other salient sounds in words. Ehri calls this a partial alphabetic phase. After they are able to fully analyze words and use vowel codings, they are in a fully alphabetic phase in which they can sound out words completely. This stage progresses to consolidated word recognition, in which children can use chunks of letters to recognize words quickly and automatically.

There are similar stages in spelling. Bear and Barone (1989) suggest that children progress from pre-alphabetic spelling to early letter name spelling, in which they use initial or initial and final letters correctly, to letter name spelling, in which they use vowels, to within-word spellings, in which they master short and then long vowels and finally to master polysyllabic spellings, including various morphological and orthographic conventions. This developmental view of the alphabetic principle suggests that children should be taught to construct their own knowledge about words, at least part of the time, in order to develop these concepts of how words are put together. Constructivist approaches involve the student in actively manipulating sounds in words.

Spelling-Based Approaches

Although the National Assessment of Educational Progress (Donahue, Voelkl, Campbell, & Mazzeo, 1999) continues to find widespread integration of spelling into reading programs, including invented spelling, there is little evidence to support the use of invented spelling. Clarke (1989) investigated the addition of invented spelling to a synthetic phonics-based reading program and found that children who were encouraged to invent spellings had better mastery of letter–sound correspondences. By 1990, this was the only study that Adams could find investigating that issue. Invented spellings have been integrated into programs differing widely from synthetic phonics, usually whole-language programs (Dahl & Freppon, 1995; Freppon & Dahl, 1991). Its practice is so widely accepted that it is difficult to find a natural control group. Any class not using invented spelling is liable to differ from the norm in many different aspects of literacy instruction.

"Making Words" is an approach to decoding instruction based on spelling but using a constrained set of letters which are manipulated to make different words. In a Making Words lesson, children are given seven or more letter squares. The teacher asks the children to make two-, three-, four-letter words, and so on, up to the total number of letters. Words are written on cards and are used in various sorting and other extension activities. Making Words is a part of Cunningham's successful "Four Blocks" program (Cunningham, Hall, & Defee, 1991, 1998) and the Emergent Reader Literacy Model (ERLI; Swann, 1997) but has not been tested by itself.

Word study was developed from observations of the developmental nature of spelling (Henderson, 1981). In word study, students examine words and word patterns through strategies such as sorting, where they categorize words and pictures according to their common orthographic features. In word study, the teacher bases instruction on word features that students are writing but are confusing (e.g., Bear et al., 2000). For example, when a child spells *rane* for *rain* and makes similar errors in other aspects of his or her writing, the teacher may begin instruction with the child on long *a* word patterns. Again, word study has been tested as part of successful tutorial programs (Invernizzi, Juel, & Rosemary, 1996/1997; Morris, Ervin, & Conrad, 1996), but I could not find research that examines its effects separately.

Compare/Contrast and Analogy Instruction

Compare/Contrast and analogy instruction is based on the observation that adults chunk words into multiletter units when decoding an unknown word. They often make analogies to known words (see (Cunningham, 1975–1976). Compare/Contrast instruction teaches children to make comparisons between unknown words and already known words. Often this instruction uses a word wall, which contains previously taught words.

There are three different types of research support for analogy based approaches. Basic research studies (Goswami, 1993, 1998; see Chapter 9) suggest that young children can use analogies before they can use other phonological information to read words. Other studies (Bruck & Treiman, 1992; Ehri, 1998; Ehri & Robbins, 1992), however, found that children need to be able to use phonetic cue reading, or initial letter–sound relationships, to take advantage of analogies in reading. The differences in findings may be attributable to differences in experimental design. (In Goswami's studies, the analogue word is always available for the child; in the other studies, the child has had to rely on memory.) In practice, analogies should be used after children can use initial sound cues, which is how they are used in Cunningham's (1995) and Gaskins et al.'s (1996) approaches.

The second line of research on analogies comes from classroom studies. Compare/Contrast instruction has been tested in small-scale studies (Cunningham, 1980; Cunningham & Foster, 1978). Both Haskell, Foorman, and Swank (1991) and Sullivan, Okada, and Niedermeyer (1971) found that an analogy approach and a synthetic approach performed equally well, and both were more effective than whole-word approaches. Fayne and Bryant (1981) found that a rime-based strategy was not as effective as teaching children initial bigrams (e.g., *co-g*). These were short-term studies. White and Cunningham (1990), in a yearlong study, found that analogy training produced significant effects on measures of both word recognition and comprehension.

Finally, analogy approaches are part of successful reading programs, including the approach used at the Benchmark School (Gaskins, 1995; see also Cunningham, 1995). The experience at Benchmark is illustrative of both the strengths and limits of an analogy-based approach. The program began as a direct adaptation of analogies with metacognitive strategy training to help children transfer the use of analogy-based decoding in their reading (Gaskins et al., 1988; Gaskins et al., 1992). This program seemed to be successful with many of the children with reading problems at Benchmark, but there were a number of children who did not succeed. In an attempt to reach more children, the program was modified to include a more thorough analysis of the words taught as anchor words (Gaskins et al., 1996), thus teaching more phonological information along with the analogy words. My conclusion is that analogies can be a powerful teaching approach but need to be taught after a child has reached the phonetic

cue level and should be taught in conjunction with other decoding approaches.

Embedded Phonics Instruction

In embedded instruction, phonics instruction is provided in the context of reading of connected text. Hiebert's (1994) program, as assessed in the Foorman et al. (1998) study is based on Reading Recovery, a tutorial program for low-achieving first-graders. Embedded instruction can also be found in whole-language classrooms (Dahl, Sharer, Lawson, & Grogran, 1999). These will be discussed below.

PHONICS IN READING RECOVERY

Lessons in Reading Recovery (Clay, 1993) are based on Goodman's (1976) model, suggesting that readers use three cuing systems to recognize words in context. Clay (1993) calls these systems visual, structural, and meaning cues. Within the lesson structure, the teacher has a number of options to teach children to better use visual cues. The individual nature of a Reading Recovery lesson enables the teacher to direct the child's attention to aspects of words relevant to their development.

The major activities involving phonics instruction are the sounding out of words during writing, often integrating the use of Elkonin boxes (Elkonin, 1973), "Making and Breaking Words," and the use of visual cues during reading. In their writing, children do invented spelling on a practice sheet. However, the final product always is spelled conventionally. Also, teachers integrate work with Elkonin boxes into spelling work, having children use the boxes to reflect on each sound in a word. A child who wants to spell "dog," for example, may be shown a set of three boxes, directed to stretch the word out, and put a counter into a box for each new sound heard. These counters are later replaced with letters.

In Making and Breaking Words, the teacher uses magnetic letters to give children practice in reading phonetically controlled words. In Making and Breaking, the teacher has the child manipulate letters to make new words, changing "dog" to "log" to "hog," for example, in order to work on initial consonants. With different goals, the teacher may ask for different manipulations. This component has been part of Reading Recovery from the beginning, but recently it has received more emphasis. Iversen and Tunmer (1993) found that they were able to help children discontinue from the program earlier by adding a phonological recoding component to the Reading Recovery lesson.

Reading Recovery teachers can also choose texts that reflect children's increasing mastery of phonics. A teacher might choose a text that requires the child to direct attention to particular visual features of words. If a child is, for example, noticing initial sound relationships, the teacher would choose a book in which the child must use these relationships to read the book successfully. When a child has a problem with a word, the teacher may choose a visual cue to aid the child. In the beginning of Reading Recovery lessons, texts are highly predictable and the pattern provides a scaffold for children's reading. As texts become less predictable over the course of the lessons, teachers decrease the amount of scaffolding they provide, encouraging children to use more visual features of words. The result of these cumulative decisions, in text reading and through other aspects of the lessons, is that children appear to advance in their word-recognition abilities and phonological awareness (Stahl, Stahl, & McKenna, 1999).

Reading Recovery has been cited by Adams (1990) as an excellent example of what good phonics instruction can be. Although children do receive a great deal of work with letters and sounds, the instruction is always integrated into the reading and writing of texts. Teachers keep track of students' increasing mastery of the visual cuing system in conjunction with the other two systems. Children spend the majority of their lesson time reading and writing connected text, with phonics embedded in reading activity.

PHONICS IN WHOLE-LANGUAGE CLASSROOMS

Phonics instruction in whole-language classrooms is embedded in the context of teaching reading and is sensitive to the child's needs. Letter–sound instruction can occur

as one of the cuing systems that children use to recognize words (e.g., Weaver, 1998) and can also occur as part of writing instruction.

Whole-language instruction varies considerably from teacher to teacher and from class to class (Watson, 1989). It may resemble the instruction described in the Reading Recovery lessons described earlier (although Reading Recovery is not a whole-language approach *per se* [see Church, 1996]). Some whole-language teachers may provide less organized phonics instruction than occurs in Reading Recovery.

Stahl et al. (1998) observed that in the accounts of phonics instruction from whole-language educators (Dahl & Freppon, 1995; Freppon & Dahl, 1991; Freppon & Headings, 1996; McIntyre & Freppon, 1994; Mills, O'Keefe, & Stephens, 1992), they did not observe the teaching of vowels. Vowels are important because research consistently shows that children make more errors on vowels than on consonants (e.g., Shankweiler & Liberman, 1972). This may be because vowels are more difficult to extract phonologically from words, because vowels can be encoded in a number of different ways in words, or because vowel rules are less consistent than consonant rules. For whatever reason, vowel knowledge emerges later than consonant knowledge in both word recognition (Ehri, 1998) and spelling (Bear & Barone, 1989). Most first-grade curricula teach consonants in kindergarten and concentrate on short and long vowels during first grade. Of course, just because lessons involving vowels or lessons involving the full examination of words were not present in vignettes does not mean that these teachers did not teach vowels. But one would expect that instruction in vowels should occur in the first grade (Anderson et al., 1985).

The lack of phonics instruction beyond consonants may be indicative of whole-language teachers' reticence to challenge their students. This may be symptomatic of a general lack of challenge in many whole-language classes. One study found that children in whole-language classrooms did not read as challenging materials as did children in traditional classes, and that the amount of challenge determined children's achievement at the end of the year (Stahl et al., 1996). Church (1994, 1996), a whole-language teacher in Nova Scotia, reported being also concerned that whole-language teachers did not sufficiently challenge their students. In short, some reading programs based on the whole-language philosophy may not encourage students to read more challenging texts and may not expose children to the types of phonics instruction they need to improve as readers and writers.

Phonological Awareness

The concept of "phonological awareness" is more recent than phonics but has been subject to much of the same controversy. Stanovich (1991) has called phonological awareness one of the major contributions that psychology has made to the pedagogy of reading over the past 25 years. Others have considered it an artifact of learning to read, inconsequential in and of itself (e.g., Smith, 1999; Taylor, 1998). Phonological awareness can be defined as the ability to reflect on units of spoken language smaller than the syllable. It may include blending, segmentation, deletion, word-to-word matching, and/or sound-to-word matching (Adams, 1990; Stahl & Murray, 1998; Yopp, 1988). Two aspects are crucial in the conventional definition. First, it involves spoken rather than written language. This is to distinguish phonological awareness from phonics. Second, it involves awareness of phonemes or onsets and rimes (Treiman, 1985, 1992). These are units that are not acoustically transparent and must be consciously analyzed to be perceived.

Stanovich (1991) and Adams (1990) suggest that a child's phonological awareness ability is a better predictor of success in reading than IQ or even knowledge of the alphabet. This is problematic because phonological awareness is intricately tied in with word recognition.

Phonological Awareness Training Studies

Although there is an abundance of evidence that phonological awareness is correlated with early reading achievement (see Adams, 1990; see also Chapter 6), the major evidence for a causal relation with learning to read comes from a series of training studies. In these studies, preschool or kindergarten children were trained in phonological awareness and tested some time later on measures of reading. If children who were trained in phonological awareness were superior in reading or had fewer instances of reading problems, it was inferred that phonological-awareness ability somehow causes reading success. The most often cited study in this area is Bradley and Bryant's (1983) study. They found that preschool and kindergarten children given training in categorizing sounds so that they would attend to sounds in spoken words were significantly better readers by the end of 3 years. What is often not cited is that the group given only sound categorization training was only 3–4 months ahead of the control group, but the group given sound categorization training in addition to training in letter recognition was an average of 9–10 months ahead of the control. Lundberg, Frost, and Peterson (1988), who developed an extensive program to train phonological awareness in kindergartners that did not incorporate letters, failed to find differences in reading achievement at the end of first grade but did find significant differences at the end of second grade.

One would assume that the effects of phonological awareness training would be stronger on measures that are more proximal to phonological awareness, such as decoding measures, than measures that are more distal, such as oral reading and comprehension. Oral reading and comprehension are affected by children's use of context, prior topic knowledge, and metacognitive strategies, as well as children's knowledge of phonological processes as reflected in accuracy of word reading. Thus we would expect stronger effects on more proximal measures than on more distal measures.

In the recent meta-analysis done for the National Reading Panel (2000), this was precisely what was found. The largest effect sizes for phonological awareness training were found on measures of decoding, of real words[1] (.60), and of nonsense words (.52 for experimenter developed and .49 for standardized). Considerably smaller effects were found on measures of word recognition (.33). Word recognition involves not only phonological knowledge but also orthographic knowledge. The same is true of spelling measures, which also involve phonological and orthographic information. Effect sizes on measures of passage comprehension were similar to the general measures of word recognition (.32) and may reflect skill in word recognition. Effects on measures of mathematics achievement, a far distal measure used to assess general effects of training as a control, were near zero (.03), as expected.

The National Reading Panel also found that the effects of phonological-awareness training were stronger when letters were used. Hohn and Ehri (1983) compared phonological awareness with and without letters and found that the use of concrete markers (e.g., letters) facilitated the development of phonological awareness. Murray, Stahl, and Ivey (1996) found that reading alphabet books to children improved their phonological awareness, even without training.

It would make sense to posit a model that phonological awareness is related to the acquisition of the alphabetic principle, or the notion that letters in words represent phonemes. This seems to be close to definitional, as phonological awareness is the understanding that spoken words can be thought of as a blending of individual sounds. This is not the whole story about decoding written English, because letters in English can also represent morphemes. (Other languages such as Spanish and Finnish are more phonological.) When letters were used in the training, The National Reading Panel (2000) found a dramatic difference, further suggesting that children were really learning to decode when letters were included in the training. The effects were less dramatic on the other measures. On measures of word recognition (often irregular words) and on measures of comprehension and spelling, the differences were even smaller.

Training effects were significantly larger for kindergarten children than for first-graders. This differential may be due to the most intensive reading instruction that the control group is getting in first grade, making the experimental group and the control group more similar. Blending training had different effects, depending on the measure used. Blending seemed to slightly facilitate word attack but produced lower scores on spelling measures.

How Does Phonological Awareness Training Relate to Reading?

These results suggest that phonological awareness, rather than being a precursor to reading, may be intricately involved in early reading acquisition. A task analysis of decoding regular words would include (1) identifying letters, (2) attaching a sound value to each letter in turn, and (3) blending the letters to form a word. Thus, teaching letters and letter sounds would enable a child to perform steps one and two, and teaching blending would enable a child to perform step three. Thus, by incorporating letter-name and letter-sound instruction into their phonological-awareness training, these authors are teaching children to decode. Thus, one would expect the larger effect sizes on measures of word attack, because such measures seem most closely related to the training. A similar analysis of spelling regular words (or invented spelling) would suggest that the child needs to (1) segment the spoken word, by stretch sounding or other means, (2) assign a letter to each sound, and (3) write down the letters in turn. There is more to spelling than decoding, because spelling involves not only phonological knowledge but also orthographic and morphological knowledge (Treiman, 1993, 1998). Thus one would expect the effect sizes to be lower. These effects are higher in studies using developmental spelling scales (e.g., Tangel & Blachman, 1992) than those using conventional spelling measures.

Another way of looking at the relation between phonological awareness and reading is to examine how word recognition develops. Recall Ehri's (1998) model of the development of word recognition and the various models of the development of spelling (e.g., Henderson, 1981). As children move from pre-alphabetic reading (and spelling) to phonetic cue spelling, they need to be able to segment the first phoneme of the word. As they become more sophisticated in their ability to use letter–sound cues to recognize and produce words, their ability to analyze spoken words should increase as well. Stahl and Murray (1998) suggest that the ability to segment an initial sound is a direct precursor to phonetic cue reading, which, in turn, leads to more advanced decoding abilities.

Murray (1998) found that the ability to segment an initial phoneme reflects an understanding of phoneme identity (Byrne & Fielding-Barnsley, 1993). Phoneme identity is the awareness of the constancy of phonemes, that the sound /s/ is the same in "sun" as it is in "bus" (or in "suspenders"). Phoneme identity can be fostered by using letters or other concrete markers, since letters readily symbolize the constancy of the phoneme. Murray trained children using phoneme identity training and more mechanical segmentation training and found that only the phoneme identity training enabled children to do phonetic cue reading. Murray argues that phonological awareness might best be though of in terms of the concept of phoneme identity and taught in a way that children learn to recognize the constancy of the different sounds in the language.

The issues involved in early reading remain the same as they were in Chall's (1967) time. Not only are the disputes the same, but the research supporting each side comes up with similar findings. From this review, as with Chall's review, the findings seem simple:

- Early and systematic phonics instruction seems to lead to better achievement than later and less systematic instruction.
- Different methods of phonics instruction, as long as they are systematic, seem to have similar results.

These were Chall's findings in 1967, but they are a paraphrase of some of the findings of the National Reading Panel in 2000. We seem to be asking the same questions as we did 40 years ago, with the same results.

Conclusion

A number of elements in a beginning reading program need to be examined. We need to understand the effects of phonics within a total reading program, to examine the unexpected effects of intensive phonics instruction. We also do not know to what extent these findings on the importance of phonics are due to teaching method or to the amount of challenge. Stahl et al. (1996) studied traditional and whole-language classrooms. Although the traditional class-

room did provide considerably more phonics instruction than the whole-language classroom, Stahl et al. (1996) found that the achievement differences were more a result of differences in the challenge of the materials used and the greater content coverage than to differences in method. It may be that phonics instruction is effective because it allows teachers to cover more material than other types of instruction.

Phonological-awareness training also seems to improve reading skill, at least on measures of word attack, and seems to be especially effective when combined with letter-name and letter-sound training. However, we do not know how much phonological awareness is needed, whether phonological awareness is an all-or-nothing phenomenon, whether it represents an aspect of phonological sensitivity (Stanovich 1991), or what the role of phoneme identities are (Byrne & Fielding-Barnsley, 1991: Murray, 1998).

Chall (1992, 2000) suggested that these divisions reflect greater divisions in the field of education. She suggests that we have had continual conflicts between a pragmatic view of education and a romantic view. The pragmatic view sees increasing achievement as a problem to be solved with scientific methodology. Those holding the romantic view focus on the individuality of the child and support approaches that foster individual development. They eschew quantitative research, such as that of Chall (1967) and Foorman et al. (1990) because this type of research treats children as part of a group rather than individually (e.g., Edelsky, 1990; Gunderson, 1997).

Resolving these controversies involves continued research, but also involves continued reflections on research, to examine how much our preconceptions and politics affect out research agenda.

Note

1. I am using the figures for experimenter-developed word tests for the word decoding measure on the assumption that these measures reflected words that were taught in the study and the figures for standardized word measure as more general measures of word recognition. The National Reading Panel did not break them out precisely like this.

References

Abt-Associates. (1977). *Education as experimentation: A planned variation model. Volume IV-B, Effects of follow-through models.* Cambridge, MA: Author.

Adams, G. L., & Englemann, S. (1996). *Research on direct instruction: 25 years beyond Distar.* Seattle: Educational Achievement Systems.

Adams, M. J. (1990). *Beginning to read: Thinking and learning about print.* Cambridge, MA: MIT Press.

Agnew, D. C. (1939). *The effect of varied amounts of phonetic training on primary reading* (Duke University Research Studies in Education No. 5). Durham, NC: Duke University Press.

Allington, R. L., & Woodside-Jiron, H. (1998). What are decodable texts and why are policy makers mandating them. *Currents in Literacy, 1*(1), 21–22.

Anderson, R. C., Hiebert, E. F., Wilkinson, I. A. G., & Scott, J. (1985). *Becoming a nation of readers.* Champaign, IL: Center for the Study of Reading.

Aukerman, R. C. (1981). *The basal reader approach to reading.* New York: Wiley.

Balmuth, M. (1982). *The roots of phonics: A historical introduction.* New York: McGraw-Hill.

Bear, D. R., & Barone, D. (1989). Using children's spellings to group for word study and directed reading in the primary classroom. *Reading Psychology, 10,* 275–292.

Bear, D. R., Templeton, S., Invernizzi, M., & Johnston, F. (1996). *Words their way: Word study for phonics, vocabulary and spelling instruction.* Upper Saddle River, NJ: Merrill.

Bond, G., & Dykstra, R. (1998). The cooperative research program in first grade reading. *Reading Research Quarterly, 2,* 5–142. (Original work published 1967)

Bradley, L., & Bryant, P. E. (1983). Categorizing sounds and learning to read—A causal connection. *Nature, 301,* 419–421.

Bruck, M., & Treiman, R. (1992). Learning to pronounce words: The limitations of analogies. *Reading Research Quarterly, 27,* 374–388.

Byrne, B., & Fielding-Barnsley, R. (1993). Evaluation of a program to teach phonemic awareness to young children: A 1-year follow-up. *Journal of Educational Psychology, 85,* 104–111.

Calfee, R. (1998). Phonics and phonemes: Learning to decode and spell in a literature-based program. In J. L. Metsala & L. C. Ehri (Eds.), *Word recognition in beginning literacy* (pp. 315–340). Mahwah, NJ: Erlbaum.

Chall, J. S. (1967). *Learning to read: The great debate.* (1st ed.). New York, NY: McGraw-Hill.

Chall, J. S. (1992). The new reading debates: Evidence from science, art, and ideology. *Teachers' College Record, 94,* 315–328.

Chall, J. S. (2000). *The academic achievement challenge: What really works in the classroom.* New York: Guilford Press.

Chall, J. S., & Feldmann S. (1966). First grade reading: An analysis of the interactions of professed methods, teacher implementation, and child background. *The Reading Teacher, 19,* 569–575.

Church, S. M. (1994). Is whole language really warm and fuzzy? *The Reading Teacher, 47,* 362–371.

Church, S. M. (1996). *The future of whole language: Reconstruction or self-destruction.* Portsmouth, NH: Heinemann.

Clarke, L. K. (1989). Encouraging invented spelling in first graders' writing: Effects on learning to spell and read. *Research in the Teaching of English, 22,* 281–309.

Clay, M. M. (1993). *Reading recovery: A guidebook for teachers in training.* Portsmouth, NH: Heinemann.

Cunningham, J. W., & Foster, E. O. (1978). The ivory tower connection: A case study. *The Reading Teacher, 31,* 365–369.

Cunningham, P. M. (1975–1976). Investigating a synthesized theory of mediated word identification. *Reading Research Quarterly, 11,* 127–143.

Cunningham, P. M. (1980). Applying a compare/contrast process to identifying polysyllabic words. *Journal of Reading Behavior, 12*(3), 213–223.

Cunningham, P. M. (1995). *Phonics they use.* New York: HarperCollins.

Cunningham, P. M., & Cunningham, J. W. (1992). Making words: Enhancing the invented spelling-decoding connection. *The Reading Teacher, 46,* 106–115.

Cunningham, P. M., Hall, D. P., & Defee, M. (1991). Non-ability grouped, multilevel instruction: a year in a first grade classroom. *The Reading Teacher, 44,* 566–571.

Cunningham, P. M., Hall, D. P., & Defee, M. (1998). Nonability-grouped, multimethod instruction: Eight years later. *The Reading Teacher, 51,* 652–664.

Dahl, K. L., & Freppon, P. A. (1995). A comparison of inner-city children's interpretations of reading and writing instruction in the early grades in skills-based and whole language classrooms. *Reading Research Quarterly, 30,* 50–74.

Dahl, K. L., Sharer, P. L., Lawson, L. L., & Grogran, P. R. (1999). Phonics instruction and student achievement in whole language first-grade classrooms. *Reading Research Quarterly, 34,* 312–341.

Donahue, P. L., Voelkl, K. E., Campbell, J. R., & Mazzeo, J. (1999). *NAEP 1998 reading report card for the nation* (Prepublication ed.). Washington, DC: U.S. Department of Education, Office of Educational Research and Improvement.

Dykstra, R. (1968). The effectiveness of code-and meaning-emphasis beginning reading programs. *The Reading Teacher, 22,* 17–23.

Edelsky, C. (1990). Whose agenda is this anyway? A response to McKenna, Robinson, and Miller. *Educational Researcher, 19*(8), 7–11.

Ehri, L. C. (1997). Learning to read and learning to spell are one and the same, almost. In C. A. Perfetti & L. Rieben (Eds.), *Learning to spell: Research, theory, and practice across languages* (pp. 237–268). Mahwah, NJ: Erlbaum.

Ehri, L. C. (1998). Grapheme–phoneme knowledge is essential for learning to read words in English. In J. L. Metsala & L. C. Ehri (Eds.), *Word recognition in beginning literacy* (pp. 3–40). Mahwah, NJ: Erlbaum.

Ehri, L. C., & Robbins, C. (1992). Beginners need some decoding skill to read words by analogy. *Reading Research Quarterly, 27,* 12–26.

Elkonin, D. B. (1973). U.S.S.R. In J. Downing (Ed.), *Comparative reading* (pp. 551–579). New York: Macmillan.

Englemann, S., & Bereiter, C. (1969). *Distar reading program.* Chicago: SRA.

Fayne, H. R., & Bryant, N. D. (1981). Relative effects of various word synthesis strategies on the phonics achievement of learning disabled youngsters. *Journal of Educational Psychology, 73,* 616–623.

Foorman, B. R., Fletcher, J. M., Francis, D. J., Schatschneider, C., & Mehta, P. (1998). The role of instruction in learning to read: Preventing reading failure in at-risk children. *Journal of Educational Psychology, 90,* 37–55.

Freppon, P. A., & Dahl, K. L. (1991). Learning about phonics in a whole language classroom. *Language Arts, 68,* 190–197.

Freppon, P. A., & Headings, L. (1996). Keeping it whole in whole language: A first grade teacher's instruction in an urban whole language classroom. In E. McIntyre & M. Pressley (Eds.), *Balanced instruction: Strategies and skills in whole language* (pp. 65–82). Norwood, MA: Christopher-Gordon.

Gaskins, I. W., Downer, M. A., Anderson, R. C., Cunningham, P. M., Gaskins, R. W., Schommer, M., & Teachers of Benchmark School (1988). A metacognitive approach to phonics: Using what you know to decode what you don't know. *Remedial and Special Education, 9,* 36–41.

Gaskins, I. W., Ehri, L. C., Cress, C., O'Hara, C., & Donnelly, K. (1996). Procedures for word learning: Making discoveries about words. *The Reading Teacher, 50,* 312–328.

Gaskins, R. W. (1995). The reciprocal relationship between research and development: An example involving a decoding strand for poor readers. *Journal of Reading Behavior, 27,* 337–377.

Gaskins, R. W., Gaskins, I. W., & Gaskins, J. (1992). Using what you know to figure out what you don't know: An analogy approach to decoding. *Reading and Writing Quarterly: Overcoming Learning Difficulties, 8,* 197–221.

Gillingham, A. (1956). *Remedial training for children with specific disability in reading, spelling, and penmanship.* Cambridge, MA: Educators Publishing Service.

Goodman, K. S. (1976). Reading: A psycholinguistic guessing game. In H. Singer & R. B. Ruddell (Eds.), *Theoretical models and processes of reading* (2nd ed., pp. 497–508). Newark, DE: International Reading Association.

Goodman, K. S. (1993). *Phonics Phacts.* Portsmouth, NH: Heinemann.

Goswami, U. (1993). Toward an interactive analogy model of reading development: Decoding vowel graphemes in beginning reading. *Journal of Experimental Child Psychology, 56,* 443–475.

Goswami, U. (1998). The role of analogies in the development of word recognition. In J. Metsala & L. Ehri (Eds.), *Word recognition in beginning literacy* (pp. 41–64). Mahwah, NJ: Erlbaum.

Grundin, H. U. (1994). If it ain't whole, it ain't language—or back to the basics of freedom and dignity. In F. Lehr & J. Osborn (Eds.), *Reading, language, and literacy* (pp. 77–88). Mahwah, NJ: Erlbaum.

Gunderson, L. (1996). Whole language approaches to reading and writing. In S. A. Stahl & D. A. Hayes (Eds.), *Instructional models in reading* (pp. 221–248). Mahwah, NJ: Erlbaum.

Harris, A. J., & Serwer, B. L. (1966). The CRAFT project: Instructional time in reading research. *Reading Research Quarterly, 2,* 27–57.

Haskell, D. W., Foorman, B. R., & Swank, P. A. (1991). Effects of three orthographic/phonological units on first grade reading. *Remedial and Special Education, 13,* 40–49.

Henderson, E. H. (1981). *Learning to read and spell: The child's knowledge of words.* De Kalb: Northern Illinois University Press.

Hiebert, E. H. (1994). A small group literacy intervention with Chapter 1 students. In E. H. Hiebert & B. M. Taylor (Eds.), *Getting reading right from the start* (pp. 85–106). Boston: Allyn & Bacon.

Hiebert, E. H., Colt, J. M., Catto, S. L., & Gary, E. C. (1992). Reading and writing of first-grade students in a restructured Chapter 1 program. *American Educational Research Journal, 29*(3), 545–572.

Hohn, W. E., & Ehri, L. C. (1983). Do alphabet letters help prereaders acquire phonemic segmentation skill? *Journal of Educational Psychology, 75,* 752–762.

Invernizzi, M., Juel, C., & Rosemary, C. A. (1996/1997). A community volunteer tutorial that works. *The Reading Teacher, 50,* 304–311.

Iversen, S., & Tumner, W. E. (1993). Phonological processing skills and the Reading Recovery program. *Journal of Educational Psychology, 85,* 112–126.

Johnston, R. S., & Watson, J. (1997). Developing reading, spelling, and phonemic awareness skills in primary school children. *Reading, 31*(2), 37–40.

Kameenui, E. J., Simmons, D. C., Chard, D., & Dickson, S. (1997). Direct instruction reading. In S. A. Stahl & D. A. Hayes (Eds.), *Instructional models in reading* (pp. 59–84). Mahwah, NJ: Erlbaum.

Kline, C. L., & Kline, C. (1975). Follow-up study of 216 dyslexic children. *Bulletin of the Orton Society, 25,* 127–144.

Leinhardt, G., Zigmond, N., & Cooley, W. (1981). Reading instruction and its effects. *American Educational Research Journal, 18,* 343–361.

Levin, H., & Williams, J. (1970). *Basic studies in reading*. New York: Basic Books.

Lovitt, T. C., & DeMier, D. M. (1984). An evaluation of the Slingerland method with LD youngsters. *Journal of Learning Disabilities, 17,* 267–272.

Lundberg, I., Frost, J., & Peterson, O.-P. (1988). Effects of an extensive program for stimulating phonological awareness in preschool children. *Reading Research Quarterly, 23,* 263–284.

McIntyre, E., & Freppon, P. A. (1994). A comparison of children's development of alphabetic knowledge in a skills-based and a whole language classroom. *Research in the Teaching of English, 28,* 391–417.

Meyer, L. A. (1983). Increased student achievement in reading: One district's strategies. *Research in Rural Education, 1,* 47–51.

Mills, H., O'Keefe, T., & Stephens, D. (1992). *Looking closely: Exploring the role of phonics in one whole language classroom*. Urbana, IL: National Council of Teachers of English.

Monroe, M. (1932). *Children who cannot read*. Chicago: University of Chicago Press.

Morris, D., Ervin, C., & Conrad, K. (1996). A case study of middle school reading disability. *The Reading Teacher, 49,* 368–377.

Murray, B. A., Stahl, S. A., & Ivey, M. G. (1996). Developing phoneme awareness through alphabet books. *Reading and Writing: An Interdisciplinary Journal, 8,* 307–322.

National Reading Panel. (2000). *Report of the National Reading Panel*. Washington, DC: National Institute of Child Health and Development (www.nationalreadingpanel.org).

Popp, H. M. (1975). Current practices in the teaching of beginning reading. In J. B. Carroll & J. S. Chall (Eds.), *Toward a literate society* (pp. 101–146). New York: McGraw-Hill.

Ogden, S., Hindman, S., & Turner, N. D. (1989). Multisensory programs in the public schools: A brighter future for LD children. *Annals of Dyslexia, 39,* 247–267.

Osborn, J., Stahl, S. A., & Stein, M. (1997). *Teachers' guidelines for evaluating commercial phonics packages*. Newark, DE: International Reading Association.

Routman, R. (1996). *Literacy at the crossroads*. Portsmouth, NH: Heinemann.

Shankweiler, D., & Liberman, I. Y. (1972). Misreading: A search for causes. In J. F. Kavanaugh & I. G. Mattingly (Eds.), *Language by eye and by ear* (pp. 293–317). Cambridge, MA: MIT Press.

Smith, F. (1999). Why systematic phonics and phonemic awareness instruction constitute an educational hazard. *Language Arts, 77*(2), 150–155.

Stahl, K. A. D., Stahl, S. A., & McKenna, M. C. (1999). The development of phonological awareness and orthographic processing in Reading Recovery. *Literacy, Teaching and Learning, 4*(3), 27–42.

Stahl, S. A. (1999). Why innovations come and go: The case of whole language. *Educational Researcher.*

Stahl, S. A., Duffy-Hester, A. M., & Stahl, K. A. D. (1998). Everything you wanted to know about phonics (But were afraid to ask). *Reading Research Quarterly, 35,* 338–355.

Stahl, S. A., & Murray, B. A. (1998). Issues involved in defining phonological awareness and its relation to early reading. In J. Metsala & L. C. Ehri (Eds.), *Word recognition in beginning literacy* (pp. 65–88). Mahwah, NJ: Erlbaum.

Stahl, S. A., Suttles, C. W., & Pagnucco, J. R. (1996). The effects of traditional and process literacy instruction on first graders' reading and writing achievement and orientation toward reading. *Journal of Educational Research, 89,* 131–144.

Stanovich, K. E. (1991). The psychology of reading: Evolutionary and revolutionary developments. *Annual Review of Applied Linguistics, 12,* 3–30.

Stanovich, K. E. (1994). Constructivism in reading education. *Journal of Special Education, 28,* 259–274.

Sullivan, H. J., Okada, M., & Niedermeyer, F. C. (1971). Learning and transfer under two methods of word-attack instruction. *American Educational Research Journal, 8,* 227–240.

Sumbler, K., & Willows, D. (1998). *Time management: Monitoring activities in* Jolly Phonics *and control classrooms*. Paper presented at the annual meeting of the National Reading Conference, New Orleans, LA.

Swann, J. M. (1997). *An investigation into the effectiveness of the Emergent Reading Literacy model*. Paper presented at the annual meeting of the American Educational Research Association, Chicago. ERIC Document Reproduction Service No. ED 404 636.

Sweet, R. W., Jr. (1997). Don't Read, Don't Tell: Clinton's Phony War on Illiteracy. *Policy Review, 38,* 38–42.

Tangel, D. M., & Blachman, B. A. (1992). Effect of phoneme awareness instruction on kindergarten children's invented spellings. *Journal of Reading Behavior, 24,* 233–262.

Taylor, B. M., Anderson, R. C., Au, K. H., & Raphael, T. E. (2000). Discretion in the translation of reading research to policy. *Educational Researcher, 29*(6), 16–26.

Taylor, D. (1998). *Beginning to read and the spin doctors of science: The political campaign to change america's mind about how children learn to read*. Urbana, IL: National Council of Teachers of English.

Treiman, R. (1985). Onsets and rimes as units of spoken syllables: Evidence from children. *Journal of Experimental Child Psychology, 39,* 161–181.

Treiman, R. (1992). The role of intersyllabic units in learning to read and spell. In P. B. Gough, L. C. Ehri, & R. Treiman (Eds.), *Reading acquisition* (pp. 85–106). Hillsdale, NJ: Erlbaum.

Treiman, R. (1993). *Beginning to spell: A study of first grade children*. New York: Oxford University Press.

Treiman, R. (1998). Why spelling? The benefits of

incorporating spelling into beginning reading instruction. In J. Metsala & L. C. Ehri (Eds.), *Word recognition in beginning literacy* (pp. 289–313). Mahwah, NJ: Erlbaum.

Vellutino, F. R., & Scanlon, D. M. (1988). Phonological coding, phonological awareness, and reading ability: Evidence from a longitudinal and experimental study. In K. E. Stanovich (Ed.), *Children's reading and the development of phonological awareness* (pp. 77–119). Detroit, MI: Wayne State University Press.

Vellutino, F. R., Scanlon, D. M., Sipay, E. R., & Small, S. G. (1996). Cognitive profiles of difficult-to-remediate and readily remediated poor readers: Early intervention as a vehicle for distinguishing between cognitive and experiential deficits as basic causes of specific reading disability. *Journal of Educational Psychology, 88,* 601–638.

Watson, D. J. (1989). Defining and describing whole language. *Elementary School Journal, 90,* 129–142.

Weaver, C. (1998). Experimental research: On phonemic awareness and on whole language. In C. Weaver (Ed.), *Reconsidering a balanced approach to reading* (pp. 321–371). Urbana, IL: National Council of Teachers of English.

White, T. G., & Cunningham, P. M. (1990). *Teaching disadvantaged students to decode and spell by analogy.* Paper presented at annual meeting of the American Educational Research Association, Boston, MA.

Yaden, D. B., Smolkin, L. B., & MacGillivray, L. (1993). A psychogenetic perspective on children's understanding about letter associations during alphabet book readers. *Journal of Reading Behavior, 25,* 43–68.

Yopp, H. K. (1988). The validity and reliability of phonemic awareness tests. *Reading Research Quarterly, 23,* 159–177.

Zutell, J., & Rasinski, T. (1989). Reading and spelling connections in third and fifth grade students. *Reading Psychology, 10,* 137–155.

23

Literature-Based Instruction in the Early Years

❖

LESLEY MANDEL MORROW
LINDA B. GAMBRELL

To support young children in developing literacy, high-quality literature including narrative and expository works are the core materials used during literature-based instruction (Scharer, 1992). This type of instruction, which has been increasingly emphasized in reading research and practice, provides authentic learning experiences and activities using literature to teach and foster literacy. This chapter focuses on the review of pertinent research about literature-based instruction and its importance in early literacy development. It is divided into three major sections: rationale and historical background, literature-based instruction in the classroom, and current perspectives and special issues in literature-based instruction.

Rationale and Historical Background

Current definitions of literature-based instruction emphasize high-quality literacy works, usually trade books, as the core instructional materials to be used to support literacy development (Harris & Hodges, 1995; Huck, 1977; Sharer, 1992). A guiding principle of the literature-based perspective is that literacy acquisition occurs in a book-rich context with an abundance of purposeful communication where meaning is socially constructed (Cullinan, 1987). Literature refers to a wide range of materials including picture books, big books, predictable books, folktales, fables, myths, fantasy, science fiction, poetry, contemporary realistic fiction, historical fiction, nonfiction informational books, and biographies (Lehman, Freeman, & Allen, 1994; Routman, 1988). A number of authorities (Cullinan, 1987; Galda, Cullinan, & Strickland, 1993; Tompkins & McGee, 1993) agree on the distinguishing characteristics of literature-based instruction in preschool, kindergarten, and first-grade classrooms:

- Literature is used as an important vehicle for language arts instruction.
- High-quality narrative and informational literature provides the basis for a consistent read-aloud program in which children are read to daily.
- Literature is the sole or primary basis for initial reading instruction or it is a significant supplement to a basal program.
- Opportunities are provided for students to listen to and read books of their own choosing.
- Students are provided with sustained time for both independent and collaborative book sharing, reading, and writing activities.
- Discussions of literature among student and teachers are commonplace.

Theoretical Framework

Although there are several theoretical orientations that support literature-based reading instruction, it is perhaps most closely associated with reader-response theory. Reader-response theory explains how readers interpret literature (McGee, 1992). According to McGee, one feature of the current literature-based reading movement distinguishing it from others in the past is the grounding in reader-response theory. Reader-response theorists posit that literature is not an object to be studied, nor does it have one correct interpretation (Iser, 1978); rather, meaning in the text is constructed by the readers' own interpretation of their experiences while they are reading (Rosenblatt, 1978). Meaning, therefore, is a two-way process that resides in the transaction that occurs between the reader and the text where the reader constructs a personal envisionment guided by the text. The reader uses prior experiences to select images and feelings that will enable him or her to shape the text at the same time that the text shapes the reader by creating new experiences (McGee, 1992; Rosenblatt, 1978, 1991).

Rosenblatt (1978, 1991) identified two stances readers might take while reading a text, depending on their purposes for reading: aesthetic and efferent. When readers take an aesthetic stance in reading a story, poem, or play, their attention shifts inward and centers on what is being created during the actual reading: personal feelings, ideas, and attitudes. While taking an efferent stance in reading informational text, such as a textbook, the readers' attention narrows in order to build up the meanings and ideas to be retained. Rosenblatt posited that it is the reader rather than the text that dictates the stance that is taken, and any text can be read either way. She also suggested that when reading any one text, readers shift along a continuum from the aesthetic to the efferent stance.

Many early literacy researchers find Louise Rosenblatt's reader-response theory to be both relevant and important in providing a foundation for literature-based instruction (e.g., Eeds & Wells, 1989; Galda, 1990; McGee, 1992). Recent research studies have explored literature-based instruction and children's responses to literature, literacy motivation, and literacy development. These studies provide insights about new ways that teachers and researchers are conceptualizing literacy development in literature-based classrooms (Allington, Guice, Michelson, Baker, & Li, 1996; McGee, 1992).

History of Literature-Based Instruction

From the 1940s through the 1990s basal programs have been documented as the dominant reading materials used for instruction in U.S. elementary classrooms (Shannon, 1989). However, during the past decade there has been a shift toward inclusion of literature in the reading curriculum due to factors including the availability of high-quality literature (Cullinan, 1989), the popularity of the whole-language movement (Fisher & Hiebert, 1990; Goodman, 1989), and the prominence of reader-response theory (Rosenblatt, 1978).

THE EMERGENCE OF LITERATURE-BASED PROGRAMS

The first literature-based beginning reading programs were created in the late 1980s for selection in California, which mandated literature programs (California English/Language Arts Committee, 1987). By 1993, all the major textbook companies had begun producing materials for the changing reading curriculum (Hiebert, 1999). To support the implementation of literature in reading programs, the state textbook guidelines in California and Texas (California English/Language Arts Committee, 1987; Texas Education Agency, 1990) called for the elimination of contrived texts and the use of text with literary merit.

The research on materials used for reading instruction documents the increasing significance of children's literature in the beginning of the 1990s. In a survey conducted in 1980, Gambrell (1992) explored the programs, approaches, and materials used in the reading curriculum. The study was replicated in 1990 in an attempt to identify shifts or changes in the reading curriculum from 1980 to 1990. In the initial study, each of the 93 teachers observed reported using a basal program as the basis for reading instruction. Only 5% of the teachers, primarily at the kindergarten level, reported that they supplemented basal instruction with other materials or approaches. These results indicate almost sole reliance on the use of basal programs in the early 1980s. The survey study was replicated in 1990 with 84 teachers from seven eastern states and the District of Columbia (Gambrell, 1992). Although 80% of the respondents reported using a basal program as the primary basis for reading instruction, more than 50% of these teachers indicated that they supplemented the basal program with children's literature—a significant increase from 1980. The most surprising finding was that the remaining 20% of the respondents reported using children's literature as the foundation for their reading program.

The most compelling evidence of widespread implementation of literature-based reading instruction in the United States comes from the findings of the 1992 National Assessment of Educational Progress (Mullis, Campbell, & Farstrup, 1993). This study revealed that teachers reported a "heavy" emphasis on literature-based instruction, and that the students of these teachers displayed higher levels of reading proficiency. Also, in 1994, Strickland, Walmsley, Bronk, and Weiss interviewed teachers in eight states and found that 18% of the teachers reported using children's literature exclusively, whereas 80% used both basals and children's literature.

EMERGING CONCERNS ABOUT LITERATURE-BASED INSTRUCTION

With the increasing growth in the use of children's literature in the classroom, however, several concerns about the implementation of literature-based instruction began to emerge. For example, Gardner (1988) speculated that without significant staff development, teachers would basalize literature by using instructional guides that have formats similar to basal manuals. Cullinan (1989) voiced the concern that few teachers kept current with the field of children's literature and lacked appropriate coursework necessary for undertaking a literature-based reading curriculum. And, currently, although some research on literature-based instruction has shown increased reading achievement levels, policymakers and educators question the use of literature-based instruction for beginning readers (Stahl, McKenna, & Pagnucco, 1994). It has been observed that some teachers focus more of their instruction time on story context, rather than on alphabetic principles, and students are not adequately acquiring essential reading skills.

Hiebert (1999) revisited the question of whether literature should be the sole material for reading instruction. She examined how young children best learn to dissect the written text and discovered that at the earliest stages of reading acquisition, especially when children are introduced to book reading in school rather than at home, careful attention must be paid to the texts they are using. She concluded that although authentic literature is vitally important, young children also need texts that are more systematic with skill development to learn to how to read; skills must be explicitly taught. She considered several different types of texts and the tasks they pose for beginning readers, concluding that literature is not the only source of materials for early literacy instruction (see Hiebert & Martin, Chapter 24). Consequently, researchers have noted that they need to continue to examine what is best for early-childhood reading instruction.

Literature-Based Instruction in the Classroom

Although few empirical studies directly compare literature-based reading instruction with alternative models, several studies do evaluate the use of literature in reading programs. This section reviews various studies exploring the effects of literature-based instruction on young children's literacy development. The role of storybook reading, literature-based reading instruction, expository text, discussion groups, and motivation to read is explored.

Storybook Reading with Young Children

In early childhood, reading to children has always been the most common practice for implementing literature-based instruction. Observations from case studies of children who have been read to frequently have described behaviors associated with early literacy development. Case studies by Baghban (1984) and others (Sulzby, 1985; Teale, 1987) demonstrate that young children who have been read to frequently know how to handle books and can identify the front of a book, the print to be read, and the appropriate direction for reading the print.

Several studies using experimental designs investigate the effects of storybook reading as a regular classroom practice on children's achievement in various aspects of literacy development. In these investigations, the children in the experimental classrooms who were read to daily over long periods scored significantly better on measures of vocabulary, comprehension, and decoding ability than did children in the control groups who were not read to by an adult (Bus, van IJzendoorn, & Pellegrini, 1995; Dickinson & Smith, 1994; Feitelson, Goldstein, Iraqi, & Share, 1993; Peterman, Dunning, & Mason, 1985; Robbins & Ehri, 1994; Senechal, Thomas, & Monker, 1995).

Experimental investigations in school settings have tried to identify specific elements of storybook reading that enhances literacy skills. Each of the studies has involved children in some type of active participation before, during, or after storybook reading. Qualitative studies, through observations and interviews, have documented how children and parents interact and participate together in reading in the home environment (Teale, 1987). Other research has focused on the influence of the teacher when reading to a whole class in school.

In experimental studies carried out in school settings where children participated with their teacher and peers in some part of the storybook reading experience, students' comprehension and sense of story structure improved in comparison to children in the control groups. The treatments involved activities implemented (1) before story reading, including previewing the story through discussion and prediction and setting a purpose for listening; (2) during story reading, which focused on ideas related to the story that were spontaneously discussed at appropriate times; and (3) after reading, including discussing predictions and purposes set, role-playing stories, retelling stories, and reconstructing stories through pictures. These activities enabled children to relate various parts of a story to one another and to integrate information across the entire story (Morrow, 1985; Pellegrini & Galda, 1982).

Although the studies cited in this section highlight the positive effects of storybook reading, Meyer, Wardrop, Stahl, and Linn (1994) suggest that reading stories is not a magical activity for literacy development; it is the quality of the interaction that occurs during reading that results in positive effects rather than just storybook reading. They reported that storybook reading sessions in classrooms are often not of sufficient quality to engage students fully and to maximize literacy growth. Reading stories as an act in itself does not necessarily promote literacy; attitudes, and interactive behaviors enhance the potential of the read-aloud event for promoting literacy development.

The primary goal of the read-aloud event is the construction of meaning from the interactive process between adult and child (Vygotsky, 1978). During story reading, the adult helps the child understand the text by interpreting the written language based on experiences, background, and beliefs (Dickinson & Smith, 1994). Teale (1984) described the interaction as being interpsychological first, that is, negotiated between adult and child together, and intrapsychological next, when the child internalizes the interactions and can function independently.

Studies focusing on teachers' interactive behaviors when reading to whole classes of children have documented the impact of teachers' reading style on children's comprehension of stories (Roser & Martinez, 1985). A series of investigations were carried out in classrooms to determine children's comprehension of stories in whole-group, small-group, and one-to-one settings (Morrow, 1987, 1988; Morrow & Smith, 1990). The interactions that occurred within these different settings were also studied. On a test of comprehension, children who heard stories in small-group settings performed significantly better than did children who heard stories read one to one, who in turn performed significantly better than children who heard stories read to the whole class. In addition, children who heard stories read in a small-group or one-to-one setting generated significantly more comments and questions than did children in the whole-class setting. Thus, reading to children in small groups offers as much interaction as one-to-one readings, and it appears to lead to greater comprehension than whole-class or even one-to-one readings.

Children's responses to read-aloud experiences, both in questions and in comments, are a critical aspect of the interactive process. When questions are asked and then answered, children receive immediate feedback, which may aid their literacy development. Children benefit by having the opportunity to regulate their own learning by questioning adults in literacy situations and such comments help teachers gain insights into the way young children attempt to construct meaning and make sense of text.

Children often request that favorite stories be read aloud, a practice that has attracted the attention of many scholars. Researchers have questioned whether lasting cognitive and affective benefits result from repeated readings of the same story. Pappas (1991) found that children's comments and questions increase and become more interpretive and evaluative when they have listened to repeated readings of the same story. Children also elaborated more often and interpreted issues in the story following repeated readings. Sulzby (1985) reported that the familiarity that comes with repeated readings enables children to reenact stories or to attempt to read them on their own. Repeated readings seem to be an important component in reading stories; the familiarity gained through the experience provides children with background information that enables them to deal with the text on various levels.

Reading aloud to children has long been advocated as a vital experience in literacy development both at home and in school, as many of the chapters in this volume highlight (see, e.g., Tabors & Snow, Chapter 12; Bus, Chapter 13; and Strickland, Chapter 21). Clearly, storybook reading to young children plays an important role in literature-based instruction.

Early Literacy Development

A number of studies suggest that the use of literature enhances children's oral and written language. This suggestion is based on the supposition that children exposed to books early and frequently become aware that printed words have sounds, and they recognize that print carries meaning. For example, Reutzel, Oda, and Moore (1989) reported the positive effects of literature-based programs on the print-awareness and word-reading acquisition of kindergarten students. Others suggest that decoding and comprehension can be enhanced through literature (Dahl & Freppon, 1995). In addition, this research found that children in the literature-based program were more strategic readers than those in a skills-based program (Dahl & Freppon, 1995).

Several studies have investigated the effects of a combination of instructional approaches consisting of time devoted to basals and children's literature. In a study conducted by Morrow (1992), second-grade classrooms were randomly assigned to one of three groups: (1) a literature-based reading and writing program that included literacy centers, teacher-directed literacy activities, and independent reading and writing periods; (2) an identical group to the one described in (1), except for the addition of a component in which parents supported the literacy activities at home; or (3) a control group that used a basal-only program. Results of the study revealed that the performance of students in the two literature treatment conditions was statistically superior to that of the control groups on the following measures: story retelling, story rewriting, and writing original stories.

Block (1993) studied the effects of a literature-based program reading program designed to teach reading and thinking strategies. In this investigation, second- and third-grade students were randomly assigned, by classrooms, to experimental or control conditions. In the literature-based classrooms students received lessons twice weekly for 32 weeks. The lessons consisted of (1) teacher explanation and modeling of thinking and reading comprehension strategy using written strategy application guides, and (2) student selection of literature and application of previously taught cognitive strategies. In the control group, students received traditional instruction that did not emphasize strategy instruction. The results revealed that the strategy/literature-based group outperformed the control group on the reading comprehension, vocabulary, and total battery sessions of the Iowa Test of Basic Skills. In addition, students in the strategy/literature-based group also outperformed controls in the ability to transfer cognitive strategies to out-of-school applications and on measures of self-esteem and critical and creative thinking.

Baumann and Ivey (1997) conducted a year-long qualitative case study to explore what second-grade students learned about reading, writing, and literature in a program of strategy instruction integrated within a literature-based classroom environment. A content analysis of the data resources—including individual student and parent interviews, videotapes of regular classroom literacy activities, artifacts of students' reading and writing, assessments of students' literacy learning, and the teachers daily plan book—revealed that students grew in overall reading performance and came to view reading as a natural component of the school experience. The students demonstrated high levels of engagement with books; developed skill in word identification, fluency, and comprehension; and grew in written composition abilities. This qualitative study provides support for the efficacy of teaching students reading and language arts strategies within a literature-based framework.

Thus, in contrast to much criticism from the press, investigations of the use of literature in reading programs have demonstrated positive effects on children's' reading development.

The Role of Discussion Groups

The increase in the use of children's literature in the elementary classroom has drawn attention to the ways in which children respond to literature during discussion groups. Literature discussion groups are typically described as involving small groups of children (three to eight) who read a story or novel over a period of time. Researchers who have explored the cognitive processes that are necessary for higher-level thinking agree that deep-level understanding occurs only through interactions with others (Almasi, 1995, 1996). This theory is in keeping with Vygotskian theories which posit that social interaction is central to the development of language and thought. Other researchers have reported that the collab-

orative nature of literature discussions appears to help students construct meaning and clarify confusions (Almasi, 1995; Eeds & Wells, 1989). Students in these studies were observed orchestrating turn taking, negotiating leadership, and drawing on various sources to clarify or agree on text interpretation.

Studies that have focused on discussion groups have used a variety of qualitative and quantitative methods to examine what happens when students engage in discussions about books they have read (Gambrell, 1996). There is evidence that prior to instruction or experience with literature discussion groups, students' responses tend to be unelaborated and their discussions involve limited interactions. For example, Eeds and Wells (1989) found that even without direct questioning by the teacher there was evidence in students' discussions that they recalled text information, drew inferences, supported their inferences, and read critically. In some studies, students sometimes had difficulty making personal connections to text before the intervention of the discussion groups; however, given opportunities to participate in discussions, these same students quickly learned to respond personally to their reading (Goatley, 1996).

The research on early elementary students' discussion of children's literature suggests that young children are capable of producing elaborate and sophisticated responses to literature, especially when supported with instruction. Across, these studies, children were able to construct meaning, share personal reactions, and demonstrate strategic reading behaviors such as hypothesizing, interpreting, predicting, and evaluating. The research clearly indicates that discussing text provides children with opportunities to explore multiple interpretations of literature and respond at higher levels of abstract and critical thinking (McGee, 1992).

The Role of Expository Text

Knowledge of the components of both narrative and expository text is part of being fully literate. A number of scholars have challenged the predominance of narrative text in early-childhood classrooms (Duke, 1998;

Kamil & Lane, 1997; Moss, Leone, & Dipillo, 1997; Pappas, 1991). These scholars argue for increased exposure and use of expository text in primary-grade classrooms.

Research has documented that even young children are familiar with the structure of narrative text (Egan, 1993; Pappas, 1993). On the other hand, evidence suggests that many children lack an understanding of expository text structure. A study by Duke (1998) provided empirical confirmation of the scarcity of informational text in the early grades. Therefore, some scholars have suggested that the problem lies in children's lack of experience with expository text (Caswell & Duke, 1998; Kamil & Lane, 1997, Pappas, 1991).

Although there are a number of possible explanations for the lack of access to expository text in the primary grades, one of the most frequently cited is that these texts are too difficult. However, a number of recent studies suggest that young children profit from exposure to expository text. Pappas (1993) conducted a study that explored kindergarten children's understanding of informational text. On several occasions, the children were asked to "read" an informational text that has been read aloud to them immediately before. The children increasingly employed linguistic features of information book language, providing evidence of their tacit understanding of expository text structure. In a study of first-graders' interactions with oral and written expository texts, Hicks (1995) found that the children were able to repond to and learn from these texts in sophisticated ways. Donovan (1996) explored first-graders' responses to narrative and expository texts and found that they were able to identify and distinguish between the two types of text in terms of a number of features.

Duke and Kays (1998) examined what young children know and can learn about expository text. They reported on 20 kindergarteners' knowledge of expository books at two points across the school year—in September, when the children first entered kindergarten, and in December, after the children had spent 3 months in a classroom in which expository books were read aloud on a daily basis. The results of this study documented that in December,

the children's pretend readings of unfamiliar wordless expository text contained far greater use of key features of expository book language as compared to the September pretend readings. According to Dukes and Kays (1998), "inattention to expository texts in early childhood settings cannot be justified on the basis that children are unable to interact productively with these texts" (p. 314).

The findings of these studies suggest that young children can learn about and from expository text and that exposure to expository text results in fast-developing knowledge of expository text structure and book language. In addition, it appears that inclusion of such texts in literature-based instruction may be well advised.

Motivation to Read

An important component of any literacy program is promoting positive attitudes toward reading to instill in children a lifelong reading habit. Early investigations on promoting interest in books and the use of literature in the classroom were mainly anecdotal and indicated that literature-based programs may enhance students' enthusiasm and foster positive attitudes toward books. Some researchers found that when classrooms are filled with trade books and teachers encourage free reading, there is an improvement in children's reading achievement, gains in vocabulary and comprehension, increased reading, and better attitudes toward reading in comparison to children in schools that do not participate in such programs (Elley, 1996). Morrow and Weinstein (1982, 1986) found that literature use increased dramatically when teachers incorporated enjoyable literature activities into the daily program, when library centers were created in the classrooms, and when recreational reading periods were scheduled on a regular basis.

Findings concerning the effects of literature-based instruction on children's attitudes toward reading have been mixed. When comparing methods, some studies have found no differences between basal reading instruction and literature-based instruction on measures of children's attitudes toward reading (McKenna, Kear, & Ellsworth,

1995; McKenna, Stratton, Grindler, & Jenkins, 1995). However, several studies using a range of quantitative and qualitative methodologies have revealed that literature-based programs positively affect children's attitudes toward reading (Goatley, Brock, & Raphael, 1995; Goatley & Raphael, 1992) and frequency of reading (Dahl & Freppon, 1995; Stewart, Paradis, Ross, & Lewis, 1996). Gambrell, Palmer, and Coding (1993) found that children seem to want to read more often when they are able to choose what they will read, have the opportunity to interact with others to discuss what they have read, and feel successful about reading.

Thus, it appears that literature-based instruction can have a positive effect on attitudes toward reading. However, it is not clear whether this instructional approach is superior to other methods of teaching reading. Consequently, there is much to be explored on the benefits of literature-based instruction on literacy motivation.

Current Perspectives and Special Issues in Literature-Based Instruction

Today's classrooms reflect overwhelming diversity. Educators are faced with the challenges of teaching second-language learners and students with special needs as well as the "typical" student. Integrating the use of technology and meeting the core curriculum content standards are issues that also must be addressed. This section explores these issues and current perspectives and discusses the roles they play in literature-based instruction.

Literature and Second-Language Acquisition

Rapidly changing demographics in society, influenced by economics and immigrant populations, are reflected in classrooms, where students speak many of the world's languages as a first language, are fluent in more than one language, speak dialects of English, and possess a varied range of reading levels (see Tabors & Snow, Chapter 12). As a result, it is important to examine how literature-based instruction relates to second-language (L2) learning.

Roser, Hoffman, and Farest (1990) investigated the effect of literature-based instruction on K–2 L2 learners in a school district on the Texas/Mexico border. Language to Literacy (LtL), a program intended to develop children's literacy skills in much the same way oral language is developed, was created to infuse literature and related instructional strategies into a traditional reading/language arts setting. Research was conducted in six elementary schools, and over the course of 18 months, 78 teachers and 2,500 students participated in the study.

Implementation of the program involved (1) getting literature into the classroom, (2) sharing books with the children, (3) collecting and recording children's responses to books, (4) encouraging writing, and (5) developing reading fluency to help children grow in language, reading, writing, and thinking and to discover their own connections with literature. The project staff developed 70 literature units and a teaching guide that rotated among teachers in the study. Literacy centers were set up in the classrooms, allowing space for reading and writing activities. The following data were collected and analyzed: teachers' reports of their students' progress, accounts of students' fluency in reading and writing, and their academic achievement on the California Test of Basic Skills. After the literature-based program was in place, five of the six schools in the study made statistically significant growth in their scores on the state-mandated test of basic skills. The results indicated that a literature-based program could be implemented successfully in elementary schools that serve primarily limited-English-speaking students from economically disadvantaged homes.

Although studies of the effects of literature-based instruction on L2 learning in early childhood are limited, certain assumptions can be made and should be considered for future research. The communicative view of language development emphasizes the meaningful interaction between language users. Thus, the classroom should be designed to facilitate many types of activities and student-centered interactions (Richard-Amato & Snow, 1992). The characteristics of a literature-based instruction program, mentioned earlier, provide L2 learners with a classroom atmosphere conducive to the acquisition of communicative competence.

Research on second-language development recommends that L2 learners receive comprehensible input and have supportive affective filters to succeed in acquiring the target language (Cummins, 1989; Krashen & Terrell, 1983). Comprehensible input contains meaning that is interesting to the learner, is about something the learner knows, and contains language that is just beyond the learner's current level. Children's literature satisfies the requirements for comprehensible input, and in many cultures, there are comparable folktales, fairy tales, and other genres that can be used as a foundation for limited-English-proficient (LEP) students to pique interest, activate prior knowledge, and enhance understanding of the children's literature familiar to mainstream students. Students' affective filters, which include factors such as self-confidence, motivation, and anxiety, are related to the students' ability to process the input properly. The classroom incorporating a literature-based instruction program presents students with choices, opportunities to interact with peers, and self-confidence building through independent reading time and computer-based literature programs that allow students to work at their own.

Further, LEP students require ample opportunities to hear and use English in various purposeful, authentic contexts that encourage and facilitate communication, social interaction, and risk taking in a low-anxiety environment. Read-alouds by the teacher or peers, book talks, story retellings, literature circles, book buddies, author studies, and other reading-response projects allow LEP students the opportunities to listen, speak, and write in the target language in a meaningful setting. These literature-based activities provide L2 learners the social interaction with native English speakers necessary to promote language acquisition.

Literature-Based Instruction and Technology

As early literacy classrooms become more technologically oriented, CD-ROMs, software, and the Internet, for example, offer teachers and students a variety of new resources using literature that was not previously available. Wepner and Ray (2000) suggest that instructional technology has potential for early literacy learning due to the interactivity and motivation associated with it. Kinzer and Leu (1997) conducted a demonstration project designed to promote literacy through the use of multimedia and literature. The Young Children's Literacy Project integrated full-motion, color video, sound, and Internet access with reading, writing, and oral language. The video-based/CD-ROM anchor story provided a common link to a shared experience among the teacher and students. As its basis, the project used the notion of the mental modeling that occurs during the comprehension process (McNamara, Miller, & Bransford, 1991). The multimedia, which included anchor video, online story sequencing, and book-making activities, supplied the framework for understanding stories. The goal was to have children understand the power, use, and importance of literacy.

Children viewed a video story and then sequenced and retold the tale. Their retellings were used to write, illustrate, and add music to their own versions of the story. When their books were published, the students placed them in the classroom and on the computer. Use of a World Wide Web home page linked students and teachers around the world to ongoing literacy activities. The Internet and the collaborative facets built into The Young Children's Literacy software optimized classroom implementation of author's circles, book-study groups, and collaborative learning. Creators of The Young Children's Literacy Project continue to study the effects of multimedia technology on young children's reading and writing in the classroom.

In a study conducted by Liaw (1997), 14 English-as-a-second-language (ESL) students in grades 1, 2, and 3 were divided into three groups based on their English proficiency level and asked to read and discuss electronic/computer books. The interactive stories—produced by Discis Knowledge Research, Inc., and chosen for the study because they were designed for both first- and second-language learning—appear on screen as actual pages of a book and include illustrations, music, voices, and sound effects. The students chose one of 10 computer books each time they visited the computer lab and could sample a book before making their decisions. During the reading, the students were encouraged to interact with the computer and discuss the book with one another. Five 30-minute computer-book reading and group interaction sessions were videotaped.

Both qualitative and quantitative analyses were performed on the data. The quantity of talk was counted in terms of the total number and average number of words per minute by book, by group, and by the amount of computer-related versus story-related talk. Computer-related talk decreased and story-related talk increased as more books were read. The quantitative data revealed how many verbal interactions occurred, and the qualitative data showed how the children used their language and what type of talk they accomplished during verbal interaction.

In the early childhood grades, regardless of their English proficiency, the LEP students used English to read, command, suggest, question, respond, explain, express emotion and opinion, and describe images and actions. They had a substantial amount of verbal interaction making comments about one another's behavior, voicing opinions about the stories, and asking one another questions. The finding that purposeful verbal interaction and various language functions of LEP children can occur in a group computer-book reading environment has significant instructional implications. Electronic/computer books promote low-anxiety discussion in English among students and encourage social interaction in an authentic context.

Although there seems to be a surge of investigation into technology's usefulness in the classroom, studies are limited regarding technology's role in literacy development and particularly in literature-based instruction. According to Leu, Karchmer, and Leu (1999), it is difficult to carry out research and publish it in recognized journals, since the technology use is often outdated by the time the paper is published. However, Wepner and Ray (2000) contend that technology provides teachers and students with enormous possibilities to use literature-based instruction programs and related activities to communicate, motivate, and sustain learning and foster literacy.

Concluding Remarks

Reading instruction in the early years has shifted dramatically during the past decade to an increased emphasis on literature in classroom instruction. Although some researchers question the appropriateness of using children's literature to teach reading instruction, studies suggest that literature has an important role in the curriculum.

If literature is to be used well, there are some clear implications for practice. Professional development opportunities are necessary for developing the extent of knowledge of literature required for effective practice. Teacher's knowledge of quality children's literature is basic to the success of literature-based instruction. Also, early-childhood classrooms should be equipped with libraries that have an abundance of print-rich materials of all genres and types. With these and other practices in place, and continued research in the area, literature-based instruction may have important benefits for early literacy development.

References

Allington, R. L., Guice, S., Michelson, N., Baker, K., & Li, S. (1996). Literature-based curricula in high-poverty schools. In M. F. Graves, P. van den Brock, & B. M. Taylor (Eds.), *The first "r": Every child's right to read* (pp. 73–96). New York: Teachers College Press.

Almasi, J. F. (1995). The nature of fourth grader's sociocognitive conflicts in peer-led and teacher-led discussions of literature. *Reading Research Quarterly, 30,* 314–351.

Almasi, J. F. (1996). A new view of discussion. In L. B. Gambrell & J. F. Almasi (Eds.), *Lively discussions!: Fostering engaging reading* (pp. 2–24). Newark, DE: International Reading Association.

Baghban, M. J. M. (1984). *Our daughter learns to read and write: A case study from birth to three.* Newark, DE: International Reading Association.

Baumann, J. F., & Ivey, G. (1997). Delicate balances: Striving for curricular and instructional equilibrium in a second grade, literature/strategy-based classroom. *Reading Research Quarterly, 32,* 244–275.

Block, C. C. (1993). Strategy instruction in a literature-based reading program. *The Elementary School Journal, 94*(2), 139–151.

Bus, A., van IJzendoorn, M. H., & Pelligrini, A. (1995). Joint book reading makes for success in learning to read: A meta-analysis on intergenerational transmission of literacy. *Review of Educational Research, 65,* 1–21.

California English Language Arts Committee. (1987). *English language arts framework for California's public schools (kindergarten through grade twelve.* Sacramento California Department of Education.

Caswell, L. J., & Duke, N. K. (1998). Non-narrative as a catalyst for literacy development. *Language Arts, 75,* 108–117.

Cullinan, B. E. (1987). *Children's literature in the reading program.* Newark, DE: International Reading Association.

Cullinan, B. E. (1989). Latching on to literature: Reading initiatives take hold. *School Library Journal, 35,* 27–31.

Cummins, J. (1989). *Empowering minority students.* Sacramento, CA: California Association for Bilingual Education.

Dahl, K. L., & Freppon, P. A. (1995). A comparison of inner city children's interpretations of reading and writing instruction in the early grades in skills-based and whole language classrooms. *Reading Research Quarterly, 30,* 50–74.

Dickinson, D. K., & Smith, M. W. (1994). Long-term effects of preschool teachers' book readings on low income children's vocabulary and story comprehension. *Reading Research Quarterly, 29,* 104–122.

Donovan, C. A. (1996). First graders' impressions of genre-specific elements in writing narrative and expository texts. In D. J. Leu, Ck. K. Kinzer, & K. A. Hinchman (Eds.), *Literacies for the 21st century: Forty-fifth yearbook of the National Reading Conference* (pp. 183–194). Chicago: National Reading Conference.

Duke, N. K. (1998, February). *Empirical confirmation of the scarcity of informational text in the early grades.* Paper presented at the Harvard Graduate School of Education Student Research Conference, Cambridge, MA.

Duke, N. K., & Kays, J. (1998). "Can I say 'once upon a time'?: Kindergarten children developing knowledge of information book language. *Early Childhood Research Quarterly, 13*(2), 295–318.

Eeds, M., & Wells, D. (1989). Grand Conversations: An exploration of meaning construction in literature study groups. *Research in the Teaching of English, 23*(1), 4–29.

Elley, W. B. (1996). Lifting literacy levels in developing countries: Some implications from an IEA study. In V. Greaney, *Promoting reading in developing countries* (pp. 39–63). Newark, DE: International Reading Association.

Feitelson, D., Goldstein, Z., Iraqi, U., & Share, D. (1993). Effects of listening to story reading on aspects of literacy acquisition in a diglossic situation. *Reading Research Quarterly, 28,* 70–79.

Fisher, C. W., & Hiebert, E. H. (1990). Characteristics of tasks in two approaches to literacy instruction. *The Elementary School Journal, 91*(1), 3–18.

Galda, L. (1990). Children's literature as a language experience. *The Advocate, 3*(4), 247–259.

Galda, L., Cullinan, B. E., & Strickland, D. S. (1993). *Language, literacy and the child.* New York: Harcourt Brace.

Gambrell, L. B. (1992). Elementary school literacy instruction: Changes and challenges. In M. J. Dreher & W. H. Slater (Eds.), *Elementary school literacy: Critical issues* (pp. 227–239). Norwood, MA: Christopher-Gordon.

Gambrell, L. B. (1996). What research reveals about discussion. In L. B. Gambrell & J. F. Almasi (Eds.), *Lively discussion!: Fostering engaged reading* (pp. 25–38). Newark, DE: International Reading Association.

Gambrell, L. B., Palmer, B. M., & Coding, R. M. (1993). *Motivation to read.* Washington, DC: Office of Educational Research and Improvement.

Gardner, M. (1988). An educator's concerns about the California reading initiative. *The New Advocate, 1,* 250–253.

Goatley, V. G. (1996). The participation of a student identified as learning disabled in a regular education book club: The case of Stark. *Reading and Writing Quarterly: Overcoming Learning Difficulties, 12*(2), 195–214.

Goatley, V. J., Brock, C. H., & Raphael, T. E. (1995). Diverse learners participating in regular education "Book Clubs." *Reading Research Quarterly, 30,* 352–380.

Goatley, V. J., & Raphael, T. E. (1992) Non-traditional learners' written and dialogic response to literature. Learner factors/teacher factors: Issues in literacy research and instruction. *40th yearbook of the National Reading Conference* (pp. 313–322). Chicago: National Reading Conference.

Goodman, Y. M. (1989). Roots of the whole language movement. *The Elementary School Journal, 90,* 113–127.

Harris, T. L., & Hodges, R. E. (Eds.). (1995). *The literacy dictionary: The vocabulary of reading and writing.* Newark, DE: International Reading Association.

Hicks, D. (1995). The social origins of essayist writing. *Bulletin Suisse de Linguistique Applique, 61,* 61–82.

Hiebert, E. H. (1999). Text matters in learning to read. *The Reading Teacher, 52,* 552–566.

Huck, C. (1977). Literature as the content of reading. *Theory Into Practice, 16*(5), 363–371.

Iser, W. (1978). *The act of reading.* Baltimore: John Hopkins University Press.

Kamil, M., & Lane, D. (1997). *A classroom study of the efficacy of using information text for first grade reading instruction.* Paper presented at the American Educational Research Association meeting, San Diego, CA.

Kinzer, C., & Leu, D. J., Jr. (1997). Focus on research—the challenge of change: Exploring literacy and learning in electronic environments. *Language Arts, 74*(2), 126–136.

Krashen, S. D., & Terrell, T. D. (1983). *The natural approach: Language acquisition in the classroom.* nglewood Cliffs, NJ: Alemany Press.

Lehman, B. A., Freeman, E. V., & Allen, V. G. (1994). Children's literature and literacy instruction: "Literature-based" elementary teachers' belief and practices. *Reading Horizons, 35,* 3–29.

Leu, D. J., Jr., Karchmer, R. A., & Leu, D. D. (1999). The Miss Rumphius effect: Envisionments for literacy and learning that transform the Internet. *The Reading Teacher, 52,* 636–642.

Liaw, M. L. (1997). An analysis of ESL children's verbal interaction during computer book reading. *Computers in the Schools, 13*(3/4), 55–73.

McGee, L. M. (1992). Exploring the literature-based reading revolution (Focus on research). *Language Arts, 69,* 529–537.

McKenna, M. C., Kear, D. J., & Ellsworth, R. A. (1995). Children's attitudes toward reading: A national survey. *Reading Research Quarterly, 30,* 934–955.

McKenna, M. C., Stratton, B. D., Grindler, M. C., & Jenkins, S. J. (1995). Differential effects of whole language and traditional instruction on reading attitudes. *Journal of Reading Behavior, 27*(1), 19–44.

McNamara, T. P., Miller, D. L., & Bransford, J. D. (1991). Mental models and reading comprehension. In R. Barr, M. Kamil, P. Mosenthal, & P. D. Pearson (Eds.), *Handbook of reading research* (Vol. 2, pp. 490–511). New York: Longman.

Meyer, L., Wardrop, J., Stahl, S., & Linn, R. (1994). Effects of reading storybooks aloud to children. *Journal of Educational Research, 88,* 69–85.

Morrow, L. M. (1985). Retelling stories: A strategy for improving children's comprehension, concept of story structure and oral language complexity. *The Elementary School Journal, 85,* 647–661.

Morrow, L. M. (1987). The effect of small group story reading on children's questions and comments. In S. McCormick & J. Zutell (Eds.), *Cognitive and social perspectives for literacy research and instruction: 37th yearbook of the National Reading Conference* (pp. 77–86). Chicago: National Reading Conference.

Morrow, L. M. (1988). Young children's responses to one-to-one story readings in school settings. *Reading Research Quarterly, 23,* 89–107.

Morrow, L. M. (1992). The impact of a literature-based program on literacy achievement, use of literature, and attitudes of children from minority backgrounds. *Reading Research Quarterly, 27,* 250–275.

Morrow, L. M., & Smith, J. K. (1990). The effects of group size on interactive storybook reading. *Reading Research Quarterly, 25,* 214–231.

Morrow, L. M., & Weinstein, C. S. (1982). Increasing children's use of literature through program and physical design changes. *The Elementary School Journal, 83,* 131–137.

Morrow, L. M., & Weinstein, C. S. (1986). Encouraging voluntary reading: The impact of a literature program on children's use of library centers. *Reading Research Quarterly, 21,* 330–346.

Moss, B., Leone, W., & Dipillo, M. (1997). Exploring the literature of fact: Linking reading and writing through nformation trade books. *Language Arts, 74,* 418–429.

Mullis, I., Campbell, J., & Farstrup, A. (1993). *NAEP 1992 reading report card for the nation and the states: Data from the national and trial state assessments.* Washington, DC: U. S. Government Printing Office.

Pappas, C. C. (1991). Fostering full access to literacy by including information books. *Language Arts, 68,* 449–462.

Pappas, C. C. (1993). Is narrative "primary"? Some insights from kindergartners' pretend readings of stories and information books. *Journal of Reading Behavior, 25,* 97–129.

Pellegrini, A., & Galda, L. (1982). The effects of thematic-fantasy play training on the development of children's story comprehension. *American Educational Research Journal, 19,* 443–452.

Peterman, C. L., Dunning, D., & Mason, J. (1985). *A storybook reading event: How a teacher's presentation affects kindergarten children's subsequent attempts to read from the text.* Paper presented at the 35th annual meeting of the National Reading Conference, San Diego, CA.

Reutzel, D. R., Oda, L. K, & Moore, B. H. (1989). Developing print awareness: The effect of three instructional approaches on kindergartners' print awareness, reading readiness, and word reading. *Journal of Reading Behavior, 21*(3), 197–217.

Robbins, C., & Ehri, L. C. (1994). Reading storybooks to kindergartners helps them learn new vocabulary words. *Journal of Educational Psychology, 86,* 54–64.

Rosenblatt, L. M. (1978). *The reader, the text, the poem: The transactional theory of literary work.* Carbondale: Southern Illinois University Press.

Rosenblatt, L. M. (1991). Literature—S.O.S. *Language Arts, 68,* 444–448.

Roser, N. L., Hoffman, J. V., & Farest, C. (1990). Language, literature and at-risk children. *The Reading Teacher,* 554–559.

Roser, N., & Martinez, M. (1985). Roles adults play in preschoolers' response to literature. *Language Arts, 62,* 485–490.

Routman, R. (1988). *Transitions.* Portsmouth, NH: Heinemann.

Scharer, P. L. (1992). Teachers in transition: An exploration of changes in teachers and classrooms during implementation of literature-based reading instruction. *Research in the Teaching of English, 26*(4), 408–445.

Senechal, M., Thomas, E., & Monker, J. (1995). Individual differences in four-year-old children's acquisition of vocabulary during storybook reading. *Journal of Educational Psychology, 87,* 218–229.

Shannon, P. (1989). *Broken promises: Reading instruction in twentieth century America.* Granby, MA: Bergin & Gavey.

Stahl, S. A., McKenna, M. C., & Pagnucco, J. R. (1994). The effects of whole-language instruction: An update and reappraisal. *Educational Psychologist, 19,* 175–185.

Stein, N. L., & Glenn, C. G. (1979). An analysis of story comprehension in elementary school children. In R. O. Fredle (Ed.), *New directions in discourse processing* (Vol. 2, pp. 53–120). Norwood, NJ: Ablex.

Sulzby, E. (1985). Children's emergent reading of favorite books: A developmental study. *Reading Research Quarterly, 20,* 458–481.

Teale, W. H. (1984). Reading to young children: It's significance for literacy development. In A. Goelman, A. Oberg, & F. Smith (Eds.), *Awakening to literacy* (pp. 110–121). London: Heinemann.

Teale, W. H. (1987). *Emergent literacy: Reading and writing development in early childhood.* Paper presented at the 36th annual meeting of the National Reading Conference, Austin, TX.

Texas Education Agency. (1990). *Proclamation of the state Board of Education advertising for bids on textbooks.* Austin, TX: Author.

Tompkins, G. E., & McGee, L. M. (1993). *Teaching reading with literature.* New York: Macmillan.

Vygotsky, L. S. (1978). *Mind in society: the development of psychological processes.* Cambridge, MA: Harvard University.

Wepner, S. B., & Ray, L. (2000). Sign of the times: Technology and early literacy learning. In D. Strickland & L. M. Morrow (Eds.), *Beginning reading and writing* (pp. 168–182). New York: Teachers College Press.

24

The Texts of Beginning Reading Instruction

❖

ELFRIEDA H. HIEBERT
LEIGH ANN MARTIN

Basal readers have been the foundation on which reading instruction has been built (Chall & Squire, 1991). While approaches to reading instruction and the materials used to support this instruction have changed over the years, what has remained constant in U.S. reading instruction is the use of prepackaged materials offered by textbook companies. In 1992, over 85% of schools reported using basal reading programs (Shannon, 1997), and this figure appears to have remained fairly stable since then (Baumann, Hoffman, Duffy-Hester, & Ro, 2000).

Although the ways in which teachers use the same textbook can vary considerably, the contents of textbooks create parameters for teachers and their students. Particularly with children who are on the cusp of acquiring independent reading proficiency, characteristics of texts such as the presence of illustrations, the nature of the language, and the number of words can influence the kinds of experiences children and their teachers can have. Our interest in this review lies with the textbooks intended for beginning readers, especially those whose literacy experiences occur primarily in school. Approximately 40–45% of an American fourth-grade cohort read so slowly that they are unsuccessful with complex literacy tasks (Donahue, Voelk, Campbell,

& Mazzeo, 1999). Aiming to improve students' reading achievement, state officials in two of three largest states in the United States—California and Texas—have used reading textbooks, primarily those intended for beginning readers, as a foundation for reform in reading achievement. In both states, the use of state monies for textbook purchases is limited to those texts that meet the state's criteria. Both states have mandated substantially different texts for beginning readers from one adoption cycle to another. When mandates have identified high-quality literature as the requisite materials for beginning readers, research has been cited as driving this mandate (California English/ Language Arts Committee, 1987; Texas Education Agency, 1990). When mandates have identified decodable text as the requisite materials for beginning readers, research has been cited as driving this mandate (California English/Language Arts Committee, 2000; Texas Education Agency, 1997).

The purpose of this review is to study the existing research on the effects that particular types of texts have on beginning readers. There were three questions of particular interest. The first considers how reading acquisition is facilitated or hindered by different types of texts. The limited number of existing studies on the effects of texts on children's reading acquisition is not surprising because isolating text effects is difficult. Even so, the policies of Texas and California—particularly those on decodable text—would suggest a much more substantial empirical foundation than currently exists.

The second question addressed in this review was how different types of words are acquired. The literature on how words are learned individually or in phrases or single sentences is fairly extensive. This learning is typically evaluated in research contexts where an individual child interacts with an investigator. Despite the limitations of the texts and contexts of these studies, these studies provide the bulk of the available evidence on how children learn to read.

Third, we examined the research on characteristics of current texts for beginning readers. Texts have changed substantially over the past two decades. Our interest lay in establishing how current texts matched the patterns from text and word learning studies.

Effects of Particular Text Types on Children's Reading Development

In light of the sizable investments publishers make in reading textbooks and the daily use of these texts in classrooms, it is surprising to find few studies on the effects of texts on beginning reading development. Most existing studies are limited in scope and often flawed in their design. The primary shortcoming is the confounding of text effects with those of instructional method. For example, when Foorman, Francis, Fletcher, Schatschneider, and Mehta (1998) investigated the effects of using a direct code approach, an embedded code approach, and an implicit code approach, each of these approaches had unique text types and instructional activities in addition to their approaches to phonics.

Hiebert (1999) identified three types of texts for beginning readers: High frequency texts, phonics texts and literature-based texts (see Morrow & Gambrell, this volume, for a discussion of literature-based programs). In one group that Hiebert described as high-frequency texts, words such as "here," "can," and "he" are overrepresented. Phonics texts support word recognition through a preponderance of decodable vocabulary. Literature-based texts emphasize the meaningfulness of the entire text, one form of which are "predictable" texts which repeat phrases or sentences. Any text can embody any of these supports to varying degrees. However, the swings in reading instruction have tended to categorize texts based on one dimension. Following proposals that predictable texts could serve as the entrée to conventional reading (Holdaway, 1979; Martin & Brogan, 1971), predictable texts have dominated the textbook programs available for beginning reading instruction. Despite their dominance over the past 15 years, the effectiveness of predictable texts in supporting reading acquisition is unclear. This review emphasizes predictable text because of the critical role it continues to have in programs for beginning readers.

In the studies of predictable text that have been conducted, the nature of miscues as a function of reading has been a particular focus. Although beginning readers display more fluency with predictable texts than texts from basal reading programs or phonics texts (Gourley, 1984; Rhodes, 1979), this fluency is an artifact of the predictable pattern of the text. When Rhodes (1979) divided each text into quarters, she found that children did well after they mastered the repetitive, patterned portion of the predictable texts. Once the text broke the pattern, children tended to experience difficulty. Similarly, Leu, DeGroff, and Simons (1986) found that once children had mastered the pattern (but not before), the contextual supports of a predictable text helped poor readers improve their reading rates and comprehension to the level of good readers. But poorer readers were less likely to attend to deviations in the pattern than good readers. Within the context of the predictable text itself, the pattern of the text offers support for beginning and poor readers but only after children have mastered the pattern. Further, these texts appear to encourage an overreliance on the pattern.

The studies of children's miscues fail to indicate how well children remember words that they have read in predictable texts. In Bridge, Winograd, and Haley's (1983) study of the effects of reading predictable or basal texts on measures of target word recognition, the predictable text group learned significantly more target words than the basal group. Although these findings suggest that the use of multiple rereadings and sentence and word activities based on the text may result in superior word learning, the exact contribution of the text to this learning is unclear as instructional activities of the groups differed substantially. The predictable text group engaged in multiple rereadings of texts, sentence and word card activities, and writing of stories, and the basal group engaged in two readings of texts (one silent and one oral) and comprehension checks.

An experiment by Boylin (1998) where one group of first-graders read decodable texts while another group read predictable texts resulted in no discernible differences between the groups. Boylin, however, observed that the children's reading of the decodable texts occurred only during twice-weekly tutoring sessions. Children's typical fare was the predictable texts that were part of the classroom program rather than the decodable texts.

While not comparing predictable and decodable texts directly, a study by Hoffman, Roser, Patterson, Salas, and Pennington (1999) examined children's reading of seven randomly ordered texts which teachers had leveled for decodability and predictability. Hoffman et al. (1999) found that the decodability of texts significantly correlated with student performance. The combined decodability and predictability index with reading levels from the Qualitative Reading Inventory were the best predictors of student performance on the texts. Although this study does not measure the impact of decodable texts on students' reading development, the results from this study indicate that the decodability and predictability of texts affect beginning readers' fluency, accuracy, and rate.

Reviews of literature typically conclude that phonics-based instruction produces reading achievement superior to approaches that emphasize high-frequency words or meaningful stories (Adams, 1990; Chall, 1995; Foorman et al., 1998), but the relative contribution of particular types of texts—especially texts that consist mainly of highly decodable words—to lessons or writing activities is unclear. One exception is

Juel and Roper/Schneider's (1985) examination of the reading development of first-graders who received the same phonics lessons but who read in texts from two different basal reading programs. The two basal series differed significantly only in the characteristics of the preprimers, with one preprimer containing easily decodable words while the other preprimer contained mostly high-frequency words. The two factors that contributed most to end-of-the-year reading performance were students' initial knowledge (scores on the Metropolitan Readiness Text) and the basal series. Students who read from the decodable preprimers were more likely to learn letter–sound correspondences early, including ones not explicitly taught, and to use decoding knowledge when encountering unfamiliar words. Use of decodable texts for a particular part of the reading acquisition period seems to help, but this study does not indicate how long this period extends.

Research on Children's Word Learning

Because the research on children's reading acquisition within texts is so limited, we turn to the more extensive research on children's word learning in word lists and phrases. In studies in which word learning individually or in phrases is investigated relative to those in which words are learned in extended texts, researchers can control numerous variables. But, because children's learning is rarely so compartmentalized in the real world of homes and classrooms, the generalizability of findings from laboratory studies of word learning has limitations. Similar findings from numerous studies, however, are suggestive for the design of reading materials and lessons. Children's learning of the three kinds of words that Hiebert (1999) identified as characterizing different text types are reviewed: highly meaningful, highly regular, or phonetically regular words and high-frequency words.

Highly Meaningful Words

Young children's first interest is in words that represent engaging and meaningful concepts. In a year-long study using children's self-chosen words (see Ashton-Warner, 1963), Hiebert (1983) found that nouns accounted for 98% of the words that young children chose and that half these nouns were proper nouns; words such as "Uncle Dan," "Magic Marker," and "Crayolas" were chosen by the young children in that study. Similar to Ashton-Warner's (1963) self-chosen vocabulary, the themes of the beginning reading textbooks from the 1930s through the mid-1980s were chosen to be familiar and relevant to young children (Gray, Monroe, Artley, Arbuthnot, & Gray, 1956). For instance, the theme of a passage in an early text from this period pertains to a child learning to roller-skate. In this passage, the words "roller skate" and "fall down" are never used. The words of interest have been substituted with high-frequency words that ostensibly convey the gist of the passage: "Look, Dick. Dick, Dick. Help Jane."

Texts with this generic vocabulary were replaced in the late 1980s with authentic literature. Rather than repetitive text about a cast of characters, the first passage in a 1993 anthology enumerated things that a young child can do, such as "brush my teeth" and "carry the groceries." The second passage also dealt with things that young children do, but all the activities were new, such as "skate on our roller skates" and "ride our bikes." The emphasis in textbook programs since the late 1980s has been on the engagingness of the text as a whole with less attention given to the repetition of meaningful words.

When many different words are introduced in passage after passage, remembering a core set of words will be difficult for beginning readers. A core set of high-meaning words, however, appears to be critical in reading acquisition. In Ehri's (1994, 1998) model of word learning, the first stage is described as "logographic reading." Children associate visual or quantitative characteristics of words with their spelling or semantic properties. The word "dinosaur," for example, may be remembered because of the height of the first letter ("The dinosaur has a long neck") and the length of the word ("A dinosaur has a long body"). At this stage, spellings of words represent the meanings of words and are not used as a cipher that represents the sounds of words. This strategy becomes difficult to maintain

as children are introduced to more and more words. At this point, they need to use the alphabetic relationships of words. These more refined representations allow children to discriminate and recognize many more words. But these first words to which children attend because of their meaningfulness in their lives ("dinosaur," "Uncle Dan") lay the foundation for the next stage where they attend to alphabetic relationships.

Laing and Hulme (1999) compared beginning readers' learning of words with high and low imagery values. Words with higher imagery values are more concrete than words with low imagery values. For example, "cake" has a higher imagery value than "food," and "food" has a higher imagery value than "things" or "it." Laing and Hulme taught target words that varied in imagery values but were similar in familiarity and number of letters and phonemes, as in "cake" and "food," to children from 4 to 6 years of age. These researchers found that young children learned significantly more highly imageable words than words with low imagery values.

In Metsala's (1999) study, phonological tasks with high-meaning words and words with consistent and common alphabetic relationships (e.g., "cat," "fat," and "hat") were compared with the same tasks using less meaningful and less decodable words. Young children performed better on the phonological tasks with words that were meaningful and alphabetic. Although the research base is small for this particular aspect of word learning, the findings support inclusion of at least a core set of meaningful, high-imagery words in beginning texts.

Highly Regular Words

Efficient word recognition in an alphabetic language depends on the beginning reader gaining insight into the alphabetic nature of the written language: that word spellings map onto word pronunciations (Adams, 1990). These mappings can occur at several levels: whole word, syllable, subsyllable, morpheme, and phoneme. For example, the word "cat" may be recognized as a whole (e.g. the sequence of "cat"), as the sequence of three phonemes (e.g., "c," "a," and "t") and as a syllable comprised of an onset "c" and rime "at." Advanced readers flexibly use any or all of these correspondences, whereas beginning readers usually rely on one mapping or even a partial mapping. Whether beginning readers should be directed in making correspondences at the level of large units (e.g., word or rime) to smaller units (phonemes) or from small units to large units remains a source of debate, but scholars agree that more advanced readers are able to recognize and use both small and large units in reading unfamiliar words (Brown, 1998; Ehri, 1994, 1998; Goswami, 1990, 1998; Thompson, 1999).

Beginning readers benefit from guidance in the alphabetic patterns of written English, but studies of text leave a critical set of questions unanswered. For example, what should the unit of the alphabetic relationship be? Examples of units of the alphabetic relationships are individual grapheme–phonemes such as the letter t and sound /t/ or a set of grapheme–phonemes that commonly appears in words such as the "at" (/at/ in "cat," "fat," or "hat"). The vowel and the consonant(s) that follow it, as in the example of "at," are called rimes.

The content of the unit is a critical issue in the current political context. The Texas and California mandates both emphasize the phoneme as the unit of learning (California English/Language Arts Committee, 2000; Texas Education Agency, 1997). One of the California criterion for acceptable beginning reading programs is quite explicit: two little books for each of 44 phonemes in both the grade 1 and grade 2 programs. According to this perspective, an individual grapheme–phoneme element becomes known once it has been taught. A word is described as having the potential for accuracy once all its elements have been taught. Take, for example, a beginning text from one of the beginning reading programs on the Texas list (Afflerbach et al., 2000). By the time children begin the first passage in the first-grade texts, these grapheme–phoneme relationships have been taught: *a, m, t, n, p, b, d, g, w.* These words appear in the first passage: "am," "nap," "at," "bat," "mat," "cat," "cap," "dad," "wag." Children should also be able to read: "Nat," "pat," "bad," "pad," "tan," and "Dan" without further instruction. The criterion of "if taught, then learned" is applied despite evidence that instructional suggestions are many and often superficial in first-grade teachers' guides (Hiebert, Menon, Martin, & Huxley, 2000).

Both the Texas and California mandates present this perspective on the phoneme as the unit of instruction as research-based. The research that indicates that children learn individual grapheme–phoneme relationships—especially those children who come to school with little conventional literacy—is less conclusive. To understand the task that confronts beginning readers in becoming fluent in alphabetic relationships, an understanding of the differences between consonants and vowels is useful.

Of the phonemes that Moats (1999) identifies as essential for a teacher of beginning readers to know, 25 are consonants and 18 are vowels. Twenty-one graphemes account for the 25 phonemes that are consonants, while 7 graphemes account for 18 vowel phonemes. Because several alphabet letters ("q," "x," "c") have no unique phonemes associated with them and seven consonants phonemes have several graphemes associated with each (e.g., f, ff, sp, gh, and lf for /f/), a stance for diversity is useful with consonants. Overall, however, consonants are fairly consistent in their grapheme–phoneme relationships. Treiman, Mullennix, Bijeljac-Babic, and Richmond-Welty (1995) reported that initial consonants are pronounced similarly in 94% of consonant–vowel–consonant (CVC) words, and final consonants are pronounced the same in 92% of CVC words.

The task of associating phonemes with graphemes is quite challenging with vowels where seven graphemes—*a, i, e, o, u, y,* and *w*—either individually or in combination (*w* always in combination with another grapheme)—account for 15 different phonemes. Further, when the consonant *r* follows the graphemes a, e, i, o, and u, three more phonemes are produced. Unlike the high percentage of consistency in consonants, vowels have the same pronunciation in only 62% of similarly spelled words (Treiman et al., 1995). When the vowel and the consonant(s) that follows it—the rime—are taken into account, however, consistency increases to 80% in CVC words (Treiman et al., 1995). Wylie and Durrell (1970) reported that 272 rimes with stable vowel sounds are contained in 1,437 words, and that 37 of these stable rimes occur in 10 or more exemplars, for a total of 500 words.

This stability of particular rimes has led investigators to compare the ease of learning rimes versus the individual grapheme–phoneme. Goswami (1990, 1998; see Chapter 9), in particular, has argued for analogies to known rime units as the point of departure for beginning readers, with later extension of this knowledge to individual graphemes and phonemes. Goswami (1986, 1988) found that prereaders could make analogies at the level of the rime to read words from a list when a clue word containing the rime was present. But, because the size of the rime analogy effect is small (prereaders identified only 1 word out of 12 in the 1986 experiment), others have investigated the question further (Bowey & Hansen, 1994; Brown, 1998; Savage & Stuart, 1998; Treiman et al., 1995). These studies indicate that facility with rime analogies increases with reading ability and is affected by phonological priming (producing a rhyming response based on the pronunciation of the clue word rather than its orthography) (Bowey & Hansen, 1998; Brown, 1998; Goswami, 1990), the presence of clue words, and the type of prompt given (Goswami, 1986, 1988, 1990; Muter, Hulme, Snowling, & Taylor, 1997; Savage & Stuart, 1998). Beginning readers have also been found to make analogies to the beginnings of words (CV-) as well as the rime units but less often to medial vowels (Bowey & Hansen, 1994; Bruck & Treiman, 1992; Savage & Stuart, 1998). When Bruck and Treiman (1992) compared the effectiveness of training beginning readers to make analogies based on rimes, consonant–vowel units, or vowels, children in the rime-based group learned the target words more quickly than did children in the consonant vowel (CV-) or vowel analogy groups but they performed the poorest on the retention test. Children in the vowel group performed the best on the generalization test. The poor performance of the rime group suggests that training in rime-based analogies may not be as effective as training to make analogies based on the vowel. Because rime-based analogies are easy to make, children who receive rime training may not have fully internalized the rime units. When training does not incorporate a clue word and uses a more rigorous criterion level, children trained to use rime-based analogies perform the same as children trained to make CV-based analogies or to phonologically recode through blending (Levy & Lysynchuck, 1997).

While the ability to phonologically detect onsets and rimes seems to interact with children's use of rime-based analogies (Bruck & Treiman, 1992; Muter et al., 1997), segmentation at the phonemic level and/or knowledge of letter–sound correspondences appears to affect beginning readers' ability to make rime-based analogies (Ehri & Robbins, 1992; Treiman, Goswami, & Bruck, 1990). Sensitivity to the consistency of rimes appears to develop with reading experience (Bowey & Hansen, 1994; Treiman et al., 1990, 1995). Because these studies were based on the frequencies of rimes or the regularity of their pronunciations, the results suggest that it is exposure to the rimes rather than the general development of decoding ability that enables beginning readers to internalize these units and make use of them. Wylie and Durrell (1970) also found that first-graders were more likely to recognize the spellings of high-frequency rimes compared to low-frequency rimes.

A two-part study by Thompson, Cottrell, and Fletcher-Flinn (1996) indicates that the frequency with which particular units appear in words influences children's acquisition of the units. Having established that *b* and *th* in the final position of words occurred significantly less often than *t* and *m*, Thompson et al. (1996) assessed 24 children on CV and VC pseudowords incorporating the target consonants. Words with *b* and *th* in the final position were read with significantly lower accuracy than *m* and *t* in the final position. In a second experiment, Thompson et al. (1996) manipulated the amount of exposure beginning readers had to words containing the consonant *b* in the final position by having children read sentences with a target word that ended in *b* or sentences in which the target words were omitted in the text but supplied orally by the investigator. The former group significantly improved in the accuracy with which pseudowords with *b* in the final position were read, whereas the latter group made no improvement.

In most studies reviewed to this point, words in training and assessment tasks appeared singly or in phrases. In two of Goswami's (1988, 1990) studies, exemplars of rimes were studied within texts. The texts varied in their inclusion of a target word in the title. By having the investigator read the title aloud, children were exposed to the target word. Significantly more words sharing the rime or the CV- unit of the target words than words that shared common letters were read by children who received the "title target word" training than children who did not. Apparently, young children can make analogies while reading text if they have learned the unit that the analogous words share. Conclusions from Goswami's studies need to be interpreted cautiously as participants were almost 7 years old—an age when many children are fluent readers. Within a recent tutoring intervention of first-graders, however, Leslie and Allen (1999) found that when rimes that had been highlighted in instruction occurred in the texts that students read, reading development was positively influenced.

To date, there is no research that supports equal attention to each of 43 or 44 phonemes. There is a research base, however, that provides directions for textbook publishers and researchers. In particular, exposure to words that encourages attention to particular grapheme–phoneme relationships supports reading development. The size of the unit is likely a function of children's existing awareness of graphemes and phonemes. Finally, as Thompson et al. (1996) and Wylie and Durrell (1970) showed, some phonemes have substantial function whereas others appear in significantly fewer words.

High-Frequency Words

One of the problems with an overabundance of instruction on highly decodable words is that much of written text consists of a small group of words—prepositions, connectives, pronouns, and articles. In an analysis of the texts used in grades 3 through 9, Carroll, Davies, and Richman (1971) found that 109 high-frequency words accounted for 50% of the total running words. The issue is muddied by the fact that many high-frequency words have irregular letter–sound relationships. While 29 of the 100 most frequent words have vowel consonant (VC) rimes, a handful of words in the group have a CVC pattern but an atypical pronunciation (e.g., "was"). Among the remaining 67 high-frequency words, 35 are either irregular in their adherence to other patterns (e.g., "have," and "some") or multisyllabic.

Believing that the irregular or ambiguous pronunciations of these words may confuse beginning readers, publishers of some phonics texts have attempted to restrict the occurrence of high-frequency words (see, e.g., Rasmussen & Goldberg, 1964). But restricting the use of irregular high-frequency words may prevent beginning readers from developing a flexible stance toward reading which can incorporate both regular spelling pronunciations and common variants (Gibson & Levin, 1975).

Readability formulas which were based on high-frequency word counts and sentence length drove textbooks through the late 1980s. Much of the justification for providing an abundance of high-frequency words in beginning texts came from studies in the 1930s. Gates (1930, Gates & Russell, 1938–1939), for example, conducted studies using first-grade materials which varied considerably in the average number of repetitions per word. Gates (1930) interpreted the results of these studies as verification that each word should be repeated an average of 35 times within a basal series.

Several decades later, Reitsma (1983) investigated how frequency of exposure to individual words affects the speed with which midyear first-graders and older, reading-disabled students recognized words. Children read sentences with the target word two, four, or six times, followed by posttests which assessed the speed of recognizing individual words. The assessments included homophonic versions of the target words, where spellings differed by only one letter such as "read" and "red" and "to" and "too." First-graders' speed of responding to target words decreased systematically with a leveling off between four and six exposures. Apparently, first-graders were recognizing words automatically at around four exposures. Further, because first-graders recognized the homophonic variants more slowly, Reitsma concluded that they were internalizing the spellings of the target words. The reading-disabled students showed only a marginally significant increase in the speed of recognizing words that had been practiced four times or the homophonic words and those practiced twice. These findings suggest that the reading-disabled students were not attending to and internalizing the spellings of the words in the same way as the first-graders.

Ehri and Wilce (1983) similarly measured the word identification speed of first- and second- grade readers. Skilled and less skilled readers were given lists of words to read, some of which were practiced either 6 or 18 times. Word identification speed increased significantly between pretest and posttest for CVC nonsense words. Skilled readers were able to recognize target words as quickly as they could name digits, an indication that the words had come to be recognized automatically as wholes (Biemiller, 1977–1978). Less skilled readers' speed increased also, but their word recognition speed still fell short of their digit naming speed, suggesting that these words had not become a fully automatic part of their sight vocabulary. Similar to Reitsma (1983), Ehri and Wilce (1983) found that additional practice did not appear to significantly increase word identification speed for familiar words by less skilled readers.

As a result of the emphasis on the "whole word" that was part of the high-frequency word method, basal readers often incorporated words which were visually dissimilar (Samuels & Jeffrey, 1966). Beginning readers learn dissimilar words more quickly than similar words (Samuels & Jeffrey, 1966). In all likelihood, beginning readers focus on one or two letters that identify a word from other words. Attending to only part of the spellings within visually dissimilar word lists may work initially, but this strategy is not particularly effective as more and more words appear in beginning reading texts.

When children are able to make use of even partial phonological cues, beginning readers acquire phonetically spelled words more quickly and accurately than visually distinct spellings (Ehri & Wilce, 1985). The more beginning readers were able to attend to phonological cues, the faster and more accurate they were at learning target words (Ehri & Wilce, 1987).

Further proof that the kind of exposure students require for words is a function of the type of word comes from Juel and Roper/Schneider's (1985) study of children's strategies as a function of their textbook program. First-graders who read a decodable preprimer were more influenced in their word recognition by the decodability of the words than by the number of repetitions. The word recognition of children who read the basal preprimer was most affected by the number of repetitions of the word, particularly if the word contained unusual letter combinations.

Research on Features of Existing Texts

While the features of beginning reading texts have been documented since at least 1930 (Hockett, 1938), features documented in the texts of one copyright are not necessarily generalizable to subsequent copyrights. There was a substantial amount of stability from the 1930s through 1960s (Chall, 1995; Hockett, 1938; Morris & Johns, 1987; Olson, 1965; Perry & Sagan, 1989; Rodenborn & Washburn, 1974), but following Chall's (1995) critique of the mainstream reading programs, vacillations in the texts over each of the subsequent decades have been considerable. Hoffman, McCarthey, et al. (1994) described substantial changes between the beginning reading texts adopted for use in Texas classrooms in 1987 and in 1993. Whereas texts in 1987 had had controlled vocabularies, the texts in 1993 were recognizable trade book selections. Since then, the 1997 guidelines of Texas, which advocated texts quite different than the 1993 copyrights, have been operationalized in the 2000–2001 copyrights that will be used in Texas classrooms in the fall of 2000. The focus of this review is on the changes in texts over the past decade, describing the changes from California's mandate for literature-based programs in 1987 (California English/Language Arts Framework Committee, 1987) to the Texas mandate (Texas Education Agency, 1997) for particular percentages of decodable text in first grade.

This review considers the characteristics of current texts on three dimensions that have received attention previously: (1) number of total and unique words in texts; (2) proportion of unique words that are phonetically regular, multisyllabic, and highly frequent; and (3) engagingness. Although researchers have yet to link these dimensions to the ease or difficulty that young children experience in reading acquisition, a compelling case can be made theoretically for each of these dimensions as a factor in reading acquisition.

Number of Total and Unique Words

Historically, the number of total words in a text or set of texts and the number of unique words among those total words have been used as indicators of the demands of reading programs on beginning readers (Chall, 1995; Hockett, 1938; Morris & Johns, 1987; Olson, 1965; Perry & Sagan, 1989; Rodenborn & Washburn, 1974). For children in their first months of formal reading instruction, the number of words that appear on a page in instructional texts can influence their willingness to read. For example, when asked to choose books to read, first-grade readers who were challenged in learning to read identified texts as easy when the number of words on a page were few and difficult when texts had more words per page (Hiebert, Lui, Levin, Huxley, & Chung, 1995).

A product of the mandate for literature-based selections has been to create greater variety across beginning reading programs in the total number of words. The first-grade anthologies of the five major programs that met the Texas guidelines for literature-based, beginning reading programs in 1992–1993 ranged in total words from 6,629 to 17,102, with an average of 12,265 (Hoffman et al., 1994). The range for total words for the 1986–1987 copyrights of these five programs that had controlled vocabulary was small in comparison: 16,865 to 17,319 words, with an average of 17,282 words. The more recent requirement of Texas that the initial texts of grade 1 comply with decodability standards may have leveled differences across programs to some degree. The range of total words for approximately 40% of four, first-grade textbook programs (10 passages from the beginning and 10 from the end) is 4,020 to 5,500 with an average of 4,270 (Hiebert, 2000).

The cohort of children who enter school while the 2000–2001 textbooks are used may be exposed to roughly the same number of words, whatever the program chosen by their state, district, or school. Even so, these children will be exposed to considerably more words than their counterparts were exposed to in the decades prior to literature-based programs. An analysis of the copyrights from one textbook program over the past 40 years (from 1960 to 2000) indicates that texts for beginning readers have gotten substantially longer from 1962 to 2000 (Hiebert, 2000). The total number of words of a selection that would provide the instruction during the first quarter of grade 1 increased from 18 words per passage in 1962 to 83 words per passage in the 2000 copyright. The three other programs with 2000–2001 copyrights, similarly, had passages that averaged 76 to 115 words.

The number of total words is a general indicator, at best, of the task posed by texts for beginning readers. For children who are at the beginning stages of reading, every different word in a passage poses an occasion for remembering a known word or, if unknown, figuring out the word. In an historical analysis of the longest published beginning reading program in the United States, Hiebert (2000) found that the total number of words for the first passages reached its highest point in 1983 with an average of 144 words per beginning passage. In its 2000 copyright, the beginning passages averaged 83 words. On the basis of total words, the 2000 passages would be described as easier, but the ratios of unique or different words per 100 running words varied substantially: 5 per 100 in 1983 and 22 per 100 in 2000. With the 1983 copyright, every 20th word that first-graders encounter was a unique word. Every fifth word that first-graders in classrooms with the 2000 copyright encounter is a unique word. Because 10 high-frequency words account for one-third of the total number of words in the sample, the other 177 unique words occur an average of three times each. Even this figure for repetition is misleading, because of these 177 unique words, 80 are what Hiebert (2000) has identified as "singletons"—words that occur only once in a set of 10 instructional passages. For beginning readers with the 2000 copyright, 5%

of the words are repeated an average of 25 times each, another 43% of the words will appear only over 10 passages, and the other 42% of the words will occur approximately five times each.

Demands for figuring out unique words remain consistent for young readers with the texts from the 2000 copyright, whether they are reading texts from the beginning or end of first grade or second grade: 21 to 22 across 10 selections at each point per 100 words in time (Hiebert, 2000). These figures differ substantially from the ratios of unique to 100 words for equivalent samples of passages from the beginning and end of grade 1 and the end of grade 2 for the 1962 and 1983 copyrights: 10, 9, and 13 for 1962 and 5, 11, and 14 for 1983 (Hiebert, 2000).

The sheer number of words and the infrequency with which all but a small group of high-frequency words appear creates a formidable task for beginning readers. The number of unique words in the 2000 copyright—187—is 10 times the number of unique words that first-graders were expected to learn over 10 passages in 1962 and 2.5 times more than in 1983 (Hiebert, 2000). The heavy repetition of high-frequency words in these pre-1993 copyrights and the lack of high-meaning words could create obstacles for beginning readers (Brennan, Bridge, & Winograd, 1986). By the same token, we have been unable to locate evidence that beginning readers can identify dozens of different words after a single exposure or even after four to five exposures.

Decodability of Words

Chall's (1995) observation that basal reading texts did not provide sufficient phonics experiences—either in the lessons or in the children's texts—spurred research into the relationship between the phonics instruction of teachers' editions and the phonics patterns in the words that appear in children's texts. Beck and McCaslin (1978) analyzed the percentages of words in eight series published in the mid-1970s that could be decoded based on previous instruction in all of a word's constituent phonic elements. According to Beck and McCaslin's (1978), lessons on the consonants "c," "t," and "n" and the short vowel "a" would mean that the words "can," "cat," and "Nat" in the

text had "potential for accuracy." If "nag" were introduced, however (and a lesson on the consonant g had not been provided previously), this word would have only a partial potential for accuracy. After applying this criterion to basal programs, Beck and McCaslin reported that texts from the first third of first grade in four phonics programs contained significantly higher percentages of decodable words (6–100%) compared to the texts from traditional basal programs (0–13%).

"Potential for accuracy" criterion was included in the guidelines for beginning reading textbooks in the most recent Texas textbook adoption (Texas Education Agency, 1997). Stein, Johnson, and Gutlohn (1999) examined the compliance of texts that were presented for the Texas textbook adoption to this criterion. Stein et al. (1998) recognized, however, that many of the high-frequency words that make up much of text are not decodable. Hence, they determined the potential accuracy of a series by adding the percentage of decodable words to the percentage of high-frequency words. Overall, they found that the potential for accuracy within some programs is low, although programs varied considerably from one another. Four programs had potential for accuracy rates that ranged from 79–100%.

In analyses of the mid-1990s copyrights of three textbook programs conducted by Menon and Hiebert (2000) and Martin and Hiebert (1999), the opportunities afforded by texts for learning about and applying knowledge of phonics was examined (1) by considering the decodability ratings of words and (2) by establishing the number and repetition of rimes. Decodability of words was established on an 8-point scale where lower points on the scale represented simple vowel patterns such as CV (e.g., "go") and VC (e.g., "at") or CVC ("cat"), middle points represented more complex vowel patterns such as CVVC (e.g., "meat," and "meet") or CVC-e (e.g., "ride"), and higher points on the scale variant vowels (e.g., "bread") and multisyllabic words (e.g., "tomorrow"). These three programs were chosen because of their differences in perspectives on beginning reading acquisition. One program has literature as its core (Literature Core); the second begins with phonics books but moves to literature by midyear of grade 1 (Phonics/Literature); and the third emphasizes phonics but has added a literary supplement (Phonics Core). Menon and Hiebert (2000) analyzed the features of the anthologies and literary components of these three programs, whereas Martin and Hiebert (1999) analyzed the features of the phonics texts as well as "little book" components that all of the programs had.

Overall, the little books and phonics texts contained higher percentages of words with simpler vowel patterns than the literature anthologies. Further, the little books and, as might be expected, the phonics texts showed a more gradual introduction of words with complex vowel patterns and multisyllabic words, whereas the literature anthologies showed a relatively stable distribution of each type of word in the beginning, middle, and final components of the program. In the literature components, the percentage of unique words that were multisyllabic stayed at a fairly consistent level of 25%, regardless of the philosophy of the program and projected time period (i.e., beginning or end of grade 1).

As has already been summarized in the review of highly regular words, learning to recognize bigger and bigger chunks of words characterizes proficient readers. The "rime" measure used by Martin and Hiebert (1999) and Menon and Hiebert 2000) establishes the opportunity children have to apply knowledge of rimes—the clusters of vowel and their subsequent consonant(s)—across words. The computer program used by these researchers indicates the number of different rimes as well as the number of "instantiations" of individual rimes. Instantiations refer to the number of different onsets that appear with the same rime. If the rime "ed" appears exclusively with the onset "r" in a program, the number of instantiations would be one. If the words "bed," "sled," "Ted," "fed," and "led" appear in addition to "red," the instantiations would be six.

Within the literature components of all three programs, Menon and Hiebert (2000) found the number of different rimes to be many. The number of different rimes per passage ranged from a high of 62 and 60 (Phonics/Literature and Phonics Core, respectively) and a low of 41 (Literature Core). The number of different rimes per passage was lower for the phonics and little books than for the literature components, an understandable phenomenon because the passages for these texts were considerably shorter. However, the average number of rimes within phonics and little book texts for the Literature Core program and the Phonics Core program were identical: 28. The Phonics/Literature program had a slightly higher average: 34 rimes per text. Rimes were represented, on average, by two instantiations, regardless of program (Literature Core, Phonics/Literature, or Phonics Core) or component within program (i.e., literature, little book, or phonics text). That is, first-grade readers would rarely encounter a rime with more than two onsets, such as "jump," "bump," "lump," and "dump," in a passage.

While texts can be judged as decodable because constituent elements have been presented in lessons in the teachers' editions (Stein et al., 1997), there is a substantial amount of phonics data that beginning readers must be able to navigate to be successful with the texts of beginning reading programs (Martin & Hiebert, 1999; Menon & Hiebert, 2000).

Text Engagingness

Alvermann and Guthrie (1993) proposed engagement as a defining construct in literacy. Wigfield (1997) notes that within the reading literature, most discussions of engagement have been restricted to a consideration of attitudes toward reading and interest in reading. Rarely have features of texts that engage readers, especially young readers, been considered. In this context, the term "text engagingness" describes the potential of a text for creating engagement. This term is distinguished from text engagement, which will occur as a result of the interaction between particular readers and particular texts, in specific instructional contexts.

Hoffman, Christian, et al. (1994) have identified three ways in which the potential of a text for engagingness can be measured: design, content, and language. Initially, children are likely to be engaged by the illustrations and the format of the book—design. Once children have begun attending to the text, other factors likely influence their sustaining interest in the text. When the content is unfamiliar, complex, or trivial, a text may not continue to be engaging. Further, if the language of the text is bland, children's interest may not be sustained. We do not intend to suggest that particular texts will be equally engaging to all children, irrespective of their race, class, ethnicity, or personal interests. Nevertheless, it is important to consider whether texts hold promise for engaging at least some of the children within a group for whom texts are being developed or selected.

Hoffman, Christian, et al. (1994) considered the engagingness of first-grade texts from four traditional basal series published in the mid-1980s with texts from five (1993) literature-based series, using these three indices. As well as using scales for the design, content, and language of the texts, these researchers used an overall 5-point holistic rating scale. Their results suggested that the newer literature basals were potentially more engaging than the older, traditional basal texts, both at a holistic level and along the dimensions of content, language, and design. However, as McCarthey et al. (1994) pointed out, while the newer texts on average are potentially more engaging, they only rated an average of 3.2 on the 5-point holistic scale (compared to 2.0 for the older basal texts), suggesting that many of the newer texts are still lacking in their potential engagingness.

Menon and Hiebert (2000) similarly had teachers rate passages from the literature anthologies of three programs, using McCarthey et al.'s (1994) scales of content, language, and design scales. The texts from the literature-based core program were rated the most highly on all three scales. The texts from the literature/phonics program were rated slightly less appealing, and the literature from the phonics core program the least appealing. Of these differences, however, only the ratings on design between literature-core texts and the phonics-core texts were significantly different. Overall, although many of the texts were highly rated, these findings similarly suggest that there is still room for improvement in the engagingness of new texts offered by basal publishers.

The texts in the Hoffman, McCarthey, et al. (1994) study were also rated by kindergartners and first- and second-graders. Pairs of texts were read aloud to children who rated each story using a smiley, neutral, or sad face. The children also commented on each story and ranked the stories within each pair. The children's ratings were similar to the researchers' ratings in 7 out of 10 pairs of texts, centering on the content, language, and design of the texts. Children attended to three additional categories: familiarity (author, text, and vocabulary), personal experience, and realism. The children's comments about the familiarity of texts and their ability to read these texts suggests that, for beginning readers, the accessibility of the text may affect its engagingness.

Next Steps

The role that the textbooks serve in beginning reading instruction and the critical role of reading acquisition in the subsequent success in school and beyond for children leads to the expectation that there would be a substantial amount of research on features of effective beginning texts. Our review of the literature indicates that this is simply not so. One of the reasons that research on textbooks has fallen between the cracks is the gulf between the publishing industry and academe. The policies on programs issued by states include the requisite "research base" (e.g., Florida Department of Education, 1999), but these investigations appear to be conducted in house by publishers (and are not available for review by scholars) or consist of reviews of related literature, some of which contains research and some of which does not. The few program evaluations that have been conducted as part of research programs (e.g., Foorman et al., 1998) are difficult to interpret when the effect of materials is confounded with critical components such as staff development. Further, the texts on which research was conducted several decades ago may have little trace in the current copyright of the program (e.g., Englemann, Becker, Carnine, & Gersten, 1988). Unlike the medical and pharmacy industries, there is neither in-house research within publishing companies nor a federal agency that provides consumers with research. Since Gray's (Elston

& Gray, 1930) affiliation with Scott Foresman, university-level educators have been involved as consultants (often given the title of "author"), but their work has been in program development and representation, not in research and evaluation.

Publishers and researchers need to collaborate in addressing critical questions on appropriate texts for beginning readers. We describe the most urgent of these questions: (1) the texts for the initial period of independent word recognition and (2) issues related to decodability.

First Books

The intent of the mainstream programs was originally to provide text on familiar, interesting scenarios to young children (Elston & Gray, 1930; Gray et al., 1956). To increase children's exposure to high-frequency words, however, the words that could be expected to interest young children—words such as "roller skates" and "crash" in a passage on learning to skate—were eliminated. The thousands of little books that now exist contain an overabundance of vocabulary on interesting topics to young children. But the vocabulary changes from book to book, with a core set of high-meaning words rarely found in more than one book in a set of books (Hiebert, 1999). A single set of concepts that is interesting to all children is not possible, but studies of little books with a shared vocabulary of highly meaningful words are needed. For example, rather than include the menagerie of one widely used beginning text—"wren," "hen," "cony," "pony," "fox," "ox," "duck," "camel," "dog," "elephant" (Pikulski et al., 1993)—the set might be "dog," "cat," "fish," and "parrot." Other words would be part of the passages, but the children who have not attained the logographic stage would have the opportunity to begin reading with a group of meaningful words.

Unresolved Decodability Issues

Mandates within Texas specify that the texts for beginning readers that will be accepted in Texas need to contain particular percentages of words that give children the "potential for accuracy," a term used by Beck and McCaslin (1978) and then by Stein et al. (1999). Potential for accuracy is defined as a word where all of the elements have been taught prior to a beginning reader's encountering of that word in a text. This definition, however, begs several critical questions:

1. What should the unit of information be?
2. How many exemplars are needed of a unit?
3. At what speed can beginning readers—especially the ones who depend most on good instruction and materials to become literate—assimilate new information?

Studies that describe the number of repetitions and rate of introduction of high-frequency word have been conducted, but these studies have not considered the viability of particular units of decodability within texts. The studies have been conducted with either lists of words or a single passage. The acquisition of decodable units alongside meaningful words and high-frequency words—some of which at least are necessary to make a somewhat coherent text—has not occurred.

A strictly laboratory approach where individual children are taught from "precise" texts disregards the role of engagingness of concepts, language, and illustrations that are part of texts and the different speeds with which children crack the code. The experiments that would be needed to isolate optimal units, instantiations of units, and the competing units at different points in a beginning reader's development—in the context of texts in which multiple forms of words are present—are sufficiently numerous to be prohibitive. But a large-scale research effort on textbooks that includes a focused number of experiments, classroom-based interventions, and descriptions of best practices is possible.

One of the questions that requires attention in a focused set of experiments has to do with the effects of treatments that give children different exposure to units. One group of children, for example, might be taught through a focused set of rimes (e.g., 8–10, with two for each of the five short vowels) that are used consistently over time. Their learning would be compared with children in groups that are taught with a more diffuse set of rimes (four or five for each short vowel). Such an experiment would take the form of Cunningham's (1990) study in which a group of kindergartners were randomly assigned to different treatment groups but came from the same classroom. The critical question that would be addressed is how quickly children generalize to other rimes. Does a focus on a particular set of rimes leave children with a limited repertoire and perspective on rimes? Or does an experience with many rimes (as is currently the case in texts that children are given) create a difficulty. Another experiment would consider the percentage of words within texts that comply with the rimes that provide the focus of instruction. Given that there are thousands of classrooms in which different textbook programs are used, it should be possible to establish general program effects as well. Even though many variables are confounded with the use of textbooks, the large-scale use of textbooks allows for establishing at least the general effect of particular programs.

Without systematic research on text features, the vacillation evident in textbooks over the past 20 years (Hiebert, 2000) will continue. The vacillations in philosophy must be negotiated by teachers at a time that they are under pressure to bring students to the high levels of literacy required for full participation in the digital age. It is imperative that the research community join teachers and publishers in ensuring that the children of the digital age are initiated into literacy with the best possible texts and the best possible experiences with those texts.

References

Adams, M. J. (1990). *Beginning to read: Thinking and learning about print.* Cambridge, MA: MIT Press.

Afflerbach, P., Beers, J., Blachowicz, C., Boyd, C. D., Diffily, D., Gaunty-Porter, D., Harris, V., Leu, D., McClanahan, S., Monson, D., Perez, B., Sebesta, S., & Wixson, K. K. (2000). *Scott Foresman reading.* Glenview, IL: Addison-Wesley.

Alvermann, D., & Guthrie, J. (1993). *Themes and directions of the National Reading Research Center* (National Reading Research Center, Perspectives in Reading Research, No. 1). Athens: University of Georgia, National Reading Research Center.

Ashton-Warner, S. (1963). *Teacher.* New York: Simon & Schuster.

Baumann, J. F., Hoffman, J. V., Duffy-Hester, A. M., & Ro, J. M. (2000). The First R yesterday and today: U. S. elementary reading instruction practices reported by teachers and administrators. *Reading Research Quarterly, 35*(3), 338–377.

Beck, I. L., & McCaslin, E. S. (1978). *An analysis of dimensions that affect the development of code-breaking ability in eight beginning reading programs* (Report No. 6). Pittsburgh: Learning Research and Development Center.

Biemiller, A. (1977–1978). Relationships between oral reading rates for letters, words, and simple text in the development of reading achievement. *Reading Research Quarterly, 13,* 223–253.

Bowey, J. A., & Hansen, J. (1994). The development of orthographic rimes as units of word recognition. *Journal of Experimental Child Psychology, 58,* 465–488.

Boylin, M. C. (1998). *Effects of predictable and decodable texts and strategy instruction on literacy acquisition.* Unpublished doctoral dissertation, University of Virginia.

Brennan, A., Bridge, C., & Winograd, P. (1986). The effects of structural variation on children's recall of basal reader stories. *Reading Research Quarterly, 21,* 91–104.

Bridge, C. A., Winograd, P. N., & Haley, D. (1983). Using predictable materials vs. preprimers to teach beginning sight words. *The Reading Teacher, 36,* 884–891.

Brown, G. D. A. (1998). The endpoint of skilled word recognition: The ROAR model. In J. L. Metsala & L. C. Ehri (Eds.), *Word recognition in beginning literacy* (pp. 121–138). Mahwah, NJ: Erlbaum.

Bruck, M., & Treiman, R. (1992). Learning to pronounce words: The limitations of analogies. *Reading Research Quarterly, 27*(4), 374–388.

California English/Language Arts Committee (1987). *English-language arts framework for California public schools (kindergarten through grade twelve).* Sacramento: California Department of Education.

California English/Language Arts Committee (2000). *English-language arts framework for California public schools (kindergarten through grade twelve).* Sacramento: California Department of Education.

Carroll, J. B., Davies, P., & Richman, B. (1971). *Word frequency book.* Boston: Houghton-Mifflin.

Chall, J. S. (1995). *Learning to read: The great debate* (3rd ed.). Fort Worth, TX: Harcourt Brace.

Chall, J. S., & Squire, J. R. (1991). The publishing industry and textbooks. In R. Barr, M. L. Kamil, P. B. Mosenthal, & P. D. Pearson (Eds.), *Handbook of reading research* (vol. 2, pp. 120–146). Mahwah, NJ: Lawrence Erlbaum.

Cunningham, A. E. (1990). Explicit instruction in phonemic awareness. *Journal of Experimental Child Psychology, 50,* 429–444.

Donahue, P. L. Voelk, K. E., Campbell, J. R., &

Mazzeo, J. (1999). *NAEP 1998 reading report card for the nation and states.* Washington, DC: U.S. Government Printing Office.

Ehri, L. C. (1994). Development of the ability to read words: Update. In R. B. Ruddell, M. R. Ruddell, & H. Singer (Eds.), *Theoretical models and processes of reading* (4th ed., pp. 323–358). Newark, DE: International Reading Association.

Ehri, L. C. (1998). Grapheme–phoneme knowledge is essential for learning to read words in English. In J. L. Metsala & L. C. Ehri (Eds.), *Word recognition in beginning literacy* (pp. 3–4). Mahwah, NJ: Erlbaum.

Ehri, L. C., & Robbins, C. (1992). Beginners need some decoding skill to read words by analogy. *Reading Research Quarterly, 27,* 12–26.

Ehri, L. C., & Wilce, L. S (1985). Movement into reading: Is the first stage of printed word learning visual or phonetic? *Reading Research Quarterly, 20,* 163–179.

Ehri, L. C., & Wilce L. S. (1983). Development of word identification speed in skilled and less skilled beginning readers. *Journal of Educational Psychology, 75,* 3–18.

Ehri, L. C., & Wilce, L. S. (1987). Cipher versus cue reading: An experiment in decoding acquisition. *Journal of Educational Psychology, 79,* 3–13.

Elston, W. H., & Gray, W. S. (1930). *Elson basic readers.* Chicago: Scott, Foresman.

Englemann, S., Becker, W. C., Carnine, D., & Gersten, R. (1988). The direct instruction follow-through model: Design and outcomes. *Education and Treatment of Children, 11,* 303–317.

Florida Department of Education. (1999). *Instructional materials specifications: Reading grades K–12 (2001–2002 adoption).* Tallahassee: Florida Department of Education.

Foorman, B. R., Francis, D. J., Fletcher, J. M., Schatschneider, C., & Mehta, P. (1998). The role of instruction in learning to read: Preventing reading failure in at-risk children. *Journal of Educational Psychology, 90,* 37–55.

Gates, A. I. (1930). *Interest and ability in reading.* New York: Macmillan.

Gates, A. I., & Russell, D. H. (1938–1939). Types of materials, vocabulary burden, word analysis, and other factors in beginning reading. *The Elementary School Journal, 39,* 27–35, 119–128.

Gibson, E. J., & Levin, H. (1975). *The psychology of reading.* Cambridge, MA: MIT Press.

Goswami, U. (1986). Children's use of analogy in learning to read: A developmental study. *Journal of Experimental Child Psychology, 42,* 73–83.

Goswami, U. (1988). Orthographic analogies and reading development. *Quarterly Journal of Experimental Psychology, 40A(2),* 239–268.

Goswami, U. (1990). Phonological priming and orthographic analogies in reading. *Journal of Experimental Child Psychology, 49,* 323–340.

Goswami, U. (1998). The role of analogies in the development of word recognition. In J. L. Metsala & L. C. Ehri (Eds.), *Word recognition in beginning literacy* (pp. 41–63). Mahwah, NJ: Erlbaum.

Gourley, J. W. (1984). Discourse structure: expecta-tions of beginning readers and readability of text. *Journal of Reading Behavior, 16,* 169–188.

Gray, W. S., Monroe, M., Artley, A. S., Arbuthnot, A. H., & Gray, L. (1956). *The new basic readers: Curriculum foundation series.* Chicago: Scott, Foresman.

Hiebert, E. H. (1983). A comparison of young children's self-selected reading words and basal reading words. *Reading Improvement, 20,* 41–44.

Hiebert, E. H. (1999). Text matters in learning to read (Distinguished Educators Series). *The Reading Teacher, 52,* 552–568.

Hiebert, E. H. (2000, April). *The task of the first-grade texts: Have state policies influenced the content?* Paper presented at the symposium The Content of Text for Young Readers in Learning to Read and Reading to Learn, at the annual meeting of the American Educational Research Association, New Orleans.

Hiebert, E. H., Liu, G., Levin, L. Huxley, A., & Chung, K. (1995, November). *First graders reading the new first-grade readers.* Paper presented at the annual meeting of the National Reading Conference, New Orleans.

Hiebert, E. H., Menon, S., Martin, L. A., & Huxley, A. (2000, April). *Teachers' guides and reading instruction: The interactions between teachers, texts, and beginning readers.* Paper presented at the symposium The Content of Text for Young Readers in Learning to Read and Reading to Learn, at the annual meeting of the American Educational Research Association, New Orleans.

Hockett, J. A. (1938). The vocabularies of recent primers and first readers. *Elementary School Journal, 38,* 112–115.

Hoffman, J. V., Christian, C., Corman, L., Elliott, B., Matherne, D., & Stahle, D. (1994). Engaging the new basal readers. *Reading Research and Instruction, 33,* 233–256.

Hoffman, J. V., McCarthey, S. J., Abbott, J., Christian, C., Corman, L., Curry, C., Dressman, M., Elliott, B., Matherne, D., & Stahle, D. (1994). So what's new in the new basals? A focus on first grade. *Journal of Reading Behavior, 26,* 47–73.

Hoffman, J., Roser, N., Patterson, E., Salas, R., & Pennington, J. (1999). *The effects of leveled texts and varying types of support on first graders' reading performance.* Paper presented at the annual meeting of the National Reading Conference, Orlando, FL.

Holdaway, D. (1979). *The foundations of literacy.* Sydney, Australia: Aston Scholastic.

Juel, C., & Roper/Schneider, D. (1985). The influence of basal readers on first grade reading. *Reading Research Quarterly, 20(2),* 134–152.

Laing, E., & Hulme, C. (1999). Phonological and semantic processes influence beginning readers' ability to learn to read words. *Journal of Experimental Child Psychology, 73,* 183–207.

Leslie, L., & Allen, L. (1999). Factors that predict success in an early literacy intervention project. *Reading Research Quarterly, 34(4),* 404–424.

Leu, D. J., Jr., DeGroff, L. J. C., & Simons, H. D. (1986). Predictable texts and interactive–compensatory hypotheses: Evaluating individual differences in reading ability, context use, and comprehension. *Journal of Educational Psychology, 78*(5), 347–352.

Levy, B. A., & Lysynchuk, L. (1997). Beginning word recognition: Benefits of training by segmentation and whole word methods. *Scientific Studies of Reading, 1*(4), 359–387.

Martin, B., & Brogan, P. (1971). *Teacher's guide to the instant readers.* New York: Holt, Rinehart & Winston.

Martin, L. A., & Hiebert, E. H. (1999, April). *Little books and phonics texts: An analysis of the new alternatives to basals.* Paper presented at the annual meeting of the American Educational Research Association, Montreal, Quebec.

McCarthey, S. J., Hoffman, J. U., Christian, C., Corman, L., Elliott, B., Matherne, D., Sthale, O. (1994). Engaging the new basal readers. *Reading Research and Instruction, 33*(3), 233–256.

Menon, S., & Hiebert, E. H. (2000). Literature anthologies: The task for first-grade readers (CIERA Report 1. 008). Ann Arbor, MI: CIERA.

Metsala, J. L. (1999). Young children's phonological awareness and nonword repetition as a function of vocabulary development *Journal of Educational Psychology, 91,* 3–19.

Moats, L. (1999). *Teaching reading is rocket science: What expert teachers of reading should know and be able to do.* Washington, DC: American Federation of Teachers.

Morris, J. A., & Johns, J. L. (1987). Are 1st grade reading books easier than 20 years ago? *The Reading Teacher, 40,* 486–487.

Muter, V., Hulme, C., Snowling, M., & Taylor, S. (1997). Segmentation, not rhyming, predicts early progress in learning to read. *Journal of Experimental Child Psychology, 65,* 370–396.

Olson, A. V. (1965). An analysis of the vocabulary of seven primary reading programs. *Elementary English, 42,* 261–264.

Perry, L. A., & Sagan, P. S. (1989). Are basal readers becoming too difficult for some children? *Reading Improvement, 26,* 181–185.

Pikulski, J. J., Cooper, J. D., Durr, W. K., Au, K. H., Greenlaw, M. J., Lipson, M. Y., Page, S., Valencia, S. W., Wixson, K. K., Barrera, R. B., Bradley, E., Bunyan, R. P., Chaparro, J. L., Comas, J. C., Crawford, A. N., Hillerich, R. L., Johnson, T. G., Mason, J. M., Mason, A. A., Nagy, W. E., Renzuilli, J. S. (1993). *The literature experience.* Boston: Houghton-Mifflin.

Rasmussen, D., & Goldberg, L. (1964). *The bad fan (Level A, Basic Reading Series).* Chicago: Science Research Associates.

Reitsma, P. (1983). Printed word learning in beginning readers. *Journal of Experimental Child Psychology, 36,* 321–339.

Rhodes, L. K. (1979). Comprehension and predictability: An analysis of beginning reading materials. In J. C. Harste & R. F. Carey (Eds.), *New perspectives on comprehension* (pp. 100–131). Bloomington: Indiana University School of Education.

Rodenborn, L. V., & Washburn, E. (1974). Some implications of the new basal readers. *Elementary English, 51,* 885–893.

Samuels, S. J., & Jeffrey, W. E. (1966). Discriminability of words and letter cues used in learning to read. *Journal of Educational Psychology, 57,* 337–340.

Savage, R., & Stuart, M. (1998). Sublexical inferences in beginning reading: Medial vowel digraphs as functional units of transfer. *Journal of Experimental Child Psychology, 69,* 85–108.

Shannon, P. (1997). Manufacturing dissent: Basal reading and the creation of reading failures. *Reading and Writing Quarterly: Overcoming Learning Difficulties, 13,* 227–245.

Stein, M. L., Johnson, B. J., & Gutlohn, L. (1999). Analyzing beginning reading programs: The relationship between decoding instruction and text. *Remedial and Special Education, 20,* 275–287.

Texas Education Agency. (1990). *Proclamation of the state board of education advertising for bids on textbooks* (Proclamation 68). Austin, TX: Author.

Texas Education Agency. (1997). *Proclamation of the state board of education advertising for bids on textbooks.* Austin, TX: Author.

Thompson, G. B. (1999). The processes of learning to identify words. In G. B. Thompson & T. Nicholson (Eds.), *Learning to read: Beyond phonics and whole language* (pp. 25–54). Newark, DE: International Reading Association.

Thompson, G. B., Cottrell, D. S., & Fletcher-Flinn, C. M. (1996). Sublexical orthographic–phonological relations early in the acquisition of reading: The knowledge sources account. *Journal of Experimental Child Psychology, 62,* 190–222.

Treiman, R., Goswami, U., & Bruck, M. (1990). Not all nonwords are alike: Implications for reading development and theory. *Memory and Cognition, 18*(6), 559–567.

Treiman, R., Mullennix, J., Bijeljac-Babic, R., & Richmond-Welty, E. D. (1995). The special role of rimes in the description, use, and acquisition of English orthography. *Journal of Experimental Psychology: General, 124,* 107–136.

Wigfield, A. (1997). Children's motivations for reading and reading engagement. In J. T. Guthrie & A. Wigfield (Eds.), *Reading engagement: Motivating readers through integrated instruction* (pp. 14–33). Newark, DE: International Reading Association.

Wylie, R. E., & Durrell, D. D. (1970). Teaching vowels through phonograms. *Elementary English, 47,* 427–451.

25

Early Literacy Development: The Case for "Informed Assessment"

❖

PETER H. JOHNSTON
REBECCA ROGERS

In the United States, since the 1930s, literacy-related assessment has occurred in the early years of schooling because of beliefs about the relationship between learning and development (Durkin, 1966). Gessell's (1925) maturational view held that children's minds must reach a certain level of maturity before they would be able to learn to read. In that context, Morphett and Washburn (1932) published a study claiming that children must reach a mental age of 6.5 (judged by an intelligence test) before which literacy instruction would be not merely wasteful but downright damaging. In their suburban Chicago school system it was common practice to put a chart on the wall highlighting when each child would be chronologically old enough to have an appropriate "mental age" to learn to read. In spite of arguments and data to the contrary, starting with Gates (1937), this "readiness" testing continues in one form or another with children being screened out of school (not the intention of early proponents). Similarly, the Gessell test continues to be one of the most popular for school readiness (Gnezda & Bolig, 1988), and prescreening

for kindergarten is mandated in 19 states, though in some (e.g., Louisiana) the tests cannot be used to withhold from children such services as proceeding to first grade (Shepard, Taylor, & Kagan, 1996).

The persistence of these practices is due, in part, to beliefs about development, to which we return presently, and in part to the downward creep of accountability and meritocratic gatekeeping. It is also due, in part, to a general increase in testing that is consistent with cultural beliefs about the value of such practices (Johnston, 1993). Consequently, as Shepard (1994) points out, "In the past decade testing of 4-, 5-, and 6-year-olds has been excessive and inappropriate . . . [encouraging] the teaching of decontextualized skills" (p. 212).

A Way of Thinking about Early Literacy Assessment

The term "assessment" is used in this chapter to refer to the broad repertoire of behaviors involved in noticing, documenting, recording, and interpreting children's be-

Editors' Note: Chapters 25 and 26 represent two contrasting views of early literacy assessment. Johnston and Rogers make a strong case for documentary assessment, whereas Salinger argues for multiple forms of evidence including standardized testing. These views characterize the current controversy in the field which is likely to become even more critical in the future.

377

haviors and performances. Testing is a subset of assessment in which performances are controlled and elicited in standardized conditions. Assessment practices are a kind of literate activity involving the representation of children's behavior, often in print, and a range of value-laden social interactions around that representation process. Assessment is part of a larger discourse about children, literacy, and learning. In other words, literacy, learning, and assessment, are fundamentally discursive practices, involving ways of knowing, believing, valuing, relating, behaving, and representing (Egan-Robertson, 1998; Gee, 1996). Two principles are attendant on this. First, assessment is fundamentally interpretive, influenced by values, beliefs, and language, and, second, assessments have consequences for children's literate development. For example, Rueda and Mercer (1985) reported that the designation of either "learning disabled" or "language delayed" was a function of whether there was a psychologist or a speech therapist on a placement committee. The designation used will have ramifications for the literacy instruction the student receives, and thus for the literacy he or she acquires, because it will change the nature and focus of the interactions that take place around text. These differences in interactions occur not just across different teachers but also with the same teacher across children designated as more or less able. For example, when a teacher asked her first-graders what someone needs to be a writer, a less able student said "eraser, pencil." When asked, "What kind of writer are you?" he said, "A printer." Other students said such things as "poet," or "scary writer." These are self-assessments—statements of identity that have implications for future participation in literate engagements. As others in this volume have pointed out, becoming literate is not simply learning to read and write in the narrow sense of converting speech to print and back again. In becoming literate, children acquire beliefs, values, and relationships that are part of their developing identities (Gee, Chapter 3), and assessment-related discourse is a central agent in this development.

These principles have implications for assessment validity. Any assessment practice will affect the discursive environment and thus alter the constructs teachers use to represent children's learning and to organize their teaching behavior (Johnston, 1992; Moss, 1998). For example, two teachers can notice a child's spelling of *candy* as *knde* and one calls it an "invented spelling" and the other a "spelling error," or even a sign of a disability. This, in turn changes the discursive environment for students, whose understandings and identities are also changed. Indeed, Mehan and others have shown the role of language in the process of children's construction as "handicapped" or "disabled," which often occurs even before a child begins school (Clay, 1987; McDermott, 1993; McDermott & Varenne, 1995; Mehan, 1993). In other words, the consequences of assessment practices are an inseparable aspect of their validity (Messick, 1994; Moss, 1998). As a further example, the impact on a child's life of being retained, including the ways children incorporate this knowledge into their daily lives and identities, is part of the validity of the assessment that produced the retention. This impact can be substantial, for, as Shepard and Smith (1989) point out, retention ranks up near a death in the family in terms of psychological trauma. Not only can pressures that follow from testing lead schools to exclude children from kindergarten but also parents, the net effect being to escalate curricula in the early years of school.

As with any interpretive practice, understandings are influenced by the circumstances in which they are made, including the assessment environment. For example, when asked for a description of the literacy development of a child they know well, teachers who work in high-stakes testing environments not only say less than teachers in less oppressive circumstances but are less likely to report on children's interests, or tastes in literature, or to mention specific books. Furthermore, the language they choose for describing students' literacy development is more distancing (Johnston, Weiss, & Afflerbach, 1993). Assessment practices are not merely objective, nonreactive applications of scientific tools. Rather, they are always social interactions, always interpretive, and always have consequences: A teacher may change her instruction; a child might be placed in a different classroom; or children, teachers, or parents may change their understanding of themselves and of what it means to be literate. Whatever tool might be involved in assessment—a test, an observation checklist, a record of oral reading—it must be interpreted by a person within an interpretive community. Two people from different interpretive communities choose different things to assess, different means to assess them, frame the data they collect differently, and use different words to describe what they observe. Even if a test yields a number, the test has been structured by people with particular views of literacy, and the number must be interpreted in order to have any meaning (Brozo & Brozo, 1994; Johnston, 1992; Tierney, 1998). Parents, teachers, and students often make different meanings from children's literate behaviors, and it is common enough for two teachers to give different descriptions of the same child's literacy development.

The purposes, forms, and interpretations involved in assessment practices are cultural artifacts. They reflect, and insist on, certain social values, beliefs, practices, and relationships. For example, not only do different cultures expect children to learn to read and write at different ages, but some include critical literacy from the start, whereas others defer it until high school or do not address it at all. Some assessment practices focus entirely on what children have learned about letters, sounds, and words, whereas others emphasize what they have learned about what literacy does and how it works (Johnston, 1997). Some assessment practices focus on normative performance, and only what can be accomplished independently, whereas others address what children can accomplish collaboratively, with normative performance being of limited relevance (Barrs, Ellis, Hester, & Thomas, 1989). These assessment practices reflect social beliefs and values; however, they also enforce them by insisting that certain behaviors are valued and by insisting on certain representations of children and their literacy. They anchor institutional discourses.

Literacy Learning and Development

At the heart of different approaches to early literacy assessment are different views of literacy, learning, and development. For example, two fundamental assumptions underlie readiness testing. The first is the roughly Piagetian view that development precedes learning such that learning cannot take place unless the appropriate prior cognitive development has occurred. For example, currently it is popular to view "phonemic awareness" essentially as a readiness feature because there are strong claims made that such awareness is a necessary precursor to literate development—anything prior to such development is viewed as prereading (Grossen, 1996).

The contrasting view of literacy assessment and development, in which readiness tests do not make sense, would be the Vygotskian position that learning leads development. In this view, children are socialized into a set of social practices, beliefs, and values, through guided, socially meaningful participation. In Rogoff's (1995) terms, we apprentice young children into literacy and they appropriate, or make their own, these social practices through a series of transformations in use. Thus, although we learn such things as the conventions of text—the organization of print, books, computer screens, and so forth—we also learn to value and to act around print in particular ways. We learn what constitutes authority, whether we should ask questions of books and authors, under which circumstances, what kind of questions, who is in charge of producing and consuming texts, how able we are, what it means to be able, the significance of ability, and who we are as literate beings. Literacy and assessment are not just "done"; they are part of a process in which children are "becoming" (Rogoff, 1995) or "being" (Gee, 1999; Lankshear, 1997) literate.

These contrasting views influence the timing and function of early literacy assessment through their implications for intervention. Marie Clay (1991, 1993), for example, has argued strongly that if long-term failure is to be prevented it must be addressed before failure experience accumulates and children develop too many confusions about the organization of print systems. But the question of *how early* to intervene continues to be problematic and centrally involves assessment. If children arrive at school with little literate experience, Clay argues that it would be premature to conclude that they are experiencing difficulty learning. Most children develop a range of literate knowledge, if not before they come to school, then in the first year at school, when immersed in a literate learning community. She proposes letting a child participate in a productive literate environment for a year before assessing with an eye toward intervention. This approach assumes, among other things, that literacy is acquired as part of participation in a literate culture. It also assumes that instruction is a productive part of assessment. In other words, part of assessment involves observing how a child responds to a particular instructional environment. More direct and detailed examination of the child-instructional-context relationship is a rare assessment practice, exceptions being found in the work of Lyons (Lyons, 1991; Lyons, Pinnell, & DeFord, 1993) as part of Reading Recovery, and in arguments made by Vellutino and his colleagues (Vellutino, Scanlon, & Sipay, 1997) following Clay (1987) (see also Vellutino & Scanlon, this volume).

Purposes of Early Literacy Assessment

Early intervention for preventing (or responding to) difficulty is one common purpose of literacy assessment. But there are two ways to approach examining the purposes of early literacy assessment: current practice and recommended practice. Starting with the latter, consider the position of the National Association for the Education of Young Children (NAEYC; 1991) on the appropriate purposes of early assessment. The first (and foremost) legitimate purpose of early childhood assessment is "to plan instruction for individuals and groups and for communicating with parents" (p. 32) (we would argue that this is really two functions). The second function is "to identify children who may be in need of specialized services or intervention" (p. 32). This function deserves some caution as it is commonly transformed into "to classify children in order to access revenue streams" (32) or "to identify children whose removal from the accountability testing pool would make the institution appear more successful" (p. 32) resulting in identification of as many children as possible. The function might better be phrased, "to identify children's strengths and appropriate, and sometimes specialized, instructional supports" (p. 32). Placing the emphasis on the identification of instructional supports rather than identification of children makes this purpose simply another example of instructional planning. A step further might be "to identify what the child knows and can accomplish independently and with particular kinds of support" (32).

The third function legitimized by NAEYC is "to evaluate how well the program is meeting its goals" (32). This function requires that goals are in fact agreed on, and that assessment practices can address those goals. Current practice relies on standardized, norm-referenced tests. But the use of these instruments with young children has been heavily criticized as we shall see, and program evaluation does not require every student to take a standardized test, or to do the same thing under the same circumstances (Clay, 1993; Johnston, 1992).

That optimizing student learning is the primary goal of assessment is a principle asserted by position papers from NAEYC (1991), the International Reading Association (IRA) and National Council of Teachers of English (NCTE) (1994), and the National Forum on Assessment (Phye, 1997). Although the purposes of assessment described previously make sense to a wide range of constituents, they are not what happens in practice. Current early literacy assessment functions include screening children for school readiness, identifying handicapping conditions, retaining or promoting children, grouping children by ability, holding teachers accountable for children's learning or holding schools accountable for funding expenditures (e.g., Goals 2000 or Title 1), and providing specific interventions for specific children. Most of these assessment practices have been roundly criticized in the literature both for the technical inadequacies of the available tests and for the serious consequences of the practices themselves (Bredekamp, 1997; Shepard & Smith, 1986; Stallman & Pearson, 1991). For example, on the matter of technical inadequacy, Shepard and Smith (1986) point out that "none of the available tests is accurate enough to screen children into special programs without a 50 percent error rate" (p. 80).

Each professional group that offers standards on assessment argues that the primary purpose of early literacy assessment is to optimize student learning. To accomplish this goal, contextual as well as cognitive issues must be addressed (Gregory, 1997; Johnston, 1997), such as the following: the funds of knowledge children bring to school, and the advantage to which they might be turned for literacy development, the languages the child brings and his or her ability to transfer one to the other, the permeability of classroom interactions around print to the language(s) and patterns of interaction in the child's home, the child's understanding of literate activity, the ways and circumstances under which the child enquires into language, what he or she can know and do under which circumstances, what the child partially understands, and can almost do, or do with support, the logic of the child's errors, how the child recruits social resources to his or her own learning. This information is substantially dependent on detailed individual observation and interaction, particularly in the classroom, making the teacher the central agent of assessment. This responsibility of the teacher is also a principle that is strongly asserted by a number of authors (Brozo & Brozo, 1994; Hodges, 1997; Johnston, 1997) and in position statements by NAEYC (1991), IRA/NCTE (1994), and the National Forum on Assessment (Phye, 1997). The principle implies that improving assessment entails investing in the development of teachers' knowledge of children and their literate development, more than investing in testing devices. However, this principle is in conflict with current practice and assessment privilege as encoded, for example, in the "formal" versus "informal" assessment contrast.

"Formal" and "Informal" Assessment

Among literacy researchers, there is considerable support for the necessity of "informal" assessment and very little support for "formal" measures of early literacy (Clay, 1993; Johnston, 1997; Stallman & Pearson, 1991; Teale, 1991). The formal assessments are afflicted with numerous shortcomings, some of which accrue from the consequences of their use. There is little argument to be made for predictive tests, such as readiness and intelligence tests, which use group performance to predict individual performance in the future—a risky business at best and self-fulfilling at worst. Such tests also do not contribute instructionally useful information. Indeed, there is little that norm-referenced, especially group, tests have to offer for the assessment of young children. As Clay (1993) points out, they are "indirect ways of informing teachers about learning. By comparison with the observation of learners at work, test scores are mere approximations or estimates, at times misrepresenting individual progress in learning, and at times presenting results stripped of the very information that is required for designing or evaluating sound instruction" (pp. 1–2). By way of contrast, the *Concepts about Print* test (Clay, 1993), a standardized assessment of how a child understands beginning literacy conventions, correlates as well with later success in reading as does an individual intelligence test at 5 years of age, and substantially better at 6 years of age (Clay, 1998). In addition, however, unlike readiness or intelligence tests, it provides clear information about what a child knows and needs to know about print conventions—information a teacher can act on. In addition, it is conducted in a manner that is, although standardized, more like the normal literacy activities in which students engage.

The alternative to "formal" assessment practices is "informal" assessment. Breaking down the privilege enjoyed by the unmarked "formal" will require replacing the distinction with terms such as "documentary," "descriptive," or "informing" contrasted with "traditional." Unlike the traditional "objective" measures, documentary assessment explicitly depends on the human expert (Johnston, 1987)—a sensitive observer (Clay, 1993) or kidwatcher (Goodman, 1978). Although young children are less able to articulate their knowledge of literacy, the more authentic the circumstance, the more literacy is a common part of community talk, and the more sensitive the observer/interviewer, the more children are able to help us understand their development (Tammivarra & Enright, 1986). For example, Scrivens (1998) provides case studies of 3- and 4-year-old children who reveal through practice, interview, and imaginative play with peers a great deal about their literate development. Indeed, children's play is a particularly good place in which to observe their literate development, especially the literate practices into which they have been socialized (Roskos & Neuman, 1993; Teale, 1991; Whitmore & Goodman, 1995) and their understanding of the functions of literacy.

A further contrast between traditional and documentary assessment lies in the relationship between assessor and student. In traditional assessment, we pretend that there is really no interaction, or at least that it is the same for everybody. In documentary assessment the interaction is an important part of the assessment because the point of inquiry is not simply what the child knows and can do independently but what the child knows and can do, partially knows and can almost do, and can accomplish with some particular social support (Feuerstein, 1979; Rogoff, 1995; Vygotsky, 1962). However, actual analysis of the interactions involved with children *as part of assessing a child's literacy* is rare (but see Lyons, 1991; Roskos & Neuman, 1993). Intervention, or changing instruction, as an assessment technique is also not common, although Clay (1987) has argued that before a child is classified as reading disabled, one should at least systematically examine the possibility that careful instruction, focused by ongoing sensitive observation and recordkeeping, will bring the child into the normal range of performance (see also Vellutino et al., 1997). Such assessment strategies foreground even more the teacher's role as the primary agent of assessment and, perhaps, interactions between the teacher and student as a primary "object" of assessment.

Teacher as Primary Agent of Assessment

When it comes to young children's literacy learning, there is substantial consensus that the teacher is the primary assessment agent (Clay, 1998; IRA/NCTE, 1994; Johnston, 1992). It makes sense because the connection between assessment and instruction is most direct. Young children are often less

articulate about their learning than are older children and thus require sensitive observation and interaction to access their literate understandings. And, data are most meaningfully collected in the course of teachers' daily interactions with students, and most meaningfully interpreted within an ongoing history. It requires a trusting relationship for students to extend themselves into areas of potential failure. It also means that the teacher needs to have a working knowledge of appropriate kinds of support and a sense of how to analyze the interactions.

The most significant reason that teachers are the primary agent of assessment, however, is that their assessments have an impact on their children's learning, on their instructional relationship, and on children's assessments of themselves as a literate individuals (Johnston, 1997; Johnston, Woodside-Jiron, & Day, 1998). For example, it is common in many places for children in kindergarten and first grade to be classified as learning disabled with respect to reading and writing. This process, which has a substantial effect on a child's literacy career (McGill-Franzen & Allington, 1993), begins with the teacher whose assessment triggers a referral. Some teachers refer many more students to special education than do others. High-referral teachers, when asked for a description of a child's literacy development, give brief and undetailed descriptions compared with those of low-referral teachers (Broikou, 1992). Although both high- and low-referral teachers notice who is having trouble, those who have a more detailed knowledge of their students appear to have a greater sense of agency with respect to the students' continued development.

The most important advances in early literacy assessment, then, involve educating teachers in observing, documenting, analyzing, and responding to children's literate behaviors (Athey, 1990; Johnston, 1993). As teachers gain control over language that allows for more, rather than less, complete and contextualized representations of children's literate engagements, they are also better able to help parents notice and make sense of children's literate development. Furthermore, as teachers become more able to help children talk about the literate activity in which they are engaged, they will also find it easier to document their development and understand their confusions. This involves the important assessment skill of listening, a skill that is often in short supply and reduced further by testing pressure. Many teachers have difficulty listening to young students for lack of time and because they feel obliged to ask known-answer questions to check comprehension. This is exacerbated with students who struggle with language or whose language is not the language of the classroom. Comprehension questions and retellings are primary assessment interactions (Brown & Cambourne, 1989; Morrow, 1990; Moss, 1997; Sulzby, 1985). These interaction patterns, and their implications, for relationships of authority between readers and text become part of the literacies children acquire (Johnston et al., 1998). As an alternative, the questions that *children* ask about books, print, and writing can be even more revealing. Arranging for them to ask such questions can be productive both for the information gained and the literate practices acquired (Commeyras, 1995).

Qualities of Assessment Practices in Early Literacy

Traditionally, two primary dimensions of quality have been applied to assessments: validity and reliability. However, these criteria have undergone considerable transformation. The consequences of the use and interpretation of assessments has come to be integral to judgments of validity (Messick, 1995; Moss, 1995). Thus, the dictum "first do no harm" has been centralized in the construct meaning that unless the assessment practice improves the quality of the child's literacy learning, it should not occur. Applying this criterion to traditional assessment practices renders them seriously problematic (Johnston, 1992; Stallman & Pearson, 1991; Taylor, 1990). Applying this framework to documentary forms of assessment, however, is not as simple because whether or not the assessment is productive depends a great deal on what the teacher knows (and the institution allows) about literacy development and the organization of literate environments, particularly ones in which children can experiment with the social uses of print, talking as they go. It also

depends on the constructs embedded in the discourse used to represent the children's literate development. Teachers can bring a discourse of disability or a discourse of assets to their documentation, consequently documenting different behaviors using different constructs, with different consequences for children's learning. Given this, the validity of the assessment cannot be considered without also examining the goals of the assessment practice. That is, of central importance is an alignment between pedagogical and assessment intentions and practices.

Reliability, also a mainstay of traditional assessment, has been similarly reworked in terms of generalizability—across time, observers, and so forth (Shavelson & Webb, 1991). In documentary assessment it is appropriate to ask: What does this performance or interpretation represent? Or, over which dimensions, or contexts, does this performance or interpretation generalize for which purpose? Reliability in this sense is usually associated with generalizing a judgment over different judges, or over time or different circumstances. Certainly one way of increasing agreement, or stability, is by increasing the number of assessments over time. This is an important strength of documentary assessment, in which assessments are part of the instructional context and occur more frequently than do more traditional measures (Gipps, 1994).

With reliability, the idea is to eliminate variability in interpretation, to get at the "true" representation, as if there were a single stable trait being measured. But because literacy is now seen as more contextualized than it is portrayed in traditional tests, some variability in performance is expected across contexts, and such variability is viewed not simply as an indicator of assessment error but as an expected source of legitimate variability in performance. Furthermore, if assessment is viewed as a vehicle for learning, some reasonable level of disagreement is less problematic because it provides space for dialogue—and hence learning—about literacy and a student's literate development. When collecting evidence of children's literacy learning in various contexts, there are more likely to be surprises in the data collected. These surprises, rather than "error," are places for further investigation into the instructional context. Whether an assessment will measure the same thing twice is less important than whether the assessment can productively focus our instruction.

Documentary assessment provides some advantages in the context of these newer views of assessment quality. For example, ongoing classroom assessments are more likely to directly affect the quality of instruction in positive ways. Similarly, because the "items" (instances of performance) in documentary assessment are more direct examples of actual reading and writing, students' work will be represented in a manner consistent with their daily performance. As teachers and students are in control of day-to-day assessments, practicing these types of assessments allows them more agency in coconstructing supportive learning contexts. Over time and across contexts, these samples are more likely to reveal patterns of student learning. In the long run, the validity and generalizability of the particular assessment *instrument* seem to be less important than the trustworthiness of the interpretations and patterns that emerge across *contexts,* and the instructional responses to these interpretations.

Although teachers are likely to use documentary language in talking with other teachers or with parents, there continue to be tensions in how they represent children's learning outside the immediate context of the child. That is, when accountability data, report card grades, or information for student placement decisions need to be provided, teachers rely primarily on information garnered from standardized measures of achievement (Hodges, 1997). A necessary effort, then, in establishing the authority and visibility of documentary forms of assessment in early childhood literacy is to establish discussions around these points of tension. Arguments against documentary assessment practices protest the potentially unsystematic and biased nature of the practices. But there is no way to avoid bias in assessment practices even with standardized tests (Johnston, 1992).

Tensions also continue to exist between "internal" and "external" assessment purposes (Wixson, Valencia, & Lipson, 1994). External assessment practices are those connected to accountability purposes, whereas internal assessments inform ongoing pedagogical decisions. These tensions revolve around what counts as evidence: how the information is reported, used, and valued and which people or groups of people get to make these decisions. The cultural disposition to regard objective, decontextualized, and deficit-driven information with more credibility and authority results in continued emphasis on normative tests, particularly with high-stakes purposes. Nonetheless, a number of attempts have been made to increase the level of credibility of teacher's ongoing "informed" assessments (Barrs et al., 1989; Wolf, 1993). Furthermore, teachers' careful observation and description of children's literacy development, even that done "on the fly," is not random or unsystematic. There are also many examples of systematic assessment instruments presented elsewhere (e.g., Barrs et al., 1989; Clay, 1993; Genishi & Dyson, 1984; Juel, 1991; Johnston, 1997). However, an example of such an assessment device might clarify important issues.

In Practice: An Example

Viewing assessment as part of a discourse around children's literacy development the question becomes, What are the implications of particular kinds of assessment practices for children's literate development? Or, more positively, how can we arrange for a most productive discourse involving children's literate learning and instruction? An example might help. Consider the Primary Language Record (PLR), developed by Barrs et al. (1989) for early literacy assessment in multilingual inner-city London. The assessment is standardized in that it has requirements of what data need to be collected in which ways, how the data should be analyzed, who should be involved, and how consistency and trustworthiness should be maintained. It is not, however, primarily norm-referenced, and neither is it a test. The principles on which the procedure is based include the involvement of parents, children (including those with special needs), and all teachers who teach the child; the importance of recording children's progress across the curriculum, in all major language modes, and in the other community languages they know as well as English; and the importance of a clear framework for evaluating progress in language. The intended use of the procedure is at different points during the year so that it informs instruction and is not simply summative paper work. It is also cumulative over the course of the child's development. The record form begins with a space for a record of the discussion with parents around work samples and observations and children's literate practices at home. The record is signed by both teacher and parent. Instructions are provided for maximizing parent participation and engagement and focus on the child's development, including ways to minimize power issues. Next is a record of a discussion or interview with the child. Teachers are provided with useful instructions on interviewing children and helping them reflect productively on their own work.

The PLR focuses on what the child *can* do, in order to "provide a positive basis for further work by parents and other teachers" (Barrs et al., 1989, p. 11). The record also emphasizes the specificity of data and source—partly a matter of building trustworthiness, but also a matter of enabling challenges to assumptions. A record is also made of any instructional procedure that has been associated with progress for the child, and any potentially useful practices, given the other information available. Similarly, the manual points out that "progress or lack of progress should always be seen in relation to the adequacy of the context" (Barrs et al., 1989, p. 18), thus moving the focus of assessment to the learning system, not simply the child. The manual also devotes considerable space to helping teachers understand the framework of reading/writing development on which it is based and what is necessary to set the stage for productive performance. This overtly recognizes the values and assumptions underlying the assessment.

The child's development as a reader is placed on two scales—independence to dependence and inexperience to experience with each point on these 5-point scales clearly defined and with potentially problematic terms further defined in the manual. These latter terms include dimensions such as "pleasure and involvement in story and reading, alone and with others," and "the

range, quantity and variety of reading in all areas of the curriculum" (Barrs et al., 1989, p. 28). Similarly, writing development is divided into compositional and transcriptional aspects. But beyond the child's command of written language conventions, also of interest are the child's ability to sustain engagement with literate processes and to engage in collaborative literate practices, the use the child makes of experience, the strategies used, and the range of genres entertained.

The complexity of the record honors the complexity of literate learning—certainly a matter of construct validity—but also places teacher knowledge at the center of assessment. This would be a worrisome psychometric property, particularly with the traditional issue of reliability, which tends to drop when authentic tasks are involved or when a range of people need to agree on complex observations. However, to reduce the process to merely increasing reliability would be to trivialize it. First, interrater reliability is a matter of getting people onto the same page, or rather into the same discourse. The PLR process works toward this goal by moderating sessions in which members of the immediate assessment community (including parents) work through cases together examining differences in judgment and their implications. This is not merely training judges, as is done for state tests; these negotiations involve more complex and wide-ranging data. Furthermore, because there are differences among participants and among the cases examined, the process extends the understanding of the individuals participating in the process. In fact, the differences that produce "unreliability" are the very places where discussions produce learning for all parties and expansion of the discourse. This moderation process is being used and developed further in other places as ways of "looking together at student work" (Blythe, Allen, & Powell, 1999). Finally, there is a place in the procedure, and on the forms, for comments from parent and teacher to assist the child's next teacher.

Aligned with the purpose of assessments, this procedure has several important features. First, it emphasizes the child's assets, which redirects conversations about student learning and instructional decisions. Second, it builds in conversations with parents, students, and teachers about the student's works, making the construction and the representation of learning a social project in which issues of power are minimized and actively addressed. Third, it uses ongoing classroom processes and performances to document children's learning. In other words, it is particularly well adapted to accomplishing the major assessment functions of optimizing learning; engaging parents, students, teachers, and others in productive conversations about learning; and shaping instructional programs and institutional supports.

Concluding Comments

Despite shifts in understandings of early childhood literacy and assessment, we continue to see traditional, norm-referenced testing and its associated language and values dominate early literacy assessment. There continue to be incentives to sidetrack children earlier, and access to institutional resources is often governed by tests which are firmly anchored in cultural assumptions. Although documentary forms of assessment are used in localized contexts, they have not gained authority. This is partly because they are not amenable to the simple numerical comparisons implicit in an accountability framework, partly because the teacher's personal involvement in the assessments makes them appear "unobjective," and partly because of the cultural assumptions about teaching, learning, and literacy.

Recognizing literacy and assessment as discursive practices means reorienting the conversation to examine the roles language plays in the construction and maintenance of traditional testing of literacy learning. Early literacy assessments as cultural artifacts of early childhood institutions and elementary schools represent the continued valuing of measuring individuals' "worth" or "potential." Even in situations in which teachers or specialists do not believe in the measurement tool, they continue to use it to talk with parents and other teachers about particular students (Brozo & Brozo, 1997). These paradoxes are also sustained by beliefs about the psychological nature of literacy development. Consistent with the competitive individualism and technological thinking endemic to the U.S. culture (Argyris & Schon, 1974; Bellah, Madsen, Sullivan, Swidler, & Tipton, 1985), we keep being drawn to a technical, cognitive view of literacy in which skills can be taught in sequence and in isolation. This view is reflected in, and reinforced by, current reading tests. Rather than ask about the circumstances in which children are noticing and theorizing about language at all levels, we become caught up in asking whether they have all the short vowels and their sounds memorized.

Literacy assessment in early childhood is essentially formative in nature. It must function to improve instruction and to communicate progress. There is no reason for high-stakes literacy testing in early childhood. There is no meritocratic function to elevate assessment to high stakes, and because accountability testing has unfortunate side effects (Johnston, 1998; Smith, 1991; Smith & Rottenberg, 1991), that, too, should be avoided. Using literacy assessments to classify children as "unready," as "disabled," or as "language delayed" also are examples of counterproductive high-stakes practices. Early interventions should be based on detailed documentation across contexts rather than on decontextualized normative testing.

There is extraordinary variation in the languages and cultures that children bring to literacy learning and in the literacies into which they are apprenticed prior to coming to school. We know, for example, that children often enter school with different expectations for ways of interacting with teachers or others in authority (Au & Jordan, 1981; Heath, 1983; Volk, 1997). Differences between these discursive environments of home and school cultures are often encountered, if not recognized, in assessment practices (Moore, 1996). Whether on the Internet or in school, using traditional or documentary practices, children's lives are transformed, for better or worse, in the process. Standardized, norm-referenced testing does not accommodate these differences well, in part because in order to allow for diversity, there need to be some adjustments in interaction, which violates the standardization and the norming. Furthermore, such tests easily lead to a discourse of deficits (Coles, 1987; Poplin, 1988; Taylor, 1990). Preferable for assessment, both before and during the early years of school, is a community of teachers who are sensitive observers/listeners and who are able to document a child's development without resorting to a discourse of disability and deficit. Because the teacher is the primary assessment agent in early childhood (as in the rest of schooling), we must look to theories of early literacy assessment that foster teacher development and contexts that make it possible for teachers and students to feel, and assert, the authority of documentary assessments.

References

Argyris, C., & Schon, D. (1974). *Theory in practice: Increasing professional effectiveness.* London: Jossey-Bass.

Athey, I. (1990). The construct of emergent literacy: Putting it all together. In L. M. Morrow & J. Smith (Eds.), *Assessment for instruction in early literacy* (pp. 176–183). Englewood Cliffs: Prentice-Hall.

Au, K., & Jordan, C. (1981). Teaching reading to Hawaiian children: Finding a culturally appropriate solution. In H. Trueba, G. Guthrie, & K. Au (Eds.), *Culture in the bilingual classroom* (pp. 137–152). Rowley, MA: Newbury House.

Barrs, M., Ellis, S., Hester, H., & Thomas, A. (1989). *The primary language record: Handbook for teachers.* London: Inner London Education Authority/Centre for Language in Primary Education.

Bellah, R., Madsen, R., Sullivan, W., Swidler, A., & Tipton, S. (1985). *Habits of the heart: Individualism and commitment in American life.* New York: Harper & Row.

Blythe, T., Allen, D., & Powell, B. S. (1999). *Looking together at student work: A companion guide to Assessing Student Learning.* New York: Teachers College Press.

Bredekamp, S. (1997). NAEYC issues revised position statement on developmentally appropriate practices in early childhood programs. *Young Children, 52*(2), 34–40.

Brown, H., & Cambourne, B. (1989). *Read and retell: A strategy for the whole-language/natural learning classroom.* Portsmouth: NH: Heinemann.

Brozo, W. G. (1990). Learning how at-risk readers learn best: A case for interactive assessment. *Journal of Reading, 33,* 522–527.

Brozo, W. G., & Brozo, C. C. (1994). Literacy assessment in standardized and zero-failure contexts. *Reading and Writing Quarterly: Overcoming Learning Difficulties, 10,* 189–200.

Clay, M. M. (1985). *The early detection of reading difficulties: A diagnostic survey with recovery procedures* (3rd ed.). Auckland, NZ: Heinemann.

Clay, M. (1987). Learning to be learning disabled. *New Zealand Journal of Educational Studies, 22*(1), 35–38.

Clay, M. (1991). *Becoming literate: The construction of inner control.* Auckland, NZ: Heinemann.

Clay, M. (1993). *An observation survey of early literacy achievement.* Auckland, NZ: Heinemann.

Clay, M. (1998). *By different paths to common outcomes.* York, ME: Stenhouse.

Coles, G. (1987). *The learning mystique.* New York: Ballantine

Commeyras, M. (1995). What can we learn from students' questions? *Theory into Practice, 34*(2), 101–105.

Durkin, D. (1966). *Children who read early.* New York: Teachers College Press.

Egan-Robertson, A. (1998). Learning about culture, language, and power: Understanding relationships among personhood, literacy practices, and intertextuality. *Journal of Literacy Research, 30*(4), 449–487.

Feuerstein, R. (1979). *The dynamic assessment of retarded performers: The learning potential assessment device, theory, instrument and techniques.* Washington, DC: Georgetown University Press.

Fletcher, J., & Lyon, G. R. (1998). Reading: A research-based approach. In W. Evers (Ed.), *What's gone wrong in America's classrooms?* (pp. 49–90). Stanford, CA: Hoover Institute Press.

Garcia-Earnest, G., & Pearson, D. (1991). The role of assessment in a diverse society. In E. H. Hiebert (Ed.), *Literacy for a diverse society. Perspectives, practices and policies* (pp. 253–278). New York: Teachers College Press.

Gates, A. (1937). The necessary mental age for beginning reading. *Elementary School Journal, 37,* 497–508.

Gee, J. P. (1996). *Social linguistics and literacies: Ideology in discourses* (2nd ed.). London: Taylor & Francis.

Gee, J. P. (1999). Reading and the new literacy studies: Reframing the National Academy of Sciences Report on Reading. *Journal of Literacy Research, 31*(3), 355–374.

Genishi, C., & Dyson, A. (1984). *Language assessment in the early years.* Norwood, NJ: Ablex.

Gessell, A. (1925). *The mental growth of the preschool child.* New York: Macmillan.

Gipps, C. (1994). *Beyond testing. Towards a theory of educational assessment.* London: Falmer Press.

Gnezda, M. T., & Bolig, R. (1988). *A national survey of public school testing of prekindergarten and kindergarten children.* Paper presented at the National Forum on the Future of Children and Families and the National Association of State Boards of Education.

Goodman, Y. (1978). Kidwatching: Observing children in the classroom. In A. Jagger & M. T. Smith-Burke (Eds.), *Observing the language learner* (pp. 9–18). Newark, DE: International Reading Association.

Gregory, E. (1997). Introduction. In E. Gregory (Ed.), *One child, many worlds: Early learning in multicultural communities* (pp. 1–8). New York: Teachers College Press.

Grossen, B. (1996). Making research serve the profession. *American Educator, 20,* 7–8, 22–27.

Hodges, C. (1997). How valid and useful are alternative assessments for decision making in primary grade classrooms? *Reading Research and Instruction, 36*(2),157–173.

IRA/NCTE Joint Task Force on Assessment. (1994). *Standards for the assessment of reading and writing.* Newark, DE: International Reading Association and the National Council of Teachers of English.

Johnston, P. H. (1992). *Constructive evaluation of literate activity.* New York: Longman.

Johnston, P. (1993a). Assessment as social practice. In D. Leu & C. Kinzer (Eds.), *Forty-second yearbook of the National Reading Conference* (pp. 11–23). Chicago: National Reading Conference.

Johnston, P. H. (1997). *Knowing literacy: Constructive literacy assessment.* York, ME: Stenhouse.

Johnston, P. H. (1998). The consequences of the use of standarized tests. In S. Murphy (Ed.), *Fragile evidence: A critique of reading assessment* (pp. 89–101). Mahwah, NJ: Erlbaum.

Johnston, P., Weiss, P., & Afflerbach, P. (1993). Teachers' evaluation of teaching and learning of literacy. *Educational Assessment, 1*(2), 91–117.

Johnston, P. H., Woodside-Jiron, H., & Day, J. P. (1998, December). *Teaching and learning literate epistemologies.* Paper presented at the National Reading Conference, Austin, TX.

Juel, C. (1991). The role of decoding in early literacy instruction and assessment. In L. M. Morrow & J. K. Smith (Eds.), *Assessment for instruction in early literacy* (pp. 135–154). Engelwood Cliffs, NJ: Prentice-Hall.

Lankshear, C. (with J. Gee, M. Knobel, & C. Searle). (1997). *Changing literacies.* Philadelphia: Open University Press

Lyons, C. (1991). Helping a learning disabled child enter the literate world. In D. Deford, C. Lyons, & G. S. Pinnell (Eds.), *Bridges to literacy: Learning from reading recovery* (pp. 205–215). Portsmouth, NH: Heinemann.

Lyons, C. A., Pinnell, G. S., & DeFord, D. E. (1993). *Partners in learning: Teachers and children in Reading Recovery.* New York: Teachers College Press.

McDermott, R. P. (1993). The acquisition of a child by a learning disability. In S. Chaiklin & J. Lave (Eds.), *Understanding practice: Perspectives on activity and context* (pp. 269–305): Cambridge University Press.

McDermott, R., & Varenne, H. (1995) Culture as disability. *Anthropology and Education Quarterly, 26,* 324–348.

McGill-Franzen, A., & Allington, R. (1993). Flunk'em or get them classified: The contamination of primary grade accountability data. *Educational Researcher, 22,* 19–22.

Mehan, H. (1993). Beneath the skin and between the ears: A case study in the politics of representation. In S. Chaiklin & J. Lave (Eds.), *Understanding practice: Perspectives on activity and contexts* (pp. 241–268). Cambridge, UK: Cambridge University Press.

Messick, S. (1994). The interplay of evidence and consequences in the validation of performance assessments. *Educational Researcher, 23,* 13–24.

Messick, S. (1995). Validity of psychological assessment: Validity of inferences from persons' responses and performances as scientific inquiry into score meaning. *American Psychologist, 50,* 741–749.

Morphet, M., & Washburn, C. (1932). When should children begin to read? *Elementary School Journal, 31,* 496–503.

Morrow. L. M. (1990). Assessing children's understanding of story through their construction and reconstruction of narrative. In L. M. Morrow & J. Smith (Eds.), *Assessment for instruction in early literacy* (pp. 110–134). Englewood Cliffs, NJ: Prentice-Hall.

Moss, P. A. (1995). Themes and variations in validity theory. *Educational Measurement: Issues and Practice, 14*(2), 5–13.

Moss, B. (1997). A qualitative assessment of first graders' retelling of expository text. *Reading Research and Instruction, 37*(1), 1–13.

Moss, P. (1998). The role of consequences in validity theory. *Educational Measurement: Issues and Practice, 17*(2), 6–12.

National Association for the Education of Young Children. (1991). Guidelines for the appropriate curriculum content and assessment in programs serving children ages 3 through 8. A Position statement of the National Association for the Education of Young Children and the National Association of Early Childhood Specialists in the State Department of Education. *Young Children, 46*(3), 21–38.

National Association for the Education of Young Children. (1998). Learning to read and write: Developmentally appropriate practices for young children. A joint position statement of the IRA and NAEYC. *Young Children, 53*(4), 30–46.

Phye, G. D. (1997). Epilogue: Classroom assessment—Looking forward. In G. D. Phye (Ed.), *Handbook of classroom assessment: Learning, adjustment, and achievement* (pp. 531–534). New York: Academic Press.

Poplin, M. (1988). The reductionist fallacy in learning disablities: Replicating the past by reducing the present. *Journal of Learning Disabilities, 21*(7), 389–400.

Rogoff, B. (1995). Observing sociocultural activity on three planes: Participatory appropriation, guided participation, apprenticeship. In J. Wertsch, P. del Rio, & A. Alverez (Eds.), *Sociocultural studies of mind* (pp. 139–164). Cambridge, UK: Cambridge University Press.

Roskos, K., & Neuman, S. B. (1993). Descriptive observations of adults' facilitation of literacy in young children's play. *Early Childhood Research Quarterly, 8,* 77–97.

Rueda, R., & Mercer, J. (1985). Predictive analysis of decision-making practices with limited English proficient handicapped students. Presented at the third annual symposium. *Exceptional Hispanic Children and Youth* [Monograph series], 6(1), 1–29.

Scrivens, G. (1998). Nursery children as emerging readers and writers. In R. Campbell (Ed.), *Facilitating preschool literacy* (pp. 169–191). Newark, DE: International Reading Association.

Shavelson, R. J., & Webb, N. M. (1991). *Generalizability theory: A primer.* London: Sage.

Shepard, L. A. (1994). The challenges of assessing young children appropriately. *Phi Delta Kappan* 76(3), 206–212.

Shepard, L. A., & Smith, M. L. (1986). Synthesis of research on school readiness and kindergarten retention. *Educational Leadership, 44,* 78–86.

Shepard, L. A., & Smith, M. L. (1988). Escalating academic demand in kindergarten: Counterproductive policies. *Elementary School Journal, 89*(2), 135–145.

Shepard, L. A., & Smith, M. L. (1989). *Flunking grades: Research and policies on retention.* New York: Falmer.

Shepard, L. A., Taylor, G. A., & Kagan, S. L. (1996). *Trends in early childhood assessment policies and practices.* Washington, DC: OERI.

Smith, M. L. (1991). Put to the test: The effects of external testing on teachers. *Educational Researcher, 20*(5), 8–11.

Smith, M. L., & Rottenberg, C. (1991). Unintended consequences of external testing in elementary schools. *Educational Measurement: Issues and Practice,10*(4), 7–11.

Stallman, A. C., & Pearson, P. D. (1991). Formal measures of early literacy. In L. M. Morrow & J. K. Smith (Eds.), *Assessment for instruction in early literacy* (pp. 7–44). Englewood Cliffs, NJ: Prentice-Hall.

Sulzby, E. (1985). Children's emergent reading of favorite storybooks: A developmental study. *Reading Research Quarterly, 20,* 458–481.

Tammivaara, J., & Enright, S. (1986). On eliciting information: Dialogues with child informants. *Anthropology and Education Quarterly, 17,* 218–238

Taylor, D. (1990). Teaching without testing. *English Education, 22*(1), 4–74.

Teale, W. (1988). Developmentally appropriate assessment of reading and writing in the early childhood classroom. *Elementary School Journal, 89,* 173–183.

Teale, W. (1991). The promise and the challenge of informal assessment in early literacy. In L. M. Morrow & J. K. Smith (Eds.), *Assessment for instruction in early literacy* (pp. 45–61). Englewood Cliffs, NJ: Prentice-Hall.

Tierney. R. J. (1998). Literacy assessment reform: Shifting beliefs, principles possibilities, and emerging practices. *The Reading Teacher, 51*(5), 374–390.

Tolbert, K. (1999, November 25). Tokyo's tots face important, early test after 2 years of cramming, kindergartners take private school entrance exams. *Washington Post Foreign Service,* pp. G01.

Vellutino, F. R., Scanlon, D. M., & Sipay, E. (1997). Toward distinguishing between cognitive and experiential deficits as primary sources of difficulty in learning to read: The importance of early intervention in diagnosing specific reading disability. In B. Blachman (Ed.), *Foundations of reading acquisition and dyslexia: Implications for early intervention* (pp. 347–380). Mahwah, NJ: Erlbaum.

Volk, D. (1997). Continuities and discontinuities: Teaching and learning in the home and school of a Puerto Rican five year old. In E. Gregory (Ed.), *One child, many worlds: Early learning in multicultural communities* (pp. 47–61). New York: Teachers College Press.

Vygotsky, L. (1962). *Thought and language* (Eugenia Hanfmann, Ed., Gertrude Vakar, Trans.). Cambridge, MA: MIT Press.

Whitmore, K., & Goodman, Y. (1995). Inside the whole language classroom. *School Administrator, 49*(5), 20–26.

Wixson, K., Valenica, S. W., & Lipson, M. (1994). Issues in literacy assessment: Facing the realities of internal and external assessment. *Journal of Reading Behavior, 26*(3), 315–337.

Wolf, K. P. (1993). From informal to informed assessment: Recognizing the role of the classroom teacher. *Journal of Reading, 36*(7), 518–523.

26

Assessing the Literacy of Young Children: The Case for Multiple Forms of Evidence

❖

TERRY SALINGER

Assessment of young children's literacy may be one of the most controversial topics in early-childhood education. It generates debate among teachers, parents, administrators, and researchers, and the debate is often impassioned, as Johnston and Rogers (this volume) clearly describe. Rather than add heat to the debate, this chapter seeks to lay out issues concerning early literacy assessment in an objective and broad-ranging way and to suggest how the favored approach, classroom-based assessments, can be improved.

Weighing in on the debate, the National Educational Goals Panel (NEGP; 1998) has suggested the following four primary purposes for assessing young children; they provide a valuable guide for thinking about both traditional tests and classroom-based assessments:

1. Assessing to promote children's learning and development.
2. Identifying children for health and special services.
3. Monitoring trends and evaluating programs and services.
4. Assessing academic achievement to hold individual students, teachers, and schools accountable.

On the surface, it would seem that the NEGP is placing its imprimatur on wide-scale testing. This is not the case at all; instead, it is trying to balance the need for data with the reality of how difficult it is to collect valid information about young children. Even though the NGEP's recommendations clearly stress the need for states and local agencies to gather information for monitoring children's living and social conditions, they also propose clear restrictions on testing of young learners. Other than testing individual children who seem at risk for referral to special services, formal testing should be done only to ensure appropriate levels of health, vision, and hearing. Observation should be the primary means of assessing children's learning and development until age 5, when "teachers [begin to] use both formal and informal assessment to plan and guide instruction" (NEGP, 1998, p. 21). For purpose three, monitoring trends and evaluating programs and services, direct and indirect measures are recommended to evaluate pre-kindergarten programs but are "not accurate enough to make high-stakes decisions about individual children" (NEGP, 1998, p. 20). Assessment of 5-year-olds is appropriate for monitoring trends; but matrix sampling, rather than testing of all children, should be used, and assessments should be administered periodically rather than every year. Essentially, these recommendations acknowledge the need to gather certain kinds of information but seek to end the frenzy of overtesting of young children. Purpose 4, assessing for accountability, provides the clearest statement of condemnation of excessive testing in the early grades:

> Before age 8, standardized achievement measures are not sufficiently accurate to be used for high-stakes decisions about individual children and schools. Therefore, high-stakes assessments intended for accountability purposes should be delayed until the end of third grade (or preferably fourth grade). (NEGP, 1998, p. 21)

The NEGP envisions an idealized world in which observant parents, caregivers, and teachers can provide information about children's academic progress with minimal use of formal measures. Even though observation may suit the needs of classroom teachers, other "stakeholders" concerned with children's learning are far too hungry for information to wait for grade 3 or 4 to collect "hard" data on individual students. School administrators, many parents, and decision makers want information to judge the success of students, teachers, and schools locally and to compare local results against state and national norms. This hunger for information has likely increased dependence on testing—and the parallel interest in classroom-based alternatives to traditional testing approaches.

Early childhood educators distrust standardized measures of early literacy (National Association for the Education of Young Children, 1988; Shepard, 1991, 1994, 1997); (see also Johnston & Rogers, this volume). Part of the frustration with early literacy assessments may stem from a hope that one assessment can be found to serve all purposes and inform all audiences. Such an instrument would satisfy the need to gather information quickly and efficiently with relatively little interruption to instruction. Attempts to find this one, ideal assessment have led state education agencies to develop their own tests. In addition, many testing companies have been motivated to provide new item types and to offer special services to education agencies that adopt their tests. (Farr, 1992). Recently, testing companies have added open-ended items to reading tests; children as early as grade 1 may now encounter both multiple-choice and con-

structed-response questions about the "passages" they read on standardized tests. Even when these "passages" are drawn from "authentic" sources, the context in which children read, think, and write is still that of a standardized test with all that it signifies.

To "customize" nationally normed tests, testing companies provide criterion-referenced interpretations of test results, specialized reports for parents, highly individualized score reports, and instructional material to help teachers "understand" how their curricular approach is reflected in a test given nationwide (Farr, 1992). Testing companies can document their tests' alignment with local and state standards so that tests such as the Harcourt Brace Educational Measurement's Stanford-9 and CTB-McGraw-Hill's Terra Nova (see Appendix 26.1) can be featured as integral parts of state or local reform efforts. However, customization of testing programs for state-level assessment, especially as part of a reform effort, has been shown to be less effective than anticipated. Large-scale assessment programs in North Carolina, Kentucky, and Arizona, which included literacy measures, were expected to motivate change in curriculum and instruction. Studies of these efforts have suggested that the tests did not provide teachers with enough guidance to bring about change, and, in Arizona especially, not enough professional development was provided to increase teachers' capacity to meet curricular mandates (Valencia & Wixson, 1999).

Customization or local development of traditional, standardized tests has not alleviated concern about the inappropriateness of tests as measures of young children's literacy development. In fact, the reverse has been true. Teachers are often encouraged to "teach to the tests" used to evaluate their students, especially if the tests are "aligned" to local standards. This practice potentially narrows the conceptualization of emergent literacy that defines teachers' instructional program and can be especially disheartening to teachers who have worked to develop a constructivist approach to early literacy learning. Teachers' realization of the mismatch between what and how their students are learning and the means by which their progress is tracked has led to a search for alternative, classroom-based assessment methods. These methods, which are discussed herein, are reasoned to provide assessment in situations that mirror the texts children read and the tasks they perform as part of their regular school literacy experiences.

It is unlikely that even the harshest critic of reading tests for young children would deny the need for information about learners' progress. But justifiable questions can be asked about the kinds of information that is gathered. Standardized measures of early reading are frequently faulted for providing information that emphasizes primarily what children need "to improve" as a reader; hence, they reflect a deficit model. Test manufacturers would counter this argument by pointing to reports that "profile" student strengths and weaknesses on numerous subcomponents of reading and possibly writing. Even if the profiles seek to present a compensatory model ("children are good in this, less good in this . . ."), deficits will undoubtedly draw more attention than strengths. A focus on deficits defies what is known about reading growth, that is, that it is impossible to find single elements or subsets of elements that are the cause of children's potential reading difficulties (Stanovich, 1984).

Further, it is the very sense of reading achievement as the accumulation of component skills that is problematic. As children learn to read and write, they progress along a developmental trajectory that includes acquisition of knowledge about literacy and numerous skills and strategies. The most valuable information is *where* children are on that trajectory, a perspective on literacy growth that cannot be provided by reports of discrete skills that have or have not been mastered.

Standardized tests are usually administered once a year. Producing a single measure of achievement is less problematic than that the measure itself may be seriously flawed. Children may do poorly on a standardized test because they find the tasks strange and inaccessible; the test then measures their confusion rather than their skills. They may do poorly because they have been asked to sit still longer than they are able; this can be especially true if a reading test is part of a larger test battery. They may do poorly because the test emphasizes microlevel tasks, such as letter–sound correspondence, and their strength is in using context clues to construct meaning from text. Situations such as these increase the error of measurement in the reports on how children have done on these tests. Their scores can be thought of as "noisy" or flawed because the tests have been influenced by extraneous variables such as confusion or disengagement. The data reported by a standardized test may also be seriously flawed simply because it is old. Results may not be reported to parents or teachers until months after the test administration, and children may have progressed far beyond the picture presented of their achievement. Even for accountability purposes, data that are flawed for individual students skew the representation of group status.

If standardized tests can be so problematic as measures of young children's reading and writing, why is their use so prevalent? Standardized tests are an efficient way to provide administrators, policymakers, concerned parents, and the public at large with normative data to facilitate comparisons of local students to students nationwide. This is, of course, a comparison derived from quantitative, not qualitative, data and is devoid of information about instructional programs or the context of students' lives.

Standardized tests also come with a tacit "guarantee" that they have been developed through according to rigorous professional standards (American Educational Research Association [AERA], American Psychological Association [APA], and National Council on Measurement in Education [NCME], 1999). This "guarantee" speaks to the needs of administrators and policymakers, if not to those of teachers, to put confidence in the tests and the data they yield. Basic tenets of sound test development have been followed so that tests measure what they say they are measuring (test validity) and do so reliably. It is assumed that items have been pilot-tested and refined prior to inclusion on an operational test, and data analyses and subsequent reporting will be objective and accurate. Appendix 26.1 provides summary tables of some of the most common standardized tests. Data have been gathered from *Buros Mental Measurement Yearbook* (Impara & Plake, 1998) and from analysis of actual test material.

Even though the NEGP advises against using standardized measures before grade 3 or 4, it is unlikely that they will disappear from the educational landscape. Policymakers and many other stakeholders consider standardized tests too important as valid, reliable, objective measures of reading progress, and test companies continue to try to respond to criticisms with innovative approaches. Farr (1992) even suggests that they can facilitate communication across audiences, especially between parents and decision makers. Understanding what tests contain and how they assess reading is essential for meaningful communication. Table 26.1 provides criteria for analyzing and understanding standardized reading tests for early grades.

The more teachers and other stakeholders understand the standardized tests children take, the more they can interpret test scores and determine how accurately test scores correspond to their own interpretation of students' progress. This is especially important when test scores seem out of line with classroom-based knowledge of students'

reading. In some cases, teachers can identify when required tests have measured skills and strategies that students have not yet mastered; in other cases, discrepancies may have more subtle causation. Although many of the concerns voiced about standardized tests refer to their inappropriateness for low income and minority children and English-language learners, Snow, Burns, and Griffin (1998), in *Preventing Reading Difficulties in Young Children,* cite the example of children whose scores are high enough to mask their potential reading problems. They refer to schools, often those serving affluent communities, where the distribution of scores is higher than the national norm.

> Many of the poorer readers (relative to their classmates) at such a school will not earn scores that are below a [locally-designated] cut point . . . based on the national average. Nevertheless, their teachers, parents, and communities consider these children to have real reading difficulties because their achievement is considerably lower than that of their classmates, despite equivalent schooling. (p. 94)

TABLE 26.1. Evaluating Standardized Tests

1. Is there evidence of test validity? Is it adequate?
2. Were norming procedures adequate? For example, was the test normed against an appropriate population?
3. Is there evidence of adequate reliability?
4. How will the test be scored? How will scores be reported?
5. What is the purpose of the test? Is it congruent with local purposes?
6. Is testing time appropriate for young children? Is the test divided into testing sessions in an appropriate way?
7. Do timing and tasks seem developmentally appropriate?
8. How are scores calculated? Will information be useful to teachers, parents, others? What do score reports tell about students?
9. How are reading and writing represented in the tests?
   - How much text do students read?
   - Is the text in individual words and phrases or in continuous prose?
   - Are the texts presented similar to those students usually read?
   - Are reading tasks similar to what students do in class? For example, are there tasks such as decoding nonsense words rather than "real" reading?
   - Are illustrations used? Are they clear and recognizable?
10. What is the focus of the test? What is the balance of item types?
    - Phonemic awareness
    - Alphabet recognition
    - Phoneme–grapheme correspondence
    - Syllables, words, phrases, sentences, paragraphs
    - Real versus nonsense words
    - Responding to pictures, as in identifying beginning sounds when cued by pictures
    - Spelling, grammar, and other basic language skills
    - Reading for comprehension in continuous text
    - Reading for specific information in content-area material

This situation speaks to what may perhaps be the most serious problem with standardized tests: They are often considered to be the single or at least the most important determinant of students' achievement. This practice defies the standards of the testing industry (AERA, APA, & NCME, 1999) and of groups such as the International Reading Association and the National Council of Teachers of English (1994). No decisions should be made about students based on one piece of evidence, especially evidence that can be so imprecise as a young child's score on a standardized test. Multiple forms of evidence or documentation are essential for sound decision making at both the instructional and the policy level, but for decisions to be accurate, the "evidence" must be of the highest quality.

Classroom-Based Assessment Systems

From the awareness of the need for multiple forms of evidence and from dissatisfaction with standardized tests has emerged the current interest in classroom-based assessment. This kind of assessment can be thought of in numerous ways. One form of classroom-based assessment serves primarily an internal purpose, what Calfee (1987) refers to as "evaluation of individual student performance, based on the teacher's decisions about curriculum and instruction at the classroom level, aimed toward the students' grasp of concepts and mastery of transferable skills" (p. 738). A second form of classroom-based assessment is represented by school-, district-, or state-wide systems that formalize procedures and seek to gather data that can serve classroom needs and can also be aggregated for external uses. Assessment systems in South Brunswick, New Jersey (Salinger & Chittenden, 1994), Bellevue, Washington (Valencia & Place, 1994), Cambridge, Massachusetts (Stuart, 1999), and Philadelphia, Pennsylvania (Chester, Maraschiello, & Salinger, 2000) exemplify local variations. New York (New York State Department of Education, 1999) and Michigan (Michigan Department of Education, 1998) have adopted similar systems as state-wide approaches to early literacy assessment.

A third form of classroom-based assessments are programs such as the Work Sampling System (Dichtelmiller) and the Primary Language Record (Falk, 1998). These approaches provide teachers with specific activities and protocols to use to gather information about children's progress. The Work Sampling System (Dichtelmiller et al., 1994) depends on developmental checklists in all subject areas, whereas the Primary Language Record helps teachers gather information about literacy growth. Both systems are marketed commercially.

Locally developed classroom-based literacy assessment systems have many common characteristics. Most draw on the theoretical perspective and research of Clay (1985), Holdaway (1979), and Sulzby (1991; Teale & Sulzby, 1986), who stress the social and constructivist nature of emergent literacy. Teachers offer tasks that invite children to show what they know and can do in situations that are similar to their everyday classroom activities. Thus, tasks such as Concepts about Print Test (Clay 1985), running records (Clay, 1985), story retellings (Morrow, 1988), invented spelling tests, and analysis of collections of student writing predominate. These tasks may be supplemented by anecdotal records, vocabulary or sight-word lists, self-assessments (McKenna & Kear, 1999), motivation inventories (Gambrell et al., 1999), and other tasks or inventories (Parker et al., 1999).

Data are collected throughout the year to provide a full profile of children's literacy growth. Classroom-based assessments allow teachers to document the range of skills and strategies students are acquiring as they learn to read and write and to gather extensive documentation of how students are orchestrating their emerging skills. Work is often kept in a portfolio and travels with children from grade to grade. Table 26.2 lists tasks proposed for the Philadelphia early literacy assessment system. They are representative of other, similar systems.

In theory, classroom-based assessments should provide a comprehensive picture of achievement and should profile students' strengths as they progress along a learning continuum (Valencia, 1997). Standardized tests suffer in comparison to classroom methods because they measure students' learning at one particular time, are rarely reflective of classroom situations, and may limit the "construct" or definition of read-

TABLE 26.2. Proposed Philadelphia K–3 Literacy Assessment

Activity	Literacy aspects assessed/observed	Model of administration	Overlap with other assessments	Comments
			Foundation abilities	
Concepts of print	Familiarity with book handling skills; purposes for reading; vocabulary of instruction	Individual	Observed in "book walks" and as children handle books	Without these basic concepts, reading progress is severely delayed.
			Prerequisite skills survey activities	
Alphabet knowledge survey	Letter recognition	Individual		These assessment tasks serve as initial screens to ensure that students possess the skills and understandings needed for reading growth. If students continue to demonstrate lack of understanding, additional diagnostic screening should be used. It is likely that these will be used *only once* for many students.
Rhyme Awareness Activity	Phonemic awareness	Small group		
			Operational use of skills and strategies	
Monster spelling test	Phonemic awareness/letter–sound correspondence	Group	Spelling observed in the context of writing activities	Consider possibility of extending use by adding additional words for advanced students: Propose to add a Spanish version.
Sight word activity	Orchestration of prerequisite skills; ability to read familiar words; decoding	Individual	Writing activities	Consider adding additional words for advanced students.
Story retelling	Listening comprehension; familiarity with story structure; ability to recall, select, organize, summarize information	Individual	Oral language; reading comprehension	Story retellings provide a quick, valid assessment of how thoroughly students have understood a text.
Running record	Reading rate and fluency; pacing in oral reading; accuracy of decoding strategies; comprehension as indicated by orchestration of text and answers to questions	Individual	Story retelling; reading comprehension	Running records provide information about decoding, pacing, and rate, all of which correlate with comprehension. Teachers record deviations from text as child reads orally.

(continued)

TABLE 26.2. cont.

Activity	Literacy aspects assessed/observed	Model of administration	Overlap with other assessments	Comments
			Operational use of skills and strategies (*cont.*)	
Reading comprehension	Comprehension; ability to orchestrate emergent and developing reading skills	Individual	Story retelling; writing	The Reading Comprehension task is the most comprehensive in that students read silently and (possibly) orally, retell the story, and answer questions. They should find the task challenging enough to require them to use multiple reading strategies. A written product may be generated.
Writing assessments	Orchestration of prerequisite skills; familiarity with story structure and conventions of writing; syntax; vocabulary	Individual	Measures of reading, spelling reflected in writing	A minimum of 12 samples should be collected each year; some samples may be collected as part of reading tasks or content area work.
On-demand tasks	Reading comprehension; problem solving; research and organization skills; writing	Individual scores; may be collaborative tasks	Reading comprehension; writing	These performance assessment tasks take 45–90 minutes to complete and are multidisciplinary.
			Surveys/affective measures	
Oral language survey	Facility with oral language	Checklist format		This may be an indicator of need for further testing.
Literacy survey	Students' out-of-school experiences	Individual or student-completed		Surveys help teachers ascertain students' understandings about literacy and ways to engage them in learning.

ing that is being assessed by sampling only small portions of the entire range of skills and strategies children acquire. The ways in which children can orchestrate complex skills can be fully reflected in classroom-based assessments that gather data over time. Information gathered through classroom-based measures can have immediate utility for teachers and more meaning for parents than do standardized tests scores.

But classroom-based assessments are not always the panacea they are supposed to be. From a measurement perspective, there is little research about the validity and reliability of classroom-based assessment measures. The local nature and relative newness of some of the assessment systems may well explain this lack of data. Chitttenden (Bridgeman, Chittenden, & Cline, 1995; Chittenden & Spicer, 1993) has documented the effectiveness of the South Brunswick, New Jersey, Early Literacy Portfolio, but his validity studies were conducted after the system had been instantiated for several years. Chittenden has also pointed out the challenges of aggregating teacher-collected data for use beyond the classroom.

Some of the challenges of implementing a classroom-based assessment system stem from the very enthusiasm with which classroom teachers have embraced the idea of becoming what Johnston (1987) called evaluation experts. Both Chittenden (1991) and Engel (1990) have written about three levels of assessment: "checking up" on a frequent basis, collecting primary data, and collecting quantified information about individuals and groups. Chittenden refers to level two as "keeping track" and level three as "finding out." Engel contends that the third level of assessment—quantifying data—is less interesting to teachers than collecting information at the two previous levels. In Engel's model, level-three data include class summaries and other information abstracted from the "keeping track" process. Engel's contention means that teachers may not become vested in collecting the kinds of systematic data needed for external purposes such as accountability. There is a logic to Engel's argument that is difficult to refute, but helping teachers to understand that classroom-based data must be collected in systematic, standardized ways is essential if an assessment system is to be taken seriously. Becoming an "evaluation expert" means taking on new levels of responsibility, new roles that standardized tests never imposed.

Further, when assessments serve the dual purpose of internal recordkeeping and external reporting, they must have the technical rigor to yield data worth aggregating to the class, school, and cluster level. Thus, the instruments serve a "keeping track" function and also provide data for external decision making about individuals, for evaluating classes, and ultimately for evaluating schools and programs.

Developing Classroom-Based Assessment Systems

When individual schools or state or local education agencies undertake the development of a classroom-based assessment system, they assume a challenge that is far more complex and nuanced than selecting a standardized test to measure early literacy achievement. Valencia, Hiebert, and Afflerbach (1994) detail many such endeavors and highlight the diversity of projects that situate assessment responsibility in the classroom. To extrapolate common experiences from programs such as those described by Valencia et al. (1994) and other ambitious early literacy programs is a worthwhile exercise, especially if these assessment systems are analyzed in terms of their validity and reliability. Validity refers to the accuracy of an assessment in measuring what it purported to measure and the extent to which interpretations of assessment data can be supported by independent evidence. Reliability refers to degree to which an assessment will produce consistent measurements across different administrations or contexts. These contexts include the extent to which different evaluators will interpret classroom-based evidence in the same way.

Determining Validity

In a well-designed test, items can be mapped back to the test blueprint or description of how the test will measure the underlying construct. For a classroom-based assessment system to be valid, it too must show clearly how instrumentation maps back to underlying constructs. The teachers who become "evaluation experts" (Johnston, 1987) must understand not only this mapping but also the constructs themselves.

Developers of the Michigan Early Literacy Assessment have stressed that their project started "with a vision" of what they want their assessment to do and what they wanted to measure (Michigan Department of Education, 1998; Weber, 1999). Teachers and administrators in the South Brunswick, New Jersey, wanted assessments that would reflect changes in their early literacy curriculum (Chittenden & Spicer, 1993). In Philadelphia, assessment work was preceded by the creation of a balanced literacy framework (School District of Philadelphia, 1999) to initiate instructional change (Chester, Maraschiello, & Salinger, 2000). In assessment terms, developers of these systems had a clear sense of the *constructs* they wanted to measure. They had determined what early reading and writing meant in their context because they had thought deeply about what students should know and be able to do as they grow as literacy users. They recognized the enormity of the construct of emergent literacy and the resultant need for multiple ways to measure its many dimensions. This process sought to ensure the *construct validity* of the assessment systems.

This preliminary step is essential for numerous reasons. At the most practical level, this step can provide extraordinary professional development. As they identify the constructs to be measured, teachers express in concrete terms the benchmarks of early literacy growth and negotiate their views with other professionals to reach consensus on what it means to move along a continuum toward literacy. Often, as in South Brunswick, a developmental continuum or scale is developed to express stages of growth, and this expression itself can go through numerous drafts before it is used as part of an assessment system. (See Table 26.2.)

Identifying the constructs underlying an assessment makes the structure of the assessment public for stakeholders such as parents. As South Brunswick, New Jersey, implemented its Early Literacy Portfolio, it announced to parents,

This method of evaluation not only gives a much broader picture of the whole child, but allows the teachers to track progress over a period of time. The portfolios that are started for the kindergarten child follow him or her straight through second grade. In short, the portfolio gives substance to our contention that we take children wherever they are when they enter our program and move them forward as they become competent readers and writers (South Brunswick, 1992, unpaged).

Knowing how children will be evaluated is important to parents, but the information is even more valuable when parents know the behaviors that constitute the evaluation. Standardized test reports to parents may try to be informative, but they frequently fall short in communicating in language parents can understand. When teachers can talk about the constructs on which children are assessed, when parents can read about them, and when assessment documentation such as running record forms are referenced directly back to the constructs, parents understand more fully what their children are learning. They are then in a far better position to support the school's efforts in what they do at home.

Yet the developers of classroom-based assessment may limit the constructs of their system by inadvertently placing ceilings on children's achievement. This can happen in several ways. For example, assessments often set aside "benchmark" or secure books to ensure that children have a "cold" read during the assessment. Unless these books are challenging enough to offer children semantic and syntactic problems to solve, they will not provide adequate measures of developing comprehension skills. Reading scores will be inflated. Children who are rated as strong readers in books at their recreational level may in fact need instruction in the strategies that allow them to learn from their reading. The writing requirements for a writing portfolio may be so formulaic that children are never asked to show how they can cope with complex rhetorical devices. In addition, the words included in a sight-word list may be so familiar that they assess children's memory rather than their decoding skills. Whereas gauging the extent of children's sight words is important, so too is a measure of how well children can marshal decoding skills independent of the contextual cues of reading. Teachers who argue that including challenging words on a sight-word list because it may lead to flash-card drill and practice or who reject measures of phonemic awareness as part of an early literacy assessment system (Chester, Maraschiello, & Salinger, 2000) often reveal their lack of understanding about assessment for use beyond the classroom walls.

A primary goal of classroom-based assessments is to ask hard questions about children's achievement to determine the upper limits of what they know and can do. Finding out what they *cannot* do and what they *have not yet* learned does not represent a deficit model of assessment. Rather, it shows the extent to which a classroom-based system can be a powerful assessment mechanism. The power rests in revealing a full picture of students' growth—including aspects of literacy learning that have not yet been mastered. If the underlying construct of a classroom-based assessment system is a developmental one, then measurement precision accrues from placing each student accurately on a developmental continuum so that his or her trajectory in literacy learning can be better understood and directed.

The process of articulating the underlying constructs of a classroom-based system helps to ensure that the assessment system will have *face validity*. When teachers say that they do not like a standardized test because it is not aligned with what and how they teach, they are saying that they disagree with the constructs on which the test is constructed; the test lacks face validity. These constructs are usually more limited than the holistic view of emergent literacy most teachers understand; this is one of the major failings of standardized tests as measures of beginning reading and writing. Emphasizing the social nature of early literacy learning also enhances face validity. Activities and tasks look like what goes on in the classroom and ask teachers and students to interact in ways that are similar to routine literacy instruction. Strong face validity can make teachers view classroom-based assessment systems as valuable, worth their time and effort, and worth the time their students spend being assessed.

What can weaken the face validity of these systems, however, is the burden of collecting information on individual students. Johnston (1987) wisely comments that "simple classroom management skills are part of evaluation expertise. Without a well managed classroom in which children have learned to work independently, a teacher cannot step back from instruction and watch the class as a whole, or work uninterrupted with particular individuals" (p. 745). Herein lies a major dilemma in classroom-based assessment and a subtle irony. Standardized tests are quick to administer; classroom-based assessments are not, especially if they seek to gather valid data that can be aggregated for external use. Assessment tasks are similar to but must be more than routine classroom activities. Significant amounts of evidence must be collected to support students' scores, evidence from tasks that are not so trivial as to be inconsequential or so ambitious as to disrupt classroom life. They must be administered at numerous times during the year in systematic, standard ways, and they must produce credible, unambiguous evidence.

But who assigns the scores to the collected pieces of evidence? And how valid will the scores be? In South Brunswick, Philadelphia, New York State, and other locales, teachers analyze student evidence to determine placement on a developmental continuum or set of scales (see Table 26.3). In the best of situations, accuracy of this assignment accrues from teachers' understanding of the constructs of the assessment, the levels of the developmental continuum, and the multiple ways students can demonstrate achievement. When assessments serve a classroom-level purpose, teachers will undoubtedly use contextual knowledge to supplement what student evidence says about performance. Teachers want their students to do well, for the sake of their students and for their own sake as well. When assessments serve an external purpose as well, scores or placement on a continuum must be reliable and objective. Here, reliability means that someone familiar with the constructs of the assessment but unfamiliar with individual children will be able to interpret student evidence in the same way as the classroom teacher. To reinforce the need for precise and objective scoring, many assessment systems use trained, external scorers who do not know the children to sec-

TABLE 26.3. K–2 Reading/Writing Scale: Development of Children's Strategies for Making Sense of Print

0—N/A

1—Early Emergent

Displays an awareness of some conventions of writing, such as front/back of books, distinctions between print and pictures. See the construction of meaning from text as "magical" or exterior to the print. Though the child may be interested in the contents of books, there is as yet little apparent attention to turning written marks into language. Is beginning to notice environmental print.

2—Advanced Emergent

Engages in pretend reading and writing. Uses reading-like ways that clearly approximate book language. Demonstrates a sense of story being "read," using picture clues and recall of story line. May draw on predictable language patterns in anticipating (and recalling) the story. Attempts to use letters in writing, sometimes in random or scribble fashion.

3—Early Beginning Reader

Attempts to "really read." Indicates beginning sense of one-to-one correspondence and concept of word. Predicts actively in new material, using syntax and story line. Small, stable sight vocabulary is becoming established. Evidence of initial awareness of beginning and ending sounds, especially in invented spelling.

4—Advanced Beginning Reader

Starts to draw on major cue systems; self-corrects or identifies words through use of letter–sound patterns, sense of story, or syntax. Reading may be laborious especially with new material, requiring considerable effort and some support. Writing and spelling reveal awareness of letter patterns and conventions of writing such as capitalization and full stops.

5—Early Independent Reader

Handles familiar material on own but still needs some support with unfamiliar material. Figures out words and self-corrects by drawing on a combination of letter–sound relationships, word structure, story line, and syntax. Strategies of rereading or of guessing from larger chunks of texts are becoming well established. Has a large, stable sight vocabulary. Conventions of writing are understood.

6—Advanced Independent Reader

Reads independently, using multiple strategies flexibly. Monitors and self-corrects for meaning. Can read and understand most material when the content is appropriate. Conventions of writing and spelling are—for the most part—under control.

Note. The scale focuses on development of children's strategies for making sense of print. Evidence concerning children's strategies and knowledge about print may be revealed in both their reading and writing activities. The scale does not attempt to rate children's interests or attitudes regarding reading, nor does it attempt to summarize what literature may mean to the child. Such aspects of children's literacy development are summarized in other forms. Rating scale developed by South Brunswick teachers and ETS staff, January, 1991.

ond-score the collected work of a sample of students. Second-scoring produces measures of interrater reliability; that is, it checks on how accurately classroom teachers have scored their own students' collected work. If individual teachers seem to be too easy or too harsh, their scores can be recalculated for use outside their classrooms, and they can be retrained to better understand assessment procedures. High levels of interrated reliability have been reported in South Brunswick (Bridgeman, Chittenden, & Cline, 1995) and in New York State (Falk,

Ort, & Moirs, 1999). In New York State, however, each collection, not just a sample, of student work is scored twice, a cost that may be prohibitive to many districts wishing to undertake a large-scale classroom-based assessment system.

Mounting a large-scale classroom-based assessment system is a costly undertaking, not just in terms of scoring. Developing such a system involves major efforts at consensus building so that the constructs to be assessed are understood and universally valued. Thus, construct validity is established.

Early literacy curriculum must be analyzed to ensure that teaching and assessment are compatible; this warrants content validity. In addition, assessment tasks must be developed to high technical standards and thoroughly pilot tested. In Philadelphia, early literacy tasks were pilot-tested to determine that grade-level designations were appropriate (Chester, Maraschiello, & Salinger, 2000). Pilot test results strongly suggested that tasks developers had anticipated to be too easy for third-grade students were in fact needed in numerous third grades. Secure, "benchmark" books leveled according to Fountas and Pinnell (1999) were in fact not challenging enough for other third-grade students and had to be supplemented with other texts. This kind of thorough pilot testing is rare.

The process of devising an assessment system provides valuable, hands-on professional development. Implementing the system demands even more extensive professional development as teachers learn how assessment tasks differ from routine classroom practice, how to manage their time to assess individuals, and how to score their students' work. The process of second-scoring selected student collections again offers professional development opportunities of great value. Researchers studying the New York State Early Literacy Profile (Falk, Ort, & Moirs, 1999) used teacher surveys to determine the value of the assessment system. They found the following:

> [B]y asking teachers to look at evidence of student learning (as it is manifested in student work) in relation to standards (as described in the Profile scales), teachers perceive themselves to have increased their knowledge of individual students, to have become better informed about the capacities of their students in relation to literacy progress, and to have received guidance about what they need to do next to support the forward development of their students. (Falk et al., 1999, pp. 40–41).

Professional development efforts must continue after initial implementation of a classroom-based assessment system because classroom-based assessment systems are neither self-evident nor self-sustaining. Ongoing efforts can help teachers refine their procedural understanding of the system and concomitantly hone their skills as interpreters of student literacy behavior. These efforts are essential because the presence of a classroom-based assessment system alone will not be enough to sustain instructional change and improvement. For example, in one extensive study researchers (Shepard et al., 1996) found that introducing a performance-based assessment system revealed that even though teachers knew about the curricular frameworks to which the assessments were aligned, instruction was not congruent with the frameworks. Thus, professional development efforts designed to introduce the new assessments had to be refocused toward instructional change. The researchers concluded that long-term professional development was needed to support both instruction and assessment innovation.

Salinger and Chittenden (1994) found that teachers in South Brunswick cited the need for ongoing professional development and focused efforts for new teachers as missing elements in the implementation over time of the Early Literacy Portfolio. Some teachers in South Brunswick expressed resentment that the system has been imposed on them by a small group of "insiders" without enough district-wide input (Salinger, 1996). In Philadelphia, the design of the Balanced Early Literacy Framework and initial work on the assessment system were undertaken by a small cohort of enthusiastic teachers who became very knowledgeable about emergent literacy principles. Implementation of the assessment system required extending knowledge and enthusiasm far beyond this central core to teachers in under-resourced schools with high student mobility (Chester, Marschiello, & Salinger, 2000). The professional development challenge inherent in introducing a classroom-based assessment system is far different in a city such as Philadelphia with 22 distinct clusters from that in a district such as South Brunswick with 7 elementary schools.

The successful implementation of a new assessment system is accompanied by comprehensive professional development that addresses several dimensions of early literacy instruction and assessment. The hard work of those individuals who developed the conceptual framework of the assessment must be transmitted in understandable ways to the teachers who will implement the assessment in their classrooms. Teachers must become knowledgeable about and take ownership of the constructs being assessed, master the instructional practices inherent in these constructs, and also learn the procedures for administering and scoring classroom-based tasks. In some ways, teachers are being asked to "take a closer look" (Hayward & Spencer, 1996; Hoffman et al., 1996) at their students than they have traditionally done: They must interpret students' responses to relatively standardized tasks and make inferences from what they see and hear. Teachers have to become data gatherers in a context that may be new to them. The validity of their inferences will rest not on their enthusiasm for the assessment system (although that is valuable) but on their understanding of the way the system reflects emergent literacy principles. Interpretations that are imprecise, superficial, or faulty about one assessment task may be ameliorated by accuracy on other tasks, but too much dependence on a compensatory scoring system will weaken the validity of the system as a whole.

Successful implementation of a classroom-based assessment system can have far-reaching effects on the early instructional childhood program. These effects are often termed "consequential validity." Collecting information systematically provides teachers a scaffold method to learn to "take a closer" look. Scoring collected evidence according to specific guidelines pushes teachers beyond their usual intuitive interpretation of what they observe. Teacher change—in practice and in belief—can accrue from professional development focused on the theoretical underpinnings of the system. Researchers studying the consequential validity of the South Brunswick Early Literacy Portfolio (Jones & Chittenden, 1995; Salinger & Chittenden, 1994) found evidence of such change among many teachers who had participated in the portfolio project. Teachers cited specific benefits, especially of their use of the Early Literacy Rating Scale. Four benefits were most striking:

1. Highlighting patterns of development among children;
2. Confirming or enhancing the process of review of student work;
3. Strengthening communication with others;
4. Supporting instructional decisions; and
5. Building consensus and common language.

But change can be superficial unless infrastructure is created to give teachers time and support to learn not only how to administer the assessment system skillfully but also how to mine its results to the fullest. Classroom-based assessments yield huge quantities of rich, descriptive data. Learning to quantify data reliably is one aspect of implementing the system, but it does not speak to consequential validity. Only deeply instantiated change will attest to consequential validity, and evidence of this level of change many not be readily apparent until long after a system is put in place. Interim evidence of change as teachers and students learn to live with the system reinforce its importance. Yet even small levels of change will not be sustained without ongoing, intense professional development. Research on school reform attests to the need for such support, and only with focused, ongoing support can classroom-based assessment of literacy fulfill its role as the agent for reform that both enhances teaching and learning and replaces more traditional measures of literacy growth.

References

American Educational Research Association, American Psychological Association, & National Council on Measurement in Education (1999). *Standards for educational and psychological testing.* Washington: American Educational Research Association.

Bridgeman, B., Chittenden, E., & Cline, F. (1995). *Characteristics of a portfolio scale for rating early literacy.* Princeton, NJ: Educational Testing Center.

Calfee, R. C. (1987). The classroom as a context for assessment of literacy. *The Reading Teacher, 40,* 738–743.

Cambridge, Massachusetts, Public Schools. (1999). *Continuum for writing.* Cambridge, MA: Office of Early Childhood Education.

Chittenden, E. (1991). Authentic assessment, evaluation, and documentation of student performance. In V. Perrone (Ed.), *Expanding student assessment* (pp. 22–32). Alexandria, VA: Association for Supervision and Curriculum Development.

Chittenden, E., & Spicer, W. (1993). *The South*

Brunswick literacy portfolio project. Paper prepared for the New Standards Project, English Language Arts Portfolio Meeting, Minneapolis, MN.

Clay, M. M. (1985). *The early detection of reading difficulties (3rd ed.)*. Auckland, New Zealand: Heinemann.

Clay, M. M. (1979). *Reading: The patterning of complex behaviours*. Auckland, New Zealand: Heinemann.

Dichtelmiller, M. L., Jablon, J. R., Dorfman, A. B., Masden, D. B., & Meisels, S. J. (1994). *The work sampling system: Teacher's manual*. Ann Arbor, MI: Rebus Planning Associates, Inc..

Engel, B. (1990) An approach to assessment in early literacy. In C. Kamii (Ed.), *Achievement testing in the early grades: The games adults play* (pp. 119–134). Washington, DC: National Association for the Education of Young Children.

Falk, B. (1998). Using direct evidence to assess student progress: How the Primary Language Record supports teaching and learning. In C. Harrison & T. Salinger (Eds.), *Assessing reading I: Theory and practice* (pp. 152–165). London: Routledge.

Falk, B., Ort, S. W., & Moirs, K. (1999, April 19–23). *Using classroom-based assessment on a large scale: Support and reporting on student learning with the Early Literacy Profile*. Paper presented at the annual meeting of the American Educational Research Association, Montreal, Quebec, Canada.

Farr, R. (1992). Putting it all together: Solving the reading assessment puzzle. *The Reading Teacher, 46*(1), 26–37.

Fountas, I. C., & Pinnell, G. S. (1999). *Matching books to readers: Using leveled books in guided reading, K–3*. Portsmouth, NH: Heinemann.

Gambrell, L., Palmer, B. M., Codling, R., & Mazzoni, S. A. (1999). Assessing motivation to read. In S. J. Barrentine (Ed.), *Reading assessment: Principles and practices for elementary teachers* (pp. 215–232). Newark DE: International Reading Association.

Hayward, L., & Spencer, E. (1989). Taking a closer look: A Scottish perspective on reading assessment. In C. Harrison & T. Salinger (Eds.), *Assessing reading I: Theory and practice* (pp. 1136–1151). London: Routledge

Hoffman, J., Roser, N., & Worthy, J. (1989). Challenging the assessment context for literacy instruction in first grade: A collaborative study. In C. Harrison & T. Salinger (Eds.), *Assessing reading I: Theory and practice* (pp. 166–181). London: Routledge.

Holdaway, D. (1979). *The foundations of literacy*. Sydney, Australia: Ashton Scholastic.

International Reading Association & National Council of Teachers of English. (1994). *Standards for the assessment of reading and writing*. Newark, DE: Authors.

Johnson, P. (1987). Teachers as evaluation experts. *The Reading Teacher, 40*, 744–748.

Jones, J., & Chittenden, E. (1995). *Teachers percep-* *tions of rating an early literacy portfolio*. Princeton, NJ: Educational Testing Service.

McKenna, M. C., & Kear, D. J. (1999). Measuring attitude toward reading: A new tool for teachers. In S. J. Barrentine (Ed.), *Reading assessment: Principles and practices for elementary teachers* (pp. 199–214). Newark DE: International Reading Association.

Michigan Department of Education. (1998). *Michigan in literacy progress portfolio*. East Lansing, MI: Author.

Morrow, L. M. (1988). Retelling stories as a diagnostic tool. In S. M. Glazer, L. W. Searfoss, & L. M. Gentile (Eds.), *Reexamining reading diagnosis: New trends and procedures* (pp. 128–149). Newark, DE: International Reading Association.

National Association for the Education of Young Children. (1988). NAEYC position statement on standardized testing of young children 3–8 years of age. *Young Children, 43*(3), 42–47.

National Educational Goals Panel. (1989). *Principles and recommendations for early childhood assessment*. Washington DC: Author.

National Research Council. (1998). *Preventing reading difficulties in young children*. Washington, DC: National Academy Press.

New York State Department of Education. (1999). *Early literacy profile*. Albany, NY: Author.

Parker, E. L., Armengol, R., Brooke, L. B., Carper, K. R., Cronin, S. M., Denman, A. C., Irwin, P., McGunnigle, J., Pardine, T., & Kurtz, N. P. (1999). Teachers' choices in classroom assessment. In S. J. Barrentine (Ed.), *Reading assessment: Principles and practices for elementary teachers* (pp. 68–72). Newark DE: International Reading Association.

Salinger, T. (1998). Consequential validity of an early literacy portfolio: The "backwash" of reform. In C. Harrison & T. Salinger (Eds.), *Assessing reading I: Theory and practice* (pp. 182–204). London: Routledge.

Salinger, T., & Chittenden, E. (1994). Analysis of an early literacy portfolio: Consequences for instruction. *Language Arts, 71*, 446–452.

School District of Philadelphia (1999). *The new Balanced Early Literacy Framework for Grades PK–3*. Philadelphia: Author

Shepard, L. A. (1991). The influence of standardized tests on early childhood curriculum, teachers, and children. In B. Spodek & O. N. Saracho (Eds.), *Yearbook in early childhood education* (vol. 2). New York: Teachers College Press.

Shepard, L. A. (1994). The challenges of assessing young children appropriately. *Phi Delta Kappen, 76*(3), 206–213.

Shepard, L. A. (1997). Children not ready to learn? The invalidity of school readiness testing. *Psychology in the Schools, 34*(2), 85–97.

Shepard, L. A., Flexer, R. J., Hieberet, E. H., Marion, S. F., Mayfield, V., & Weston, J. T. (1996). Effects of introducing classroom performance assessments on student learning. *Educational Measurement: Issues and Practice, 15*(3), 7–18.

South Brunswick Township Public Schools (1992).

Early childhood education in South Brunswick schools: A guide for parents and children. South Brunswick, NJ: Author.

Stanovich, K. E. (1984). The interactive–compensatory model of reading: A confluence of developmental, experimental, and educational psychology. *Remedial and Special Education, 5,* 11–19.

Sulzby, E. (1991). Assessment of emergent literacy: Storybook reading. *The Reading Teacher, 44*(7), 498–500.

Teale, W. H., & Sulzby, E. (Eds.). (1986). *Emergent literacy: Writing and reading.* Norwood, NJ: Ablex.

Tierney, R. J. (1999). Literacy assessment reform: Shifting beliefs, principles possibilities, and emerging practices. In S. J. Barrentine (Ed.), *Reading assessment: Principles and practices for elementary teachers* (pp. 10–29). Newark DE: International Reading Association.

Valencia, S. W., Hiebert, E. H., & Afflerbach, P. P. (Eds.), (1994). *Authentic reading assessment: Practices and possibilities.* Newark, DE. International Reading Association.

Valencia, S. W., & Place, N. A. (1994). Literacy portfolios for teaching, learning, and accountability: The Bellevue Literacy Assessment Project. In S. W. Valencia, E. H. Hiebert, & P. P. Afflerbach (Eds.), *Authentic reading assessment: Practices and possibilities* (pp. 134–156). Newark, DE. International Reading Association.

Valencia, S. W., & Wisxon, K. K. (1999). *Policy-oriented research on literacy standards and assessments* (CIERA Report # 3-004). Ann Arbor: University of Michigan Center for the Improvement of Early Reading Achievement.

Assessment	Subtests/skills assessed	Stated purpose	Standardization	Reliability/validity
Analytical Reading Inventory—6th edition (Prentice-Hall)	Oral reading (oral reading errors, fluency, retelling, comprehension); silent reading, retelling, comprehension; listening comprehension (retelling, comprehension). Also measures respondent's processing strategies as print is encountered, estimates respondent's reading levels.	Designed to measure a constellation of skills/abilities believed to comprise total reading ability; recommended primarily for use with students grades 2 through 9; used in classroom settings.	Criterion-referenced	No reliability information reported. Grade-level validation of the reading level of each passage was established through the use of the Spache and the Harris–Jacobson readability formulas and computer analysis of the text. Test authors report that there is evidence of construct validity in both the narrative and expository passages.
Bader Reading and Language Inventory–3rd edition (Prentice-Hall)	Graded word lists (one list per grade, K–12); graded reading passages (oral reading accuracy, silent reading comprehension, and listening comprehension); spelling (phonetic spelling list, nonphonetic spelling list, and spelling list to test knowledge of rules and conventions); visual discrimination (literary concepts, phoneme blending, phoneme segmentation, letter knowledge, hearing letter names in words, and syntax matching); phonics and structural analysis test (initial single consonants, consonant blends, consonant digraphs, short vowel sounds, long vowel sounds, vowel digraphs, reversal, inflectional suffixes, derivational suffixes, prefixes and compound words); semantic and syntactic evaluation (semantic/syntactic cloze test, semantic cloze test, and grammatical cloze test).	Placement of students in instructional material; can also be used as an English as a second language screen.	Criterion-referenced	
Basic Reading Inventory (BRI-7) (Kendall/Hunt)	Graded word naming (decoding skills); oral reading accuracy (miscue analysis); reading comprehension (oral and silent reading through retelling and comprehension items); reading rate. In appendix are other assessments: alphabet knowledge (letter names); literacy knowledge (concepts about print); storytelling (respondent generates a story and story structure is evaluated); auditory discrimination (test of phonology); spelling (mostly high frequency, regular words), phoneme segmentation.		Criterion-referenced	

405

(continued)

Assessment	Subtests/skills assessed	Stated purpose	Standardization	Reliability/validity
Botel Reading Inventory (Modern Curriculum Press)	Four subtests: Decoding (measures 12 decoding skills: letter naming, awareness of initial consonant sounds, rhyming words, and 9 levels of decoding words of various phonetic and spelling patterns); spelling; word recognition; and word opposites.	Used to place students at appropriate levels of reading instruction and for checking progress and mastery of reading skills throughout the school year.	Normed on 659 students in one elementary school in Pennsylvania in 1968.	Alternate form reliability for Word Recognition and Word Opportunities subtests: .94 to .99 (grades 1 to 6). Correlations between placement scores for grades 1 to 3 were generally high. Internal consistency was determined by correlating Word Opposites and Word Recognition subtests (correlations from .86 to .95). Criterion-related validity: used teacher/principal judgments as well as other reading tests. Correlations were between .57 and .95 for scores with BRI and actual student placement in grade equivalents. Concurrent validity established by correlating the BRI with other unspecified reading tests (coefficients .80 to .93 for grades 2 and 3). Correlations between Standard Reading Inventory and BRI were .78 to .95 (grades 1 through 6).
Brigance Comprehensive Inventory of Basic Skills (CIBS-R) (Curriculum Associates)	Readiness (27 subtests, e.g., recognizing colors, drawing a person, visual motor skills, visual discrimination, letter/number writing); listening comprehension (5 subtests: auditory discrimination, sentence memory, following oral directions, language comprehension, listening vocabulary); recognition grade-placement test (test of decoding skill); reading oral (graded passages); reading and listening comprehension (2 subtests: vocabulary comprehension, grade placement test); word analysis (one subtest: auditory discrimination, reading		Normed on a representative nationwide sample of 1,121 children.	Test–retest reliability in lower grades was approximately .85. Interrater reliability, alternative forms reliability, and internal consistency measures all also uniformly high. Validity assessed using the Iowa Test of Basic Skills, the Stanford Achievement Test, and the California Achievement Test.

Test	Skills/Subtests Assessed	Purpose	Standardization	Reliability/Validity
	rhymes, and reading words in word families; subtest also includes other nonvalidated assessments); functional word recognition (basic sight vocabulary, direct words, number words, warning/safety signs, info signs, warning and food labels); spelling (spelling grade placement).			
Burns/Roe Informal Reading Inventory—4th edition (Riverside)	Word naming (decoding); oral reading–graded reading passages (accuracy and comprehension assessed).	Provides information about the reading skills, abilities, and needs of individual students in order to plan an appropriate program of reading instruction.	Criterion-referenced	
California Achievement Tests (CAT-5) (CTB-McGraw-Hill)	Varies different grades, e.g., for level K, Visual recognition (letter-name knowledge, upper–lower case matching; matching letters within words; and matching words); Sound recognition (matching picture of object with same initial sound as dictated word, and rhyming); Vocabulary; Comprehension. For level 11 (first grade): Language mechanics (capitalization and punctuation); Language expression (syntax).	Measures students' educational development in reading, spelling, language, mathematics, study skills, science, and social studies.	Normed in spring and fall of 1991 on a large nationwide representative sample of students (K–12).	Internal consistency reliability (KR30s) for total battery (.94 to .98); for content area totals, Complete Battery (.86 to .96 range), for survey (.79 to .91), subtests of Complete Battery (.63 to .94, with mean of .78) ; alternate forms for subtests (.25 to .90, mean of .75), content-area totals (.27 to .93, mean of .82). Content validity: comprehensive sample of curriculum materials from around the country, textbooks, and major basal series were analyzed and test questions were developed to assess achievement within specific domains. Construct validity: reviews of previous CAT editions have found substantial overlap between the CAT and its companion ability measure, the Test of Cognitive Skills.
Comprehensive Test of Phonological Processing (CTOPP) (PRO-ED)	Elision, Blending words, Sound matching, Memory for digits, nonword repetition, Rapid color naming, Rapid digit naming, Rapid letter naming, Rapid object naming, Blending nonwords, Phoneme reversal, Segmenting words, segmenting nonwords.		Normed on a representative nationwide sample of more than 1,600 students.	Reliability coefficients were in the .70 to .90 range; validity measures are available from the publisher.

(continued)

APPENDIX 26.1 *cont.*

Assessment	Subtests/skills assessed	Stated purpose	Standardization	Reliability/validity
Comprehensive Tests of Basic Skills—4th edition	Grades K.0 to K.9: reading (visual recognition, sound recognition, vocabulary, comprehension, total); mathematics; concepts and applications; total. Grades K.6 to 1.6: reading (word analysis, vocabulary, comprehension, total); Mathematics; Concepts and applications; Total. Grades 1.0 to 2.2: reading (same as previous); language (mechanics, expression, Total); Mathematics (computation, concepts and applications, total); Science; Social studies; Total. Grades 1.6 to 3.2: same as previous plus spelling. Grades 2.6 to 4.2: same as previous.	Measures academic achievement		
Developmental Reading Assessment (DRA) (Celebration Press/Scott Foresman)	Prediction of story content, oral and silent reading, story retelling, comprehension, student performance on EALRs. Student performance in terms of fluency and accuracy is also assessed. Word identification and phonetic knowledge is also assessed.	Frequently used as part of classroom-based assessment; has been augmented in Vermont for statewide use by the addition of comprehension questions.	Criterion-referenced	Authors report evidence of construct validity.
Diagnostic and Achievement Reading Tests (Modern Curriculum Press)	66 subtests presented in 10 different test booklets; subtests range from asking children to identify, from an array, the picture that corresponds to a stimulus picture in subtest 1 to asking children to identify from an array the dictionary syllabication of a stimulus word in subtest 66; other subtests assess children's knowledge of words, letters, and phonemes and phoneme–letter correspondences, as well as their ability to read silently and comprehend sentences, contractions, synonyms, antonyms, and homonyms.	Designed to allow teachers to assess certain word recognition skills that they have taught their students.	Criterion-referenced	Publishers do not indicate that any validity or reliability studies were performed on its subtests.

Test	Skills/Content	Purpose	Standardization	Reliability/Validity
Diagnostic Assessments of Reading with Trial Teaching Strategies DARTTS (Riverside)	The assessment component comprises tests in six areas of reading and language (word recognition, word analysis, oral reading, silent reading comprehension, spelling, and word meaning).	Provides individual diagnostic information in essential areas of reading and language, and to deliver trial teaching strategies for students reading at any level.	Criterion-referenced	
Durrell Analysis of Reading Difficulty—3 (Harcourt Brace Educational Measurement)	Oral reading (reading accuracy, reading rate, and oral reading comprehension); Silent reading (reading rate and reading comprehension); Listening comprehension; Word recognition; Word analysis; listening vocabulary; Sounds in isolation (letters, blends and digraphs, phonograms, initial affixes, final affixes); Spelling; Phonic spelling of words; Visual memory of words (primary, secondary); identifying sounds in words (letter-sound knowledge); prereading phonics abilities inventories (optional, including syntax matching, identifying letter names in spoken words, naming lower-case letters, writing letters from dictation).	Estimates general reading ability, and in particular an individual's instructional, independent, and capacity reading levels. Can be used as a screen for reading problems.	Normed on a nationwide sample of 1,224 children (200 children per grade, grades 1 to 6).	Predictive validity of several of the subtests at the prereading level was assessed by correlating the results of measures administered to first-graders in September with reading achievement the following June (.55 to .65).
Ekwall—Shanker Reading Inventory—3 (Allyn & Bacon)	Skills assessed include knowledge of letters, phonics, basic sight words, vowel rules, syllable principles, and contractions. The reading passages are also designed to measure students' oral and silent independent, instructional, and frustration reading grade levels. Test description appears to outline the following sections (or subtests): Graded-word list, Oral and silent reading, Listening comprehension, Basic sight words and phrases test, letter Knowledge, Phonics, structural analysis, knowledge of contractions test, el paso phonics survey, quick survey word list, Reading interest survey.	Designed to assess the full range of students' reading abilities.	Not nationally standardized	A product-moment coefficient was calculated between the A and C (oral) forms and found to be .82. The same calculations between the B and D (silent) forms produced a correlation coefficient of .79. Because of the process by which tests were administered, these coefficients are considered to be a measure of intrascorer reliability. Validity was not reported.

(continued)

409

APPENDIX 26.1 *cont.*

Assessment	Subtests/skills assessed	Stated purpose	Standardization	Reliability/validity
Gates–MacGinitie—4 (Riverside)	Level PRE (preschool) has four subtests: literacy concepts, relational concepts (under, first, middle, etc.), oral language concepts (phoneme sequencing, phoneme matching, phoneme segmentation, word length), and letter-sound knowledge (matching letters, naming letters, identifying letter sounds); Level R (K) has three subtests: Letter-sound knowledge, vowels, sentence context (syntax); Levels 1 and 2 (grades 1 and 2) has two subtests: Vocabulary, Reading comprehension.	Measures reading achievement	Normed on a representative sample of 77,413 students in grades K–12.	Reliability: fall administration (stability): Vocabulary: .92; comprehension: .93; total: .96; spring administration: internal consistency (Cronbach's alpha); Vocabulary: .92; Comprehension: .93; total: .96. Validity: subtest intercorrelations (Vocabulary and Comprehension) for level two: .83 (fall) and .81 spring. Stability for the fall and spring correlations—total test: .83. Correlations with other tests range from .53 to .56 on Vocabulary, .74 to .83 on the Comprehension subtest, and .81 to .85 on the total test. Correlations between the Gates–MacGintie total and subtests and grades in Reading and Language range from .61 to .82. Correlations of the students' total grade point average and the Vocabulary subtest: .65, the Comprehension subtest: .66, and Total test: .63.
Gray Oral Reading Test—3 (GORT-3) (PRO-ED)	Info from GORT-R: test measures oral reading accuracy, oral reading comprehension, total oral reading ability, and oral reading miscues (meaning similarity, function similarity, graphic/phonemic similarity, multiple sources, and self-correction).	Assesses reading strengths and weaknesses, assesses abilities of students who are significantly below their peers, identifies those who may benefit from intervention, documents progressfollowing intervention.	Standardized on 1,485 children residing in 18 states whose demographic characteristics closely approximate 1990 US Census data.	Cronbach's alpha for internal consistency (range from .87 to .93 for the subtests, and .96 to .97 for Oral Reading Quotient); alternate form (range from .62 to .82). Criterion-related validity: used GORT-3 in combination with group achievement tests (range of .22 to .89). Construct validity: correlations of GORT-R and age (median .81), subtest intercorrelations (median .68), other language scores (median .57), other achievement tests (median .55), and intelligence (median .58).

Test	Subtests/Content	Purpose	Norming	Reliability/Validity
Metropolitan Achievement Test—8 (Psychological Corp.)	At the preprimer/primer level, there are four prereading subtests: Understanding print—preprimer only (primarily test of letter knowledge), Auditory discrimination, Phoneme/grapheme relationships (letter-sound knowledge), Word reading—primer only (test of decoding skill). Also at the preprimer/primer level there are two language subtests: Listening vocabulary (match dictated words with pictures) and Listening comprehension (listen to a passage and answer content questions. At the primer/elementary level there are three reading subtests: Word recognition—primary level only, Reading vocabulary (match synonyms or antonyms), and Reading comprehension (passages followed by comprehension questions). Also at the primer/elementary level there are two language subtests: listening comprehension and spelling.	General purpose achievement test battery designed to assess school curriculum from K to 12, used for large-scale assessment.	Normed on national samples of 100,000 and 79,000 students (Spring and Fall 1992, respectively). Approximately one-third were in grades K–2.	Test–retest and alternate form reliability coefficients were found to be in excess of .80 for all reading related subtests on the preprimer- to elementary-level tests. Validity was assessed with a comparison with the Otis–Lennon School Ability Test.
Mini Battery of Achievement (MBA) (Riverside)	Four subtests: Reading (word recognition, sight recognition, reading comprehension, and vocabulary), Writing (dictation spelling, punctuation, usage, and proofreading), Factual knowledge (general information in science, social studies, and the humanities), Mathematics.	Initial screening of new students; screening for special education referrals.	Normed on a national sample of more than 6,000 students.	According to publisher, reliability: mid .90s for reading, writing, mathematics, and the basic skills cluster; high .80s for factual knowledge. Validity: the Basic Skills cluster consistently correlated in the .80s with the total or composite scores from other achievement batteries.
Multilevel Academic Survey Test, Primary Form (MAST) (Psychological Corp.)	Four subtests: Letter-sound knowledge (phonics skills), Reading comprehension (both Oral and silent reading), Oral reading accuracy (miscue analysis), Oral reading rate.	Intended for use by school personnel who make decisions about student performance in reading and mathematics.	Normed on more than 1,600 students	Test–retest reliability correlations were found to be in the .80 range. Validity was assessed in a study of 300 children using the Iowa Test of Basic Skills

411

(continued)

APPENDIX 26.1 *cont.*

Assessment	Subtests/skills assessed	Stated purpose	Standardization	Reliability/validity
Norris Educational Achievement Test (NEAT) (Western Psychological Services)	Two subtests: Reading readiness (fine motor skills, letter matching, letter names, and letter-sound knowledge), Achievement (word naming, spelling, oral reading accuracy, and comprehension); battery also includes subtests in math and composition/writing.		Normed on a nationwide representative sample of 3,000 students	Test–retest reliability and equivalent-form comparison scores were in the .90 range. Validity was assessed using the Wide Range Achievement Test—Revised (for the achievement test). Validity of the readiness portion was assessed using the achievement portion of the test.
Peabody Individual Achievement Test (PIAT)—R/NU (normative update) (American Guidance Service)	Five subtests: General information (knowledge of facts), Reading recognition (readiness skills for young children, such as letter and word matching and initial phoneme matching, and word naming for older children), Reading comprehension (choose picture that best illustrates the passage), and Spelling and Written expression (from dictation), Mathematics.	Measures academic achievement; a screening measure (not diagnostic).	Normed again in 1997 using over 3,000 individuals (NU in test title refers to normative update)	Split-half reliability measures were reported to be in the .95 range, and test–retest reliability was found to be in the .90 range. Internal consistency coefficients were .60 to .69 (Level I) and .69 to .91 (Level II) Criterion validity was assessed using the Peabody Picture Vocabulary Test (.50 to .72).
Peabody Picture Vocabulary (PPVT-3) Test (American Guidance Service)	Receptive vocabulary (matching spoken words with pictures).	Test of vocabulary.	Normed on white children living in and around Nashville.	Validity evaluated in 122 separate studies (summarized in manual). Five test–retest reliability studies with various populations resulted in coefficients ranging from .69 to .92, and 18 studies assessing alternate form reliabilities resulted in coefficients ranging from .54 to .91.
Qualitative Reading Inventory—2 (Addison-Wesley/ HarperCollins)	Reading (oral reading accuracy, rate, strategies, and comprehension of graded reading passages), Word identification—a decoding test (naming words from graded word lists); second source adds that this test assesses prior knowledge related to passage topic, unaided retell, automaticity, prediction.	Informal reading inventory designed to assess reading ability at emergent through middle school levels; frequently used as part of classroom-based system.	Not nationally standardized	Interrater reliability in the .98 range; alternate form reliability measures were in the .90 range. Criterion-related validity was assessed using the Woodcock Reading Mastery Test (revised).

Test	Skills/Content measured	Purpose	Standardization	Reliability/Validity
Slosson Oral Reading Test (SORT-R) (Slossan Educational Publications)	Word recognition—a test of decoding skill	Designed as a quick estimate to target word recognition levels for children and adults.	Standardized on 1,331 individuals (preschool to adult) from 24 states in 1990.	All measures of reliability (internal consistency, Rulon, Kuder–Richareson, and test–retest) were in the .98 range. Criterion validity scores were assessed using the Woocock–Johnson Tests of Achievement—Letter Word Identification and the PPVT Reading Comprehension (both correlate over .90 with SORT-R). Passage Comprehension (WJTA) and Reading Comprehension (PIAT)—correlate w/ SORT-R .68 and .83, respectively. SORT-R also correlates w/ Slosson Intelligence Test—Revised (.87)—may indicate two tests do not assess independent constructs.
Standardized Reading Inventory (SRI-2) (PRO-ED)	Prior knowledge related to passage topic, oral reading miscues, oral reading accuracy, unaided retell, comprehension, word recognition, strategic reading skills, prediction.	Evaluates students' reading abilities; for children with reading ability not exceeding eighth-grade level.	Normed on 1,099 children residing in 28 states; sample stratified using 1997 U.S. Census figures.	Reliability: correlation coefficients ranged from .88 to .97. Criterion-referenced validity studies correlated SRI-2 with Gray Oral Reading Test—3, Gray Silent Reading Test—2, Comprehensive Test of Phonological Processes, and Otis–Lennon School Abilities Test with favorable results. In addition, evidence of construct validity is presented showing that the SRI-2 discriminates between good readers and the following groups: poor readers, students with learning disabilities, and students with speech–language disorders.
Stanford Achievement Test—Abbreviated Version—8th edition (Harcourt Brace Educational Measurement)	Word study skills, reading vocabulary (grades 2.5 to 3.5), Word reading (grades 1.5 to 2.5), Reading comprehension, total reading, Language/english, Spelling, Listening, Concepts of number, mathematics computation, Mathematics applications, Total mathematics, Environment.			

413

(continued)

APPENDIX 26.1 *cont.*

Assessment	Subtests/skills assessed	Stated purpose	Standardization	Reliability/validity
Stanford Achievement Test—9 (Harcourt Brace Educational Measurement)	Sounds and letters; Word study skills; Word reading, Reading vocabulary; Sentence reading; Reading comprehension. Open-ended reading (narrative selections each followed by nine open-ended questions (questions measure of three processes: initial understanding, interpretation of relationships, and critical analysis, as well as one of three content skills: character questions, setting and plot questions, theme/writer's craft).	Measures student achievement in reading, language, spelling, study skills, listening, mathematics, science, and social science; frequently used for large-scale assessment.	Normed on stratified random samples of 250,000 students from 1,000 school districts during spring of 1995, and another 200,000 students in the fall, from 49 states and District of Columbia.	Reliability: K-R20 coefficients (.80s to .90s) for most tests/subtests of multiple-choice battery. Listening, Language, Science, and Social science: 70s to low .80s; open-ended assessments (Reading, Mathematics, Science, and Social science): low .60s to low .80s.; combined multiple-choice and open-ended assessments: mid .80 –.90s. Alternate forms coefficients: multiple choice coefficients: .80s; most of Total reading, Total math, and Language tests: in the .70s or less for remaining tests and Reading and Language subtests; Open-ended assessments: .60s and .70s for most except Writing (.30s to .60s); interrater correlation coefficients: .50s to .80s, and Spearman–Brown: .70s to .90s. Validity: criterion-related: for majority of tests and subtests, the multiple-choice and open-ended assessments have less than 60% in common in terms of content measured.
Stanford Diagnostic Reading Test— 4th edition (SDRT-4) (Harcourt Brace Educational Measurement)	Four subtests: Phonetic analysis, Vocabulary, Comprehension, Scanning (grades 4.5 to 13.0 only); in addition, there are three optional informal assessment instruments: Reading strategies survey (identifies strategies student understands and use in various situations), Reading questionnaire (surveys student's attitudes toward reading, his/her reading interests and familiarity w/ concepts appearing in the Comprehension subtest), and Story retelling (to evaluate comprehension as student retells in own words).	Program placement, determine strength/ weakness for instructional planning, identify trends in achievement, measure change over time, evaluate effectiveness of instructional program.	Normed on a nationally representative sample of students.	Publisher reports that SDRT (all four subtests) have been statistically equated to the Stanford Achievement Test–9, as well as to the SDRT-3.

Test	Subtests/Content	Description	Norms	Reliability/Validity
TerraNova Reading (CTB McGraw-Hill)	Four subtests: Comprehension (listening and silent reading) Vocabulary (includes multimeaning words and words in context), Reference skills, Word analysis (decoding phonologically, structurally, and reading high-frequency words).	General achievement test, frequently used for large-scale assessment.	Normed in 1996 on over 1 million test administrations to over 172,000 students nationwide.	Validity studies were not yet completed when the 1996 prepublication *Technical Bulletin* was published. Types of validity being assessed included: content-related, criterion-related, construct, convergent, and divergent.
Test of Academic Performance (Psychological Corp.)	Three subtests: Spelling (from dictation), Reading recognition—a test of decoding skill (word naming of high-frequency words), Reading comprehension (assessed with comprehension questions on vocabulary, facts and inference).		Normed on 3,216 students in all grades.	Interrater reliability was found to be in the .75 range, and test–retest reliability measures were in the .60 range for third-grade students.
Test of Early Reading Ability-2 (PRO-ED)	Three subtests: Construction of meaning (knowledge of environmental print, categorical vocabulary, and reading comprehension), Alphabet knowledge, Conventions (book handling, punctuation, proofreading).	Measures actual reading ability of young children	Normed on a national sample of 1,454 children, ages 3 to 10 in 15 states.	Both internal consistency and test–retest reliability coefficients approach or exceed .80. Validity measures, assessed using the Basic School Skills Inventory, were found to be in the .55 range.
Test of Phonological Awareness (PRO-ED)		Measures young children's awareness of the individual sounds in words; can be used to identify children in kindergarten who may profit from instructional activities to enhance their phonological awareness in preparation for reading instruction.	According to publisher, the test has been standardized.	
Test of Reading Comprehension (TORC-3) (PRO-ED)	Eight subtests grouped under the General Reading Comprehension Core and Diagnostic Supplements. The General Reading Comprehension Core includes General vocabulary, Syntactic similarities, Paragraph reading, Sentence sequencing; Diagnostic Supplements include measures of content-area vocabulary in Mathematics, Social Studies, and; last subtest is Reading the directions of schoolwork.	TORC-3 represents the operationalization of a constructivist orientation that focuses on holistic, cognitive, and linguistic aspects of reading.	Normed on 1,962 students from 19 states; publisher provides info on the sample by region, gender, residence, race, ethnicity and disabling condition stratified by age and keyed to the 1990 census data.	On web site, publisher indicates existence of research supporting reliability and validity, but no further information.

(continued)

Assessment	Subtests/skills assessed	Stated purpose	Standardization	Reliability/validity
Test of Word Knowledge (Harcourt Brace Educational Measurement)	Level 1 (ages 5–8) has five subtests: Expressive vocabulary, Receptive vocabulary, Word opposites, Word definitions, Synonyms.			Test-retest reliability over 1 to 4 weeks was assessed on Level 2 of this assessment and was found to be in the .90 range. Validity was assessed using the Clinical Evaluation of Language Fundamentals—Revised.
Test of Word Reading Efficiency (PRO-ED TOWRE)	Monitors growth of two kinds of word-reading skills: the ability to accurately recognize familiar words as whole units (sight words) and the ability to sound out words quickly. Contains two subtests: sight-word efficiency (number of printed words that be accurately identified within 45 seconds) and Phonetic decoding efficiency (number of pronounceable printed nonwords that can be accurately decoded within 45 seconds).	Measures word reading accuracy and fluency	Normed on over 1,500 individuals from 6 to 24 years old in a nationwide sample.	Alternate forms reliability (.90); test-retest (ranged from .83 to .96). Publisher claims that, extensive evidence of the validity of TOWRE test scores is provided for content-description validity, criterion-prediction validity, and construct-identification validity.
Wechsler Individual Achievement Test (WIAT) (Psychological Corp.)	Screener includes Basic reading, Mathematics reading, Spelling, Screener composite. WIAT-3 subtests: Basic reading, Reading comprehension, Total reading, Mathematics reasoning, Numerical operations, Total mathematics, Listening comprehension, oral expression, Total language, Spelling (from dictation), Written expression, Total writing, Total composite.	Intended to be a comprehensive individually administered achievement battery; particularly suited to investigate ability–achievement discrepancies in children ages 6 to 16.	Normed on 4,252 children, ages 5 to 19 enrolled in K to 12, (demographically very closely matched to 1988 U.S. Census).	Split-half reliability coefficients: .59 to .94. Test-retest reliability coefficients .76 to .94 for subtests. Interrater reliability mean r = .98 for dichotomously scored subtests; the multipoint criteria scoring of the Oral and Written Expression subtests (intra-class correlations: .79 to .93). Content validity: use of curriculum experts to ensure WIAT test specifications paralleled Stanford Achievement Test—8. Construct validity demonstrated by intercorrelations among subtests, correlation with various IQ tests, and patterns of inc. scores with age and grade observed in Standard and Achievement Tests. Criterion validity was assessed by

Instrument	Subtests/components	Purpose	Norming	Reliability/validity
				correlations between WIAT and other standardized assessments, resulting in correlations coefficients ranging from .42 to .90.
Wide Range Achievement Test—3 (Wide Range)	Three subtests: Reading (recognizing and naming letters and naming high-frequency words), Spelling (writing name, writing letters from dictation, writing words from dictation), Arithmetic (providing written answers to arithmetic problems on a page).	To measure the skills needed to learn reading, spelling, and arithmetic.	Normed on a national, stratified sample of 4,433 people (ages 5 to 75).	Reliability claimed from three measures of internal reliability consistency (coefficient alpha, alternate form, and person separation indices) and a test–retest study. However, small sample size ($n = 142$) and sample mean age (10.5 years) a problem. Author claims that because items range in difficulty, this supports content validity.
Woodcock–Johnson Psycho-educational Battery—Revised (Riverside Publishing)	Tests of Achievement: Letter–word identification, passage comprehension, Calculation, Applied problems, Dictation, Writing samples, Science, Social studies, Humanities; supplemental battery: Word attack, Reading vocabulary, Quantitative concepts, Proofing, Writing fluency, Punctuation and capitalization, Spelling, Usage, Handwriting; Tests of Cognitive Ability: Memory for names, Memory for sentences, Visual matching, incomplete words, visual closure, picture vocabulary, Analysis–synthesis, broad cognitive ability; Supplementary battery: Visual–auditory learning, Memory for words, Cross out, Sound blending, Picture recognition, Oral vocabulary, Concept formation, Delayed recall (Memory for names, Visual–auditory learning), Numbers reversed, Sound patterns, Spatial relations, Listening comprehension, Verbal analogies.	Measures cognitive abilities, scholastic aptitudes, and achievement.	Standardized on 6,359 individuals (ages 2 to 90+) nationwide.	Internal reliability consistency coefficients for WJ-R fall in the mid .90s for the major clusters on the Cognitive and Achievement scales; internal consistency for subtests on the Achievement scale (.80s and low .90s) except for Written fluency subtest (.76); for subtests of Cognitive Batteries—standard and supplemental (mid .70s to low .80s).

(continued)

417

Assessment	Subtests/skills assessed	Stated purpose	Standardization	Reliability/validity
Woodcock–Johnson Language Proficiency Battery—Revised (Riverside Publishing)	Five subtests in oral language test: Memory for sentences, Picture vocabulary, Oral vocabulary, Listening comprehension; Verbal analogies. Four subtests in the reading test: Letter–word identification, Passage comprehension, Word attack, reading vocabulary, Dictation (letter formation, spelling, punctuation, capitalization and word usage are assessed).		English version was nationally normed on more than 6,300 students; Spanish version was nationally normed on more than 2,000 students.	Internal reliability measures for the early grades are mostly above .80, and the test–retest reliabilities were in the .90 range. Validity was assessed using the PIAT, the WISC-R, the BASIS, the K-ABC, the K-TEA, the WRAT-R, and the Stanford Binet (4th).
Woodcock–Johnson Reading Mastery (norms revised in 1997) (American Guidance Services)	Six subtests: Visual–auditory learning , letter identification, Word identification, Word attack (a test of the ability to read regular words), Word comprehension (a test of vocabulary), Passage comprehension, Form G has two letter-identification tests providing the option of testing the respondent's letter–sound knowledge.		Standardized on 4,201 students (K to 12) nationwide.	Split-half reliability measures were found to be in the .95 range. Validity was assessed using the Iowa Test of Basic Skills, the PPVT, and the WJ-R.

Note. Information from test reviews or test publisher prepared by Terry Salinger and Janet Voight.

VI
SPECIAL INTERVENTION EFFORTS

27

Preschool Education for Economically Disadvantaged Children: Effects on Reading Achievement and Related Outcomes

❖

W. STEVEN BARNETT

Children's abilities at school entry are highly predictive of their later learning and school success, and children from lower-income families enter school with less developed academic abilities, on average than do more advantaged children and tend to fall further behind as the years pass (Alexander & Entwisle, 1988; Deutsch, 1965; Stevenson & Newman, 1986; White, 1982). Emergent literacy at school entry may be viewed as particularly important because of its association with later reading skills and the importance of reading for school success generally. Thus, one avenue for improving the reading abilities and school success of disadvantaged children may be through preschool education that increases their abilities at school entry.

Many studies have found that preschool programs can produce immediate gains for disadvantaged children on tests of academic abilities and intelligence. However, scholars disagree about the nature of these effects and whether the effects persist after children leave the preschool program and enter school. Some argue that short-term effects are merely the temporary results of "hothousing" that does not lead to long-term gains in cognitive abilities (Herrnstein &

Murray, 1994; Locurto, 1991; Rowe, 1997; Spitz, 1991). Others suggest that preschool education's influences on test performance may be produced by changes in motivation or through effects on parents' beliefs and behavior (Haskins, 1989; Seitz, 1990; Zigler & Muenchow, 1992). Finally, some propose that short-term effects increase early school success, which increases later abilities directly and indirectly by affecting opportunities to learn and parent and teacher expectations (Barnett, Young, & Schweinhart, 1998; Entwisle, 1995). This chapter reviews research on the effect of preschool education on the reading achievement, other cognitive abilities, grade repetition, and special education placement of disadvantaged children and assesses the extent of its long-term impact on reading. This chapter also sheds light on how preschool produces beneficial effects. (For related reviews, see Zill, Chapter 18; Dickinson & Sprague, Chapter 19, and Wasik et al., Chapter 29).

Studies of Short-Term Effects

Two largely separate streams of res⸍ containing hundreds of studies have

421

ined the short-term effect of early-childhood programs. One stream consists of studies of the effects of child care on children from a variety of backgrounds. The other is research on the effects of intervention programs specifically designed to serve children from low-income families. These two streams of research began with different concerns and a tendency to focus on children at different ages (with much child-care research focusing on infants and toddlers) but have begun to converge in recent years. Child-care research initially emphasized the potential for negative effects on the mother–child relationship and on social development with distinctly less attention to the possible effects on cognitive development (Belsky, 1988; Scarr, 1998). In the last two decades, child-care researchers have attended more to the effects of variations in the quality of care and increased their attention to effects on cognitive development (Scarr, 1998). Research on preschool education interventions for children in poverty initially emphasized effects on cognitive development, especially as measured by IQ. Over time, interest grew in the effects of these interventions on other aspects of cognitive development and academic success, on motivation and attitudes toward school, on socialization, and on parents and other family members (Benasich, Brooks-Gunn, & Clewell, 1992; Lazar, Darlington, Murray, Royce, & Snipper, 1982).

Overall, child-care research has found little evidence that child care per se is harmful to child development regardless of the age at which a child enters care, though there continue to be some concerns about negative effects from long hours in child care (Lamb & Sternberg, 1990; NICHD Early Child Care Research Network, 1999; Zaslow, 1991). There is evidence that the consequences of care vary with its quality, though the effects of quality seem to vary with child and family characteristics (Peisner-Feinberg et al., 1999; Scarr, 1998). Higher quality is associated with better cognitive and social development contemporaneously and into the first few years of school, but the estimated effects are small and appear to weaken over time (Helburn & Culkin, 1995; Lamb & Sternberg, 1990; Peisner-Feinberg et al., 1999; Phillips, McCartney, & Scarr, 1987; Scarr, 1998; Zaslow, 1991).

Two recent studies typify the results. Caughy, DiPietro, and Strobino (1994) employed a large national data set to investigate the effects of age at entry or years of experience and type of care on the reading achievement of children at ages 5 and 6. For children in poverty, child care had positive effects, and earlier entry produced a larger effect. Conversely, for children in the highest-income families, child care had negative effects. These interactions appear to be due to differences in the home environment and not current income per se. Children whose home environments were relatively poor, as measured by the Home Observation for Measure of the Environment (HOME; Bradley & Caldwell, 1979), gained the most from child care, whereas children whose home environments scored highly had lower reading scores if they had been in child care. In a multistate longitudinal study, child-care quality was found to be associated with children's abilities and behavior during the preschool years and into the first years of school, with somewhat larger effects for disadvantaged children (Peisner-Feinberg et al., 1999). However, even for disadvantaged children, effects on language and early reading skills appeared to fade by second grade.

Research on the immediate and short-term effects of preschool education programs for children in poverty, including Head Start and public school programs, has been summarized in both quantitative meta-analyses and best-evidence syntheses. These summaries find immediate effect sizes for IQ, reading achievement, and other cognitive measures of about half a standard deviation (McKey et al., 1985; Ramey, Bryant, & Suarez, 1986; White & Casto, 1985). Averaged across studies, the estimated effects decline over time and are negligible several years after children exit the programs. Some programs produced sizable gains that persist to school entry and beyond for IQ and achievement and for school success variables that one would expect to be highly dependent on reading ability, such as grade repetition and special education placement. However, a limitation of these studies is that the vast majority of effect sizes are for IQ-type measures. A variety of different approaches produced positive effects, but some reviewers conclude that the magnitude of effects is roughly related to a program's intensity, breadth, and duration (Ramey et al., 1986).

New Evidence from Randomized Trials

Most studies have relied on natural variation in program participation, making it difficult to accurately estimate the effects of programs or program quality. The results of these nonexperimental studies can be biased by differences in the characteristics of children and families that influence program enrollment decisions (e.g., children's abilities and behavior, parents' income, socioeconomic status, education, and attitudes toward education and childrearing). Experiments in which children are randomly assigned to preschool programs are extremely valuable because their estimates are not subject to this sort of bias. Results from several new randomized experiments have become available in the last few years that greatly add to our knowledge.

The Carolina Approach to Responsive Education (CARE) study randomly assigned children ($n = 57$) to three conditions: a high-quality full-day year-round educational child-care program and home visits for parent education from shortly after birth to age 5, home visits alone, and a control group (Roberts et al., 1989; Wasik, Ramey, Bryant, & Sparling, 1990). At age 5, the child-care-program-plus-home-visits group had higher IQs and better language skills but did no better on a reading test (perhaps because of a lack of sensitivity at that age) than the other two groups despite substantial participation of the others in community child care.

The Infant Health and Development Program (IHDP) study is an eight-site randomized trial ($n = 985$) of early care and education from birth to age 3 for low-birthweight infants primarily, but not entirely, from low-income families (Brooks-Gunn et al., 1994; IHDP, 1990). The program offered weekly home visits during the first year of life directed at both parents' and children's needs, followed by biweekly home visits and full-day educational child care from age 1 to age 3. The program was not taken up by everyone in the treatment group and the control group had access to other programs up to age 3 (e.g., early intervention under Part C of the Individuals with Disabilities Educa-

tion Act) and later. By age 3, the treatment group had IQs that were 13 points higher and had fewer behavioral problems as measured by the Child Behavior Checklist. Unfortunately, at the age 5 follow-up, effects on the children were no longer apparent (Brooks-Gunn, McCormick, Shapiro, Benasich, & Black, 1994).

The Comprehensive Child Development Program (CCDP) employed home visitors as case managers to increase and improve social, health, and education services for families with young children (St. Pierre & Lopez, 1994). Families ($n = 4,411$, 21 sites) entered the study with a child under 1 year of age and were to receive visits twice monthly. The CCDP substantially increased mother's participation in parenting education, mental health services, and education; slightly increased children's use of health services; and substantially increased children's participation in early-childhood programs. Yet, after several years, only extremely small effects were found for mothers and children.

Even Start provides parenting education, adult education, and preschool education plus a variety of supporting services. In an evaluation of Even Start, St. Pierre, Swartz, Murray, Deck, & Nicke, (1993) found that the extent and duration of services varied considerably among families, though nearly all children received some preschool education. An experimental substudy at five sites with 164 3- and 4-year-old children found small positive effects on a measure of school-readiness skills 2½ years after program entry (St. Pierre et al., 1993). Small effects also were found on one aspect of home environment (reading materials) and on parents' expectations for children's academic success.

Parents as Teachers (PAT) provides parenting education to the general population through home visiting that, among other goals, seeks to improve child development and school success through improved parenting. Two randomized trials have been conducted on PAT, one with a primarily Latino population in the Salinas Valley and the other with teenage parents in four California cities (Wagner & Clayton, 1999). In Salinas, monthly home visits began before the child was 6 months old and continued until the child turned 3. In the teenage-parent study, participants were randomly assigned to receive PAT, case management, PAT plus case management, or no treatment. Services to teenage parents continued until the child turned 2. Researchers found no evidence of effects on parenting. In Salinas and for the case management group in the teenage study, small effects were found on parental reports of child development. However, the Salinas study also had two independent measures of child development, and no effects were found on either the Bayley Scales or the Peabody Picture Vocabulary Test.

Summary of Short-Term Findings

Preschool programs can have an important short-term impact on general cognitive development and academic abilities including reading achievement. Effects appear to be larger for intensive, high-quality educational programs targeting children in poverty. Ordinary child care, parent education, and case management programs that seek to increase the use of existing health, social, and educational services have, at best, small effects on reading achievement and related outcomes. Some, but not all, studies report that effects decline after children leave the programs, and programs that cease serving children several years prior to school entry cannot be counted on to produce effects that last until school entry.

Research on Long-Term Effects

Studies were included in the long-term studies review if they met four criteria: (1) children entered the program as preschoolers (in Head Start this could include some 5-year-olds prior to the availability of kindergarten), (2) the program served economically disadvantaged children, (3) at least one measure of reading achievement or school success was collected at or beyond age 8 (third grade), and (4) the research design identified treatment and no-treatment groups from program records. The requirement for follow-up through third grade allowed sufficient time to observe fadeout in effects (Caldwell, 1987).

Thirty-seven studies were identified that met the review criteria. They fall into two distinct categories. Fifteen are studies of the effects of small-scale exemplary programs. Twenty-two are studies of the effects of large-scale public preschool programs. Twelve of these studied Head Start programs, seven public school programs, and four a mix of Head Start and public school programs.

Small-Scale Program Studies

Table 27.1 decribes the 15 small-scale program studies. Generally, these programs provided more intensive, higher-quality services than did the large-scale public programs. Public preschool programs have never been funded at the level required to replicate these small-scale "model" programs. Higher funding levels made it possible to hire highly qualified staff, maintain small class sizes and low child–staff ratios, and provide extensive support and supervision to the teachers. Children in these studies were economically disadvantaged, as indicated by mother's education which averaged less than 12 years in all studies and less than 10 years in five studies. Many studies were motivated by concerns for inequalities in school success across ethnic groups, and in all but one study the majority of children were African American.

Three model program studies limited their samples in ways that might have affected their results. The Harlem Training Project served only boys. The Perry Preschool study selected children based on low IQ scores, and its sample had substantially lower IQs at age 3 than children in other studies. The Milwaukee study selected children whose mothers had IQs below 75.

As can be seen from Table 27.1, the model programs varied in entrance age, duration, services provided, and historical context (1962 to 1980). Most comparison children began formal education at kindergarten. However, in the later studies it is likely that many children in the comparison groups attended another preschool or child care program. For example, in the Abecedarian study, which enrolled newborns between 1972 and 1980, two-thirds of the control group attended a child-care or preschool program for 12 months or more by age 5 (Burchinal, Lee, & Ramey, 1989). Thus, it is important to consider the

TABLE 27.1. Small-Scale Preschool Education Programs and Their Long-Term Results

Program name (years program provided) (source)	Program description and ages of participation	Research design/methodological concerns	Sample size[a]	Time of follow-up	IQ results[a,b]	Achievement and other results[a]
1. Carolina Abecedarian (1972–1985) (Campbell & Ramey, 1993, 1994; Campbell, 1997)	Full-day child care Entry: 6 weeks to 3 months Exit: 5 years	Randomized.	Initial E = 57, C = 54 Follow-up Age 8 E = 48, C = 42 Age 15 E = 48, C = 44	8, 12, 15, and 21 years	Age 12: E > C E = 93.7 C = 88.4 Age 15: E = C E = 95.0 C = 90.3	Achievement tests: E > C at age 15 and age 21 Special education: E < C at age 15: E = 24%, C = 48% Grade retention: E < C at age 15: E = 39%, C = 59%
2. Houston Parent–Child Development Center (1970–1980) (Andrews et al., 1982; Johnson & Walker, 1991)	Home visits Full-day child care Center-based program for parents Entry: 1 to 3 Years Exit: 3 to 5 Years	Randomized. High attrition.	Initial E = 97, C = 119 Follow-up School data E = 50, C = 87 IQ data E = 39, C = 78	Grades 2 to 5	Not measured	Achievement tests: E > C Grades: E = C Bilingual education: E < C E = 16%, C = 36% Special education: E = C, grades 2 to 5 E = 27%, C = 31% Grade retention: E = C, grades 2 to 5 E = 16%, C = 23%
3. Florida Parent Education Project (1966–1970) (Jester & Guinagh, 1983)	Home visits Twice weekly part-day preschool (ages 2 to 3 years) Entry: 3 to 24 months Exit: 3 years	Initially randomized with one group, and additional control group members added at 24 months. Not randomized. High attrition. School-administered tests.	Initial E = 288, C = 109 Follow-up E = 83, C = 24	Grades 4 to 7	E = C (grades 4 to 7) E = 83.1 C = 79.8	Reading achievement: E = C Math achievement: E > C Special education: E < C, grade 7 E = 23%, C = 54% Grade retention: E = C, grade 7 E = 28%, C = 29%
4. Milwaukee Project (1968–1978) (Garber, 1988)	Full-day child care Job and academic training for mothers Entry: 3 to 6 Months Exit: 3 years	Groups of 3 to 4 children assigned alternately to E and C groups. Small sample.	Initial E = 20, C = 20 Follow-up E = 17, C = 18	Grade 4 Grade 8	Grade 8: E > C E = 101 C = 91	Achievement tests: E = C, but positive trend Grades: E = C Special education: E = C, grade 4 E = 41%, C = 89% Grade retention: E = C, grade 4 E = 29%, C = 56%

(continued)

TABLE 27.1. *Continued*

Program name (years program provided) (source)	Program description and ages of participation	Research design/methodological concerns	Sample size[a]	Time of follow-up	IQ results[a,b]	Achievement and other results[a]
5. Syracuse Family Research Program (1969–1975) (Lally, Mangione, & Honig, 1988)	Home visits Full-day child care Entry: 6 months Exit: 5 years	Matched comparison group selected at 36 months. Not randomized.	Initial E = 82, C = 72 Follow-up Parents E = 52, C = 42 Children E = 49, C = 39	Grades 7 to 8	E = C, age 5 on Stanford–Binet	Teacher ratings: E > C, but for girls only Grades: E > C, but for girls only Attendance: E > C, but for girls only
6. Yale Child Welfare Research Program (1968–1974) (Seitz, Rosenbaum, & Apfel, 1985; Seitz & Apfel, 1994)	Home visits Full-day child care Pediatric care Developmental screenings Entry: Prenatal Exit: 30 months	Two comparison groups for same neighborhoods for first follow-up. Matched comparison group selected for follow-up at 30 months. Not randomized. School-administered tests.	Initial E = 18, C = 18 Follow-up Age 7 to 8 E = 17, C1 = 33, C2 = 31 Age 10 E = 16, C = 16	Age 7 to 8 and age 10	E = C at age 10	Achievement tests: E = C Attendance: E > C Teacher ratings: E = C, but positive trend for boys only Special education: E = C E = 25%, C = 50%
7. Verbal Interaction Project (1967–1972) (Levenstein, O'Hara, & Madden, 1983)	Home visits Entry: 2 to 3 years Exit: 4 years	Six groups with three matched comparison groups. Not randomized.	Initial E = 111, C = 51 Follow-up E = 79, C = 49	Grade 3	E > C at grade 3 E = 101.9 C = 93.6	Achievement tests: E > C Special education: E < C, grade7 E = 14%, C = 39% Grade retention: E = C, grade 7 E = 13%, C = 19%
8. Early Training Project (1962–1967) (Gray, Ramey, & Klaus, 1982, 1983)	Home visits Summer part-day preschool program Entry: 4 to 5 years Exit: 6 years	Randomized. School-administered tests.	Initial E = 44, C = 21 Follow-up E = 36, C = 16	Post high school	E = C at age 17 E = 78.7 C = 76.4	Achievement tests: E = C Special education: E < C, grade 12 E = 5%, C = 29% Grade retention: E = C E = 58%, C = 61% High school graduation: E = C E = 68%, C = 52%

Study	Program	Design	Sample	Last assessment	IQ	Findings
9. Experimental Variation of Head Start (1968–1969) (Karnes, Shwedel, & Williams, 1983)	Part-day preschool program Entry: 4 years Exit: 5 years	Post-hoc comparison group from same communities. Not randomized. School administered tests.	Initial E = 116, C = 24 Follow-up E = 102, C = 19	Post high school	E < C at 13 E = 85.0 C = 91.0	Achievement tests: E = C, but positive trend Special education: E = C, grade 7 E = 13%, C = 15% Grade retention : E = C, grade 7 E = 10%, C = 16%
10. Harlem Training Project (1966–1967) (Palmer, 1983)	One-to-one tutoring or child-directed play Entry: 2 to 3 years Exit: 4 years	Comparison group recruited from children born 1 to 2 months later. Not randomized. School-administered tests.	Initial E = 244, C = 68 Follow-up E = 168, C = 51	Grade 7	E = C at 12 E = 92.1 C = 88.9	Reading achievement: E < C Math achievement: E > C Grade retention: E < C, grade 7 E = 30%, C = 52%
11. High/Scope Perry Preschool Project (1962–1967) (Barnett, Young, & Schweinhart, 1998; Schweinhart, Barnes, Weikart, Barnett, & Epstein, 1993; Weikart, Bond, & McNeil, 1978)	Home visits Part-day preschool program Entry: 3 to 4 years Exit: 5 years	Randomized.	Initial E = 58, C = 65 Follow-up E = 58, C = 65	Post-high school	E = C at age 14 E = 81.0 C = 81.0	Achievement tests: E > C Grades: E > C Special education: E = C, grade 12 E = 37%, C = 50% Grade retention: E = C, grade 12 E = 15%, C = 20% High school graduation: E > C E = 67%, C = 49%
12. Howard University Project (1964–1966) (Herzog, Newcomb, & Cisin, 1974)	Part-day preschool program Entry: 3 years Exit: 5 years	Comparison group from neighboring tracts. Not randomized.	Initial E = 38, C = 69 Follow-up E = 30, C = 69	Grade 4	Not measured	Grade retention: E = C E = 33%, C = 47%
13. Institute for Developmental Studies (1963–1967) (Deutsch, Deutsch, Jordan, & Grallo, 1983; Deutsch, Taleporos & Victor, 1974)	Home visits Part-day preschool program Parent center school (K–3) Entry: 3 years Exit: 9 years	Randomized. High attrition. School-administered tests.	Initial E = 312, C = 191 Follow-up E = 63, C = 34	Grade 7	E = C, age 8 E = 96.7 C = 91.4	Achievement tests: E = C, grade 3 Special education: E = C E = 0%, C = 13% Grade retention: E = C E = 23%, C = 43%

(continued)

TABLE 27.1. cont.

Program name (years program provided) (source)	Program description and ages of participation	Research design/methodological concerns	Sample size[a]	Time of follow-up	IQ results[a,b]	Achievement and other results[a]
14. Philadelphia Project (1963–1964) (Beller, 1983)	Home visits Part-day preschool program Entry: 4 years Exit: 5 years	Matched comparison group from same kindergarten classes. Not randomized. School-administered tests.	Initial E = 60, C = 53 Follow-up E = 44, C = 37	Post-high school	E > C at age 10 on Stanford–Binet E = 98.4 C = 91.7	Achievement tests: E = C, but positive trend Special education: E = C, grade 12 E = 5%, C = 6% Grade retention: E = C, grade 12 E = 38%, C = 53%
15. Curriculum Comparison Study (1965–1967) (Miller & Bizzell, 1983, 1984)	Part-day preschool program Kindergarten program Entry: 4 years Exit: 5 or 6 years	Post-hoc comparison group from original pool. Not randomized. School-administered tests.	Initial E = 244, C = 68 Follow-up E = 168, C = 51	Post high school	Not measured	Special education: E = C, grade 12 E = 32%, C = 63% Grade retention: E = C, grade 12 E = 26%, C = 58% High school graduation: E = C E = 67%, C = 53%

[a]Throughout Table 27.1, E refers to the experimental or intervention group, and C refers to the control or comparison group. Outcomes listed as E > C or E < C were statistically significant at the $p < .05$ level.

[b]IQs were measured using the WISC or WISC-R unless otherwise noted.

extent to which preschool program participation by comparison-group children may lead to underestimation of the effects of preschool education in some studies.

Head Start and Public School Programs

Table 27.2 describes the 22 studies of Head Start and public school preschool programs. None of these programs took children before age 3. Most served children part-day for one school year at age 4. Class size and child-teacher ratio are likely to have been higher than in model programs. Head Start has broader missions than most other programs, including improving health and nutrition, and providing services to parents and the community (Zigler & Styfco, 1993). In three studies, preschool program participation was linked with a school-age program. In the Cincinnati Title 1 study, most full-day kindergarten students had attended preschool while most half-day kindergarten students had not. In the two Child–Parent Center (CPC) studies, services began in preschool and continued as an enhanced educational program through third grade.

Research Design

Tables 27.1 and 27.2 describe key elements of research design. These include (1) initial setup (including how comparison groups were formed) and procedures with such limitations as lack of a pretest and high rates of attrition, (2) initial and follow-up sample sizes, and (3) length of follow-up. All have important implications for the validity and interpretation of study findings.

SMALL-SCALE PROGRAM STUDY DESIGNS

Seven model program studies formed comparison groups by randomly assigning children to experimental and control groups. Doing it this way increases confidence that estimated effects in these studies are due to the program rather than to preexisting and, perhaps, unmeasured, differences between groups. However, the benefits of random assignment can be lost as a result of severe attrition or small sample size, and small sample size can severely limit the power of a study to detect important effects. Only two experiments began with sample sizes larger

than 30 per group and maintained low attrition throughout follow-up—the Abecedarian and Perry Preschool studies. Two other experimental studies—Milwaukee and the Early Training Project (ETP)—began with such small sample sizes that they had little power to detect even fairly large effects without attrition. The other four experimental studies suffered substantial attrition that could have invalidated the initial random assignment and reduced the power to detect program effects in long-term follow-up.

The remaining eight small-scale or model program studies constructed comparison groups, usually at a later date. Some of the approaches to constructing comparison groups seem likely to have created group differences that favored the preschool program groups. The two curriculum studies formed comparison groups after the fact by selecting children who had not attended another preschool program. This eliminated from the comparison group any children whose parents sought out preschool education experiences for their children. Parents who did not seek a preschool education for their child might be expected to differ in other ways with respect to their attitudes about education and efforts to support their child's educational success. In the Harlem Training Project, attrition during a waiting period prior to entry at age 3 may have introduced differences favoring this later entry group as it had a higher IQ prior to treatment than did the control group (Lazar et al., 1982). The Yale Child Welfare Research Program study obtained a control group 30 months after it selected the program group using the same clinic records it had used to identify the program group. However, the program group was invited to receive child care and other services while the comparison group was invited to participate in data collection. Moreover, researchers needed three times the number of months of clinic records to obtain subjects for the program group as they did to obtain the comparison group (Seitz, Rosenbaum, & Apfel, 1985).

HEAD START AND PUBLIC SCHOOL
RESEARCH DESIGNS

All the large-scale public program studies employed quasi-experimental designs. Some

TABLE 27.2. Head Start and Public School Preschool Education Programs and Their Long-Term Results

Program name[a] (years attended) (source)	Ages of participation	Research design/methodological concerns	Sample size[b]	Time of last follow-up	Results[b]
1. Child–Parent Center (1965–1977) (Fuerst & Fuerst, 1993)	Entry: 3 or 4 years Exit: 9 years	Compared former CPC children with non-CPC children from same feeder schools. Not randomized. No pretest. School-administered tests.	Initial E = 684, C = 304 Follow-up E = 513, C = 244	Post-high school	Achievement tests: E > C at grade 2, E = C at grade 8 High school graduation: E > C E = 62%, C = 49%
2. Child–Parent Center II (1983–1985) (Reynolds, 1993, 1994a, 1994b)	Entry: 4 or 5 years Exit: 9 years	Compared former CPC children with several other groups. Not randomized. No pretest. School-administered tests.	Initial Unknown Follow-up E = 757, C = 130	Grade 7	Achievement tests: E > C for grades K to 7 Special education: E < C, E = 12%, C = 22% Grade retention: E < C, E = 24%, C = 34%
3. Cincinnati Title I Preschool (1969–1970; 1970–1971) (Nieman & Gastright, 1981)	Entry: 4 or 5 years Exit: 6 years	Compared children who attended full-day kindergarten and mostly had preschool with children who attended half-day kindergarten and mostly had no preschool. Not randomized. No pretest. School-administered tests.	Initial E = 688, C = 524 Follow-up E = 410, C = 141	Grade 8	Achievement tests: E > C for grades 1, 5, and 8 Special education: E = C, grade 8 E = 5%, C = 11% Grade retention: E = C, grade 8 E = 9%, C = 12%
4. Maryland Extended Elementary Pre-K (1977–1980) (Eckroade, Salehi, & Carter, 1988; Eckroade, Salehi, & Wode, 1991)	Entry: 4 years Exit: 5 years	Compared attenders to nonattenders, including only children continuously enrolled in school district (kindergarten to grade 5). Not randomized. Not pretest. High attrition. School-administered tests.	Initial Unknown Follow-up E = 356, C = 306	Grade 8	Achievement tests: E > C for grades 3, 5, and 8 Special education: E < C, grade 8 E = 15%, C = 22% Grade retention: E < C, grade 8 E = 31%, C = 45%

Study	Entry/Exit	Description	Sample	Grade	Results
5. New York State Experimental Prekindergarten (1975–1976) (State Education Department, University of the State of New York, 1982)	Entry: 3 or 4 years Exit: 5 years	Compared attenders with children in same district on waiting list and with children in other districts with no prekindergarten program. Not randomized. High attrition.	Initial 1,800[c] Follow-up E = 1,348, C = 258	Grade 3	Achievement tests: E > C in kindergarten E = C in grade 1 Special education: E = C, E = 2%, C = 5% Grade retention: E < C, E = 16%, C = 21%
6. Florida Prekindergarten Early Intervention Cohort 1 (King, Cappellini, & Gravens, 1995)	Entry: 4 years Exit: 5 years	Compared Pre-K early intervention children with children from same schools who qualified for free/reduced lunch. Not randomized. High attrition. School-administered tests. Pre-K EI children attended schools in poorer communities. First year of program operation.	Initial Unknown Follow-up E = 350, C = 352	Grades 3 and 4	Achievement tests: E > C in kindergarten E = C in grades 1 to 3, E < C in grade 4 Special education: E = C, E = 25%, C = 25% Grade retention: E = C, E = 3%, C = 3% Disciplined: E < C, E = 11%, C = 32%
7. Florida Prekindergarten Early Intervention Cohort 2 (King, Cappellini, & Rohani, 1995)	Entry: 4 years Exit: 5 years	Compare Pre-K early intervention children with children from same schools who qualified for free/reduced lunch. Not randomized. No pretest. High attrition. School-administered tests.	Initial Unknown Follow-up E = 983, C = 1,054	Grades 3 and 4	Achievement tests: E > C in kindergarten E = C in grades 1 to 4 Special education: E = C, E = 17%, C = 15% Grade retention: E < C, E = 9%, C = 13%
8. Florida Chapter I (King, Rohani, & Cappellini, 1995)	Entry: 4 years Exit: 5 years	Compared children screened into with those screened out of Chapter I pre-k based on a test (DIAL-R). Not randomized. High attrition. School-administered tests.	Initial E = 103, C = 121 Follow-up E = 54, C = 65	Grade 8	Achievement tests: E > C in grades 1,2,4,7,8 E = C in grades 5,6 (no data for grade 3)

(continued)

TABLE 27.2. cont.

Program name[a] (years attended) (source)	Ages of participation	Research design/methodological concerns	Sample size[b]	Time of last follow-up	Results[b]
9. Detroit Head Start and Title 1 Preschool (1972–1973) (Clark, 1979)	Entry: 4 years Exit: 5 years	Compared children who had attended Head Start or Title 1 preschool with children who were eligible but did not attend. Not randomized. No pretest. School-administered tests.	Initial Unknown Follow-up Unknown	Grade 4	Achievement tests: E > C in grade 4
10. DC Public Schools and Head Start (1986–1987) (Marcon, 1990, 1994)	Entry: 4 years Exit: 5 years	Compared children who attended public school preschool or Head Start with children in same kindergartens who had not. Not randomized. High attrition.	Initial E = 372, C = 89 Follow-up E varies, C varies	Grades 4 and 5	Achievement tests: E = C in grades 3 to 5 Special education: E = C, grade 4 E = 10%, C = 9% Grade retention: E = C, grade 4 E = 31%, C = 38%
11. Philadelphia School District Get Set and Head Start (1969–1970; 1970–1971) (Copple, Cline, & Smith, 1987)	Entry: 4 years Exit: 5 years	Compared children in enriched K–3 program (follow-through) who had and had not attended preschool. Not randomized. High attrition. School-administered tests.	Initial E = 1082, C = 1615 Follow-up E = 688, C = 524	Grades 4 to 8, varies by cohort	Achievement test: E = C Grade retention: E < C
12. Seattle DISTAR and Head Start (1970–1971) (Evans, 1985)	Entry: 4 years Exit: 5 years	Compared children who had attended Head Start and DISTAR with matched children from same school and grades. Not randomized. No pretest High attrition. School-administered tests.	Initial E = 92, C = unknown Follow-up E = 44, C = 20	Grades 6 and 8	Achievement tests: E = C, but positive trend, in grades 6 and 8
13. Cincinnati Head Start (1968–1969) (Pinkleton, 1976)	Entry: 4 years Exit: 5 years	Compared third graders who had attended Head Start with those who had not. Not randomized. No pretest.	Initial Unknown Follow-up Unknown	Grade 3	Achievement tests: E = C in grade 3

Study (citation)	Entry/Exit	Description	Sample size	Grade at follow-up	Results
14. Detroit Head Start (1969–1970) (O'Piela, 1976)	Entry: 4 years Exit: 5 or 6 years	Compared children who had attended Head Start with children in Title 1 elementary programs. Not randomized. School-administered tests.	Initial Unknown Follow-up Unknown	Grade 4	Achievement tests: E > C in grade 4
15. ETS Longitudinal Study of Head Start (1969–1970; 1970–1971) (Lee, Brooks-Gunn, Schnur, & Liaw, 1976; Shipman, 1970, 1976)	Entry: 4 or 5 years Exit: 5 or 6 years	Compared children who went to Head Start with children who went to other preschools or no preschool. Not randomized. High attrition.	Initial 1,875 Follow-up 852	Grade 3	Achievement tests: E > C in grade 1, E = C in grades 2 and 3
16. Hartford Head Start (1965–1966) (Goodstein, 1975)	Entry: 4 years Exit: 5 years	Compared children who had attended Head Start with those who had not. Not randomized. No pretest. High attrition. School-administered tests.	Initial 293 Follow-up E = 148, C = 50	Grade 6	Achievement tests: E = C in grade 6 Special education: E = C, E = 5%, C = 10% Grade retention: E < C, E = 10%, C = 22%
17. Kanawha County, West Virginia Head Start (1973–1974) (Kanawha Board of Education, 1978)	Entry: 4 years Exit: 5 years	Compared children who had attended Head Start with low-income children who had not. Not randomized. School-administered tests.	Initial Unknown Follow-up Unknown	Grade 3	Achievement tests: E = C in grade 3
18. Montgomery County, Maryland Head Start (1970–1971; 1974–1975; 1978–1979) (Hebbeler, 1985)	Entry: 4 years Exit: 5 years	Compared children who had attended eight or nine months with those who had attended 1 month or less. Not randomized. High attrition. School administered tests.	Initial E = 1,915, C = 619 Follow-up E = 186, C = 112	Grade 11	Achievement tests: E = C, but negative trend in most grades, E > C in grade 11
19. New Haven Head Start (1968–1969) (Abelson, 1974; Abelson, Zigler, & DeBlasi, 1974)	Entry: 4 years Exit: 5 years	Compared children who attended Head Start with those who had not. Not randomized. No pretest. High attrition.	Initial E = 61, C = 48 Follow-up E = 35, C = 26	Grade 3	Achievement tests: E > C in grade 1, E = C in grade 3 Grade retention: E < C, E = 18%, C = 35%

(continued)

TABLE 27.2. *Continued*

Program name[a] (years attended) (source)	Ages of participation	Research design/methodological concerns	Sample size[b]	Time of last follow-up	Results[b]
20. Pennsylvania Head Start (1986–1987) (Reedy, 1991)	Entry: 3 to 5 years Exit: 5 to 6 years	Compared children who attended Head Start with children who had applied but had not been admitted. Not randomized. No pretest.	Initial E = 98, C = unknown Follow-up E = 54, C = 18	Grade 3	Achievement tests: E = C, but positive trend in grades 2 and 3
21. Rome, Georgia Head Start (1966) (McDonald & Monroe, 1981)	Entry: 5 years Exit: 6 years	Compared children who attended Head Start with all children in first grade in disadvantaged schools in 1966. Not randomized. No pretest. School-administered tests.	Initial E = 130, C = 88 Follow-up E = 94, C = 60	Post-high school	Achievement tests: E > C in grade 5, E = C in grades 6 and above Special education: E < C, E = 11%, C = 25% Grade retention: E = C, E = 51%, C = 63% High school graduation: E > C, E = 50%, C = 33%
22. Westinghouse National Evaluation of Head Start (1965–1966) (Westinghouse Learning Corporation and Ohio University, 1969)	Entry: 4 or 5 years Exit: 5 or 6 years	Compared children who attended Head Start with those who did not (matched within grade). Not randomized. No pretest.	Initial Unknown Follow-up E = 1988, C = 1992	Grades 1 to 3	Achievement tests: E > C in grade 1, E = C in grades 2 and 3

[a]Programs are grouped such that public school program studies are listed first, followed by program studies involving both public school programs and Head Start, and then all Head Start studies.

[b]Throughout Table 27.2, E refers to the experimental or intervention group, and C refers to the control or comparison group. Outcomes listed as E > C or E < C were statistically significant at the $p < .05$ level.

[c]The numbers of children in experimental and comparison groups were not reported separately.

constructed comparison groups from waiting lists or other groups of children thought to be similar to program children. Others relied on natural variation in program attendance. In both approaches comparability problems can result from self-selection and administrative selection. Self-selection can create differences between groups because some parents exert more effort to educate and obtain educational opportunities for their children. The educational success of their children is likely to exceed that of children whose parents exert less effort, even without preschool education. The results of administrative selection are less clear. Programs may enroll the most needy, those easiest to recruit, or those thought most likely to gain from the program. Head Start and public school program studies are at a disadvantage in dealing with the potential biases introduced by selection because not only did they not use random assignment, but they rarely have pretest measures of children's cognitive abilities to verify that the groups were initially the same or to adjust for initial differences.

Long-Term Findings

Findings with respect to general cognitive ability, reading achievement, math achievement, and school success are reported by study in Tables 27.1 and 27.2. Results for measures other than reading tests provide a context that may assist in interpreting effects on reading. IQ scores can be viewed as measures of general cognitive abilities rather than subject-matter-specific knowledge and skills, though this distinction can be difficult to maintain, and many IQ tests have a strong verbal ability component. School success (primarily grade repetition and special education placement) is dependent on verbal abilities, particularly as reading plays an important role in accessing new knowledge from textbook reading and other schoolwork.

IQ EFFECTS

Initial IQ effects are ubiquitous in the small-scale program studies, and in most studies IQ gains were sustained until school entry. At age 5, 10 studies found effects between 4 and 11 IQ points, the Milwaukee study found a 25-point gain, and the Syracuse study found no effect. Three studies did not measure IQ at school entry. The two experimental studies that enrolled infants in full-day educational child-care programs found the largest initial effects and that some IQ gain persisted at least into adolescence. The other studies that enrolled infants did not find persistent effects, but both were quasi-experimental and one ceased serving children before age 3. The latter result is similar to that of the IHDP study reported earlier.

None of the large-scale program studies obtained data on IQ tests comparable to those used in the model program studies. A few studies employed the Peabody Picture Vocabulary Test (PPVT), which is sometimes considered a "quick" test of IQ, and one study administered the Illinois Test of Pyscholinquistic Abilities (ITPA). Although questions can be raised about the comparability of these measures to IQ tests generally, the results were quite comparable. No effects are found on these measures after school entry.

ACHIEVEMENT EFFECTS

Five of 11 model program studies with achievement data found statistically significant positive effects on reading test scores beyond grade 3. Evidence of effects was strongest in the six studies that randomized assignment to program and control groups. The Abecedarian and Perry Preschool studies found effects on reading and literacy scores persisting into early adulthood. The Houston Parent Child Development Center (PCDC) study found reading effects to the time of last follow-up, grades 2 to 5. The Florida Parent Education study found some effects on reading scores through grade 7 for children with at least 2 consecutive years in the program. The Milwaukee study found that effects were statistically significant only to grade 2, and the ETP found no significant effects on reading by grade 4, but both studies had little power to detect lasting effects due to small samples ($N < 50$). Of the quasi-experimental model program studies, only one found persistent effects on reading achievement.

Achievement test results varied among the Head Start and public school studies, but the vast majority report positive effects at some time during elementary school. Of 22 studies, 14 found significant effects, including 7 with positive effects in their last follow-up. Studies with significant effects on achievement found them across the board rather than in a single area so that effects on reading are accompanied by effects on math.

A simple interpretation of the results would be that most preschool programs for disadvantaged children produce initial gains in reading achievement as part of a general pattern of increased cognitive abilities, but that these gains generally do not last through the primary years. However, a closer look at the evidence indicates that the apparent fadeout in effects on reading achievement may result from problems with research design and procedures that bias estimated effects toward zero and attrition in achievement test data that decreases statistical power.

Many studies relied on the standardized tests routinely administered by schools for their reading achievement data. This is a low-cost approach, but it has several unfortunate consequences. First, greater random error can be expected when testing is done for entire classes by teachers rather than individually by specialists. Second, tests are administered by grade so that children who repeat a grade are not tested with their age cohort. Third, children expected to perform poorly on the tests often are excluded, as the use of test scores to hold districts and schools "accountable" creates pressures for school administrators to remove poor performers from the test pool at each grade level (McGill-Franzen & Allington, 1993). Many schools do not test children in special education classes, for example.

At best, studies relying on school-administered tests have reading test data with lower reliability and sample sizes that decline over time, both of which would reduce their ability to detect long-term program effects. At worst, such studies systematically lose the more poorly performing students from year to year as the cumulative percentage of children retained in grade, placed in special education, or otherwise omitted from testing grows. The result is that any differences between program and comparison groups are gradually hidden as grade level rises because the children for whom achievement tests are available become more similar across the two groups.

Some studies had idiosyncratic flaws that led to similar biases in achievement test data, even though tests were specially administered for the studies. For example, the New Haven Head Start study individually administered achievement tests, but only to children at expected grade level. The Educational Testing Service (ETS) Head Start study tested only children in classes in which at least 50% of the children were study participants. As children move through school, those placed in special education classes or who repeated a grade would be lost from the sample. The Westinghouse national evaluation of Head Start formed its comparison group by matching former Head Start children in grades 1, 2, and 3 with other children in their grade levels. This automatically equated the two groups on grade level and generated comparison groups that included children from older cohorts who had been retained. In the second and third grade when effects appear to "fade out," the Head Start groups are significantly younger than the comparison.

Studies that found persistent effects on reading achievement generally did not suffer from these design and procedure problems. The two experimental studies that provide the strongest evidence for long-term effects on reading administered individualized achievement tests and maintained adequate sample sizes. The second CPC study obtained and analyzed test scores for children who repeated. The Cincinnati Title 1 study had low rates of grade repetition and special education placement that were unlikely to introduce much difference between groups.

The results of the Abecedarian and High/Scope Perry Preschool studies deserve special attention. These studies are the strongest with respect to internal validity and provided measures of effects of reading from the early primary grades to the early adult years. The Abecedarian study found statistically significant effects on reading achievement, from age 8 through age 21. From age 8 to age 15, the Abecedarian study provides data on total reading achievement and subscales from the Wood-cock–Johnson Tests of Academic Achievement (Woodcock & Johnson, 1977). Statistical analyses were conducted with a repeated-measures ANOVA (analysis of variance) testing for effects of group (preschool vs. control), time, and group-by-time interaction (Campbell, 1997). Results indicate that the program's effects on reading achievement were large (.75 to .50 standard deviations) and across all subscales— word identification, word attack, and passage comprehension. It appears that size of the effects may have decreased over time on the passage comprehension subscale but not on the other reading subscales. At age 15, the Abecedarian program increased the average reading score roughly from the 30th to the 40th percentile. These reading gains are reported to have been sustained until age 21 (Carolina Abecedarian Project, 1999).

The High/Scope Perry Preschool study provides reading or literacy test scores from age 7 to age 27. The tests employed are the California Achievement Test (CAT; Tiegs & Clark, 1971) through age 14 and the Adult Performance Level (APL; American College Testing Program, 1976) at ages 19 and 27. The Perry Preschool program found significant effects (one-tailed test, $p < .05$) on the CAT total score beginning at age 8, and on the reading and language subtests by age 9 (Schweinhart, 1996; Schweinhart, Barnes, Weikart, Barnett, & Epstein, 1993). The strongest results are at ages 14 and 19 (Schweinhart, 1996; Schweinhart et al., 1993). Significant effects are no longer found at age 27. Standardized effect sizes in the Perry Preschool study suggest the possibility that effects on reading grew throughout the school years. However, it is also possible that the pattern results from differences in the sensitivity of the tests over time (and similar concerns can be raised about the pattern in the Abecedarian reading scores). The Perry Preschool program's effects on reading tend to be somewhat smaller than the Abecedarian effects, one-third to one-half of a standard deviation. Of course, caution is required in making comparisons because of differences in the tests and in the samples (the Perry Preschool

sample was selected based on low IQ test scores). In percentiles the average gain in reading achievement at age 14 was from the 9th to the 15th percentile (Schweinhart et al., 1993).

EFFECTS ON SCHOOL SUCCESS

School success was most commonly measured by grade repetition and special education placement. Evidence of positive effects on these outcomes was quite uniform across the studies. All but one of the small-scale program studies reported grade repetition and special education rates, and everyone of these reported lower rates for the preschool program group. Five studies found statistically significant differences. In the large-scale program studies, statistically significant effects were found in 10 of the 13 studies with data on grade repetition or special education.

As these school success effects are all measured as percentages, effect estimates can be pooled to estimate average effects across studies and to compare the results of different types of programs. Table 27.3 presents means and standard deviations of estimated effects for grade repetition and special education separately for small-scale and large-scale program studies. Average effects are substantial for both types of programs, though effects are significantly larger for small-scale programs (two-tailed t-test, $p < .05$). Differences in results between the two types of program studies could be due to differences in samples and contexts, and higher rates of grade repetition and special education for the control groups in the small-scale program studies permit larger effects.

Two studies provide direct comparisons of effects between the two types of programs on IQ and achievement test scores (but not on school success measures, unfortunately). Both indicate that the more intensive, higher quality, small-scale programs produced larger effects. The Abecedarian study found the effects of the comparison group's participation in child care that met federal guidelines for quality to be no more than half the size of the Abecedarian program effects (Burchinal et al., 1989). A comparison of the Learning-to-Learn pro-

TABLE 27.3. Long-Term Effects (Percentage Point Changes) on School Success by Type of Program

Outcome measure	Model programs			Head start/public School		
	Mean	(SD)	n	Mean	(SD)	n
Special education	19.6**	(14.6)	11	4.7**	(5.3)	9
Grade repetition	14.9*	(9.8)	14	8.4*	(5.4)	10

**p < .01, two-tailed t-test with unequal variances
*p < .05, two-tailed t-test with unequal variances

gram with Head Start and Title 1 public school classrooms found that children who attended the small-scale program scored higher on IQ and achievement tests from the end of the preschool year through third grade (Van de Reit & Resnick, 1973).

DO LONG-TERM EFFECTS REQUIRE SCHOOL-AGE INTERVENTION?

The evidence reviewed previously establishes that preschool programs can produce long-term effects on achievement and school success for children in poverty *without* school-age follow-up interventions, as these were not present in most studies. This is not evidence for an inoculation model of early intervention. It is consistent with the view that children are active learners who draw on resources in their environments in and out of school. It is also consistent with the view that the first few years of schooling have an important influence on future school success, for example, by affecting reading group placements and other ability tracking, teacher expectations, parental expectations, and the child's sense of self-efficacy, motivation, and classroom behavior (Barnett et al., 1998; Entwisle, 1995). None of this suggests that society should abandon efforts to improve the elementary education of disadvantaged children whether by such structural changes as decreased class size or through improved pedagogy (Allington & Walmsley, 1995; Levin, 1987; Mosteller, 1995; Ross, Smith, Casey, & Slavin, 1995). Preschool education hardly obviates the need for other educational reforms and interventions. There is ample room for further improvements in the reading achievement and school success of disadvantaged children who have received even the most intensive preschool education programs.

Discussion

Preschool education in a variety of forms improves general cognitive abilities during early childhood and produces long-term increases in reading achievement. In most cases, persistent reading gains are not accompanied by persistent gains in general cognitive abilities as measured by IQ tests but are accompanied by increases in language and math achievement and in school success as measured by grade repetition and special education placement. Although a substantial number of studies fail to find persistent effects on reading achievement, these results can be explained by flaws in study design and follow-up procedures (which have less effect on measures of school success) and are contradicted by the results of well-implemented true experiments.

Why IQ effects generally fade out while effects persist on reading and other subject-matter specific achievement tests is unclear. Some equalization of IQs is expected when children who did not attend preschool programs enter school, but the primary cause of the fadeout in IQ effects is not a subsequent rise in IQs for the comparison group (Campbell & Ramey, 1995; Ceci, 1991; Husen & Tuijnman, 1991; Schweinhart et al., 1993). Nevertheless, initial effects on general cognitive abilities seem to be the source of early effects on achievement. Possibly these early effects set in motion a cycle of effects on motivation, school behavior, expectations, opportunity to learn, and achievement (Barnett et al., 1998; Entwisle, 1995). It is also possible that these results are an artifact of measurement; that when children are young, IQ tests primarily assess the specific knowledge and skills that provide a foundation for learning reading, writing, mathematics, and other subject matter, but as children become older the tests assess more general abilities (Barnett et al., 1998).

Cross-study comparisons indicate that some types of programs are more effective than others. Several popular home-based approaches appear to be ineffective (see also Boutte, 1992), though other approaches to working with parents have been found effective (e.g., Barnett, Escobar, & Ravsten, 1988; Whitehurst et al., 1994). Most child-care programs produce relatively small effects. However, highly intensive full-day, year-round educational child care beginning in infancy and continuing to school entry seems to produce the greatest long-term cognitive and academic gains for children in poverty, including large improvements in reading achievement. Research on this hypothesis ought to have a high priority.

Head Start and public school programs produce smaller gains in reading achievement and school success than do better-funded model preschool education programs. This suggests that underfunding of public preschool programs may seriously limit the magnitude of the improvements produced in disadvantaged children's learning and development. One response to this is additional research, perhaps using true experiments to produce more rigorous evidence on the issue. However, weighing the potential costs of the alternatives, it would be less risky to increase funding for these programs now rather than wait for additional research (Barnett, 1993). Finally, public programs could benefit from additional research on learning and teaching in the early years that could provide more guidance for teachers regarding the most productive approaches to the development of abilities and dispositions that facilitate later achievement in reading and other subject-matter areas.

References

Abelson, W. D. (1974). Head Start graduates in school: Studies in New Haven, Connecticut. In S. Ryan, (Ed.), *A report on longitudinal evaluations of preschool programs* (vol. I, pp. 1–14). Washington, DC: U. S. Department of Health Education, and Welfare.

Abelson, W. D., Zigler, E., & DeBlasi, C. L. (1974). Effects of a four-year follow through program on economically disadvantaged children. *Journal of Educational Psychology, 66*(5), 756–71.

Alexander, K. L., & Entwisle, D. R. (1988). Achievement in the first two years of school: Patterns and processes. *Monographs of the Society for Research in Child Development, 53*(2), (Serial No. 218).

Allington, R. L., & Walmsley, S. A. (1995). *No quick fix: Rethinking literacy programs in America's elementary schools.* New York: Teachers College Press.

American College Testing Program. (1976). *User's guide: Adult APL Survey.* Iowa City, IA: Author.

Andrews, S., Blumenthal, J., Johnson, D., Kahn, A., Ferguson, C. Lasater, T., Malone, P., & Wallace, D. (1982). The skills of mothering: A study of parent–child development centers. *Monographs of the Society for Research in Child Development, 46*(6,. Serial No. 198).

Barnett, W. S. (1993). Benefit–cost analysis of preschool education: Findings from a 25-year follow-up. *American Journal of Orthopsychiatry, 63*(4), 500–508.

Barnett, W. S., Escobar, C. M, & Ravsten, M. (1988). Parent and clinic early intervention for children with language handicaps: A cost-effectiveness analysis. *Journal of the Division for Early Childhood, 12,* 290–298.

Barnett, W. S., Young, J., & Schweinhart, L. J. (1998). How preschool education contributes to cognitive development and school success: An empirical model. In W. S. Barnett & S. S. Boocock (Eds.), *Early care and education for children in poverty: promises, programs, and long-term outcomes* (pp. 167–184). Buffalo, NY: State University of New York Press.

Beller, K. (1983). The Philadelphia Study: The impact of preschool on intellectual and socio-emotional development. In Consortium for Longitudinal Studies, (Ed.), *As the twig is bent . . . lasting effects of preschool programs* (pp. 133–170). Hillsdale, NJ: Erlbaum.

Belsky, J. (1988). The "effects" of infant day care reconsidered. *Early Childhood Research Quarterly, 3,* 235–272.

Benasich, A. A., Brooks-Gunn, J., & Clewell, B. C. (1992). How do mothers benefit from early intervention programs? *Journal of Applied Developmental Psychology, 13,* 311–362.

Boutte, G. S. (1992). *The effects of home intervention on rural children's home environments, academic self-esteem, and achievement scores—A longitudinal study.* Unpublished dissertation, UMI Dissertation Services.

Bradley, R., & Caldwell, B. M. (1979). Home observation for measurement of the environment: A revision of the preschool scale. *American Journal of Mental Deficiency, 84,* 235–244.

Brooks-Gunn, J., McCormick, M. C., Shapiro, S., Benasich, A. A., & Black, G. W. (1994). The effects of early education intervention on maternal employment, public assistance, and health insurance: The Infant Health and Development Program. *American Journal of Public Health, 84*(6), 924–930.

Burchinal, M., Lee, M., & Ramey, C. (1989). Type of day-care and intellectual development in disadvantaged children. *Child Development, 60,* 128–37.

Caldwell, B. M. (1987). Sustaining intervention effects: Putting malleability to the test. In J. J. Gallagher & C. T. Ramey (Eds.), *The malleability of children* (pp. 115–126). Baltimore: Brookes.

Campbell, F. A. (1997). Unpublished analyses of Abecedarian data.

Campbell, F. A., & Ramey, C. T. (1993, March 26). *Mid-adolescent outcomes for high risk students: An examination of the continuing effects of early intervention.* Paper presented at the biennial meeting of the Society for Research in Child Development, New Orleans.

Campbell, F. A., & Ramey, C. T. (1994). Effects of early intervention on intellectual and academic achievement: A follow-up study of children from low-income families. *Child Development, 65,* 684–698.

Campbell, F. A., & Ramey, C. T. (1995). Cognitive and school outcomes for high-risk African-American students at middle adolescence: positive effects of early intervention. *American Educational Research Journal, 32*(4), 743–772.

Carolina Abecedarian Project. (1999). *Executive summary. Early learning, later success: The Abecedarian study.* Chapel Hill, NC: Frank Porter Graham, University of North Carolina. Available: www. fpg. unc. edu/~abc/executive_summary.htm

Caughy, M. O., DiPietro, J., & Stobino, M. (1994). Day-care participation as a protective factor in the cognitive development of low-income children. *Child Development, 65,* 457–471.

Ceci, S. J. (1991). How much does schooling influence general intelligence and its cognitive components? A reassessment of the evidence. *Developmental Psychology, 27,* 703–22.

Clark, C. M. (1979). *Effects of the project Head Start and Title I preschool programs on vocabulary and reading achievement measured at the kindergarten and fourth grade levels.* Unpublished doctoral dissertation, Wayne State University.

Copple, C. E., Cline, M. G., & Smith, A. N. (1987). *Path to the future: Long-term effects of Head Start in the Philadelphia School District.* Washington, DC: U. S. Department of Health and Human Services.

Deutsch, M. (1965). The role of social class in language development and cognition. *American Journal of Orthopsychiatry, 25,* 78–88.

Deutsch, M., Deutsch, C. P., Jordan, T. J., & Grallo, R. (1983). The IDS Program: An experiment in early and sustained enrichment. In Consortium for Longitudinal Studies (Ed.), *As the twig is bent . . . lasting effects of preschool programs* (pp. 377–410). Hillsdale, NJ: Erlbaum.

Deutsch, M., Taleporos, E., & Victor, J. (1974). A brief synopsis of an initial enrichment program in early childhood. In S. Ryan (Ed.), *A report on longitudinal evaluations of preschool programs* (Vol. I, pp. 49–61). Washington, DC: U.S. Department of Health Education, and Welfare.

Eckroade, G., Salehi, S., & Carter, J. (1988). *An analysis of the midterm effects of the extended elementary education prekindergarten program.* Baltimore: Maryland State Department of Education.

Eckroade, G., Salehi, S., & Wode, J. (1991). *An analysis of the long-term effect of the extended elementary education prekindergarten program.* A paper presented at the annual meeting of the American Educational Research Association, Chicago.

Entwisle, D. R. (1995). The role of schools in sustaining early childhood program benefits. *The Future of Children, 5*(3), 133–144.

Evans, E. (1985). Longitudinal follow-up assessment of differential preschool experience for low income minority group children. *Journal of Educational Research, 78*(4), 197–202.

Fuerst, J. S., & Fuerst, D. (1993). Chicago experience with an early childhood program: The special case of the Child Parent Center Program. *Urban Education, 28,* 69–96.

Garber, H. L. (1988). *The Milwaukee Project: Prevention of mental retardation in children at risk.* Washington, DC: American Association on Mental Retardation.

Goodstein, H. A. (1975). *The prediction of elementary school failure among high-risk children.* Unpublished paper, Connecticut University.

Gray, S. W., Ramsey, B., & Klaus, R. (1982). *From 3 to 20: The Early Training Project.* Baltimore: University Park Press.

Gray, S., Ramsey, B., & Klaus, R. (1983). The Early Training Project, 1962–1980. In Consortium for Longitudinal Studies, (Ed.), *As the twig is bent . . . lasting effects of preschool programs* (pp. 33–70). Hillsdale, NJ: Erlbaum.

Haskins, R. (1989). Beyond metaphor: The efficacy of early childhood education. *American Psychologist, 44,* 274–282.

Hebbeler, K. (1985). An old and a new question on the effects of early education for children from low income families. *Educational Evaluation and Policy Analysis, 7*(3), 207–16.

Helburn, S., & Culkin, M. L. (1995). *Cost, quality, and child outcomes in child care centers: Executive summary.* Denver: Economics Department, University of Colorado at Denver.

Herrnstein, R. J., & Murray, C. (1994). *The bell curve: Intelligence and class structure in American life.* New York: Free Press.

Herzog, E., Newcomb, C. H., & Cisin, I. H. (1974). Double deprivation: The less they have, the less they learn. In S. Ryan, (Ed.), *A report on longitudinal evaluations of preschool programs* (Vol. I, pp. 62–76). Washington, DC: U. S. Department of Health, Education, and Welfare.

Husen, T., & Tuijnman, A. (1991). The contribution of formal schooling to the increase in intellectual capital. *Educational Researcher, 20*(7), 17–25.

Infant Health and Development Program. (1990). Enhancing the outcomes of low-birth-weight premature infants. *Journal of the American Medical Association, 263*(22), 3035–3042.

Jester, R. E., & Guinagh, B. J. (1983). The Gordon Parent Education Infant and Toddler Program. In Consortium for Longitudinal Studies (Ed.), *As the twig is bent . . . lasting effects of preschool programs* (pp. 103–132). Hillsdale, NJ : Erlbaum.

Johnson, D., & Walker, T. (1991). A follow-up evaluation of the Houston Parent–Child Development Center: School performance. *Journal of Early Intervention, 15*(3), 226–236.

Kanawha County Board of Education. (1978). *Kanawha Count Head Start evaluation study.* Unpublished report.

Karnes, M. B., Shwedel, A. M., & Williams. M. B. (1983). A comparison of five approaches for educating young children from low-income homes. In Consortium for Longitudinal Studies (Ed.), *As the twig is bent . . . lasting effects of preschool programs* (pp. 133–170). Hillsdale, NJ: Erlbaum.

King, F. J., Cappellini, C. H., & Gravens, L. (1995). *A longitudinal study of the Florida Prekindergarten Early Intervention Program, Part III.* Tallahassee: Educational Services Program, Florida State University.

King, F. J., Cappellini, C. H., & Rohani, F. (1995). *A longitudinal study of the Florida Prekindergarten Early Intervention Program, Part IV.* Tallahassee: Educational Services Program, Florida State University.

King, F. J., Rohani, F., & Cappellini, C. H. (1995). *A ten-year study of a prekindergarten program in Florida.* Tallahassee: Educational Services Program, Florida State University.

Lally, J. R., Mangione, P., & Honig, A. (1988). The Syracuse University Family Development Program: Long-range impact of an early intervention with low-income children and their families. In D. Powell (Ed.), *Parent education as early childhood intervention: Emerging directions theory research and practice* (pp. 79–104). Norwood, NJ: Ablex.

Lamb, M., & Sternberg, K. (1990). Do we really know how day care affects children? *Journal of Applied Development Psychology, 11,* 351–379.

Lazar, I., Darlington, R., Murray, H., Royce, J., & Snipper, A. (1982). Lasting effects of early education: A report from the Consortium for Longitudinal Studies. *Monographs of the Society for Research in Child Development, 47*(2–3), (Serial No. 195).

Lee, V. E., Brooks-Gunn, J., Schnur, E., & Liaw, F. R. (1990). Are Head Start effects sustained? A longitudinal follow-up comparison of disadvantaged children attending Head Start, no preschool, and other preschool programs. *Child Development, 61,* 495–507.

Levenstein, P., O'Hara, J., & Madden J. (1983). The Mother–Child Home Program of the Verbal Interaction Project. In Consortium for Longitudinal Studies (Ed.), *As the twig is bent . . . lasting effects of preschool programs* (pp. 237–263). Hillsdale, NJ: Erlbaum.

Levin, H. M. (1987). Accelerated schools for disadvantaged students. *Educational Leadership, 44*(6), 19–21.

Locurto, C. (1991). Beyond IQ in preschool programs? *Intelligence, 15,* 295–312.

Marcon, R. A. (1990). *Early learning and early identification: Final report of the three year longitudinal study.* Washington, DC: District of Columbia Public Schools.

Marcon, R. A. (1993). *Early learning and early identification follow-up study: Transition from the early to the later childhood grades 1990–93.* Washington, DC: District of Columbia Public Schools, Center for Systemic Change.

Marcon, R. A. (1994). Doing the right thing for children: Linking research and policy reform in the District of Columbia Public Schools. *Young Children, 50*(1), 8–20.

McDonald, M. S., & Monroe, E. (1981). *A follow-up study of the 1966 Head Start program, Rome City schools.* Unpublished paper.

McGill-Franzen, A., & Allington, R. L. (1993). Flunk 'em or Get Them Classified: The contamination of primary grade accountability data. *Educational Researcher, 22*(1), 19–22.

McKey, R., Condelli, L., Ganson, H., et al. (1985). *The impact of Head Start on children, families, and communities. Final report of the Head Start Evaluation, Synthesis, and Utilization Project.* Washington, DC: U. S. Department of Health and Human Services.

Miller, L. B., & Bizzell, R. P. (1983). The Louisville Experiment: A comparison of four programs. In Consortium for Longitudinal Studies (Ed.), *As the twig is bent . . . lasting effects of preschool programs* (pp. 171–200). Hillsdale, NJ: Erlbaum.

Miller, L. B., & Bizzell, R. P. (1984). Long-term effects of four preschool programs: Ninth and tenth grade results. *Child Development, 55*(6), 1570–1587.

Mosteller, F. (1995). The Tennessee study of class size in the early grades. *Future of Children, 5*(2), 113–127.

NICHD Early Child Care Research Network. (1999). Child care and mother–child interaction in the first 3 years of life. *Developmental Psychology, 35*(6), 1399–1413.

Nieman, R. H., & Gastright, J. F. (1981). *The long-term effects of ESEA Title I preschool and all-day kindergarten: An eight-year follow-up.* Cincinnati, OH: Cincinnati Public Schools.

O'Piela, J. M. (1976). *Evaluation of the Detroit public schools Head Start program, 1975–1976.* Detroit, MI: Detroit Public Schools.

Palmer, F. (1983). The Harlem Study: Effects by type of training, age of training, and social class. In Consortium for Longitudinal Studies (Ed.), *As the twig is bent . . . lasting effects of preschool programs* (pp. 201–236). Hillsdale, NJ: Erlbaum.

Peisner-Feinberg, E. S., Burchinal, M. R., Clifford, R., Culkin, M., Howes, C., Kagan, L., Yazejian, N., Byler, P., Rustici, J., & Zelazo, J. (1999). *The children of the Cost, Quality, and Outcomes Study go to school: Technical report.* Chapel Hill: University of North Carolina at Chapel Hill, Frank Porter Graham Child Development Center.

Phillips, D. A., McCartney, K., & Scarr, S. (1987).

Child-care quality and children's social development. *Developmental Psychology, 23,* 537–543.

Pinkleton, N. B. (1976). *A comparison of referred Head Start, non-referred Head Start and non-Head Start groups of primary school children on achievement, language processing, and classroom behavior.* Unpublished doctoral dissertation, University of Cincinnati.

Ramey, C. T., Bryant, D. M., & Suarez, T. M. (1986). Preschool compensatory education and the modifiability of intelligence: A critical review. In D. Detterman (Ed.), *Current topics in human intelligence* (pp. 247–296). Norwood, NJ: Ablex.

Reedy, Y. B. (1991). *A comparison of long range effects of participation in Project Head Start and the impact of three differing delivery models.* Unpublished paper for the Graduate Program in School Psychology, Pennsylvania State University.

Reynolds, A. J. (1993). One year of preschool intervention or two: Does it matter? *Early Childhood Research Quarterly, 10,* 1–33.

Reynolds, A. J. (1994a). Effects of a preschool plus follow-on intervention for children at risk. *Developmental Psychology, 30,* 787–804.

Reynolds, A. J. (1994b, February 4). *Longer-term effects of the Child–Parent Center and Expansion Program.* Paper presented at the annual meeting of the Chicago Association for the Education of Young Children.

Roberts, J., Rabinowitch, S., Bryant, D. M., Burchinal, M., Koch, M., & Ramey, C. T. (1989). Language skills of children with different preschool experiences. *Journal of Speech and Hearing Research, 32,* 773–86.

Ross, S. M., Smith, L. J., Casey, J., & Slavin, R. E. (1995). Increasing the academic success of disadvantaged children: An examination of alternative early intervention programs. *American Educational Research Journal, 32*(4), 773–800.

Rowe, D. C. (1997). A place at the policy table? Behavior genetics and estimates of family environmental effects on IQ. *Intelligence, 24*(1), 133–158.

Scarr, S. (1998). American child care today. *American Psychologist, 53*(2), 95–108.

Schweinhart, L. J. (1996). *Unpublished analyses provided to the author.* Ypsilanti, MI: High/Scope.

Schweinhart, L. J., Barnes, H. V., Weikart, D. P., Barnett, W. S., & Epstein, A. S. (1993). *Significant benefits: The High/Scope Perry Preschool study through age 27* [Monographs of the High/Scope Educational Research Foundation No. 10]. Ypsilanti, MI: High/Scope Press.

Seitz, V. (1990). Intervention programs for impoverished children: A comparison of educational and family support models. *Annals of Child Development, 7,* 73–104.

Seitz, V., & Apfel, N. H. (1994). Parent-focused intervention: Diffusion effects on siblings. *Child Development, 65,* 677–683.

Seitz, V., Rosenbaum, L. K., & Apfel, N. H. (1985). Effects of family support intervention: A ten-year follow-up. *Child Development, 56,* 376–391.

Shipman, V. C. (1970). Disadvantaged children and their first school experiences: ETS—Head Start Longitudinal Study. *Preliminary description of the initial sample prior to school enrollment* (ETS Technical Report Series, PR-70-20). Princeton, NJ: Educational Testing Service.

Shipman, V. C. (1976). *Stability and change in family status, situational, and process variables and their relationship to children's cognitive performance.* Princeton, NJ: Educational Testing Service.

Spitz, H. H. (1991). Commentary on Locurto's 'Beyond IQ in Preschool Programs?' *Intelligence, 15,* 327–33.

State Education Department, University of the State of New York. (1982). *Evaluation of the New York State experimental prekindergarten program: Final report.* Albany, NY: New York State Education Department. (ERIC Document Reproduction Service No. ED 219 123)

Stevenson, H. W., & Newman, R. S. (1986). Long-term prediction of achievement and attitudes in mathematics and reading. *Child Development, 56,* 646–659.

St. Pierre, R., & Lopez, M. (1994, December 16). *The comprehensive child development program.* Paper presented at the National Research Council, Board on Children and Families, Washington, DC.

St. Pierre, R., Swartz, J., Murray, S., Deck, D., & Nicke, P. (1993). *National evaluation of the Even Start Family Literacy Program, report on effectiveness.* Washington, DC: U.S. Department of Education, Office of Policy and Planning.

Tiegs, E. W., & Clark, W. W. (1971). *California Achievement Tests. 1970 ed.* Monterey Park, CA: McGraw-Hill.

Van de Reit, V., & Resnick, M. B. (1973). *Learning to learn: An effective model for early childhood education.* Gainesville: University of Florida Press.

Wagner, M. W., & Clayton, S. L. (1999). The Parents as Teachers Program: Results from two demonstrations. *Future of Children, 9*(1), 91–116.

Wasik, B. H., Ramey, C. T., Bryant, D. M., & Sparling, J. J. (1990). A longitudinal study of two early intervention strategies: Project CARE. *Child Development, 61,* 1682–1696.

Weikart, D. P., Bond, J. T., & McNeil, J. T. (1978). *The Ypsilanti Perry Preschool Project: Preschool years and longitudinal results through fourth grade.* Ypsilanti, MI: High/Scope Press.

Westinghouse Learning Corporation and Ohio University. (1969). *The impact of Head Start: An evaluation of the effects of Head Start on children's cognitive and affective development* (vols. 1 and 2) (Report to the Office of Economic Opportunity). Athens, OH: Westinghouse Learning Corporation and Ohio University.

White, K. (1982). The relation between socioeconomic status and academic achievement. *Psychological Bulletin, 91,* 461–481.

White, K., & Casto, G. (1985). An integrative review of early intervention efficacy studies with at-risk children: Implications for the handicapped.

Analysis and Intervention in Developmental Disabilities, 5, 7–31.

Whitehurst, G. J., Epstein, J., Angell, A., Payne, A., Crone, D., & Fischel, J. (1994). Outcomes of an emergent literacy intervention in Head Start. *Journal of Educational Psychology, 80*(4), 542–555.

Woodcock, R. W., & Johnson, M. B. (1977). *Woocock-Johnson Psycho-Educational Battery.* Hingham, MA: Teaching Resources Corp.

Zaslow, M. (1991). Variation in child care quality and its implications for children. *Journal of Social Issues, 47*(2), 125–139.

Zigler, E., & Muenchow, S. (1992). *Head Start: The inside story of American's most successful educational experiment.* New York: Basic Books.

Zigler, E., & Styfco, S. J. (1993). Using policy research and theory to justify and inform Head Start expansion. *Social Policy Report, 8*(2).

28

Intergenerational Family Literacy: Concepts, Research, and Practice

❖

BARBARA HANNA WASIK
DIONNE R. DOBBINS
SUZANNAH HERRMANN

The study of literacy and language in families is not a new phenomenon. Sociologists, anthropologists, psychologists, linguists, and others who examine family life have a long history of exploring the uses of language among family members. The concept of family literacy, though rarely discussed in educational arenas until the 1980s, has come to refer to a wide range of beliefs and practices about the roles and transfer of literacy within families, children's literacy, adult literacy, early-childhood education, parenting education, and home–school links related to literacy. As a result of these various uses, questions have been raised about definitions and models of family literacy, and several frameworks have been proposed for organizing the multiple uses of the concept family literacy. For example, Morrow and Paratore (1993) developed a model that includes three categories: (1) the uses of literacy within families, (2) home–school partnerships, and (3) intergenerational literacy intervention program.

Before examining family literacy, we first consider definitions of literacy and family because of their centrality to family literacy. Literacy is conventionally defined as one's ability to read and write (see Whitehurst & Lonigan, Chapter 2). In the 1998 report by the National Academy of Science, *Prevent-ing Reading Difficulties in Young Children,* a more inclusive definition was proposed. In this definition literacy is described as including reading, writing, other creative or analytic acts, and knowledge and skill in specific subject matter (Anderson & Pearson, 1984; Snow, Burns, & Griffin, 1998). During the past decade, as researchers and program developers have examined the mechanisms of social support for the development of "literacy," the term has become recognized as a more complex process than previously believed (Snow & Tabors, 1996). Literacy can be seen as a set of complex multidimensional skills that improve over the life of an individual from childhood to adulthood. Both the complexity of literacy and its developmental nature have direct implications for how literacy is examined (Snow, Barnes, Chandler, Goodman, & Hemphill, 1991) and how intervention programs are implemented.

Literacy is also described as a social practice, not simply a skill learned through formal schooling and detached from other social contexts (Delgado-Gaitan, 1994; Street, 1984; in particular also see Gee, Chapter 3, and Pellegrini, Chapter 5). Viewing literacy as a social construct takes into the account variables such as the family's socioeconomic level, social and political relations, beliefs, and relationships to other organizations in the family's environment (Delgado-Gaitan, 1990, 1994). For example, asking questions is described as a sociocultural activity because how questions are formulated and responded to varies as a function of the family's social class (Delgado-Gaitan, 1990).

Also important in discussing family literacy are definitions of family. Broad definitions of family that take into account changing social and demographic conditions as well as cultural differences are essential. Family may refer to a unit including a father, a mother, and two children. But it may also refer to a mother and child, a grandparent, and three children; two unmarried adults with children; or related individuals across three generations.

Family literacy in this chapter is framed as a concept that includes naturally occurring practices within the home, family, and community and as a formal activity, exemplified by organized instruction usually linked with educational settings. We believe these are not mutually exclusive categories. Literacy practices change within and across generations as a function of family members' interactions with their environment, especially educational institutions. In our present society, how educational programs influence a family's literacy practices has been at the center of a major debate in the field of family literacy and one we discuss in this chapter.

We see the study of family literacy as a broad one that is inclusive of (1) descriptive studies of literacy and language practices within families; (2) studies of family and parent influences on children's literacy, language, and reading; and (3) studies on family literacy interventions, including children, parents, and the family as a whole. Family literacy includes studies about specific intervention procedures, such as adult education, early-childhood education, and parenting education, as well as programs for learners of English as a second language. Family literacy may also encompass studies of emergent literacy, reading, and school performance.

In this chapter we examine the ways that family literacy has been conceptualized, assumptions that have influenced the development of intervention programs, and empirical findings related to children's literacy and language. We conclude with recommendations for research.

Conceptualization of Family Literacy

In this section we describe conceptualizations of family literacy using the framework of family literacy as both a naturally occurring practice and a formal activity. Under the naturally occurring practice, we discuss both literacy practices in the family and family influences on children's literacy.

Naturally Occurring Literacy Practices in the Family

Studies of naturally occurring literacy activities within families and communities have been conducted in part to examine differences in literacy practices among families of different cultures and income levels and to study the relationship between family activities and later school success. The first use of the construct "family literacy" to study family practices appears to be by Taylor (1983) in her early work *Family Literacy: Young Children Learning to Read and Write*. This ethnographic work of middle-class families provided insight into the ways children learn to read and write through their participation in the day-by-day experiences of family life.

In a follow-up study, Taylor and Dorsey-Gaines (1988) explored the literacy development of children in low-income African American families. Even when facing poverty and other unfortunate circumstances, these families provided literacy experiences for their children in their everyday lives. There were, however, differences in the ways families used literacy experiences. Literacy experiences in low-income families focused more on practice experiences, such as applications for financial assistance.

Heath (1983) has also explored children's literacy development in her classic study of children in the rural south. She used ethnographic methods to study the language of children in different communities—a white working-class community of textile mill workers, a black working-class community of older farmers and younger textile mill workers, and a community of middle-class townspeople. From her intensive examination, she described the deep cultural differences among the groups and how these cultural differences affect language and literacy patterns. She suggested that some family language and literacy patterns that are developed from family activities tend to be more compatible with instruction and curriculum in the school system than those of other families.

Other significant work on family literacy has been conducted by Voss (1996), who observed and interviewed children in their home and school settings using participant–observer methodology. From her work she concluded that multiple forms of literacy must be taken into account when teaching children. Purcell-Gates (1995), through a case study of a family facing the consequences of low literacy, followed a mother and son as they learned to read and write together. In examining their progress, she concluded that an understanding of the learning process of individuals must take into consideration the context of social, cultural, and cognitive factors.

A number of empirical investigations have documented relationships between specific family characteristics and children's literacy, language, and reading. Evidence for the role of parents in children's language and literacy comes from the long history of research that has shown a correlation between parental storybook reading with children and later success with literacy in school (Bus, van IJzendoorn, & Pellegrini, 1995). Although some have questioned the predictive strength of parent storybook reading (Scarborough & Dobrich, 1994), recent reviews of research reaffirm the importance of shared book reading (Lonigan, 1994). Furthermore, these more recent research findings suggest that the interactions between adult and child during reading and during other parent–child activities are more predictive of literacy outcomes than simply reading to children. Research shows that discussing predictions, making elaborations, and linking to ideas to previous experiences during mealtime and during dyadic reading is predictive of language and literacy outcomes (Beals, DeTemple, & Dickinson, 1994; Snow, 1994). Parents of good readers use expansions, including graduated support and scaffolding; the parents of poor readers use reductionism strategies such as

decoding and criticism (Lancy, Draper, & Boyce, 1989). Other characteristics in the home also influence children's literacy levels, including the number of books in the home and the use of print.

Other research has examined characteristics such as income level, language, and culture. Despite evidence that lower-income families value "growing up literate" and provide opportunities for literacy experiences in the home (Fitzgerald, Spiegel, & Cunningham, 1991; Gadsden, 1993; Heath, 1983; Taylor & Dorsey-Gaines, 1988; Teale, 1986), socioeconomic differences in literacy and language have been and continue to be documented (Hart & Risley, 1995; National Assessment of Educational Progress, 1994, 1995). In addition, low-income children are likely to have multiple risk factors related to literacy development, such as low-literate parents, poor educational opportunities, and home language other than English or nonstandard English that serve to further compound their poor literacy outcomes (Snow et al., 1998).

Consequently, researchers interested in understanding socioeconomic differences have examined the family in a process-oriented fashion, providing evidence that family interactions around literacy are different between low- and middle-income families (Delgado-Gaitan, 1987; Gadsden, 1995; Teale, 1986). Baker, Serpell, and Sonnenschein (1995) compared literacy opportunities in low- and middle-income families and children. Middle-income parents reported a good deal more play with print and independent reading by children and were more likely to view literacy as a source of entertainment. On the other hand, low-income parents were more likely to view literacy as work and emphasized more reading practice and homework (e.g., flash cards and letter practice). Ninio (1980) found similar effects along with correspondingly smaller productive vocabularies for lower-income children. The ethnographic work by Taylor and Dorsey-Gaines (1988) and Heath (1983) referred to earlier summarizes examples of literacy behavior in the home environments of families from varying economic circumstances and reports that although behaviors could be categorized similarly, the use of print varied to fit the context of the family situation.

Gadsden (in press), in reviewing relationships between literacy and children within families across diverse cultural, social, and community contexts, reported on several studies conducted in the 1960s that have relevance for literacy intervention programs. These studies include Goodman's (1965, 1968) work on the language-experience approach, Labov's (Labov, Cohen, Robins, & Lewis, 1968) study of Black dialect with children and families in New York, and Durkin's (1966) research on parent–child interactions around reading in poor, urban communities in Chicago. Gadsden concluded that the cultural and social settings in which children learn and develop language and literacy are important supports for all children across ethnic and social lines who experience difficulty in learning to read and write regardless of ethnic or social lines. In other writings, she has noted that variability exists in the approaches to literacy among families and that the historical and social circumstances in which literacy acquisition occurs are important to consider (Gadsden, 1995, 1996). (For a review reflecting similar concerns see Fegans et al., Chapter 14, and Goldenburg, Chapter 15).

Children growing up attending schools in which English is the dominant language but whose parents use a different language clearly have different home experiences around literacy than do children in homes in which English is the primary language. In writing about the literacy needs of immigrant families, Durán (1996) noted the important differences among those with extensive formal education, economic resources, and familiarity with English in contrast to those without these resources. He also stressed the importance of going beyond the assessment of skills in reading and writing English to an understanding of the "full range of cultural, linguistic, and social knowledge that families need to acquire in order to survive" (p.2 6).

These studies of practices related to literacy and language within families have brought about an appreciation for the importance of beliefs, values, and traditions in developing interventions that are responsive to the family. These findings indicating differences in literacy and language behaviors across socioeconomic level, language, and culture also raise questions about the best way to help parents expand their own literacy skills and give their children the support they need to become successful readers. These questions are also at the heart of considerable tension in the field on whether and how to provide literacy interventions for families. They are addressed later in this chapter.

Studies of Family Literacy Interventions

Beginning in the 1980s and 1990s, when some of the ethnographic and descriptive studies described previously were ongoing, a different set of initiatives provided educational services for parents and their children related to literacy and language skills. Some of these family literacy interventions developed more from perceived beliefs about low-literacy adults and their children than from a clearly articulated theoretical base or a strong empirical base. Several of these beliefs also guided the development of early-intervention programs that began in the 1960s and 1970s (i.e., Campbell & Ramey, 1994; Schweinhart, Barnes, Weikart, Barnett, & Epstein, 1993; St. Pierre & Layzar, 1998). St. Pierre and Layzar (1998) identified three assumptions about child development and poverty influential to the development of these early-intervention programs. First, child development is a complex, dynamic process influenced by multiple interacting that is part of a larger ecosystem (Brofenbrenner, 1979). Second, a child's early experiences are critically important for healthy development (Bowlby, 1973). Finally, poverty adversely affects a child's early development through multiple mechanisms and threatens chances for success in life (Sameroff & Chandler, 1975). Several strategies have followed from these assumptions, including (1) providing direct services to children in the form of center-based programs, (2) providing parenting education, and (3) developing programs that provide adult education as well as two-generation programs (St. Pierre & Layzer, 1998). (For similar reviews, see Barnett, Chapter 27.)

Before examining the outcomes of interventions that combine these strategies, we briefly examine evidence on each separately. Providing direct high-quality center-based services to children has been repeatedly demonstrated to be of benefit to children

(Burchinal, Campbell, Bryant, Wasik, & Ramey 1997; Campbell & Ramey, 1994; Wasik, Ramey, Bryant, & Sparling, 1990). Both short- and long-term effects have been found for children's cognitive performance as well as other measures of school success. Evaluations of parenting education programs have found mixed results in bringing about changes in child performance (Barnett, 1995; Bryant, & Maxwell, 1997; Gomby, Culross, & Behrman 1999). Positive outcomes have been found for child performance, but results vary by study. The data on adult education shows some positive outcomes for adults, such as attaining the general equivalency diploma (GED), but the outcomes for children's development is less clear. Furthermore, St. Pierre and Layzer (1998) note that any influences on children from adult education will most likely be long term, not immediate.

Several programs that provide direct parenting education as a means of improving children's literacy and language are referred to as family literacy programs, including the Parents as Teachers (PAT) program and the Home Instruction Program for Preschool Youngsters (HIPPY). PAT is an early-childhood family education and support program created in 1981, based on the beliefs that infants are born to learn and that parents play a critical role from the beginning of the child's life. Currently implemented in over 2,000 sites in 49 states and 6 countries, the PAT program offers home visits in conjunction with parent group meetings, annual developmental screenings, and referrals to other community resources. In home visits, a certified parent educator helps families apply child development and childrearing information. Two recent evaluations revealed small positive effects on parent knowledge, attitudes, and behavior and no gains in child development or health when compared to a control group. (Wagner & Clayton, 1999).

Originally developed in 1968 in Israel and first implemented in the United States in 1984, HIPPY offers a 2-year, home-based early-childhood education and parent-involvement program for parents with limited formal education (Baker, Piotrkowski, & Brooks-Gunn, 1998). The program features bimonthly home visits and bimonthly group meetings in which parents use HIPPY story-books and educational activities with their preschool children. In a study of this program, a two-cohort experimental design with a randomized control group was implemented. Children were assessed at baseline, at the end of the program, and 1 year later on cognitive skills, adaptation to the classroom, and standardized achievement. HIPPY children from cohort 1 performed significantly better than did comparison-group children on all measures of school performance both at the end of the program and 1 year later. However, no effects were found for cohort 2. Similar mixed findings occurred from a second study.

Comprehensive Family Literacy Programs

Comprehensive family literacy programs as defined here combine three major components: early-childhood education, parenting education, and adult education. Although some two-generation family literacy programs have been implemented before the 1980s, most of these efforts began less than 15 years ago. Two systems theories are particularly relevant to family literacy programs: Bronfenbrenner's ecological model and family systems theory.

THEORIES

Bronfenbrenner's ecological model frequently has framed many early-intervention efforts (Bronfenbrenner, 1974; 1986; Bronfenbrenner & Crouter, 1983). His early writings promoted a shift toward recognizing the family itself as a more appropriate focus for intervention rather than the child only (Bronfenbrenner, 1974). Based on a detailed review of existing intervention programs, Bronfenbrenner (1974) concluded that "the family seems to be the most effective and economic system for fostering and sustaining the child's development. Without family involvement, intervention is likely to be unsuccessful, and what few effects are achieved are likely to disappear once the intervention is discontinued" (p. 300). His ecological theory envisioned the child as nested within a set of increasingly complex environments, beginning with the family and nesting, in turn, within the neighborhood, the community, and finally the larger social structure. His theory predicts that the most enduring child outcomes occur from interventions that encompass a variety of significant people and settings in the child's life. Given the model's inclusion of families, preschools, adult and parenting education, relationships with community colleges, social services, employment opportunities, and local jobs, it becomes especially relevant to family literacy educational programs. These programs are also influenced by and influence government policies and procedures related to literacy programs for families.

Family systems theories also have relevance for family literacy interventions. Most early theories of parenting addressed the parent influence on the child. Family systems theories, developed initially to provide a framework for understanding and providing services to families (Bateson, 1972; Jackson, 1957; Minuchin, 1974), takes us beyond parental influences on children to a more in-depth examination of the ways individuals in a family influence and are influenced by others in the family. The family itself is seen as a social system with interaction patterns that have been developed and maintained over time (Minuchin, 1985). Use of family systems theories within family intervention programs provides a framework for identifying influences beyond direct program services that are essential to take into consideration when working with families (Minuchin, Colapinto, & Minuchin, 1998). In family literacy programs, assumptions about what parents may be able to do with their child need to take into consideration the home environment and the resources and needs of other family members.

The federal Even Start Family Literacy Program is one of the most visible programs offering educational services for the child and parent (or parent substitute), including early childhood education, parenting education, and adult education. This program originated in two Kentucky programs. In the early 1980s, the Parent and Child Education Program (PACE) program served both parents with low-literacy skills and their young 3- and 4-year-old children (Brizius & Foster, 1993). Designed to directly address the literacy needs of each, this program provided opportunities for learning more about parenting and parent–child in-

teractions. The National Center for Family Literacy, building on this work, developed a three-component model frequently referred to as the Kenan model (Brizius & Foster, 1993; Darling & Hayes, 1989).

The following criteria must be met for a family to participate in Even Start: (1) the adult of the family is eligible for Adult Basic Education (ABE), (2) the family has a child under 8 years of age; and (3) the family lives in the catchment area receiving funds for Even Start services. Services provided by Even Start may include classes, meals, transportation, home visits, case management, transition services, and child care.

The purpose of the early-childhood education component is to provide developmentally appropriate services to prepare children for regular school programs. Three types of classrooms characterize early childhood education: child care for infants and toddlers, the preschool classroom, and the elementary school classroom. The purpose of the adult education component is to provide instruction to promote adult literacy and education. Adults may receive services in the form of ABE, Adult Secondary Education, English as a Second Language, a GED certificate, or a high school diploma (Tao, Gamse, & Tarr, 1998). The third component, parenting education enables parents to support their children's educational growth. Even Start also requires time for parents and children together (PACT) time, classroom time for parents and children under the guidance of the program staff (Powell, in press).

The assumptions that guided the development of programs based on only one of these components, early-childhood education, parenting education, or adult education, are also included within comprehensive family literacy programs. However, family literacy programs build on these assumptions in ways that are distinct from programs that offer only one component. Furthermore, there are also assumptions related to the combination of these components. A major assumption of these comprehensive family literacy programs following from systems theories is that intervention will be more effective if it is focused on the family rather than just the parent or the children (St. Pierre & Layzer, 1998). For parenting education, it is assumed that having structured time for parents and children in an instructional setting is important for promoting parent–child interactions focused on literacy activities as well as for promoting positive parent–child relationships. Another assumption is that children who are participating in early-childhood education and whose parents are participating in adult education will have value added to the benefits of providing only direct services to children. Empirical support has not been established for this premise, though it is one of the major reasons for combining program components in reference to children's outcomes. Other assumptions relate to the need for multiple services by low-income families, and as a result programs are encouraged to aid families in accessing the help they need within their community. Although the need for multiple services has been documented (Tao et al., 1998), the assumption that these services are available in the community is only partially supported, and the assumption that families need help in accessing these services is not supported (St. Pierre & Layzer, 1998).

OUTCOMES

The federal legislation requires Even Start evaluation at the local and national levels. The first national evaluation took place from 1989–1990 to 1992–1993 (St. Pierre et al., 1995); the second evaluation took place from 1993–1994 to 1996–1997 (Tao et al., 1998). Each of the national evaluations of Even Start had two parts. The first part collected descriptive information on participants, participant outcomes, and program processes along the lines of the three components; the second part collected more comprehensive information on parent and child outcomes.

Results from these studies show that although adults in Even Start gained in literacy skills, similar gains were found in a control group not participating in Even Start. In addition, more adults in Even Start earned a GED than those in the control group. The evaluations also concluded that based on the normal expectations for development, Even Start children learned school-readiness skills significantly faster than would be expected. In the first evaluation, when Even Start children were compared to a control

group, they initially showed greater gains in their readiness skills during the intervention, but the control group caught up with Even Start children after receiving school services. Children also showed gains with receptive vocabulary during the intervention, yet a control group showed similar gains. In the second evaluation, children who remained in Even Start for more than 1 year developed at a faster than expected rate for school readiness and language.

The evaluations also looked at parenting outcomes. In the first evaluation, limited effects were seen in the areas of parents' personal skills, the home learning environment, parent–child reading tasks, and parental expectations. Even Start participants did show positive gains in the home learning environment. Though the control group had similar gains in area of the home learning environment, Even Start participants had a wider range of different kinds of reading materials in the home. In the second evaluation, gains were found on cognitive stimulation and emotional support provided to Even Start children by their families (St. Pierre et al., 1995; Tao et al., 1998).

Despite the extensiveness of these evaluations, many questions still remain. For example, with the Even Start evaluation, according to Tao et al. (1998), although children and adult outcomes were better in the second evaluation, relationships between the amount of instruction, participants, program characteristics, and outcomes measures demonstrate few clear trends and directions. At this point we do not have consistent patterns of positive outcomes for children and their families from these evaluations.

Several evaluation efforts have been conducted by the National Center for Family Literacy (Darling & Hayes, 1989, 1996; Philliber, Spillman, & King, 1996). These evaluation efforts have shown positive outcomes for children. Children have performed higher than expected on the Peabody Picture Vocabulary Test (PPVT) and the Child Observation Record (COR). Teachers rated these children as above average on variables such as academic performance, motivation to learn, and classroom behaviors. In another study of programs following the National Center for Family Literacy model—the Toyota Families for

Learning Program—positive effects on the COR were found for participating children. Although comparison children make similar gains, gains by the children in the Toyota family literacy programs were significantly higher (Philliber et al., 1996).

In Purcell-Gates' review of family literacy research, she uses three of the four categories in the system proposed by Nickse (1990) in which programs are defined according to whether services are delivered directly or indirectly to parents and/or children. Purcell-Gates reviewed programs offering direct services to both children and parents (i.e., Even Start); programs offering parenting education, and services provided directly to children, including home-school programs. From her review she drew somewhat more positive conclusions than did reviewers of comprehensive family literacy programs, stating that the documentation from the literature shows "clear benefits to children of family literacy programs of all types" (Purcell-Gates, 2000, p. 863). We draw a more cautious conclusion. We believe there are promising early results and that these results point to ways of enhancing program effectiveness. For example, program intensity and direct child services are often supported as important aspects of family literacy programs. However, we believe we need considerably more empirical information to help us understand for whom, when, and how these programs are most effective.

Conflicting Beliefs and Intervention Procedures

Though questions have been raised since the 1960s on the beliefs underlying many early-intervention programs, the debate on interventions for family literacy programs appears especially intense. We believe this intensity has arisen from theoretical differences about the role of pedagogy and becomes more visible as the number of programs increase. One approach to developing interventions for families follows from empirical studies demonstrating a positive relationship between certain parenting practices related to literacy and children's literacy, language, and reading. Much of this research comes from studies with middle-income families. It is believed that low-literacy families do not engage in these same practices or that other literacy practices in the home do not promote later academic success. Consequently, critiques of this approach believe such procedures impose on families, especially low-income, minority, or immigrant families, mainstream beliefs about the roles of parents and families in promoting both child and family literacy. Challenges suggest that this approach derives from a lack of congruence between home and school literacy (Auerbach, 1989; Paratore & Harrison, 1995) and from a lack of understanding about literacy experiences in linguistically and culturally diverse families (Paratore & Harrison, 1995). An alternative approach, sometimes referred to as a sociocultural approach, calls for building on parents' strengths and including parent ideas in intervention efforts.

We refer to the first approach as the coaching approach that emphasizes the possibility of teaching effective strategies, including didactic training. Proponents of coaching, noting the poor literacy outcomes for children from low-income families, have provided these parents with opportunities to learn strategies demonstrated to be successful for middle-income parents and children. For example, this approach to reading intervention emphasizes training parents to learn and use new "scripts" when reading to their child. Depending on the intervention, coaching strategies can include book management, book modeling, questioning techniques, language proficiency, or the importance of positive affect. Advocates of coaching reason that low-income parents want to learn how to help their children, seek intervention, deserve assistance (Darling, 1988; Edwards, 1994) and should be offered access to practices that have been successful.

Coaching techniques are common in literacy interventions targeting low-income families (e.g., Edwards, 1991, 1994; Neuman & Gallagher, 1994; Whitehurst, Arnold, et al., 1994; Whitehurst, Epstein, et al., 1994). One example is the Parents as Partners in Reading program (Edwards, 1991; 1994). Edwards acknowledges the controversy surrounding coaching but suggests that many low-income and low-literate parents are seeking explicit directions. Her program provides parents with needed knowledge and skills as well as opportunities for peer modeling and practice.

Neuman and her colleagues have conducted extensive research on literacy interventions. One study examined the effects of coaching on six teenage mothers' literacy play with their children (Neuman & Gallagher, 1994). In this study each parent was coached to use the following strategies during play: labeling, scaffolding, and contingent responsivity. After coaching, all mothers were found to use the strategies more often. During the maintenance condition, the coached behaviors decreased but not to baseline levels.

The Dialogic Reading Program developed by Whitehurst and colleagues is a well-known literacy intervention using the coaching model (Whitehurst, Arnold, et al., 1994; Whitehurst, Epstien, et al., 1994). The goal of dialogical reading is to make children active participants in book-reading interactions rather than passive listeners. During a 20-minute videotaped training session, adults learn the acronym CROWD to help them remember to use completion, recall, open-ended, wh- words (what, who, where and why), and distancing questioning strategies when reading to children. In addition, the acronym PEER helps adult readers remember to imbed those questions using the following types of interactions: prompting, evaluating, expanding, and repeating. Adults role-play with one another and practice with their children using commercially available books supplemented with strategy hints.

Dialogical reading has had a significant effect on preschool children's expressive language, mean length of utterance, writing, linguistic awareness, and print concepts (Whitehurst et al., 1988; Whitehurst, Epstein, et al., 1994). Whitehurst and colleagues have also found that the dialogical reading intervention has a greater effect on child language when both teachers and parents actively use the technique with children (Whitehurst, Arnold, et al., 1994; Whitehurst, Epstien, et al., 1994b).

The second school of thought in the area of parent literacy intervention is influenced by the sociocultural theory of literacy that emphasizes an understanding of family culture and world view in developing interven-

tions. It includes reciprocal teaching and conversation between parents and a facilitator. The sociocultural theorists characterize literacy is a social activity in which learners attempt to derive meaning from text and incorporate their own life experiences into learning (Ada, 1988; Delgado-Gaitan, 1994; Neuman, 1996). Neuman (1996) explains that "parents teach more than the mechanisms and strategies of reading during storybook activity with their children; rather, they impart sociocultural knowledge" (p. 824). This model is also referred to as a facilitating model.

Proponents of sociocultural parenting interventions call for building on parental strengths and including parent ideas in intervention efforts (Auerbach, 1989; Taylor, 1997). Neuman, Hagedorn, Celano, and Daly (1995) have implemented an intervention consistent with this approach. In their study, adolescent mothers in a family literacy program participated in peer discussion groups consisting of no more than five mothers. They were asked to comment, explain, share experiences, and provide insights on their beliefs about learning and early literacy. Sessions were audiotaped and later transcribed. The results indicated that although these mothers did not share a common world view of literacy and learning, they did express some shared goals. For example, parents mentioned that they learned about parenting but had little time to link what was learned to their interactions with their children. In response to this information, the staff invited parents to spend time in the child-care program with their children as part of their intervention. The results demonstrated how collaborative relationships between parents and professionals can influence intervention efforts.

Parent–child literacy interventions influenced by the sociocultural theory include instructor facilitation, demonstration, interaction and reciprocal teaching (Ada, 1988; Delgado-Gaitan, 1994; Handel & Goldsmith, 1994; Neuman, 1996). The Family Reading Program demonstrates one example of including learners in the process (Handel & Goldsmith, 1994). This project, geared toward poor readers, sought to build on learner strengths in parent workshops using the following framework: (1) introduction activities, (2) presentation of book,

(3) demonstration of strategy, (4) practice in pairs, (5) group discussion, (6) preparation for reading at home, and (7) optional adult reading. The authors have found that the majority of participants learn to use interactive strategies and have positive experiences with the program.

Delgado-Gaitan (1994) developed a parent–child book-reading intervention for Spanish-speaking parents with elementary students identified as poor readers. Following a model set forth by Ada (1988), parents participated in discussion groups in which they were introduced to four questioning strategy categories. Then parents were encouraged to create questions about the storybooks reflecting their own personal experience and knowledge. Delgado-Gaitan found that the intervention increased parent's self-perception and efficacy in being able to help their children. In addition, when parents considered the text in relation to their own experiences, they were more interactive in their reading with their children.

Neuman (1996) extended the work of Delgado-Gaitan (1994) and Ada (1988) in an intervention with Head Start parents and their children. Parents participated in hour-long weekly book clubs lasting 12 weeks. A parent leader and a bilingual teacher from the community facilitated the book clubs. Each session began with a choral reading of a children's book by the facilitator, who would dramatize the action, emphasize repetitive phrases, and ask questions during the reading. The facilitator would engage the parents in discussion with guiding questions. Parents were expected to become actively involved in these discussions and to derive strategies for reading based on their experiences. Then parents practiced with one another and eventually read to their child in his or her classroom.

We have described this debate on pedagogy not simply because of its frequent appearance in discussion on family literacy intervention programs but because we believe this debate can lead to a series of important research studies in which various combinations of instructional approaches are used and multiple outcomes are assessed. Both approaches are part of a larger set of pedagogical knowledge and it is important to make available to families resources from both approaches from which they can benefit.

Research Directions

Both theory and research can guide future research directions. Ecological systems theory and family systems theory both provide a broader base for conceptualizing future research directions. They prompt consideration of a wider range of variables than is usually studied, including such variables as community supports, employment opportunities, transportation, and child care. Research needs to focus on specific individual characteristics, family variables, and setting variables, such as the classroom and the community in relation to outcomes. The effects of program variables such as intensity, duration, teaching strategies, and integration of program components need to be explored in more depth.

Beliefs arising from the studies of family literacy practices also need to be considered in developing research agendas. What are ways to meaningful involve parents as collaborators in the development of intervention programs? How can we ensure that program procedures are sensitive to family needs? How do we move beyond rhetoric into empirical investigations of the value of different theoretical approaches to parenting education and family literacy interventions? The debate identified earlier on alternative approaches to working with families needs to be directly addressed. Parent preferences and satisfaction with the program need to be addressed.

Family systems theories can take us into unexplored areas within family literacy. Concerns with the ways participating in such programs influence families need to be explored empirically. There is a need to study child, parent, family, and community characteristics within designs that take into consideration relationships, environmental settings, and both short- and long-term program effects. We need to ask what the effects are of participating in these programs on family dynamics, marital relationships, and interactions with older and younger siblings who are not receiving direct services.

Specifically, additional information on

ways of providing opportunities for developing children's emergent and early literacy skills is needed. Recent literature on strategies to promote early language and literacy skills (e.g., phonemic awareness and print concepts) appears promising for young children (International Reading Association and National Association for the Education of Young Children, 1998; Snow et al., 1998). We also need to examine how to encourage children's emerging literacy skills within a program that is also attentive to children's social, emotional, and developmental needs.

The setting characteristics of the early-childhood classroom are important. We know that quality programs are more likely to have positive child outcomes than are other programs (Burchinal et al., 1997). However, measures of the quality of preschool classroom such as the Early Childhood Environment Rating Scale (ECERS) (Harms, Clifford, & Cryer, 1998) typically take a broad look at the environment and do not assess in depth the literacy richness of the early-education component. Within our own research project, the Carolina Family Literacy Studies (Wasik, Herrmann, Dobbins, & Roberts, 2000), we developed a more specific observational measure of the literacy richness of the preschool classroom. New instrument development such as this is essential for research to progress.

Family literacy programs offer unique opportunities to examine parent education in more depth. Comprehensive family literacy programs provide parents with many occasions to observe their children in learning situations and staff with many opportunities to assist parents in promoting their child's abilities and competencies. Staff make home visits to families, providing additional opportunities to individualize the program in response to family characteristics and needs. Although the purpose of home visits is to promote literacy, we need to know the range of issues discussed during these visits, how parents value them, what needs other than parenting education they serve, and the value added from home visiting.

PACT time is unique within early-intervention programs. Parents do not simply receive content about parent education, they participate in interactions with their child as part of the overall program. As such, this component provides an excellent opportunity to foster positive parent–child interactions and increase parent knowledge about their children's skills and needs. PACT time allows for family literacy staff to model and prompt positive and constructive ways of interacting with children, to demonstrate positive child-management procedures, and to demonstrate strategies to develop children's social and problem-solving skills. Parents can learn by trying out and practicing new roles and having supportive feedback from staff, consistent with adult learning strategies. We believe that PACT time is so significant that we recommend considerable attention be devoted to the study of this component.

In summary, future research needs to focus on a combination of experimental and descriptive studies. Each has a role in providing information for practice and policy decisions. As part of future experimental research, we believe program components need to be studied separately, in combination, and in comparison studies.

Conclusions

Family literacy programs have brought together a set of intervention components that include early-childhood education, adult education, and parenting education. A consideration of these various components can lead to instructional approaches and program procedures that are responsive to concerns related to family culture, family strengths, socioeconomic levels, language diversity, family dynamics, school success, and family independence. The study of family literacy is, however, much more than a combination of these individual components. It has emerged as a domain of study in itself and consequently is in need of conceptual models and research methods that can advance the field. It is clearly a complex, multifaceted, and intellectually challenging area of study.

Family culture, beliefs, and practices around literacy need to be considered in any intervention effort. Programs should meet the family where they are and collaborate with parents with respect to adult educational needs, support for parent–child interactions around literacy, language and socialization, and family needs. We believe this collaboration needs to involve parents in planning and provide them with choices about parent–child interactions and opportunities to try out different options.

Family literacy programs are at the juxtaposition of some of the most important values and beliefs in our society—families, children, education, school success, home–school linkages—as well as current political issues of employment, welfare, immigration, and language diversity. The fact that these programs do involve such basic values and beliefs makes it even more important to extend our empirical investigations of these programs so that we can collaborate with families on the best that society has to offer.

Acknowledgments

Preparation of this chapter was funded in part by a grant from the Office of Educational Research Initiatives to the Frank Porter Graham Child Development Center at the University of North Carolina at Chapel Hill. The National Center for Early Development and Learning is supported under the Educational Research and Development Centers Program, PR/Award No. R307A60004.

References

Ada, A. F. (1988). The Parjaro Valley experiences. In T. Skutnabb-Kangas & J. Cummins (Eds.), *Minority education* (pp. 224–248). Cevedon, PA: Multilingual Matters LTD.

Anderson, R. C., & Pearson, P. D. (1984). A schema-thematic view of basic processes in reading comprehension. In P. D. Pearson, R. Barr, M. L. Kamil, & P. Mosenthal (Eds.), *Handbook of reading research* (pp. 255–291). New York: Longman.

Auerbach, E. R. (1989). Toward a social–contextual approach to family literacy. *Harvard Educational Review, 59,* 165–181.

Baker, A. J. L., Piotrkowski, C. S., & Brooks-Gunn, J. (1998). The effects of the Home Instruction Program for Preschool Youngsters (HIPPY) on children's performance at the end of the program and one year later. *Early Childhood Research Quarterly, 13,* 571–588.

Baker, L., Serpell, R., & Sonnenschein, S. (1995). Opportunities for literacy learning in homes of urban preschoolers. In L. Morrow (Ed.), *Family literacy: Connections in schools and communities* (pp. 236–252). New Brunswick, NJ: International Reading Association.

Barnett, W. S. (1995). Long-term effects of early childhood programs on cognitive and school outcomes. *The Future of Children, 3*(5), 25–50.

Bateson, G. (1972). *Steps to an ecology of mind.* New York: Ballantine.

Beals, D. E., DeTemple, J. M., & Dickinson, D. K. (1994). Talking and listening that support early literacy development of children from low-income families. In D. K. Dickinson (Ed.), *Bridges to literacy: Children, families and schools* (pp. 19–40). Cambridge, MA: Blackwell.

Bowlby, J. (1973). *Attachment and loss.* New York: Basic Books

Brizius, J., & Foster, S. (1993). *Generation to generation: Realizing the promise of family literacy.* Ypsilanti, MI: High/Scope Press.

Bronfenbrenner, U. (1974). Is early intervention effective? *Teachers College Record, 76*(2), 279–303.

Bronfenbrenner, U. (1979). *The ecology of human development.* Cambridge, MA: Harvard University Press.

Bronfenbrenner, U. (1986). Ecology of the family as a context for human development: Research perspectives. *Developmental Psychology, 22*(6), 723–742.

Bronfenbrenner, U., & Crouter, A. C. (1983). The evolution of environmental models in developmental research. In P. H. Mussen (Ed.), *Handbook of child psychology: Vol. I. History, theory and methods* (pp. 357–414). New York: Wiley.

Bryant, D., & Maxwell, K. (1997). The effectiveness of early intervention for disadvantaged children. In M. J. Guralnick (Ed.), *The effectiveness of early intervention* (pp. 23–46). Baltimore: Paul H. Brookes.

Burchinal, M. R., Campbell, F. A., Bryant, D. M., Wasik, B. H., & Ramey, C. T. (1997). Early intervention and mediating processes in cognitive performance of children of low-income African-American families. *Child Development, 68,* 935–954.

Bus, A. G., van IJzendoorn, M. H., & Pellegrini, A. D. (1995). Joint book reading makes for success in learning to read: A meta-analysis on intergenerational transmission of literacy. *Review of Educational Research, 65*(1), 1–21.

Campbell, F., & Ramey, C. (1994). Effects of early intervention on intellectual and academic achievement: A follow-up study from low-income families. *Child Development, 65,* 684–698.

Darling, S. (1988). *Family literacy education: Replacing the cycle of failure with the legacy of success.* Washington, DC: Office of Educational Research and Improvement (ERIC Document Reproduction Service No. ED 332749)

Darling, S., & Hayes, A. E. (1989). *The William R. Kenan, Jr. Charitable Trust Family Literacy Pro-*

ject. *Final Report 1988–1989.* Louisville, KY: National Center for Family Literacy.

Darling, S., & Hayes, A. E. (1996). *The power of family literacy.* Louisville, KY: National Center for Family Literacy.

Delgado-Gaitan, C. (1987). Mexican adult literacy: New directions for immigrants. In S. R. Goldman & K. Trueba (Eds.), *Becoming literate in English as a second language* (pp. 9–32). Norwood, NJ: Ablex.

Delgado-Gaitan, C. (1990). *Literacy for empowerment: The role of parents in children's education.* London: Falmer Press.

Delgado-Gaitan, C. (1994). Sociocultural change through literacy: Toward empowerment of families. In B. Ferdman, R. M. Weber, & A. Ramirez (Eds.), *Literacy across languages and cultures* (pp. 143–170). Albany, NY: State University of New York Press.

Durán, R. (1996). English immigrant language learners: Cultural accommodation and family literacy. In L. A. Benjamin & J. Lord (Eds.), *Family literacy: Directions in research and implications for practice* (pp. 25–30). Washington, DC: US Department of Education.

Durkin, D. (1966). *Teaching young children to read.* Boston: Allyn & Bacon.

Edwards, P. A. (1991). Fostering literacy through parent coaching. In E. H. Hiebert (Ed.), *Literacy for a diverse society; Perspectives, practices, and policies* (pp. 199–214). New York: Teachers College.

Edwards, P. A. (1994). Responses of teachers and African-American mothers to a book-reading intervention program. In D. K. Dickinson (Ed.), *Bridges to literacy: Children, families, and schools* (pp. 175–208). Cambridge, MA: Blackwell.

Fitzgerald, J., Spiegel, D. L., & Cunningham, J. W. (1991). The relationship between parental literacy level and perceptions of emergent literacy. *Journal of Reading Behavior, 23,* 191–213.

Fuligni, A. S., & Brooks-Gunn, J. (in press). Early childhood intervention and intergenerational literacy programs. In B. H. Wasik (Ed.), *Synthesis of research in intergenerational literacy programs.* Washington, DC: U.S. Department of Education.

Gadsden, V. L. (1993). Literacy, education, and identity among African Americans: The communal nature of learning. *Urban Education, 27,* 352–369.

Gadsden, V. L. (1995). Representations of literacy: Parents' images in two cultural communities. In L. Morrow (Ed.), *Family literacy: Connections in schools and communities* (pp. 287–303). New Brunswick, NJ: International Reading Association.

Gadsden, V. L. (in press). Family literacy and culture. In B. H. Wasik (Ed.), *Synthesis of research in intergenerational literacy programs.* Washington, DC: US Department of Education.

Gomby, D. S., Culross, P. L., & Behrman, R. E. (1999). Home Visiting: Recent Program Evalua-tions—Analysis and Recommendations. *The Future of Children, 9*(1), 4–26.

Goodman, K. S. (1965). *A linguistic study of cues and miscues in reading.* (ERIC No. ED011 482).

Goodman, K. S. (1968). *Words and morphemes in reading.* (ERIC No. ED020 686).

Handel, R. D., & Goldsmith, E. (1994). Family reading-still got it; Adults as learners, literacy resources, and actors in the world. In D. K. Dickinson (Ed.), *Bridges to literacy: Children, families and schools* (pp. 150–174). Cambridge, MA: Blackwell.

Harms, T., Clifford, R. M., & Cryer, D. (1998). *Early childhood rating scale (ECERS) revised edition.* New York, NY: Teachers College Press.

Hart, B., & Risley, T. R. (1995). *Meaningful differences in the everyday experiences of young American children.* Baltimore: Brookes.

Heath, S. B. (1983). *Ways with words.* Cambridge, MA: Cambridge University Press.

International Reading Association and the National Assocation for the Education of Young Children. (1998). Learning to read and write: Developmentally appropriate practices for young children. *Young Children,* 30–46.

Jackson, D. D. (1957). The question of family homeostasis. *Psychiatric Quarterly Supplement, 31,* 79–90.

Labov, W., Cohen, P., Robins, C., & Lewis, J. (1968). *A study of the non-standardized English of Negro and Puerto Rican Speakers in New York City. Volume I: Phonological and grammatical analysis.* New York: Columbia University.

Lancy, D. F., Draper, K. D., & Boyce, G. (1989). Parental invluence on children's acquisition of reading. *Contemporary Issues in Reading, 4*(1), 83–89.

Lonigan, C. J. (1994). Reading to preschoolers: Is the emperor really naked? *Developmental Review, 14,* 303–323.

Minuchin, S. (1974). *Families and family therapy.* Cambridge, MA: Harvard University Press.

Minuchin, P. (1985). Families and individual development: Provocations from the field of family therapy. *Child Development, 56,* 289–309.

Minuchin, P., Colapinto, J., & Minuchin, S. (1998). *Working with families of the poor.* New York: Guilford Press.

Monsour, M., & Talan, C. (1993). *Library-based family literacy projects.* Chicago: American Library Association

Morrow, L. M., & Paratore, J. (1993). Family literacy: Perspective and practices. *Reading Teacher, 47,* 194–200.

Morrow, L. M., Tracey, D. H., & Maxwell, C. M. (Eds.). (1995). *A survey of family literacy in the United States.* Newark, DE: International Reading Association.

Morrow, L. M., & Young, J. (1997). A family literacy program connecting school and home: Effects on attitude, motivation, and literacy achievement. *Journal of Educational Psychology, 89,* 736–742.

National Assessment of Educational Progress.

(1994). *The NAEP 1992 technical report.* Princeton, NJ: Educational Testing Service.

National Assessment of Educational Progress. (1995). *The NAEP reading: A first look-Findings from the National Assessment of Educational Progress* (rev. ed.). Washington, DC: U.S. Government Printing Office.

National Research Council. (1999). *Starting out right: A guide to promoting children's reading success.* Washington DC: National Academy Press.

Neuman, S. B. (1996). Children engaging in storybook reading; The influence of access to print resources, opportunity, and parental interaction. *Early Childhood Research Quarterly, 11,* 495–513.

Neuman, S. B., & Gallagher, P. (1994). Joining together in literacy learning; Teenage mothers and children. *Reading Research Quarterly, 29*(4), 382–401.

Neuman, S. B., Hagedorn, T., Celano, D., & Daly, P. (1995). Toward a collaborative approach to parent involvement in early education: A study of teenage mothers in an African-American community. *American Educational Research Journal, 32*(4), 801–827.

Nickse, R. S. (1990). Family literacy programs: Ideas for action. *Adult Learning,* 9–13 and 28–29.

Ninio, A. (1980). Picture-book reading in mother–infant dyads belonging to tow sub-groups in Israel. *Child Development, 51,* 587–590.

Paratore, J., & Harrison, C. (1995). A themed issue on family literacy. *Journal of Reading, 38,* 516–517.

Philliber, W. W., Spillman, R. E., & King, R. (1996). Consequences of family literacy for adults and children: Some preliminary finds. *Journal of Adolescent and Adult Literacy, 39,* 558–565.

Powell, D. R. (in press). Parenting Education in Family Literacy Programs. In B. H. Wasik (Ed.) *A synthesis of research on intergenerational family literacy programs.* Washington, DC: U.S. Department of Education.

Purcell-Gates, V. (1995). *Other people's words: The cycle of low literacy.* Cambridge, MA: Harvard University Press.

Purcell-Gates, V. (2000). Family literacy. In M. L. Kamil, P. B. Mosenthal, P. D. Pearson, & R. Barr (Eds.), *Handbook of reading research* (vo. 3, pp. 853–870). Mahwah, NJ: Erlbaum.

Sameroff, A., & Chandler, J. (1975). Reproductive risk and the continuum of caretaking casualty. *Review of Child Development Research, 14,* 187–244.

Scarborough, H. S., & Dobrich, W. (1994). On the efficacy of reading to preschoolers. *Developmental Review, 14,* 245–302.

Schuele, C. M., Roberts, J. E., Fitzgerald, J., & Moore, P. L. (1993). Assessing Emergent literacy in preschool classrooms. *Day Care and Early Education, 21*(2), 13–21.

Schweinhart, L. J., Barnes, H. V., Weikart, D. P., Barnett, W. S., & Eptein, A. S. (1993). Significant benefits: *The High/Scope Perry Preschool study through age 27* [Monographs of the High/Scope Educational Research Foundation No. 10]. Ypsilanti, MI: High/Scope Educational Press.

Smith, S. (Ed.). (1995). *Two generation programs for families in poverty: A new intervention strategy. Advances in applied developmental psychology, volume 9.* Norwood, NJ: Ablex.

Snow, C. E. (1994). Enhancing literacy development: Programs and research perspectives. In D. Dickinson (Ed.), *Bridges to literacy* (pp. 267–272). Cambridge, MA: Basil Blackwell.

Snow, C. E., Barnes, W. S., Chandler, J., Goodman, J. F., & Hemphill, L. (1991). *Unfulfilled expectations: Home and school influences on literacy.* Cambridge, MA: Harvard University Press.

Snow, C. E., Burns, M. S., & Griffin, P. (1998). *Preventing reading difficulties in young children.* Washington, DC: National Academy Press.

Snow C. E., & Tabors, P. (1996). Intergenerational transfer of literacy. In L. A. Benjamin & J. Lord (Eds.), *Family literacy: Directions in research and implications for practice* (pp. 73–81). Washington, DC: U.S. Department of Education.

St. Pierre, R. G., & Layzer, J. I. (1998). Improving the life chances of children in poverty: Assumptions and what we have learned. *Social Policy Report, 12*(4), 1–25.

St. Pierre, R. G., Swartz, J., Gamse B., Murray, S., Deck, D., & Nickel, P. (1995). *National evaluation of the Even Start Family Literacy Program: Final report.* Bethesda, MD: Abt Associates.

Street, B. (1984). *Literacy in theory and practice.* Cambridge, UK: Cambridge University Press.

Tao, F., Gamse, B., & Tarr, H. (1998). *National Evaluation of the Even Start Family Literacy Program, 1994–1997. Final report.* Washington, DC: U.S. Department of Education, Planning and Evaluation Service.

Taylor, D. (1983). *Family literacy: Young children learning to read and write.* Portsmouth, NH: Heinemann.

Taylor, D. (Ed.). (1997). *Many families, many literacies: An international declaration of principles.* Portsmouth, NH: Heineman.

Taylor, D., & Dorsey-Gaines, C. (1988). *Growing up literate: Learning from inner-city families.* Portsmouth, NH: Heinemann.

Teale, W. H. (1986). Home background and young children's literacy. In W. H. Teale & E. Sulzby (Eds.), *Emergent literacy: Reading and writing* (pp. 173–205). Norwood, NJ: Ablex.

Voss, M. M. (1996). *Hidden literacies: Children learning at home and at school.* Portsmouth, NH: Heinemann.

Wagner, M. M., & Clayton, S. L. (1999). The Parents as Teachers Program: Results from two demonstrations. *The Future of Children, 9*(1), 91–115.

Wasik, B. H., Herrmann, S., Dobbins, D. R., & Roberts, J. E. (2000, Fall). *Family Literacy: A promising practice for the twenty-first century.* North Carolina Association for Supervision in Curriculum and Development, 7–19.

Wasik, B., Ramey, C., Bryant, D., & Sparling, J. (1990). A longitudinal study of two early intervention strategies: Project CARE. *Child Development, 61,* 1682–1696.

Whitehurst, G. J., Arnold, D. H., Epstein, J. N., Angell., A. L., Smith, M., & Fischel, J. E. (1994). A picture book reading intervention in day care and home for children from low-income families. *Developmental Psychology, 3*(5), 679–689.

Whitehurst, G. J., Epstein, J. N., Angell, A. L., Payne, D. A., Crone, D. A., & Fischel, J. E. (1994). Outcomes of an emergent literacy intervention in Head Start. *Journal of Educational Psychology, 86*(4), 542–555.

Whitehurst, G. J., Falco, F. L., Lonigan, C. J., Fischel, J. E., DeBAryshe, B. D., Valdea-Menchaca, M. C., & Caulfield, M. (1988). Accelerating language development through picture book reading. *Developmental Psychology, 24*(4), 52–59.

29

The Complex World
of One-on-One Tutoring

❖

MARCIA A. INVERNIZZI

Uniqua, a rising second-grader reading on a late preprimer–early primer level, is totally dependent on school to learn to read. Her mother is a single parent who works two part-time jobs at minimum wage and has with three children under the age of 6. She has no car, so she wakes her children before dawn, carries them to the babysitter down the street, then catches the bus for work that begins at 6:00. When she comes home, she must fix meals, do laundry, and get her children ready for bed. She is counting on school to teach Uniqua how to read; it's all she can do to send her to school clean and ready to learn.

According to the National Research Council (NRC), one in five children is estimated to have difficulty learning to read in school; other researchers estimate that as many as 45% of our children are having difficulty learning to read (National Institute of Child Health and Human Development [NICHD], 1999). The NRC report asserts that reading problems are more likely to occur among children who are poor, are minorities, attend urban schools, or arrive at school not speaking English (Snow, Burns, & Griffin, 1998). The exigency of these realities are further underscored by longitudinal research that suggests that poor readers at the end of first grade are likely to remain poor readers by the end of fourth grade (Clay, 1985; Juel, 1988). Worse, this lack of achievement is associated with a declining

spiral of negative side effects (Stanovich, 1986), including persistent academic difficulty, frustration, and loss of self-esteem. These difficulties tend to persist throughout school and even into adulthood. In the words of Reid Lyon, "If you don't learn to read and you live in America, you do not make it in life" (National Institute of Child Health and Human Development, 1999).

Given the importance of reading, the following questions are important to consider: What works in helping struggling readers learn to read? Is one-on-one tutoring the most effective way to go? Can volunteers be effective tutors? What other factors influence the effectiveness of tutoring programs?

Research funded by the National Institute of Child Health and Development (NICHD) has demonstrated that most reading problems can be prevented when indicators are detected early and intervention is implemented immediately. In fact, recent evidence suggests that the percentage of children with reading difficulties can be reduced from current levels between 20% and 45%, to 5% or fewer when children are provided comprehensive, systematic, and intensive reading intervention (O'Connor, 2000; Scanlon & Vellutino, 1996; Torgesen, 2000). Many reading interventions involve one-on-one tutorials.

This chapter traces the broad context of one-on-one reading tutorials as they relate to differential outcomes in the literacy development of young children. After an examination of the broader issues involved in implementing quality tutorials, the chapter focuses on alternative delivery models within the ecological context of home, school, and community (Shanahan, 1998). Finally, the feasibility of one-on-one tutorials in terms of cost-effectiveness, longevity, and diffusion of knowledge and skill among practitioners, community members, and parents is discussed, with an emphasis on the future direction of tutorial models.

The Historical Roots of Tutoring

Tutoring at Home and in the Nearby Community

Prior to the institution of public schools, literate parents, relatives, and neighbors used an apprenticeship model to help struggling readers at opportune occasions throughout the year. Teaching methods consisted of modeling and whatever made sense to the master. Books were not written for children; therefore, reading materials came from what was at hand or could be written from memory. Reading apprentices built fluency through repeated reading of familiar content such as bible verses, prayers, proverbs, songs, or poems. They taught the alphabet and phonics directly, collecting pictures from newsprint and labels to illustrate beginning sounds. They showed students how to connect letters to sounds, first by verbalizing and writing single sounds, then two sounds, and then three. Connections were built not only between letters and sounds but also between mother and child and between familiar life routines and unfamiliar text (Heath, 1991).

Tutoring in Reading Clinics

The advent of public schools did not condemn the tutorial apprenticeship to a relic of the past. The upper class retained private tutors to teach their children to read at home. As public and private schools flourished, tutoring became the safety net for both institutions because of the difficulty of moving 100% of their students into reading. Schools tended to refer struggling readers to reading clinics for individualized instruction. University reading clinics used a master-apprenticeship model in which a master, usually a knowledgeable professor, educator, or researcher, provided guidance and feedback to the tutors before, during, and after the tutorial session. Tutoring conducted in university clinics simultaneously fulfilled several functions: service to children experiencing reading difficulty, professional development for special education and reading teachers in training, and research on the nature of reading difficulties. Much of what we know today about effective reading interventions comes from the tutoring case studies generated from these early reading clinics (Kibby & Barr, 1999).

Tutoring in the Schools

One-on-one tutorials moved out of the clinic and into the schools primarily through Reading Recovery, the prototype of modern reading tutorials. In a meta-analysis of Reading Recovery studies, Shanahan and Barr (1995) found that "children who receive Reading Recovery instruction make sizable gains in reading achievement during the first grade year [comparing] favorably with those of higher achieving first graders who receive only classroom instruction, or such instruction along with compensatory support" (p. 973). Most researchers also agree that early intervention aimed at preventing problems yield more powerful benefits than does later remediation (Slavin, Karweit, & Wasik, 1994).

Research on the Effectiveness of One-on-One Tutoring

In response to the recognized need for early intervention, Reading Recovery research spawned a renewed interest in one-on-one tutorials. Several studies demonstrated that tutored students faired better than did comparable students who did not receive tutoring services. Wasik and Slavin (1993) reviewed 16 studies of five first-grade-reading tutorials to compare instructional components and effect size. Studies were included in their review if they evaluated one-to-one instruction supplied by adults for first-graders learning to read for the first time and if they compared tutored children to nontutored children in school settings over at least a 4-week period. Their best-evidence synthesis reported effect sizes in the range of .55 to 2.37 for one-on-one tutorials using certified teachers and effect sizes in the range of .20 to .75 for the programs using paraprofessionals (p. 181). Effect sizes above .50 are worth considering and gains above .70 would likely make a significant difference (Lloyd, Forness, & Kavale, 1999). If students reading below grade level were to gain an additional 71% of a standard deviation in reading achievement over and above what they would otherwise gain without tutoring, conceivably they would eventually catch up.

Importance of Instructional Design

Simply providing one-on-one tutoring in reading does not always guarantee such success. Wasik and Slavin's (1993) review suggested that programs with a more comprehensive instructional design reaped greater gains than did programs with a more narrow focus. Effect sizes were higher for enriched tutorials such as Reading Recovery and Success for All, which included more components of the reading process. In contrast, effect sizes were considerably smaller for more restricted tutorials that focused on a narrow set of skills to the exclusion of the reading of connected text. The enriched tutorials were found to include contextual reading for fluency, comprehension strategies, and sound, letter and word-level instruction in phonemic awareness, alphabet, phonics, and spelling (Mantzicopoulous, Morrison, Stone, & Setrakian, 1992).

Importance of Knowledge of the Reading Process

Wasik and Slavin (1993) also found that programs using certified teachers as tutors obtained larger average effect sizes than those using paraprofessionals and volunteers. They concluded that certified teacher/tutors deliver comprehensive, quality instruction because of their knowledge of the reading process and their ability to implement a sound reading curriculum, presumably knowledge which paraprofessionals and volunteers lack. However, the volunteer programs of this study used rote, programmed instructional methods within a narrowly defined curriculum, whereas teacher/tutor models used a more responsive approach that relied on teacher judgment and knowledge of how children learn to read.

Promising Work with Volunteers

Promising work with paraprofessionals and volunteers, however, has been reported. The key to successful volunteer efforts appears to be the training and mentoring given to the tutors in an apprenticeship model similar to those originating in university clinics.

Howard Street, Juel's cross-age tutoring program, and Book Buddies provide examples of volunteer and paraprofessonal efforts that effectively use an apprenticeship model. The Howard Street program uses trained and supervised volunteer tutors in an after-school tutorial. Similar to the teacher/tutors in the comprehensive models reviewed by Wasik and Slavin (1993), volunteer tutors of this program deliver a comprehensive instructional plan that includes fluency, comprehension, alphabet, and phonics. Morris, Shaw, and Perney (1990) reported significant gains in reading graded basal passages (from .5 to 1.5 grade levels) for the tutored group compared to matched controls. These gains suggest that nonprofessional volunteers can deliver effective intervention when trained and supported by a professional reading coach who is knowledgeable about how children learn to read.

Juel's cross-age tutoring program using undergraduate student athletes, who were themselves poor readers, also yielded positive results. Juel mentored the student athletes both on-site and through a Psychology of Reading course they took concurrent to the tutoring program. The mean score of the tutored children on the reading comprehension subtest of the Iowa Tests of Basic Skills was at the 41st percentile, compared to a mean score at the 16th percentile for nontutored controls (Juel, 1996). Serendipitously, the tutors improved their own reading skills.

The Book Buddies program (Invernizzi, Juel, & Rosemary, 1996) has yielded positive results as well. This program uses unpaid community volunteers solicited by a volunteer recruiter to tutor first-grade non-

readers. Reading specialists who write individualized lesson plans and provide guidance and feedback before, during, and after
each lesson mentor the volunteer tutors on
site. Program evaluations for the first three
cohorts reported effect sizes of 1.24 for
word recognition (Invernizzi, Rosemary,
Juel, & Richards, 1997), and results have
showed consistent improvement from one
year to the next. Book Buddies also has
been evaluated using a random-assignment
control-group design in a replication study
in the South Bronx. Children who received
40 Book Buddies lessons significantly sur-
passed students in the control group on
measures of letter identification, word
recognition, and reading in context (Meier
& Invernizzi, 1999).

Whether intervention services are delivered by teachers or volunteers, the pattern
of effect sizes reported by intervention researchers may vary according to the interrelatedness among components of the instructional plan. Tutor knowledge, and the
guided apprenticeship of those who do not
possess such knowledge are critical. The
benefits to the tutor and to the child can
vary significantly depending on the strength
of connections made among these contextual factors.

The Interrelatedness
of Tutoring Components

Research on the effectiveness of one-on-one
tutoring has focused on the following attributes: (1) the structure and content of the lesson plan; (2) the consistency, frequency, and
duration of the lesson; and (3) the guidance,
knowledge, and skill of the tutor. There is a
trade-off among attributes of effective tutoring models. Less knowledge on the part
of the tutor requires more effort on the part
of the master teacher to provide guidance
and feedback within the context of a more
structured lesson plan. A critical tension
among tutoring elements can lead to positive or negative outcomes for children.

Structure and Content of the Lesson Plan

The structure of the lesson plan may vary
from program to program, but according to
the Report of the National Reading Panel

(NRP; 2000), all beginning reading instruction should contain a balanced diet of oral
reading for fluency, alphabetics (phonemic
awareness and phonics), and comprehension. These elements of the reading process
are among the components included in the
lesson plans of the most effective tutoring
programs reviewed by Wasik and Slavin
(1993), and they corroborate recommendations articulated by NICHD (1999).

Oral reading fluency refers to accuracy,
speed, and expression. It is one of the critical ingredients necessary for reading comprehension and is cultivated primarily
through practice. The advantages of repeated oral reading practice guided by feedback
from a tutor or teacher has been well documented by educators and researchers from a
variety of theoretical orientations. Re-
hearsal of the same text cultivates reading
fluency and yields other benefits such as automatic word recognition (Samuels, 1979),
improved comprehension (Dowhower,
1987), and improved reading expression.
Many educators espouse the benefits of
warming up with repeated readings. The
rereading of familiar books is a hallmark
beginning activity for many one-on-one tutorials (Pikulski, 1998).

Interestingly, the kinds of texts used for
repeated oral reading instruction have not
received much attention in the literature;
rather, the emphasis has been to use texts on
the right level of difficulty for the child.
Reading Recovery and another one-on-one
tutorial intervention, Early Steps, use natural-language storybooks. In contrast, Success
for All uses a series of "phonetically regular
but meaningful and interesting minibooks"
(Slavin, Madden, & Wasik, 1996, p. 5).
Book Buddies and Howard Street use phonetically regular, natural-language storybooks, as well as carefully graded texts featuring well-written stories and a moderate
amount of vocabulary control (e.g. *Ready
Readers* series; Englebert, Heibert, & Juel,
1998).

Regardless of the series, effective tutoring
programs rely on a set of carefully graded
materials. Careful leveling of books allows
children to be placed according to their "instructional level" in reading and advanced
gradually through the graded reading curriculum with "all deliberate speed" (Morris,
1999a, p.29).

Alphabetics refers to instruction in phonemic awareness, the alphabet, and phonics and spelling. Here again, the two most widely known one-on-one tutorials use vastly different approaches to the teaching of phonemic awareness and phonics. Success for All employs direct instruction including one-minute drills in letter–sound correspondences. Reading Recovery has been criticized for using a more incidental, student-centered approach to phonics, seizing opportune moments to squeeze in a minilesson in the context of sentence writing. Iverson & Tumner (1993) improved on Reading Recovery's track record by incorporating more direct instruction in phonics and spelling patterns. Howard Street, Early Steps, and Book Buddies all incorporate direct instruction in the systematic correspondences between sounds, letters, and spelling patterns through sorting tasks known as word sorts (Bear, Invernizzi, Templeton, & Johnston, 1999). Word sorts are direct in that there is a systematic scope and sequence of phonics and spelling patterns to be learned, but they are also student centered in that the curricular entry point and the pace of instruction are determined by what the child knows about an alphabetic orthography. Regardless, effective one-on-one tutorials all encourage and monitor their student's use of letter–sound and orthographic cues in the act of reading and phoneme awareness in the act of writing.

Comprehension is a complex cognitive phenomenon that depends on vocabulary knowledge as well as thoughtful interaction between the reader and the text (NRP, 2000, p. 13). Vocabulary can be learned directly or indirectly. Reading Recovery features an indirect approach through incidental exposure to new words through a tutor-directed new-book introduction. The book introduction may also include repeated exposures to a new vocabulary word by encountering it in various contexts on different pages. Success for All demonstrates a more direct approach to vocabulary instruction by using new words in "meaningful sentences." Howard Street, Early Steps, and Book Buddies rely on more incidental approaches to vocabulary instruction similar to Reading Recovery. Book Buddies adds "concept sorts" in which children sort words and/or pictures into semantic categories and verbalize what the exemplars have in common. One-on-one tutoring affords an optimal context for rich tutor–child interaction replete with all manner of scaffolding in conversation about vocabulary, words, ideas, and concepts.

Comprehension also entails active engagement through intentional interaction between the reader and the text. Probably the best way to intellectually engage a child is through casual conversation between the tutor and the student as they read a story together. The intimacy of the one-on-one setting spawns a natural interaction between the tutor, the tutee, and the text they share, much like the scaffolded conversation between mother and child while reading storybooks (Juel, 1998). Still, effective tutorials use multiple strategies to keep their students actively engaged with the text. Question answering is probably the most common technique, where students answer questions posed by the tutor and receive immediate feedback. Howard Street, Early Steps, and Book Buddies also uses variations of question generation, where students anticipate upcoming events or information based on what they already know. Writing is also a useful medium for interacting with text; students may pause during reading to make notes on a graphic organizer or semantic map. Often tutors write with their students, perhaps writing predictions before they read, taking notes during the reading, and summarizing what was read after reading. In all successful tutorials, active engagement is essential to maintaining interest, motivation, and promoting understanding.

The Consistency, Frequency, and Duration of the Lessons

In addition to including daily practice in guided oral reading, alphabetics, and comprehension strategies, balanced lessons include a routine structure to accommodate the content. The daily routine of Reading Recovery is as follows: rereading familiar books, working with letters, writing a sentence, and learning a new book. Howard Street, Early Steps, Book Buddies, and other tutorial models are variations of this basic routine. Children respond positively to the habit-forming routine and they eagerly anticipate the next activity.

The frequency and duration of tutoring is an important program consideration. Reading Recovery lessons are 30 minutes in duration and continue every day from 12 to 20 weeks. Children are "discontinued" when they reach a level of performance consistent with that of their classmates in the middle reading group and when they show characteristics of problem solving with new words and independent processing of texts (Clay, 1992, p. 77). Success for All tutoring occurs for 20 minutes daily in 8-week cycles. Depending on the results of the 8-week assessment, students may be circulated in or out of tutoring. In Success for All, tutoring is "relentless"; children are tutored for as long as they need it (Slavin et al., 1996). Early Steps teachers tutor one-on-one for 30 minutes a day for most of the academic year (Santa & Hoien, 1999). In Book Buddies, supervised volunteers tutor for 45 minutes, twice a week, from the end of September to the end of May. Despite their differences in frequency and duration, all these programs have yielded significant effects compared to matched controls.

Some controversy exists, however, regarding the stability of these effect sizes. The effect sizes of Reading Recovery, for example, diminish substantially by the end of third grade and continue to decline at fourth (Hiebert, 1994). The erosion of effect sizes as children advance upward through the grades has also been demonstrated with Success for All. Whereas Success For All studies conducted by the program originators illuminate positive aspects of the intervention, nearly every replication study possesses less-than-glowing results, more quietly spoken. In a Memphis study, for example, the effectiveness of Success for All decreased as grade level increased (Ross & Smith, 1994). Furthermore, Success for All has not always met its goal of all children achieving at or near grade level by grade 3 (Walberg & Greenberg, 1998).

Regardless of the intensity of early-intervention efforts, some children require continuous support to ensure academic success (Vellutino et al., 1996). Juel (1996) found that many of the children her student athletes tutored failed to meet grade-level expectations at the end of the first year. When these students were offered an additional year of one-on-one in second grade, however, they demonstrated substantial gains in reading. Likewise, in a study of Book Buddies who did not achieve end-of-year, first-grade reading levels after 1 year of tutoring, all the tutored children achieved grade-level expectations after a second year of one-on-one intervention. Tutored group means were consistently higher than matched controls across all outcome measures (Fowler, Lindemann, Thacker-Gwaltney, & Invernizzi, 2000).

These results reinforce the notion that schools should consider connected, ongoing systems of intervention to address individual student needs throughout the elementary school years (Snow et al., 1998). To borrow a popular saying from phonological awareness research, 1 year of intervention may be "necessary, but not sufficient" for students to achieve grade-level expectations in reading.

Guidance and Knowledge of the Tutor

Some tutoring programs, such as Reading Recovery, use highly trained professionals who are mentored for a full year by a certified Reading Recovery trainer in an apprenticeship model behind a one-way mirror. Through this daily apprenticeship, Reading Recovery tutors learn to make ongoing decisions about tutoring tasks that are responsive to the knowledge and interests of the child. Clay insists that it is the "reciprocity" and the manner in which "independent control of a task is passed to the child" that accounts for the quality of the one-to-one interaction (Clay, 1992, p. 76). In essence, success depends on the knowledge of the tutor who is specially trained to make instructional decisions based on day-to-day changes in the response of the child.

In contrast, Success for All tutors receive only 2 days of training (along with all other beginning reading teachers in the school) on the Success for All beginning reading curriculum, and another 4 days of training on assessment and instruction. Success for All tutors, who are all certified teachers, work closely with the classroom teacher and teach a reading group in the same classroom every day. The tutoring sessions are a carbon copy of the classroom lesson in shorter form. In Success for All, the master is the curriculum. A program facilitator ensures the quality and pace of instruction.

Reading Recovery and Success for All tutors are opposites on the theoretical continuum of tutor knowledge. In Reading Recovery, success depends on the decision-making prowess of tutors, which in turn, depends on the knowledge gained through extensive training in becoming responsive to student literacy behaviors. In Success for All, success depends on the fidelity and congruence of the curriculum. The curriculum is scripted and does not vary. Although Clay maintains that Reading Recovery develops links and interrelationships between what is to be learned and the child's understanding of what is to be learned, the emphasis on tutor knowledge is decidedly student centered. In contrast, Success for All is decidedly teacher centered and emphasizes knowledge of the curriculum.

Early Steps (Santa & Hoein, 1999), an early-intervention one-on-one tutorial program formerly known as First Steps (Morris, 1995), represents a middle ground on this issue. Early Steps uses an apprenticeship model in which first-grade and Title 1 teachers are released from the classroom for 30 minutes a day to provide one-on-one instruction for their lowest readers. A reading specialist provides ongoing feedback and guidance about the details of their tutoring sessions and mentors them. On a regular basis, the reading specialist/mentor provides the Title 1 and classroom teacher/tutors group seminars that offer an opportunity for reflection and planning. As a result of this ongoing support, Early Steps teacher/tutors become deeply involved in the learning-to-read process and develop a sense of urgency for tending to individual needs in their own classrooms. Early Steps is student centered; the teacher/tutors are responsive to the child's understanding of particular literacy concepts and the tutoring is paced accordingly. The tutoring model is also teacher directed; the teacher/tutors follow a specific scope and sequence of phonics and spelling skills and move the children through an organized sequence of leveled books. The entry point into the curricular plan is determined by assessing the knowledge of the child in the areas of phonological awareness, decoding, fluency, and comprehension. The major goal for the training of Early Steps tutors is to invest in teacher knowledge of specific literacy domains (e.g. phonological awareness, decoding skill, fluency, and comprehension) in relation to a properly timed scope and sequence of instruction. According to Morris (1999b), tutoring is the optimal context for learning how to teach reading, because the one-to-one format allows the tutor to give his or her full attention to "observing, interpreting, and intervening purposefully in a student's reading development" (p. 90).

Reading Recovery, Success for All, and Early Steps all use certified teachers as tutors; however, more recent research on the effectiveness of volunteer tutorials suggests that tutors do not have to be teachers to be effective as long as they are mentored in a model of continuous support. Howard Street and Book Buddies both use community volunteers, but both programs have demonstrated their effectiveness against a comparable control group that did not receive tutoring. Both programs operate under an apprenticeship model in which tutors learn by doing under the watchful eye of an experienced practitioner. Volunteer tutors can experience unsettling problems in the details of their daily tutoring. Everyday questions (e.g., "Should I immediately correct Dante when he makes a mistake?") present enormous uncertainties for novice tutors. But with the guidance of an experienced coach or mentor on hand, these uncertainties become fodder for growth in knowledge and understanding.

Although a reading specialist coach or mentor costs a tutoring project extra money, the consequences of an unsupervised program can result in wasted time and money, as well as wasted instructional time for the child. One program, funded by more than $1 million in federal work–study grants, placed more than 1,300 federal work–study students, volunteers in national service, and community volunteers in 16 schools in a high-poverty urban city. Believing that a reading specialist supervisor was too expensive, untrained VISTA members wrote the lesson plans. Observation and evaluation of the program revealed inappropriate lesson plans and questionable instruction. A newspaper reporter recorded the following tutoring interaction:

> During one session, a community volunteer asked a first-grader to complete the spelling of the word "panda." The student's guesses at the final vowel included o, r, d, e, o, u, d, and o again. The tutor followed up each wrong

guess with "No," or "How did I tell you to spell this?" or "Now, what would that make it? pan-dOOO." There was no lack of effort of the part of the student or affection from the tutor. But neither had a clue about how to get over that phonetic hurdle. Better training and supervision are now at the top of the agenda for their comprehensive evaluation. (Chaddock, 1998, p. A1)

There appears to be a trade-off between the high labor intensity of an apprenticeship model that invests in knowledge versus highly structured and scripted direct instruction models such as Success for All. Apprenticeship models are harder to implement and even harder to replicate, as Chaddock (1998) has shown. However, the Book Buddies in the Bronx study has demonstrated that replicability of an apprenticeship model is possible. The payoff is down the road as the knowledge spreads. Conversely, scripted models are easier to implement and easier to replicate, but they may never make an impact on the prevalence of new crops of struggling readers because they do not invest in teacher knowledge.

An examination of the interrelatedness of critical tutoring components leads to a discussion of intrinsic and extrinsic factors that also affect student literacy achievement.

Making Connections

The place of one-on-one tutorials in the larger scheme of literacy instruction is a complex issue, confounded by political expectations. While the goal of having all children read independently and well by the end of third grade is a noble one, all children will not be reading on grade level despite relentless efforts to provide continuous support. This is true for many reasons.

Risk factors associated with illiteracy cut across the three worlds of the child: the home, the school, and the community. Children come to kindergarten and first grade from all walks of life, in various configurations of sickness and health, varying degrees of familiarity with the culture of school, diverse experiences with books and print, and disparate understandings of the English language and alphabet. Children also differ from one another in emotional fortitude and cognitive abilities that interact in myste-

rious ways with learning to read. The personal lives of many children are full of drama and upheaval. Children who did not have preschool experiences need those experiences when they start school. Yet, teaching to an established curriculum creates further differences in their rates of progress. Rigorous, often mandated curricular demands drive the pace of instruction and the children who are the least prepared often struggle and are left behind.

Ensuring that every child will learn to read independently and well by the end of third grade will require meaningful home–school partnerships as well as partnerships between the research community and school districts. These partnerships would work together to assess student progress, invest in staff development, and target instructional resources to children with the greatest need.

Within the tutoring environment, connections must be made between the skills and content of the lesson plan and the cultural and emotional needs of the child. At the same time, these ties cannot sacrifice the cognitive connections necessary for reading success. For example, an effective tutor would connect isolated skill work in phonics and spelling to its usefulness for decoding when reading in context. Similarly, an effective writing prompt would connect to phonics and spelling instruction and/or the content of the reading.

Within the school environment, assessment and instruction must be inextricably intertwined to advance student achievement in reading. When classroom teachers and tutors all use different assessments, valuable instructional time is lost to overtesting, communication is restricted by the lack of common parlance, and the connection to instruction gets lost in the shuffle. Curricular congruence between the tutoring and classroom instruction will never be achieved if the one-on-one tutorial is marginalized to the fringes. Consideration should be given to using common assessments to inform teachers, tutors, and specialists alike, and to determine whom to serve with which intervention, where, when, and how.

Much has been written about the importance of paralleling the content and pacing of reading/language arts instruction in the classroom and in the tutorial (Allington,

1983). Unfortunately, this connection assumes that the instruction in each context is appropriate for an individual child. Often, this is not the case. Classroom observation data suggest that many Book Buddies students are placed in books that are too difficult for them to read and that the phonics instruction they receive is beyond their current understanding of how the written system works. For example, the teaching of long vowel patterns that involve silent letters is not effective when a child is grappling with basic letter–sound correspondences. Until greater congruence is achieved between intervention programs and classroom instruction, we may be spinning our wheels (Walmsley & Allington, 1995). Congruence is achieved through shared understandings about how children learn to read.

To design programs for children who are struggling to read, schools must develop intersecting plans and work to build connections that actualize the shared responsibility among families, communities, teachers/tutors, and supporting school staff. Each of these allies has unique and overlapping responsibilities toward a child's success.

Jefferson Elementary, a K–4 school in an urban community in central Virginia, is experimenting with making connections through intersecting plans. The school, guided by a strong instructional principal and literacy coordinator, operates with the knowledge that all the Jefferson faculty, staff and community are responsible for the education of Jefferson students.

The school's efforts begin with prevention, with a pre-K, 4-year-old program that targets not only basic oral language competencies, numeric concepts, and the like but also phonological awareness, alphabet, and basic print skills. Jefferson's 4-year-olds chant nursery rhymes and play sound awareness games such as those found in *Phonemic Awareness in Young Children,* (Adams, Foorman, Lundberg, & Beeler , 1998).

Jefferson has evolved its own phonemic-awareness training program for their 3 kindergarten classrooms. Jefferson's kindergartners are aggressively taught reading skills using a combination of oral language, children's storybooks, phonemic-awareness activities, and phonics. This is made possible by parallel scheduling so that half the

children are at computers, physical education, and art, while the other half remain in small groups for reading instruction. Kindergarten children lagging in phonemic awareness and alphabet knowledge work in small groups with the reading specialist again in the afternoon. These short, small-group lessons provide additional instruction in phoneme segmentation, letter recognition, and letter sounds.

Ongoing staff development and university–school partnerships provide the shared knowledge necessary for excellent classroom teaching. Teachers determine their professional development needs as they work toward a common goal. Graduate reading courses are taught on site by the school's literacy coordinator who is also an adjunct university professor in reading education. The courses are designed specifically to meet Jefferson's needs.

Jefferson kindergarten families are targeted as top priority for the "Families Learning Together" program which provides intergenerational support for reading, writing, homework, parenting skills, and classes for the general equivalency diploma (GED) during the schoolday and in the evening. The principal can be found in classrooms, or in the family literacy center, working with children and their parents, observing instruction and classroom management, and providing constructive feedback. By February, 83% of the kindergarten cohort is already reading.

Follow-up support awaits kindergartners who are not already reading in first grade in the form of two different compensatory programs: (1) one-on-one and small-group reading instruction in Title 1, and (2) Book Buddies, the community volunteer one-one-one tutorial. The Title 1 teacher and the Book Buddies coordinator, both reading specialists, work together in planning the best-intervention services for each and every child. Common assessments are used throughout the building, and the data generated from these assessments drive instruction in the classroom, in Title 1, and in Book Buddies, the one-on-one tutorial.

Further support exists in second grade in the form of a Book Buddies tutorial extension using federal work–study (FWS) education students as tutors. FWS students work under the supervision of the Book

Buddies coordinators, who write the lesson plans, and guide the FWS students in the act of tutoring. Book Buddies coordinators also meet regularly with classroom teachers to share assessments and discuss instructional pacing in light of assessed student needs.

Meanwhile, the entire Jefferson faculty and staff reconfigure themselves to achieve instructional-level, cross-program reading groups for 110 minutes of uninterrupted, direct reading instruction 4 days a week. Called RISE (Reading Initiative for Student Excellence), each reading group has 12 students and two adults. Librarians, special education teachers, classroom teachers, instructional aids, administrators, and America Reads volunteers all avail themselves for this sacrosanct period of instruction. Some semesters, university education students join yet another effort during content instruction in the afternoon, working with third- and fourth-grade teachers to ensure that children also read in science, social studies, and health.

There is much work yet to be done to ensure that classroom teachers, specialists, Book Buddies coordinators, and tutors work together so that all children learn to read; but Jefferson Elementary is making a start. Starting before kindergarten, Jefferson offers a diverse range of intervention services across the grades, including small-group and one-on-one tutorials. In addition, their intervention efforts include the family, the community, one-on-one tutorials, and classroom instruction.

Many researchers are calling for a hierarchy of intervention services similar to Jefferson's, starting in kindergarten, or sooner (Scanlon, Vellutino, Small, & Fanuele, 2000). Vellutino maintains that improving classroom instruction must be the first line of attack. Instead of waiting until failure occurs, schools must provide additional instruction in literacy-related skills immediately. Some children may be helped in small groups, in kindergarten, if the small-group instruction is over and above what is offered in classroom. Others need more intense, one-on-one instruction. One thing is clear: One-on-one tutorials cannot fix it all. It takes a teacher within a classroom, within a school, within a village, to teach a child to read.

Currently, an estimated 2.5 million school-age children are diagnosed with learning disabilities (United States Department of Education, 1999). This does not have to be. Research on the effects of ongoing tutoring suggests that by continuing to support struggling readers with additional reading instruction across the grades, the current proportion of children who experience reading difficulty can be reduced to 5% or less (Scanlon & Vellutino, 1996; Torgesen, 2000). Vellutino suggests that "labor-intensive remedial reading, tailored to the child's individual needs "should always precede psychometric testing for special education" (Vellutino et al., 1996, p. 32). If response to one-one-one intervention became a prerequisite for such referrals, new evidence suggests that the current incidence of specific learning disability could be reduced to only 1 to 3% (Vellutino, Scanlon, & Tanzman, 1998).

With 40% of our nation's fourth-graders unable to read at even a basic level on the National Assessment of Educational Progress, the sheer numbers of children in need of one-on-one instruction is daunting; however, trained and supervised paraprofessionals and volunteers can add significantly to the cause. One-to-one tutoring can provide direct, systematic, intense instruction that also is responsive to the knowledge and interests of the child. As Juel (1996) concluded, tutors working one on one can provide "verbal interactions, instructions, and written materials that [are] on the right level and at the right time," a task often difficult to accomplish in a whole-class situation (p. 288). Other researchers in the area of preventing and remediating reading disabilities concur: "It may indeed be the case that the only way to provide opportunities for some children to acquire normal reading skills is to provide one-on-one instruction over a significant period of time" (Torgesen, Wagner, Rashotte, Burgess, & Hecht, 1997, p. 153).

Building on rich interpersonal relationships, reading tutors can provide individualized instruction, elaborated explanations, specific instructions, and written materials on the right level, at the right time, and for the right child–a task often difficult to accomplish in a classroom context. By enlisting the human resources inherent in every home, school, and community, we can ensure that every child learns to read, one child at a time.

References

Adams, M. J., Foorman, B., Lundberg, L., & Beeler, T. (1998). *Phonemic awareness in young children*. Baltimore: Brookes.

Allington, R. L. (1983). The reading instruction provided readers of differing reading ability. *Elementary School Journal, 83,* 584–559.

Bear, D., Invernizzi, M., Templeton, S., & Johnston, F. (1999). *Words their way: Word study for phonics, vocabulary, and spelling instruction*. Englewood, Cliffs, NJ: Prentice-Hall.

Bock, C. (1998). *Why Children Succeed or Fail at Reading*. Monograph prepared for NICHD by Robert Brock, Public Information and Communications Branch, NICHD. NICHD Clearinghouse, Rockville, MD.

Chaddock, G. R. (1998, April). What happens when they teach the ABCs? *The Christian Science Monitor*, p. A1.

Clay, M. M. (1985). *The early detection of reading difficulties*. Auckland, New Zealand: Heinemann.

Clay, M. M. (1992). A second chance to learn literacy by different routes to common outcomes (The Reading Recovery Programme). In T. Cline (Ed.), *The assessment of special education needs: International perspectives* (pp. 69–89). New York: Routledge Press.

Dowhower, S. L. (1987). Effects of repeated reading on second grade transitional readers' fluency and comprehension. *Reading Research Quarterly, 22,* 389–406.

Englebert, R., Heibert, E., & Juel, C. (1998). *Ready Readers*. Parsippany, NJ: Modern Curriculum Press.

Fowler, M., Lindemann, L., Thacker-Gwaltney, S., & Invernizzi, M. A. (2000). *A second year of one-on-one tutoring: An intervention for second graders with reading difficulties*. Manuscript submitted for publication.

Heath, S. B. (1991). The sense of being literate: Historical and cross-cultural features. In R. Barr, M. L. Kamil, P. B. Mosenthal, & P. D. Pearson (Eds.), *Handbook of reading research* (vol. 2, pp. 3–25). White Plains, NY: Longman.

Hiebert, E. (1994). Reading Recovery in the United States: What difference does it make to an age cohort? *Educational Researcher, 23*(9), 15–25.

Invernizzi, M. A., Juel, C., & Rosemary, C. A. (1997). A community volunteer tutorial that works. *The Reading Teacher, 50*(4), 304–311.

Invernizzi, M., Rosemary, C., Juel, C., & Richards, H. (1997). At risk readers and community volunteers: A three year perspective. *Scientific Studies of Reading, 1*(3), 277–300.

Iverson, A. J., & Tumner, W. E. (1993). Phonological processing skills and the Reading Recovery

program. *Journal of Educational Psychology, 85,* 112–126.

Juel, C. (1988). Learning to read and write: A longitudinal study of fifty-four children from first through fourth grade. *Journal of Educational Psychology, 80,* 437–447.

Juel, C. (1996). What makes literacy tutoring effective? *Reading Research Quarterly, 31,* 268–289.

Juel, C. (1998). What kind of tutoring helps a poor reader? In C. Hulme & R. M. Joshi (Eds.), *Reading and spelling: Development and disorders* (pp. 450–471). Mahwah, NJ: Erlbaum.

Kibby, M. W., & Barr, R. (1999). The education of reading clinicians. In D. H. Evensen & P. B. Mosenthal (Eds.), *Reconsidering the role of the reading clinic in a new age of literacy, vol. 6*. (Advances in Reading/Language Research series) (pp. 3–40). Stanford, CT: Jai Press.

Lloyd, J. W., Forness, S. R., & Kavale, K. A. (1999). *What special education practices are effective?* [On-line]. Available: http://curry.edschool.virginia.edu/go/cise/ose/information/mega/index.html/

Mantzicopoulous, P., Morrison, D., Stone, E., & Setrakian, W. (1992). Use of the SEARCH/TEACH tutoring approach with middle-class students at risk for reading failure. *Elementary School Journal, 92*(5), 573–586.

Meier, J., & Invernizzi, M. A. (in press). Book Buddies in the Bronx: Testing a model for America Reads and national service. *Journal for the Educational Placement of Children Placed at Risk, 6*(4).

Morris, D. (1995). *First Steps: An early reading intervention program*. (ERIC Documentation Reproduction Service No. ED 388956)

Morris, D. (1999a). Preventing reading failure in the primary grades. In T. Shanahan & F. V. Rodriguez-Brown (Eds.), *National Reading Conference Yearbook, 48,* 17–38.

Morris, D. (1999b). The role of clinical training in the teaching of reading. In D. H. Evensen & P. B. Mosenthal (Eds.), *Reconsidering the role of the reading clinic in a new age of literacy, vol. 6*. (Advances in Reading/Language Research series) (pp. 69–100). Stanford, CT: Jai Press.

Morris, D., Shaw, B., & Perney, J. (1990). Helping low readers in grades 2 and 3: An after-school volunteer tutoring program. *The Elementary School Journal, 91*(2), 133–150.

National Institute of Child Health and Human Development. (1999, November). *When stars read.* [Video].

O'Connor, R. (2000). Increasing the intensity of intervention in kindergarten and first grade. *Learning Disabilities Research and Practice, 15*(1), 43–54.

Pikulski, J. J. (1998). Preventing reading failure: A review of five programs. In R. L. Allington (Ed.), *Teaching struggling readers* (pp. 35–46). Newark, DE: International Reading Association.

Report of the National Reading Panel. (2000, April). *Teaching children to read: An evidence-based assessment of the Scientific Research Liter-*

ature on reading and its implications for reading instruction. (NIH Pub. No. 00–4769). Washington, DC: National Institute of Child Health and Human Development.

Ross, S. M., & Smith, L. J. (1994). Effects of the Success For All model on kindergarten through second-grade reading achievement, teacher's adjustment, and classroom-school climate at an inner-city school. *The Elementary School Journal, 92*(2), 121–138

Samuels, S. J. (1979). The method of repeated readings. *The Reading Teacher, 32,* 403–408.

Santa, C., & HØein, T. (1999). An assessment of early steps: A program for early intervention of reading problems. *Reading Research Quarterly, 34*(1), 54–73.

Scanlon, D. M., & Vellutino, F. R. (1996). Prerequisite skills, early instruction, and success in first grade reading: Selected results from a longitudinal study. *Mental Retardation and Developmental Disabilities, 2,* 54–63.

Scanlon, D. M., Vellutino, F. R., Small, S. G., & Fanuele, D. P. (2000, Spring). *Severe reading difficulties—Can they be prevented? A comparison of prevention and intervention approaches.* Paper presented at the annual meeting of the American Educational Research Association, New Orleans.

Shanahan, T. (1998). On the effectiveness and limitations of tutoring in reading. *Review of Research in Education, 23,* 217–234.

Shanahan, T., & Barr, R. (1995). Reading Recovery: An independent evaluation of the effects of an early instructional intervention for at-risk learners. *Reading Research Quarterly, 30,* 58–996.

Slavin, R. E., Karweit, N. L., & Wasik, B. A. (1994). *Preventing early school failure: Research, policy, practice: The first comprehensive, direct comparison of programs designed to prevent failure in the early grades.* Boston: Allyn & Bacon.

Slavin, R., Madden, N., & Wasik, B. (1996). *Success for all/roots and wings: Summary of research on achievement outcomes. Center for Research on the Education of Students Placed at Risk.* Baltimore: Johns Hopkins University Press.

Snow, C. E., Burns, M. S., & Griffin, P. (Eds.).

(1998). *Preventing reading difficulties in young children.* Washington, DC: National Academy Press.

Stanovich, K. E. (1986). Matthew effects in reading: Some consequences of individual differences in the acquisition of literacy. *Reading Research Quarterly, 21,* 360–406.

Torgesen, J. K. (2000). Individual differences in response to early intervention in reading: The lingering problem of treatment resisters. *Learning Disabilities Reseachers and Practices, 15*(1), 55–64.

Togesen, J. K., Wagner, R. K., Rashotte, C. A., Burgess, S., & Hecht, S. (1997). Contributions of phonological awareness and rapid automatic naming ability to the growth of word-reading skills in second- to fifth-grade children. *Scientific Studies of Reading, 1*(2), 161–185.

United States Department of Education (1999). *21st Annual Report to Congress. The Implementation of the Individuals with Disabilities Education Act.* Washington DC, Author.

Velluntino, F. R., Scanlon, D. M., Sipay, E. R., Small, S. G., Pratt, A., Chen, R., & Denckla, M. B. (1996). Cognitive profiles of difficult-to-remediate and readily remediated poor readers: Intervention as a vehicle for distinguishing between cognitive and experiential deficits as basic cause of specific reading disability. *Journal of Educational Psychology, 88,* 601–638.

Velluntino, F. R., Scanlon, D. M., & Tanzman, M. S. (1998). The case for early intervention in diagnosing specific reading disability. *Journal of School Psychology, 36*(4), 367–380.

Walberg, H. J., & Greenberg, R. C. (1998, April). The Diogenes Factor. *Education Week On the Web* [On-line]. Available: http://www. edweek. org/ew/vol–17/30walber. h17

Walmsley & Allington (1995). Redefining and reforming instructional support programs for at-risk students. In R. Allington & S. Walmsley (Eds.), *No quick fix* (pp. 19–44). New York: Teachers College Press.

Wasik, B. A., & Salvin, R. E. (1993). Preventing early reading failure with one-to-one tutoring: A review of five programs. *Reading Research Quarterly, 28,* 178–200.

30

Title 1 and Special Education: Support for Children Who Struggle to Learn to Read

❖

ANNE McGILL-FRANZEN
VIRGINIA GOATLEY

Special education and compensatory education exist to help the neediest children achieve their fullest potential. Special education and remedial reading operate under the purview of the Individuals with Disabilities Education Act (IDEA) and Title 1 of the Elementary and Secondary Education Act (ESEA) respectively and both have a history that spans several decades. Although the two programs were originally conceptualized as two distinct categorical programs, serving different students, the boundaries between these categories have blurred, particularly in reference to children with reading disabilities (Birman, 1981; McGill-Franzen, 1987; Stanovich, 1991).

Research has established few psychometric distinctions, if any, between young, struggling readers who have been identified as handicapped and those who participate in Title 1 or remedial reading programs (Algozzine & Ysseldyke, 1983; Scanlon & Vellutino, 1996; Shaywitz, Escobar, Shaywitz, Fletcher, & Makuch, 1992;). Distinctions reside in Title I and IDEA oversight and funding, not in the instructional needs of children served by the programs. Whether special education teachers or remedial reading teachers serve struggling readers depends on the resources and ethos of particular school communities. Although instruction in Title 1 and special education does not differ (Allington & McGill-Franzen, 1989), the labels assigned to children may influence the beliefs of teachers and administrators (Allington, McGill-Franzen, & Schick, 1997; McGill-Franzen, 1994;). Nonetheless, over the past decade, researchers in the fields of special education and reading have found common ground and shared expertise and, in service of helping all children be all they can be, have created a substantive body of knowledge on effective interventions for struggling readers (National Research Council, 1998).

In this chapter, we provide brief histories of Title 1 and Special Education. Research in literacy areas associated with these laws and policies have shifted to include a greater focus on teacher education, early interventions, and instructional methods. Thus, we explore the configurations of services most often provided to children who struggle in reading: pullout, inclusion, retention, and extended learning time. We examine exemplary interventions within these differing service models and identify what might be learned from each. Finally, we look ahead to the millennium and raise issues for the future, informed by experience in the past.

Title 1 of the ESEA: From Redistribution of Resources to Leverage for Reform

Lyndon Johnson signed Title 1 of the ESEA into law in 1965 as the centerpiece of his War on Poverty. The ESEA significantly increased the federal role in education. Title 1 is a categorical program, basically a financial subsidy (National School Boards Association, 2000), aimed at supporting the education of disadvantaged children. Although the focus on helping the poorest children is virtually unchanged since its inception, Title 1 has evolved as a program (McGill-Franzen, 2000).

Today, Title 1 serves children in over 90% of school districts. It has a current appropriation of over $8 billion, with most of the money supporting teachers and teaching aides. Over 70% of Title 1 students participated in services to improve reading; another 24% participated in services to improve language arts (U.S. Department of Education, 1999).

Early Years of Title 1: Emphasis on Regulatory Compliance and Add-on Remediation

Initially, Title 1 was concerned with little more than resource allocation, with districts and schools receiving funds to make educational resources more equitable in poorer communities. Because the early emphasis of Title 1 was on resource distribution, or inputs, school districts receiving federal funds needed to be able to show that those funds were spent in ways that conformed to federal regulations. To be able to demonstrate compliance with federal regulations, districts differentiated Title 1 programs from those of the regular classroom by establishing "pullout" or other clearly supplemental services, usually remediation of basic reading skills.

During the Reagan years, funding for Title 1 diminished somewhat. Proponents of Title 1 successfully countered the Reagan administration's push to consolidate Title 1 with other federal programs into block grants for states to use as they saw fit. With the passage of the Education Consolidation and Improvement Act (ECIA) in 1981, federal regulation over Title 1, now Chapter 1, was reduced, but the goals of the original legislation remained.

Also, during the Reagan administration, A Nation At Risk (National Commission on Excellence in Education, 1983) and other commission reports were published, setting in motion unprecedented interest and activity in educational policy and the achievement of America's schoolchildren. The National Governors Association coordinated state efforts to improve education, ultimately leading to the Education Summit in 1989 and the establishment of the National Education Goals by George Bush. Thus, by the time of the Clinton administration, education reform was front and center on the policy agenda, where it remains through the millennium and into the next presidential administration.

Hawkins–Stafford Amendments: Toward School Capacity and Improved Achievement

The reform movement influenced Chapter 1 as well. During this period, several studies of Chapter 1 suggested that remedial programs were unrelated to the regular classroom and unlikely to improve children's achievement in the regular curriculum (Allington & McGill-Franzen, 1989; Carter, 1984; Rowan & Guthrie, 1989). In 1988, the Hawkins–Stafford Elementary and Secondary School Improvement Act Amendment (Public Law 206-297, 1988) attempted to improve compensatory education for disadvantaged students by introducing more flexibility into the ways that districts could use federal Chapter 1 funds. The Hawkins–Stafford amendments moved compensatory services away from the pullout model and toward more coordination with the regular classroom, away from basic skills and toward more challenging curriculum. In addition, although schoolwide projects were theoretically possible as early as 1978, few districts were able to meet the matching funds requirement of the federal legislation. The Hawkins–Stafford amendments removed that requirement, opening the door to more schoolwide improvement in high-poverty schools in place of the add-on programs of the past.

Nonetheless, evaluations of the Chapter 1 programs in the 1990s found that these programs differed little from those of the previous decades (Puma, Jones, Rock, & Fernandez, 1993). Despite the loosening of federal regulations by the Hawkins–Stafford amendments, Chapter 1 remained a marginal intervention. The final report on the congressionally mandated study of student outcomes, *Prospects* (Puma et al., 1997), noted that Chapter 1 added only 10 minutes of additional instruction each day, typically taught by an aide, not a certified teacher, and in a pullout program. As in the past, Chapter 1 programs often pulled students out of their regular classroom instruction in reading, thereby diminishing the effects of extra instruction and further removing disadvantaged students from opportunities to participate in grade level curriculum.

Under the Hawkins–Stafford amendments, Chapter 1 funds could be used more easily for schoolwide programs in schools with high concentrations of poverty. Studies of achievement in high-poverty schools suggested little additional progress, however. The average achievement of all students in high-poverty schools was approximately the same as the achievement of Chapter 1 students in low-poverty schools. Not only had Chapter 1 not closed the gap in achievement between advantaged and disadvantaged students, but "the observed lockstep pattern of student growth clearly demonstrated that where students started out relative to their classmates is where they ended up in later grades" (Puma et al., 1997, p. vi). Despite some "relatively smaller school factors" (p. vi) that may contribute positively to student growth, in general, it appeared that the longer students received Chapter 1 services, the further they lagged behind their peers.

On a more positive note, later analyses of national achievement data confirmed that at least some schools do make a difference. For example, even though the 1970s and 1980s were a time of increasing poverty for many families, the gap in achievement between white children and minorities on the National Assessment of Educational Progress (NAEP) declined. This phenomenon has been attributed in part to such federal educational interventions as Chapter 1 (Grissmer, Kirby, Berends, & Williamson, 1994).

Improving America's School Act: A Focus on Standards-Based Reform and Assessments

Reflecting a growing concern on the part of the states about the achievement of all America's children, the Goals 2000: Educate America Act was passed by the Congress in 1994, providing federal support for states to develop new standards and assessments. Also in 1994, the Congress reauthorized ESEA. In keeping with the tenor of the times, the reauthorization called for disadvantaged children to participate in more challenging curriculum and standards-based reforms. When Congress reauthorized ESEA in 1994 with the passage of the Improving America's Schools Act (IASA), again Title 1, it did so with the intention of reforming instruction for poor children. IASA made Title 1 congruent with the national move toward excellence and accountability (U.S. Department of Education, 1996). According to the provisions of IASA, disadvantaged students were to participate in standards-based curriculum and assessments to the same extent that all other children participate. Further, IASA encouraged more flexibility in the ways that schools and districts were able to use Title 1 funds to support school improvement, including teacher development and parent-education activities and extended learning time for students. Finally, IASA mandated the National Assessment of Title 1 (NATI) to evaluate progress toward meetings its goals. Rather than supplemental remediation outside mainstream curriculum and instruction, the revised Title 1 was intended to be integral to national, state, and local standards-based reform and systems of accountability. IASA was intended to leverage change in educating poor children.

The most recent NATI (U.S. Department of Education, 1999), in fact, did report improved reading achievement—almost a whole grade level—among 9-year-olds in high-poverty schools between the 1992 and 1996 administrations of the NAEP. Further, NATI reported that several states with standards-based reforms in place improved significantly in reading among 9-year-olds on the 1998 NAEP (U.S. Department of Education, National Center for Education Statistics, 1999). Similarly, several of the country's largest and most troubled urban school districts reported improvements in reading on the NAEP (Council of Great City Schools, 1999). Although research on the effectiveness of the revised Title 1 is still emerging, the U.S. Department of Education attributed recent progress to the 1994 changes in Title 1 and argued for Congress to continue to support these reforms (U.S. Department of Education, 1999).

During Title 1 reauthorization proceedings in Congress, various constituents weighed in on the effectiveness of IASA in improving achievement for poor children and what changes should be made in the 35-year-old program. Clearly, the new direction for Title 1 is toward greater flexibility in use of Title 1 funds and greater accountability to students and families for results.

Special Education: Public Law 94-142 and the Individuals with Disabilities Education Act

Although ESEA was the first federal legislation to provide direct financial subsidies to a targeted category of children, it provided money only for handicapped students who attended special schools operated by the states (Martin, Martin, & Terman, 1996). Advocates for the handicapped lobbied Congress intensively for an educational entitlement, separate from the ESEA, and following the early lead of several states, in 1975 Congress passed and Gerald Ford signed the Education for All Handicapped Children Act (Public Law 94-142). Public Law 94-142 entitled all children with disabilities to a free and appropriate public education. Public Law 94-142 was amended in 1983 and again in 1990 and renamed the Individuals with Disabilities Education Act.

Although special education was never a fully funded mandate, the cost of the program has risen from approximately $250 million at its inception to a total estimated at $32 billion by the mid-1990s (Reschly, 1996). *The 20th Annual Report to Congress on the Implementation of the Individuals with Disabilities Education Act* documented the increasing numbers of students and preschool students who are identified as disabled (Sack, 1999; U.S. Department of Education, 1998). Each year, from 1994 to 1997, the latest year for which data are available, the number of students identified with disabilities has increased by 3% over the previous year. The total number of children from 3 to 21 years of age now identified as handicapped is almost 6 million. The largest single category of disability is "specific learning disability," accounting for over 3 million children. The majority of children identified as learning disabled have deficits in reading (Lyon, 1996).

IDEA Amendments of 1997: An Emphasis on Achievement Outcomes and Accountability

The IDEA Amendments of 1997 (IDEA 1997) represented the first major revision to Public Law 94-142, Education of All Handicapped Children Act of 1975. IDEA 1997 amended the provisions for disabled children in two important ways: by requiring that disabled children have access to regular curriculum and by introducing a measure of accountability for their progress. In the words of the IDEA final regulations, "IDEA 1997 provides a new and heightened emphasis on results" (Office of Special Education and Rehabilitative Services, 1999). Prior to IDEA 1997, little attention was given to students' achievement in regular education. Now, each disabled student's individualized education plan (IEP) must provide the following: (1) a statement describing the student's present level of functioning and how the student's disability relates to his or her participation and success in the general curriculum; (2) a statement of measurable annual goals and accompanying benchmarks to document progress in the regular curriculum; and (3) a statement of related services and program modifications to help the child with disabilities attain the annual goals set for him or her, participate and progress in the general curriculum, participate in extracurricular activities, and be educated in settings with children who have disabilities and those who do not.

Prior to IDEA 1997, classroom teachers were not required to participate in IEP development. Now, according to the Director of the Office of Special Education Programs (OSEP), the IEP team must include the classroom teacher so that his or her judgment and expertise can be brought to bear on discussions of the participation and progress of students with disabilities in the regular curriculum. The classroom teacher is expected to participate as well in decisions about the supplementary support needed for handicapped students to succeed in the regular environment (Hehir, 1999). Similarly, IDEA 1997 was designed to strengthen parent involvement in the education of children with disabilities.

Second, IDEA 1997 required that children with disabilities be included in general state and district assessments and reported to the public in the same manner as for students without disabilities. Accommodations must be detailed in the IEP. It was anticipated that relatively few children will require an alternative assessment, but in those cases, the alternative assessment must have been in place by July 2000. In addition, IDEA 1997 required that states establish performance standards to document how well special education students are doing in the general education curriculum. A decade ago, fewer than 10% of students with disabilities were participating in national, state or local assessments (Allington & McGill-Franzen, 1992; McGill-Franzen & Allington, 1993). Currently, 50 to 80% of students with disabilities are participating in large-scale assessments. However, major issues of accountability for students with disabilities remain to be worked out. States vary in the standards they have set for students with disabilities, the assessments and assessment accommodations allowed for students with disabilities, and the way the results of the assessments are publicly reported.

Relating Funding to Classification and Early Intervention: An Unresolved Issue of the IDEA

IDEA 1997 does not address the definition of learning disability as defined in the statute as significant discrepancy between achievement and ability (Office of Special Education and Rehabilitative Services, 1999). However, in contrast to prior special education legislation, IDEA 1997 may discourage the classification of students with "invisible disabilities" such as learning dis-

abilities or attention-deficit/hyperactivity disorder. By the same token, IDEA 1997 also may not have allocated sufficient funds to support early intervention in kindergarten and grade 1 for students who are at risk of failing to learn to read before their failure is so profound that they are candidates for special education services (Kolmeir, 1999). At the current time, IDEA provides minimal funds for districts to implement mandated special education services. For example, the Chair of the Advisory Commission on Special Education in California noted in the satellite conference series transcript of the U.S. Department of Education Broadcast on ConnectLive.com News (Riley, 1999) that the federal government provided only $400 million to support current programs. On the other hand, according to this report, the state of California provides $2 billion and the districts another $1.2 billion, making it unlikely that districts in California, as elsewhere, will be able to fund early-intervention services in addition to those services already mandated by law.

However, one change in IDEA 1997, opening the door to earlier intervention before failure becomes acute, was the revision in the definition of "developmentally delayed" to include children between the ages of 3 and 9 (Office of Special Education and Rehabilitative Services, 1999). States can opt to use the expanded definition, thus providing an opportunity to address the needs of children, such as intensive remediation in reading, without giving the child one of the 13 labels under IDEA. Similarly, preschool and kindergarten interventions may also circumvent the need for further special education services when these children reach school age. In addition, under the IDEA 1997, special education teachers may work with any children in inclusion classrooms, not just already identified children. Thus, children who are struggling but not labeled could receive extra support from the special education teacher in an inclusion classroom.

According to Heumann (1999), the Clinton administration and the U.S. Department of Education wanted fewer students referred for extensive special education services. Through improved teacher education in reading, for example, she believes that regular education teachers would understand "the variety of types of methodologies that could be utilized to begin to assist a child in learning how to read." Recent reviews of research support the assertion that students with reading disabilities may need the same kind of effective instruction as students without disabilities (National Research Council, 1998; Swanson & Hoskyn, 1998).

Education Secretary Riley (1999) admonished the field to rethink special education. Rather than "a place" for children with disabilities, "it is a set of important services." In the sections that follow, we examine examples of successful support for Title 1 students in pullout and push-in interventions in the regular classroom and students identified for special education services in inclusion classrooms or special education settings.

Early Literacy Instruction for Students in Title 1/Special Education Programs

Currently, students qualifying for Special Education and Title 1 services receive support through a range of programs, from extra instruction within the regular education setting to extra instruction in pullout programs, that is, in resource rooms and one-to-one tutoring, and in self-contained special education classrooms (see, e.g., Hiebert & Taylor, 1994; Pinnell, Lyons, Deford, Bryk, & Seltzer, 1994; Vellutino et al., 1996). In addition, different locations within the community, including the home, schools, public libraries, day care, and churches, may become the social settings within which children experience literacy. All these interactions have an impact on children and their uses of literacy, particularly given the importance of language opportunities for young children's literacy development. Although there are many potential areas of concern in any discussion of research relevant to the development of instructional support for struggling readers, our review in this section centers on two main issues from the literature on Title 1 and special education. First, literate activity should be more prominent in early-childhood instruction for all children, and for children who need support beyond participation in effective early-literacy classrooms,

intensive learning opportunities must be provided. Second, we believe that teachers of reading, early-childhood or elementary classroom teachers, Title 1 reading specialists, or special education teachers, must be proficient in appropriate pedagogy for learners at diverse levels of development and able to coordinate learning opportunities for children across settings.

Good First Teaching Is the Most Effective Intervention

The belief that excellent instruction for young children is the best way to prevent later reading difficulties is consistent with recent Title 1 and IDEA legislation and the National Research Council report of the National Academy. For all children of preschool age and children in kindergarten, and particularly for children eligible for Title 1 or special education services, literacy activities should be not only available but *prominent*. Recent research has demonstrated that access to books, opportunities to write, oral language play, instruction in letter-sound correspondences, and storybook reading can significantly accelerate the literacy development of very young children at risk (McGill-Franzen, 1993; McGill-Franzen, Allington, Yokoi, & Brooks, 1999; Neuman, 1999; Neuman & Roskos 1997; Scanlon & Vellutino, 1996).

Likewise, in recognition of the importance of early intervention in the prevention of reading difficulties, there has been a shift in the use of Title 1 money and, to a lesser extent, special education support to the early grades. This early grade focus on prevention typically extends from preschool to kindergarten and first grade. Currently, a range of services support children in the early grades who are already identified as experiencing difficulty with learning to read.

Interventions may take the form of specialized instruction within the classroom by the regular education teacher, extra instruction within the classroom by a Title 1 or special education teacher, and pullout programs such as self-contained special education or reading resource classrooms. Often, the debate focuses on which of these settings is the most effective, rather than the actual instruction that occurs in the various locations. It is important to think about literacy instruction across settings rather than assuming that a particular location always will be best for a particular student. Indeed, children's competence may vary, depending on the interaction of the individual with the social setting (Rueda, Gallego, & Moll, 2000). Thus, particular settings may facilitate or impede development, depending on children's personal levels of knowledge and agency and the social or institutional opportunities available for children to participate in different learning communities.

In the sections that follow, we discuss teachers' knowledge of literacy development, coordination and collaboration of instruction across social settings, and extended learning opportunities for children—all issues of utmost importance for young students experiencing difficulty learning to read.

Teachers' Knowledge of Literacy Development

A joint statement by the International Reading Association and National Association for the Education of Young Children (1998) emphasized the need for teachers of young children to be particularly knowledgeable about literacy issues: "Teachers of young children, whether employed in preschools, childcare programs, or elementary schools, have a unique responsibility to promote children's literacy development, based on the most current professional knowledge and research" (p. 38). Some states, such as New York, have changed reading teacher certification guidelines to reflect the importance of the period between birth and school rather than only the elementary school years.

Certainly, state licensure and hiring requirements can profoundly influence reading achievement. The Center for the Study of Teaching and Policy (CTP) found that teacher qualifications ("fully qualified" teachers of reading were defined in the study as having a major in reading coursework) accounted for approximately 40 to 60% of the variance across states in reading achievement among 9-year-olds on the National Assessment of Educational Progress (NAEP) (Darling-Hammond, 1999). This relationship held even among students with

backgrounds of poverty and limited English proficiency—students who are the least likely to have fully certified teachers. An area not addressed by the CTP study was the lack of reading credentials among teachers and teacher aides who likely teach the lowest-achieving children.

Too often, education certification programs for special education teachers, for example, may have few requirements for courses in how to teach reading, yet this is the academic area most often a problem for students in special education settings. Similarly, studies have shown that regular education teachers do not feel they have the necessary understandings to teach students who are identified with reading disabilities (Minke, Bear, Deemer, & Griffin 1996; Vaughn, Reiss, Rothlein, & Hughes, 1999). Recognizing the importance of well-prepared teachers, the International Reading Association (IRA) has recently established the Commission on Teacher Preparation (CTP) in order to examine undergraduate teacher education and link features of exemplary preservice programs to successful practice in the teaching of reading (Roller, 2000). The IRA has also taken a strong stance in the reauthorization of ESEA, recommending, for example, that (1) those assigned to teach the neediest children be fully qualified teachers of reading, not unqualified paraprofessionals, as is frequently the case now; and (2) teachers of reading have access to ongoing professional development and the findings of current research (International Reading Association, 1999).

Often even modest professional development opportunities can influence teachers' knowledge and, ultimately, children's achievement. A case in point is the urban kindergarten literacy initiative reported by McGill-Franzen et al. (1999). Kindergarten teachers were assigned to one of three conditions. Some teachers received a 200-book classroom library; others received the books and professional development on effective ways to read to children, develop print knowledge, and provide parent and classroom access to books. The third condition was a control group, and these teachers received neither books nor professional development. Kindergarten children of teachers who received both books and professional development outperformed the children in the other classrooms on every measure of print knowledge and vocabulary development. Of particular significance is the finding that the teachers who received the 200 books only—that is, no professional development on the instructional use of these materials—performed no better than the teachers who had no books.

Recent reviews of experimental research with readers with disabilities support a view of effective treatments (and effective teachers) that combine direct instruction and strategy instruction in an interactive and opportunistic way, depending on task demands (Swanson & Hoskyn, 1998). In early literacy, the most effective interventions develop teachers' knowledge of appropriate levels of task and text difficulty, explicit instruction in strategy use such as phonemic segmentation, matching sound to print, summarizing, or interpreting and creating complex texts (Pikulski, 1994).

Literacy Instruction within and across Various Settings

Literacy instructional programs designed for specific groups of learners vary widely. These range from one-to-one tutoring sessions, as in the Howard Street tutoring program (Morris, Shaw, & Perry, 1990) and Reading Recovery (Pinnell et al., 1994), small-group guided reading instruction (Fountas & Pinnell, 1996), multiple forms of grouping such as Four Blocks (Cunningham, Hall, & Defee, 1998), and schoolwide initiatives such as Success for All (Madden, Slavin, Karweit, Dolan, & Wasik, 1993).

The congruence of instruction across social settings within a school is critical in terms of both the nature of the literacy instruction and the way in which participation connects to learning in other settings. Whether or not it is effective to pull students from one school setting for instruction in another is a concern, particularly if the instruction is not consistent across locations (Pugach & Wesson, 1995). In response to earlier arguments about the deleterious effects of instruction for students in special education settings (Allington, 1983), several researchers have described effective literacy practices outside the regular classroom and in more "restrictive" environments (Englert,

Raphael, & Mariage, 1994; Pinnell & McCarrier, 1994).

The Early Literacy Project, for example, developed contextualized literacy instruction within special education settings, involving 10 self-contained special education classrooms serving 88 students in grades 1–4 (Englert, Mariage, Garmon, & Tarrant, 1998; Englert et al., 1994). Rather than focusing on only one area of literacy, this intervention viewed literacy as a whole and focused on making connections across reading, writing, and discussion instead of treating these processes in isolation. The main purpose of the project was to develop a literacy curriculum for special education classrooms based on a sociocultural perspective and one that was similar to effective literacy instruction for students in regular education classrooms. The project was based on four major principles: (1) teaching to self-regulation, (2) responsive instruction, (3) building literate communities, and (4) meaningful and holistic literacy activities. The literacy curriculum included independent/silent reading, sharing chair, story response/discussion, thematic units, supported partner reading/writing, morning news, choral reading, journal writing, and author's center. Although these activities are all components of the program, the intervention focused on the language used by teachers and students and the ways classroom discourse led to constructing meanings around texts for preconventional readers and writers. Englert et al. (1994) suggested that "new understandings evolved through a classroom discourse in which teachers guided children's thinking, apprenticed them in new ways of talking about texts, and scaffolded their performance so that students could progressively assume more responsibility for self-regulation" (p. 2).

Further, the intervention itself supported the learning of teachers as well as students, increasing their knowledge of literacy pedagogy, and relatedly, the performance of their students. Achievement tests indicated that the students in the classrooms of the teachers in their second year with the project performed better than the first-year or control-group students (Englert et al., 1995). This finding applied to several areas of literacy, including writing, oral reading, comprehension, and metacognitive knowledge. For example, areas of writing that improved included organization of texts, awareness of audience, and writing more words. The study suggests three main hypotheses about the success of the program: (1) the more experienced teachers were more willing to relinquish control to their students, (2) student success seemed connected to teachers' knowledge of their student in relation to the curriculum, and (3) teachers needed an extended period to develop conceptual understandings associated with the curriculum (Englert, et al., 1995). Thus, the Early Literacy Project not only supported the authors' assertion that highly effective instruction can take place in self-contained special education settings as well as in regular classrooms, but the study also demonstrated that students' improved performance is directly related to special education teachers' developing expertise in literacy pedagogy.

Although the expertise of individual teachers is arguably the most important element in effective teaching of at-risk learners, the realities of day-to-day life in schools suggest the salience of organizational issues as well—that is, the grouping, scheduling, and monitoring of services provided by specialists, aides, volunteers, or tutors from any number of programs. Some Title 1 and special education studies specifically have addressed collaboration issues, examining the instruction provided within and across settings to determine the consistency in the curriculum experienced by struggling readers (Goatley, 2000; Goldfarb & Salmon, 1993; Richek & Glick, 1991). Goatley (2000), for example, conducted a case study on Mrs. Casey, a remedial reading teacher, and the ways in which Mrs. Casey's communication with regular classroom teachers created congruency in instruction across social settings. Mrs. Casey knew the factors that can negatively influence pullout instruction, including allocation of less instructional time, less engaged instructional time, instructional emphases on low-level skills, quantity and mode of assigned reading, and teacher interruption behaviors. Mrs. Casey directly targeted her own practice, making changes in these areas to avoid problems. In addition, she developed relationships with other teachers, collaborations that seemed to be conducive to supporting and reinforcing the students' learning. These collaborations developed, in part, because of Mrs. Casey's expertise in reading instruction. Teachers asked her for suggestions to help struggling readers, and Mrs. Casey, in turn, made genuine attempts to learn more about her Title 1 students' experiences with the regular reading curriculum from classroom teachers. These collaborations involved written and oral communication, shared instructional plans, specific literacy demonstrations, and performance-based assessments of individual students' progress. These formal and informal collaborations enabled Mrs. Casey to share her reading instruction expertise with other teachers. In her documentation of the practices of the case study teacher, Goatley observed that instruction for Title 1 students was congruent across social settings. Title 1 students, for example, demonstrated familiarity with vocabulary in the regular education classroom that had been carefully introduced and used in the resource room the previous week.

Both the teachers in the Early Literacy Project (Englert et al., 1995) and Mrs. Casey (Goatley, 1995) provided instruction in a pullout setting that was intended to reinforce and improve on the instruction found in regular education classrooms. Rather than focus on isolated skills, these teachers emphasized extended reading and rereading of connected texts, writing opportunities, word study, response activities, and critical talk between teachers and students and among students, providing a wide range of learning opportunities for struggling readers. Thus, the teachers avoided the problematic nature of pullout programs characterized by earlier research, and the collaborations across settings made the best use of the professional knowledge of the teachers.

Extended Learning Opportunities for Children: Issues of Retention and Increased Instructional Time

Retention is often the first intervention that schools use when students struggle with reading or show signs of immaturity, especially at the kindergarten and first-grade level. However, there is overwhelming research that suggests retention is not a useful alternative (Allington & McGill-Franzen, 1995; Shepard & Smith, 1989). Long-term studies of students who have been retained show that retention may have short-term benefit but students quickly fall behind again as they progress through the grades.

Of particular interest to us is the reanalysis of Prospects data conducted by Karweit (1999) to examine the relationship between retention and student achievement among Title 1 students. The 1988 Chapter 1/Title 1 legislation initiated the collection of longitudinal data on a cohort of first-graders (Puma et al., 1997). First-graders (51.8% of retentions occur in grades K through 3) are more likely than students in other grades to repeat their grade or to attend a transition room.

Karweit's (1999) analysis identified Chapter 1 participation as one characteristic of students more likely to be retained. Students were more likely to be retained if they had the following characteristics: "male, being of race/ethnicity Other, mobility during the school year, disability and health status which are poor, larger family size, living in the South, attending a high poverty school, and being a Chapter 1 student" (p. 22). White students were more likely to be retained in kindergarten than were black students, who were more likely to be retained in first grade or later. Karweit also examined the data on retained children in connection to Title 1 services. She found that "of the students who repeated first grade, 58 percent received Title 1 services the first time they were in first grade while only 34 percent received services in the repeated year" (p. 64). These findings suggest that children in retention situations may receive less support the second year, and one-third of the students did not receive Title 1 service in either year of first grade. This finding is important in that it suggests that some schools are using retention as an intervention or treatment rather than providing extra reading instruction that would likely benefit the student.

Although retention does not appear to be an effective means of improving the achievement of students needing special services, other initiatives have been developed to extend the learning time offered to struggling readers. The most well-known and well-researched of these initiatives is Reading Recovery, a specific program of intensive, one-to-one tutoring by an expert teacher of reading. Although Reading Recovery, a model based on the work of New Zealand educator Marie Clay (1972), is extremely expensive to implement (Shanahan & Barr, 1995), it has served as a model for tutorial programs and other interventions across the country (National Research Council, 1998). Wasik (1998) reviewed 17 volunteer tutoring models and identified four common features of the tutorial instruction—reading new books, rereading, word analysis, and writing—that are typical elements of Reading Recovery tutorials. Just as teachers' knowledge and ability to communicate across settings are concerns in instruction by teachers, Wasik found similar issues in the effectiveness of volunteer tutors: Tutors varied in their competence and in the number of hours provided for their training; more effective volunteer programs provided ongoing support and supervision for tutors; and, not surprisingly, there was virtually no coordination between the tutoring and the classroom instruction. Wasik recommended, and we concur, that effective volunteer programs, many funded under the America Reads initiative (2000), can extend the learning time of struggling readers, but the costs and benefits of programs to children should be scrutinized.

Beyond the one-to-one tutorial programs, other initiatives have been proposed to provide extra instruction to students in need of early literacy support. Several of these initiatives may be eligible for the more flexible funding under IDEA 1997 and the reauthorized ESEA. Newly designed support services to struggling learners include kindergarten extensions from half-day to whole-day and other extended-day programs wherein students arrive early or leave later in order to participate in focused, small-group instruction. Likewise, there is renewed interest in summer school to compensate for the reported reading loss experienced by low-achieving children and children from low-income families (Entwisle, Alexander, & Olson, 1997; McGill, Franzen, & Allington, in press). We need long-term research on many of these extended day programs and extra services to determine their effectiveness.

Summary and Conclusions

Research on the agenda-setting process holds that in order for policy issues to come to the fore, that is, to reach the point at which government takes action on them, there needs to be a fortuitous coming together of problem, solution, and support (McGill-Franzen, 1993, 2000). An issue first has to be perceived as a problem that deserves the attention of government. The problem must be labeled in a way that gains the public's attention. Government, in turn, must believe that there is a solution to the problem, and that the public wants government to act to resolve the problem. Education is the top priority among voters, with both Republican and Democratic candidates hoping to convince the public that he or she has done or will do more than the opposition to improve education in this country. Given the direction of recent IDEA regulations and the debates around the current reauthorization of ESEA, the plight of young struggling readers is clearly on the policy agenda. It is not clear whether the solution lies in developing teachers' expertise in reading pedagogy, in more efficient structures for program coordination across professional affiliations, or simply in more money. What is clear is that these evolving programs may be very different from past Title 1 and special education services.

In any case, Title 1 and special education will continue to evolve as programs that support needy children. What form the support services will take is an open question. Thus far, federal support services have not closed the persistent achievement gap between advantaged children and those from poor families or those children whose achievement lags so far behind their peers that they are identified as "disabled." At this juncture in time, after decades of federal support for compensatory and special education, we must ask what we know and what we need to know (to paraphrase the Director of IRA Research & Policy Division; Roller, 2000, p. 634) to make every child a reader, child by child.

References

Algozzine, B., & Ysseldyke, J. (1983). Learning disabilities as a subset of school failure: The oversophistication of a concept. *Exceptional Children, 50*, 242–246.

Allington, R. L. (1983). The reading instruction provided readers of differing abilities. *Elementary School Journal, 83*, 548–559.

Allington, R. L., & McGill-Franzen, A. (1989). Different programs, indifferent instruction. In A. Gartner & D. Lipsky (Eds.), *Beyond separate education* (pp. 75–98). Baltimore: Brookes.

Allington, R., & McGill-Franzen, A. (1992). Unintended effects of educational reform in New York State. *Educational Policy, 6*, 396–413.

Allington, R. L., & McGill-Franzen, A. (1995). Flunking: Throwing good money after the bad. In R. L. Allington & S. A. Walmsley, (Eds.), *No quick fix: Rethinking literacy programs in America's elementary schools* (pp. 45–60). New York: Teachers College Press.

Allington, R. L., McGill-Franzen, A., & Schick, R. (1997). How administrators understand learning difficulties: A qualitative analysis. *Remedial and Special Education, 18*, 223–232.

America Reads Program. (2000). [Online]. Available: www.ed.gov/init/americareads

Birman, B. F. (1981). Problems of overlap between Title 1 and PL94–142: Implications for the federal role in education. *Educational Evaluation and Policy Analysis, 3*, 5–19.

Carter, L. F. (1984). The sustaining effects study of compensatory and elementary education. *Educational Researcher, 13*, 7.

Clay, M. (1972). *Reading: The patterning of complex behaviour.* Auckland NZ: Heineman Educational Books.

Council of Great City Schools (1999). *Closing the achievement gaps in urban schools: A survey of academic progress and promising practices in the great city schools.* [Online]. Available: http://www.cgcs.org

Cunningham, P. M., Hall, D. P., & Defe, M. (1991). Nonability-grouped, multilevel instruction: A year in a first grade classroom. *The Reading Teacher, 44*, 566–571.

Darling-Hammond, L. (1999, December). *Teacher quality and student achievement: A review of state policy evidence.* Stanford, CA: Center for the Study of Teaching and Policy.

Englert, C. S., Garmon, M. A., Mariage, T. V., Rozendal, M., Tarrant, K. L., & Urba, J. (1995). The early literacy project: Connecting across the literacy curriculum. *Learning Disabilities Quarterly, 18*, 253–275.

Englert, C. S., Mariage, T. V., Garmon, M. A., & Tarrant, K. L. (1998). Accelerating reading progress in early literacy project classrooms: Three exploratory studies. *Remedial and Special Education, 19*(3), 142–149.

Englert, C. S., Raphael, T. R., & Mariage, T.

(1994). Developing a school-based discourse for literacy learning: A principled search for understanding. *Learning Disabilities Quarterly, 17,* 3–33.

Entwisle, D., Alexander, K., & Olson, L. (1997). *Children, schools and inequality.* Boulder, CO: Westview Press.

Fountas, I., & Pinnell, G. S. (1996). *Guided reading: Good first teaching for all children.* Portsmouth, NH, Heinemann.

Goatley, V. J. (1995). *The literacy communities of emergent readers and writers: A sociocultural perspective.* Unpublished doctoral dissertation, Michigan State University.

Goatley, V. J. (2000). Exploring school learning communities: Students' early literacy transformations. *Reading and Writing Quarterly: Overcoming Learning Disabilities, 16,* 337–360.

Goldfarb, L., & Salmon, S. (1993). Enhancing language arts for special populations: Librarians and classroom teachers collaborate. *Language Arts, 70,* 576–572.

Grissmer, D., Kirby, S., Berends, M., & Williamson, S. (1994). *Student achievement and the changing American family.* Santa Monica, CA: RAND.

Hehir, T. (1999, March 18). Satellite conference series transcript. *The U. S. Department of Education Broadcast on ConnectLive. com News Network "IDEA '97 Regulations."* [Online]. Available: http://www.ideapolicy.org

Heumann, J. (1999, March 3). *Satellite conference series transcript.* The U. S. Department of Education Broadcast on ConnectLive. com News Network "IDEA '97 Regulations." [Online]. Available: http://www.ideapolicy.org

Hiebert, E. H., & Taylor, B. (1994). *Getting reading right from the start: Effective early literacy interventions.* Boston, MA: Allyn & Bacon.

International Reading Association and National Association for the Education of Young Children. (1998). Learning to read and write: Developmentally appropriate practices for young children. *Young Children, 53,* 30–45.

International Reading Association. (1999, August). *Title 1 reauthorization.* [Online]. Available: www.reading.org

Karweit, N. (1999). *Grade retention: Prevalence, timing, and effects. Technical Report #33.* Baltimore: Johns Hopkins University, Center for Research on the Education of Students Placed At Risk (CRESPAR).

Kolmeir, L. (1999, March 18). *The U.S. Department of Education Broadcast on ConnectLive. com News Network "IDEA '97 Regulations"* [Online]. Available: www.ideapolicy. org/IDEA%20Satellite%20Conf/march_18th_satellite_conference_.htm

Lyon, G. R. (1996). Learning disabilities. *The Future of Children: Special Education for Students with Disabilities, 6,* 54–76.

Madden, N. A., Slavin, R. E., Karweit, N. L., Dolan, L. J., & Wasik, B. A. (1993). Success for All: Longitudinal effects of a restructuring program for inner-city elementary schools. *American Educational Research Journal, 30,* 123–148.

Martin, E. W., Martin, R., & Terman, D. L. (1996). The legislative and litigation history of special education. *The Future of Children: Special Education for Students with Disabilities, 6,* 25–39.

McGill-Franzen, A. (1987). Failure to learn to read: Formulating a policy problem. *Reading Research Quarterly, 22,* 475–490.

McGill-Franzen, A. (1993). *Shaping the preschool agenda: Early literacy, public policy, and professional beliefs.* Albany, NY: State University of New York Press.

McGill-Franzen, A. (1994). Is there accountability for learning and belief in children's potential? In E. Hiebert & B. Taylor (Eds.), Getting reading right from the start: Effective early literacy interventions (pp. 13–35). Boston: Allyn & Bacon.

McGill-Franzen, A. (2000). Policy and instruction: What is the relationship? In R. Barr, M. Kamil, P. Mosenthal, and P. D. Pearson (Eds.), *Handbook of reading research* (vol. 3, pp. 889–908). Mahwah, NJ: Erlbaum.

McGill-Franzen, A., & Allington, R. (1991). The gridlock of low-achievement: Perspectives on policy and practice. *Remedial and Special Education, 12,* 20–30.

McGill-Franzen, A., & Allington, R. L. (1993). Flunk 'em or get them classified: The contamination of primary grade accountability data. *Educational Researcher, 22,* 19–22.

McGill-Franzen, A., Allington, R., Yokoi, L., & Brooks, G. (1999). Putting books in the room seems necessary but not sufficient. *Journal of Educational Research, 93,* 67–74.

McGill-Franzen, A., & Allington, R. (in press). Lost summers: Few books, few opportunities to read. *Classroom Leadership* [online]. Available: www.ascd.org/readingroom/classlead/

Minke, K. M., Bear, G. B., Deemer, S. A., & Griffin, S. M. (1996). Teachers' experiences with inclusive classrooms: Implications for special education reform. *The Journal of Special Education, 30*(2), 152–186.

Morris, D., Shaw, B., & Perry, J. (1990). Helping low readers in grades 2 and 3: An after school volunteer tutoring program. *Elementary School Journal, 91,* 133–150.

National Commission on Excellence in Education. (1983). *A nation at risk.* Washington, DC: U. S. Department of Education.

National Research Council. (1998). *Preventing reading difficulties in young children.* Washington, DC: National Academy Press.

National School Boards Association. (2000). *Exploring new directions: Title 1 in the Year 2000.* Alexandria, VA: Author.

Neuman, S. B. (1999). Books make a difference: A study of access to literacy. *Reading Research Quarterly, 34,* 286–311.

Neuman, S. B., & Roskos, K. (1997). Literacy knowledge in practice: Contexts of participation for young writers and readers. *Reading Research Quarterly, 32,* 10–32.

Office of Special Education and Rehabilitative Services. (1999, March). *IDEA Part B Final Regulations. [Online].* Available: www.ideapolicy.org/ IDEA%20Satellite%20Conf/march_3.htm

Pikulski, J. J. (1994). Preventing reading failure: A review of five effective programs. *The Reading Teacher, 48*(1), 30–39.

Pinnell, G. S., Lyons, C. A., Deford, D. E., Bryk, A. S., & Seltzer, M. (1994). Comparing instructional models for the literacy education of high-risk first graders. *Reading Research Quarterly, 29,* 8–39.

Pinnell, G. S., & McCarrier, A. (1994). Interactive writing: A transition tool for assisting children in learning to read and write. In E. H. Hiebert & B. M. Taylor (Eds.), *Getting reading right from the start: Effective early literacy interventions* (pp. 149–170). Boston: Allyn & Bacon.

Pugash, M. C., & Wesson, C. L. (1995). Teachers' and students' views of team teaching of general education and learning-disabled students in two fifth grade classes. *Elementary School Journal, 95,* 279–295.

Puma, M., Jones, C., Rock, D., & Fernandez, R. (1993). *Prospects: congressional mandated study of educational growth and opportunity—interim report.* Washington, DC: U. S. Department of Education, Office of Planning & Evaluation Services.

Puma, M., Karweit, N., Price, C., Ricciuti, A., Thompson, W., & Vaden-Kiernan, M. (1997). *Prospects: Final report on student outcomes.* Washington, DC: U. S. Department of Education, Office of Planning & Evaluation Services.

Reschly, D. (1996). Identification and assessment of students with disabilities. *The Future of Children: Special Education for Students with Disabilities, 6,* 40–54.

Richek, M. A., & Glick, L. C. (1991). Coordinating a literacy support program with classroom instruction. *Reading Teacher, 44,* 474–479.

Riley, R. (1999, March 18). *Satellite conference series transcript. The U.S. Department of Education Broadcast on ConnectLive. com News Network "IDEA '97 Regulations"* [Online]. Available: http://www.ideapolicy.org

Roller, C. (2000). The International Reading Association responds to a highly charged policy environment. *The Reading Teacher, 53,* 626–636.

Rowan, B., & Guthrie, L. (1989). The quality of Chapter 1 instruction: Results from a study of 24 schools. In R. Slavin, N. Karweit, & N. Madden (Eds.), *Effective programs for students at risk* (pp. 195–219). Boston: Allyn & Bacon.

Rueda, R., Gallego, M., & Moll, L. (2000). The least restrictive environment: A place or a context? *Remedial and Special Education, 21,* 70–78.

Sack, J. (1999, March 17). Report charts rise in special education enrollment. *Education Week.* [Online]. Available: www.edweek.org/ew/vol-18/27/ idea.h18

Scanlon, D., & Vellutino, F. (1996). Prerequisite skills, early instruction, and success in first grade reading. *Mental Retardation and Developmental Disabilities: Research and Review, 2,* 54–63.

Shanahan, T., & Barr, R. (1995). Reading Recovery: An independent evaluation of the effects of an early instructional intervention for at risk learners. *Reading Research Quarterly, 30,* 958–996.

Shaywitz, S. E., Escobar, M. D., Shaywitz, B. A., Fletcher, J., & Makuch. (1992). Evidence that dyslexia may represent the lower tail of a normal distribution of reading ability. *New England Journal of Medicine, 326,* 145–50.

Shepard, L., & Smith, M. L. (Eds.). (1989). *Flunking grades: Research and policies on retention.* Philadelphia: Falmer.

Stanovich, K. E. (1991). Discrepancy definitions of reading disability: Has intelligence led us astray? *Reading Research Quarterly, 26,* 7–29.

Swanson, H. L., & Hoskyn, M. (1998). Experimental intervention research on students with learning disabilities: A meta-analysis of treatment outcomes. *Review of Educational Research, 68,* 277–321.

U.S. Department of Education, National Center for Education Statistics. (1999, March). *NAEP 1998 reading report card for the nation and the states.* [Online]. Available: http://nces.ed.gov

U.S. Department of Education. (1996). *Mapping out the national assessment Title 1: The interim report.* Available: http://www.ed.gov/pubs/NatAssess/

U.S. Department of Education. (1998). *The twentieth annual report to Congress on the implementation of Individuals with Disabilities Education Act.* [Online]. Available: http://www.ed.gov/offices/OSERS/OSEP/OSEP98AnlRpt/

U.S. Department of Education. (1999). *Promising results, continuing challenges: The final report of the national assessment of Title I.* [Online]. Available: http://www.ed.gov/offices/OUS/eval/exsum. html

Vaughn, S., Reiss, M., Rothlein, L., & Hughes, M. T. (1999). Kindergarten teachers' perceptions of instructing students with disabilities. *Remedial and Special Education, 20*(3), 184–191.

Vellutino, F., Sipay, E., Small, S., Pratt, A., Chen, R., & Denckla, M. (1996). Cognitive profiles of difficult-to-remediate and readily remediated poor readers: Early intervention as a vehicle for distinguishing between cognitive and experiential deficits as basic causes of specific reading disability. *Journal of Educational Psychology, 88,* 601–638.

Wasik, B. A. (1998). Volunteer tutoring programs in reading: A review. *Reading Research Quarterly, 33*(3), 266–291.

Index

❖